Resources for Te

Ways of Reading

AN ANTHOLOGY FOR WRITERS

D1086440

Resources for Teaching

Ways of Reading

AN ANTHOLOGY FOR WRITERS

TENTH EDITION

Prepared by

David Bartholomae

UNIVERSITY OF PITTSBURGH

Anthony Petrosky

UNIVERSITY OF PITTSBURGH

Stacey Waite

UNIVERSITY OF NEBRASKA–LINCOLN

BEDFORD/ST. MARTIN'S

BOSTON ◆ NEW YORK

Copyright © 2014, 2011, 2008, 2005 by Bedford/St. Martin's

All rights reserved.
Instructors who have adopted *Ways of Reading: An Anthology for Writers*, Tenth Edition, as a textbook for a course are authorized to duplicate portions of this manual for their students.

Manufactured in the United States of America.

8 7 6 5 4 3

f e d c b a

For information, write: Bedford/St. Martin's, 75 Arlington Street, Boston, MA 02116 (617-399-4000)

ISBN: 978-1-4576-4883-0

Acknowledgments

Cathy Birkenstein. "We Got the Wrong Gal: Rethinking the 'Bad' Academic Writing of Judith Butler" in *College English*, Vol. 72, No. 3, January 2010. Used by permission of the National Council of Teachers of English.
Richard E. Miller. "Coda: On the Teacher's Zone of Efficiency." from *Professing in the Contact Zone: Bringing Theory and Practice Together*, edited by Janice M. Wolff. Copyright © 2002.
Richard E. Miller. "Fault Lines in the Contact Zone." in *College English*, Volume 56, No. 4 (April 1994): 389–409.
Thomas Recchio. Reprinted with permission from *Taking Stock: The Writing Process Movement in the '90s*, edited by Lad Tobin and Thomas Newkirk, Editors. Copyright © 1994 Boynton/Cook Publishers, Inc. Published by by Heinemann, Portsmouth, NH. All rights reserved.

Preface

•••••

Ways of Reading is designed for a course in which students are given the opportunity to work on what they read, and to work on it by writing. This manual is a guidebook to such a course. We cannot begin to imagine all the possible ways that the selections might (or should) be taught. The best we can do is to speak from our experience in such courses. If we seem at times to be dogmatic (to be single-minded in saying what should be done or how it should be done), it is because we are drawing on our practices as teachers, and they are grounded, finally, in our beliefs about what it means to read, write, and teach. We don't mean to imply that we have a corner on effective teaching or that there is no other way to help young adults take charge of what they do with texts.

In part I of this manual, you will find a brief introduction to the textbook and the opportunities it offers a teacher. A second section addresses the questions instructors often ask us about teaching with *Ways of Reading*, and a third details how the book is used in the training program for Teaching Assistants and Teaching Fellows at the University of Pittsburgh. Part II of the manual is composed of individual discussions of the selections and the three sets of questions that follow each selection, "Questions for a Second Reading," "Assignments for Writing," and "Making Connections." Part III provides a similar discussion of the "Assignment Sequences." We have also included additional "Assignment Sequences" to give you even more options in the classroom. In part IV, we have reprinted papers by instructors who have taught with *Ways of Reading*. Many were written by graduate students or former graduate students in our department who developed their work in a seminar on the teaching of composition. Also included are several essays written by experienced instructors who have used *Ways of Reading* for many years. Part V features an interview with Jean Ferguson Carr, a colleague of ours who has taught a version of the sequence "History and Ethnography: Reading the Lives of Others," included in previous editions of *Ways of Reading*. She talks about the logistics of preparing both students and local librarians for an archival project.

The tenth edition of *Ways of Reading* comes with e-Pages. We've marked those selections appearing in the e-Pages with the following icon: **e**. To access the e-Pages, visit **bedfordstmartins.com/waysofreading.**

v

Contents

• • ● • •

Part III. Working with the Assignment Sequences 161

SEQUENCE ONE   EXPLORING IDENTITY, EXPLORING THE SELF   **161**

This sequence engages students in urgent questions about race, gender, sexuality, ethnicity, nation, and selfhood. The assignments invite students to consider particular questions of identity and to think about those questions in specific relation to the responsibilities and challenges writers face in trying to represent, speak for, and understand themselves and others.

ASSIGNMENTS
1. *Narrative and Identity* [APPIAH]   **162**
2. *Identity and Representation* [SAID]   **162**
3. *The Concept of Human* [BUTLER]   **163**
4. *The Politics of Dehumanization* [BUTLER]   **163**
5. *Interconnectedness and Identity* [GRIFFIN]   **163**

SEQUENCE TWO   THE AIMS OF EDUCATION   167

The writing assignments in this sequence provide an opportunity for students to test the arguments in the individual essays by weighing them against scenes and episodes from the students' own schooling.

SEQUENCE THREE   THE ARTS OF THE CONTACT ZONE   172

This sequence asks students to work closely with the argument of Mary Louise Pratt's "Arts of the Contact Zone," not so much through summary (repeating the argument) as through extension (working under its influence, applying its terms and protocols).

SEQUENCE FOUR   AUTOBIOGRAPHICAL EXPLORATIONS   178

What is suggested by the title of this sequence is a use of writing (and the example of one's experience, including intellectual experience) to investigate, question, explore, inquire.

SEQUENCE FIVE   EXPERTS AND EXPERTISE   183

These assignments give students the chance to think about familiar settings or experiences through the work of writers who have had a significant effect on contemporary culture. In each case, students will be given the opportunity to work alongside these thinkers as an apprentice, carrying out work they have begun.

SEQUENCE SIX   READING CULTURE   187

In this sequence, students will be reading and writing about culture — the images, words, and sounds that pervade our lives and organize and represent our common experience.

Additional Sequences included in the e-Pages

ADDITIONAL SEQUENCE ONE   DELIBERATE ACTS OF DISCOVERY   192

This sequence invites students to study the ways in which writers use research and specific references to enrich their essays.

ADDITIONAL SEQUENCE TWO   ON DIFFICULTY   **196**

The assignments in this sequence invite students to consider the nature of difficult texts and how the problems they pose might be said to belong simultaneously to language, to readers, and to writers.

ADDITIONAL SEQUENCE THREE   THE USES OF READING (I)   **201**

This sequence focuses attention on authors as readers, on the use of sources, and on the art of reading as a writer. It combines technical lessons with lessons on the practice and rhetoric of citation.

ADDITIONAL SEQUENCE FOUR   THE USES OF READING (II)   **204**

This sequence is similar to the preceding one but provides an alternative set of readings.

ADDITIONAL SEQUENCE FIVE   THE ART OF ARGUMENT   206

The assignments in this sequence ask students to focus on arguments in terms of form and content, asking them to identify and explore writers' arguments and also to explore the assumptions that led to these kinds of arguments in the first place.

ADDITIONAL SEQUENCE SIX   WORKING WITH METAPHOR   208

The assignments in this sequence ask students to write about the metaphors in these selections as a way to think about how metaphors work.

Additional Sequences included in *Resources for Teaching Ways of Reading*

WRITING WITH STYLE   212

Assignments in this sequence focus on style. Most provide (or ask students to select) a sample sentence or paragraph from the text, one that is characteristic or exemplary of the author's style. It asks them to imitate that sentence or paragraph (that is, to write in parallel). And it asks them to describe sentences, not through textbook terms (subject, predicate, direct object), but in terms of what the sentence *does*.

WIDEMAN   *Our Time*
APPIAH   *Racial Identities*
BERGER   *Ways of Seeing*
GRIFFIN   *Our Secret*
WALLACE   *Authority and American Usage*
BORDO   *Beauty (Re)discovers the Male Body*

EXPERIMENTS IN READING AND WRITING   218

Each of the writers in this sequence is experimenting, pushing against or stepping outside of conventional ways of writing and thinking. This is an opportunity to learn about these experimental ways of writing from the inside, as a practitioner, as someone who learns from doing the very thing that he or she is studying.

GRIFFIN   *Our Secret*
SAID   *States*
WIDEMAN   *Our Time*
ANZALDÚA   *How to Tame a Wild Tongue*

ALTERNATIVE SELECTIONS
WALLACE   *Authority and American Usage*
BECHDEL   *The Ordinary Devoted Mother*
MILLER   *The Dark Night of the Soul*

ASSIGNMENTS

ALTERNATIVE ASSIGNMENTS

WAYS OF SEEING (I)   225

This sequence works closely with John Berger's "Ways of Seeing" and his argument about the relationship between a spectator (one who sees and "reads" a painting) and knowledge—in his case a knowledge of history.

BERGER   *Ways of Seeing*
BORDO   *Beauty (Re)discovers the Male Body*

ASSIGNMENTS

WRITING PROJECTS

The purpose of this sequence is to invite students to work closely with pieces of writing that call attention to themselves as writers, that make visible writing as a problem, a fundamental problem of representation and understanding.

READING WALKER PERCY

This sequence is designed to provide students with a way of reading Walker Percy's essay "The Loss of the Creature." There are six assignments in this sequence, all of which offer a way of rereading (or revising a reading of) Percy's essay; and, in doing so, they provide one example of what it means to be an expert or a critical reader.

A WAY OF COMPOSING 240

This sequence is designed to offer a lesson in writing. The assignments stage students' work (or the process they will follow in composing a single essay) in a pattern common to most writers: drafting, revising, and editing.

WAYS OF SEEING (II) 245

This sequence calls for an examination of the claims that John Berger makes about our ways of seeing art.

WORKING WITH FOUCAULT 249

This sequence asks students to work their way through "Panopticism" by summarizing Foucault's argument, by interrogating the summary (as it does and doesn't "capture" Foucault), and by putting Foucault to work in a Foucauldian analysis of primary materials.

Part IV. On *Ways of Reading* 255

Part V. Research and *Ways of Reading*

Part I. Teaching with *Ways of Reading*

· • ● • ·

INTRODUCTION

Some time ago, we were asked by the dean of the University of Pittsburgh to put together a course that combined instruction in reading and writing. The goal was to make students proficient users of the varieties of texts they would encounter in undergraduate education. When we began working on this course, we realized that the problems our students had when asked to write or talk about what they read were not "reading problems," at least not as these are strictly defined. Our students knew how to move from one page to the next. They could read sentences. They had obviously been able to carry out many of the versions of reading required for their education—skimming textbooks, cramming for tests, strip-mining books for term papers.

Our students, however, felt powerless in the face of serious writing, in the face of long and complicated texts—the kinds of texts we thought they should find interesting and challenging. We thought (as many teachers have thought) that if we just, finally, gave them something good to read—something rich and meaty—they would change forever their ways of thinking about English. It didn't work, of course. The issue is not only what students read, but what they can learn to *do* with what they read. We have learned that the problems our students had lay not in the reading material (it was too hard) or in the students (they were poorly prepared) but in the classroom—in the ways we and they imagined what it meant to work on an essay.

In the preface and introduction to *Ways of Reading*, we provide an extended glimpse into that classroom. The preface is addressed to teachers; it speaks of the design of the book and the assumptions about reading, writing, and teaching that have informed our work. The introduction is addressed to students. It is also, however, a demonstration of how we have learned to talk to our students about reading and writing, about their work and ours. If you haven't read the preface and introduction, we suggest that you begin there before working with this manual. Many instructors assign the introduction as one of the "readings" for the course. Some have asked students to reread the introduction later in the semester—perhaps after reading the essays by Wideman or Freire—and to write a response to it, to provide a student's introduction to *Ways of Reading*. This is a way for students to reflect on the work they have been doing and to articulate a sense of the course in terms that can stand alongside or outside of the terms that dominate the book. It is a way for students to have a conversation with Bartholomae, Petrosky, and Waite, to imagine us as writers or as characters, to represent the book as having a point of view.

1

What follows is a brief additional list of tips and afterthoughts—the sorts of things we find ourselves saying to each other over coffee or in the staff room.

Be Patient. We remind ourselves of this more often than anything else. The argument of this text is that students should be given the very types of essays that are often denied them—those that demand time and attention. The purpose of the course, then, is to teach students how to work on those essays and, in particular, how to work on them by writing. There is work for a reader to do. It is important work and part of the process of a liberal arts education. And yet, because the essays cannot be quickly handled, students' first efforts with them are often halting. You cannot expect to walk into class and have a dazzling discussion of Percy's "The Loss of the Creature," or to pick up a set of papers and see commanding readings of that essay. At least not all at once. You have to teach students to do this. As we have taught such courses, the rhythm goes something like this: Students write papers on "The Loss of the Creature" that are beginning attempts, footholds on a difficult essay. It is only through further discussion and revision that students will begin to shape these early drafts into more confident and impressive performances. With time, students will learn to take great pleasure in their accomplishments. They will see that they are beginning to be able to enter conversations, to do things with texts, that they never imagined they could do. If you move too quickly from one work to the next, however, students will experience frustration more than anything else. They will sense what they might have been able to do, without getting a chance to show their best work.

Write First or Write Later? When students are working regularly from essays, much depends on whether they write before or after those essays are discussed in class. The issues are these: If you talk through an essay in class, there is a way in which the students' papers are prewritten. If a teacher takes a strong line and speaks convincingly about how he or she reads Percy, it is a rare student who will do anything but say back what the teacher has already said. This student has not been in a position to author, or take responsibility for, a reading. The enabling moment for a reader is the moment of silence, when the student sits down before a text—a text that must remain silent—and must begin to write and to see what can be made of that writing. Even if a teacher is skilled at being slippery in front of class, even if a teacher avoids taking a stand and serves primarily to encourage and orchestrate the various comments of the students, there is still a way in which the pressure to write is taken from a writer by discussion. One student may sit down to write about Percy and find that whatever she says sounds just like what she heard others say in class. Another student may sit down with the intention of doing no more than trying to piece together what went on in class. In many cases, it is best to let students write first. And then, after a discussion of their papers and perhaps a discussion of the selection, let them go back to those papers to work on them again.

This is not cut-and-dried, however. While all this makes sense, we have often felt that we would have given students a real head start by anticipating problems in students' readings of the essays before they wrote, and so we often hold discussions before they begin. The discussion to have *before* students write is the discussion that will enable students to be better readers of the essays—a discussion preparing students to deal with Foucault's language or to anticipate the temptation to ignore the difficult sections and stick to the familiar in "The Loss of the Creature." We will often speak directly to these special requirements in the discussions of each selection in the first part of the manual.

Be Patient. This is worth repeating. Students will learn to take charge of the work they do as readers and writers when they are given a chance to go back to the work—when they are given opportunities to reread and revise. If they have a chance to go back to a paper on "The Loss of the Creature," they can see themselves as readers in what they have written; they will be able to work on the reading by working on the essay. The act of revision we are thinking of, then, is not just a matter of tightening or correcting a paper; it is a matter of going back to the primary text and reworking what one might say about it. Students will not learn the same lesson by jumping ahead to a new assignment. Students will learn more if they can spend time working again and again on a single essay than they will if they start a paper on one subject and then jump forward to something new. If you think of your course as a course in reading and writing, there is no pressure to cover material. There is pressure to read and write, but it makes no difference whether you cover three selections in the textbook or eleven.

On Revision. Revision has been a standard part of the courses we teach—and by that we mean that revision is part of the weekly schedule of work. It is not an afterthought or something students might do on the side. It is part of the assigned work from class to class. Our students, in other words, know that they can expect to work their way toward a final draft. And they can expect to receive help from us through written comments or conferences, and from their colleagues through class discussions of sample photocopied papers and through group conferences. Since revision is a group process in our classes, we find that we have to make a point of ensuring that revision is not (at least necessarily) a drive toward consensus. When students write first drafts on, for example, "The Loss of the Creature," we will get quite a variety of responses. When we discuss these papers in class, we call attention to the variety of responses—particularly the strongest ones—in order to demonstrate that there are ways of reading "The Loss of the Creature," not just one way, and that these ways of reading are driven by different strategies and serve different ends. We want students, in other words, to see their papers as evidence of choices they made in talking about the text. And we want them to see those choices in the context of choices made by other writers. The purpose of revision, then, is to enable students to take their approach to a text and to make the most of it. We do not want students to revise in order to say what we would say, or what the group has said about "The Loss of the Creature." Our goal as teachers has always been to try to bring forward the paper that seems to be struggling to be written. That's the paper we want the student to work on in revision. These revisions should show again the variety of the first drafts. We do not want students to rework their papers so that they all say the same thing. We want students to work on readings of an essay; we do not insist that they come to a common point of view.

Background Information. There are classes where it is a teacher's job to know all that he or she can about the backgrounds to the texts under discussion. These are not necessarily composition classes, however. We would be paralyzed if we felt we had to be specialists on Freire, Foucault, and Berger before we could walk into our classes. It would keep us from teaching what we want to teach. So what do we want to teach? We want to teach students how to make what they can out of essays that don't lend themselves to quick summary. We want to show students, or lead them to show one another, how to work with what they have. We want to teach them how to draw on their own resources. As a consequence, we have avoided *Norton Anthology*–like footnotes (the footnotes you find are in the original texts), and we have avoided headnotes that cast the essays in the context of the history of ideas. Readers read outside of their areas of professional expertise. And they take pleasure and instruction from reading unfamiliar material. We don't want students to get the notion that because they lack specialized knowledge, they are unable to read essays like "Panopticism." The essay may be difficult, but we don't want students to imagine the difficulty in those terms. If they do, then there is nothing to do but give up. The argument of the textbook, then, is that readers and writers make use of what they have. No reader catches all the allusions or understands all the words or translates all the foreign phrases — yet readers can make texts meaningful by what they do with them when they act as though they had the ability to make a text meaningful. Your students will learn most as they discover how to deal with complex or unfamiliar material. They will be learning about learning.

So What Is This Course About? It is about composing — reading and writing. You are not teaching Berger or Pratt, art history or anthropology. You are teaching reading and writing. You stand for a method, a way of working with texts, and not for a set of canonical interpretations, a series of approved statements used to represent an understanding of those texts. Your authority as a teacher in this course comes from your ability to do things with texts, not from your experience with all the fields of inquiry represented by these essays. The best way to prepare for your teaching is to imagine the varieties of ways these texts might be read. Then you will not be surprised by what your students want to do when they read, and you will be better able to encourage them to work out the potential of their own approaches to the essays. The worst thing to do is to come to class ready to expound or defend a single reading, one that all your students are expected to speak back to you by the end of the day. Then students will sit back and wait to be told what the essays say; they won't feel empowered to forge a reading on their own. You need to be able to monitor and assist your students as they work on these essays. To do that, you will have to be able to enter into their ways of reading. You must do more, that is, than tell them whether they are wrong or right.

Who's the Boss? You are, of course. But this means that you are responsible for evaluating the performance of your students. You may ask the class an open question, one reasonable people can disagree on. This is not, however, the same thing as saying that everyone has a right to his or her opinion. Some opinions are phrased powerfully, some work closely with material from the text, some acknowledge and represent counteropinions, some push against easy commonplaces and clichéd thinking. Whether they are writing or speaking, students are composing ways of talking about these essays, and the job of a teacher is to encourage, monitor, and evaluate those performances. There is nothing worse than a class where discussion is an end in itself — where a lively fifty minutes is its own justification. Whether students are discussing Percy's essay or an essay of their own, the point of the conversation should be to bring forward a textual problem and to demonstrate how, with care, attention, rigor, and precision, a person might work on it.

Reading against the Grain. We have tried to write a book that leaves plenty of room for a student to move around in, one that is strongly voiced, or as strongly voiced as the conventions of textbook publishing will allow. In the introduction and headnotes, in the questions and assignments, we wanted students to get a sense of two characters speaking. We did not want them to hear the disembodied voice of Truth or Reason. We wanted, in other words, to encourage students to read the text *as* a text, to see it as representing a point of view, to argue with it, to take it as a prompting to respond in a voice of their own.

Students can read with or against the text—with it by participating in its form of instruction, against it by seeing its bias or limitations. Students are asked to read not only with but against the grain of the authors represented in *Ways of Reading*. While it is important for students to pay generous attention to what they read—to give in, to think through someone else's words—it is also important that students feel what it is like to step outside a text in order to ask questions about where it might lead, what it leaves out, and whose interests it serves and why. We wanted students to imagine that they could read in the name of a collective set of interests. Students need to feel their power to step outside a text, and they need to learn how and why it is OK to ask difficult questions or to resist the forces of tradition, power, and authority.

Using This Book. And we have tried to write a book that leaves plenty of room for a teacher. You'll notice that the teaching materials are placed both after the selections and at the end of the book. There are second-reading questions and writing assignments after each piece and assignment sequences at the end. This is not to insist that a teacher use either one set of materials or the other. All the assignments in the sequences, for example, assume that students will reread the selections, and the second-reading questions are designed to help students imagine where to begin and how to proceed—so that they are not just reading the words one more time. We hope that students will work back and forth between the questions at the end of an essay or a story and the writing assignments in the sequences. Many instructors have found the assignment sequences a powerful way of representing writing as a tool for learning and inquiry, particularly inquiry as it involves the close and critical reading of texts. The assignment sequences are meant to suggest possible courses of instruction, but they are not meant to be limiting. We have used the book for many years at the University of Pittsburgh, teaching different sequences each year. We always revise the sequences at the end of the book by leaving out some readings and adding others, using the "Assignments for Writing" in place of the writing assignments in the sequence. We have also known several instructors who put together semester-long sequences out of a combination of questions in "Assignments for Writing" and "Making Connections."

Reader's Journal. A reader's journal can serve as a useful adjunct to the more formal writing students do. We think of a reader's journal as both a commonplace book and a double-entry notebook. We encourage students, in other words, to copy out and reflect on passages that grab them in what they read. There are powerful lines and phrases in these essays, and this is one way of acknowledging to students that readers grab on to the minute specifics as much as they do the general argument in what they read. The journal can also serve as a way for students to record the process of reading. They can, for example, make two columns in the journal, using one to note puzzles or problems or reactions after a first reading and the other to comment on those entries after a second reading.

And, Finally. Assume that students will need to read each selection at least twice before they do any of the assignments. First readings should give a sense of the selection and its language; subsequent readings should be focused by the questions or directions in the assignment.

Tell students there are no quick-and-easy ways to read these selections. They will need to reread and pay attention to the passages and moments in each selection that allow them to address the questions in the assignments.

Ask students to take notes and mark passages on their second and third readings of the selections.

Use class discussions of the "Questions for a Second Reading" to help students prepare for the writing assignments.

Ask students to come to class prepared to discuss the "Questions for a Second Reading." They should have notes and numerous references to the selection for each question.

Discuss writing with students before they do any of the writing assignments. Use examples of past students' papers to demonstrate such things as note-taking, drafting, revising, and editing.

Duplicate students' papers for class discussions. Use complete papers and parts of papers to demonstrate students' work on such matters as interpretation, critical commentary, text references, paraphrase, and risk-taking.

Encourage students to take notes from the texts and to record their thoughts, other students' comments, class discussions, and their responses to your comments on their papers.

Encourage students to reread their drafts, paying attention to what they say and how they use the selection, and to redraft whole drafts or parts of drafts before they hand in their papers.

Accept students' drafts as drafts. Allow them the opportunity to use drafts and revisions to think through the problems posed by the assignments.

Encourage or require revisions for the assignments that warrant them, especially if a student is particularly involved in an assignment.

Respond to students' writing in stages. Respond first to their completion of the task, then to what they have to say and how they use (or don't use) the text, then to editorial matters.

Write comments and raise questions on students' papers. Press them back into the texts and push against their generalizations and quick summaries.

Limit the number of comments you write on students' papers. Pick two or three things to focus on, and avoid mixing comments for revision with editorial suggestions.

Teach students to edit their papers. Show them how to use a ruler and a red pencil and to read line by line through their final revisions.

Teach students to work in peer editing groups. Ask them to read one another's papers and to explain to one another the errors that they find.

Try to avoid grading individual papers. Ask students to be responsible for keeping all their papers, including all their drafts, in a pocket folder or portfolio, and grade the portfolio of work at mid-semester and at semester's end.

Hold two or three twenty- to thirty-minute conferences with each student during the semester. Go over papers and note what you would like each student to work on during that semester. Keep a record of these conferences for your files, and use your notes to help with grading.

QUESTIONS WE ARE OFTEN ASKED

The writing assignments are often long and difficult, even confusing. Why is this? How do you prepare students to read and work with the assignments in *Ways of Reading*?

Let's take the last question first: "How do you prepare students to read and work with the writing assignments?" It's true that the assignments are long. In comparison to what students are used to (test questions, for example, or writing assignments that look like test questions), they take time to read. This is part of the design of the assignments. Even in their format, we want them to challenge or call into question the assumption that the project before students, their writing, is simple or simply a matter of following instructions.

Our goal, rather, is to set a context, to define the outlines or possibilities of a project (we say to our students) within which students can find interesting work to do. Our students say, "Just tell us what you want." And we say, "We want you to do something interesting, something you care about." But, as teachers, we also want to help our students imagine unimaginable projects, work they couldn't do without our help.

From our point of view, the worst way to read the assignments is to find one sentence or one question and to say, "Aha, *here* is what this assignment is *really* about," as though the rest of the words were simply distraction, a smoke screen. This is a version of the standard technology of mastery, similar to reading an essay for its main idea. You find one passage you can control, and you let it stand for the whole essay. You find one question you can answer quickly, and you let it stand for the whole assignment. We want our assignments to open up a process of questioning for students, not to present a single question or to signal a routine school task.

The other problem we have observed, and again we can link this to the history of American education, is that students are tempted to take the questions in the assignments and answer them one by one, thus using them to structure their essays. One reason there are several questions in each assignment is to suggest that there are several ways in, several ways to begin to think about a response. They are not meant to serve as a checklist for a writer to follow, item by item. A question, for many students, becomes a straitjacket, an order, a command, a test. We want our questions to be an exercise in questioning.

Most of the questions are designed to turn against what we have taken as the flow of the assignment, to open it up and to suggest a new direction. As we just said, we don't want students to think of writing as following a series of orders. In any case, the questions (at their best) don't function that way. They *aren't* a series but a set of interruptions. They are designed to frustrate the very patterns the assignment has set into play.

The writing assignments, then, are meant to suggest a project. This project usually asks students to do two things: to reread the essay, this time with a specific problem in mind; and to write an essay as a way of thinking through an answer to that problem. Our goal is to set some specific limits on students' work—the assignment might direct students to perform a close reading of passages or to apply the terms of one essay to examples of their own choosing or to read one essay as it is framed by another. At the same time, we want to provide room for students to move around; we want to make the assignments "readable" in the sense that there is room for interpretation. We want students to be able to find *their* work in *our* assignments. Now, we're realists. Sometimes they do and sometimes they don't. We realize that. If we have done our work well, students will often find ways of making the work their own. In our own classes, we certainly never set ourselves up as assignment police. We expect our students to read the assignments carefully. We expect them to be able to explain how they read the assignments and how their work constitutes a response. But we do not have a specific answer in mind to our questions, and we do not have a particular essay in mind as a response to our assignments. When students ask us, "What do you want?" we answer, "What do *you* want to do?" In a class of twenty-two students, our goal is to get as many different kinds of response as we can. We use the assignments as starting points. They suggest an approach to the readings ("Look at the poems in 'When We Dead Awaken'—a selection by Adrienne Rich in the eighth edition of *Ways of Reading*—and think about how they might represent a series"), and they suggest a project ("Write an essay describing what you consider to be the most significant pattern of change in Rich's poems. When you are done, compare your account with Rich's account"). Because as teachers we can begin with what our students imagine to be the most profitable (or possible) directions to take with this (their sense of what the assignment might mean for them as they prepare to write), our discussions about the work they might do have a focus and a motive they would not have if students were left to determine projects on their own. We think that our assignments intervene in productive ways and enable students to want to do things they would never have imagined doing on their own.

Perhaps it might help to look closely at a couple of assignments. Because we have begun using Rich as an example, we have chosen another assignment from "When We Dead Awaken" and, for the sake of comparison, one of the assignments that followed Virginia Woolf's "A Room of One's Own" in the fifth edition of *Ways of Reading*. The discussion will treat them paragraph by paragraph (or section by section).

> In the opening of her essay, Woolf says that the "I" of her text "is only a convenient term for somebody who has no real being." And at the beginning of the last chapter (in reference to a new novel by "Mr. A"), she says,
>
>> But after reading a chapter or two a shadow seemed to lie across the page. It was a straight dark bar, a shadow shaped something like the letter "I." One began dodging this way and that to catch a glimpse of the landscape behind it. Whether that was indeed a tree or a woman walking I was not quite sure. Back one was always hailed to the letter "I." One began to be tired of "I." (p. 766)
>
> It's hard to know what to make of this, as an argument about either the position of women or writing. Read back through Woolf's essay, noting sections you could

use to investigate the ways an "I" is or is not present in this text and to investigate the argument that the text makes about a writer's (or speaker's) presence. (See the third "Question for a Second Reading.")

Write an essay in which you examine the ways Woolf, a writer, is and is not present in this piece of writing. Where and how does she hide? And why? Whom do you find in her place? How might this difficulty over the presence of the writer be said to be a part of Woolf's argument about women and writing? And what might this have to do with you and the writing you are doing, either in this class or in school generally?

The first paragraph was written to prompt a close reading and to resituate a student in relation to the text of "A Room of One's Own." We focus on a passage, making it a key passage. When students reread, they will be reading for the definition of both the authorial I (the writer) and the presentation of the character who speaks in the first person throughout the essay. And, following the passage, we do what we often do. We take something that we suspect students might feel to be straightforward and announce that it is strange, mysterious, or problematic ("It's hard to know what to make of this"). In a sense, the writing assignment sets students the task of making something out of the ways in which Woolf, both in what she says and in what she does as a writer, challenges the standard notions governing the status and presence of a "Person" in writing.

The first paragraph, then, defines the project as a directed rereading of "A Room of One's Own." The last paragraph turns specifically to the essays students are to write. The first few questions are there for students who can't quite figure out where to begin ("Think about how and why Woolf might hide. Think about where she is present."). The remaining questions are there to complicate this project: first, by asking students to think about the connections between the argument in "A Room of One's Own" and the argument represented in its style or method; second, by asking students to think about how this essay might be written for them, as writers, how it might have a bearing on the work they are doing in a composition course. In most of our assignments, we try to find a way of saying to students, "Hey, this isn't just academic; it is speaking directly to you about the way you think and write, about how you live your life."

There is a similar pattern in the Rich assignment:

Rich says, "We need to know the writing of the past, and know it differently than we have ever known it; not to pass on a tradition but to break its hold over us." That "us" includes you too. Look back over your own writing (perhaps the drafts and revisions you have written for this course), and think back over comments teachers have made, textbooks you've seen; think about what student writers do and what they are told to do, about the secrets students keep and the secrets teachers keep. You can assume, as Rich does, that there are ways of speaking about writing that are part of the culture of schooling and that they are designed to preserve certain ways of writing and thinking and to discourage others.

One might argue, in other words, that there are traditions here. As you look at the evidence of the "past" in your work, what are its significant features? What might you name this tradition (or these traditions)? How would you illustrate its hold on your work or the work of students generally? What might you have to do to begin to "know it differently," "to break its hold," or to revise? And, finally, why would someone want (or not want) to break its hold?

This assignment defines a different kind of project from the Woolf assignment. The Woolf assignment asked for a close reading of the text. This one asks students to use a text (its terms, its interpretive frame, its motives) to "read" their own experience, including the material record of that experience.

The opening paragraph sets the terms for this project. The "we" of Rich's essay, it says, is also "you." It suggests where students might go to begin to gather material to write about (not just memory but also old textbooks, old papers). And the end of the paragraph returns to frame their work in Rich's terms, terms that would remain hidden or lost or invisible in the text if we did not bring them forward and make them key terms. We want students to think not just about "*my*" school or "*my*" teacher, but about the past, about tradition, about patriarchy (a word we wish we had featured more prominently in the assignment), and about culture.

The final paragraph restates the goal of the project and then tries to question or complicate students' (or any reader's) desire to say — "Oh, I get it, what they want is simply this." We want to forestall the desire to see it "simply." We do this by pointing, again, to the larger social, historical, and cultural context of the examples students will be writing about, a context we know from experience will be lost without our prompting. We do this by turning, again, to the words of the text. Our goal is to make this essay also a reading of "When We Dead Awaken." We are hoping that students will refer to Rich and use some of her terms in their discussion ("Nothing in this textbook even suggests, as Rich does, that I might need to not only write a topic sentence but 'know it differently,' even 'break its hold' on my writing"). And, finally, we want students to imagine that the essay speaks to them directly as students in a writing course — that, in a sense, "When We Dead Awaken" can be read as a lesson in writing.

How do you construct assignment sequences?

We always begin with the readings. Our teaching is driven, in other words, by what we want to teach — that is, what we want students to read. The process of selection is described in both the preface and the introduction, but we begin by locating challenging readings, readings with some currency in the academy. We look for work in writing that we think can provide important examples to young writers, that can provide interesting work for a required course, and with authors, ideas, terms, and subjects that can be useful in the education of young scholars. Each selection, then, must be something students can profitably write from and about; it must also, itself, be a lesson in writing.

Once we have decided on the readings, the key question becomes one of how to engage writers with the material over an extended period of time. How might these readings define a project and not simply serve as independent units to be processed and then left behind? It is important to us that the semester be defined by a project, an evolving body of work that asks students to think of one text in terms of another, usually with some general subject or question in mind, and, by thinking about them, to revise, extend, and rework earlier essays and earlier positions. The assignments, then, are written to broker that engagement, to call attention to certain problems in the text that students might otherwise overlook, and then to move from that piece of reading to the next, both to focus attention on its ways of thinking and writing and to invite students to see it in relation to what they have read before. They move into one piece and then back to the general project in a pattern that will include revision as well as addition. Because we know how easy it is for students to be overwhelmed by the readings, the sequences are generally punctuated by assignments that ask students to stop, take stock, and find a place to enter, as writers, into the discussions begun by others, by the authors they have read.

How many readings do you teach in a semester?

This is an easier question to answer than the first. Usually four. Sometimes three, sometimes five, but never more than that. We could imagine assigning more essays and using them for discussion, in groups or in class, but only if students' writing was limited to three, four, or five essays.

Our semester has fourteen weeks. We spend at least two weeks on every essay and generally leave time for what we call "retrospective" essays. These essays, assigned at mid-term and at the end of the term, are designed to give students time to reflect on the work of the course (and to give us a sense of what students are thinking).

We give students at least two weeks to work on the readings they write about. There is a simple and standard pattern here. Students write a draft in the first week and revise it in the second. The readings are difficult enough to warrant giving students the extra time, particularly the time to reread and revise, tasks we have come to think of as almost identical. We also want students to feel their achievement as readers and writers. If we were moving quickly from one essay to the next each week, we would worry that students would feel only frustration at their failure to understand. Each first draft would give them a sense of what they might be able to do with an essay, but they would never be able to complete that work—or at least take it to its next stage.

What are your courses like? What is the daily routine?

The first thing to say is that even at the University of Pittsburgh, where a large staff has been teaching this or similar material for a long time, there is a surprising range of differences in the shape of the courses and in the daily routine. Teachers need to teach from their strengths. They need to believe in their courses. Most teachers who work with us make regular revisions in the sequences or in individual assignments, both before the semester begins (to create a different emphasis, for example) and once it is under way (to respond to issues that have come up in class).

There are some generalizations to make, however. We regularly reproduce student essays and use them (often in pairs) as the center of class discussion. Instead of having a general discussion of "When We Dead Awaken," for example, we would focus on two specific readings by two students. Rather than talk about revision generally, we would use those same two papers to discuss how and where and why they might usefully be revised. As we have already stated, revision is a central part of the course. Students revise as part of their weekly schedule of assignments, not on their own or for extra credit; they do one of the writing assignments one week, receive our comments, then revise it the next week. Revision in this case is represented as something other than "fixing" an essay. We ask students to put in the same amount of time as they did on the first draft. Their goal is to rethink the essay they have begun and to take it to its next step.

Perhaps the best way to illustrate one of our classes is to present an example of a course description and a syllabus. The following course description comes from one of Bartholomae's courses taught from an earlier edition. (You should feel free, by the way, to take any of this and use it in your courses. Good teachers borrow from other teachers all the time.)

Sample Course Description
David Bartholomae

COURSE DESCRIPTION

Introduction. The subject of this course is writing. Writing, as I think of it, is an action, an event, a performance. It is a way of asserting one's presence but, paradoxically, in a language that makes the writer disappear. No matter what you write, the writing is not yours; it's part of a larger text, one with many authors, begun long ago. And its end is outside your control. In spite of what you think you are saying, your text will become what others make of it, what they say you said.

One of my goals in this course is to arrange your work to highlight your relationship (as a writer) to the past and to the words of others (to history and culture). This is the reason for the assigned readings, and this is the primary role reading will play in this writing course. You will be asked to read a series of assigned texts and to write in response to what you have read. I want to foreground the ways in which your writing takes place in relation to the writing of others. My goal, as your teacher, will be to make that relationship interesting, surprising, and productive. These meetings between the past and the present, writing and a writer, those places in your essays where you work with someone else's words and ideas to my mind represent the basic scene of instruction; they are the workplaces, the laboratories, the arenas of what is often called a "liberal" education. It is there, on the page, that the key work of a student is done and not in some private, internal mental space. This is why a writing course is fundamental to undergraduate education.

The Course. I have asked you to think of a writing course as the representative workplace of a liberal arts education. You might also think of our course as a studio course, like a course in painting or sculpture or composition. You will be practicing your art by working on specific projects. I will be looking over your shoulder, monitoring your progress, and, at various points in the semester, assessing the work you gather together in a portfolio.

In this sense, the course is one where you practice writing. You can expect to write regularly, at least one draft or essay each week. You will need to develop the habits and the discipline of a writer. You will need a regular schedule, a regular place and time for writing. There is nothing fancy about this. You need to learn to organize your time so that there is time for writing, so that it becomes part of a routine.

You'll need to learn to work quickly but also to keep your attention inside sentences for hours at a time. This requires discipline, a kind of physical training I can best describe as athletic. Writers need to be able to sit in one place and to think inside of sentences for long periods of time. You'll have to set your own goals. I would suggest four hours a week in two two-hour sessions. These are writing times, when you will be sitting in one place and working closely with words, yours and others'. You should do nothing else during these sessions. You should work in the same place at the same time every week.

I can insist on this kind of care and attention, but I can't teach it. I can, however, teach you ways of working on your writing. I have come to believe that the most important skill I can teach in a writing course is reading—the ability to read closely and critically. In this sense, a writing course is like any other course in an English department. There is one difference, however. In a writing course, we are interested in how you can apply criticism to production, to the production of your own writing, your texts. In a course on Shakespeare, you may write about Shakespeare, you may be said to "produce" Shakespeare's plays by interpreting them and writing about what you have read. But there is a fundamental difference in what you produce, in your writing, and how your writing is valued. In a writing class, it is your work that is the center of critical attention, not Shakespeare's. The pressing question is what your writing might say about our culture, about language and imagination, not what his might say. Writing requires the skills of endurance and attention. In revision, it requires critical reading, a form of practical criticism, a protocol that will allow you to read your own writing in order to go back to work.

I have learned that the essential work of any writing course is revision. There is more to writing than first thoughts, first drafts, and first pages. A writer learns most by returning to his or her work to see what it does and doesn't do, by taking time with a project and seeing where it might lead. This class is a place where you will practice writing, but it is also a place where the writing is expected to change. You will be writing regularly, but I will also be asking you to revise—to step outside your writing, to see what it might represent (not just what it says), and to make changes. I will teach you how to read your own writing, how to pay close and critical attention to what you have written, and I will teach you how to make this critical attention part of the cycle of production, part of your work as a writer.

The course will be organized so that you will work a single essay through several drafts; each essay will be a part of a larger project. When I assess your writing, I will be looking primarily at the progress from draft to draft.

Schedule and Routines. I have planned for fourteen weeks and divided the semester into three units, each with a particular focus.

You should plan to read each assigned reading twice before I begin to discuss it in class. The first time through, you should read quickly, to get a general sense of what the writer is doing, what the piece is about. Then you should read through a second time, this time working more closely and deliberately with the text, focusing on those sections that seem difficult or puzzling or mysterious. You should read with a pen or pencil, marking the text in a way that will help you when you go back to it (particularly when you go back to it as a writer). If you can't bring yourself to write in your book, you should begin to develop a system using note cards or Post-it notes.

Each week you will write one essay and/or revise one essay, both as stages in a larger project. Each week you should make two additional copies of everything you have written, one for me and one for a peer reader. My graded copy of *everything* you write for this course must be placed in your portfolio. Keep backup copies in a separate folder. In order to monitor your progress, I will review your portfolio at three points in the term—around the fifth week, the tenth, and at the end of the term. Your final grade will be based on my final reading of your portfolio. It will be an assessment of your work in the course over the term. I will be particularly interested in the development I see in revision and across the portfolio. I will be looking for evidence of your involvement with the course and of your willingness and your success in working on your writing. I will *not* add together and average the grades from the earlier reviews.

I will also read individual essays carefully each week and write comments on them. I spend a lot of time on these comments, and I will expect you to take time to read what I have written. If you find that I have written much on your paper, you should take this as a sign of love, not of desperation. It means I was interested, engaged.

The best way to read my comments is to start at the beginning of your essay, reread what you have written, and stop to read my comments along the way. This is how I write the marginal comments, while I am reading. They show my reactions and suggestions at that moment. The final comment is where I will make a summary statement about your essay. Be warned: I tend to be blunt and to the point. If I sound angry, I probably am not. I want to get your attention, I want to be honest, and I see no reason to beat around the bush.

If your work seems thoughtless or quickly done, I will notice. I have taught writing for many years, and I know when writers are working hard and when they are fooling around. I will tell you if I think you are fooling around.

I will not put grades on individual essays. I will grade your performance over fourteen weeks, but I see no reason to grade each and every piece you write. In many cases, I will be asking you to extend yourself and to do what you cannot do easily or with grace. It would make no sense for me to grade everything you do. (Please see the separate handout titled "Error and Plagiarism." I will expect you to consistently and successfully proofread all papers, including first drafts.) I will be available to answer questions or to look at an essay immediately before and after class. I know that my handwriting can be a problem. I will not be embarrassed if you ask me to decipher what I have written. I will, however, be heartbroken if you simply skip over what is hard to read.

Class Participation. I will regularly reproduce your papers (with names removed) and use them for class discussion. Most of our class time will be spent discussing copies of your essays. This is as important to your education as the time you spend alone working on your writing. I expect you to attend all classes. If you are absent, you are not taking the course, and I will ask you to drop or give you a failing grade. Similarly, all written work must be completed on schedule. Because you will be writing every week, and because one week's work will lead to the next assignment, you cannot afford to fall behind. I will not accept work that is late. If you are not doing the writing, you are not taking the course, and I will ask you to drop or give you a failing grade.

Writing Groups. I will divide the class into groups of three. Few writers work alone; they rely on friends and colleagues to listen to ideas, to read drafts, and to help with copyediting. You will be responsible for commenting on one group member's essay or draft each week. When you do, you are to sign your name to your comments. (See the handout "Working as a Reader and Editor.")

Workshop. Throughout the semester you can receive free tutorial help at the Writing Workshop, CL 501. It is open Monday through Friday, with evening hours Tuesday through Thursday. I will also set aside three or four class sessions as tutorial workshops. I will meet with you individually and ask you to work together in your writing groups.

End of Term. I will not put comments on the work in the final folders. You will have heard plenty from me throughout the semester, and I don't want to waste time writing comments that won't be read. This does not mean, however, that I am not interested in talking with you about your work. If you would like to review the folder or individual essays, come see me first thing at the beginning of the next semester. There is no final exam.

Materials. You will need:

A handbook (I have ordered one for the course)

A dictionary (there are copies of *The American Heritage Dictionary* at the Bookcenter)

Ways of Reading, Fourth Edition, Bartholomae and Petrosky

Photocopied handouts

You will need a sturdy folder with pockets to hold your work and everything I hand out in class. This will become your portfolio.

A Word to the Wise. All work for this course must be typed. If you have not yet begun to use a word processor, now is the time to begin. In a course like this, where you are expected to revise and to revise regularly, you will make your life a lot easier if you can do your revisions on a computer screen. Typing papers over and over again is tiresome and inefficient. If you need help getting started with a computer or a program, see me immediately.

COURSE SCHEDULE Readings: Pratt, Anzaldúa, Wideman, Said, Jamie (Sequence Two: The Arts of the Contact Zone)

Writing and Revising: "Long, intense absorption," "logic and imagination," "practical criticism"

Sept. 3	Introductions
Sept. 8, 10	Read Pratt, "Arts of the Contact Zone"
Sept. 15, 17	Assignment 1 due: The Literate Arts of the Contact Zone [Pratt]
Sept. 22, 24	Revise Assignment 1; Read Anzaldúa, "How to Tame a Wild Tongue"
Sept. 29, Oct. 1	Assignment 2 due: Borderlands [Pratt, Anzaldúa]; Portfolios due 9/29

Working with Texts: "Historical awareness"

Oct. 6, 8	Revise Assignment 2; Read John Edgar Wideman, "Our Time"
Oct. 13, 15	Midterm retrospective writing assignment
Oct. 20, 22	Assignment 3 due: Counterparts [Wideman]; Read Said, "States"
Oct. 27, 29	Revise Assignment 3
Nov. 3, 5	Assignment 4 due: A Dialectic of Self and Other [Pratt, Said]; Portfolios due 11/3

Fine-Tuning: "Linguistic precision"

Nov. 10, 12	Assignment 5 due: A Dialectic of Self and Other [Pratt, Said]

Nov. 17, 19	Revise Assignment 5
Nov. 24	Assignment 6: Producing Place [Jamie]
Dec. 1, 3	Revise Assignment 6
Dec. 8, 10	Final retrospective essay
Finals week	**Final Portfolios Due** Friday, December 18th, 4:00 P.M.

Aren't these readings too hard? What do you do with students who claim that they can't read them or that the work is boring? What do you do with students who become angry or who give up?

We get this question all the time. Or people say, "Maybe you can teach this stuff at Pitt, but it would never work on our campus."

The course represented by *Ways of Reading* began a number of years ago, prompted by our sense that students were being cheated. Textbooks and courses were founded on the assumption that students would be bored or frustrated or angry with the intellectual materials that we ourselves found most interesting, fascinating, compelling, or important. And so, ostensibly to protect students, composition courses gave them simple things to work with. ("Don't worry your pretty little heads," the profession said. "Work on simple essays for simple minds.")

We designed our course, as we say in the preface, to teach students *how* to work with difficult materials. We wanted to bring them into the conversation, to give students a way to begin to work with the materials that mattered to us, that we valued.

We don't hide the fact that these essays are difficult and frustrating. They were for us when we read them the first time. Our goal is to give students a course to show them how and why they might negotiate the difficulty. This is why rereading is such an important feature of our courses. This is why the writing assignments are designed to help students work with the readings.

Nevertheless, the questions about the difficulty of the texts are valid, and we don't ignore them. Even if you make difficulty one of the acknowledged features of the course, how do you keep students interested? How do you allow them to believe that they can do the work? One way is to show your enthusiasm and pleasure in the work they are doing. It is important, we've said, for teachers to be patient. If students are going to work on these essays, that work will take time. There will be halting steps along the way. Even at the end, a student's account of Berger's "Ways of Seeing" will most likely not reproduce the level or intensity of the lecture that you or a colleague might be able to give. The point of a course like this is to give students a chance to work on the materials and concerns important to the academy. They will not, however, all attain the eloquence or the conclusions of their professors. So patience is more than a matter of waiting. It requires a willingness to value and show enthusiasm for work that is partial, unfinished, the work of novices, work that we have been prepared to call "error."

The book also offers a protocol for dealing with difficulty. It says indirectly (and we say directly in our classes), "Read through quickly as though it all made sense, get the big picture, get a feel for what the piece is about. Then go back to read more closely, taking time to work on passages that seem difficult or mysterious. Assume that these passages are hard for you because they are indeed difficult and would be hard for any reader, not because you are stupid." We offer questions to help direct this rereading. Students should also think of this stage as pencil work, writing in the margins, connecting sections of the text, working out provisional responses and definitions. We've also found that it is important to help students know when and where to use a dictionary.

The other approach we often take is to use class time to model ways of working on difficult passages. We will begin a discussion by asking students to identify passages that they would like us to work on together, as a group. Then we will use the discussion to work out possible readings and to chart, on the blackboard, the strategies that have enabled them. We will also do this in our discussion of students' essays, asking students to notice how a writer has made sense of a difficult section or (often early in the semester) where a writer has carefully avoided dealing with the parts of text that resisted his or her reading.

Your course seems to put so much emphasis on reading. Where is there time for writing instruction? How is your course a writing course?

We have never thought of our course as anything *but* a writing course. As we interpret reading (working on a text, working out a response), it becomes almost synonymous with writing. Reading, too, is a way of working with meaning and language. We also feel that writing students can learn some of the most important lessons only by writing from readings. By doing so, students learn that their ideas aren't simply their own. They learn about convention and context. They learn that they don't invent a subject. They learn what it means to work in the context of a history of writing that comes into play when they sit down to write. This is how we make sense of the metaphor of the "conversation of humankind." There are other speakers already speaking. You enter this moment not alone but in the company of others.

But we are avoiding the crux of the question: Where and how do we give the kinds of instruction traditionally associated with the writing course? There are two answers to this question. The first is simple. The work that surrounds the production and revision of students' essays each week, in class, in groups, in conference, and in our comments on their papers represents our most immediate intervention with the students' writing. In this sense, our writing courses follow the standard pattern of "workshop" courses. The one major difference is the degree to which revising here also requires rereading. As we have said elsewhere in *Resources*, the one surprising feature of our classes is the small amount of time we spend, as teachers, talking about the readings. Almost all of our discussion of the readings takes place *through* the discussion of student essays, which we reproduce and use to represent specific acts of reading and writing. Most of the questions we address to the assigned texts, in other words, are delivered through questions we ask about writing. Rather than talk generally about introductions, for example, we would talk about the ways a writer has introduced a project or a text or a quotation. Rather than talk about examples in the abstract, we would discuss the use of examples in a student essay — what examples were chosen from the assigned reading; what examples were ignored; what use was made of the examples; what counterexamples there might be; where and how the writer might bring in examples not prefigured in the assigned text.

The second "writing lesson" is represented in the readings themselves. Because we have chosen readings that are about writing, they offer lessons to writers, some directly and some indirectly. And the assignments ask students to consider the readings as having immediate import on their work as writers.

The sequences—how do you write them? How do you use them? Why put so much emphasis on the broad sweep of a course?

These are questions we have tried to address in the introductions to the textbooks and to the sequences. The brief section of the textbook just before the sequences begin ("Working with the Assignment Sequences," pp. 465–68) explains the idea of a sequence to students. You might want to ask your students to read this before they begin their work, perhaps at the same time as you ask them to read the introduction. Many teachers have found both these introductions to be useful.

Why do we put so much emphasis on the broad sweep of a course? Writers work differently if they are working on single, discrete weekly exercises than if they are working on longer, academic projects. We think of our course as a project course; and we want our students, as writers, to see and pace their work for the long haul. This requirement is not just a matter of endurance, although endurance counts. Students need to learn that *the* subjects that matter aren't quickly exhausted, that the best ideas come when you think there is nothing else to say, that it is important to turn from the security of newfound conclusions to consider alternative points of view. Students also learn to imagine drafts and revisions differently when they are in service of a longer project. In particular, they learn to imagine revision as a way of opening up an issue rather than finishing it, closing it down, and getting it out of the way. We want to teach our students to imagine intellectual life differently than they have imagined it before (with the pieces they read and the pieces they write standing alone, as single exercises), and we want them to imagine reading and writing as they serve in the long term and not just the short.

The best way to work with the sequences is to imagine that they suggest the possibilities for a project students can begin to believe in and imagine as their own. This approach requires flexibility. We have never taught a sequence, whether in the textbook or not, without making changes along the way. We go into a course with a sense of how to put together some interesting readings, readings that speak back and forth to one another in productive ways, readings that we feel we can use to enable students to think about reading and writing. Once we are into that course, however, and get a chance to watch how our students are reading and working with our assignments, we begin to make revisions. Sometimes, when students are not doing what we want, we revise to get better control of the class; sometimes, when students are doing productive work we hadn't imagined them doing, we revise to respond to directions they have taken.

You need to be flexible, to adjust assignments and readings so that they make sense to you and your students as the semester goes along. In this sense, you and your students are readers. The sequences won't automatically make sense. There is no guaranteed payoff if you only follow from step to step. They represent a plan and, in almost every case, a course we have taught. But during the course of the semester or quarter, you will need to feel that you and your students have begun to take the sequence over, so that it begins to make your kind of sense.

As mentioned earlier, we also have found it useful to ask students at midterm and at the end of the term to write a "retrospective" assignment. This short essay, in which students stop to reflect on the course and its materials, has a double benefit. It allows us to hear our students' versions of the course they are taking. More important, however, it formalizes our concern that students take an active role in making sense out of the course. We don't want the course to just happen to them; we want them to see it as something they can use to frame and enable their work in school.

The question of how we put the sequences together is a bit harder to answer. This process has changed, actually, since we began to work on *Ways of Reading*. Initially, we would get together with our friends and colleagues to design a course we would teach in the upcoming year. Often we would begin with a single book or essay that had knocked us out over the summer. We would start to gather readings to surround this core text, provide interesting ways of going back to it. In most cases, we would look for readings that would profitably counter the piece we began with.

We continue to use these same principles when we design the sequences for *Ways of Reading*. We collect pieces we would like to teach; we then find other pieces suggested by those we have collected. And then we think about teachable combinations. The biggest difference now is that we will have three or four courses going in a semester, Tony teaching one, Dave another, some of our students teaching the third and fourth.

So we gather materials that we think can be profitably read together. A good example is the "Arts of the Contact Zone" sequence. We loved the Pratt essay, and Pratt's work generally, and found pieces that could be used to put her argument to the test. In a sense, we looked for essays that could stand as alternatives to the Guaman Poma example Pratt employs. When we wrote the assignments, we wanted them to represent a stage to various uses of Pratt's texts; we wanted students to work closely with Pratt's text, to apply the metaphor of the "contact zone" to local scenes, and to use her interpretive scheme to look at alternative examples of writing that could be said to be produced by the contact zone.

The general pattern in most of the sequences takes students into one of the readings (asking them to work closely with the text and to produce a "close reading"). Then students are asked to apply and test a set of terms (and, sometimes, an argument) by turning to alternative examples. Finally, students are asked to step back from what they have done to take a position of their own, adding their voice to the conversation among authors, making space in their essays where they speak and speak at length.

We like to think of the sequences as projects and not as arguments. We would be disappointed, for example, if people saw the sequence "The Aims of Education" as an argument we are making about American education. It would be wrong, to our minds, to work through the sequence asking what point it makes or what the correct final position might be. We would hate students to be trying to guess *our* version of the "right" answer to the implied question, "What are the appropriate aims of education?" The sequence is offered not as an argument but as a way of raising questions about education. Now these selections are not neutral or value-free, of course, but we have tried to offer a variety of positions. The questions have their own thrust and direction. But we have written many questions; and we try to turn the issues back to students and to their understanding (in the case of their sequence) of their own participation in the history and culture of schooling. The argument of the textbook is that readers can read both generously and critically and that such reading does not happen naturally but rather requires work, labor. The argument extends to the sequences. To our minds they would be misread if used as a series of fixed steps or seen as representing an argument students are bound to reproduce.

How do you know your class is going well? What are the signs that a class is working?

It sounds corny to say it, but we can feel it when a particular class works well, or when class meetings have gone well. When they do, it almost always means that students feel comfortable—they talk about the examples of writing before them, and they get involved responding to one another and commenting on one another's remarks. We invariably conduct our classes around two or three examples of students' writing, and we always work from examples that demonstrate students' successes or admirable struggles with particular "moves" in their writing. We tend to focus on what we call "moves" that occur in students' writing; they depend, of course, on the particular assignment and the student work, but generally we look at papers to see how closely students are reading, speculating about, or interpreting sentences and passages from their readings. We also look at how students use others' sentences and language in their writings, and we pay attention to how students create and use such things as summary statements and paraphrases. And, of course, we look for the "moves" that students make when they revise passages in their papers or whole papers. Such examples of typical "moves" in student writing represent the kinds of student work that we would bring into class for discussion, given, of course, our particular agenda for the class and for the assignment at hand. Our classes generally run for ninety minutes twice a week, and this allows us enough time to work with two or three student papers or excerpts from papers during each meeting. We focus the discussions with our own questions, even though we invite students to respond and ask questions, because we don't want students' comments to be haphazard. We want them to discuss the work in front of them for the reasons that we've brought it into class. We might, for example, bring into class excerpts from two students' papers that show the students interpreting particular passages from a text. We might ask the class then to discuss these excerpts by first restating what each student seems to be saying that the text says. How, in other words, does each student author read his or her passage? We might, then, after that initial discussion, ask the class to comment on these readings. At this point, the class would be working well if the students were involved, if they were talking and speculating and commenting and drawing conclusions about the excerpts from the students' papers in front of them. And the discussion would seem truly accomplished if students were speaking substantively about particular sentences in the work before them rather than talking in general, abstract terms ("I think she makes her point well," "He has a lot of evidence to back up his point") about why a student's paragraph seems good or strong. These discussions are going well, of course, when students are involved, participating, but it takes more than enthusiasm for a class to work well. Students have to be doing the detailed work of writers, and that means that they have to be commenting on sentences and chunks of prose in the examples of writing before them, whether those examples be from students' papers or from the essays or stories they are reading and writing about. This is the "local," important work of talking about writing, and when students do it in class discussions, we feel good.

What do you do about sentence errors?

We approach sentence errors in a number of ways. First, we make distinctions between "accidental errors" that students can and do catch and fix when they proofread carefully and "error patterns" that students regularly make and don't notice, or notice but don't know how to fix. We have a routine for dealing with both kinds of errors that involves individual work with students' papers and whole-class instruction. The key, at least for us, to working on sentence errors has to do with the atmosphere and rhythm of the class. We want to encourage students to experiment with sentences, and we want them to proofread. Both of these tasks can be accomplished without heavy-handed attention, as a part of the regular routine of the class. Five or fifteen minutes here and there throughout the semester seems much more effective than large blocks of time or whole days of instruction given over to sentences and errors.

Before we describe what we do in class, we would like to make a few comments about how we encourage our students to experiment with complex sentences. Generally, we do this in two ways. First, we like to bring interesting sentences to students' attention. Sometimes this exercise is as casual as reading sentences aloud in class and commenting on why they are interesting or compelling, and other times we might put sentences on the chalkboard and study them more closely for the work that's taking place in them. We use examples from the readings and from students' writing for this kind of casual attention drawing. Occasionally, we might conduct a whole class lesson on a particular kind of sentence (e.g., those that use conjunctions to show causal relationships) or sentence construction (e.g., complex, related sentences joined by a semicolon). Here again, we work from examples in the readings and from students' writing. Tony, for instance, regularly asks his students to use embeddings and appositives to qualify and specify subjects and nouns in sentences. He sees this kind of instruction as a way of helping students understand how qualifications that modify nouns and subjects can help wring vagueness and generality out of sentences. When we do this kind of instruction and attention drawing, we feel it's important for students to realize that they'll make errors as they try kinds of sentences they aren't yet familiar with. Such experimentation can give writers another dimension or plane to work on, but they need to feel there's room for it, and this feeling depends a great deal on how we establish the work of the class when it comes to editing and errors.

From the start of the semester, we ask students to buy and use a writer's handbook. They must proofread their papers, including their drafts. We want them to get into the habit of using a handbook and of proofreading as a regular part of writing. Sometimes we ask them to proofread using red pencils so that we can see which errors they catch and which they don't, in other words, those that are accidental and those that might indicate regular error patterns. If students are proofreading, catching what we call accidental errors, but still having problems identifying or correcting recurring errors, then we step in and help. Usually, for students struggling with errors that repeat from one paper to the next, we'll place a check mark in the margin next to the lines where errors occur. We explain to students that when they get their papers back with these check marks, they should find and fix the errors by turning to their handbooks, getting help from friends, and by going to the English Department's Writing Workshop for help. As part of this work, we ask the students who have persistent errors in their sentences individually to keep logs or error journals where they record their errors, explanations of why they made them, and then the corrected sentences. We seldom ask whole classes to do this kind of error journal, but we have. It's important to conduct this kind of error work individually, as a part of the rhythm of the class, and not to make a big deal of it. If students are proofreading and working to correct their errors, we feel that we can show them how to help themselves.

At times, when it seems appropriate, we conduct whole-class lessons, using students' sentences and paragraphs as examples, on the conventions of punctuation and the more common usage errors we see in our students' writing (e.g., noun-verb agreements, noun-pronoun agreements). We don't belabor this kind of instruction, which we do on the chalkboard as graphically as possible, using circles around phrases and clauses and boxes around the punctuation as part of a visual demonstration of how commas, for example, or semicolons or colons work in sentences. Of course, students can always turn to their handbooks for additional help, but we don't assign exercises. When we conduct whole-class instruction like this, we always center it on discussions and demonstrations involving students' work. We work toward establishing an atmosphere in which students get a feel for sentences as plastic and malleable, as language that can be shaped and formed with the help of a few conventions and procedures.

What about the research paper?

Our students regularly write assignments and work on projects that ask them to read various kinds of texts closely, to study texts for particular purposes, and to work across texts. These ways of reading and studying prepare them for the intellectual work of academic research and writing, which historians, scientists, anthropologists, engineers, and market researchers, among others, must be able to do. As part of their work on these assignments and projects, they learn to use quotations and paraphrases; they learn, that is, to use the writings of others in their research. A number of the instructors who use our book ask their students to cite references and document sources in their papers in one of the commonly used styles (that is, MLA, APA) as yet another way of preparing them for academic research.

We don't, however, teach what might be called the traditional research paper in which students compile research on a subject or an issue, although many of our assignments ask students to conduct library research, observations, and interviews. Assignments, for example, for Mary Louise Pratt's selection, offer students opportunities to do both observations and interviews as part of their work on individual texts and larger projects involving multiple texts.

WAYS OF READING AS PART OF A TA/TF TRAINING PROGRAM

TA/TF Training and *Ways of Reading*

The readings and assignments (and assignment sequences) in *Ways of Reading* have served for many years as the central documents in the TA/TF training program at the University of Pittsburgh. Perhaps it would be useful to begin by briefly describing that program and its history. (See also the essay by our colleagues, Paul Kameen and Mariolina Salvatori, "The Teaching of Teaching: Theoretical Reflections," in *Reader*, Spring/Fall 1995, pp. 103–25.)

At Pittsburgh, all new Teaching Assistants (TAs) and Teaching Fellows (TFs) teach a common set of materials in the first year. It is called the "staff course." The faculty design a new course each year, a sequence of assignments engaging students with a long-term writing project organized through a set of readings. We write a new course each year not only to finesse the plagiarism problem but also as a way of paying attention and remaining closely involved with this area of the curriculum.

The new TAs/TFs, as is the case with any large program, bring a wide variety of preparation and professional goals to their first year of teaching at Pitt. They are MA, MFA, and PhD students; some are teaching for the first time; some bring with them considerable experience. Some plan for careers in colleges and universities, and so see their teaching as essential to their professional preparation; but this is not the case with all, particularly with the MFA students, many of whom go on to work outside the academy. All new TAs/TFs are sent materials over the summer (including the readings and assignment sequence); there is a brief orientation before classes begin in August. This is largely a welcome session, an introduction to the faculty, the office staff, and the facilities in support of instruction. It serves also as an introduction to policies and procedures, and, particularly for the new teachers, it provides a way of imagining the first week or two of classes. We often have previous years' TAs/TFs lead sessions and give papers. (Some of these are collected in *Resources for Teaching Ways of Reading*.)

During the first semester, the work of the first-year staff is supported by a Teaching Seminar (more on this later) and by a committee charged to run staff meetings, to provide one-on-one support, and to organize classroom observations (called CEAT, or the Committee on the Evaluation and Advancement of Teaching). The committee is made up of advanced graduate students and faculty. Ideally, there is close communication between the faculty running the Teaching Seminar and CEAT.

The Teaching Seminar began in 1974 and has been a regular part of the program ever since. Most members of the composition faculty have taught it; it is often team taught, sometimes with a member of the literature or writing faculty. CEAT was developed in the 1980s in order to increase the opportunities for making teaching visible and for providing occasions for the staff to talk together about their work.

Perhaps the most distinctive feature of this program is the insistence that all new TAs/ TFs teach a common, core set of materials, no matter their prior training. After the first year, graduate students have much more freedom to develop their own courses (and to teach courses in other programs: film, literature, creative writing); it is often the case that they will make some revisions to the core course in preparation for the second semester of the first year (revising the core either individually or as a group). In the first year, however, we have two concerns: that our graduate students work with a course that represents our common practice and history as a faculty, and that all students in the first year have a common point of reference as they work to develop ways to talk about (and to think about) teaching.

We feel that there is something distinctive about composition at the University of Pittsburgh. While the course changes from year to year, and changes as it is designed by different members of the faculty, there are features and concerns that represent both a tradition of teaching and our determination to work together as a collective: the assignment sequences, the sets of readings, an emphasis on revision, a desire to represent students as intellectuals, a respect for difficulty. The core course also provides a common point of reference for the Teaching Seminar and the staff meetings (and the informal conversations in the hallways and offices) throughout the year.

We have learned that there is much to be gained with discussions of teaching that are grounded in reference to common (and therefore specific) readings, assignments, materials, and practices. The discussions, then, are not about general topics ("teaching revision") but about what specific, representative students are doing in the first papers they are writing on John Edgar Wideman's "Our Time," about what they have written, and how and why they might reread and revise. Because all are working with the same assignments, the staff can trade student papers, looking for examples that can help to open up discussion and focus attention on a particular problem. TAs/TFs and faculty can (and will) argue and take different positions on these papers and what they represent, leading to different next steps, and the results of those next steps, too, can be presented and shared. The approaches to particular pedagogical problems will differ, as they must, but everyone's teaching is shaped by their participation in a common project and in relation to the rest of the staff. A common set of materials enables teachers, as Bill Coles used to say, to put their cards on the table. It is a way of making teaching visible. And it is a way of enabling individual teachers to define themselves in relation to a faculty and a program, its ideas and history.

The Teaching Seminar

The Teaching Seminar is a regular, full, three-credit graduate seminar. It meets during the fall semester. It is one of the distinctive features of our graduate program and has a long and colorful history.

From the beginning, the seminar was designed to place the freshman course and its materials (materials in *Ways of Reading*, for example) in relation to the problems central to

English studies as represented in the work graduate students would be doing in other graduate courses. The Teaching Seminar has never, then, served as an "Introduction to Composition Studies." It does not survey approaches to the freshman course, theories of composition, or major books and figures in the field. There are other courses to do that work and to do it for graduate students who elect advanced work in composition.

The Teaching Seminar, rather, is organized around three sets of texts: the readings in the freshman course (selections in *Ways of Reading*, for example), student papers, and a selection of books and articles from the professional literature designed to focus theoretical attention on fundamental problems of language, writing, reading, and reception. It is to our advantage to choose readings likely to be present and important to the graduate students as they prepare for conferences and for other courses. This part of the reading list, then, looks similar to what you would expect in an "Introduction to Graduate Studies" or any introduction to theory and method. The seminar gives the graduate students a chance to work through these materials slowly and in relation (often surprising relation) to the "everyday" concerns of the first-year writing class.

In a year that we are teaching the selections by Wideman, Pratt, Griffin, and Foucault (for example), the Teaching Seminar would organize the students' work in the following ways.

1. The seminar would be the place to work on these as primary texts (and for some of the students, this will be the first time). As in any graduate seminar, this is a matter of discussion, writing, research, and group presentation. The seminar, however, asks students always to think about these texts as they might serve writers and writing courses. What do you need to know to prepare writers to make the best use of these texts? What does it mean to read these texts as a writer? What writing lessons do they contain? As a result, the work on Foucault or Wideman is very different than it would be for another graduate seminar.

2. There is work on the texts as texts. There is also work on the texts as they are read and understood by our students. Student papers, then, are some of the central materials for the Teaching Seminar. How might we understand the ways of reading Wideman, Pratt, Griffin, or Foucault as reading is represented in sample student papers drawn from the course, the course everyone is teaching (including the faculty member teaching the Teaching Seminar)? And, from those student papers, how might we best understand revision—the next step, whether that next step be a class discussion of one or two sample papers, or directions for rereading and revision? We have long felt that the central skill for a writing teacher is knowing how to read student writing. Student writing is not a genre we are prepared to read or to value. Learning to read student writing has immediate and practical consequences, providing a context for evaluation or for marginal, editorial commentary, for example; but it is also crucial for understanding the first-year writing course as a course. First-year writing not only names a spot in the curriculum; it names a genre, a subject position, a way of reading and writing. You can't teach student writing unless you have an informed and determined sense of what student writing is and what it is good for. And, of course, Wideman, Pratt, Griffin, and Foucault provide powerful tools to think about the writing produced by the students in the course. The readings can be turned to, used as tools to examine the work of students as writers. Wideman provides a powerful way for thinking about "beginnings" or for thinking about who speaks in an essay and how and why. Wideman writes wonderful sentences, sentences that provide a way of talking

about sentences. Pratt provides terms for analysis, terms like "rhetoric of sincerity," and for imagining the position and practice of the student writer. Griffin provides a powerful counterexample for the classroom pieties about unity, order, and coherence. Foucault we have used often to think about the paragraph and about examples.

3. And, finally, there are the "outside" readings, critical and theoretical texts drawn from the standard reading lists in graduate education in English. They are brought into the mix in order to demonstrate that the work on language, literature, literacy, and culture is also always about writing and schooling, about the work of students in any given term in a first-year writing class as they try to represent themselves and others, to represent knowledge, tradition, and authority. We have taught, for example, Gates, Spivak, Said, Foucault, Butler, Bove, Williams (Patricia and Raymond), Fish, Clifford and Marcus, Spillers, Gallop, and Tompkins. Their work (and that of others) becomes surprisingly appropriate to the course. The specific selections are suggested by the readings from *Ways of Reading* and by whatever is pressing and in the air at a given moment.

In this sense, the seminar is an argument that writing is writing and that student writing can be read into the theoretical literature; it is also an argument that pedagogy is a theoretical concern and can be well served by books and projects that don't specifically name the classroom as their topic. We always also bring in a work from the field of composition. Again, the seminar is not an "Introduction to Composition Studies"; composition, however, has much to offer our discussions. We want to make that clear, while also making clear that composition doesn't have to stand alone. And we have been concerned to bring in material from creative writing and its representations of writing, the problems of writing, and the process of learning to write.

Ways of Reading

Ways of Reading argues for the connection between students' work and some of the most interesting writing of our time. This is, finally, how it serves a TA/TF training program; it argues that the first-year writing course is connected to the general concerns of English studies and its graduate students. The textbook provides the occasion for graduate students to think about teaching and about student writing in relation to some of the key figures and arguments in their field. For some of our students, the textbook has been a safe space to think for the first time about Foucault and/or the death of the author and what these arguments might say to a young scholar trying to find a way of thinking about writing, teaching, and a career. For others, it has been the surprising occasion to think from theory into practice, not only the practice of teaching but writing practice as well, including their own.

When we hear from graduate students, we tend to hear that they appreciate the book for providing a course that they can take seriously (and that will allow them to take their students seriously). We also hear, however, that it has made a difference to their own writing. It seems an odd thing to say, but advanced students in English, including MA and PhD students, have a very limited sense of what they can and can't do as writers. The "experimental" assignments in *Ways of Reading* have provided the invitation to write like Griffin or Wideman or Anzaldúa—not just about them. And the MFA students are given a sense of the power and range of the essay (and of academic writing) beyond what they had learned to expect, including within the domain of "creative nonfiction."

TOOLKIT

Some Strategies for Working with *Ways of Reading*

Writing about Teaching. Advice often carries unwarranted baggage. Since what follows offers advice on designing and teaching a course in composition, I (Tony) would like to frame it with a caveat. This is one person's thinking about teaching, but it does emanate from many years of teaching and thinking about teaching. Experience matters, but only if it is inscribed in a stance on teaching that has been theorized and thought about, not simply enacted over and over. That theory is situated in *Ways of Reading* (and in Bartholomae and Petrosky, *Facts, Artifacts, and Counterfacts* [Boynton/Cook, 1986]) as it presents a pedagogy through the kinds of selections it brings before students for extended work and the teaching apparatus that it uses to engage them in that work. So while what follows occupies the pedagogical space formed by *Ways of Reading*, it also offers a set of pedagogical intentions and "moves" derived from teaching composition with *Ways of Reading* for many years. This is, then, my pass at codifying, generally and in certain particulars, the kinds of work students do in my classes when they prepare to read and write, work in pairs and groups, study their own writing, and learn to imitate sentences and use conventions. My intention is to offer some of these classroom moves, which you should feel free to use and adapt in the context of your own pedagogy.

Designing a Course

Before I say anything about course design, it is important to acknowledge that even the best course design shifts, changes, and unravels over a semester, if only because it has to respond to what actually happens in a class with students. There are the times when assignments fall flat, when readings or student writings take longer or diverge in unexpected, perhaps productive directions (or perhaps not), and when the work of the class simply takes more or less time than anticipated. With that said, students and teachers need to begin a semester with a carefully designed course.

Beginning to design a course, though, as most of us know, isn't a matter of moving from a reading to a writing assignment to the next reading assignment and so on. I begin by imagining a project that might engage me as much as it might engage students. In other words, make sure that the course is going to engage you yourself; your enthusiasm (or lack thereof) will be evident. There are several ways to approach course design. I switch among them when designing different courses, often to tap into my own particular interests at the time. Here are several ways to start.

Start with a Sequence. Often, I'll proceed by reading through the assignment sequences in *Ways of Reading*, trying to locate my interest as well as imagining what might be compelling to my students. I may use a sequence as published, or I may take a chunk of a sequence and play with it by altering it or by adding to it. You should feel free to alter or combine parts of sequences as you see fit.

Start with a Theme. Other times, I'll have a clearer sense of a nominal theme, such as "Autobiographical Explorations," than of the readings or the project, so I might imagine that I'd like my students to study autobiography and their relation to the past, for example. I might then begin designing a sequence of readings that would allow students to read autobiography as both example and occasion for critique or study and to write autobiography as an occasion for explorations into its workings as a genre and into the ways it shapes thinking about the past. For me, then, it is a matter of beginning by imagining a course where students write about something, critique it, and write in imitation of it. So if the subject is autobiography, they write about particular autobiographies, they critique these, and they write their own autobiographies. All of this work is on the table for study and critique.

Start with a Set of Key Readings. To start this way, I begin by imagining a framing reading selection—a text used as a lens through which later texts are read. Lately, this has meant work with documentary writing that poses questions about nonfiction, fiction, and poetry. Over the past couple of years, this has been dramatically different at different times. A few semesters ago, the course frame was set by short stories, one by Flannery O'Connor and the others by Lydia Davis. The project that I had in mind by juxtaposing these had to do with the differences in the ways these stories imagine reality and what those differences mean for how they're written—and for how students imagine reality, especially the realities they re-create from their pasts. From there, I wanted to open up a discussion about fiction and nonfiction, including the ways authors re-create the past, so we moved to Robert Coles's essay "The Tradition: Fact and Fiction" (in an earlier edition of *Ways of Reading*).

More recently, my course design began with the Coles essay to open up the conversation on documentary writing; then it complicated his notions by turning to John Wideman's discussion of doing documentary work on his brother Robbie in "Our Time." After these readings, and my students' writings about them, we moved to their writing documentary work of their own as a way to test the claims made by Coles and Wideman. From there, we studied fiction and nonfiction by returning to both of these essays in light of two short stories and their own writing of a fiction piece. Finally, we read "Our Secret" by Susan Griffin as a way of complicating the distinctions between fiction and nonfiction, and the ways writers re-create the past, in a nonfiction work.

There are multiple ways to begin and proceed but, at the same time, I follow my own set of predilections.

The Syllabus. Once my course is charted, I produce a lengthy syllabus (four to six single-spaced pages) for students in which I present detailed explanations of the reading selections, the writings students will be doing, and the way the course will be conducted.

I tell them why I think the work we'll do is important, and I tell them what I think they'll learn by doing this work. Here are some areas I cover:

- *Keeping a Notebook.* In the syllabus, I ask students to keep a notebook because they'll want to remember points brought up in discussions, and there will also be technical reviews of such things as punctuation conventions that I expect them to study and for which they will be held accountable.

- *Using Portfolios.* I have never taught a composition course in which I put grades on individual papers, so I explain portfolio grading to students in the syllabus.

- *Conferences.* I make it clear that I plan to meet with each student in an individual conference twice during the semester—once midway and the other time at the end of the semester—to discuss work and possible grades for all the work done so far.

All of this said, when we take thirty minutes of the first class meeting to read and discuss the syllabus, I'm quick to assure them that the plan of readings and writings outlined in the syllabus will undoubtedly change, so they shouldn't be concerned about that, and that change will be the result of the direction the work takes.

Classroom Pedagogical Moves

You'll want to develop a set of pedagogical moves that can be used at different moments in a particular class, as variations on a theme, and at different times during the semester. Here are some suggestions.

Pair Work. Pair work is my favored way of proceeding, although we do use groups of three or four after the midpoint of the semester, when students are accustomed to one another and the intellectual work of the class. I often assign pair work on the "Questions for a Second Reading," for preparations for a whole-group discussion, and for work on students' own papers. I keep the work on their papers sharply focused. We are always working on a particular intellectual move—creating explanations of "points" or interpretations or "constructions"; contextualizing ideas or characters; summarizing, paraphrasing, or quoting others' writings; explaining quoted material; connecting ideas across two or three reading selections; studying students' interpretations for similarities and differences; and so on. By keeping their work focused, and by always presenting them with written directions or assignments, even for in-class work, we make a ground to which we can refer before work begins and a written track record of the work they were asked to do over the semester (my students keep all their handouts in their sectioned and tabbed portfolio binders along with all their notes, drafts, and so on).

In-Class Writing. Another pedagogical move involves asking students—working alone—to take out a sheet of paper and write or rewrite in class. Five minutes of in-class writing offers the opportunity for students to say again, for themselves, what they have done in pairs or in a whole-class discussion, taking the assignment for the pair or the discussion as the topic for the quick writing. They often rewrite paragraphs from their own papers. I might ask them, for example, to go back to a paragraph in their papers where they have quoted a passage from a reading selection. If we were working on introducing or explaining quotations, I would ask them to rewrite the paragraph taking into consideration the work we just did in class on those particular moves. Most likely I'd follow up their five or ten minutes of writing with a request for volunteers to read their "before and after" versions. If we had time, we might open these up to discussion, but it's difficult to do, especially with longer rewrites, so we most often simply read the before-and-after versions so that everyone gets a sense of what others have done with the work we did as a whole class or in pairs. It is also good to let them see again and again the generative nature of writing because they don't have time to plan much or make outlines, so they get to see what they're capable of producing on the spot. Quick-writing assignments are also useful summary pieces to help students re-form a class discussion in their own words, especially if it has been a particularly important discussion or one that developed complex threads or complicated notions.

Asking students to read and comment on before-and-after papers can be a useful pedagogical move, especially if the papers demonstrate compelling revisions, yet even if they present only minimal changes, the papers still offer an occasion for a potentially useful teaching moment, one grounded in a discussion of both what the minimal changes mean for the work (including what those revisions do to the paper—for better or worse) and what others might suggest as further revisions. One of the most productive uses of before-and-after papers ties them to in-class on-the-spot writing, writing in which students enact a strategy or revision based on class discussion and examples. Often this kind of work can happen in five to ten minutes of students' writing a new version of a paragraph or moment in their papers.

A Variety of Moves. Keep this in mind when thinking about these suggestions for pedagogical moves: students engage with difference. Similarity quickly becomes routine from which it is relatively easy to disengage. This view has led me to think of classes as compositions, somewhat like musical scores, so while I see each as a whole with particular directions, each also seems to me to require variation. This means that I deliberately design each class so that students do a variety of work. For instance:

- We might begin a class with a five-minute review of the conventions for punctuating quoted material followed by students' rereading papers they are about to hand in for the use of these particular conventions. That would take ten to fifteen minutes.

- I might follow that with thirty minutes' work on selections from student writing. This thirty minutes would focus on student critiques of two or three passages from their essays. Most likely I'd ask them to work in assigned pairs, and I would have the assignment ready for them written out on a sheet of paper, so that they all have the same set of directions before them. We'd take three to five minutes to review the assignment before they move into their assigned pairs.

- The class could conclude with a report by the pairs to the group. We might reconvene in a discussion circle, or students might simply report from wherever they're sitting. I track the reports with notes on the board, and I ask them to take notes on the reports and on my notes. If there is time, I might ask everyone to take out a sheet of paper and write a one-paragraph response to the task at hand by writing about one of the examples of student writing that the pairs critiqued.

- Other times, I might skip the pair work and ask students to review the examples of students' writing, take out a sheet of paper, and write a critique.

- We might then follow that with a discussion drawn from their critiques.

- Or I might ask three or four students to read their critiques aloud and take their work as the entry point for a group discussion.

- For other classes, I might begin the class directly with the assigned pairs and save the editing work until the end of class or place it at the midpoint.

Teaching Grammar. I regularly teach grammatical conventions, drawing my focus from the errors I see in the students' writing in that class, so every class involves some sort of work for five to fifteen minutes on conventions of language usage. So that this has weight in our work, students know ahead of time from my constant explanations that they are accountable for editing their papers for all of the conventions we cover in class. This is one of the reasons I ask them to keep notebooks, which I regularly, informally check as they're working in pairs or alone during class time. (See the section on sentences and conventions, on page 37, for more on this topic.)

Review and Practice. Yet another move would be brief reviews of conventions (see below), followed by students' practicing what they have reviewed in their own papers (most often ones they are about to hand in). The review without the practice doesn't carry much weight. The move without accountability doesn't, either, yet it's not worth the frustration to be heavy-handed and require absolute accountability. I think of it as a sort of loose accountability; I continually—but gently and humorously—nag them.

Preparing to Read and Write

When David and I talk about our teaching from *Ways of Reading*, people always ask how we handle the sequence of reading, discussion, and writing. Generally, we turn to a discussion of the readings only after students have had opportunities to write about them, although both of us often turn students to "Questions for a Second Reading" to prepare them for a writing assignment. As I mentioned above, I frequently assign students to pairs for fifteen or twenty minutes of discussion and note-taking focused on a "Question for a Second Reading." When my students prepare to discuss a selection, after they have written about it, I give them the discussion question in writing and ask them to take ten minutes to review the reading selection and to take notes with references to particular pages and moments in the text from which they can speak. I also ask them to take notes on the discussion. Often my students will take a first pass at the question on their own as a homework assignment, and lately, I have been asking students to work in assigned pairs as study groups outside class. In these study groups, they can do a great deal of preparatory work, and if they are asked to come to class with notes on this work, they can review these before any whole-class discussion.

Give Written Assignments. Regardless of the kinds of work students might be asked to do—in pairs, in groups, as individuals, in study groups, in whole-class discussions—they must have the assignment or directions in front of them in writing, and time must be given to them in class to demonstrate their understanding of the assignments and to ask questions. So I always give students reading, writing, and discussion assignments or directions in writing. Generally, my students have told me that they appreciate the opportunity to work on discussion and writing assignments in pairs either before going on to work alone or before a larger class discussion.

Becoming Familiar. In the first month, students need time and repetition to become familiar with the work of our readings and discussions and their writing. Using assigned pairs to introduce them to challenging work—such as "Questions for a Second Reading" or critiques of the explanations of particular points or interpretations in their peers' writing—gives them a more comfortable, cooperative ground from which to enter the almost always unfamiliar work they are being asked to do. Assigning students to pairs is guesswork at first, but as we get to know one another, it becomes easier to rotate students so that by the end of the semester everyone has worked in a pair with everyone else.

Group Work

As I observe novice teachers using groups of all sorts in their classes, I am usually struck by how much they ask students to accomplish (generally far too much) and how unfocused their requests for work are. Over the years, I've learned that students in groups handle one or two tasks best and that these tasks should be presented to them in paragraph-long assignments or sets of directions that allow them to see the focus of the work and that also briefly explain why they are being asked to do it. The same guidelines are enormously helpful for conducting whole-group discussions of reading selections and students' papers. It is important, I think, to keep the discussion focused on one or two questions and to present the questions in writing with brief explanations of their relation to the work at hand to everyone.

The Instructor's Role. My role in a whole-class discussion is generally to listen carefully, take notes, ask follow-up questions for clarification and substantiation, and help the students see the connections (so that they can comment on them) among their remarks. My tendency is to lay back in these discussions, to pose questions rather than respond to them. I seldom call on people and often explain that it is their responsibility to enter discussions and to learn how to do that. If I call on them, then they expect me to do so regularly, and it is an easy way for them to sidestep their responsibility to learn such strategies. Toward the end of the semester, once students have established a sense of themselves and feel confident in their abilities, I step into discussions, often taking a different point of view on a question, to complicate matters or to open up another way into a critique. I also do this when we discuss students' papers.

Pairs versus Groups. It takes practice to be able to work well with a group of people on questions of reading and writing. For this reason, I have begun to ask students to first work in pairs. I assign pair work to be sure that people have opportunities to work with different people, and I assign it when I think a particular problem requires a particular mix of students. There is no way that I know of to codify this; it seems to me that this method is a response to the moment and to a particular class. I do keep records, though, noting who has worked with whom, so that I can be careful about not creating the same pairs again and again. After the first meeting, once my students are oriented to their work, we begin immediately, and with almost every class meeting, to work in pairs for anywhere from ten to thirty minutes.

Larger groups of three or four students working together pose different problems. It is more challenging to place students in these larger groups, and if left to their own devices, they will gravitate toward those they know. For these reasons, my classes work in these larger groups only after they have worked together in pairs for at least a month. This gives me time to get to know them and their work habits, and it gives them time to grow accustomed to working closely and quickly with others.

My students, as I said earlier, often take the "Questions for a Second Reading" as their focus in their pair and group work. At other times I'll give them a question that follows from our class discussions of a particular selection, and I've learned that at most they can handle two or three well-focused, significant questions in thirty minutes. And again, they can generally handle no more than two student papers in the same amount of time, especially if they are being asked to both critique and suggest specific revisions to the pieces. In this vein, my students have found it very helpful to both study and practice particular intellectual moves such as constructing explanations for points they want to make or suggesting interpretations of reading selections. When they study such things in the works of professional writers, the pair work gives them opportunities to tell each other how they understand the work and to then create their own examples that they can share with the class. The same sort of work can be asked of them when they critique and interpret each other's papers. Lately, I've taken to asking them, in pairs, to locate moments in their papers that I have duplicated for everyone that strike them as admirable or compelling and, using their notes, to say why. And, of course, they share these with the class in the final fifteen minutes of our meeting.

Rewriting with Partners. My students like to rewrite moments in their papers with partners, so we use pairs for this as well. If, for example, we have been working as a class on crafting compelling explanations of interpretations, perhaps with sets of overheads from their papers and from passages in the selections we are reading, then I might ask them to turn to specific moments in their papers and to rewrite them along the lines of what we just went over. They can do this in pairs, and after they have had twenty or thirty minutes to work, they can read their before-and-after versions to the whole class without comments from others so that everyone gets to hear as many as possible. Generally, I like to follow up such class work by duplicating some of the before-and-after passages to discuss as a whole class at the next class meeting, so I'll begin the following class this way.

Developing Key Terms. It is important to me as well as to my students that the language of reading and writing, the language of the profession, be available to them, so that they can use it to name and explain the work they're doing. And it's not that we sit around memorizing terms such as "contextualizing a reading" or "constructing the past" or "locating a position," because we do not. But I do use the language of the profession in class as it is appropriate, and I expect them to as well, if only because it places all of us in a similar discourse.

Working with Multiple Selections. If students are working on "Making Connections" questions or working in some way with their writings on one selection to read or test another selection's ideas or methods, it seems obvious that they'll need to reread both selections and will need to do some preliminary work with the selection just being introduced to them. I generally ask students to respond to the second-reading questions for this kind of work, and I almost always use assigned pairs for this, followed by a whole-class discussion drawn from that pair work.

Incorporating Quotations. My students will almost always do this kind of spontaneous writing when they are learning how to use others' language, including quotations, in their papers. Generally, they don't have much experience with this, so they simply drop quotations or paraphrases into papers where they imagine that they fit or add to an argument by presenting information or by giving authority to something they have written. We take time out to learn how to use others' writing in papers, and this begins with the study of how the professional authors and their peers use others' writing. We discuss examples from both sources, usually nothing longer than a paragraph or two, and almost always examples that they can learn from rather than simply critique as being inadequate. They are presented in the form of duplicated papers or overhead presentations, and we generally follow the pattern of the work itself. That is, we ask, first, Why in this case use others' writing? Then, if some reason is established that seems compelling, we go on to discuss the example in detail by focusing first on how the writing or quotation is introduced by the writer. How does the author prepare his or her text to move into a quotation or paraphrase? I ask them, as out-of-class work, to study this further and to come to class with a list of the kinds of moves and language writers use to introduce quotations in a couple of professional essays so that during the next class, we can share these and I can ask students to write on the board what they found, allowing everyone to take notes on it.

The second thing we focus on is the actual quotation or paraphrase. Is there enough? too much? How might it be edited? Is it punctuated correctly? If we are working with quotations, we review editing with ellipses and brackets, and then we review punctuation conventions that pertain to quotations. This is usually new to most of my students, so we take this as a piece of ongoing work for the semester even though I do hold them accountable for it once they have studied and practiced it.

The third thing we focus on is the way the cited language or paraphrase is explained or linked to the text that surrounds it. Although there is no set way of thinking about these connections, my students usually try to codify the relation of the cited text to their own as one of explanation, example, or authority, so they initially imagine that the cited text stands on its own, is self-evident, or by its inclusion gives their text outside authority or confirmation. Usually, of course, none of these assumptions pan out, and they learn from examples that cited texts almost always have to be explained and conceptually linked to their texts. We practice, then, writing these explanations and conceptual links both before and after the cited text appears in their writing. I usually ask: How do you imagine the cited text plays into, elaborates, supports, or diverges from what you've written around it? Is what you imagined explained so that a reader will get it?

Reporting. As a general rule, when my students work together in pairs or groups, they always have time in that class to report their work to the larger group in an informal discussion about the same questions or topic that occupied the students in their pairs or groups. If this doesn't happen, then the groups quickly lose their focus, energy, and memories, even if they have taken notes as I asked them to, so it seems to me that work in groups generally needs to be brought forward to the class as a whole.

Students' Writing as Examples

One way to think about student writing is to imagine what they read as the examples from which they work. My students come to me with enormously limited repertoires. They most likely will have read no contemporary essays and little fiction. They will have spent their high school careers writing three- and five-paragraph essays that were presented to them as templates for all kinds of writing. Most of the examples that have been put before them were from these kinds of school writing, so they have little experience with academic essays and probably no experience with contemporary essays. It seems to me, then, that they have had enough exposure to poor models, so I take the responsibility to present them with interesting and compelling models of writing from professionals and from their peers. It is in this spirit that I made the decision, as a general rule, not to present my students with examples of poor writing, although this does not mean that I prevent them from studying examples that illustrate writers struggling, perhaps making a mess of things, to write about difficult or complex ideas.

Show Good Writing. By reading only examples that are in some way admirable, students develop a clear sense of themselves as capable writers, as writers who lack experience but who have the intelligence to take on challenging readings and writings. This is enormously important, I think, for students have almost always been positioned as incapable. The relentless insistence on formulaic essays in high school tells them that since they aren't capable of writing on their own, they should follow these simple-minded templates. That means years of negative, demeaning experience to push against in one semester, so the student work that I use as examples always makes it possible for me to say what I admire about the pieces.

A large part of their work with an essay such as "Our Secret" will be their writings about it, so as soon as they have finished their first draft of a writing assignment, generally for the beginning of their second week's study, they will be studying excerpts of their own writings alongside the Griffin essay. I might start, for instance, with a set of beginning paragraphs from two or three students' papers as a way of focusing their work on beginnings—of openings as a way of doing something other than rephrasing the writing assignment, for instance. Or I might take a set of paragraphs from different papers in which students are making claims for the essay's arguments, saying what they think Griffin is trying to convince us about. Or, if we are somewhat farther along into the Griffin piece, we might be studying her use of others' writing, the ways she signals facts from things she imagines, for example, so I would present them with a few paragraphs from their papers in which writers make these distinctions by citing her examples.

Limit the Models. It is important to consider the examples we put before students, especially those taken from their papers. A part of this consideration also has to do with how much writing we ask students to study and comment on in detail. When my students read professional essays such as "Our Secret," they need about a month's worth of classes to get into it in any depth, and that includes a month's worth of work in pairs, writing together and individually, and class discussions of various sorts. That essay has a lot to teach them about using others' writings in one's essay, but it isn't until the third week of work with it that we generally get to a close study of Griffin's methods—some of which allow her to introduce "fiction," what she imagines rather than what she knows, alongside factual information—for citing others' texts. By the fourth week of their study, they are usually using what they know about her methods to write their own Griffin-like essays.

Work with Small Pieces. When working with student writing, we work from paragraphs and moments in their papers and seldom from complete papers. Only by semester's end are my students ready to focus on complete papers of two pages or so in length, and even then, we limit our work to no more than two papers per class meeting, with the entire class given over to a focused study of them in pairs followed by a whole-class report and discussion of their work in pairs. Until then, we work exclusively from excerpts, passages that offer interesting or compelling models even though they still may be incomplete or messy. When we work like this, usually from overheads, my students also have paper copies of the examples on which they can take notes.

Generally, until they have found language for beginning such discussions, I begin by telling them what I think the writer is trying to do and why I think it's an example worth sharing; then I ask for their comments. At about mid-semester, when they have had experience discussing numerous examples from their own papers, I gradually turn over some of these discussions to students and only comment at the end. It's their turn, I tell them—they have done this enough to take responsibility for themselves.

Harness the Power of Imitation. Imitation holds an ambivalent place in writing instruction. Students reach for originality and profundity; at the same time, many instructors cringe when they think of themselves teaching their students to imitate the writing of others. Yet we all imitate, appropriate, and transform others' writing. In the space that language provides us, we apprentice continually to cultural discourses, to what we read, and to the talk in which we immerse ourselves. When we invite students to consciously, carefully imitate the writing of others, we invite them to participate in the performance of language, and this enlarges their repertoires of language use. When we work with the Anzaldúa piece, for instance, we have opportunities to appropriate her terms, to understand that we do so, and to bring that understanding into our class discussions and individual intellectual spaces. We can, for instance, imagine borderlands other than those she writes about, while studying those she does write about, and we can learn to create sentences with her rhythms and syntax for our own purposes while studying how they inflect her purposes.

If one is to take imitation, as I do in my teaching, as a major piece of the work students do, then it is important to present it to them, to explain its significance, and to give them examples of its effects. I like to point to moments in essays in *Ways of Reading* as well where authors take on aspects of other authors' projects. Generally, we take thirty minutes early in the semester, usually during the second week of class, to discuss the place of imitation, along with examples of such things and of the kinds of assignments they'll be asked to take on that pose problems of imitation. And once we have done enough writing, I'll turn their attention to the ways in which they imitate the selections they're studying, including the writings of their peers, by duplicating moments from their papers and conducting a five- or ten-minute lesson in which I'll explain the imitation that I see at work in their writing. With this kind of ongoing discussion, imitation can become a part of the class discourse on reading and writing, and this contributes to my students' willingness to experiment with it, to step out of the discourse with which they feel comfortable and try on others.

Sometimes I will ask my students to read and study a particular selection and to then deliberately write in the genre and spirit of that selection—what I refer to as a form of loose imitation. It also is important to me that students take their own writings as subjects for study and critique, exactly in the ways that they study the work of professional writers, so I duplicate whole papers, often bundling two or three in a packet for the whole class, and I regularly make overheads and copies of compelling paragraphs and moments from students' papers to use as both models of good writing and occasions for students to talk and write about their own writings. I often ask them, for instance, to talk or write about what strikes them as admirable in particular paragraphs, given the focus of the work we have been doing (for example, using others' writing in their essays), and why it strikes them as it does. This sort of work opens up the playing field by showing students that as writers we learn from our work as well as from the work of professional writers.

I discussed above the ways students can imitate Griffin's various methods of mixing factual descriptions gleaned from research with fictional ones that she imagines. Initially, students study her methods to uncover the ways she works, and then they turn to doing the same sorts of things in papers of their own. I mention this again here because it seems important to me to make clear that there are many levels of imitation that we can ask students to engage. They can imitate complete pieces by extending authors' projects or by working in their footsteps. Anzaldúa's essay, for example, gives students a way to think about the borderlands they inhabit and the languages that are particular to those spaces. They can research these and write about them in the spirit of extending Anzaldúa's work. They can step into Griffin's shoes by researching family history, for instance, and writing a Griffin-like essay in which they report on that and its relation to their personal histories and the cultural events of their times, all the while using Griffin's methods by interweaving factual reporting with fictional imaginings of figures and events that they feel compelled to create as a part of their re-creation of this history.

Sentences and Conventions

My students, of course, also often imitate the work of professional writers and their peers. Such assignments ask them to imitate a specific set of sentences or a paragraph that I present to them as a writing assignment. I ask them to try out Griffin's sentences, for example, keeping as close as they can to her syntax and rhythms but using their own subjects for their sentences. When I choose passages for this exercise, I focus on those that are stylistically typical of Griffin and that, from what I've seen of the students' sentences, might give them experience with sentences with which they are unfamiliar. After they have had an opportunity to try their hand at this imitation, which usually takes place at least twice during their work with a particular reading selection, we turn to similar assignments that ask them to imitate passages from the writings of their peers. Generally, we'll work from a paper they are presently writing, and I'll give them an assignment sheet with two or three student sentences to imitate by transforming or editing one of the sentences in their own paper. The emphasis, again, is on their staying as close as they can to the syntax, punctuation, and rhythms of their peers' sentences.

From Imitation to Grammar and Conventions. When we take time to read aloud the before-and-after sentences, we'll stop—when there is time to plan it as part of a class meeting—to talk about the sentences. If it is early in the semester and students are unsure of the language to use to explain how sentences work, then I'll explain one or two of the sentences they were asked to imitate. I'll use the board to write out the sentence, and I'll put boxes around the independent and dependent clauses, marking the subject with an S and the verb with a V, and I'll mark the punctuation conventions as well. The marking of these helps me draw attention to them, and it gives me a way to explain how chunks of sentences come together to form relations with the other sentence chunks. I'll also quickly review the rules for the punctuation conventions I've marked and note them in a shorthand on the board. Once that's done, I ask for volunteers to do the same sort of explanation with a sentence of theirs.

As I said, my students expect to learn sentence conventions, grammar, and usage. The short list of what we generally work on covers all of the punctuation conventions, with particular emphasis on punctuating quotations. It also includes basic sentence boundary work—dependent and independent clauses, appositives, prepositional phrases (particularly those at the beginnings and ends of sentences), subject and pronoun agreement, noun and verb agreement, and dashes and hyphens. It's not that this work proceeds completely from a preset agenda, although in a sense it does, because over the years I've noticed that these happen to be the things with which students continually struggle. And I take a loose approach, knowing that these are learned more by habit than by memorization or admonishment, so as we study each in turn, my students log the class work into their notebooks, and I hold them responsible for editing their papers for the conventions and points of grammar and usage we have formally studied in class. And it's not that we give over a great deal of time in class to this study. Generally, I'll take fifteen or twenty minutes in every other class to deal with these issues (if it seems to me that we actually need to), including taking five or six sentences with errors from their papers, reproducing them for everyone, and asking them to fix the sentences, first working as pairs and then later in the semester working individually.

Here again I take the lead in explaining corrections, setting up a model for them to follow; then, once that is established, I ask for volunteers to explain the errors and the corrections. We do this quickly, and they are responsible for taking notes (which I monitor and check). After a month, it is clear to everyone that this kind of work is required of them, but it is also clear that they'll have plenty of opportunities to find and fix these errors, often during the first five or ten minutes of a class. I hand out warning after warning on papers until about three-quarters of the way into the semester, when I begin handing back papers unread because of errors. I don't take off points for any of that, but at that point I won't read a paper until it is edited and proofread, and if I don't read a paper, then it doesn't go into the portfolio, and the grade, of course, is based on a complete portfolio. It doesn't help anyone to be uptight about sentence-level errors in work, though at the same time, it doesn't help anyone to ignore them, and experience has led me to carefully and deliberately teach and require this kind of work in a somewhat relaxed way. I have more faith, that is, in slow, patterned redundancy and practice than in memorization and strict adherence to rules.

We've included on the following page a helpful handout on comma usage that you may wish to distribute and go over with your students.

The Comma

I will assume that you know about the use of commas in a list (peas, beans, and carrots) or in dates, addresses, and titles. With that in mind:

1. Do *not* assume that there is a relationship between the comma and a pause. There are many occasions to pause when reading or writing sentences. Not all of them indicate a place for a comma.

2. Understand that the comma is related to the structure of the sentence. Its primary function is to provide information to a reader, to let a reader know where she is in relation to the larger structure of the sentence. The use of the comma is determined by the structure of the sentence.

Here is a brief demonstration. (I am working with a sentence from the "Prologue" to Stephen Greenblatt's lovely book, *Hamlet in Purgatory*.)

Take this as a base or kernel sentence: <u>The little children were told by their teacher to stand around the mangled corpse and to recite the psalms.</u>

2a. If you add an introductory clause or phrase, you need to set it off with a comma. This lets a reader know when the introduction is over and the kernel sentence begins. Readers need a sense of where they are going in order to negotiate all those words on the page.

On a normal school day, after being taken to the apartment of a Jewish railway worker who had been struck and killed by a train, <u>the little children were told by their teacher to stand around the mangled corpse and to recite the psalms.</u>

The first comma (between "day" and "after") is required under the principle of the list. That list could have been extended indefinitely: *On a normal school day, when the sun was high in the sky, late in the month of September, after the celebration of Yom Kippur, and after being taken to the apartment of a Jewish railway worker. . . .*

The second comma indicates that the introductory phrase is complete and the core or kernel sentence is about to begin: *After being taken to the apartment of a Jewish railway worker who had been struck and killed by a train,* <u>the little children were told. . . .</u>

There is some leeway here. If the opening phrase is quite short, some writers will leave off the comma. (*On a normal school day the little children were told. . . .*) With long opening phrases or clauses, readers will most likely be confused and annoyed if the comma is missing.

2b. When you separate subject and verb, you put a comma before and after the unit that interrupts the subject and verb.

On a normal school day, after being taken to the apartment of a Jewish railway worker who had been struck and killed by a train, <u>the little children</u>, **six of them,** <u>were told by their teacher to stand around the mangled corpse and to recite the psalms.</u>

2c. The same is true, actually, of any parenthetical expression (like the "actually" in this sentence). Just as you need to open and close a parenthesis (like this), you need commas at each end of the parenthetical.

On a normal school day, after being taken to the apartment of a Jewish railway worker who had been struck and killed by a train, <u>the little children were told by their teacher</u>, **whom I can only imagine as a madman**, <u>to stand around the mangled corpse and to recite the psalms</u>.

The principle here is simple: a reader needs to know that you are taking time off before completing the base sentence.

There is no leeway here. If you break the conventions represented by 2b and 2c, readers will be confused and annoyed. In these cases, you will have made a stupid mistake.

2d. Use a comma in certain cases when you are adding a phrase or clause to the *end* of a base sentence. If you add a *non-restrictive* element at the end of the base sentence, you indicate that with a comma. A *non-restrictive* element is something you've added because you felt like it. You use a comma to let a reader know that this is an addition. A *restrictive* element is a piece of language required to complete the meaning of the sentence, so you do not include a comma. In the case of a restrictive element, readers need to know that their work is not over yet.

On a normal school day, after being taken to the apartment of a Jewish railway worker who had been struck and killed by a train, <u>the little children were told by their teacher</u>, whom I can only imagine as a madman, <u>to stand around the mangled corpse and to recite the psalms</u>, **while the man's wife wailed inconsolably in a corner**.

On a normal school day, after being taken to the apartment of a Jewish railway worker who had been struck and killed by a train, <u>the little children were told by their teacher</u>, whom I can only imagine as a madman, <u>to stand around the mangled corpse and to recite the psalms</u> **in order to complete the act of mourning as required by the Torah**.

You get the greatest leeway with additions to the end of a sentence. You can also hang something onto the end of a sentence with a dash—like this.

3. Here is the actual sentence from Greenblatt. Notice how he uses dashes in order to situate one more parenthetical. The dash is a useful additional signpost for a reader who has already been busy processing commas:

My father was born in the late nineteenth century. I was the child of what I used to think of as his old age but that I have now, at my point in life, come to think of, rather, as his vigorous middle age. I saw him, in any case, as embodying the life experience not of the generation directly behind me but of two generations back. His own childhood memories seemed to have a quite unusual, almost eerie distance from my life-world. Hence, for example, he told me that when he was very young, he was taken, along with the other boys in his Hebrew school class (his *cheder*) to the apartment of a Jewish railway worker who had been struck and killed by a train. **The little children were told by their teacher, whom I can only imagine as a madman, to stand around the mangled corpse—which was placed on great cakes of ice, since it was the summer in Boston and very hot—and to recite the psalms, while the man's wife wailed inconsolably in a corner.** Initiated, perhaps, by this traumatic experience, my father was obsessed throughout his life with death. (6)

Part II. Working with the Readings

$\cdot\cdot\bullet\cdot\cdot$

GLORIA ANZALDÚA

How to Tame a Wild Tongue (p. 26)

Anzaldúa's book *Borderlands/La frontera* is a compelling example of postmodern, fragmented writing that can introduce students to the plasticity of writing, to its possibilities beyond the tired, rationally argued essay that they (and everyone else) have been forced to write for all their academic years. This chapter from Anzaldúa's book captures the spirit, style, and argument of the book and demonstrate that it is possible, feasible, and perhaps desirable to compose in "montage," presenting complex subjects like identity, sexuality, and religion in understandable, passionate, and compelling writing while allowing for the inherent contradictions and paradoxes of such subjects and such writing. We loved teaching Anzaldúa, and for our students, this kind of text was both new and challenging (and fun, once they allowed themselves to work with it rather than trying to "get it"). It's a genuine "assemblage" or "montage," a "crazy dance," as Anzaldúa calls it, made up of sections written in a variety of styles (prose poems, endnotes, stories, anecdotes) and languages. Its argument is unconventionally cast. Rather than logically presenting a case for her mixed identity and languages as a *mestiza*, Anzaldúa juxtaposes passionate statements on her heritages, identities, sexualities, religions, and cultures with stories, poems, and anecdotes. The effect is jarring, powerful, but students will need to spend time sorting out the text's mixed style and arguments.

Immediately, questions will arise about the Spanish interspersed in the text. Students will want to know whether they need to read Spanish to understand Anzaldúa's argument. It might be difficult for them to understand, at first, that they don't, that the text reveals its use of the Spanish sections as a part of its style and argument, that they'll be able to work through it as they come to see the text as a representation of Anzaldúa's mixed identity. The best advice for students, then, is to read as if the Spanish passages will defy any attempts at a complete understanding but, at the same time, will offer up sentences, phrases, and larger stylistic patterns that they'll be able to make sense of and connect to the rest of her writing.

QUESTIONS FOR A SECOND READING (p. 35)

1. This is an important discussion question to pose for students, especially since this kind of text will be new and challenging (and fun) for most of them. The central question (So how do you read this text if you don't read Spanish?) is a natural one for breaking the ice before any other discussion or writing assignments. It allows students to relate how they read the selection, how they worked with it, and it serves beautifully as an opening to other questions about Anzaldúa's style and arguments.

2. The idea of an author inventing a reader as she writes gives students a way of understanding a text's creation aside from (or alongside) notions of arguments and "points" being put forward. If students begin their work with this text through the first question in this section on how they read the chapter, then they are ready to consider how Anzaldúa invents a reader or a way of reading and what her expectations or demands might be. A number of sections, like the one quoted in this question, obliquely reveal Anzaldúa's expectations, and students shouldn't have trouble finding and working from them. They should be encouraged, especially, to work from their own experiences reading the chapters. What kinds of readers were they? How would they describe the ways in which they read?

3. This question prompts students to discuss Anzaldúa's arguments, but its primary emphasis is on asking students to explain the arguments' connections across the chapters. Anzaldúa's key terms involve issues of identity, sexuality, religious experience, and consciousness, especially what she refers to as *la facultad*, the ability to see deeper realities in surface phenomena. It's fair to say that there is no specific number of correct terms that students must identify and explain; but some terms and arguments and examples do carry across the chapters, and students would do well to look to these for their discussions of Anzaldúa's arguments and how they're connected across the chapters. It's critical to place the emphasis on *arguments*, as opposed to argument, because Anzaldúa makes numerous arguments, some of which contradict others — this is not a unified text, nor a unified, seamless argument.

ASSIGNMENTS FOR WRITING (p. 36)

1. This is a wonderful writing assignment that allows students to experience the creation of a mixed style from their various positions, voices, and backgrounds. Of course, as the assignment points out, students have not been prepared to write this kind of text, but Anzaldúa's example is strong enough to enable them to do so. The key moment in the assignment is the one that asks students to consider the different positions they occupy. What does this mean? Resist the temptation to tell them. Let them come to see that they are students, sons and daughters, friends, authorities, novices, swimmers, skateboarders, lovers, bikers, enemies, ballplayers, music listeners, concertgoers, inheritors of particular cultures and traits, and so on. Let them realize that these various selves have voices, often contradictory, that students can bring forward in writing, as Anzaldúa does, when they set out to explain who they are, how they understand their experiences, and, in particular, what their key or significant experiences are and in what form or style they might be presented.

2. Like the first of the "Questions for a Second Reading," this writing assignment asks students to tell the story of their reading of the chapter, but the assignment goes beyond the simple recounting of a reading. It asks students in addition to consider themselves as readers who feel at home in the text and then lost in it, who occupy a position in relation to the text, and, especially, who read or don't read as Anzaldúa expects. Some passages in the text, like the one quoted in the assignment, voice Anzaldúa's expectations about her readers, and they ask to be answered. Students

may align themselves with Anzaldúa's expectations or be put off or angered by them; or they might have different responses at different times in their reading. The goal for this assignment is to let students speak back to Anzaldúa's expectations of them as readers and to use their experiences reading these chapters in that essay.

3. This assignment would work well with the first writing assignment, which asks students to write a mixed text like Anzaldúa's. Students might write this assignment first. It's straightforward in its request to students to locate and define Anzaldúa's woman's voice, her sexual voice, and her poet's voice, to work from specific passages to do this locating and defining, and to speculate how these voices differ from one another and from what Anzaldúa imagines a "standard" voice to be. Although the assignment is straightforward, the task is challenging. It opens up the discussion of what constitutes a voice, where voices come from (the self? language?), and how they're defined. It's not unusual for students to see these voices mixing into one another or to begin naming the voices by the emotional reactions they elicit. The goal of this assignment is to open up the conversation for students to the idea of voice, not to have them find rock-solid examples of one kind of voice or dictionary or literary definitions of voice. The text offers students plenty to work with, and they should puzzle these voices out from it and from their own reactions to the various shifts in style and tone.

4. This assignment is a slightly different version of the first writing assignment. Like that first assignment, it asks students to write in different voices that are a part of them or a part of an argument they want to make. Unlike the first assignment, this one focuses specifically on students creating an argument (rather than expressing their own selves or their understandings of their situations). For this assignment to work well, students will need to write an argument about which they feel passionate, yet one on which they can see themselves taking various positions, given the different roles (students, sons and daughters, friends, skateboarders, lovers, bikers, swimmers, enemies, and so on) they hold in relation to the argument. In other words, students need to make an argument in which they allow their various voices to speak, as Anzaldúa does; they shouldn't expect to have a logical, unified, seamless case.

The second part of this assignment, the two-page assignment on why a student's argument is worth a reader's attention, serves as a way for students to consider the importance of their arguments. It's a way of asking students to think of their readers and their writing in order to present arguments worth a reader's attention, which will teach, challenge, or show readers something rather than simply reiterating commonplace clichés or generalities. In short, the two-page coda is a way of forcing the issue of asking for writing that is worth a reader's time and attention. If this assignment is to work, students will have to invest the time and energy to create arguments that they care about, that they feel confused or uncertain about, as Anzaldúa does (even though she comes across at times as certain), that they can actually explain in terms of being worth a reader's attention. If the explanation turns to clichés or generalizations, then the argument is most likely not worth a reader's attention. The two-page coda can be used, then, as a way to begin the discussion of the arguments that students produce. The first question might be, "Is this argument worth our attention? Why or why not?"

MAKING CONNECTIONS (p. 38)

1. Students will need to have read both the Pratt essay and the Anzaldúa chapter before working on this assignment. It would be worthwhile for students to work with at least one other assignment (either a second-reading or writing assignment) for each selection before they turn to this one. The key terms and notions for this assignment reside in Pratt's use of autoethnographic or transcultural texts as writing in which the writer engages in some way the representations others have made of him or her. Anzaldúa continually refers to and critiques various representations of her identity, sexuality, religion, and culture, and students will need to locate those two or three representations that they would like to work from. But the task they face is larger than simply presenting Anzaldúa's text as autoethnographic or transcultural, because they are also being asked to present Pratt's argument for autoethnographic texts and Anzaldúa's text to readers who haven't read either. In other words, they are being asked to represent both texts and to use Anzaldúa's as a further example for Pratt's discussion of autoethnographic or transcultural texts. Students, of course, will have to produce some sort of summary or paraphrase of both texts in order to complete the assignment, but that summary or paraphrase is only the frame. They must then go on to present Anzaldúa's writing as part and parcel of Pratt's argument. The summary or paraphrase of these texts serves the purpose of orienting readers unfamiliar with either Pratt's essay or Anzaldúa's text, and this assignment offers a good opportunity for students to test their drafts against readers outside their class.

2. We find that students often have had exposure to metaphor in similar contexts — meaning most students have some sense of what metaphors are and how they are different from, for example, similes or other what might be called "literary devices" or "figurative language." But we also find that students recognize metaphor most readily when it is obvious (like: love is a piano) and less readily when the metaphor is part of a larger project or is implied in dialogue, echoes, or images in readings. This assignment invites students to first expand and complicate their own notions of metaphor. Once they've done that work as readers, the assignment invites them to write about that experience. A few students, surprisingly, have been really playful with this assignment — using, for example, metaphor to talk about metaphor. The final question in this prompt is perhaps the most important question for students to think through as they work on the assignment. Our goal is for students to understand that metaphor is not just for "fancy-ing" up one's prose or making it more vivid (though it can certainly do those things), but that it can also be used for layering and complicating the subject at hand like Griffin does in her treatment of the missile alongside the cell. We have noticed also that after students have completed this particular assignment, there is often an increase in their own experimentation with metaphor and noticing of metaphor in other readings from the book. This is especially useful for helping students become readers of all the readings in the collection.

3. Students will need to have read both the Anzaldúa essay and the Butler essay in order to complete this particular assignment. Both Butler and Anzaldúa are deeply concerned with the relationship between language and being. During first readings, students may tend to fixate on Anzaldúa's focus on language and Butler's focus on being, but we ask

that in subsequent examinations of both essays they take note of the connections the authors make *between* identity and being. Helping students (through class discussion or small group discussion) see what it means to explore two essays side by side is often useful before asking them to think about the specific questions they feel are key for both authors.

For many students, writing essays that raise questions rather than answer them is new territory. We sometimes spend a class meeting talking about what makes a productive question that demands inquiry, as opposed to a question that just wants a definitive answer. Learning to raise and sustain questions is one of the most significant processes student writers need to learn at the college level. Students can work together to generate questions from both readings and to discuss which of those questions seems to have the most potential for further investigation in an essay.

KWAME ANTHONY APPIAH

Racial Identities (p. 42)

This selection was taken from the book *Color Conscious: The Political Morality of Race* (1996; coauthored with Amy Gutmann), winner of the 1997 Ralph J. Bunche award from the American Political Science Association. (Amy Gutmann is currently president of the University of Pennsylvania. Previously, she was the Laurance S. Rockefeller University Professor of Politics at Princeton.) *Color Conscious* is drawn from the lectures Gutmann and Appiah gave as the Tanner Lectures on Human Values at the University of California at San Diego in 1994. The book is organized as follows: After a long introduction by David B. Wilkins (Kirkland and Ellis Professor of Law and director of the Program on the Legal Profession at Harvard), Appiah offers a long discussion titled "Race, Culture, Identity: Misunderstood Connections." It is divided into two parts: "Part 1. Analysis: Against Races" and "Part 2. Synthesis: For Racial Identities." The selection we have reprinted is Part 2.

Here is how Part 1 of the essay opens:

Imagine yourself on Angel Island in the 1920s. You are helping an inquisitive immigrant from Canton to fill in an immigrations form. *Name,* it says. You ask her name. She tells you. You write it down. *Date of birth.* She gives it to you (according to the Chinese calendar, of course, so you have to look up your table for translating from one system to another). Then there is an entry that says *Race.* This you do not have to ask. You write "Oriental." And your interlocutor, because she is inquisitive, asks politely: "What are you writing now?" (After all, until now everything you have written has been in response to her answers.)

Disingenuously, you say: "I am writing down where you are from."

"Ah yes," she replies helpfully, "Canton, I was born in Canton. How did you know?"

"No. Actually, that's the next question I was going to ask. Place of birth."

"So what have you written already?"

How do you answer this question? Seventy years ago, how would you have explained to someone from outside the modern West what our English word "race" meant? Or how would you have explained to a Sicilian across the continent on Ellis Island, thirty years earlier, why the right answer for him was "Caucasian"? (Where he came from, the people of the North of Italy, the ancestors of the modern Lombard league, think of him, as he very well knows, as of a different, darker, *razza* than theirs: how do you explain that here he is going to become white?) And would you give the same explanation today?

Or, again, imagine yourself in North Carolina, in the later nineteenth century, as Reconstruction is coming to an end. You are in a small town, out of the way, where there are families that come in all shades of skin color, milk through chocolate. A message comes through from the state capitol in Raleigh. Everyone now has to be white or colored. If you're white, step this way; colored, go the other. You are talking to Joe, a teenager, whose skin is milky white, whose eyes are blue, but whose grandmother, Mary, is a brown-skinned woman who remembers *her* mother's stories of Africa. "I was gonna go with my grandma," he tells you. "But then I saw my Uncle Jim was gonna be with her, so I'm gonna cross to the other side of the room. 'Cause one thing I know for sure; I don't want to be anywhere my Uncle Jim's gonna be."[1]

Is Joe making a conceptual mistake? Or is he unintentionally making what will turn out to be a lucky choice for him and his descendants; a choice that will leave him and them with a vote, better schools, better jobs? Can you imagine someone like Joe, in the nineteenth-century South, born after emancipation but raised before the high-water mark of the strange career of Jim Crow, who doesn't know that in America, or at least in the Carolinas, even white-skinned people with black grandmothers are Negroes?

My preliminary aim in this essay is to explore the concept of race that is at work in these cases—an American concept, though also, of course, one that draws on and interacts with ideas from elsewhere. I will go on to argue for three[2] analytical conclusions. First, I want to explain why American social distinctions cannot be understood in terms of the concept of race: the only human race[3] in the United States, I shall argue, is *the* human race. Second, I want to show that replacing the notion of race with the notion of culture is not helpful; the American social distinctions that are marked using racial vocabulary do not correspond to cultural groups, either. And third, I want to propose that, for analytical purposes, we should use instead the notion of a racial identity, which I will try to explore and explain.

Finally, I will argue for an ethical conclusion: that there is a danger in making radial identities too central to our conceptions of ourselves; while there is a place for racial identities in a world shaped by racism, I shall argue, if we are to move beyond racism we shall have, in the end, to move beyond current racial identities.

The remainder of this section of the essay traces the concept of race as it evolved in the English-speaking world in the nineteenth century, partly through developments in science (Darwin and Mendel), but primarily through the development of a discourse on race that was taken to be true and self-evident. For these cases, Appiah turns primarily to Thomas Jefferson and Matthew Arnold. In all these cases, attempts to distinguish human biological types slide quickly into statements about fundamental qualities of character and mind. Jefferson, writing on behalf of emancipation, also argues that African Americans will have to be moved out of the country. Jefferson says,

> the real distinctions which nature has made; and many other circumstances, will divide us into parties, and produce convulsions which will probably never end but in the extermination of the one or the other race.—To these objections, which are political, may be added others, which are physical and moral. (44)

African Americans, he observes, are inferior in regard to reason and imagination.

Appiah turns, as well, to Matthew Arnold's discussion of the fundamental distinction between Celts and Saxons in his *On the Study of Celtic Literature*, and to Arnold's conclusion (an example of what Appiah calls "racialism") that the genetic legacy of Britain (which he takes to be Celtic, Norman, and Germanic) has produced differences beyond biological inheritance. There is something quite brilliant in turning to Arnold, since the distinctions he draws seem much more immediately goofy to an American reader, someone well prepared to think about essential differences between blacks and whites but not at all used to thinking about Celts.

But Appiah returns from Arnold to American "racialism":

> Arnold's discussion in *On the Study of Celtic Literature* makes it plain that he believes that the racial essence accounts for more than the obvious visible characteristics of individuals and of groups—skin color, hair, shape of face—on the basis of which we decide whether people are, say, Asian- or Afro-Americans. For a racialist, then, to say someone is "Negro" is not just to say that she has inherited a black skin or curly hair: it is to say that her skin color goes along with other important inherited characteristics—including moral and literary endowments. By the end of the nineteenth century most Western scientists (indeed, most educated Westerners) believed that racialism was correct, and theorists sought to explain many characteristics—including, as we see here, the character of literatures—by supposing that they were inherited along with (or were in fact part of) a person's racial essence. (56)

Appiah ends Part 2 with a brief section titled, "In Conclusion." It might be useful to provide a summary. He begins, "Much of what I have had to say in this essay will, no doubt, seem negative." He offers, however, these "positive proposals":

- live with fractured identities;
- engage in identity play;
- find solidarity, yes, but recognize contingency;
- and, above all, practice irony. (p. 62)

In short, he says, "I have only the proposals of a banal 'postmodernism.'" He imagines this response:

> It's all very well for you. You academics live a privileged life; you have steady jobs; solid incomes; status from your place in maintaining cultural capital. Trifle with your own identities, if you like; but leave mine alone. (p. 63)

To which he answers: "my job as an intellectual is to call it as I see it."

Appiah's essay is followed by Amy Gutmann's "Responding to Racial Injustice." And Appiah provides an "Epilogue," in which he says:

> In the academy, where race is the topic of discussion in almost every department of the humanities and social sciences, controversies proliferate. We in the academy are sometimes angry, also; but even when we are not, we are adversarial, argumentative, disputatious. Our debates, too, can seem divided and divisive. (p. 41)

And so, in the four pages that follow, he points to "common ground" between the positions he represents and those represented by Amy Gutmann. In an era when discussions of race are often angry, rigid, and strident, Appiah and Gutmann's book provides the best possible example of careful, thoughtful, and constructive debate.

When we first read *Color Conscious*, we were struck by what a teachable book it is. It not only models careful, thoughtful inquiry and debate, but it is so generous in the ways it invites and engages and imagines a reader. From the opening paragraphs, Appiah assumes a reader ready and willing to work seriously as he moves quickly to the example of W.E.B. Du Bois in 1911. But it is also a prose that teaches—preparing a student to read Du Bois's prose and to see Du Bois's "autobiography of a race concept" as not just "moving," but also as "misleading." And, because it will take time to establish this case, Appiah positions the reader in relation to the evolving text:

> For reasons I shall be able to make clear only when I have given my account, Du Bois's own approach is somewhat misleading. So instead of proceeding with exegesis of Du Bois, I must turn next to the task of shaping a sociohistorical account of racial identity. Still, as it turns out, it is helpful to start from Du Bois's idea of the "badge of color." (42)

This is exemplary prose. As the chapter goes on, Appiah works his way through key terms—identity, identification, authenticity—familiar terms, comfortable terms, common terms whose dangers and difficulties he slowly teaches a reader to understand.

"Racial Identities" offers an argument against the usual commonplaces about racial identity, an argument that is difficult, challenging, and unsettling. It says, in effect, that we have fallen into a thoughtless way of speaking, thinking, and writing about race, culture, and identity. Students will struggle with this. It will require them to write and to think beyond what they are accustomed to writing and thinking. This problem is useful and instructive. Students can feel intimately the difficulty in thinking and saying something they are not prepared to say, a difficulty that is enacted in Appiah's prose. He is inviting them into a philosophical experiment.

As we taught this selection, we found that we needed to foreground the key terms and to invite students to work with them out loud in discussion. What identifications are thrust upon you? What ones do you invite? Can you imagine identifications that have "gone imperial"? And we found that we needed to foreground the unusual strategy of a philosopher, someone who will enter into an argument to see where it will lead, even if (or perhaps especially if) it needs to finally be rejected. Where, we would ask, can you find Appiah in this essay? Where is he speaking on his own? These moments often come in relation to autobiography—to personal examples—and the urgencies of his own beliefs are nicely present in the concluding section, where he speaks out from the chapter to imagine its consequences—actually, to invite a reader to imagine its consequences.

While this is a very teachable selection, it is not necessarily an easy selection to teach. It can provide anxiety and concern—on both sides of the table—not because of its internal strategies but because it directly addresses the topic of race. Still, it is important to find ways to teach work like Appiah's, and it is important for students to learn to talk together about race. After years of experience, we can offer these two pieces of advice. First, don't let African American students in your class be forced into speaking on behalf of all African American people. Be careful and respectful of their silences, as well as their interventions. They occupy a difficult position. You are not asking for (or expecting) testimony; you are trying to find a way for a group of readers to have a conversation about something they have read, a conversation that can help them as writers. And this leads to our second piece of advice.

When someone tells a difficult story or takes a difficult stand in the class, it can be helpful to remind students that you (and they) are working on and with a text. This is not a talk show or talk radio—where everyone is an authority by virtue of their willingness to speak with the voice of authority. Nor are we experts on "the political morality of race," the subtitle of *Color Conscious*. As a teacher and as a class, you are working together to become experts on what Appiah has written, to become expert readers of this text, and to be able to write with authority on the basis of what you have read. As questions come up about race in relation to personal experience or in current (or past) U.S. history, it is entirely appropriate to use them as the occasion to return to the text. You might ask: "How does this relate to Appiah's concerns? What part of the text might provide terms or arguments that might be useful? What is Appiah's position on this? If he doesn't have one, why not? Why wouldn't this be something he would bring into the discussion?"

You aren't going to settle the question of racial identity in the United States in one day, one week, or one semester. The goal of the class should be for individuals to consider different positions on the issue, including (and ideally) ones they had not encountered before. If there are to be conclusions, they should be voiced and phrased in the manner of Appiah's discussion. (It can be helpful, in fact, to read a paragraph or two to get a sense of tone and rhythm.) Appiah has initiated and provided the context for the conversations you are hoping to promote.

QUESTIONS FOR A SECOND READING (p. 65)

1. It has always been our concern that students see the selections as offering writing lessons—lessons as well as topics or ideas or arguments. And so we try to highlight features in the text as examples of "technical" achievement, something a student writer can bring into his or her own texts. Here we focus attention on the ways Appiah engages and addresses his readers, the ways he brings them into the text or prepares them to work with difficult ideas or passages. And we insist that this is not magic or inspiration or brain surgery, but a relatively simple technique. The key is to know how and when and where to apply it, how not to be cloying or patronizing, but these are lessons learned through experience, through trial and error. You can develop a working list of these strategies, perhaps online or on the blackboard or in a handout. In our experience, you'll see the effects of this lesson in student papers for the rest of the semester.

2. This assignment sends students out on a mini–research project. They are asked to follow up on some of Appiah's references and to highlight and to develop working definitions

of some of his key terms or technical references—to be a little more knowledgeable about the context within which a writer like Appiah is working.

For investigating his references, we often combine this exercise with a trip to the library and a session with a reference librarian on how to use a university library and its resources. A university library is a special and daunting place; it has tools well beyond what students will have encountered in their high schools and communities. And students often quite literally need someone to take them across the threshold. For developing glosses of key or technical terms, we have found it useful for students to think of themselves as translators rather than as dictionary makers. If they see the task as translation, they are imagining the problem as one of understanding rather than of definition. How does one make sense of, or come to understand, a phrase like "semantic deference"? It puts the student on the inside, speaking from a position of (earned) understanding and facing a common writing problem, finding a way to address an audience not yet in the know.

3.   Voice. In all of our teaching, we spend a fair amount of time in class asking students to notice, to think about, to argue about "voice." Thinking about voice is a way of thinking about the prose as situated (rather than god-like). It is a way of thinking about address—about what the voice invites or assumes or demands in a reader. Usually, students are thinking about differences in register—and it is useful to invite students to pair passages—passages where Appiah writes as a philosopher and passages where Appiah assumes different roles. The difficulty here, as we noted above, is that Appiah will often follow out lines of thought that are *not* his, that he doesn't endorse, because he wants to highlight the implications or the consequences of certain ways of thinking and speaking. We provide an example in this prompt. You might ask students to bring examples of their own—from Appiah and from other things they are reading.

4.   For years, we have used paraphrase—short paragraphs written in class or outside class—as "exercises in understanding." And we have had students follow the development and deployment of key terms. Here, we are asking for paragraphs that translate key moments in Appiah's text. Of course, they are also exercises in close reading, and they serve as excellent preparation for the extended discussion of a passage, an idea, or a block quotation when the students are working on their own essays. Although it is tempting to assign a common passage for paraphrase, we have found it more useful to send students back to the text to search for a passage that they found to be particularly "interesting or challenging," as we say. This is a way to invite a purposeful second reading. And, most likely, you will find some overlap—that is, some students will write about the same passage. We routinely prepare copies of two to four paraphrases for class discussion. This opens up discussion of the text and provides the opportunity to talk about difficulty—about what it is that makes a passage perplexing or challenging, and about what a reader can do with such a textual moment. And it can provide the opportunity for a discussion of technique, everything from the use and punctuation of a block quotation (including highlighting sections through italics) to the tough questions of selection (what is appropriate and complete) and representation (what is the difference between a good paraphrase and a bad one, one that misrepresents or oversimplifies).

5.   This long list is both shocking and thrilling.

>   In policing this imperialism of identity—an imperialism as visible in racial identities as anywhere else—it is crucial to remember always that we are not simply black or white or yellow or brown, gay or straight or bisexual, Jewish, Christian, Moslem, Buddhist, or Confucian but that we are also brothers and sisters; parents and children; liberals, conservatives and leftists; teachers and lawyers and auto-makers and gardeners; fans of the Padres and the Bruins; amateurs of grunge rock and lovers of Wagner; movie buffs; MTV-holics; mystery-readers; surfers and singers; poets and pet-lovers; students and teachers; friends and lovers. Racial identity can be the basis of resistance to racism; but even as we struggle against racism—and though we have made great progress, we have further still to go—let us not let our racial identities subject us to new tyrannies. (62)

In the argument for freedom, or in the argument against "tyranny," we hear the cadences of Martin Luther King Jr. The list is seductive and inviting. And, perhaps shockingly, Appiah insists on the leveling of categories—that being a Christian, say, is no more fundamental to one's identity than being a fan of the Bruins.

This list is qualified by the list in the concluding section: "So here are my positive proposals: live with fractured identities; engage in identity play; find solidarity, yes, but recognize contingency, and, above all, practice irony." Here the invitation is different. Above, we are asked to fill in our own favorite tags. ("Penguins" rather than "Bruins.") Here, readers are asked to stop and consider terms like "contingency" and "irony," terms that become technical terms, crucial to thinking about identity formation. (Where, for example, might you find "irony" in Appiah's list? Or in his own self-representations in the essay?)

In our teaching, we turn early to these final pages. There is an energy here that is inviting. Students find it both easy and challenging to construct parallel lists of their own. And we insist on the formal arrangement (and the "always"): "It is crucial to remember always that we are not simply . . . but that we are also. . . . " These concluding passages have offered students new ways back into the text and its difficulties. And this exercise has brought home Appiah's argument about identity and identification and authenticity.

Note: you might also consider a similar exercise in relation to Appiah's discussion of "life scripts" in the section "Beyond Identity." Students can list the scripts that have been offered to them at home, by the culture, the scripts that they have found compelling or seductive or inevitable (or odious). Once a list begins to form, the power and seductiveness of listing will provoke others to add new items.

ASSIGNMENTS FOR WRITING (p. 67)

1.   We don't often give assignments that ask, primarily, for summary. We do this when we believe the summary can function strategically to enable students to think thoughts that are difficult or that run against habit and the commonplace. That is the goal here. Students will need to present a rich and textured account of Appiah's argument that "American social distinctions cannot be understood in terms of the concept of race." This might even function as a suitable first draft. The most difficult part of the task will be making the turn to a discussion of the "consequences" of our current ways of thinking

and acting. To make this essay work, students will need to have something to write about here. It can certainly be helpful to use class discussion to think about ways of representing examples of how American social distinctions are currently thought of in terms of race, examples from the news, from experience, from the distinctions central to our national discourse, from distinctions present in popular culture—movies, novels, music, art. You need to work hard to make this a project for your students, one where they are responsible for bringing examples or materials to the table, something to study, something beyond opinions. Formally, it is useful to ask students what they might bring to the discussion that could be equivalent to Appiah's use of Arnold or Jefferson. We have found it useful to invite students to think that they are bringing materials relevant to their world, their cohort, their collective, or their generation. "Here, Mr. Appiah," we invite them to think, "here is where the language of race is most striking for us."

2.   This has been one of the most interesting and productive assignments in our teaching in the last few years. We often ask students to extend the argument of an essay to materials or narratives central to their own lives. Here, the focus is more clearly on the narrative itself. Although our students aren't familiar with terms like "narrative nonfiction" or "creative nonfiction," we encourage them to write as though they were writing a story—with an emphasis on scene, character, and dialogue. The more people speaking, we say, the better. And we have received impressive papers in return—impressive in their length, their ambition, and their seriousness. This assignment always leads to a revision, and so we are quick to bring the most ambitious papers to class for discussion. Their example has provoked impressive revisions from students whose first drafts were mechanical or perfunctory.

      We also, however, think of this as a critical exercise. We don't demand (or even prompt) direct reference to Appiah in these papers. In the assignment, however, we make it clear that this is an Appiah-like exercise. It is not an open invitation to a personal essay. It is an invitation to think through, as we say, the "competing demands of a life and a 'script,' of the personal and the collective, of individual freedom and the politics of identity."

3.   This kind of writing assignment is common in *Ways of Reading*. It asks students to consider consequences of what they have read—to assume that what they have read is directed to them and that what it says matters, matters to them and to people like them, to their generation, perhaps. Here, students are asked to respond to Appiah's conclusions, to be in conversation with him. And to be in conversation, they will need to turn to the text—to summary, quotation, and paraphrase—but only in service to something they want to say. Summary here is not servile but strategic. The quality of work will certainly be improved if students have a chance to revise this essay. Their energies in the first draft will be directed to the account of Appiah and the presentation of the example. After students have formally completed the project, the essay will feel complete—or it has felt complete to our students. They have filled in the empty spaces. And so we have found it very useful to send them back to revise—not simply to improve what they have done (to make it more correct or self-contained) but to write new pages and develop new sections to the essay, particularly ones where they are speaking on their own and on behalf of what they understand (and feel) to be at stake in this project — for them and for their generation.

MAKING CONNECTIONS (p. 69)

1–3. We regularly feature assignments that ask students to read one essay in light of, or in reference to, another so that they can imagine that they are engaged in an ongoing project rather than just a little of this and a little of that—Appiah one week, and Wideman the next.

Assignment 1 asks students to use Appiah's account of racial identity (and identification) to think about John Wideman's family history. For Wideman, the difficulties of representation are present in the text as acts of memory and invention, and they are there as polemic, in his argument about the usual representation of African American male identity.

Assignment 2 asks students to think about voice and persona, about the styles of adult prose, by working back and forth between representations of the intellectual in the David Foster Wallace essay and the Appiah essay. Both writers are performative. Both are compelling stylists. Most students will take Wallace as exemplary. The most striking feature in his essay is the way the figure of the writer, as evidenced in the text, does and does not inhabit the style of scholarly writing exemplified by a writer as distinguished, elegant, and magisterial as Kwame Anthony Appiah. The assignment asks students to think about the difference in relation to their own intellectual styles and ambitions, current and future.

Assignment 3 is somewhat similar in that it asks students to think about the writing as writing, here thinking through Schulz's discussion of evidence and of evidence as a key to thought. We have always made it a point to insist that students use assignments like these to take a step beyond "compare and contrast," a method already (most likely) a part of their toolkits. There is a technical side to using one text as a lens through which to view the other. One way to make this act of reading materialize on the page is to bring a paragraph or block quotation from one text, from Schulz, say, to a discussion that also requires a paragraph or block quotation from Appiah. What do you hear in each? Where and how do they speak to each other? Or not? As we ask students to visualize the page, we ask them also to imagine a space in the essay where they, the student writer, speaks, where they take a position and make an evaluative judgment about what they have read. (What is your favorite moment in all of this? Which text is most persuasive?) And we ask them to strike out on their own, either to develop an idea or to apply what they have found to a new situation or set of examples.

JAMES BALDWIN

Notes of a Native Son 🄴

We are of the generation who read Baldwin, and particularly *The Fire Next Time* (1963), while neighborhoods were burning in our home cities: Akron, Ohio, and Buffalo, New York. He was one of the figures we turned to with the hope that he could explain and understand what we could not, and that he could explain it with a force and eloquence that would make a difference, particularly to our fathers.

"Notes of a Native Son" is a remarkable piece of writing—to us it is one of the key documents in the history of writing in the United States. In the headnote and in the assignments, we try to situate it between *Native Son* (which we suspect students will not yet have read) and rap and hip-hop, each as attempts to give voice to anger and desire in an urban, African American setting. As our students read "Notes of a Native Son," we want them of course to pay attention to the family story at its center, a frank and powerful story of men of two generations, one that allows identification across race. We have always wanted to insist, however, that "Notes" must be read with regard to the specific location of its narrator—a young, African American man in Harlem in the early 1940s. Determined context is one of the greatest achievements of this essay. The story of Baldwin and his father is to be read in relation to slavery, to the black migration to northern cities, to World War II and the ways the experience of black soldiers changed race relations in the United States, and, finally, to the riots in Detroit and in New York. The father and son, who they are, their love, hatred, and despair, are part of this history, produced by it. This is not the story students are prepared to read—a story about individuals, self-determined, defined primarily in relation to narratives of love, marriage, and professional ambition. To teach this essay, we've found, we need to ask students to reread in order to pay attention to background and context, to all (and it is most of the essay) that is not just the "universal" story of father and son.

We've also learned that students need help placing the "voice" of the narrator. Our students are products of a moment when "black voices" are represented (thought to be equivalent to) a standard "black" urban vernacular common to contemporary music, film, and advertising. Baldwin doesn't "sound black," and this is often said by students to be problematic. (The voices of John and Robbie in John Wideman's "Our Time" can help to name this problem—or to bring it to the next generation. Martin Luther King is another common point of reference.)

It is important, then, to help students to place the voice in "Notes of a Native Son." We usually begin with the scene of the funeral in section 3, where the narrator slips easily into the language of the preacher and of eulogy:

> Only the Lord saw the midnight tears, only He was present when one of His children, moaning and wringing hands, paced up and down the room. When one slapped one's child in anger the recoil in the heart reverberated through heaven and became part of the pain of the universe. And when the children were hungry and sullen and distrustful and one watched them, daily, growing wilder, and further away, and running headlong into danger, it was the Lord who knew what the charged heart endured as the strap was laid to the backside; the Lord alone who knew what one *would* have said if one had had, like the Lord, the gift of the living word.

It is such a remarkable passage, and from it students can begin to hear biblical cadences throughout the text and see the degree to which a mode of analysis which might be said to be (loosely) "sociological" is accompanied by a language of explanation that relies on references to pride, hatred, rage ("a pounding in the skull and fire in the bowels") and the deep truths of the heart. The body represented here is not the body of pop psychology (where there are issues to be resolved) but of the Old and New Testaments, where souls are won and lost and where sacrifice can be redemptive. We can also ask students to examine the way of thinking through narrative that places family stories in relation to the story of the nation; and the way of thinking represented by the other language of argument, perhaps best represented in the penultimate paragraph, where Baldwin (the writer) sets the narrative voice in relation to the language and rhetoric of the sermon—"All my father's texts and songs, which I had decided were meaningless, were arranged before me at his death like empty bottles, waiting to hold the meaning which life would give them for me." The concluding paragraph is quite remarkable for the way it moves from argument to sermon to narrative:

> It began to seem that one would have to hold in the mind forever two ideas, which seemed to be in opposition. The first idea was acceptance, the acceptance, totally without rancor, of life as it is, and men as they are: in the light of this idea, it goes without saying that injustice is a commonplace. But this did not mean that one could be complacent, for the second idea was of equal power: that one must never, in one's own life, accept these injustices as commonplace but must fight them with all one's strength. This fight begins, however, in the heart and it now had been laid to my charge to keep my own heart free of hatred and despair. This intimation made my heart heavy and, now that my father was irrecoverable, I wished that he had been beside me so that I could have searched his face for the answers which only the future would give me now.

Moving from "two ideas" carefully held in counterpoise to a battle in the heart and a new covenant—"and it now had been laid in my charge to keep my own heart free of hatred and despair"—Baldwin returns in the final sentence to his father, earlier referred to as "an old man dead." "Why," we ask our students, "does he wish to search his face for answers? Why doesn't he wish for words, for what his father could say?" With all the talk of the heart, this is not a sentimental narrative. It is not *that* language of the heart that drives this essay.

"Notes of a Native Son" is an extraordinarily rich text. It is distant enough from contemporary culture to be an important history lesson, including a lesson in the history of writing. That is the challenge it brings to the classroom, the challenge of teaching students to read it as strange rather than as familiar. If they can, it teaches as well a lesson in how autobiography can be a rich genre, serving more than trivial celebrations of the local and the personal.

QUESTIONS FOR A SECOND READING 🄴

1–2. These questions ask students to reread in order to think about the writing as writing, to think about form and style. Question 1 asks about form or arrangement and phrases the question in terms of the way prose organizes a reader's time and attention. Why are there two sections? What is gained by this arrangement—what are the two parts and how might they serve a reader? Within each section, how might you chart the development of ideas and/or story? What are the key transitions? Are there moments of climax or conclusion (or provisional conclusion)? The order of this essay is nothing like the textbook definition of an essay's order (the march from thesis to conclusion). It is important for students to be able to carry away a visual or verbal representation of the order of "Notes"—so that this essay can serve as a formal model and not simply as evidence of Baldwin's "genius" or "inspiration."

The second question refers to style, defined here as "voice." We spoke at length about how we direct students' attention to voice in the introduction. The key part of the exercise is for students to choose characteristic passages and to be prepared to report on them. We prompt the question of whether and how "voice" can or should be racialized only because we know from experience that this is an issue students will bring to the classroom (and yet fear that it is out of place). Does it make sense, does it matter, whether we can define Baldwin's voice as a "black" voice? He is certainly quick to speak for the black experience: "There is not a Negro alive who does not have this rage in his blood—one has the choice, merely, of living with it consciously or surrendering to it." As we say above, the voice in "Notes" is significantly (and importantly) different from the standard urban black voice as it is produced for and reproduced by popular music, film, and advertising.

3. We have wanted more and more to focus students' attention on sentences. Baldwin is a remarkable writer of sentences. One of the characteristic sentence patterns is represented in the example:

    He was not a young man when we were growing up and he had already suffered many kinds of ruin; in his outrageously demanding and protective way he loved his children, who were black like him and menaced, like him; and all these things sometimes showed in his face when he tried, never to my knowledge with any success, to establish contact with any of us. When he took one of his children on his knee to play, the child always became fretful and began to cry; when he tried to help one of us with our homework the absolutely unabating tension which emanated from him caused our minds and our tongues to become paralyzed, so that he, scarcely knowing why, flew into a rage and the child, not knowing why, was punished.

    For discussion, we like to ask, "What do these sentences do?" We are not looking for a formal description (or a formal description alone). We want students to note the length of the sentences and the use of commas and semicolons in relation to an expressive project—as a necessary or determined way of doing something with words. Baldwin is not, for example, being dismissive even though he is being critical. This is not the rhetoric of simple statement: "He was outrageous and demanding with his children. He never established contact. He caused his children to become paralyzed with a fear of his rage." Thus the long elaborated sentences. The semicolons insist on the link and proximity of utterances: the father's experience as a child and adult; the form of his love; his failure to establish contact. And the forward movement of the sentences, their inevitability, are regularly interrupted with qualifications and secondary statements. It is not "he flew into a rage and the child was punished." Rather than simply resting agency in the father, both the father and the child are products of a moment (a family moment, a national moment) that neither can understand or control.

4. We have been increasingly careful to remind students that research is part of reading and writing. While learning to work *with* the text is crucial and important, it is not the

only kind of work a scholar performs. Or, while a reader has the responsibility to read closely and carefully, there are other responsibilities to the text. Here we are asking students not only to have more information about the riots in Detroit and Harlem in 1943, but also to look for newspaper accounts. This is another way for students to understand that there were different ways of thinking about and talking publicly about race in the 1940s. This is a way of situating Baldwin's essay (written in 1955) in a history of racial discourse.

ASSIGNMENTS FOR WRITING e

1. The assignment begins with an extended passage from Richard Wright's *Native Son*. It is unlikely that first year students will have read the novel; we wanted to give some sense of Bigger Thomas and how he is represented. The assignment says, "The speaker in 'Notes of a Native Son,' like 'Thoreau' in *Walden*, is one of the exemplary characters of American letters." And it asks students to write an essay on the character of the speaker, or narrator, in "Notes of a Native Son." It is important to help students to distinguish between the character of the narrator (represented by a way of speaking) and the character James Baldwin, who is part of the narrative. The essay is not asking students to summarize a series of actions and events but to write about a way of thinking about and representing family, nation, and race. The assignment may not put enough emphasis on the question, "How does he think and speak?" You might need to call attention to it as you prepare students to write. And the assignment asks students to think about a "comparable voice today, in the twenty-first century." Comparable does not have to mean similar. We are looking for students to turn to an example of a contemporary text (our students tend to write about Spike Lee movies or sitcoms). These are not likely to be similar. In fact, it might be useful to prompt students to think about differences.

2. In many ways, this assignment is a reworking of the first. The point of this assignment is a comparison with a contemporary text, and it makes the question of the style and method of "Notes of a Native Son" a secondary concern. The success of this assignment will depend upon the time and care students give to presenting and developing examples. It is not easy to write about music or a music video or a film or a television show. Students should not underestimate the task. In fact, if you are working with draft and revision, it will most likely be the case that the work of revision will be to further develop the examples and to further articulate the comparison with Baldwin.

3. This assignment asks students to write about "Notes" as a representative essay, an example of style and method that can serve as a model (or whose usefulness can be questioned for contemporary purposes). Irving Howe referred to Baldwin as a writer whose essays represented an art form, "a form with possibilities for discursive reflection and concrete drama." And, he said, "The style of these essays is a remarkable instance of the way in which a grave and sustained eloquence . . . can be employed in an age deeply suspicious of rhetorical prowess."

    Our age is not deeply suspicious of rhetorical prowess. It is either blind to it or drawn by it. Because our age is preoccupied with autobiography, testimonial, and life stories, we do, however, have much to learn about the possibilities for "discursive reflection and concrete drama." Students do not, however, need to feel bound by the terms of Howe's appreciation. The crucial thing is that they find ways of describing and naming the key features of "Notes" as an example of the genre of the essay. It is useful, we have found, if they think of this essay in relation to what they have heard or learned about the essay (usually something about importance of thesis and "logical" order). And it is important for students to take the final set of questions seriously. The temptation will be to say that Baldwin is a great writer and thus everyone should be allowed a similar freedom of expression—or something like that. Students should feel the pressure (or students will benefit, we've found, from the pressure) to think seriously about what an essay like this can and can't do, the purposes and occasions it can and cannot serve.

4.   We have had great success with assignments like these. This one asks students to consider the style and method of "Notes of a Native Son" and then to write an essay that is in direct imitation or to write as an act of homage. The first step, of course, is crucial. Students need to develop a sense of what Baldwin does and how he works before they can try to write from inside his example. They key here, we've found, is for students to think primarily about method rather than subject. They don't have to write about fathers, in other words. They should think about a family story that can be written against the story of nation, state, city, or community.

   And you should take time to think with your students about voice and style. We would recommend some short, in-class exercises in writing Baldwin-like paragraphs as starting points. You need to have the Bible deeply in your history to write Old Testament narrative or to work within a sermonic style. It is perhaps a more useful instruction to ask students to work from within the discursive world of the central secondary character in their narrative (the figure occupying the father slot) and to move into and out of that discursive frame.

5.   This assignment was prompted by our students' frequently phrased concern for the appropriateness (or the ethic) of Baldwin's treatment of his father. It is an appropriate question, rooted more (we think) in what students are used to reading than in a different experience or sense of obligation, child to parent. The text provides the frame for this question—Baldwin invites it, that is, in the way he presents the funeral and in the extended discussion of eulogy. We direct students' attention to this section, although we don't suggest (in the wording of the assignment) that their response should be based on a reading of this section. A reading of this section, however, might be useful as a form of preparation. You could read from this section aloud in class (or invite readings). It is brilliantly readable. And then you could ask students to discuss how he might be using this section to address a reader and to answer questions a reader might harbor.

   The students' essays, though, should ideally reach beyond this section to address "Notes" more generally. The essay begins, "I had inclined to be contemptuous of my father for the conditions of his life, for the conditions of our lives." The essay does not idealize the father; it struggles against simple sentimental narratives (or simple dismissal); it is not, however, contemptuous. That is a position marked in the past tense: "I had inclined to be." In fact, *inclination* is an important word here, since it pushes the reader to ask who or what had put the speaker in a position to take this attitude. In our teaching, we have found it important to ask students to think of the essay in its completion—from beginning to end—at some point in their papers.

MAKING CONNECTIONS 🄴

1.   The first of these assignments points to the obvious connections with another selection written by an African American writer, John Edgar Wideman, that, in one way or another—and in relation to a particular period and audience—has tried to think through what Baldwin refers to as "the American Negro problem."

   The Wideman connection is particularly promising as an example of another generation of writers considering a common project, since it too places a family narrative against the larger questions of race in America. As always, the success of this assignment will depend on students taking time to present and to develop examples from the texts. Certainly summary and paraphrase will be required strategically to prepare the comparison. You can help students feel the pressure, however, to turn to block quotation and to specific and extended points of comparison.

2.   This assignment asks students to think about "Notes of a Native Son" in relation to Susan Griffin's "Our Secret," an essay that uses autobiography and family history to think about large questions—race, patriarchy, nation, war. Students could also write about Anzaldúa, Rodriguez, or Wideman. In Howe's terms, all their work combines discursive reflection and concrete drama.

   As we said before: The success of the writing to this assignment will depend on students taking time to present and to develop examples from the texts. Certainly summary and paraphrase will be required strategically to prepare the comparison. You can help students to feel the pressure, however, to turn to block quotation and to specific and extended points of comparison.

   And, again: It is important for students to take the final set of questions seriously. The temptation will be to say that these are great writers and of course everyone should be allowed a similar freedom of expression—or something like that. Students should feel the pressure (or students will benefit, we've found, from the pressure) to think seriously about what an essay like this can and can't do, the purposes and occasions it can and cannot serve.

ALISON BECHDEL

The Ordinary Devoted Mother (p. 73)

For this edition of *Ways of Reading*, we made a significant investment in selecting a piece of graphic work to include. Graphic novels, graphic essays, and graphic memoir have such great promise for illuminating how we interpret texts. Bechdel's work more specifically calls attention to its own making, thereby turning a reader's attention to the ways a writer's decisions influence readerly movements and reactions. Bechdel's rich layering (of autobiography, theory, and art) also offers students unique opportunities to read more deeply and with close attention both to language and to image. Students respond well to Bechdel's work—both to its graphic form and its intriguing personal family story. This selection is taken from her 2012 book *Are You My Mother? A Comic Drama*. As we mention in the selection's headnote, Bechdel begins with an epigraph from Virginia Woolf that reads: *For nothing was simply one thing.* That sentiment effectively captures Bechdel's project and also opens up numerous possibilities for working on the piece as a writer.

We have found that students are split in terms of their confidence about reading a graphic memoir. Some students feel very at home reading in images and cartoons, while others struggle to pay attention to the text and the image at once. We've designed assignments that guide struggling students by allowing them to teach themselves how to read Bechdel's genre. The assignments also invite more comfortable students to think about the process of making graphic memoir and its connection to the other kinds of texts in this book.

QUESTIONS FOR A SECOND READING (p. 109)

1. This question is intended to help students orient themselves to the experience of reading graphic memoir. In asking students to concentrate on a single frame, we hope they will begin to notice specific details about the way that frame is drawn, narrated, and arranged. It is also interesting for students to discuss what is left out of the frame. Asking students to think about the form of a frame as opposed to the form of a paragraph, for example, calls on them to articulate how paragraphs work and what similarities exist between the two modes. At times, students are able to read frames successfully; many of them are used to reading memes, online forums, and digital compositions. Every time we've taught Bechdel so far, we've found that students find rich discussions in thinking about digital compositions and their relationship to this graphic memoir.

2. While some students will, of course, possess better drawing skills than others, this question invites students to learn about graphic work by trying it out. So many of our assignments value imitation as a way for writers to see what is possible in their own writing, and Bechdel's work is no exception. Some students will find it very difficult (or even comical) to try to design their own frames. This exercise is not only fun for students (especially the part where they share their frames with others students), but it also engages them in thinking through the kinds of challenges and decisions Bechdel faced in her process. Interestingly, a few students found that composing graphic frames was easier for them than writing paragraphs, and the discussion of this subject proved fruitful (especially for these students) in articulating what exactly is difficult about writing itself.

3. The most apparent goal of this assignment is to expose students to the *Oxford English Dictionary*, something we often find opens productive conversations about language, meaning, and the histories words carry with them, whether we are aware of them in our usage or not. This assignment also engages students in thinking about what an author says she values and how that valuation shows up in the work itself. It has often sparked promising class discussion and essays that send students outside the piece of writing in order to return to the piece with a new angle or approach. This investigation

into the words Bechdel uses to talk about her investments provides the impetus for that new approach to reading her work.

4. Similar to our first question in this section, this question seeks to orient student readers to the genre by asking them to perform close readings of a set of frames. This work helps them explore the movement of a graphic work and furthers the work they completed in Question 1.

ASSIGNMENTS FOR WRITING (p. 109)

1. In some ways, Bechdel's comments about telling her story are linked to the ones Wideman makes in his essay. When we choose readings that might be characterized as "autobiographical," we always seek to select readings that complicate the notion of telling a story or telling "the truth" of what happened. Bechdel's comments illuminate this kind of complexity. In a way, the story Bechdel wants to tell, a story of a mother-daughter relationship, is a very familiar story. So this assignment invites students to think of Bechdel's narrative as a genre and to look for other examples of the genre.

    Some students have latched on to the mother-daughter genre, while others think of Bechdel's work as being in a genre of art that is self-conscious about its own making. One student remarked, "Reading Bechdel is like watching one of those movies where someone narrates the story the movie tells, as though the movie was separate from the voiceover." When students recognize connections between the pieces we focus on in class and the narratives with which they are already familiar, they often see new things about the piece they are writing about. Learning how to read in order to write means always trying to find multiple entry points into a text, to open up a new way of seeing Bechdel so that readers might also experience that viewpoint.

2. In some ways, this assignment is quite rhetorical, calling students to locate a kind of argument in Bechdel's work, an argument for a theory of composing, a case for how things are (or should be) made. In teaching this assignment, students have raised questions about whether the genre of autobiography, or what they sometimes call "personal experience," has arguments built in and how we, as readers, are to recognize those arguments if they don't happen in traditional ways. This is tricky work at times, which is why we give students the line of inquiry, leading them to look for specific arguments or suggestions about reading and writing as they are rereading Bechdel's piece. We have found that students, once they are looking for the subject, find something about the process of writing or reading in *most* of Bechdel's frames. In teaching Bechdel's piece, students have had some interesting discussions, particularly with regard to author intention, as many of the students wondered how many of these references or allusions to reading and writing were conscious. They ultimately wondered whether that mattered. Students connected this to their own writing, making references to essays they had written earlier in the semester and explaining how the class workshop noticed something they had done in their writing that they were not conscious of doing. To treat student writers as serious writers means to pursue these kinds of questions together.

3. We considered for a long time whether to include a more imitative assignment in this section of the assignments. Imitation is always a difficult writerly task, and imitating Bechdel is even more difficult. However, students overwhelmingly chose this assignment when given a choice of essays. Even students who thought of themselves as "terrible artists" wanted to try their hand at graphic composition.

    Perhaps the most fruitful aspect of this assignment is the students' opportunity to write about their process. A few students talked about the challenge of keeping track of the words and the images or about how the images seemed to "take over" the text, rendering the text secondary to the image. These discussions did, in fact, bring us back to other texts in *Ways of Reading*, texts that make use of the visual image. One of our "Making Connections" questions takes up these connections.

MAKING CONNECTIONS (p. 111)

1. Reading, as we suggest in our Introduction, is not only a matter of text; several of the readings in *Ways of Reading* contain images, photographs, and, in Bechdel's case, drawn cartoons. In this assignment, we challenge students to think about the different kinds of images (or different uses for images) they see in each of our selections that have visual representations.

    We began this assignment by having students look, first, at the images out of context. We used a document reader in the classroom to project only the images from each of the texts, inviting students to make lists of descriptions—how the images made them feel, what sorts of images they were, and what the images seemed to suggest on their own. This was a useful exercise before students actually got to the work of thinking about the text around the images, what each of the authors *does* with the images. Of course, they noticed right away that, in Bechdel's work, there is (most of the time) no separation between text and image. They are one and the same. This realization alone produced an interesting discussion of the differences between graphic work and work that happens to use visual images. We find that beginning many of the assignments with what the students notice is a generative strategy for helping them gather ideas for writing.

2. We've found that students enjoy thinking about family relationships, and perhaps that's not entirely surprising, since all of us have some sort of upbringing that constitutes the way we understand what it means to be a parent or a child. Of course, part of the difficulty with assignments like these is helping students make productive use of their pasts and experiences. Many instructors we talk to tell us about the difficulty of personal writing in the first-year composition classroom, but its difficulty is what led us to compose some assignments that ask students to blend their experience with a theoretical discussion of a subject. Learning how to make sense of our experiences in relation to intellectual ideas and concepts is part of learning to become a writer. Very few writers (or few good ones) *don't* think about their lives as connected to ideas.

    One way to invite students to think in more complicated ways about this connection is to ask them to make what our students called "webs," which in practice just meant spatial lists of moments from the texts (in this case Bechdel and Griffin), moments from their own lives, and then some kinds of intellectual questions that arise out of these moments. This seemed to help students see their thinking as steps having to do with textual analysis, personal narrative, *and* intellectual inquiry.

3. This is a very difficult and theoretical assignment. It requires that students sift through Butler's essay again, first in order to develop their own working definition of being "beside oneself." Once they've completed this work, they examine Bechdel through the lens of this working definition. Both of these steps ask students for some challenging, careful reading and the ability to move a concept from one text to another. Part of the challenge as a teacher is to help students feel prepared to do this work. In one course, we found it helpful to try this kind of work first with a concept that is more familiar to students, asking them questions about how they've come to know what a certain concept or theory *means*. The students reported that they felt they had a strong knowledge of the "theory of relativity," so we spent some time talking about that theory and brainstormed with students about films or books they've read where they feel like this theory is reflected, played on, or used. This work of moving an idea is difficult writerly work, but students are ready to do this work if they have some guidance about what the moves are in getting there.

JOHN BERGER

Ways of Seeing 🄴

As the headnote says, this selection is the first chapter of a book, *Ways of Seeing*, drawn from John Berger's television series with the BBC, the relevant episode of which is reproduced in the e-Pages along with a set of assignment questions. The book actually has five authors—or, as the page opposite the title page says, it is "a book made by" John Berger, Sven Blomberg, Chris Fox, Michael Dibb, and Richard Hollis. Both the spine and the title page, however, carry Berger's name only. For convenience, we refer to the essay as his. Possession and ownership, as Berger argues in the essay, are difficult and problematic concepts.

Berger creates books that are hard to classify, and this one is certainly no exception. Some chapters in *Ways of Seeing* have no words, only pictures. In the chapter we've included, there are pictures that are clearly part of the text (the argument instructs the reader to look at them), but other pictures are included as well, and they have a less official status. Some could be said to be illustrations of points in the text. Others have to be worked into the chapter.

We were attracted to this piece by the way it allowed us to extend the concept of reading beyond written texts (to the way one "reads" paintings or images, to the way one "reads" one's culture), and for the act of reading it requires. There is a strong argument in the essay, to be sure, particularly in the discussion of the paintings by Frans Hals, and students can reproduce it without great trouble. But there is still much work left for the reader. There are paintings and pictures that go without discussion. There are moments when a common word like *history* is wrenched out of common usage. Berger wants to take common terms and make them problematic, just as he wants to take familiar images and give us a new way of seeing them, yet he is not pushy about definitions; terms remain open to discussion. The structure of the essay also presents a challenge to its readers. While students can begin through discussion to work out the argument of various sections in the essay (his reading of the Hals paintings, the example of mystification, his argument about reproduction, the section on the use of museums), there is no single answer to how these various parts should fit together in a single discussion.

This, then, is one way to teach the essay. Students can begin by focusing on individual sections in order to figure out what Berger is saying and what, as a group, they feel it means. (How do you make sense out of the "yet" in "Yet, although every image embodies a way of seeing, our perception or appreciation of an image depends also upon our own way of seeing" [e-Pages para. 8]?) As teachers, we are willing to be a resource at this point: to say what we see in the painting by Magritte or the figures on museum attendance, or to help students see the lines of demarcation that underlie their various points of view on, for instance, what it means to say that the prose in e-Pages para. 8 is mystification. We are unwilling to tell our students everything we know about Magritte or Benjamin—at least not until very late in the discussion, when this section of the course is over. We don't want the textual problems in an essay to seem like problems of information. The question is not what students can be told about Magritte but what they can make out of that painting, placed as it is in the text. The issue is not how much they know about Walter Benjamin, but that they know that Berger felt the need to bring forward Benjamin's name and one of his books.

The fun of the discussion comes when students find they have gained a foothold on various sections of the essay and you ask, "How does it fit together? How do you put together the section on the *Virgin of the Rocks* with the section on Van Gogh and Hals? What does this have to do with what you've learned to say about history or about the relationship between a person, an image, and ways of seeing?" These are questions that don't have any quick answer. The uncertainty they create can only in a limited sense be resolved by returning to the text. Berger, in other words, loses his capacity as the authority here. Students might test what they have to say by talking about the charts in e-Pages paras. 45–46 or the painting that follows, but they won't find answers. These are answers that they must create, present, and defend both for themselves and for their colleagues, and in discussion as a prelude to work they might do as writers.

QUESTIONS FOR A SECOND READING e

1. These questions are designed to take one of the key terms of this essay, "history," and to make its possible meanings the central textual problem for students as they read back through the text. For Berger, who is both an art historian and a Marxist, history is something of a technical term, and he uses it to frame his argument. He puts pressure on the term and forces it to mean more than it does when it is used loosely in conversation. The job for students is to see how they might make sense of these sentences—what, for a reader of Berger, might it mean to be "situated" in history or to be "deprived" of history?

    Students are directed to pay attention to Berger's use of this term. Once they begin to develop a way of accounting for that use, the remaining questions ask them to put their sense of the term "history" to the test by using it in sentences that discuss the Hals paintings. Students are asked to develop a specialized use for a common term and then to use that term to enable a discussion of an example they share with their colleagues in class (and with Berger, their author). They are asked, that is, to produce a Berger-like discussion, or a discussion that demonstrates their way of reading Berger.

2. This question is intended to allow students to imagine a position outside of Berger's, one from which they can critique Berger's argument. On the one hand, Berger argues that mystification hides that which is "really" there. The assumption, at least at a first reading, seems to be that there are some people who can see with that kind of clarity. On the other hand, Berger argues that we see what we have learned to see. Students are asked, then, to work out Berger's position on the relationship between seeing and understanding, between the individual and the culture, and to turn the terms of that discussion back on Berger himself. Could you say that he sees the truth in the Hals paintings? Is his perception "shaped" or pure? If you find that you can say that Berger, too, sees what he has learned to see, does that discredit his argument?

ASSIGNMENTS FOR WRITING e

1. This first assignment is an opportunity for students to closely study Berger's essay to resay his arguments about what gets in the way when we look at paintings and what we might do to overcome the barriers. Berger claims, in a broad sense, that culture gets in the way of our readings of paintings and history, but his examples are examples of culture as it appears in different enacted forms—in the machinery of "mystification," for example, and in the social positioning of experts or critics. So students will need to work closely from Berger's examples of things and people getting in the way and to use these examples as the grounds for making their claims for his argument. With this assignment, students also are asked to imagine that they are writing to an audience unfamiliar with Berger's essay.

2. Accepting the implied invitation of the essays, this assignment asks the reader to see what he or she can make of one of the paintings that is given a prominent position in the text. While Berger has something to say about *Woman Pouring Milk*, he does not give it a full discussion. The problem posed is, "What can you make of this painting, if you work on it in Berger's spirit?" One way of framing a discussion of these papers or of preparing students for revision is to turn to Berger's own words: "What we make of that painted moment when it is before our eyes depends upon what we expect of art, and that in turn depends today upon how we have already experienced the meaning of paintings through reproductions" (e-Pages para. 62). Students might begin by considering what the authors of the papers under consideration expect of art, how they might have experienced the meaning of paintings through reproductions. What, in those papers, might be attributed to the authors' work with Berger? What might be attributed to our general culture? What might be taken as a sign of some individual or idiosyncratic vision?

   In our experience, the key features for students who have worked on this painting have been the identity of the box and pot on the floor behind the woman, the woman's relationship to this room—is it hers, for example?—and the nature of the task she is performing. One question for a teacher here is the degree to which this project could, or should, involve research. It would be a good idea to decide beforehand whether to provide additional information about Vermeer; to provide art historians' readings of the painting; to suggest that students make use of the library; or to allow students to work without secondary sources.

3. We've had a good deal of success with this assignment. Ideally, students should have ready access to a museum. Berger talks about the ways we have come to experience paintings in museums, and a trip to a museum to look at a painting will give students a way of adding to or reflecting on Berger's argument. But he also talks about reproductions, so we felt justified in adding the option of using art books. If you can reasonably expect your students to get to a museum, however, we think the trip will hold some interesting surprises for you. We usually schedule a class meeting at the museum—just to get the students walking around to think about which painting might be "theirs." Warn students against docents and taped tours—for your purposes, prepared readings of paintings will be a real barrier to writing.

   The students who have had the most success with this assignment have been fairly literal in their sense of what it means to have a "conversation" with a painting. Their essays do not read like museum-guide interpretations but rather like more open-ended and speculative pieces, sometimes cast as a narrative with dialogue, sometimes as pure dialogue. The key is to invite students to talk to the painting, to ask questions, and to imagine rich and ambiguous responses. You want to avoid papers in which students begin with an idea of what a picture is about and simply impose that reading on the material. The paintings need to be imagined to talk back, to counter or open up a student's desire to master and control.

   For revision: In some cases, we've found that we needed to send students back to the painting and the original assignment, usually because they were more concerned to push through a single reading than to have a conversation with their material. In most cases, however, we have used the revision as the occasion to send students back to the Berger essay. As they became involved with the museum assignment, students forgot about Berger, so we used the revision to send them back to see what use they could make of his way of talking about paintings or the museum. "How, for example, could you use the example of your essay to explain what Berger might mean when he talks about 'history'?" The idea is to engage students in a conversation with Berger, where they can draw on their expertise to enter his argument.

4. Berger offers interesting and compelling readings of Rembrandt's *Woman in Bed* and Caravaggio's *The Calling of St. Matthew* as ways to talk with his lover. Students will see a slightly different Berger in these two pieces than in "Ways of Seeing," and this assignment offers them both the opportunity to use these readings to clarify and elaborate on Berger's claims that he makes in "Ways of Seeing" for what it means to "read" paintings and the opportunity to see readings of paintings created in a meditative space as a part of a long love letter. How, they might be asked, does this kind of reading differ from the readings in his essay? What would account for those differences? What, in other words, are these readings able to accomplish that the readings in the essay do not or cannot?

MAKING CONNECTIONS 🄴

1. The assignment points to the common starting point in Percy's and Berger's essays: both work with the assumption that people see what they have learned to see—we

don't "naturally" or "truly" receive scenes in nature or pictures in a museum. Both argue that, if this is the case, one ought to think about ways of seeing, worry about one's habitual understanding of the world, and plan strategies or approaches to improve one's vision. With this Percy/Berger sense of the problem, students are asked to put themselves (and the essays) to the test by imagining approaches to a painting in a museum (although there is no reason why a teacher should insist on a museum—it would be possible to use slides or handouts or the images in the text). Students must step back from what they have done and use what they have written in their essays to compare and evaluate the two essays.

The only real difficulty in this assignment is the number of steps: grasp the argument of the essays, write a series of approaches, and evaluate what you have done. There is no reason why these steps can't be separate stages as students work on this essay. Each might be written individually and discussed in class or in groups. All three might then be put together into a single essay in a final revision.

2. Before writing this assignment, students will undoubtedly need to do some preliminary work with the Foucault selection and would certainly be helped by preliminary work with the Berger piece. The second-reading questions for class discussions of both the Foucault and the Berger selections will help students orient themselves to these challenging texts.

Neither Berger nor Foucault directly defines what he means by power. However, Berger is more direct in his attribution of power to the ruling class and invites us to imagine how power relations might change if people were to understand history in art, whereas Foucault presents power as a force of production in culture that, in a sense, has a life of its own. If students approach this assignment as a single project to explain theories of power, rather than to make a critical judgment about either theory, they'll have a clearer sense of purpose as they reread the texts and mark passages that they can use to represent each author's notions of power. Students will find it more challenging to write about Foucault's arguments about power, which he invests not in people or classes of people but rather in culture as a force that those knowledgeable enough about power can use to channel and manipulate people. But it is difficult to say from either Foucault's or Berger's arguments how power works and how you might know it when you see it. Students will be frustrated if they think that they can get either author's arguments about power down pat, and they will need to write this assignment in an atmosphere of experimentation so that they can acknowledge and write about the sections of both texts that they have trouble understanding. It helps our students to know that anyone reading these texts will have a challenging time of trying to come to grips with the discussions of power, and that this difficulty is an opportunity to speculate and venture explanations that are tentative and uncertain.

3. To use Bordo's essay in a reconsideration of Berger's, students will obviously need to work with both essays before framing Berger in terms of Bordo. This is the kind of assignment that makes considerable demands on students, particularly of their close readings of Bordo's and Berger's examples as representatives of their respective arguments on the readings and uses of images. Because this is the case, students will need to do preliminary work in both discussions of their readings of each essay and in at least one

piece of writing for each in which they work through a set of two or three images and the ways each author uses those images to promote arguments and positions. What, then, are each author's arguments and positions on readings and uses of images?

From this preliminary work, students will be ready to put the two essays next to each other to consider whether they're doing the same work and saying the same things. The key, of course, is to be certain that students are working from at least two images for each text, so that their arguments will be grounded in those and develop, then, as minicases. When students consider the relationship of Bordo's work to Berger's, they'll need to imagine that Bordo is in some way extending and transforming Berger's. Berger came first, but it's not a cause-and-effect relationship. Bordo uses Berger, so students will need to imagine that she is on her own trajectory through the reading of the images that have caught her attention. Berger offers her a way to read and understand them. What of Berger does she use? How does she transform Berger's ideas? How, finally, might their work be understood to be similar and different?

JOHN BERGER

Ways of Seeing: Episode 1 🄴

Students will need to read Berger's text before they watch this video. There are a number of reasons for doing this. The text has more to say. It presents more examples and other extended arguments about art and reproductions that the video only touches on or alludes to. The text, in other words, adds complexity to the subject matter as presented in the video. The BBC episode, meanwhile, makes use of the kinds of things that only videos can—quick shifts, visual juxtapositions, zoom and pan, and that sort of self-awareness of itself as a medium that Berger relishes in manipulating.

If you do ask students, as we're suggesting, to read the text first, there's opportunity for a Berger assignment in that. How, students might be asked, did their reading of the text influence their "seeing" the video? How, in other words, did the text situate their first takes on the video? What did they expect, given the reading? What didn't they expect? What does each—the text and the video—do that the other doesn't?

QUESTIONS FOR A SECOND VIEWING 🄴

1. Berger likes video as a medium. It allows him to juxtapose and situate images, with his voiceovers and the images of himself, in the blink of an eye. He takes images from galleries and places them instantly in rooms, on T-shirts, next to other images, including images of him talking to viewers. He's an expressive lecturer, and he knows he's using himself, his facial and bodily expressions, in the mix of all the other images. It's these juxtapositions and situations of images of which students should take note. They'll need to find a set that seems significant in their arrangements, a set that Berger seems to be using to make a particular argument. To do this, they'll need to watch the video with this assignment in hand; then they'll need to watch it at least one other time to take notes and identify the set of images with which they'd like to work.

2. This question is all about contexts for the paintings that Berger presents in the video. Students will need to watch the video at least twice before doing this work. The first time, they should be watching with an idea towards identifying the paintings Berger presents and the various contexts in which he presents them, especially the moments in which he changes the contexts for the same paintings. He's making a point with the contexts and their changes. What is that point, other than the obvious one that contexts matter? What happens to us as we see these paintings in different contexts? What happens to our perceptions of the paintings? Berger appears to be making an argument about the seen and the perceiver in this part of the video. How does he begin that argument? Where does he end up by the end? How do the paintings and their contexts contribute to the argument?

3. This is a challenging assignment that invites students to work across the first and third video sections and the texts in the book. The heart of the assignment is its focus on the way in which the video, taking the camera as an eye, narrates an argument about paintings and their reproductions. Berger manipulates the eye; he controls what viewers see and the order in which they see images, including the images of him as a narrator and instigator. Students will need to identify moments in the video that allow them to describe Berger's narrative by thinking of the camera as an eye. What is the eye focusing on? What does it draw us to? What does it want us to see? What's the story it's telling about paintings and reproductions, including its own reproductions?

   Once students have worked with the camera as an eye narrating a story about paintings and their reproductions in these two video sections, they can turn to the essay in the book. The big question here has to do with what the video camera as narrating eye allows Berger to do in the video that he doesn't or can't do in the essay. What examples from the video and the essay would make this clear to readers? Students will need to work from those video and essay examples or else their thinking and writing will lift off the page into untethered abstractions.

4. This is a great assignment to pair with the first writing assignment. Both invite students to study Berger's presentations of the Franz Hals painting. He has a lot to say about it, the way it has been mystified by art critics, and the way they seem to carefully sidestep the expressions on the subjects' faces and their relationship to Hals. How does Berger with his camera as a narrating eye make use of the camera to develop his argument about the Hals painting? Students will need to view this section of the video a number of times to see what Berger is doing by juxtaposing Hals's painting with details of the painting, for instance, and how he uses the camera along with his voiceover and narrative persona to play out the thread of his argument about this painting.

ASSIGNMENTS FOR WRITING ⓔ

1. This assignment begins with the assumption that both the video and the essay are manipulating how we see the Hals painting. If students have worked with the fourth "Question for a Second Viewing," they're ready to think about the ways in which text works differently from the video on us as readers of the Franz Hals painting. What

does Berger have to do with the essay that he doesn't have to with the video? What advantage does the essay have over the video in its presentation and discussion of the Hals painting? What are the advantages and constraints of each presentation of the Hals?

2. Students will be asked to do multiple pieces of work for this essay. They might think of it as a case report of peoples' perceptions of the Caravaggio painting. First, they'll need to study the painting themselves without turning to art critics or other sources. They might think of it as a thought or perception experiment.

The first part of the experiment is their own two- to three-paragraph explanation of what the painting means to them. To be clear, they need to write about what they see in the painting, but they also need to attribute meaning to what they see. The assumption here is very much from Berger—that viewers make meaning of paintings.

The second part of the experiment is to imitate Berger's discussion of the painting with a small group of people. The video example seems to take a heavy hand in framing or perhaps leading the children to see things in certain ways. Students can do better than this by asking their small group of three or four people to do what they did. What do they see in the painting? What catches their attention? How do the details cohere into a whole from which they can take or draw meaning? What is that meaning?

Finally, after working on these two aspects of the experiment, students can write their essays in which they report on their study of their perceptions of the Caravaggio and the meanings they attributed to it and their groups' perceptions of the painting and the meanings they drew from it. Do they agree with Berger about the way the Caravaggio speaks to people based on their study? What would they conclude about what the others saw and they didn't and vice versa? Finally, what would they conclude about what it means for a painting to speak to its viewers? Would they agree with Berger on this?

SUSAN BORDO

Beauty (Re)discovers the Male Body e

Bordo's work is compelling. Few students will read this essay and remain silent. It's the kind of work that prompts students to speak back, although not necessarily in agreement. Bordo reads what seems so obvious to us—advertisements having to do with male bodies, clothes, and lifestyles—and she sees more at play in these than capitalistic desires to make money. She sees representations of male gender that have remained largely unspoken in our culture against a backdrop of very vocal and visible representations of female gender. As a part of her reading of the history of advertising involving the male body, she argues that the popular displays of the male body and various notions of masculinity in media and ads became possible first through the gay community, where cultural taboos against the male body broke their silence. Her documentation of the opening of cultural space to the male body will fascinate readers, and after work with this essay, it will be difficult for students to imagine representations of the male body, particularly of ads peddling clothes, without also imagining the positions they take on what it means to be male and masculine. This is the beauty of Bordo's essay. It gives students an accessible route into thinking of ads and media representations of the male as promoting particular notions of masculinity. And although we have long been saturated with such promotions of what it means to be female, it is unlikely that students will have played out a parallel awareness of what it means to be male.

It's odd (but then it isn't) how our culture has kept the male body under wraps, so to speak, for so long while freely unveiling and using the female body. You might expect that students, especially the male students, will be somewhat uncomfortable initially with this essay and the work it asks of them. The male body, as much as it is presented and used around us, still carries taboos for many men. There are at least two obvious ways to frame this work, then, to open it up. One is to point to the parallel work that has been done on women in advertising and how freely we critique and speak back to those representations. The other is to frame it, of course, as academic work and let the resistance dissolve as students read the essay. Bordo is candid, smart, and funny. Her writing can disarm even the most uptight and resistant readers; so although there might be initial reluctance, students will loosen up once they are into the reading. At least that's been our experience with readers of this work.

And Bordo is a generous writer. In the opening chapter of *The Male Body*, she offers her readers their own perspectives on the images she reads. She says, "You may not see the same things in this ad that I do. Representations of the body have a history, but so too do viewers, and they bring that history—both personal and cultural—to their perception and interpretation. Different viewers may see different things. In pointing to certain elements in ads, or movies, or fashion, I'm not ignoring the differences in how people may see things, but deliberately trying to direct your attention to what I see as significant" (p. 29). In the essay included here, she extends this invitation by opening up the notion of "subject position," so that readers can understand the positions she occupies and those that they occupy. The concept is central to her work, as is her use of "gaze," so it's worth students' time to take this essay as an opportunity to understand and work with these two terms, which represent key concepts in culture studies. A number of our assignments, including the third of the second-reading questions and the first, third, and fourth writing assignments, offer students opportunities to become familiar with them.

Whatever work you invite students to do with this essay, it is important to keep them close to Bordo's examples of ads and media representations. With an essay such as this, it is all too easy for discussions to drift off the page into abstract, overgeneralized arguments about what she does and what she says. The first assignment for writing offers students the opportunity to extend Bordo's work by thinking and writing about their own set of examples or counterexamples, so students can learn her strategies both by closely reading them and by writing with and through them.

QUESTIONS FOR A SECOND READING 🄴

1. One of the pleasures of Bordo's text has to do with the ways in which she lingers over her examples and arguments. At times, she writes about the pleasures this gives her, and she's not shy at all about telling us how much she enjoys particular images and moments in ads. This kind of lingering will be unfamiliar to students accustomed to steamrolling through their writing to simply get it done, so it will take some effort for

them to notice how Bordo does this and when she does it. This is a good time for students to mark the moments in the text when she takes pleasure in playing out threads. First, though, students will need to have an overall sense of her pacing. There are a number of ways for them to get this, and perhaps the easiest is the most direct. They can think about how much time and space she gives moments in relation to their relative importance to her work. Where are the big chunks? What does she treat at length? Where does her pace pick up? Students can invent their own way of marking these moments in the text, and it would be interesting to have them share their work, perhaps in pairs or groups of three, with the class. This can also be an interesting question to return to once students have written their own essays, perhaps after they've done a draft or two of the first writing assignment, where they take on and extend Bordo's project with their own examples. Once they have given time to studying Bordo's pacing, they can then turn to their own work with the same questions. Over what do they linger? Why? Where does the pace pick up? How might they change the pace by rewriting or cutting back?

2.   This is another question about form that follows nicely from the first, and as such, it would also be a good piece of work for students to do with their own essays (or with the essays of their peers). The attention here is on the subsections that Bordo marks and uses. As with the first question, students can invent their own ways of marking these and of referring to them. We use the language of rhythm and tonality. What is the slowest section, for example? Or which one is the loudest? And what would they mean by that? How is it loud? Any such discussion will have to place sections in context since slow is always slow in relation to something else and loud is loud in relation to quiet sections. It would be interesting to hear students speculate as to why they think particular sections are slow or loud or quiet. And, of course, it would be even more interesting to hear them discuss their own essays and the essays of their peers using these same terms and strategies.

3.   This question offers students an opportunity to do an important piece of work in an area that has come to define a critical structure of culture studies—subject positioning. Bordo takes various subject positions and also defines those she takes and those taken by others to whom she refers. She's smart about how she uses the notion of subject position, and since she writes directly about it, students can read critically for the various positions she takes (that of a historian, for example, or coyly seduced voyeur or cultural critic), and then, in response to her work, they can take various positions that they imagine both as a part of their argument and as a part of just having fun with the ability to take various positions (even if one doesn't hold or believe in them). There is also interesting work here for students with the ways in which a subject can be defined by another's gaze and, of course, the ways in which one's gaze can be said to define others. Students can begin this work with Bordo's discussions of gaze. They also can imagine how their own gazes at the others presented in ads define them and inscribe the others in such a definition.

Subject positions that are compelling, one might argue, hold up differently from those that are not, and a good way for students to become familiar with why this is so is to first turn to Bordo's various positions (we suggest making a list). After they have had some experience reading critically, they can turn to creating their own positions, and as a class or in pairs, they can assess them as they did hers. The final suggestion in the assignment asks students to speak back to Bordo from what they take to be their own positions, and hopefully this would complicate students' work because seldom do readers hold monolithic positions toward such a shifting and complex piece of reading. It would be interesting to hear students articulate their positions in relation to the changing landscape in Bordo's text.

4. This question prepares students to extend Bordo's project and write their own essay (for the first "Assignment for Writing") in which they study a set of ad examples or counterexamples. The key piece of work here is for students to collect examples of ads that they believe are also, as Bordo puts it, "advertisement[s] for a certain notion of what it means to be a man." As students collect these, they might invent ways to annotate them that serve as shorthand for their readings, and they might also imagine what language they would use to classify or categorize the ads. This could easily be a class or group project that would materialize, then, as work that the entire class could benefit from seeing and hearing. Inventing terms and language for categorizing imitates the intellectual moves that mark academic work grounded in building cases and generalizing from them.

ASSIGNMENTS FOR WRITING e

1. The invitation to students is to extend Bordo's project, to present readers with at least the outlines and fundamental terms of her work in this essay, to read a set of ads as she does, using her methods, and to locate themselves as subjects with positions that are relative to them. It's a challenging piece of work, and you will want to begin it by giving students opportunities to discuss the assignment itself. You might ask students: "What are you being asked to do? What do you need to do in your essay? How do you identify and write from your subject position?"

   If students have already completed the fourth of the second-reading questions, they will have collected the examples from which they can work. If not, then they'll need to set about doing this with an eye to identifying ads that allow them to make claims for the ways the ads promote specific notions of "what it means to be a man," as Bordo puts it. It would be fun to extend this project beyond the boundaries of representations of the male by asking students to complete a second part in which they do a similar Bordo-like study of ads that represent particular ways of being a woman. Their methods of working would be similar, and once they had done both, they could imagine, for instance, the ways in which their own gazes define their subject positions toward men and women in these ads. How much of this defining is being manipulated by the ad? How much of it do they bring to the ad?

2. The pleasures of the text, this assignment claims, can be in the ways it directs and organizes a reader's (and a writer's) attention. The key move for students when writing to this assignment is in their identification of key moments in the text from which they can write, from which they can make their own claims about what is pleasurable and what is not in Bordo's writing. We suggest that students begin with the first second-reading question, which asks them to imagine the rhythm and pace of the selection, the tone and volume of the voice speaking, and to note what in these gives them pleasure and

poses problems. It would be interesting to encourage students to take note of the same types of moves in other texts they are reading or have read recently, so that they can move back and forth between texts, using the same methods or approaches for each, to point to issues of pace, rhythm, tone, phrasing, and so on. The obvious complexities—is a certain pace or rhythm or structure always pleasurable or problematic?—present themselves, then, if students have the opportunity to work across texts. That would be a great occasion to raise questions about the relations of the content of the text to the structures that define its form and offer it up as pleasurable or problematic.

3. This assignment invites students to read and write about ads directed primarily at men and women as an occasion to think through, while using Bordo's terms and methods, the role of gender in the design, presentation, and reading of these ads. What, we might ask, in the ads makes them gender specific or appealing to a particular gender? And, then, of course, how do students read and react differently to ads directed at men and those directed at women? What, in other words, might they say that the designers of these ads are counting on from men? from women? What assumptions are the ad designers making about their audiences? the audiences' predispositions? their acculturations? their predictable reactions?

    Students will need to find ways to include the images from which they work in their essays, and they'll also need to find ways to refer to Bordo's work, to contextualize their studies, so that readers unfamiliar with Bordo's essay would understand the ground from which the students' work proceeds. How might their essays refer to Bordo's claims? her examples? her methods of gathering her examples and information? Then, too, students will need to learn to cite her essay.

4. Students have an opportunity with this assignment to work with a comparison of Bordo's position on two of her examples and their own. Since the focus of this essay is on the development of subject positions, they'll need to carefully select examples for which Bordo has an articulated subject position or where she speaks from another's position. The work of the essay, then, is to explain Bordo's position toward the examples and, at the same time, for students to define their own position toward the same examples. How, they might ask, would they account for Bordo's position toward these examples? And how would they account for their own position toward the same examples? What is it about the examples? about Bordo's history and preparation? about their own backgrounds and preparations?

    A more challenging version of this assignment would ask students to work from examples in which Bordo imagines the subject positions of viewers she imagines as the audience for the ads. How, we'd want to ask, does she imagine these positions? In what ways are her imaginings similar to and different from those of ad designers? And, finally, how do the ad designers' positions on these same examples stand alongside those that Bordo imagines for others? What's influencing theirs? hers?

MAKING CONNECTIONS 🄴

1. To use Bordo's essay in a reconsideration of Berger's, students will obviously need to work with both essays before framing Berger in terms of Bordo. This is the kind of assignment that makes considerable demands on students, particularly of their close

readings of Bordo's and Berger's examples as representatives of their respective arguments on the readings and uses of images. Because this is the case, students will need to do preliminary work in both discussions of their readings of each essay and in at least one piece of writing for each in which they work through a set of two or three images and the ways each author uses those images to promote arguments and positions. What, then, are each author's arguments and positions on readings and uses of images?

From this preliminary work, students will be ready to put the two essays next to each other to consider whether they're doing the same work and saying the same things. The key, of course, is to be certain that students are working from at least two images for each text, so that their arguments will be grounded in those and develop, then, as minicases. When students consider the relationship of Bordo's work to Berger's, they'll need to imagine that Bordo is in some way extending and transforming Berger's work. Berger came first, but it's not a cause-and-effect relationship. Bordo uses Berger, so students will need to imagine that she is on her own trajectory through the reading of the images that have caught her attention. Berger offers her a way to read and understand them. What of Berger does she use? How does she transform Berger's ideas? How, finally, might their work be understood to be similar and different?

2. This is a standard *Ways of Reading* assignment. You have two scholars, two projects; the assignment asks students to think of them together, as though they are speaking back and forth. (It helps, we have found, to invite students to speak from the point of view of a Kipnis or a Griffin or a Bordo, and to do so even when the gesture is tentative: "I think what Griffin is saying is this. . . ." or "My sense of Bordo is such that she would agree, or disagree, with Griffin about this. . . .") The real test is to keep the assignment from becoming an empty formal exercise in comparing and contrasting. This is why we emphasize audience ("keep in mind a reader familiar with neither essay"). Students, then, have to think about translating ideas and presenting key terms and examples. This is why we insist upon some kind of argument: "Who speaks most powerfully to you?" We want students to read one essay through the lens of the other—and we have found that asking them to take sides is a convenient way to do this. The danger, of course, is that in order to prefer Griffin, students need to make Bordo into a cartoon figure. It is up to you to keep that from happening. A revision, in fact, is often a way to invite students to work on the section of their essay that was too slick or too easy to write the first time around.

JUDITH BUTLER

Beside Oneself: On the Limits of Sexual Autonomy (p. 114)

We are excited to include Judith Butler among the writers in this edition of *Ways of Reading*—not only because she is one of the most significant intellectuals of the past twenty years, but also because the presence of a scholar working explicitly in the discipline of queer theory will expose students to a set of concerns and rhetorical complexities that are part of the richness of this field. Students may find Butler very difficult to read and understand at first. They may even be frustrated on their first readings, wondering why the sentences feel so dense or even convoluted. And the fact that Butler discusses sexuality and gender politics does not make this frustration and difficulty any easier for students. As with most difficult texts, we found that what students seemed to need most in order to be able to engage with Butler is a way in—a path through which they can start to work on the essay as they would on clay or painting, making moves here and there to see what unfolds. The assignments that follow, particularly the "Questions for a Second Reading," aim to offer these ways in, allowing students to revisit Butler in smaller, more manageable pieces that may unlock the whole of the essay as they return to it a second and third time.

We think it is worth mentioning that instructors need not understand every word of Butler's essay to teach it. Such a rich and complicated philosophical text continues to make new meanings even for the most experienced and most educated reader. We cannot imagine what *mastery* of a text such as this would look like. Like a poem or an experimental piece of literature, Butler's essay is meant to engage us in the very problems she is working through, problems that do not have easy resolutions, problems that do not necessarily have answers. We have found that it is useful to lead students through sentences one by one, thinking along with them about what one turn of phrase or syntactical shift might mean. It was helpful to write individual sentences on the board in class, creating a kind of diagram of Judith Butler sentences. (See Cathy Birkenstein's "We Got the Wrong Gal: Rethinking the 'Bad' Academic Writing of Judith Butler," p. 265.) We spent several classes doing this work, and it allowed students to return to the essay with more confidence, trusting that they could, in fact, make meaning out of even the most difficult passages.

QUESTIONS FOR A SECOND READING (p. 132)

1. We think it is important to remind students that reading theory or philosophy is difficult work for any reader, regardless of the reader's intelligence or level of education. Encountering a new theoretical essay, or an essay outside our field of expertise, can feel like reading an entirely new language. Its key terms feel strange and empty. The assumptions and subtext are hidden from us, at first. In a sense, we begin reading as if in the dark, feeling around for something that is familiar, for something that evokes an image, a point of reference, a moment of connection. And then, we hang on to that moment as we read on, waiting for another. This assignment offers students one way to approach the difficulties of reading a highly theoretical work. Reading theoretical work, we think, is productive not just for its ideas, but for the ways that it defamiliarizes language, making it strange and new all over again. This is an important experience for students because of the way it makes them aware of their blind spots and assumptions. When students begin to write their own essays engaging with Butler, they too have the burden of defining and contextualizing their concepts and key terms for their readers. They cannot simply take a word like *agency*, for example, for granted, even if they think they know what it means. Reading philosophy reminds us that language attains meaning through its usage, through its repetition in context.

2–3. Students seemed to need to move through Butler's essay slowly. We spent a good deal of time in the first few classes after students had read the essay asking them to identify passages from the essay that were particularly difficult to understand or follow, so that we could move through them together and linger on their difficulties. This assignment works to complement the spirit of that close reading. Taking Butler's sentences one phrase, or sometimes one word, at a time helps students not only to make meaning from that specific sentence but also to learn how to read a Judith Butler sentence. One of the challenges with reading Butler and with the density of her work is that students can lose sight of the reading's connection to LGBTQ realities. This question also asks students to consider the political and personal implications of their close reading of Butler, calling attention both to Butler's project as a whole and to the significance of that project in context.

4. Students, in their own essays, often struggle to find ways of using questions—and yet, Butler provides a number of productive possibilities, using questions as a way to introduce an issue, as a hypothetical, or as a way of grappling with an unsolvable problem. In this assignment, we ask students to focus on the style of Butler's questions, on her rhetorical moves as an intellectual. In looking at the ways Butler asks questions, and sometimes answers or asks another, students can focus on this particular way of meaning making as a thinker and as a writer. Locating questions and lingering on their implications is another way of reading Butler, giving students something to *do* with Butler's essay, and something they will likely have immediate success in doing.

ASSIGNMENTS FOR WRITING (p. 134)

1. As we say in response to the fourth "Question for a Second Reading," Butler provides a number of productive questions, as ways to introduce issues, as a hypothetical, or as a way of grappling with an unsolvable problem. Locating questions and lingering on their implications is a way of reading Butler, giving students something to *do* with Butler's essay, and something they will likely have immediate success in doing.

2. One way of reading and understanding Butler's work is to write about it, as the first "Assignment for Writing" asks of students. This writing assignment calls attention to Butler's work in another way—pointing to one of the ways she organizes and structures her essay around the possibilities and meanings of the idiomatic phrase *beside oneself*. This assignment asks students to do some Butler-like thinking of their own, to try to mimic the kinds of meditations of language that Butler uses to make her arguments. In a sense, this assignment is an intense assignment in close reading, giving students the challenge of writing an essay focusing on a single phrase and theorizing about its figurative meanings. An assignment like this highlights Butler's creativity and calls students to do this kind of creative thinking on their own. We don't often think of interpretation and close reading as creative skills, but we find it productive to think of these challenges in those terms, as problems to be tackled with imagination as much as reasoning.

MAKING CONNECTIONS (p. 135)

1. Because Foucault is a large part of Butler's lineage of theoretical influence, in this assignment students are enacting a kind of archaeological textual dig in which they are asked to hear and discover in Butler the echoes of Foucault's understanding of power, knowledge, and regulation. This assignment will be very challenging for students as

they try to grapple with two particularly difficult texts—ones whose complexities are reflected in the very nuances and movements of their sentences. This difficulty is part of the reason that we have given the students so much text to work with in the actual question. In fact, it may be productive to give students the option of working only with the quotes we have given them in the text of this assignment. Even these passages alone will offer students opportunities to practice both interpreting and articulating the ideological relationships between two complex philosophical texts.

The concept of surveillance alongside the metaphor of the prison seemed to help our students understand more about Butler's project and perhaps even what is at stake in her writing. And this assignment, through analysis, invites them into this conversation through the metaphor of the prison, giving them a grounding from which to begin their own theorization of culture, power, and identity.

2. This writing assignment, in some ways, asks students to do something that may already be familiar to them—to focus on the common themes between two texts. The prompt itself even outlines for students the common threads of exile, existence, and, as Butler puts it, "the question of the human." But the assignment also asks students to think of the implications of these intersections between Butler and Said. What we like about this assignment is the possibility for students to reflect on their own experiences of "otherness." These experiences will not necessarily emerge in narrative or personal essay form, but instead as a way of understanding, or sometimes challenging, the claims Butler and Said make about alienation, identity, and exile.

3. This assignment offers students the unique opportunity to turn to Butler as a way of understanding and engaging with Miller's essay. For students, engaging in a Miller-like project of reflecting on Butler through reading will be a material way of pointing to the challenges, problems, and intricacies of Miller's project of moving between text and self. Students may recognize part of this assignment as a kind of personal essay, but our intention is for the genre of the personal essay to be disrupted by the requirement that students use Butler to help keep the essays situated and focused on literacy practices rather than exclusively on life experience. We like this assignment because of the way that it draws students into a critique of the work we are doing in the composition classroom. In this regard, it makes them collaborators and coauthors in the work of the course itself by asking them to explore the reasons why we talk about reading and writing in the first place. This assignment, then, leads us into a discussion of what we take for granted about the value of reading and writing; and, in doing so, students become conscious of these values in ways that allow them either to invest in them or to interrogate them. And, both investment and interrogation are significant scholarly practices.

JUDITH BUTLER

Your Behavior Creates Your Gender e

Judith Butler is always a difficult reading experience—her prose is dense and complicated. She has a winding and ever-qualifying grammar that makes her arguments intricate and circular. We've found that one way of helping students engage more confidently with Butler's essay is to engage them with Butler herself speaking about her work more broadly. In the video "Your Behavior Creates Your Gender," Butler explains some of her most groundbreaking and circulating ideas about gender, ideas that are the foundation for work that comes later, work like the essay we've included in *Ways of Reading*. Since bringing video materials into the classroom, we've noticed the ways that author videos can remind students that there *is* an author, a human voice behind the ideas they respond to and read in their writing course. We have designed questions that engage the video alongside Butler's essay, allowing students to move back and forth from the reading to the video. In the end, the video has the potential to enrich students' reading experience and make the essay seem more approachable to readers.

QUESTIONS FOR A SECOND VIEWING 📧

1. Listening to Butler talk about gender and identity requires the same close attention to particular terms needed when reading her writing. The difference between (or even the overlapping possibilities between) *fact* and *phenomenon* are at the heart of Butler's selections in *Ways of Reading* and at the center of her work as a writer more broadly. This question can help students develop an understanding of the ways that a phenomenon is *produced* rather than preexistent. When we work with students on particular terms, we find it's always useful to have students discuss their associations with those terms as a beginning point. In what context have they heard the terms *fact* and *phenomenon* used before? How might Butler's use of those terms build on or challenge the meanings they currently have for them? Finally, why might some people (or even some students) not want to shift their understandings of these terms?

2. This question invites students to think through some real-world applications and possibilities for Butler's claims about the ways gender is regulated and to posit some of their own theories about why this regulation takes place. While this question has its more leading components (for example, the question leaves little room for students to say that gender is *not* policed), we've found that most students find it easy to recall personal examples of gender policing. The concept itself is often not new to them, but the theoretical language or the nuance of that language is very new—and, at times, hard to follow. This question works particularly well when we first ask students to compose a list of policing examples and then launch a class discussion after students have written their lists.

3. This question invites students to use some of Butler's theoretical notions of performance *and* some of their own close-reading skills on the video itself. It's useful to remind students that videos or photographs are constructed just as texts are constructed—with decisions about angle, edits, visual effects, etc. And if identities are constructed in many of the ways Butler suggests, it's often interesting for students to discuss how identities are formed—by clothing, by haircut, by posture, by word choice. Many of our students have talked about Butler's *performance* of "scholar." In one particular class, the question prompted a discussion of the students' performances of "scholar" in their own writing. This sparked, for those students, a fascinating question about when performance stops seeming like performance and starts appearing natural. These discussions, to us, seem

not only important in understanding theoretical ideas about gender but also important in exploring some key performative aspects of writing itself.

ASSIGNMENT FOR WRITING 🄴

1.   We imagine this assignment as very much an extension of the work students begin in all of the "Questions for a Second Viewing," but it is most connected to our first question in that section. We have found that one of the most productive ways for students to engage with difficult texts is through that text's key terms and those terms' relationships to one another. The terms offer students some fence posts, some markers around which to construct their essay and some ways of entering the text with a specific thread. The relationship between being and doing is, of course, in both Butler's writing and in the world, extremely complex. And perhaps the most difficult part of this assignment is composing an essay that honors the complexity rather than trying to simplify it. For example, one instinct some students might have is to create a binary distinction whereby *being* is who you *really* are and *doing* is something you "put on" or "perform." Without a close reading of Butler, this is likely the kind of analysis we might find someone putting forth. So preparing students for this writing assignment goes beyond having them read the essay and watch the video; it requires us to do the work of helping students to unpack some of Butler's terms so that they can envision those terms with complexity, and with a tolerance for contradiction.

ANNE CARSON

Short Talks (p. 140)

When we first read Anne Carson's *Short Talks* for *Ways of Reading*, we were struck by both its originality and its sense of surprise. After all, what reader can experience Carson's *Short Talks* without wondering where we are, what Carson wants from us, what these meditations might mean? While none of the assignments in the textbook make reference to the "short talks" as meditations, it might be useful to use this term as you discuss with students what Carson might be after. Why, for example, write a meditation "On Trout"? Why meditate on anything for that matter? Considering these questions together as a class may give students an angle from which to read Carson's writing and interact with her talks as meditations, reflections, and even intellectual arguments.

Carson's *Short Talks* will become more familiar with repeated readings, particularly if you ask students to read aloud—in class or in small groups—the same short talk more than once. These readings will help students notice new things about Carson's writing each time, giving them the opportunity to both hear and speak Carson's poem. It might be useful for students to see what it feels like to speak aloud in Carson's voice, to consider how she makes the usual strange or perhaps is trying to make the strange more usual. It is likely that students will have some difficulty with Carson because her writing may at first feel arbitrary, strange, or even nonsensical. The assignments that follow offer students a pathway toward the work of cultural critique, scholarly inquiry, and narrative analysis.

QUESTIONS FOR A SECOND READING (p. 143)

1. This question will work well if instructors decide to assign names to different students or different groups of students. References that students don't recognize—to Sylvia Plath, Elektra, the Nuremberg Laws, or Kafka—can be barriers not only to their understanding but also to their willingness to enter into dialogue with a text. Having a class discussion after students have looked up this information might help all the students navigate *Short Talks* more confidently.

    Once the class has done this work, it may be useful for students to consider the effects of knowing this new information. Anne Carson's *Short Talks* is certainly difficult to read in terms of form and content—it is part poem, part flash fiction, and part essay. This second-reading question engages students in folding back some of the first layers of meaning. The follow-up questions then try to help students dig through other layers.

2. We find it useful to acknowledge with students from the beginning that Carson's *Short Talks* might be quite difficult to read and that they might even experience fading in and out of the reading as they move through it. Having them focus on the personal aspects of Carson's work may give students the confidence to talk about what they noticed or found puzzling. Asking students for single lines or sentences that compelled them or spoke to them gives students a way to engage with Carson's work. Ideally, this question will enable students to work from what they do understand as a way of sorting through what they don't understand or what seems impossible to understand. Carson does ask that we think of sense-making or understanding in different ways. More so than any other essay in *Ways of Reading*, Anne Carson's *Short Talks*, at times, resists understanding, resists the very notion that text is meant to be understood in traditional ways. The "Questions for a Second Reading" aim to help students consider the ways of knowing that Carson opens and resists for her readers.

3. Although Carson's brief pieces appear simple, their structures are not. She makes some obvious stylistic moves such as addressing the reader—or someone referred to as "you"—and writing sentences that aren't sentences, but noticing her methods of writing will require students to do some close reading. One of the best ways for students to get close to her methods is to reread the pieces over and over. We've noticed, too, that students can get close to the language if they actually write out each piece as a part of their rereadings, noting those sentences or moments where she is making structures within the pieces. It's not important that the students know formal names for her methods. It is important that they name her ways of writing themselves, that they imagine language that will represent these ways to others.

ASSIGNMENTS FOR WRITING (p. 144)

1. Students will more than likely have difficulty with Carson, perhaps viewing her genre-bending and experimentalism as random, arbitrary, or even impenetrable. Carson is playful, even when she explores deep grief or heartbreak. This first writing assignment asks students to explore Carson's work using Carson's terms and rules. One way to

help students engage with this kind of writing is to find ways that students might see the writing on its own terms. Carson's introduction offers a potential pathway through which students might feel more able to discuss and interpret the work. In this sense, Carson provides us with the language we might use to talk about her writing. Students have the opportunity both to interpret that language and to discover how Carson's statements about writing unfold in the craft of the talks themselves.

2. This kind of assignment is not uncommon in *Ways of Reading*—assignments that ask students to imitate, mimic, or work in the spirit of another writer in order to learn something about that particular writer's project or sensibility. However, Carson's collection of short talks is not exactly an essay. In fact, we are not quite sure what it is. Some teachers may even feel nervous about this assignment because students will produce writing that is not measurable as an essay, per se. But, of course, we find this ambiguity to be one of the joys and possibilities of both Carson's work and the work students will do in trying to take on a short talks project of their own. Students will likely surprise you and themselves with their creativity. An assignment like this allows for the kinds of writing that emerge when the process itself is so strange and unfamiliar.

MAKING CONNECTIONS (p. 145)

1. Before students begin trying to tackle this assignment, it is useful for instructors to guide students through how they might look for "distinctive features" of a given piece of writing and how they might name those features. We have found that a large class discussion in which students have a chance to practice finding features and naming them is really useful. Oftentimes, we have supplied students with short passages from other selections in *Ways of Reading* in order to practice before sending them off to do their own work on Doyle and Carson. Through identifying and naming these features, this assignment asks students to then consider the genre of the essay through the lens of those features they noticed. Students usually put the examples they notice in Doyle and Carson in conversation with what they've previously learned about the essay as a genre. This assignment can be really productive at the beginning of a course when instructors might be interested in having students look beyond the traditional conventions and typical understandings of an essay.

2. This assignment works against the assumption that facts are automatically true and objective statements that inform or instruct. This assignment aims to complicate notions of "fact" through an examination of how writers engage with the facts they present in their essays. After having worked with Doyle, whose essay reiterates numerous facts about hummingbirds, blue whales, and mammal hearts, students will then consider additional essays to think about facts in the context of a critical essay. As students begin writing their own analysis, they might notice themselves becoming self-conscious as they make declarative statements about the "facts" they are writing about. Assignments that provoke this kind of self-consciousness are productive because of the ways they illuminate critical thinking and writerly decisions, making students aware not only of what they are saying but also of how they are saying it.

BRIAN DOYLE

Joyas Voladoras (p. 147)

We think this essay is stunning, intelligent, and radiating with possibilities for writing prompts. In our experience, students respond well to it—perhaps because something about it feels familiar. It provides readers with facts at some level of certainty and also offers readers a profound conclusion, some kind of message or life philosophy that resonates at the end. Our assignments are connected by two primary concerns. First, Doyle's essay offers compelling ways to think with students about form and movement. It is certainly difficult to teach writers how they might talk about one thing while also pointing to another. Doyle is a wonderful example of how writers might do this work, how they might move their essays from one idea to the next without explicit transitions or connections. Second, Doyle's piece is made up primarily of facts: its basic building blocks are "facts" about hummingbirds, blue whales, and hearts. And yet, Doyle's piece does not read like a reporting of information. Focusing students' attention on these facts illuminates this piece of writing as something other than a report, instead as a series of writerly decisions that lead and shape our reading experience. We hope, then, that these assignments will make students' writing more conscious and deliberate.

QUESTIONS FOR A SECOND READING (p. 149)

1. This question seeks to focus students' attention on how Doyle's essay works on them, how the essay points to somewhere outside of itself, or away from its apparent subject. Students might select sentences such as "We all churn inside" or "You fry the machine." They might notice that "we" seems to include them and thereby moves them away from the discussion of the hearts of mammals; or they might notice how "you" works in the second set of sentences as both a general "you" and as a direct address to the reader. This question provides students with the opportunity to articulate how language works in addition to what that language is saying.

2. When students see writing only as a way of reporting information or conveying facts, they miss the infinite possibilities of language. This can stifle writing but can also lead to uncritical readings of the texts we encounter every day in the form of television commercials, news media reports, or school assignments. And while many of the selections in *Ways of Reading* trouble notions of stable or singular truths (Griffin and Wideman, for example), Doyle seems to offer a concise illustration of how facts can be used to do something other than provide information. Students might be puzzled at first to think of Doyle's "facts" about hummingbirds and blue whales as having little to do with hummingbirds and blue whales, but this question can be useful for beginning a conversation about how this might be so. The essay, after all, does not have hummingbirds or whales as its central concern, even though it spends most of its sentences referring to them. This question is designed with the idea that learning to write means, partly, opening to the possibilities of what a writer can do. And Doyle's essay offers an intriguing opportunity to see and to experiment with what facts might accomplish beyond the literal and obvious.

3.   This question asks students to pay close attention to the ways in which they are addressed and implicated in Doyle's essay. One of the reasons we are so drawn to this piece is that *how* Doyle writes is as inspiring and interesting as *what* he writes about—indeed the how and the why are integrally linked. Students have often given little thought to the figures they may strike on the page; it can be exciting to discover that one can craft (and inhabit) a voice that is more personal and intimate than the voice one might expect to use in an academic setting. This assignment implicitly invites something the textbook as a whole enacts and encourages—that students imagine themselves as thoughtful, engaging intellectuals, people who read and think and write not just because their teachers or bosses expect it of them but because they have ideas and knowledge and something to say and expect that their readers might willingly go along for the ride. Doyle provides a model of such a figure. The final part of the assignment turns to ask students to experiment with Doyle's style, trying on more remote voices and examining the effects that such remoteness produces.

4.   This kind of assignment is not uncommon in *Ways of Reading*—assignments where students are asked to imitate, mimic, or work in the spirit of another writer in order to learn something about that particular writer's project or sensibility. Doyle's "Joyas Voladoras" is not exactly an essay. But, of course, we find this ambiguity to be one of the joys and possibilities of Doyle's work and the work students will do in trying to imitate his sentences. Students will likely surprise you and themselves with their creativity. An assignment like this allows for the kinds of writing that emerge when the model itself is strange and unfamiliar.

ASSIGNMENTS FOR WRITING (p. 150)

1.   This writing assignment follows from the final "Question for a Second Reading," and we invite students to use that work in preparation for this piece of writing. As we say in response to that question, this kind of assignment is not uncommon in *Ways of Reading*—assignments where students are asked to imitate, mimic, or work in the spirit of another writer in order to learn something about that particular writer's project or sensibility. Students will likely surprise you and themselves with their creativity. An assignment like this allows for the kinds of writing that emerge when the model itself is strange and unfamiliar.

Students will need to be in conversation with Doyle while describing the features and conventions of the "experimental" essay as they understand them. Students' work should be in conversation with Doyle but also in service of something the student writer has to say. The quality of the work will be improved if students have a chance to revise the essay.

2.   In one sense, this question is quite traditional; it asks students to point to a main idea, or main sentence, and to argue for this sentence as the most significant in the essay. These are two tasks students may feel familiar with—finding main ideas and making definitive arguments. However, the question tries to remind them that even though they are making an argument, the argument is already *not* definitive. It exists as a

possibility among many. In order to write this essay, then, students need to approach the question in terms of what makes them choose the sentence they do. Of course, this has as much to do with their interpretive experience of the essay as it does with the essay itself. This writing assignment also asks students to work with the essay as a set of materials, searching the essay for ways to support and confirm their sense of its project.

MAKING CONNECTIONS (p. 151)

1. This assignment works against the assumption that facts are automatically true and objective statements that inform or instruct. This assignment aims to complicate notions of "fact" through an examination of how writers engage with the facts they present in their essays. After having worked with Doyle, whose essay reiterates numerous facts about hummingbirds, blue whales, and mammal hearts, students will then consider additional essays to think about facts in the context of a critical essay. As students begin writing their own analysis, they might notice themselves becoming self-conscious as they make declarative statements about the "facts" they are writing about. Assignments that provoke this kind of self-consciousness are productive because of the ways they illuminate critical thinking and writerly decisions, making students aware not only of what they are saying but also of how they are saying it.

2. In this assignment, students are asked to "test out" one of Halberstam's ideas on Doyle's essay. They begin with Halberstam's version of a common theme: that we humans frequently use animals in our movies, writing, and advertising in order to convey human objectives and logic. While many students may not have previously thought about this phenomenon in such a way, they often seem interested in this idea and enjoy identifying other examples in popular culture where they see Halberstam's idea playing out. We find it is helpful to lead a class discussion that addresses the first part of this question so that students can together flesh out Halberstam's idea. Once they have a grasp of what "penguin logics" might mean and how unknowable those logics might be, we send students off to work on the Doyle essay. Students may or may not have read this essay before taking on this assignment. Because the Doyle essay is quite short, they can read it on their own as they think about the question.

    This assignment can prove fascinating once students have written their essays. Because the Doyle essay can be very compelling and beautiful in its composition, launching a critique of Doyle's essay can seem "mean" or "wrong," as some students have put it. Students have even found out that some of Doyle's "facts" about hummingbirds aren't even true or are exaggerated. This can lead not only to further productive discussions of Halberstam's point but also to complex discussions about truth. Students can further consider questions such as: What is so wrong with using "human logics" to understand animals? Can we know what is "true" about hummingbirds—or about ourselves for that matter? At first glance, the Doyle essay and the Halberstam essay seem very different—in one case, a queer theorist works on animation films, and in the other, a creative writer muses about nature. But, in the end, that seeming difference is the productive location for this assignment.

RALPH WALDO EMERSON

The American Scholar 🅴

When Bartholomae first read and taught "The American Scholar," it always disappeared into what he had read or felt he had to say about transcendentalism and American literary history. This was the case until he taught the essay to Spanish students at the University of Deusto in Spain. They were galvanized by this essay. They came to class all in a buzz and wanted to know if this—meaning (we think) the attitudes toward reading, writing, and authority in the essay—was what it was like at an American university. In particular, they were taken by Emerson's claim that sentences could be "doubly significant," and they wanted to know if that meant that there could be more than one interpretation of a single text. They were students in a system that insisted in its exam structure that this could not be the case. Professors told them what poems or stories "meant." Students wrote the meanings down in their notes and were expected to repeat these interpretations in their exams. Feelings were high enough about all this that for a month there was concern that the students might go out on strike!

For us, this occasion wrenched the essay out of American literary history and made it again a piece directed to students and teachers about the nature and consequences of the educational process. And this is how we have continued to teach it when we use it in a composition class. We want students to move section by section, trying to image how this man, a man speaking over a gap of 150 years in such a strange voice, might be speaking to them about their courses, their teachers, and their situation as students. We want them, in other words, to find ways of taking these grand or arcane sentences seriously—sentences about the use of libraries or books or time in and out of the classroom. When they have begun to do this—when they have a way of talking about place or nature or books or action in their own education (both in practice and in theory)—we ask them how they might bring the sections of the essay together into an overarching theoretical statement about education, one they might attribute to Emerson.

We also find it important to spend some time on Emerson's style; particularly useful is the first paragraph under section I on text page 00. We want students to imagine a person who would speak this way, not to assume that this is just the way everyone talked in 1837. And we want them to consider how such sentences want to be read. If Emerson is talking about the proper use of books, or various ways of reading, we want our students to put Emerson to his own test and to consider what kind of relationship seems to be required between a reader of these sentences and their author.

QUESTIONS FOR A SECOND READING 🅴

1. This is always an eye opener for students. Emerson carries the weight of being a major figure in American literature; and it is easy for students to assume that he is difficult to read because he is a genius or his prose is "art" or they (the students) are simply too far from the mid-nineteenth century to understand the prose. It is an interesting and useful exercise for students to think of Emerson's prose as strategic and as embodying strategies at odds with the classroom rhetorics of the later twentieth century. One way

of approaching the assignment is to ask students to use the tools available to them (outlining, diagramming, clustering, spider-webbing) to try to chart Emerson's sentences, paragraphs, and the larger sections of the essay. They can, then, invent names for Emerson's prose. It is important that they also think about style as strategy and ideology—as a way of seeing and organizing the world. If the topic sentence/example/restatement paradigm enables students to force the world to yield evidence to prove what is given (if, that is, it asks students to begin with whatever it is they want to say and then to find examples to justify that commonplace), what assumptions about truth, order, the individual, and the world are represented in Emerson's prose? The assignment then asks students to tell a story of reading. This is a phrase we have used for years with some success. It allows students to cast themselves as readers negotiating a text, and it allows them to define a dramatized and narrativized relationship with a character called "Emerson."

2–5. All of these are designed to encourage students to reread the essay as though Emerson meant what he said, and as though they had a reason to listen and pay attention. Emerson's sentences, in our experience, will sound either elegant and sermonic or weird and impenetrable to students, and they will assume that you pay attention to them the way you pay attention to a convocation speaker—you let the words roll over you and take pleasure in a lofty occasion, but you don't need to focus in and pay attention. It is probably a good idea, then, to spend some class time preparing students to read Emerson, particularly after students have read through once without such preparation.

The central textual problem, according to these questions, is how these characteristically Emersonian terms might be situated in the context of a pressing modern conversation about college education. Emerson's appeal to instinct might become a question of who gets to make the rules and take authority for what stands as knowledge in a classroom. The same approach might be taken to Emerson's references to nature, or to books and the "mind of the past."

The third question is meant to call attention to the double role of Emerson's essay. Emerson talks about teaching and reading, but he stands, at the same time, as a teacher and a writer. This same doubleness is represented in the role of the scholar in the essay—the scholar is a person who must be a student but, at another point, serve as a teacher or a model for others. We're not sure how it is possible for one person to play both roles and remain, as Robert Frost says, the same person.

ASSIGNMENTS FOR WRITING e

1. These assignments extend the project of the "Questions for a Second Reading": They ask students to give an Emersonian reading of their own position as students. This first assignment will not work well unless students have contemporary documents to work from: a college catalogue, a list of courses, statements for majors, and some general discussion of the curriculum and the distribution of studies requirement. It can be quite striking to look through Emerson's eyes at a list of available courses or at a distribution requirement.

2. This assignment zeroes in on what students usually find the most provocative section of the essay—Emerson's account of the proper use of books and the "mind of the past." The assignment asks students to imagine that they are teaching in Emerson's spirit and that they are using this textbook. What, from that point of view, might they do with it? And, of course, what might they say about the way we have packaged the essays with our questions and assignments? An interesting variation on this assignment is to have students prepare an Emersonian assignment and write the paper that they would hand in to Emerson. Instead of writing an account of how an Emersonian teacher might teach reading and writing, they would demonstrate in practice what his students might be expected to do.

3. We like to include at least one assignment like this in every course we teach—an assignment that asks students to take their experience as readers, turn it into narrative, and reflect upon what they have written. Following Culler in *On Deconstruction*, we have called these "stories of reading."

    The purpose of this assignment is to bring forward what students suspect they must hide—their sense that Emerson's writing is weird, difficult, and, at times, incomprehensible. Students may believe that we—or any competent reader—would read this the same way we read Stanley Fish's essay, that it makes sense to us in just the same ways. Of course, this is not so. When students acknowledge the difficulty of the essay and use it as a way of talking about Emerson's writing rather than as a sign of their failure as readers, they are in a position to think about the argument *enacted* in Emerson's text. They can begin to talk about how the style of the essay imagines a reader who might be called, in Emerson's terms, an American scholar.

    When we have taught the essay, we have worked with section II. With very few exceptions, the difficulties here cannot be attributed to history or vocabulary, to big words, or to a change in what we say and how we say it. It is interesting to ask students to mark sections where the meaning is lost to a modern reader or where Emerson uses words impossible to understand. There are few of the former, and they lead to an interesting discussion of what is involved in trying to imagine the past. In most cases of the latter, Emerson goes on to try to make the meaning clear in the text. If you look at the paragraph beginning, "Undoubtedly there is a right way of reading,—so it be sternly subordinated," you can find many of the characteristic features of Emerson's style—paragraphs that develop by piling epigram upon epigram, clarifying statements that mystify ("A fig tree looking on a fig tree, becometh fruitful"). It is interesting to ask, "Who is speaking here?" and "What is the writer doing in crafting these sentences in these ways?"

    We think it is important for students to write this essay before there is any class discussion of section II. We generally have a kind of warmup discussion of a passage drawn from anywhere else in the essay. "Take us to a passage that seemed weird, difficult, or impossible," we'll say and begin there, leading students through a close reading of the passage. Our goal is to give them a way of talking about difficulty as a strategy or a feature in the text and not as a sign of their failure.

    For revision: when students revise this paper, we send them in two directions. We deliberately confused genre in writing the assignment—at one point, we ask for an essay, at another we say "tell a story"—as a way of opening up the formal possibilities for student writers. Often the narrative is dull and spare, and we encourage students to develop character and action. Some of the most successful papers we have received break the conventions of the essay as students imagine them. We also find that we need to send students back to look at "The American Scholar" as an argument, to see how Emerson's style could be said to run with or against his ideas about the relationship between readers and writers. If his style could be said to create a reader, in what ways is that reader like and not like the reader he calls for in the paraphrasable argument of the text?

4. This assignment asks students to look at how Emerson figures gender. The first part of the assignment is an occasion for students to look at "The American Scholar" to examine Emerson's "natural" construction of gender, to question his unstated assumptions. We have found that it can be a challenge for students to construct a reading of Emerson's assumptions given the difficulty they often have with his prose, so it is important in this assignment that students work closely with a few specific passages in order to ground their essays in Emerson's text. The second part of this assignment asks students to extend and enrich their project by locating at the library or through the Internet other texts by Emerson that deal with education and culture.

MAKING CONNECTIONS e

1. This is an invitation for students to locate themselves (their expectations, their experience, their education) in relation to a history of thinking about the distinctive qualities of American education. As phrased by Emerson, this is not a question about civics class or a class in American literature, about being formed *as an* American by American schools. It is a question about the conditions of life in the United States, about U.S. history and culture, about the history of our democracy and its current formations, and about how each shapes the intellectual foundations and possibilities for an "American" scholar.

   Whomever a student may choose from this list—Gloria Anzaldúa, Joshua Foer, Richard Miller, Walker Percy, Richard Rodriguez, Kathryn Schulz, or David Foster Wallace—they will need to consider some version of the present, usually (although not always) conceived of as a problem. Students will need to be reminded that two writers need to be represented in their essay, Emerson and someone else, and that they need to be brought into conversation.

   We have always made it a point to insist that students use assignments like these to take a step beyond "compare and contrast," a method already (most likely) a part of their toolkits. There is a technical side to using one text as a lens through which to view the other. One way to make this act of reading materialize on the page is to bring a paragraph or block quotation from one text, from Richard Miller, say, to a discussion that also requires a paragraph or block quotation from Emerson. What do you hear in each? Whom do you hear? Where and how do these texts (and these persons) speak to each other, if they do?

   As we ask students to visualize the page, we ask them also to imagine a space in the essay where they, the student writer, speaks, where they take a position and make an evaluative judgment about what they have read. (What is your favorite moment in all of this? Which text is most persuasive?)

And, finally, we ask them to strike out on their own, either to develop an idea or to apply what they have found to a new situation or set of examples. "And what about you—where do you locate yourself in this discussion? How do you understand the influences today, for good or for ill, that will shape the American scholars of your generation?" Ideally, the essay should end with the student taking center stage. Because of the demands of the assignment, and because this moment comes at the end of the essay, that doesn't always happen. Or it happens far too quickly or mechanically or dutifully. In all of our courses, essays go through more than one draft. When we prepare students for the revision of an essay like this one, we tend to focus on two areas: 1.) More completely representing the authors—attending to paraphrase, rereading with an eye to what was lost from the text, attending to the presentation of the block quotation; and 2.) Taking time at the end to fully present a writer with something to say, someone worth standing next to Emerson and (perhaps) Anzaldúa.

2. In Emerson and Freire, we have two radical American educators—a North American from the nineteenth century and a Brazilian from the twentieth. The assignment asks students to take note of this and to consider, primarily, the differences. There are, of course, similarities, but these are easier to find, and they tend to make two interesting individual minds blur into one general set of fuzzy statements about the individual's need to be free and express himself or herself, and so on. These are not the sorts of sentences students should be encouraged to write, since they have no edge to them and don't require much attention. As with the first assignment in this set, students who write their essays without working from one or two specific sections in the essays will probably write dreadful papers. The advice in assignment 1 holds here as well: Be careful not to prewrite these papers, leaving no pressure for students to adopt the perspective discussed in class. It is still a good idea to help students see what it means to return to the texts to work on a problem.

JOSHUA FOER

The End of Remembering (p. 160)

At first glance, Joshua Foer's "The End of Remembering" seems journalistic in genre. After all, Foer's idea for the book started as a journalism assignment. But in reading the piece, we found it to be a layered and complicated theorizing of memory itself—conceptually, narratively, and historically. We have discovered that students are very interested in Foer's work and fascinated by the notion of "mental athletes." In fact, several student athletes in the class felt a particular resonance in their readings—many times illuminating for their peers the connection between exercising one's memory and exercising one's muscles. A few students even recognized Foer from *The Colbert Report* on Comedy Central.

One of the most valuable aspects of Foer's work is the way his piece asks questions without necessarily providing an answer or argument. It is clear that Foer values memory, but he seems more interested in getting us to think *about* memory, to raise questions about its implications, rather than to think in one particular way about memory. We've found that Foer's essay really helps students imagine essays that don't merely make a persuasive argument but that conduct an intellectual inquiry into a particular subject. Because of Foer's journalism background, students said, they felt that he approached his writing as an explorer rather than someone "with something to prove," as one student put it. Our questions about Foer's work try to lead students to think about how Foer raises questions just as much as which questions he raises.

QUESTIONS FOR A SECOND READING (p. 175)

1. This question sparked a lot of discussion in our classes. Students seemed to relate to reading and forgetting, but they also seemed interested in *not* forgetting, in talking with each other about how Foer's piece might help them become better readers. Some students tentatively (likely because they were in English class) confessed to "not reading very much" or "hating to read." In turning their attention back to Foer's text, students discovered passages they had missed the first time through the essay and came to the conclusion that some of their characterizations of themselves as readers were far more common than they thought. We returned during our discussion of this question to the Introduction to *Ways of Reading* (p. 1) as a way of thinking through what reading means and its connection to memory.

2. Like many other "Questions for a Second Reading," here students are asked to move through the steps of a careful and close reading—first to look closely at and articulate the meaning and implications of a particular passage; second, to put that passage in conversation with other passages in Foer's work; and third, to think about the relationship of those passages both to each other and to Foer's larger project. These steps must be practiced—not because they are rhetorical or even perhaps literary, but because they help students to practice an essential thinking pattern that makes for complex writers and thinkers: the pattern of finding the web of connections in what they are reading or looking at in order to understand the larger picture.

3. Students can work together in small groups to make lists of the questions Foer might be raising—directly or indirectly—in his work. We found that this question is particularly useful in early discussions of "The End of Remembering," specifically when we want to highlight Foer's work as an enactment of intellectual and personal inquiry, an enactment that students might model and imagine for their own writing later.

ASSIGNMENTS FOR WRITING (p. 176)

1. While many students will have had discussions about metaphor prior to our particular writing course, we find it especially useful to prepare students for this assignment by conducting a class discussion on the topic. Students will usually know, literally, what a metaphor is and will be familiar with other terms connected to metaphor like "simile" or "figurative language," but it is often necessary to illuminate precisely *how* metaphor works to think through a problem or question. Short poems that use one central metaphor can be helpful in leading this kind of discussion. We have used poems such as

Yehida Amichai's "Like a Ship's Captain" or Ruth L. Schwartz's poem "The Important Thing" to this end.

Fully understanding what metaphor makes possible and what limitations it might have sometimes requires pulling a specific metaphor apart and seeing how it works. When students get to that final question about why Foer chose the palace as opposed to another metaphor, oftentimes they actually begin thinking about metaphors Foer might have used instead, and this work is critical as well as creative.

2. This assignment produced some very interesting essays from students in our classes. The question of being an expert in memory seemed to intrigue them. On the one hand, they find the memory work Foer describes quite impressive. On the other hand, they raised questions about whether merely remembering facts or details makes one an expert in something. One student asked, "Doesn't being an expert mean you not only remember stuff but you fully understand the way things work? Just because you know a bunch of dates and facts doesn't mean you know how or why stuff is connected."

Students, like many of us, feel implicated at times by Foer's inquiry. After all, part of the experience of reading Foer's piece is to understand ourselves as forgetters. So certainly part of their impulse in challenging the idea that memory champions are experts is something of a defensive posture, but there is something more to it—an articulation of the distinction between remembering details and understanding connections. And that articulation, particularly in the context of the project of *Ways of Reading*, is an important one.

MAKING CONNECTIONS (p. 176)

1. In this instance, students return to some of the work they started in the first "Questions for a Second Reading" assignment. We've been told by teachers and by reviewers of *Ways of Reading* that many instructors *do* make use of the Introduction to the book as a way of preparing students for the kinds of reading and writing they will be asked to do in a course that is focused on essay writing. So in this edition, we've designed a few prompts that make use of the Introduction as it connects to the selections in the book. Students have commented that moving back to the Introduction for a later writing assignment helped them to see why they had read the Introduction in the first place. All of us would likely agree that when reading the introduction to something we identify as a textbook, we sometimes experience that reading as merely introductory, and we perhaps skim the text because we see ourselves as ready to read what's "really the book." We found that in returning to the Introduction again later in the course, students had more to say about it and had more reading experience to connect back to the piece.

2. As many instructors might know, proponents of critical pedagogy are often critiqued by feminist and queer scholars because of their assumptions about power and gender. This assignment opens up the possibility of thinking about Freire through the lens of two queer theorists whose work is concerned with similar conceptual frameworks but is applied very differently. This doesn't mean, of course, that we expect students to launch this particular critique in response to this assignment, but it does mean that

students are invited to see the essays as having similar conversations decades apart. It is sometimes helpful to remind students about the dates and contexts for the essays as they begin, helping them keep those contexts in their minds as they work. This assignment is very much about exploring specific terms like "marginal" and "structure" and "oppression." While it might be safe to assume that students know basic definitions of these terms, it can be very useful to walk them through the process of what it means to understand a term *within the context* a reading provides. It might help your students to understand definitions as unstable rather than stable, so that they can open up their own definitions to the meanings suggested by Freire, Halberstam, and Butler. We often ask students questions like: What does Freire mean by "structure" and how can you tell what he means? You might ask, then, the same question of the other two essays so that students can begin a dialogue about the places in the texts where these terms come up and how each author understands and makes use of them.

3. Students will need to have read both the Griffin essay and the Foer essay in order to take on this assignment. At first glance, Foer's piece can be read as being more *literally* about memory than Griffin's in that he discusses memory champions remembering poems and decks of cards. So it can be useful for students to begin with a discussion of how Foer's discussion of memory might extend beyond just what we can literally recall. This can lead to a meaningful class discussion about remembering—about its various connotations and definitions. But in both Griffin's and Foer's essays, most readers can recognize that there is a fear of forgetting, a fear of erasure that seems to thread through time. Many students hear this fear in their own historical moment—when, for example, older individuals might complain about their inability to remember phone numbers or their own dependence on Web search engines—so these questions of memory are often resonant for students.

    In assignments that, like this one, ask students to locate and focus on particular passages in the text, we find it's helpful to dedicate class time to activities that might enable students to practice and discuss the process of reading through a text with a goal in mind and also how to use the passages they find as part of an essay. Making meaning of another writer's text and incorporating that meaning into a larger project is not only part of what it means to learn to be a writer but also a skill we feel translates to particular habits of mind—paying attention to one's own interpretative strategies, being empowered to make meaning, and bringing seemingly disparate ideas together into a whole picture.

MICHEL FOUCAULT

Panopticism (p. 181)

We've taught Foucault over several semesters, and, as surprising as it may seem, he always emerges as one of the most revisited figures in the course. When students are given the option of going back to an essay, they often go back to their Foucault essays. When asked which selection we should be sure to retain in the course, they often choose Foucault.

The reading is difficult and frustrating, to be sure, but students take great pleasure in working with this text, and, for reasons that should not be so surprising, they are eager to have an analytical tool (and a fancy vocabulary) they can use to think about power, about the "disciplinary mechanism" at play in the academy and in their lives. We have heard this story over and over again: students and teachers who approached Foucault with hesitation end by finding that the work with Foucault is among the most memorable ever. Most recently, the story came from a group of instructors teaching extension courses in Oregon, who talked with great pleasure about the work of students in a technical curriculum who love to quote Foucault to each other in the shop or the hallway.

Foucault offers students surprising examples and dramatic new ways of thinking about and talking about power, knowledge, and life in the midst of institutions, ominous institutions quick to define themselves as benign and benevolent. There is something very seductive, too, about Foucault's willingness to write prose that always attempts to be all-inclusive. His essays, and his sentences, are thick, qualified, and, it seems, always moving to the edge of abstraction.

Some of the ways our students have found "Panopticism" difficult or daunting are predictable. You will find that students will want to begin with (rather than work toward) definitions, including a definition of the title word. The key with Foucault is to allow students to work within their own limits and uncertainty. We find we have to school students to write sentences that are tentative—that say, for example, something like, "While I don't completely understand what Foucault means by a 'disciplinary mechanism,' it seems to me that. . . ." In writing and in discussion, students need to acknowledge what they don't understand. And they need to feel the invitation to try to translate the difficult phrases or to work toward examples of their own. We have found it useful to get a class to come up with a list of what they take to be the key phrases in "Panopticism," then to type the list for use as a kind of toolkit during the weeks they are working on, and with, the essay.

In this selection, length functions as more of a barrier than in, say, Griffin's "Our Secret," where it at least makes some remote sense to say that the length extends our fascination with the piece. With Foucault, since his prose does not follow structures of elaboration familiar to American students, readers have to simply make their way from beginning to end. The apparatus we provide can help with this, but it is worth making the point that work on this essay requires fortitude and endurance. We've asked students to chart, and to account for, the structure of the piece as an alternative to the structures they have learned to take for granted. This motivates them to think about Foucault's argument or about the way he imagines the work of the historian.

Finally, in our teaching (and in the assignments in *Ways of Reading*), we have tried to invite students to make connections between the technologies of power revealed by Foucault and those common to the classroom and its practices, turning attention, for example, to the *controlling* idea of the standard classroom rhetoric or to the ways in which writing is normalized by American instruction. The summary assignments, for example, ask students to think of "mastery" as both an achievement and a problem, and to connect writing techniques with other techniques of political control.

Foucault makes these connections in *Discipline and Punish*. Among the illustrations in the book are pictures from students' penmanship guides. We found it an extremely useful exercise, in fact, to ask students to think both inside and outside English as a system designed to discipline language and language use—that is, to think both generously and critically about English as a scene of discipline and control. This provided a parallel to the prison as an organizing term. The technology of control in English was readily available in ways that the technology of control in the law was not. It was easy for students to play the role of the professor and to speak for English. In fact, there was some subversive pleasure in this act of ventriloquism—where students could "correct" a piece of writing and then think about how and where they had made it worse—more predictable, less interesting, less "personal," and so on. These discussions gave students a sense of the basic oppositional move in Foucault; and it gave them a sense of how he ignores traditional historical or disciplinary boundaries (connecting schools and prisons, the seventeenth century and the twentieth).

These were our goals in teaching Foucault. We did not use the word "poststructuralism"; we did not make any attempts to connect this chapter to the body of Foucault's work or to the larger critical project he has inspired. That, to our minds, would be the work of a different kind of course. We wanted students to work with the peculiar difficulties of Foucault's text and to put into lay terms what they could imagine to be his critical project. We did not bring in terms from his earlier or later work. For our classes, Foucault was only the figure represented in "Panopticism."

QUESTIONS FOR A SECOND READING (p. 209)

1. Like the questions that follow, this one is designed to give students a way of working back through the essay to make connections, to see it as an evolving project rather than as an assortment of interesting or arresting moments. Here the question is designed to have students make an inventory of the various instances of the "dream" of order and to think about how Foucault accounts for the differences between present and past. It might make sense to invite students to extend their inventory to even more contemporary instances—items they might add to Foucault's list.

2. We have found it useful for students to try to imagine the kind of work Foucault is doing in relation to their sense of academic traditions. Like Griffin, Foucault can be thought of as a historian who is unwilling to write the usual kind of narrative history. If he doesn't do what he is supposed to do, what *does* he do, and how might one generously account for what he does?

3. The numbered sections can be imagined as parodic—Foucault is calling attention to the poverty and the inevitability of the desire for ordered "sense," for a 1, 2, 3—but they can also be seen as straightforward summary gestures, places where the text alludes to other forms of order or to the more conventional needs of readers. This question uses those sections as reference points and asks students to chart the chapter as an argument.

ASSIGNMENTS FOR WRITING (p. 210)

1. Although this assignment presents itself as an opportunity for students to write an essay that summarizes "Panopticism," it is important that students take the position of presenting Foucault's arguments and key terms to other readers, perhaps to members of their class who are also trying to figure out what Foucault is saying. It is equally

important that they understand this as work in progress on a text that will refuse to be mastered or re-presented in a summary. Most likely students will attend to the discussion of Bentham and the prison and shy away from everything else — from the difficult terms and connections that define what Foucault *does* with Bentham and his design for a prison. In other words, Foucault will likely be left *out* of the summaries or perhaps made to stand as the same figure as Jeremy Bentham. You can, in advance, direct students to draw on three different sections of the text in their account of the text, or you can ask them to account for the unfolding of the text (for where it begins and where it ends and for the key steps along the way). And (or) you can make this the work of revision, where students go back to think about what they have left out or ignored, about the consequences of their desire to master the text.

2–3. These are fairly standard *Ways of Reading* assignments. Whereas the first assignment asks students to work closely with the text, its terms and examples, these two ask students to extend the argument to examples of their own selection.

MAKING CONNECTIONS (p. 211)

1. Students will need to reread both selections, taking notes toward this essay. In their notes, students will need to identify passages that represent how each author thinks about (talks about) power — where it comes from, how it works, and so on. Berger thinks power comes from privileged positions, from individuals with the wealth and heritage to mystify art and to turn it into a commodity. Basically, he allows members of the ruling classes to hold power as a form of control over others and their perceptions, but he also makes it possible for ordinary people, without wealth and privilege, to have power when they learn to demystify the art of the past and thereby come to "see" that art is situated, opinionated, not in any way "objective," and always, then, a commentary on the relationship of its subjects and its creators. Foucault, working from examples of how punishment changes (rather than progresses), thinks of power in terms of social relations, but where there is no single, identifiable agent (like the "ruling class"). For Foucault, people like jailers, priests, and psychiatrists use and direct power by virtue of their control over others. It is harder to think with Foucault, since he does not think in terms of the usual narratives of domination and revolt.

   Of the two authors, students will find Foucault's notion of power new and compelling, but they'll have to work to unpack abstract sentences where he describes power in terms of its technologies and filiations. It is important, we have learned, to push for differences, since the easiest tack is to collapse both into a familiar accounting of antiestablishment thinking.

2. Does Freire imagine an alternative to education that would be something other than panoptic, something other than a system of surveillance? There are obvious demonstrations of this surveillance and registration — the physical architecture of schools and classrooms, the regulated movement in them, and the educational architecture of testing and observation. Freire doesn't write about these, although he does propose a problem-solving education, one that allows students to identify the problems they need to solve and that takes consciousness-changing as its aim rather than knowledge accumulation. So are both men thinking along the same lines? Are Freire's notions of change

embedded in a system that can only be panoptic, or does he offer an alternative that would require a change in the panoptic architecture of surveillance and registration?

Clearly, students will need to do preliminary work with the Freire selection before dealing with the questions posed by this assignment, and they'll only benefit from a close reading of Foucault, perhaps with the help of second-reading questions. This is one of those assignments that will take careful grounding in both texts to be compelling to readers, so students will want to locate moments in Freire that give them ground from which to imagine Freire's educational alternative in terms of Foucault's arguments about the panoptic nature of such institutions. Another way into this assignment, along with the questions about panopticism, would take Foucault's notion of power as the fulcrum for considering the kinds of changes Freire's changes to education would bring about. How do power relations shift in Freire's educational architecture? Would these changes undo or reconstruct the panoptic nature of education as we know it?

3.   This essay question is an expansive one, giving students the opportunity to think about how writers turn to each other to think through problems and to challenge each other's (and in some cases their own) notions of epistemology. This question also presents the possibility for thinking of research in new ways, suggesting to students that they might look through the books of Butler and Foucault—and those who write about them—to develop a sense of their work. This aspect of the assignment can also be done in group work by giving each group of students several of these texts, asking them to look around in the books and note what strikes them, how it might be connected to their assignments. This also allows for a kind of collaborative research—putting students in dialogue with one another not only about what they find in these texts but also about the meaning of what they find.

4.   Perhaps it is not surprising that while students often find Foucault's essay extremely dense and difficult to read, they also find the concept of discipline very productive to talk through. This discussion can sometimes begin with a more common understanding of the term *discipline*: conversations about parenting, laws they find absurd, or school policies they have experienced. For this assignment, it can be particularly useful to begin with students' experience of discipline. Foucault's essay is theoretically challenging, and Griffin's piece is "before their time" in terms of its historical examination, so beginning with what students *know* or think about discipline can be a productive launching point for what Foucault knows about discipline and how his theories might be reflected in Griffin's essay as well. Griffin, after all, discusses some of the examples students might offer—German parenting manuals, laws, control. Like many of our assignments, the first part might offer you some ways to have students collaborate on the assignment. They might, for example, reread "Our Secret" in several small groups—each group taking a set number of pages to reread and "mine" for quotes from Griffin. If each small group generates a list of passages from Griffin where they see an interesting connection to Foucault's ideas on discipline, this list can be shared on the board or online with the other groups in the class. Students would then be able to use these lists as a resource as they begin their individual essays. We find, in teaching first-year writing especially, that students need help learning to "mine" an essay, to dig up its useful pieces for a specific line of inquiry. Doing this work collaboratively helps students see connections they might not have otherwise seen on their own.

PAULO FREIRE

The "Banking" Concept of Education (p. 216–230)

This essay provokes students. Either they feel strongly sympathetic to Freire's condemnation of "banking" education, where students are turned into "containers" to be "filled" by their teachers or they feel strongly that "banking" education is the very education they need to be competitive and successful.

Assume that your students will need to reread this selection a number of times as it poses challenging conceptual problems, and Freire's terms, like "problem-posing" and "creative transformation," are usually part and parcel of the conceptual problem. The essay has momentum, though, and once students begin to follow his argument—that education that only transmits information, that is conducted through teacher narratives and student silences, stands opposed to "problem-solving" education, which is conducted by teachers and students working together to solve genuine problems—they'll react to it, largely because their personal experiences serve as quick validations of Freire's central concepts.

QUESTIONS FOR A SECOND READING (p. 227)

1. This discussion assignment is designed to allow students to "problem-pose" Freire's concepts by testing them against their own experiences and by imagining them in classes and subjects with which they are familiar. You will want to move slowly, perhaps allowing two or three class sessions to work your way through the assignment's questions. Students will need to be constantly moving between the essay and examples they come up with. When they discuss problem-posing in English, for instance, they'll need to turn to Freire to put his concept in their own language. Then they'll need to imagine an English class where reading, writing, and discussion are used by the teacher and students to "work" a problem that has some significance to them—for example, growth and change in adolescence. When they turn to Freire's examples, as the second half of this assignment asks them to, they'll need to pay particular attention to what he means when he discusses students as spectators and students as re-creators. You can make connections between their examples and his by asking them to include a discussion of students as spectators and students as re-creators in their examples of problem-posing classes in the various subjects.

2. This assignment focuses students on two important concepts that Freire borrows from Marxist thought, and it serves as a good follow-up discussion to the first assignment. Because of its narrow focus, it's not good as an opening assignment, although a discussion of praxis and alienation could certainly be broadened to include Freire's concepts of banking education and problem-posing education.

    Students will need to stay close to the text to discuss these terms, and you'll want to ask them to reread to find those passages and moments that present Freire's use of the terms. Once they've located and noted those, they're ready to put them into their own words and create what I. A. Richards calls a "radical paraphrase."

3.   There is a way in which Freire's voice and his explanations invite response. Readers often mention their inclination to talk back as they read and reread Freire. Although some of this can be explained by his accessible subjects (education and teachers and students) and his accessible metaphors (banking and working together in problem-posing), he takes a stance that both gives information and invites response by posing education as a problem for readers to work on. Although he frames the question with descriptions, explanations, and a few examples, he doesn't offer definitive solutions. Instead, he insists through his posture and commitment that readers begin to examine their experiences from this problem-posing perspective. Still, he does offer information, and it is quite strong stuff, raising the question of whether banking and problem-posing are as clear-cut as Freire would have us believe. Students will need to speak from his text, so they'll need to reread to find those moments when Freire can be said to be both depositing information and allowing for a dialogue. You might turn your students' attention to his voice by asking them to characterize the kinds of voices that speak in banking education and the kinds that speak in problem-posing. Ask them to recall those times when they experienced each. Where, you might ask, would Freire's voice put him—in banking or in problem-posing? What passages or moments in the text lead them to make this appraisal?

ASSIGNMENTS FOR WRITING (p. 227)

1.   This challenging writing assignment offers students the opportunity to see a significant learning experience of their own through Freire's eyes. You might consider turning to this assignment after some extended discussion of the essay, perhaps after spending two or three class sessions working with the questions for the first of the "Questions for a Second Reading." Students will then be familiar with the essay and with framing their own experiences in its terms.

You might consider asking students to identify a rich and illustrative incident in which they learned something from their own experience, without paying much attention to whether it fits or doesn't fit in Freire's view of education. Once they have identified the incident—and it should be one that they can write quite a bit about—they can begin the work of seeing it through Freire's terms. They'll need to reconstruct the incident with as much detail as they can, and they'll need to pay attention to conversations and what specific people did during or as a result of the incident. If the incident involved school experience, they'll want to write about what they worked with (textbooks, assignments, etc.) and how they worked (what they did, what other students did, what teachers did). Once they've reconstructed the incident, you'll want to turn their attention to a Freirian reading of it. They might consider whether it could be said to be a banking experience or a problem-posing one. What about the experience allows them to talk about it as one or the other? Was it an experience that would allow them to write about an "emersion" of consciousness? or perhaps a submersion?

For revision: In their first drafts for this essay, students often tell lively stories of an individual's experience in school or provide a tightly organized demonstration that their experiences show that Freire was right. The goal of revision, we feel, should be to open these accounts up, to call them into question.

Perhaps because they are young adults, and perhaps because they are, by and large, Americans, students translate Freire's account of social, political, and historical forces into a story of individuals—a mean teacher and an innocent student. One way to pose problems for revision, then, would be to send students back to Freire's essay to see how he accounts for "agency"—who is doing what to whom in Freire's account of education. Once students have reread the essay with this in mind, they can go back to their own pieces, making this story of individuals a story of *representative* individuals. Here, teacher and student play predetermined roles in the larger drama of American education and are figures through which the culture works out questions of independence and authority, production and reproduction of knowledge, and the relationship of the citizen to society.

The first drafts often make quick work of Freire. We asked one of our students how he was able to sum up in three tidy pages everything Freire said. He replied, "It was easy. I left out everything I didn't understand and worked with what I did." This is a familiar strategy, one that is reinforced by teachers who have students read for "gist." Another strategy for revision is to have students go back to the sections of Freire's essay that they *didn't* understand, or couldn't easily control, and to see how they might work those sections into what they have written. This is an opportunity for a dialogue with Freire—not a debate, but a chance to put his words on the page and to say, in effect, "Here is what I think you are saying." This revision will put pressure on students' resources for including quotations and representing and working on text. It makes a big difference, for example, whether a student uses Freire to conclude a point or uses Freire's language as material to work on. These different approaches to Freire provide handy illustrations for a discussion of problem-posing education.

2.   This writing assignment would follow nicely from two or three class sessions devoted to a discussion of the first of the "Questions for a Second Reading." You might also consider using the third question as part of prewriting discussions.

Students will have to imagine themselves as teachers determined to adapt Freire's practices to a class working with his essay. They'll have to enact problem-solving through a writing assignment or a set of discussion questions, guidelines, or instructions for this essay. You might consider asking them to examine the questions and assignments in the book to see which, if any, they think fit Freire's notions of problem-solving tasks. They'll need to engage in some discussion of the questions and assignments to say why the tasks do or do not reflect Freire's thinking about problem-solving, and this could help them begin to conceptualize criteria for translating his theory into learning tasks. Once they've participated in these discussions, they'll be ready to write their problem-solving tasks. Then they'll have to complete their own assignments. You might consider a follow-up discussion on what students thought their tasks were asking of them. From there, they could go on to revise their tasks.

MAKING CONNECTIONS (p. 228)

1.   Students need to use one of the essays in the book as a starting point for posing a Freirian problem. Then they need to begin working on that problem, responding to it in

writing. It's difficult to say ahead of time which essays or stories will trigger students' thinking about a genuine problem that interests and involves them. You might go through the text table of contents and comment on the essays and stories with an eye toward presenting their subjects or issues so students can pinpoint essays to consider. The introductions to each selection will give you a sense of what each one touches on.

When students have posed their problems, you might consider conducting two or three class discussions to examine those problems so students can revise them before they write. They'll have to present their problems, including brief summaries of the selections they have worked from, and they'll need to explain why, in Freire's terms, their problems are Freirian. Consider using questions about how this writing differs from what they are accustomed to doing. Another assignment might ask them to look back on the essays they wrote in response to their own problems or questions.

2. Students will need to have read Rodriguez's essay and to have spent some time discussing it, perhaps in response to the "Questions for a Second Reading," before they can write this imagined dialogue between Freire and Rodriguez. You might suggest that they begin by imagining questions Freire and Rodriguez might ask each other. They could also reread the Rodriguez selection and note passages or moments that they think Freire would comment on, and they can do the same for the Freire selection by rereading from Rodriguez's point of view. It's important for the dialogue that students avoid turning this into a debate in which someone challenges someone. The stance should be conversational—two people from different backgrounds and different sets of beliefs talking with each other about education. They ask questions and comment on things each has said in the essays, and try their best to answer and further explain their comments.

3. As many instructors might know, proponents of critical pedagogy are often critiqued by feminist and queer scholars because of their assumptions about power and gender. This assignment opens up the possibility of thinking about Freire through the lens of two queer theorists whose work is concerned with similar conceptual frameworks but is applied very differently. This doesn't mean, of course, that we expect students to launch this particular critique in response to this assignment, but it does mean that students are invited to see the essays as having similar conversations decades apart.

It is sometimes helpful to remind students about the dates and contexts for the essays as they begin, helping them keep those contexts in their minds as they work. This assignment is very much about exploring specific terms like "marginal" and "structure" and "oppression." While it might be safe to assume that students know basic definitions of these terms, it can be very useful to walk them through the process of what it means to understand a term *within the context* a reading provides. It might help your students to understand definitions as unstable rather than stable, so that they can open up their own definitions to the meanings suggested by Freire, Halberstam, and Butler. We often ask students questions like: What does Freire mean by "structure" and how can you tell what he means? You might ask, then, the same question of the other two essays so that students can begin a dialogue about the places in the texts these terms come up and how each author understands and makes use of them.

SUSAN GRIFFIN

Our Secret (p. 233)

Our students were overwhelmed, knocked out, or, as they said, "blown away" by this selection. Its methods are unusual, to be sure, and our students had never read anything like it, and as much as Griffin's methods took them by surprise, so did her passion and commitment to her subjects. And our students saw many subjects, all interconnected in this surprising reading: the effects of childhood upbringing on adult behaviors, the relations of violence to cultural patterns, the cultural patterns—like childhood habits—that seem related to Nazi hatreds, the effects of familial and national secrets, the Nazi manipulations of science and media, the intertwining of personal and cultural habits, and so on. This is a rich and deep selection, and the more we worked with it in discussions and through writings, the more its subjects, its layers, and its connections became visible to us. One of the joys of working with this selection was our continual discoveries of the connections between the personal and the cultural with and through it.

Most of our students weren't accustomed to reading a selection as long as this, so we approached it by first asking them to read four or five pages in class. We then conducted a discussion of the reading, touching on Griffin's methods and where students saw connections among the various sections. We encouraged them to speculate about the connections, for example, between cell chemistry and rocketry, as Griffin lays them out in the opening pages, so that students could become somewhat familiar with the way Griffin asks readers to read between the sections and subjects to make connections that she does not explicitly bring forward. It's important, we think, that students be encouraged to find their own point of organization or reference when they read to make connections between the essay's fragments. Some will take secrets, fascism, Himmler, childhood, or sexuality as their point of departure. No single point is the "right" one, and the more ways students have of organizing their reading of this selection, the more it will open up to them.

After this class session on reading Griffin, we asked students to read the selection in one sitting, to time their readings, and to come to class prepared to talk about what it was like reading the whole thing. From there, we went to class discussions with the "Questions for a Second Reading" and then to the "Assignments for Writing," although we can easily imagine students working directly with writing assignments after some discussion of their readings of the selection.

QUESTIONS FOR A SECOND READING (p. 264)

1. Here, again, the point is that there is no one "right" way into this selection, no one "right" way of organizing a reading of it. The more ways students organize their readings, the more and more varied points of departure they explore, the fuller their understanding of its subjects and layers will be. When we encouraged this position toward the selection, we often heard students begin their discussions with something like, "Well, if I take secrets as a subject and connect it to families and child-rearing, here's what I make of them." As our discussion progressed and students became more

comfortable with the selection, we encouraged them to look for connections among multiple subjects in the piece. How, we asked, for example, do you connect Griffin's writing about "secrets," "child-rearing," and Himmler's adult behaviors? How then do you figure the selections on RNA and DNA into your reading of those examples? What, in other words, does Griffin seem to be making of them, as examples, and the sections on secrets and child-rearing and Himmler? There are, of course, many more connections that can be made by students as they reread and work on this text, and we let the connections unfold in discussions and drew students back into them by layering them into multiple connections.

2. In many sections in this piece, Griffin writes about the work she is doing, the way she imagines her research project, and the reasons she is so passionately involved with it. Students can locate those passages and speak from them in discussions of the project. They can also use her definitions of her project as a way to define all of its pieces. Why, for example, does she write about V-2 rockets? RNA and DNA? her childhood? And why does she put all of these various subjects or pieces together? What seems, then, to be her intention? It has also been interesting for our students to imagine the kinds of research Griffin had to do to write the various sections. She mentions traveling, interviewing people, and research, but the particulars of that work are left to our imagination. In our experience, students have little experience thinking through the kinds of research one would need to do to write a selection like this. They have had little exposure to this kind of research; at most, they'll have a limited sense of it from writing out three-by-five cards for high school research papers.

ASSIGNMENTS FOR WRITING (p. 265)

1. This assignment is useful for teaching students to chart a trajectory through a complex piece of reading that allows them to re-present it to their readers. It also gives students an opportunity to describe text that doesn't proceed logically or chronologically but makes its connections and arguments through association and metaphorical relationships. There is no way, students might be warned, that they could represent all of Griffin's work in this essay, so they need to chart a trajectory of their reading, but they also need to acknowledge that it is *their* reading and to point to at least some of the other possible readings or some of the aspects of the selection they leave out or only briefly touch on.

    This is also a good assignment for students to revise once they have the opportunity to think through and discuss other students' first drafts. When using this assignment, we are careful to choose paragraphs and pages from students' essays that allow the class to see writers at work charting their readings, acknowledging other possible readings, indicating the way the piece is written and the kinds of work it asks of readers, and indicating what their readings leave out.

2. Although the work students must do for this essay echoes the work they are asked to do in the second-reading questions, it is more determined, more focused. Students receive an invitation here to take a given trajectory through Griffin's text, and it's a key one: to understand her claims for the ways we are all connected in a matrix or a field or a common past.

In order to do this work, students will need to reread the selection, looking for those moments when Griffin directly writes about interconnectedness or the key terms that the assignment presents them. They will also need to reread the "white spaces" between her fragments for the implications, the connections, that she implies. She never tells us, for example, how she thinks through RNA and DNA as metaphors that stand for growth or change, for instance, but she clearly implies that these metaphors have something to do with her thinking about these subjects and, too, about secrets. This has been the most difficult work for our students. They aren't accustomed to reading for implications or inferring between the lines, and they need to participate in discussions in class that seem to us like occasions for them to convince themselves that it's legitimate to infer or speculate about what something in the text, say Griffin's use of the DNA metaphor, might stand for or represent. These discussions seem to be essential, a part of the work of learning to read between the lines, and we encourage them whenever students appear skeptical or uncertain about their right to do such reading.

It's a difficult assignment because it steps right past the kinds of questions students will want to begin with — What is "Our Secret" about? What is Griffin saying? — and moves immediately to questions about the project as a project — What is she doing? Why does she write this way? It may be best to assign a preliminary writing assignment or to work with some of the "Questions for a Second Reading." Or it might be useful to precede or follow this assignment with one that asks students to write like Griffin, where students are allowed to think about her project in terms of their own practice as writers. This assignment worked best for us when we made it clear to students that they should think about Griffin's writing in terms of the usual education offered young writers in the United States. They should begin, that is, not with the language of literary analysis ("image" or "metaphor") but with the language of the composition classroom ("topic sentence," "paragraph," "organization," "footnotes," and "three-by-five notecards").

3. Our students had a great time with this assignment, and it produced some of the most interesting writing of the semester. They chose topics that ranged from parental influences; the relationship of machines and thinking; the struggle to be, as one young woman called it, in an unfriendly environment of violence; the replication of behaviors in men from different generations of the same family; and the various metaphors for space. The key to students having a successful experience with this assignment seems to lie in the subjects they choose to write about and the stories they tell. We have told them to write about stories they know or would like to research because they are curious about them, because they sense connections to other stories or examples that they may or may not need to research. The students' involvement in the writing will push them to do the kinds of thinking through and connecting that imitates Griffin's work. This assignment demonstrates to them the kind of planning and care that Griffin's work required, and our students found that they could help themselves with outlines and charts or maps of the territories they wanted to cover. We allowed them class time, also, to test their plans with other students and with us. This proved to be time well spent, for it helped students see connections that others saw and it prevented anyone from being lost at sea for anything but a brief period. In this assignment, we also took students through multiple drafts, and we assigned students

to pairs at different points so that they could continually test their work against the readings of others.

MAKING CONNECTIONS (p. 266)

1. The subjects that students chose to work on with this assignment focused on surfaces and depths, visible and invisible, secret and apparent, hidden and exposed, control and surveillance. These are very abstract notions, especially for students who are unaccustomed to writing about abstractions and grounding them in particulars. In order to prepare them to work on this project, we took a considerable amount of time discussing the second-reading questions for each selection, and we asked them to write one assignment on each selection before we presented them with this project. As a part of this project, students need to reread the two selections (that seems obvious), but they also benefit from class discussions in which they point out the ways they could use ideas from one to critique or "investigate" the other. There is a strong pull for students to transform this project into a compare-and-contrast assignment. We used the project after students had some experience writing critiques, where they took ideas or sets of ideas from one reading selection and used them as a frame or a lens to analyze or critique another reading or other examples. That's the basic move in this project, so it's important for students to be able to identify those subjects or ideas that they could use from one selection to read or analyze or investigate another.

    This also turns out to be a project that poses challenges for students as they summarize and present it to their readers. The writing assignment that we used for each before we turned to this project asked them to re-present the selection's key examples and ideas to readers who had read the essay but didn't have it in front of them. We then discussed examples from these papers in class as ways of showing students how their colleagues handled the task. When we did this, we presented students with examples that could stand as interesting or compelling models of presentation that included both examples and the ideas they were meant to illustrate. This coupling of examples and ideas is particularly important for a project like this one, because it's so easy for students to get lost in the abstractions of the selections. Keeping sight of the examples that illustrate those abstractions gives them a way to think of the project at hand. What examples and ideas, then, we asked, could you use, for instance, from Foucault's selections to investigate the workings of secrets, for example, in Griffin's?

2. Students will need to have read both the Griffin essay and the Foer essay in order to take on this assignment. At first glance, Foer's piece can be read as being more *literally* about memory than Griffin's in that he discusses memory champions remembering poems and decks of cards. So it can be useful for students to begin with a discussion of how Foer's discussion of memory might extend beyond just what we can literally recall. This can lead to a meaningful class discussion about remembering—about its various connotations and definitions. But in both Griffin and Foer's essays, most readers can recognize that there is a fear of forgetting, a fear of erasure that seems to thread through time. Many students hear this fear in their own historical moment—when, for example, older individuals might complain about their inability to remember phone

numbers or their own dependence on Web search engines—so these questions of memory are often resonant for students.

In assignments that, like this one, ask students to locate and focus on particular passages in the text, we find it's helpful to dedicate class time to activities that might enable students to practice and discuss the process of reading through a text with a goal in mind, and also how to use the passages they find as part of an essay. Making meaning of another writer's text and incorporating that meaning into a larger project is not only part of what it means to learn to be a writer but also a skill we feel translates to particular habits of mind—paying attention to one's own interpretative strategies, being empowered to make meaning, and bringing seemingly disparate ideas together into a whole picture.

3.   This assignment asks students to think about "Our Secret" in relation to another essay that uses autobiography and family history to think about large questions—race, nation, war. The assignment identifies Wideman's "Our Time."

As always, the success of this assignment will depend on students taking time to present and to develop examples from the texts. Certainly summary and paraphrase will be required strategically to prepare the comparison. You can help students feel the pressure, however, to turn to block quotation and to specific and extended points of comparison.

It is important for students to take the final set of questions seriously. The temptation will be to say that these are great writers and of course everyone should be allowed a similar freedom of expression—or something like that. Students should feel the pressure (or students will benefit, we've found, from the pressure) to think seriously about what an essay like this can and can't do, the purposes and occasions it can and cannot serve.

4.   Miller's essay has several striking connections to Susan Griffin's "Our Secret." The first of these connections has to do with the kinds of projects they both perform and also with the reasons they seem to engage with these projects. This question calls students' attention to the ways Miller and Griffin study their respective "characters"—with particular attention to those who have done violence to others. In some ways, students will find Miller's and Griffin's subject matter familiar—World War II narratives, school shootings, and stories of violence are certainly a part of both their educational and personal experiences. Something they might find unfamiliar is an author's desire to understand the behavior of those involved, an author's intention to learn from or theorize out of these atrocious events and controversial figures.

Students will then be asked to notice the nuances of both Miller's and Griffin's projects, and they will need to perform some careful close reading of both the passages here and their contexts in order to articulate not only the tensions between Miller and Griffin but also how these two authors seem interested in some of the same questions. This assignment might illuminate for students how two writers—making no direct reference to each other and having written their respective pieces fifteen years apart—might be engaged in an intellectual conversation that began long before them and will continue long after; hopefully, students might be able to see themselves as engaged in this conversation as well.

JUDITH HALBERSTAM

Animating Revolt and Revolting Animation (p. 271)

This selection, taken from Halberstam's book *The Queer Art of Failure*, asks readers to revisit and rethink some relatively popular films like *March of the Penguins*, *Chicken Run*, and *Finding Nemo* in order to critique common notions of success and failure, which, for Halberstam, are tied to normative constructions of sexuality and family. There is something deceptively familiar about "Animating Revolt and Revolting Animation," because many students recognize the films that are the focus of Halberstam's inquiry. At first glance, this familiarity seems to offer the perfect opening to the piece, but sometimes it can also be a challenge whereby Halberstam's engagement with popular culture obscures for students the bold social critique at the center of the argument.

Many of the reading and writing exercises we have designed for this selection begin by asking students to look more closely at what seems familiar, and to then look for what might be unfamiliar. These kinds of questions help students illuminate for themselves what they might have taken for granted or missed in their initial readings of the essay. We've also had instructors raise questions about the difficulty of talking about sexuality or gender in writing courses. But just as some texts are difficult because of their denseness or vocabulary (like Foucault's, for example), other texts are difficult for readers because they ask us to revise (to see again) the conventional or normalizing practices and ideas that circulate in our culture. We have found that many students really want to learn how to talk about these subjects in intellectual ways because they are subjects that students care deeply about.

Halberstam also gives us the chance to talk with students about the ways in which seeing a film is *like* reading, to discuss how films are read and what kinds of strategies viewers use (or don't use) when watching movies. Part of learning to write essays is learning to think in unconventional ways, learning to put seemingly divergent ideas side by side, and learning to pose difficult questions about taken-for-granted ideas. Halberstam serves as an engaging model for learning this practice.

QUESTIONS FOR A SECOND READING (p. 293)

1. Because it is easy for students to get lost in the pop-culture familiarity of Halberstam's references, this first question asks them to pay attention to what is *un*familiar. We then ask students not only to research unfamiliar ideas or terms but to think about why they have not had exposure to these terms before. This question can spark interesting discussions about how our personal experiences shape our reading practices and the ways our environment shapes what we know. Students choose terms like "Marxist" or "animal husbandry" or even "human exceptionalism." These terms provide another entry point to Halberstam's essay, an alternative to taking the familiar route of the films themselves.

2. We and our students are often told that it is important for writers to directly examine the sources other writers utilize — to not always take the writer's interpretation of them at face value. So this assignment invites students to look closely at one of Halberstam's

objects of study and to think about how Halberstam is reading the film and also how it might be read differently. Because *Ways of Reading* is so invested in how we read and its connection to our writing, assignments like this one are crucial in our classes. Of course, many instructors in a traditional English department setting like students to be able to go to a primary source, to see for themselves what an essay, novel, or film might be doing. But this is not the only reason the practice is important. Teaching students to examine sources for themselves, to weigh their experience alongside the voices of others (and to thereby join a conversation) also teaches students to engage the world rather than hear about it, to experience their own readings and viewings rather than only see what they see through the eyes of others. This assignment has often sparked class discussions about the idea of what one student has called "mediated experience."

3. Sometimes students can have difficulty entering into the discipline of Queer Theory without context. We have found that part of this is because some students still associate the word "queer" with something derogatory, something they should not say. For some students, this may be the first time they have heard the word "queer" used academically or intellectually. But we have also found that this is a productive conversation to have—about language, and about the vocabularies that give us access to pieces written for that particular disciplinary audience. We have also discovered that this assignment helps students to address a potential challenge with the piece as they are first working on it. As instructors, of course, we must be prepared to facilitate some perhaps controversial or difficult discussions. It can be useful to connect Foucault to this field of study as well and to illustrate to students that the study of identity is at the center of intellectual work in the twenty-first century.

4. This question invites students to both perform a close reading of a specific passage of Halberstam's piece and also to consider the possible responses to the question Halberstam poses once they understand (through that close reading) her question. We find this question useful as an in-class activity. It's particularly helpful to go through the passage one phrase at a time and invite the class to comment about meaning as you move through it. Then, once the class has come to an understanding by working collaboratively on the passage, they can brainstorm in small groups about the second part of the question, considering what the answer to Halberstam's question might be.

ASSIGNMENTS FOR WRITING (p. 294)

1. One way to get inside the meaning of an author's project is to take on his or her project, to move its methods to another object of study. Students have taken on some complex critical lenses as they watch the film they choose to analyze, and they've had fun doing so.

    One student, taking his cue from Halberstam, performed an interesting exploration of the film *Brave*, concluding that the film is not a symbol of revolution and challenging Halberstam's claim by writing, "Anything can look revolutionary, but that doesn't mean it is." This student, rather than reading for revolution, read for the normalizing functions of the film *Brave*. The class workshop focused on his paper and engaged in a fascinating discussion about whether something "counts" as queer or revolutionary if some aspects of its story are quite traditional. In short, the class was doing the kind of work Halberstam invites them to do, thereby taking on Halberstam's way of reading texts and employing some of their own strategies as well.

2. Many assignments ask students to focus on the central or main idea of an essay, and doing so is certainly a useful way of reading. But this question focuses on the peripheral ideas in Halberstam's essay, inviting students to read for what isn't at the center. Students can sometimes find assignments like this one difficult because they are so used to looking for and reading for that main idea. But once they go searching (and perhaps this is work you might do collaboratively as a class by making a list of subjects *other* than the films), students often find subjects that interest them and assumptions that Halberstam makes in order to construct that central argument in the first place. This is a key learning experience in how essays are made, and often students begin to see possibilities for their own writing or the assumptions they, too, make when they compose.

3. Perhaps the most difficult of the essay questions related to Halberstam's piece, this question asks students to engage in one of the central philosophical questions of Queer Theory: the question of being and the question of knowing. We often get questions about whether first-year writing students or undergraduate students in general can take up questions and epistemology and ontology the way the assignment invites them to do. And, of course, this textbook offers a resounding *yes* to that question. There is no denying the difficulty of these questions, but their difficulty is precisely the point. Students always surprise us and often surprise themselves with the kinds of challenging questions they find they can take on in their writing.

MAKING CONNECTIONS (p. 295)

1. Schulz's and Halberstam's texts are an engaging combination—both writers value the concept of *going against the grain*. This assignment asks students to see the ways the two authors think about "evidence that challenges our beliefs." As readers, we don't necessarily notice that we are responding to a text in a given way because it moves against our most basic logics or assumptions. In completing this assignment, students will have to think about the ways Halberstam might move against common belief systems. And because the question asks them to consider Schulz as well, students are invited to value rather than resist evidence that challenges their beliefs.

    It is conventional for readers who are reading in order to write to see their reading as a means of looking for "evidence" that *supports* their beliefs. That rhetorical strategy is something many of our students are familiar with from their writing experiences thus far. Reading for kinds of evidence that might challenge their beliefs is likewise an important exercise not just for reading but for writing as well. The best writers are able to see many dimensions and contradictory ideas at once, and they learn to recognize and engage with how our beliefs affect our reading and writing practices.

2. In this assignment, students are asked to "test out" one of Halberstam's ideas on Doyle's essay. They begin with Halberstam's version of a common theme: that we humans frequently use animals in our movies, writing, and advertising in order to convey human objectives and logic. While many students may not have previously

thought about this phenomenon in such a way, they often seem interested in this idea and enjoy identifying other examples in popular culture where they see Halberstam's idea playing out. We find it is helpful to lead a class discussion that addresses the first part of this question so that students can together flesh out Halberstam's idea. Once they have a grasp of what "penguin logics" might mean and how unknowable those logics might be, we send students off to work on the Doyle essay. Students may or may not have read this essay before taking on this assignment. Because the Doyle essay is quite short, they can read it on their own as they think about the question.

This assignment can prove fascinating once students have written their essays. Because the Doyle essay can be very compelling and beautiful in its composition, launching a critique of Doyle's essay can seem "mean" or "wrong," as some students have put it. Students have even found out that some of Doyle's "facts" about hummingbirds aren't even true or are exaggerated. This can lead not only to further productive discussions of Halberstam's point but also to complex discussions about truth. Students can further consider questions such as: What is so wrong with using "human logics" to understand animals? Can we know what is "true" about hummingbirds—or about ourselves for that matter? At first glance, the Doyle essay and the Halberstam essay seem very different—in one case, a queer theorist works on animation films, and in the other, a creative writer muses about nature. But, in the end, that seeming difference is the productive location for this assignment.

3. Part of the challenge of this assignment is that there are so many ways to think about the "realm of the possible" and so many ways to read Halberstam as engaged with this realm. Students are sometimes intimidated by questions like these. After all, how do they know what Butler means when she wrote that? But part of learning to be an active reader and writer means learning to construct webs of meaning of your own. There is no set answer to what Butler means by this phrase, but through reading and rereading her essay in this collection, we can construct our own potential meanings within the context Butler constructs. Students, of course, know what the words "realm" and "possible" mean, but what do they mean in the context of Butler and Halberstam? How do these words gather new meaning through the writers' projects? Answering this question helps students think also about themselves as writers, about how they can give meaning to language that seems already defined.

KATHLEEN JAMIE

Shia Girls 🄴

Our students enjoyed working with this essay. They lingered over it. They also puzzled over it. Few of them had more than a handful of received ideas about Pakistan and its cultures. Few of them could picture the landscape, even though Jamie dwells on it at times. One of the challenges for them, then, had to do with using the terms and language of the essay to piece together accurate understandings of the country, its cultures, and its traditions, including the situations of women. For this reason, we recommend beginning with the first Question for a Second Reading. We worked alongside our students to do our own research using this question, so when we took a complete class meeting to report amongst ourselves on our findings, we were all working from definitions, Web pages, and images. This important work prepared all of us with common understandings and images.

The other challenge students encountered with this essay has to do with its structure. Jamie's piece is not "point" or thesis driven, although it does, as many students said, seem to be making an argument. The nature of that argument, what that argument might be said to be, provided our students with opportunities to do their most interesting writing of the semester, so don't miss the first Assignment for Writing. There's plenty of other work for students to do before they take this on, and they will benefit from digging into two or three of the second-reading questions before attempting the first Assignment for Writing.

QUESTIONS FOR A SECOND READING 🄴

1. This is the question that all students should complete. It will result in a tapestry of discoveries that coheres when the entire class discusses their findings for a class meeting. Students had images on their computers and phones that they shared, definitions from multiple sources, and out of all these, we concluded our discussion with a reflection on what we could say that we learned to prepare us for our next reading of "Shia Girls."

2. Most of our students thought that the essay made a case for the effects of change that Jamie observes, although few of them could point to the text to locate those moments when Jamie observes and reports on change. This question allowed them to step outside of their initial understandings and misunderstandings about what Jamie sees and thinks about change. And the picture that Jamie paints complicates the idea of change. She observes and notes changes, but it's much more difficult than students think it is to attribute judgments to Jamie about the changes she observes and reports.

3. Rashida marks her writing to Jamie as important, and so does Jamie. The paragraphs situate the essay immediately from Rashida's perspective. They are both a frame and an invitation to Jamie, and our students wondered how Jamie's essay might be a response to those two paragraphs. Others thought that Jamie used the paragraphs as a frame to allow her to make contrasts between her experiences and Rashida's. Since Jamie has made the decision for us by using the paragraphs to open her essay, it's then a matter of allowing students to think of their rereading in terms of these paragraphs.

4. Jamie notices the talk and actions of both men and women, but one could make the case that she observes and reports on women, including those she meets on the bus trip, with attention or access that's not so obvious with the men she observes. Is this because she's more interested in the women? The essay is, after all, titled "Shia Girls." Or is this because she "sees" them in more intimate or telling situations, including in their long conversations together? How might Jamie's seeing or her focus on women be thought of as an argument about the situations of women and her own position as a woman? This is challenging work for students, but, like the second and third second-reading questions, it's an engaging close reading.

ASSIGNMENTS FOR WRITING 🄔

1. This assignment produced some of the best writing from students during the semester. Students wrote multiple revisions of it after studying examples from their work in class. The challenge for them was in identifying a single point of reference that they could use to organize their reading of Jamie's essay. Some chose metaphors and images, while others chose passages. At first, students wanted to work from multiple points of reference, but they had difficulties keeping the focus on the single or most significant point of reference. In class, we studied examples of paragraphs from their essays in which the writers took different types of points of reference and different paths into using them to frame their readings of the Jamie essay. Because they worked from different points of reference, they wrote about different understandings of what Jamie's project might be. Those who took, for instance, passages from the conversations among the women or lines from Rashida found ways into writing about Jamie's project as either a study of herself amongst the Shia women or a study of the Shia women through their conversations. Those who took a line about change as a point of reference committed themselves to seeing Jamie's project as a kind of travel account of past and present, of the changes brought forward by looking at the past and present, or of the impending changes from development and tourism. Between these two readings of Jamie's projects, there was a range of points of reference and readings of her project. One particularly compelling student paper took a metaphor of a spreading flower as a point of reference and developed a perspective on Jamie's project that positioned her as concerned about the spreading influences working their ways through the traditions of the Shia women.

2. Jamie's written conversations feature prominently in "Shia Girls." Our students commented on the ways in which they were unaccustomed to reading essays with many long conversations. They wanted to make sense of them quickly, to imagine that those conversations could be said to be making specific points, but that's not the nature of Jamie's presentations of the conversations. During class discussions of the conversations that they identified, we kept coming back to the question of why. Why does Jamie include them in such detail? What do they allow her to accomplish? After these discussions, students began to imagine that the conversations are her project, that they allow her to present her subjects in ways more complex than if she simply reported on them or on what they said. The conversations, as one student said, paint pictures of the people as people, as people with things to say about their situations and those of others they know.

    This writing assignment pairs wonderfully with the fourth writing assignment that invites students to try their hands at imitating Jamie's creation of conversations. That too, though, has its challenges, since it asks students for more than just copied-down conversations. It asks them to interweave observations and comments into the conversations, as Jamie does, to present talkers as a journalist might.

3. Although students felt certain that Jamie had a political position after rereading her essay, few could develop compelling explanations for anything but the most obvious. That has to do with Jamie's position on change—that to know someone or some place is to see them through change. The leap from that idea to political awareness caught students in knots of their own thinking. Some wanted to say that Jamie is against

change or for it—taking a simple dichotomy as a thinking machine. Others wanted to say that Jamie is against the Westernization of Pakistan and its traditions, while still others thought she favored such change. Students used the notion of egalitarianism as a hinge for making all of these claims—Jamie favors equality for women, some said, while others thought that she favors change because it affects traditions, such as the separate treatment of men and women, that should be changed. So while this is an assignment that will ask students to think close to the text for those examples of political awareness that might speak to an atmosphere of egalitarianism, it will take considerable discussion to test their claims against Jamie's passages and sentences. It's not an assignment to do cold and is best thought of as a follow-up to either the first or second writing assignment.

4. As we mentioned earlier, this imitation of Jamie's conversations pairs well with the second writing assignment that invites students to study those conversations. We ask students to work from a specific passage that shows Jamie integrating description and commentary into her presentation of a conversation, but we could imagine that other passages would work just as well and that students would benefit just as much from working only with conversations at first. They could add description and commentary as a revision to the conversations or not add it at all. Our students had fun with this assignment, but they didn't revise their conversations. They did their imitations as a follow-up to their studies of Jamie's conversations for the second writing assignment.

MAKING CONNECTIONS

1. This is a challenging assignment. Students will need to read and work with Mary Louise Pratt's essay on the "Arts of the Contact Zone" before they take on this assignment. They'll need to have a good understanding of her ideas about writing and pedagogy in the contact zone. Jamie presents her conversations, one could argue, as examples of the ways people use oral rhetoric to communicate across lines of difference. One can also argue, of course, that Jamie herself is using writing as a cultural mediation to instruct her readers about how to understand differences among those on which she reports and on herself as the reporter. If students assume that Jamie is writing from a political awareness, from an atmosphere, as she says, of egalitarianism, and if her writing can be thought of as an art of the contact zone, how might students then describe the contact zone? How is such a contact zone shaped by her writing, by her presentation of others in conversations, and by her interests in instructing her readers? What, then, might she want to teach her readers?

2. Our students brought strong preconceived notions to "Shia Girls." Work on the first "Question for a Second Reading" went a long way in improving their understandings of this particular region in Pakistan and its various cultures and traditions, but these understandings didn't push back against their preconceived notions about such things as gender differences and the situations of the women presented in "Shia Girls." Studying Walker Percy's essay gave our students language for explaining preconceived notions. The hard work of identifying such notions in their own essays fell to numerous small group discussions in which students worked in pairs or trios to identify sentences and passages in their essays that seemed to be carrying assumptions and preconceived ideas about Pakistan, its cultures, and the gender differences often

presented in Jamie's essay. Students benefited enormously from a couple of rounds of such close readings of their essays (which had been produced for the writing assignments) before going on to write this reflective essay. The students first wrote multiple drafts of two different essays for two of the writing assignments. Once these were completed, they studied Percy's essay. After that, they went back to their essays from the writing assignments to study them for "symbolic complexes," preconceived notions, and assumptions that they brought to reading and studying Jamie's essay. After two rounds of small group work on their own essays from Percy's framework, they then took a first pass at the reflective essay for this assignment.

JONATHAN LETHEM

The Ecstasy of Influence 🄴

"The Ecstasy of Influence." I think the challenge of teaching this piece is to get students to believe in the "ecstasy" of it all. The essay is a tour de force—the surprise at the end, the discussion of theft, gift, and influence presented as an act of theft, gift, and influence. It certainly make sense to have students read the essay without any advance knowledge of what they are about to read. That way, they get the chance to feel the essay's effects. Unfortunately, one of the effects for a first-time reader is a sense of aimlessness and repetition. As an essay, the piece has lovely moments but not much in the way of forward momentum. It makes sense, then, to offer this essay as an exercise in organizing (or invention) by "section." When we taught it, that is where we began. We asked students to look page by page to see how the essay was divided into sections with subheadings. And we asked them to be prepared to talk about how the sections worked—how they worked for Lethem, how they worked for a reader. This gave them a motive to keep reading, to try to discern the logic or internal force that moved from one section to the next.

Rereading, then, becomes a very different act. If (as I think they should) students reread with the "Key" as a guide (and use it closely for at least a couple of the sections), they are reading this time to try to get a feel for the poetics of a mash-up. We added the afterword, "The Afterlife of 'Ecstasy,'" which Lethem prepared for the book that collected a number of essays under this essay's title, for two reasons. We wanted students to hear Lethem's account at the end on the "somatics" of influence—on the energy behind it, on the fun of it all. And we wanted Lethem to prompt a stepping back to think about the essay not just as an essay but as an action, as a way of doing something with words, something linked to traditions of U.S. literary and popular culture. We realized early on that we would want students to come to class prepared to present and to talk about collages or borrowings or mash-ups from their own private inventories. And we realized early on that we would want them to track down some of Lethem's references (like, say, "The Wasteland") that could be both interesting and useful to them as points of reference somewhere down the line.

And, finally, from our experience, there is much to be gained by having two writing assignments—one that thinks about the essay and another that carries out its project, that does something similar. It is only by constructing a "plagiarism" that students can feel the pleasure of such a transgression.

QUESTIONS FOR A SECOND READING 🄴

1. As we say above, the classroom discussions were advanced by having students track down some of Lethem's examples — "The Wasteland," for instance, and any commentaries on the work as borrowing or appropriation or plagiarism. This assignment sends students out on a mini-research project. We often combine an exercise like this with a trip to the library and a session with a reference librarian on how to use a university library and its resources. A university library is a special and daunting place; it has tools well beyond what students will have encountered at the libraries in their high schools or neighborhoods. And students often quite literally need someone to take them across the threshold.

    Remember, though, that although it is important to have students track down, explain, and defend examples that lie beyond their immediate range of reference, it is equally important to have them come to class with examples that are close to them, that mean something to them, that are part of their own immediate cultural experience.

2. As we said above, this assignment became a way for us to get past the fact that the essay, given its construction, lacks a narrative or argumentative forward energy. By asking students to think about sections (and "sectioning") and to think from section to section, we were giving them a way to think ahead without our spilling the beans on where it all would end.

    It is also the case that, for some time now, we have been teaching students to "punctuate" their essays by marking sections. We teach this practice regularly and with essays that are more conventionally made. It remains a remarkable and often liberating discovery for students to learn that they, too, can divide their essays into numbered sections, with or without subheads. We teach this as a way of assisting the reader (which is how we teach all forms of punctuation). But we also teach it as a way of assisting the writer. The subsections provide places where a writer is able to stop and take stock, or to mark progress and direction, or to pause to catch a breath — and to pause not only to rest but to see what has been left out, what counterexamples are possible, what new directions are hidden by the current track. Each pause offers a moment to think about readers and what they might be thinking or where they might be confused.

3. It is interesting: Students often read past (or feel alienated by or affronted by or offended by) technical terms, key terms. And yet, as we understand the discursive world of the academy, these are the equivalents of the money shots — this is where it is happening; this is the payoff. And, of course, one way to describe the larger coherence of nonfiction texts is as a movement from one organizing term to another. It is important, we have found, to call attention to key terms, to ask students to think about how they work (as well as what they might mean). And we urge them to use

the key terms of others—and, beyond that, to coin or to introduce key terms of their own.

This is also, however, a brief writing exercise. For years, we have used paraphrase—short paragraphs written in class our outside class—as exercises in translation and in understanding. These open up a discussion of the text and of meaning; they also provide the opportunity to talk about difficulty—about what it is that makes a passage perplexing or challenging and about what a reader might do at such a moment.

4–5. These two questions are the prompts that invite students to step out of the essay to ask questions about what the essay *does* as opposed to what it *says*. The first asks students to think about the writer of this essay: What is he doing? Why is he doing what he is doing? What problems does he face—what "writing" problems, that is? And does he pull it off?

Assignment 5 turns the dial and asks students to think about the "Lethem" in this essay as a reader—as representing the figure of the reader. "Active reading." "Critical reading." These are dead terms, classroom clichés. The example of this essay (and the discussion in "The Afterlife") provides new, precise, and provocative definitions.

ASSIGNMENTS FOR WRITING   e

1. As we say above, there is much to be gained by having students work with two writing assignments—one that thinks about the essay and another that carries out its project, that does something similar. It is only by constructing a "plagiarism" that students can feel the pleasure of such a transgression. The first is an invitation to a Lethem-like project.

   Please note that we focus attention on Lethem's sense that his project is "urgent" and "ecstatic." We are inviting students to feel that what they are doing is powerful, inspiring, fun, dangerous. Not all will agree, of course, which we acknowledge. And we ask for a "key." The real danger in teaching this assignment is that a student will miss or ignore Lethem's necessary acknowledgement that he had been (is) working with other people's material, with other writers' sentences. We would be pleased for students to begin to understand how difficult it is (how counterintuitive it can be) to draw the line between "my" work and yours, between a source and an idea. We would not, however, want to be taken to be endorsing cheating. Students know what it means to cheat. Lethem may complicate the relationship between tradition and the individual talent, but he is not giving license to turn in an essay by T.S. Eliot as though it were one's own.

2–4. These assignments ask students to engage with the essay as an essay—to enter the conversation Lethem has begun (or joined or appropriated or highjacked!). The second assignment invites students to think of plagiarism in relation to schooling and the usual (and usually unexamined) language of official statements on plagiarism. It is not a difficult context to imagine—a student has read Lethem, thought about influence and the use of prior texts, and then wants to write something, say, for the student newspaper, on the university's plagiarism statement.

Assignment 3 is a more conventional assignment. It asks students to represent Lethem's essay through summary, paraphrase, and quotation (to represent it for readers who have not yet read it), to establish Lethem's position, and then to respond. We never offer assignments that rely on summary alone. We want summary to function strategically, and that is our goal here. Students will need to provide a rich and textured sense of what Lethem says in this essay (and what Lethem does there). This alone is a job of some complexity—and it might constitute a first draft. The most difficult part of the assignment, however, comes when the student writer needs to take center stage. We represent that moment in two ways—as a need to bring a new example to the table, something close to the student and his or her world, and as an invitation to extend or challenge Lethem's argument.

Assignment 4, which builds on the first "Questions for a Second Reading," turns attention to just one of Lethem's examples, one which the student can then research in detail. If assignment 3 asks the student to bring a new example to the table, assignment 4 asks the student to take a closer look at something already there.

MAKING CONNECTIONS e

1. See the commentary on the first Assignment for Writing (above). This "Making Connections" assignment invites a student to produce a Lethem-like plagiarism using selections from *Ways of Reading* as sources.

2. We regularly feature assignments that ask students to read one essay in light of, or in reference to, another so that they can imagine that they are engaged in an ongoing project rather than just a little of this and a little of that—Emerson one week, and Lethem the next.

   The assignment provides a long list of selections in *Ways of Reading* that raise questions about the relation of the individual to tradition, to history, to the words and the work of others: Berger, Butler, Emerson, Freire, Rodriguez, Miller, and Percy. With Rodriguez, we provide a section from Richard Hoggart's *The Uses of Literacy* so that students can see his much more conventional act of citation.

   We have always made it a point to insist that students use assignments like these to take a step beyond "compare and contrast," a method already (most likely) a part of their toolkits. There is a technical side to using one text as a lens through which to view the other. One way to make this act of reading materialize on the page is to bring a paragraph or block quotation from one text—from Lethem, say—to a discussion that also requires a paragraph or block quotation from Emerson. What do you hear in each? Where and how do they speak to each other? Where do they not? As we ask students to visualize the page, we ask them also to imagine a space in the essay where they, the student writer, speaks, where they take a position and make an evaluative judgment about what they have read. (What is your favorite moment in all of this? Which text is most persuasive?) And we ask them to strike out on their own, either to develop an idea or to apply what they have found to a new situation or set of examples.

RICHARD E. MILLER

The Dark Night of the Soul 🄴

In the context of the composition classroom, this becomes a highly metatextual essay, one that is interrogating the very work we so often take for granted as students and teachers of writing. Dare we ask, with our students, whether the work we do in the classroom has any value? In doing so, we ask our students to engage with us, and with Miller, as intellectuals who are thinking through the same problems that he is thinking through in "The Dark Night of the Soul." In this piece, Miller is asking not just about the value of writing but about the tenuous relationships between text and meaning, between language and reality. The assignments here will make this intellectual work explicit to students and will direct their attention to the places where they are *already* doing this work in class discussion and in their writing.

Most likely, some students may already feel skeptical about the value of writing, and we like the way that Miller both appeals to this skepticism and pushes against it, drawing students into the reading but resisting points of identification. On the other hand, some students may identify with the idealism Miller is questioning. And yet Miller makes it difficult to resolve the problems he is raising with either faith or dismissals; this text requires a more complicated way of looking at things. Regardless of students' relationships to reading, whether they have been lifelong or reluctant readers in the past, Miller's essay offers them a way in, a way to engage with questions about the values and dangers of writing and reading in the modern world.

Note: Miller's "Fault Lines in the Contact Zone" is included in Part IV, page 355.

QUESTIONS FOR A SECOND READING 🄴

1. This is a standard assignment for us, one that opens up numerous formal possibilities for students' writing.

2. Please see the entry for "Assignments for Writing," #3.

3. This assignment leads us into a discussion of what we take for granted about the value of reading and writing. In this discussion, students become conscious of these values in ways that allow them either to invest in them or to interrogate them.

4. Miller's "critical optimism" energized our students, but many of them wondered out loud whether so many authors were necessary to his argument. No doubt this is a legitimate and important observation. In their questioning, students were marking a significant difficulty of the text, and by rereading with this difficulty in mind, students investigated the connective tissue of the argument without which the core, the critical optimism Miller seeks to outline, would disintegrate. After working through these connections, we have found that students used Miller's own reading to articulate a fuller sense of critical optimism, which gave them increased freedom when discussing his argument as writers. Articulating these connections also requires students to imitate aspects of Miller's own project, to ponder why he reads who he reads and what he

does with those readings. This line of questioning also sets up the groundwork for the first and third "Assignments for Writing."

5.   It's not enough for students to make their own argument about the value of (or problems with) the electronic technologies that are reshaping literacy; they need to place their ideas in conversation with Miller's, responding to his claims. And given the difficulty of seeing outside the new media that have shaped them, we suggest you ask students to begin by taking a skeptical stance toward those media, if only to suggest that students consider Miller's position carefully before leaping to a defense of technologies that combine sound, image, and text.

ASSIGNMENTS FOR WRITING 🔲

1., 4. Our students took these assignments personally, many making a case for a piece of writing either that they had loved for years or that had recently knocked them down. Because Miller is so focused on what kind of difference writing can make in school, in our public, these essays expressed a moving mixture of personal investment and public concern. Students chose a myriad of genres—children's books, song lyrics, magazine articles, novels, memoirs—and though different genres presented different challenges, the choice itself was central to the assignment's success. Many students were surprised by how much they needed to reread Miller despite the fact that the assignment asked them to focus on an outside source. Students must possess a deep understanding of Miller's definition of critically optimistic writing in order to make a case for the piece that they choose. The "Questions for a Second Reading" may help students develop this understanding, but this particular writing assignment asks them to move from broad argumentative strokes to specific aspects of writing. For example, what kinds of moves does Miller want authors to make? And what purposes does he hope underlie these moves? Thinking about Miller's writing style itself—his persistence in asking difficult questions, his refusal to shy away from "why" and "could"—can help students translate Miller's big ideas into writerly actions. Students tended to use Miller to discover the set of questions that they thought were most important to Miller's project and most relevant to the piece they had chosen. With the set of questions or concerns that they brought from Miller, students recast writing that they had enjoyed privately as publicly relevant: besides my liking this book, they asked, what could it be said to be good for?

2.   This assignment offers students the unique opportunity to turn to some of their own materials and texts as a way of understanding and engaging with Miller's essay. For students, engaging in a Miller-like project of reflecting on themselves or others through reading will be a material way of pointing to the challenges, problems, and intricacies of Miller's project of moving between text and self. Students may recognize part of this assignment as a kind of personal essay, but our intention is for the genre of the personal essay to be disrupted by the requirement that students use a text of some kind—the texts students choose help to keep the essays situated and focused on literacy practices rather than exclusively on life experience. We like this assignment because of the way that it draws students into a critique of the work we are doing in the composition classroom. In this regard, it makes them collaborators and coauthors in the work of the course itself by asking them to explore the reasons that we talk about reading and writing in the first place. This assignment, then, leads us into a discussion of what we take

for granted about the value of reading and writing. In this discussion, students become conscious of these values in ways that allow them either to invest in them or to interrogate them. And both investment and interrogation are significant scholarly practices.

3. While some of the other questions in this section focus on the texts that Miller examines and discusses, this question focuses on the reader, on the kind of reader Miller seems to be in his essay, and the kinds of readers students might be as they read both Miller and the texts Miller interprets. This question also points students to the problem of what a reader does with a text when he or she writes about it. Students will be able to consider that once we start writing, we are revising the text we have read, following our own agendas, speaking in place of the author. This, of course, as the question suggests, is part of the broader project of *Ways of Reading* itself and a part of our understanding that reading and writing are intimately bound. This assignment blurs the distinctions between reading and writing and hopes to open an opportunity for students to explore that blurring.

MAKING CONNECTIONS   🄴

1. This is a variation on the first "Assignment for Writing." That assignment will be good preparation for the work that students do with this one. Instead of taking school violence as an entry point into Miller, it asks students to work with both Miller and Rodriguez. The assignment asks students to think of two scholars, two projects, together, to imagine that they are speaking back and forth. (It helps, we have found, to invite students to speak from the point of view of a Miller or a Rodriguez and to do so even when the gesture is tentative: "I think that what Miller is saying is this...." or "My sense of Rodriguez is that he would agree, or disagree, with Miller about this....") The real test is to keep the assignment from becoming an empty formal exercise in comparing and contrasting. We insist that students make themselves present in the conversation. A revision, in fact, is often a way to invite students to do so.

2. This assignment asks students to engage in work with a key term, to follow a grounding conceptual term and uncover it in new places. What might a shared term reveal about disparate projects or investments? How could it change our reading of each piece? Though Miller is the inspiration, his essay may not appear in your students' essays. Instead, you might use Miller as a model during discussion. How does he read for desire in his examples (Karr, Descartes, Harris), and how does he express his own desires? Because Rodriguez uses "desire" so prominently, spending time with his title in its original context (Hoggart's *The Uses of Literacy*) will help to flesh out the paradox in their shared usages. It is important that discussions include how writing continually plays into these usages—students will expect that desire fuels authors' works, but how does it emerge in their writing? And how does it build or change throughout?

    It is possible that students will lean too heavily on the idea of "good" desire, simplifying the essay assignment to each writer's search for the "right" set of wants. Though rightness has a foundational place in this assignment (Miller makes it clear that he hopes for a certain set of desires and not others), Griffin should prove a powerful corrective to this oversimplification, opening up other ways of imagining desire's importance. In returning to Griffin, students will notice that she continually looks, wonders, listens, and probes, and through her various fragments, asks us to do the same. In fact, arriving at the right desires seems antithetical to her very project.

It's important to note that this assignment has no predictable structure. By giving students the option to reflect on their desires as they write, we are asking them to pause their metacognitive moments, to recognize and comment on connections between their own practices and the desires that they are interpreting textually. Immediately the possible voices and structures for their essays expand.

3. Miller's essay has several striking connections to Susan Griffin's "Our Secret." The first of these connections has to do with the kinds of projects they both perform and also with the reasons they seem to engage with these projects. This question calls students' attention to the ways Miller and Griffin study their respective "characters"—with particular attention to those who have done violence to others. In some ways, students will find Miller's and Griffin's subject matter familiar—World War II narratives, school shootings, and stories of violence are certainly a part of both their educational and personal experiences. Something they might find unfamiliar is an author's desire to understand the behavior of those involved, an author's intention to learn from or theorize out of these atrocious events and controversial figures.

Students will then be asked to notice the nuances of both Miller's and Griffin's projects, and they will need to perform some careful close reading of both the passages here and their contexts in order to articulate not only the tensions between Miller and Griffin but also how these two authors seem interested in some of the same questions. This assignment might illuminate for students how two writers—making no direct reference to each other and having written their respective pieces fifteen years apart—might be engaged in an intellectual conversation that began long before them and will continue long after; we hope that students might be able to see themselves as engaged in this conversation as well.

4. Questions of representation and truth are writing problems, problems that all writers must wrestle with at some point. Wideman's writing might be considered to be more explicitly engaged with these questions, while Miller's piece is more implicitly engaged, suggesting through its particular movement the problem of representation and reality. Miller, like Wideman, makes the stories he tells his own, bending and molding them for the purposes of "The Dark Night of the Soul." Whether we're writing about ourselves or someone else, we must always choose what to include and exclude, where to begin and end, what portrait we will paint for our readers. On what basis do we decide, and what are the consequences of our decisions? We are always faced with the limits of language and representation, the limits of our perspective, the limits of any piece of writing to capture the complexities of identity. What kinds of ethical dilemmas do we face when we decide to write about others? What can we ever claim to really *know* about others? Are some representations more true, just, or valuable than others? By what means can we make such judgments responsibly? This assignment asks students to consider the difficulties of representation. In this essay, not only will students have a chance to offer an analysis of what Wideman and Miller suggest about representation and truth, but they will also have the opportunity to offer their own theories of truth, thinking carefully about the term, its definitions and its relevance to their own writing.

5.   Engaging students in a Miller-like project of reflecting on Butler through reading will be a material way of pointing to the challenges, problems, and intricacies of Miller's project of moving between text and self.

ERROL MORRIS

Will the Real Hooded Man Please Stand Up? 🔲

I don't believe that students need to know much about Abu Ghraib in order to be readers of "Will the Hooded Man Please Stand Up?" When I taught this selection, though, I felt the urgency to give them some background, which I did by asking them to read the coverage of the event found in the Abu Ghraib "Times Topics" archive of the *New York Times.* I brought some of these images and headlines up in class, which seemed important for two reasons: the essay references the position of these images in the media, including the *New York Times,* whose photos we regrettably were unable to reproduce. I didn't want to lecture or to force home a point about the war and the consequences of the Bush administration's decisions about torture and detention. In fact, I worried that time spent in that direction would move Morris (and his concerns for the image) to the background. I did, however, want students to have some details and some sense of what the *Times* said and did. I found that not all students had much direct memory of this moment in our history.

The other problem you need to anticipate is the problem of the text itself. It is, as we say in the Questions for a Second Reading, a "documentary" essay. It includes photographs, notebook entries, pieces of journalism without much framing or commentary. By categorizing the prose as "documentary," we wanted to anticipate students' sense that the text was odd, that something was missing. Morris is a very good and very interesting writer, but he is, before anything else, a filmmaker, and his style comes close to montage.

QUESTIONS FOR A SECOND READING 🔲

1.   The first question points attention to the text as a text, to its methods and its organization and its use of image. Here we refer to it as a "documentary" text, for all of the reasons stated above.

2.   There is a narrative in this text—a kind of mystery story. Who IS the hooded man? And, we learned, students are drawn to this narrative at the expense of the argument it entails—that believing is seeing and "not the other way around." This is a complicated argument, delivered more (as we say) through sound bites and memorable phrases than through a carefully developed demonstration or chain of reasoning. We wanted to alert students to this and to ask them to solve the other textual problem—what is Morris saying about seeing and believing, about the image, in this discussion of the hooded man at Abu Ghraib?

3.   We often include a prompt that sends students out from the essay to the library for additional research—here about the status of the "iconic" image from Iwo Jima. Morris treats this image in the book, but we insisted that students find other sources as well.

It is not a bad idea to use an exercise like this as the occasion to schedule a trip to the library and a session with a reference librarian on how to use a university library and its resources. A university library is a special and daunting place; it has tools well beyond what students will have encountered in their high school or neighborhood libraries. And students often quite literally need someone to take them across the threshold.

4. The previous Questions for a Second Reading sent students back to the text. This one wants to remind them that this essay addresses them personally, particularly. It has something to say to them—and they may or may not feel the urgency or importance of this address. What the questions point to is what they might make of the encounter. Not, "Did you get what he said about the image?" but "What difference might any of this make to you? What might you recall? Where are you with this piece?" The answer, of course, can be "Nowhere; it means nothing to me." But we are always surprised by the students who speak with feeling about something we would never have known or imagined.

ASSIGNMENTS FOR WRITING

1. This is a standard type of assignment in *Ways of Reading*. Students are asked to extend Morris's argument to an example, in this case, a photograph that they bring to the table. Much will depend upon the care they take in choosing an image. They should have a sense that care and selection are part of the project. It is easy to grab an image and find that it provokes little but silence or the usual stuff, familiar sentences about scantily clad women or the horrors of war. Students aren't, most likely, going to be able to contextualize an image (and its history) as Morris does. They just don't have access to the information. They can, however, certainly think about cropping and selection and location, and they can speak to how the images circulate and, perhaps, how they are written about or spoken about by others.

   The assignment also requires students to represent Morris's essay through summary, paraphrase, and quotation (to represent it for readers who have not yet read it), to establish Morris's position, and then to respond. We never offer assignments that rely on summary alone. We want summary to function strategically, and that is our goal here. Students will need to provide a rich and textured sense of what Morris says in this essay (and what Morris does there). This alone is a job of some complexity—and it might constitute a first draft. The most difficult part of the assignment, however, comes when the student writer needs to take center stage. We represent that moment in two ways—as a need to bring a new example to the table, something close to the student and his or her world, and as an invitation to extend or challenge Morris's argument. This last is the hardest. The student must take center stage, and the student must take center stage at (usually) the end of the essay—when they are tired and out of time. I always teach through revision. In fact, my assessment is always and only an assessment of what happens from draft to draft, where (as I say to my students) I can actually see them at work.

2. See my comments on the fourth Question for a Second Reading (above). And see what I say in relation to the first Assignment for Writing on representing Morris. When I taught

Morris, I offered the option of these two writing assignments. Most students chose to write about an image. The one student who wrote a response to the prompt had been in the army and stationed in Iraq. His essay spoke powerfully of the difficulty, even the impossibility, of bringing home the news of the war or the experience of the war.

I've received essays from veterans who have seen action before. These are always difficult to respond to as a teacher/editor—partly because I find myself asking, *Who am I to say that this paragraph doesn't work?* and partly because the discourse of war is so over-determined as to make it very difficult for a student to reinflect or to revise the standard lines about courage and sacrifice. Courage and sacrifice are real, and testimony is often sufficient.

MAKING CONNECTIONS e

1–3. The "Making Connections" questions all ask students to use Morris to reread another text in *Ways of Reading*. Questions 2 and 3 send students to texts that also consider the status of photographic images: Edward Said's "States" and Susan Bordo's consideration of advertising in "Beauty (Re)discovers the Male Body." The first question uses Schulz's essay to consider the status of the photograph as "evidence" and its relation to error.

We regularly feature assignments that ask students to read one essay in light of, or in reference to, another so that they can imagine that they are engaged in an ongoing project rather than just a little of this and a little of that—Morris one week and Bordo the next.

We have always made it a point to insist that students use assignments like these to take a step beyond "compare and contrast," a method already (most likely) a part of their toolkits. There is a technical side to using one text as a lens through which to view the other. One way to make this act of reading materialize on the page is to bring a paragraph or block quotation from one text—from Schulz, say—to a discussion that also requires a paragraph or block quotation from Morris. What do you hear in each? Where and how do they speak to each other? Or not? As we ask students to visualize the page, we ask them also to imagine a space in the essay where they, the student writer, speaks, where they take a position and make an evaluative judgment about what they have read. (What is your favorite moment in all of this? Which text is most persuasive?) And we ask them to strike out on their own, either to develop an idea or to apply what they have found to a new situation or set of examples.

ERROL MORRIS

We've Forgotten That Photographers Are Connected to the Physical World e

As you prepare to teach the prose selection, "Will the Real Hooded Man Please Stand Up?" you should take time to watch this *Guardian* video, even if you don't plan to assign it. It is a nice introduction to the larger themes of Morris's book *Believing Is Seeing: Observations on the Mysteries of Photography*. It opens with Crimean War photographs taken by the British photographer Roger Fenton, photographs of what became known as "the valley of the shadow of death." It is a quick introduction to the larger issues Morris raises about the connection of the photograph to the physical world. And it is a useful counterpoint to the image of the hooded man at Abu Ghraib.

QUESTIONS FOR A SECOND VIEWING

The "Questions for a Second Viewing" point students to what we took as the key terms of the video—key terms for Morris: the "connection" between photography and the physical world, "remembering" (or "forgetting") that connection, the ontology of the photograph (to talk about photographs as either "true" or "false" is, he says, "nonsense talk"), and, finally, the "icon." (How and why has history chosen certain images as unforgettable?)

ASSIGNMENT FOR WRITING

The writing assignment is designed to bring attention back to the written text, which we take to be the primary text for a writing course. Our students, however, couldn't *not* comment on what an odd character Morris seemed to be once they met him "in person" through YouTube! For more of Morris, be sure to check out his Web site: http://errolmorris .com/

WALKER PERCY

The Loss of the Creature (p. 298)

In the assignments, we define Percy's method in "The Loss of the Creature" as an enactment of his argument: The world is disposed of by theory; to strive for a more immediate experience of the "thing," one must resist packages and packaging; the job for the writer is to resist the desire to translate examples into generalizations; the job for the reader is to attend to the varied richness of detail, not to search for the hard outline. Percy talks about the value of the indirect approach and shows how it works and how it feels once you climb inside.

Percy does his best to unsettle his readers, to keep them from turning his argument into a fixed, abstract statement. Students, to be sure, will try to sum up the essay—to tame it and make its weirdness manageable—by saying something like "Percy says that we have to work hard to be individuals" or "We must try to live every day to the fullest." When you place these sentences against Percy's own ("The layman will be seduced as long as he regards beings as consumer items to be experienced rather than prizes to be won, and as long as he waives his sovereign rights as a person and accepts his role of consumer as the highest estate to which the layman can aspire," text p. 310), or when you place them against those wonderful, almost parable-like anecdotes (the weary, sophisticated tourist who seeks out the Greyhound package tour with the folks from Terre Haute), you sense the degree to which this writing resists a reader's desire to put it into a box and tie it up with a bow.

The terms of the argument resist summary or translation into common terms. The examples seem almost to deflect, rather than to support or to illustrate, the argument. Sometimes, in fact, the argument seems playfully, or willfully, absurd: Are we really to believe that Cárdenas saw the Grand Canyon without any preconceptions? that he didn't see it as an example of God's grandeur or as property for his queen? And what about the bogus precision of assigning a fixed value *(P)* to the experience of seeing the Grand Canyon? And the examples, as they accumulate, seem to say to readers not that they are getting closer to a final, summary statement but that they are going to somehow have to find the point of all this somewhere in the spaces between the examples. They all approximate something that is ultimately beyond saying.

We find students alternately puzzled, frustrated, and entranced by this essay. Percy doesn't do what a writer is supposed to do. Yet he seems to be upbeat, and on the side of students, in favor of freedom and against dull courses. "What if we wrote like that?" we have been asked. "Give it a try," we've said. When students talk or write about the essay, we have found it important for them to focus on the examples, particularly on those that seem mysterious, that defy their efforts as readers. When students talk about the tourists at the Grand Canyon, they inevitably turn to the examples of tourists who get off the beaten track ("That's what Percy is saying—we have to take the road less traveled") and ignore the difficult talk about dialectic and the complex soul who sees through the predicaments of others. The former comes to students without effort; the latter is hard to explain (or there is no ready explanation). The complexities become invisible or unimportant to students unless a teacher brings them into the foreground.

When we teach this essay, we are interested in keeping track—for the class—of what students notice and what they fail to notice, of what they take as significant and what they allow to disappear from attention. Then we can ask why they read the essay as they do and how their difficulties with the essay fit into Percy's argument about the problems of seeing the Grand Canyon or a dogfish. Students, we've found, read on the assumption that the examples are equivalent, that they all illustrate the same thing. It is harder to look for differences, or to imagine why Percy has piled example on example ("If they are all the same, then why wouldn't one or two do the trick?"). We insist that they work on a phrase like "dialectical movement," both because it is a powerful phrase—in the academy and in this essay—and because it marks a point at which Percy's essay makes an argument with more precision and rigor than the version students will offer in everyday language ("Be yourself! Don't fall into the same old rut!"). Percy talks about elaborate packages and coverings; students will want to talk about hidden meanings. The problem of translation is a central one in the essay. We want students to go back and *work* on this essay—to do more than just take pleasure in its anecdotes. We want them to see the demands the structure of the essay makes on them as readers; we want to call attention to the difference between the language of the essay and the language students will bring forward to represent and displace it.

The discussion and writing assignments begin with particulars and move outward. There is a point at which we want students to work on the largest structural problem in the essay—the relation between the first and second sections. An appropriate question would ask students, given their reading of the essay and their sense of its method and agenda, what sense it makes to compare the experience of the tourist with that of the student. The essay insists on the comparison—or contrast—without coming forward and making it, without speaking directly of the relationship between parts I and II. Students will have to fill in this silence, and at the risk of making fixed and simple that which is presented as open and complex.

There is a way in which this essay is a trap. It is extraordinarily difficult to write about it without packaging it and thereby becoming a consumer or a theorist and wearing the Percian badge of shame. Still, it is extraordinarily powerful to feel the problem of knowledge and representation in just this way. If you are concerned about leading students down this shady lane, then perhaps the most appropriate writing assignment is one that asks students to imitate Percy's project rather than write *about* it, hence the seeming indirection of the two "Assignments for Writing" on text pages 128–29.

If we can lead students to sense that there is a trap in this essay—or that Percy is playing a slippery role, having his theories and denying them at the same time—we will have some successful classes. The difficulty is getting a class to move beyond the certainty that Percy is simply telling them, if elegantly, what they already know.

QUESTIONS FOR A SECOND READING (p. 310)

1. The first of these directs students to what we referred to earlier as Percy's method. It asks students, as they reread, to think about what it is like to read this essay or to think about the demands it makes upon them. We've found that this distinction is a surprising but often an enabling one for students. When students consider that the essay is, in a sense, teaching them how it wants to be read, they suddenly have a very different sense of what an essay is and what it means to be a reader. They are not, in other words, receiving information the way they might receive it from a textbook. The essay makes different assumptions about the nature of information and the roles of both reader and author.

2. Students are asked to imagine that the essay is not just performance—that Percy has an argument to make, however indirect the presentation, and that the argument has bearing on the life of a student. It is, for that matter, an essay *about* the life of the student. The problem with inviting students to reread the essay with the argument in mind is that it can be an invitation to misread if students are not given advance warning that Percy is trying to undo them as readers. Without a warning, many students will read the essay as though it were no different from a piece in *Reader's Digest* and see it as saying exactly what they have learned to say to each other: Be yourself, beware of school, count every daisy, don't lose the trees in the forest. With the warning, a rereading with these questions in mind can give students a way of beginning to talk back to Percy. Once students can make Percy's terms work for them, they can begin to imagine what it would take to stand outside that argument and speak back: Why must the "thing" be beyond words? What is the argument against this theory of education? (Rodriguez, in "The Achievement of Desire," offers one counterargument.) What about the people who can't afford trips or Sarah Lawrence—do they have an equivalent loss? What would be the consequences for a person who could step outside his or her culture and

see the Grand Canyon? If such a thing is impossible, and if people nonetheless care about seeing natural phenomena, then what else might we struggle for or worry about?

3.   This question is intended to make it possible for students to imagine the essay as the demonstration of a method, and to imagine how that method might be said to be problematic. There are written accounts of first encounters with the Grand Canyon dating back at least two centuries. And, of course, there are Native American accounts of the canyon. It would be possible to conduct a scholarly analysis of what actual people have actually said. Percy's essay can be read as a deliberate rejection of the archive, the interview, and the survey. Once students begin thinking about the essay in these terms, it is interesting to ask what is gained and what is lost. It is surprising that an essay about the limits of cultural packaging deals largely in stereotype and caricature—in the quick, representative example (his tourist, his islander, his student, and his "great man"). At the same time, one could argue that the figure of the novelist or artist, while not named directly in the essay, stands behind Percy's essay as the expert who stands outside time and culture. This is a familiar longing, and the essay can be used as a way of examining a general desire to imagine such a position.

ASSIGNMENTS FOR WRITING (p. 128)

1.   Here is a writing assignment that frees students from the burden of theorizing about an essay that condemns theorists. It asks them, rather, to do a Percian thing—to carry out a Percian project. The assignment points students in two directions. On the one hand, they will have to be good storytellers; whether they should tell Percian anecdotes is another issue. On the other hand, they will have to arrange and comment on their stories using Percy's terms and methods. This is the occasion to work on the use and meaning of a word like "dialectic" (and to work on the use and meaning of the word as Percy uses it and makes it meaningful). It is not the occasion to "forget all that stuff" and turn naively to personal experience. The experience is important, but the way it is shaped and phrased by a writer who is carrying out Percy's project is equally so.

We don't want to underplay the difficulty of this, and it is a difficulty that can be represented in a cycle of drafts and revisions. Students will have access to related stories, and they will care about those stories well before they sense the attention that is required to work on them in Percy's spirit. Such Percian work may make more sense to students when they are working on a later draft, particularly if you direct comments or discussions of sample papers in class toward the relationships between the stories and the shape of the essays or the presence of a voice that speaks in general terms.

A note on the final sentence: It seems rather weak to say "Feel free to imitate Percy's style and method," as there is much teaching to be done if students are to take up the invitation. One issue, however, is whether students will ground their papers in "real" stories from their own experience or representative anecdotes crafted to serve the occasion. The latter is much harder for students to do well, but to realize this is to realize something telling about Percy in this essay. In this apparent guidebook to daily living, he never turns to the detail of his own life, and this allows him a purity and status that students won't have if they bring forward memories of family trips or favorite teachers.

2. This assignment takes the central metaphor of the common and the complex and asks students to use it to imagine that there is more than one way of reading "The Loss of the Creature," that reading can be imagined as a matter of struggle and strategy. Students are asked to imagine a common reading and to write an essay showing what it might look like. Then they are asked to plan and to put into action a strategy to enable another form of reading, one they would be willing to label complex. Finally, they are asked to step back and comment on what they have done.

    The all-at-onceness of this assignment is hard for students. This, too, is an assignment that benefits from stages. If students work on one reading before the other, they are more likely to develop essays on "The Loss of the Creature" that are real essays—in length and seriousness—than if they are preparing miniatures. The same could be said for the final section of the essay. If it is to serve as the occasion for reflection, that reflection can be greatly assisted by time and by group discussion of sections I and II.

MAKING CONNECTIONS (p. 313)

1. Our students brought strong preconceived notions to Kathleen Jamie's "Shia Girls." Work on the first Question for a Second Reading for this selection went a long way in improving their understandings of this particular region in Pakistan and its various cultures and traditions, but these understandings didn't push back against their preconceived notions about such things as gender differences and the situations of the women presented in the piece. Studying Walker Percy's essay gave our students language for explaining preconceived notions. The hard work of identifying such notions in their own essays fell to numerous small group discussions in which students worked in pairs or trios to identify sentences and passages in their essays that seemed to be carrying assumptions and preconceived ideas about Pakistan, its cultures, and the gender differences often presented in Jamie's essay. Students benefited enormously from a couple of rounds of such close readings of their essays (which had been produced for the writing assignments) before going on to write this reflective essay. The students first wrote multiple drafts of two different essays for two of the writing assignments. Once these were completed, they studied Percy's essay. After that, they went back to their essays from the writing assignments to study them for "symbolic complexes," preconceived notions, and assumptions that they brought to reading and studying Jamie's essay. After two rounds of small group work on their own essays from Percy's framework, they then took a first pass at the reflective essay for this assignment.

2. Here students are asked to add to the repertoire of representative anecdotes, to use their story as a response to the stories featured by Percy and Rodriguez. The key to students' success will be time spent working with the stories in "The Achievement of Desire" and "The Loss of the Creature." Rodriguez's essay, like Percy's, depends on anecdotes—the scholarship boy, Rodriguez's parents, his life in England, and so on. Rodriguez's anecdotes, however, are drawn from recollected experience, not invented for the occasion, as are Percy's. Rodriguez is clearly creating a figure of himself in this presentation on his schooling, one that we can hold alongside Percy's great man with the grubby thumb. You will want your students to think not only about the story they will tell but also about storytelling, or about themselves as storytellers and the figures

they create to stand alongside the textual Rodriguez and Percy's great man. One decision you will face with this assignment is whether you want it to stand as a commentary on Rodriguez and Percy, whether you want your students to name Rodriguez and Percy and to allude to their work in their essays. When we have taught versions of this assignment, we have made this an issue for revision, since we do not want the students to acknowledge Percy and Rodriguez as sources in their work. Without any reminders, the first draft will most likely be primarily a story. This, we think, is a fine place for students to begin — thinking about their story and about the type of story they want to tell. In revision, we remind them of the other context — the relationship of their story to Percy and Rodriguez. We ask them to make it clear to the reader when they revise how their account is a commentary on those prior essays.

MARY LOUISE PRATT

Arts of the Contact Zone (p. 317)

For a long time, we felt that Pratt's work — particularly her essay "Linguistic Utopias" and her book *Imperial Eyes* — had much to offer those interested in writing and the teaching of writing. So much of the work on writing pedagogy was, in her terms "utopian," assuming as its end a common language commonly valued; and while we understood why teachers were prone to utopian beliefs, often expressed in the name of "community," we felt that the current version of the promised land worked against those conceptions of writing and teaching that gave priority to the social, historical, and political contexts of the classroom (and the individual act of writing). We had been greatly helped by Pratt's representation of writing and the classroom, and we had been looking for a piece of hers we could use in our undergraduate courses. We finally settled on "Scratches on the Face of the Country; or, What Mr. Barrow Saw in the Land of the Bushman" (first published in *Critical Inquiry;* a version of it appears in *Imperial Eyes*).

We taught this, we felt, with considerable success. The essay is a wonderful demonstration of close reading (Pratt is reading excerpts from eighteenth- and nineteenth-century accounts of travel in Africa), which makes it very hard for students to write the conventional paper about exotic others (travel essays, essays about roommates, and so on). "Scratches on the Face of the Country" was on our list for inclusion in the third edition of *Ways of Reading.* However, the essay was also very difficult reading, particularly the first five pages, which are written in the style of 1980s poststructuralism (with puns on "sight" and "cite," for example).

We heard "Arts of the Contact Zone" when it was first delivered at a literacy conference in Pittsburgh and then saw it in *Profession 91.* Partly because it was written as a lecture (and partly, we believe, because Pratt had been working on this project for several years), its argument (about "contact zones" and the clash of cultures as represented in the production and reception of written texts) was similar but much more direct and would certainly put fewer roadblocks in the way of undergraduates. Parts of "Arts of the Contact Zone" appear in the introduction to *Imperial Eyes,* which we also considered, but that piece removes the references to education and the undergraduate curriculum. It was these references, we felt, that made obvious the connections we wanted to make in our classes between colonial expansion, travel writing, a letter to King Philip III of Spain, and the contemporary American classroom.

The teaching problems the essay presents are fairly straightforward. We don't get to see much of Guaman Poma's text, so the demonstrations of close reading come with the discussion of the illustrations (which are wonderful). In our teaching, we have supplemented this discussion with a photocopy of a page from "Scratches on the Face of the Country," in which Pratt works with the text of an early travelogue. It is important to get students to feel that they can talk about Guaman Poma (and not just Pratt's kids and baseball cards). Students will be thrown a bit by "autoethnography" and "transculturation," which is the point. Turning these into working terms requires going back to the essay (not the dictionary). It was important to some of our students to note that Guaman Poma was himself a member of the elite. We can cast him as the subaltern in his relation to King Philip, but on his home turf, who knows what role he played in representing the lower castes of the Inca empire? (Positions, in other words, are situated, not pure.) The passages that provoked the most pointed discussion are those we point to in the assignments. They include those in which Pratt defines her alternative (for many students, counterintuitive) sense of community and culture, as well as those in which she lists the arts of the contact zone. The lists were extremely useful in prompting discussion, helping students to think out instances of the "rhetoric of authenticity," for example, or to imagine "unseemly comparisons" and how they might function for a student writer.

QUESTIONS FOR A SECOND READING (p. 33)

1. It is interesting for students to imagine the intellectual context in which one might turn quickly from children's talk, to the *New Chronicle*, to the undergraduate curriculum. On the one hand, there is a training or sensibility evident here that erases what seem to be obvious barriers of time and place, of personal and professional. On a second reading, we want students to try to imagine Pratt's imagination—her way of thinking about and reading the material around her as she prepares to write. On the other hand, we want students to go back to the argument of the essay and to its key terms (like "community" and "contact") to see how they hold together the pieces Pratt presents for discussion.

2. We've found that both students and teachers are sometimes frustrated by this essay. Teachers wish there were more work within the text—more on the pictures, more on Guaman Poma. That textual work appears in Pratt's book *Imperial Eyes*, although even that book, despite its extensive readings of the work of European travelers, has only a few examples of "native" texts. The reading of texts was simply not part of Pratt's original lecture, which serves as the text for "Arts of the Contact Zone." Students are frustrated because they don't see the connection between the opening section (about Pratt's son) and the later discussion. Nor do they have the sense of which texts she may be alluding to when she talks about the texts of the contact zone. One way we have found for students to question the text is to imagine places within the flow of its presentation (or its delivery, if they imagine it as a public lecture) where they might have questions for the author.

3. This is, for us, a standard application question. We want to direct students' attention to the material that they can command and use to extend Pratt's project—in this case, the classroom. As a frame for rereading, the question asks students to look for passages and terms they could bring to bear in an examination of their own educations.

4. This question emerged from our experiences in class, specifically concerning the obviously difficult terms. We wanted to acknowledge that the difficulty is strategic—part of the text, not part of students' "poor" preparation—and we wanted to suggest when and where and how a dictionary can be useful. But we also wanted to point to what is for our students the hardest term to get a handle on: "culture." In particular, we wanted to focus attention on the ways in which Pratt revises the essay's usual use for her readers (making the "unnatural" definition the operative one, arguing against utopian thinking). To this end, we wanted students to think from both positions (a linguistic version of the "face and cup" pictures that appear in psychology textbooks).

ASSIGNMENTS FOR WRITING (p. 331)

1. The first assignment is an "inventory" assignment, asking students to collect documents that could stand, like the *New Chronicle*, as evidence of the literate arts of the contact zone. Pratt's essay provides a frame to organize the search. Students should imagine that they can break this frame; that is, they can take it as a challenge to find the document that would surprise Pratt, that she would overlook or never think of. Her essay thus provides the terms for a discussion of the material, or representative examples from that material that they collect.

    This assignment offers two options. The first sends students to a library (or historical society) to find documents from the past. We tried to suggest the many possible moments of contact in local history (between slaves and owners, workers and management, women and men, minority and majority). This assignment was prompted by Jean Ferguson Carr's teaching at Pitt (her courses almost always include some kind of archival project) and Pat Bizzell's teaching at Holy Cross (where she has students research local accounts of European settlements written by Native Americans). We were frustrated by the degree to which students feel removed from library archives and the degree to which our teaching (and the textbook) seemed to enforce that remove. Needless to say, this option will seem to be the harder of the two, and students will need some prompting or challenge or rewards to choose it. One thing to remember is that an assignment like this will take more time than usual, since it takes time to find the library and spend enough time in the stacks to make the experience profitable, more than a quick search for the one book that will get you through the assignment. We've also found that we needed to make the process of search and selection an acknowledged part of the work of the course. We ask students to collect folders of material, to present them to others (to the class, to groups), and, in their essays, to talk about how they chose the material they chose to write about.

    The second option sends students out into their local culture to look for the "documents," which can be defined loosely to include music (like rap), transcripts of talk shows, films, documentaries, and so on. Students should feel that they can follow Pratt's lead and turn to their brothers and sisters (or their children) and to educational materials, including papers they are writing or have written recently. You should think carefully about whether or not you would want students to choose papers from your course. It is an interesting possibility, but it will be hard for students to write about you and your class as anything *but* a utopia, paradise on earth. You may be disappointed if you invite students to take your classroom as an example.

With either option, students are asked to present their material as part of a project Pratt has begun. We have found it important to remind students that they need to *present* "Arts of the Contact Zone," even to their fellow students who have read it. You cannot assume, we remind our students, that readers have it freshly in mind or that they will be willing to get the book off the shelf and turn to pages. And we have found it important to help students imagine the role they will play in this text. They will need, in other words, to do more than simply cite from or summarize what they have gathered in their inventories. They will need to step forward as Pratt does to teach, translate, make connection, explain, comment, discuss, think this way and that. Students, at least our students, are often too quick to let the wonderful material they gather speak for itself.

2. Whereas the other assignments in this set ask students to use Pratt's term "contact zone" in an intellectual project, this assignment asks them to write an autoethnography from the contact zone, to show how they understand Pratt's argument through their practice.

    It is important, as a starting point, to ask students to imagine how this task might be different from writing an autobiography. In a sense, autobiographies have historically been read as autoethnographies. But as these terms define a *writer's* motive, it will be important for many students to imagine from the outset that they occupy a position likely to be ignored or unread or misread. It can be useful to think of the ways writers signal that they are "engaging with representations" others make of them ("many people would say . . . ," "I have been called . . . ," "some might refer to this as . . . ," "from a different point of view . . ."). This is also a good time to return to the lists Pratt offers of the literate arts of the contact zone ("parody," "unseemly comparisons," "bilingualism," "imaginary dialogue," and so on). These lists can serve as a writer's toolkit or, perhaps, as a way of beginning to imagine revision.

3. This assignment is the most straightforward of the three. It asks students to use Pratt's key terms in an essay in which they provide the key examples, in this case, examples of "scenes" of education (assignment 1 asked for examples of texts). We have found it useful to ask students to provide parallel accounts of a scene (the utopian and antiutopian, the pre- and post-Pratt). You could cut this if it seems too arbitrary or distracting. We added it not just as an exercise in thinking from alternative points of view but also as preparation for the final question, which asks students to think about the consequences of this shift—the practical consequences as well as the consequences to one's sense of the order of things. As we usually do, we try to phrase assignments asking students to take a position in such a way as to remind them that their "position" is not autonomous but links them, whether they choose the connections or not, with a more generalized interest, a "group."

MAKING CONNECTIONS (p. 333)

1. This assignment requires something of a leap from students, since "Arts of the Contact Zone" does not provide an example of a close reading of a text. It provides the terms that can organize a close reading (and the grounds for evaluation), but the only extended example is the reading of the images from the *New Chronicle*. There are plenty of examples of close reading in Pratt's book *Imperial Eyes*. It might be useful to photocopy a page or two—pages where she works closely with a block quotation. (This can help students get a sense of the format and mechanics of a written close reading.) Whether you provide this supplement or not, it is interesting to ask students to begin to rework another selection from *Ways of Reading* by trying to organize passages under the terms Pratt uses to describe the arts of the contact zone. Pratt's terms give them an angle on the ideology of style—thinking about parody or autoethnography or comparisons or the rhetorics of authenticity. It is crucial that students spend time looking over possible examples from the texts but, when they begin to write, that they limit themselves to two or three. The goal should be to work closely with extended passages in block quotation, not simply to provide a list of passages organized under Pratt's headings.

2. Said's "States" is, for this assignment, a case to further develop and test Pratt's notions of a contact zone in her "Arts of the Contact Zone" as social and intellectual space that is not homogeneous or unified and where understanding and valuing difference can occur. The object, then, is to read "States" as a project in light of Pratt's notions. Is there a way to write about Said's writing and other writings represented in "States" as contact zones where difference is valued and understanding is the point? Is there a way to think about the culture represented in "States," through Said's writing, as such contact zones? To figure this assignment, students will need to reread both essays. They'll need to work from moments in both as well. It is particularly important that students identify examples in "States" that they can use to test and further develop Pratt's ideas about the contact zone and what might happen there socially and intellectually and, of course, in writing.

    This is a challenging assignment. Students will need to read and work with Mary Louise Pratt's essay on the "Arts of the Contact Zone" before they take on this assignment. They'll need to have a good understanding of her ideas about writing and pedagogy in the contact zone. Jamie presents her conversations, one could argue, as examples of the ways people use oral rhetoric to communicate across lines of difference. One can also argue, of course, that Jamie herself is using writing as a cultural mediation to instruct her readers about how to understand differences among those on which she reports and on herself as the reporter. If students assume that Jamie is writing from a political awareness, from an atmosphere, as she says, of egalitarianism, and if her writing can be thought of as an art of the contact zone, how might students then describe the contact zone? How is such a contact zone shaped by her writing, by her presentation of others in conversations, and by her interests in instructing her readers? What, then, might she want to teach her readers?

RICHARD RODRIGUEZ

The Achievement of Desire (p. 338)

Part of the power of Rodriguez's essay in an undergraduate class is the way it allows students to frame, even invent, a problem in their own lives as students. Throughout *Hunger of Memory*, Rodriguez argues that his story is also everyone's story. It takes some work on the part of a teacher to make this connection work, however. Students will read Rodriguez with either sympathy (because he is an oppressed person) or annoyance ("What's he got to complain about—he got good grades, he went to a good school, he was offered a good job"). But it is not at all uncommon to hear students claim that their situations are different: "Well you see, I'm not on a scholarship. I'm not a scholarship boy." It takes some teaching, then, to get students to imagine "scholarship boy" or "scholarship girl," as a metaphor representing a complex relationship among a student, his or her past, and school and teachers.

Those who praise Rodriguez's book often praise it in just these terms, by saying that Rodriguez's story is "everyone's story," that he has identified a universal in human experience. This is a problematic reading of the text, since it erases the ethnic and class distinctions that could be used to explain and describe Rodriguez's position. Those who are not sympathetic to the book say that Rodriguez not only turns his back on his parents and his Hispanic roots, he also writes a general justification for this act of turning away. (Note the two reviewers in the headnote.) If Rodriguez's story is everyone's story, then there is no reason to investigate the particular determinates of ethnicity and class in America. Rodriguez's conclusion to "The Achievement of Desire" reflects this thematic displacement of class. He talks about the tradition of pastoral: "The praise of the unlettered by the highly educated is one of the primary themes of 'elitist' literature." But the relationship of high to low, of Hispanic laborers to this graduate of Berkeley, is defined finally not in terms of an elitist culture but in terms of the difference between the "passionate and spontaneous" and the "reflective" life.

We need to find a way of enabling students to read the essay, as Rodriguez says he read Hoggart's *The Uses of Literacy*, to frame their experiences—as a tool, that is, to enable a certain form of analysis and understanding, both in the terms and metaphors it offers and in the example it provides of a process of self-examination. In graduate and undergraduate classes, this essay has inspired some of the best personal essays we have ever read.

Students read the essay to frame experience and as an example of the process of self-examination—we can use this claim to describe two approaches to the essay. We have had students write a kind of "framing" exercise for ten minutes or so at the beginning of a class. We have asked them to go to a phrase or a scene, to write it out, and to use it as the starting point for a kind of reverie drawing on their own memories. The same opening move can function in discussion or in more formal writing assignments. The basic assumption is this: something in this essay will grab you, and often for reasons you can't begin to describe. For us it is the phrase "middle-class pastoral," the story of the "hundred most important books of Western civilization," and the ambiguity of the final phrase "the end of education." One can begin here, in the manner of a preacher working from a text, to draw forward and shape (or "frame"—as in "frame" a house, "frame" a painting, and "I was framed") the recalled (or invented) stuff of one's experience. This is a way of paying attention to the text—if not to its argument then to its richest moments—and of drawing a connection between it and oneself. It is also a Rodriguez-like thing to do.

We are also interested, as in the case of many of these essays, in having students turn to rich examples, like the story of the boy's reading program, and moving back and forth between their own and Rodriguez's ways of accounting for them. We want students to see Rodriguez's stories as open texts, but we also want them to feel the difference between his characteristic ways of interpreting those stories and their own.

Students, as we have said, can read the essay as an example of a process of self-examination. We like to make this a minute, textual issue. One of the most characteristic features of Rodriguez's style, for example, is his use of parentheses. They are a sign of his desire to speak in two voices at once—what he might call a public and a private voice—or to say contradictory things and mean both at the same time ("I wanted to be close to my parents, I wanted to push away from my parents"). If you ask about the characteristic features of Rodriguez's sentences, students will turn to the parentheses or to the sentence fragments and the sentences that trail away to nothing. Once you gather together three or four examples, you can start a conversation about what they represent. Why are they there? What's the effect? What do they tell you about Rodriguez as a writer? about his skill? about the problems he has as a writer? We think the parentheses, in other words, are a method in miniature, a way of using language to shape experience. They provide a tool that Rodriguez uses again and again. Our students begin relying on parentheses in the papers that follow their reading of Rodriguez.

We will give one more example of a close-up look at Rodriguez's method. Students generally have difficulty working quoted material into their essays. On the one hand, this is a mechanical problem, and students have to learn about punctuation, ellipses, and the conventions of block quotation. But the concerns a writer faces in using someone else's words are not just mechanical ones. It is interesting to consider Rodriguez's use of Hoggart. He first quotes Hoggart on text page 000. As you look at the block quotations, you find an interesting variation in the relationships between the words that are quoted and those that surround the quotations. There are occasions when the two become indistinct, as though Hoggart could speak for Rodriguez and Rodriguez for Hoggart. On other occasions, Rodriguez insists on a position beyond the quoted passages—a position from which he can claim his authorship, that allows him to comment, to disagree, to put Hoggart into perspective. Since the essay is about the relationship between students and teachers, or about the relationship(s) of mimicry, imitation, and identity, the small scene in which Rodriguez struggles to define his relationship to Hoggart's words represents a larger issue, in which Rodriguez struggles with his parents, his teachers, and the public world of middle-class, English-speaking America.

QUESTIONS FOR A SECOND READING (p. 355)

1.   This essay is not ostensibly difficult, so students will not feel the need to reread to bring it generally under control. Our purpose for sending students back to the essay is to allow them to complicate matters. The purpose of this question is to have students read as though the story could serve as a means of framing their own experiences, as though

Rodriguez could stand to them as Hoggart does to Rodriguez. This is an invitation to call Rodriguez's bluff—to say "Wait a minute" to his desire to place the burden of his sadness on all of us, to offer his story as everyone's story.

2. In the preface to *Hunger of Memory*, Rodriguez speaks about the double nature of his text: it is both essay and autobiography. He refers, in fact, to his refusal to grant his editor's wishes and make it more of a series of personal sketches (his editor has asked for more stories about Grandma). He refused because he felt he had an important argument to make—about education in general and about bilingual education in particular. This question asks students to reread the chapter in order to pay attention to the argument it contains both in the exposition ("His story makes clear that education is a long, unglamorous, even demeaning process—*a nurturing never natural to the person one was before one entered a classroom*") and in the arrangement of anecdotes and argument.

ASSIGNMENTS FOR WRITING (p. 356)

1. These assignments represent, in written exercises, the two concerns raised in the opening discussion. The second asks students to frame their story in Rodriguez's terms and style. This one asks them to turn Rodriguez's argument about education—about the relationship between students and teachers—back on the essay by considering the relationship between Rodriguez and Hoggart as a case in point. The general question is this: Is Rodriguez still a scholarship boy? Is he still reading "in order to acquire a point of view"? The earlier general discussion explains why we send students to look at the use of quotations. There are other ways of talking about the relationship between these two writers, but our concern is to make these problems textual problems—problems that hold lessons for readers and writers.

    This can be a more complicated question than it appears, depending on how far you want to push it. Some students will argue that Rodriguez is still a blinkered pony. Some will take his argument on its own terms and argue that he rejects Hoggart in the end for being "more accurate than fair" to the scholarship boy. There is the larger question of Rodriguez's use of Hoggart's book *The Uses of Literacy*, a book about the class system, which strives to speak in the general and not to sentimentalize individual stories. It is possible, if you and your students have the time, to send students to Hoggart's book in order to construct a more complicated and comprehensive account of this reading.

2. Here, students are asked to reinvest their lives by framing their stories in Rodriguez's terms. It becomes a more powerful exercise if students try to do it in Rodriguez's style. As an opening exercise, they might write out a paragraph of his, using the shape of his sentences but filling in the names and details from their own experience. There is no reason, however, why students cannot write a personal essay that is more loosely suggested by Rodriguez's. They might lay a Rodriguez-like commentary over it, or include one with it.

    The revision process will differ in each case. If students are concerned first with telling their own stories and then with speaking of them in Rodriguez's terms, then that commentary may be the focus of revision. If the essay is more completely a stylistic revision, then we would reverse the emphasis. The first thing students want to attend to is the form that will enable the writing—sentences and paragraphs and the relationship of anecdote to commentary. Then, in revision, they can best attend to the richness and detail of their own stories. As Scholes says about autobiography, the tension is between beauty and truth. You want to shape a story but also to honor the details of memory and investigation. In the revision we would ask students to try to honor the truth of the stories they are telling.

3.   Essentially, this assignment asks students to locate and characterize Rodriguez's methods, his "ways of speaking and caring," his ways, that is, of presenting and valuing what he presents. He's making an argument about being a scholarship boy and, finally, about the differences between the reflective and the "passionate and spontaneous" life. Students need to consider how he presents his arguments and his materials (Hoggart, his recollections, and so on) and how he thinks through them on the page. They need, too, to name and characterize the ways he "speaks" and to figure out what it is he cares about now, in this text, and what he cared about during the various stages of his education. What can he do now, in writing and in his thinking, that he says he couldn't do earlier, in other moments of his evolution into a "speaking and caring" guy?

MAKING CONNECTIONS (p. 357)

1.   Freire spent much of his life teaching peasants. There are many reasons why Rodriguez should not be considered a peasant. But Freire also speaks generally about the relationship between students and teachers and the way that that relationship determines the nature and status of knowledge in the classroom. At first glance, Rodriguez seems to offer both a perfect example of oppression (an ape and a mimic) and, in his success, an example of the conservative counterpoint to Freire's plan for a democratized education. If students can work out a Freirian critique of Rodriguez in such black-and-white terms, we are not sure that they are violating the spirit of Freire's project. We are not convinced, however, that Rodriguez can so easily be labeled a conservative and Freire a liberal, or that Rodriguez as a child received little more than deposits from his teachers. And we would want to push against students' attempts to organize their essays in such set terms.

2.   This assignment requires something of a leap from students, since "Arts of the Contact Zone" does not provide an example of a close reading of a text. It provides the terms that can organize a close reading (and the grounds for evaluation), but the only extended example is the reading of the images from the *New Chronicle*. There are plenty of examples of close reading in Pratt's book *Imperial Eyes*. It might be useful to photocopy a page or two—pages where she works closely with a block quotation. (This can help students get a sense of the format and mechanics of a written close reading.) Whether you provide this supplement or not, it is interesting to ask students to begin to rework Rodriguez's text by trying to organize passages under the terms Pratt uses to describe the arts of the contact zone. Pratt's terms give them an angle on the ideology of style—thinking about parody or autoethnography or comparisons or the rhetorics of authenticity. It is crucial that students spend time looking over possible examples from

the text but, when they begin to write, that they limit themselves to two or three. The goal should be to work closely with extended passages in block quotation, not simply to provide a list of passages organized under Pratt's headings.

3. This assignment asks students to think about "The Achievement of Desire" in relation to other essays that use autobiography and family history to think about large questions—race, family, nation, war. The assignment identifies Griffin's "Our Secret" and Wideman's "Our Time."

As always, the success of this assignment will depend on students taking time to present and to develop examples from the texts. Certainly summary and paraphrase will be required strategically to prepare the comparison. You can help students feel the pressure, however, to turn to block quotation and to specific and extended points of comparison.

It is important for students to take the final set of questions seriously. The temptation will be to say that these are great writers and of course everyone should be allowed a similar freedom of expression—or something like that. Students should feel the pressure (or students will benefit, we've found, from the pressure) to think seriously about what an essay like this can and can't do, the purposes and occasions it can and cannot serve.

4. This is a variation on the first "Assignment for Writing" under Miller. That assignment will be good preparation for the work that students do with this one. Instead of taking school violence as an entry point into Miller, it asks students to work with both Miller and Rodriguez. The assignment asks students to think of two scholars, two projects, together, to imagine that they are speaking back and forth. (It helps, we have found, to invite students to speak from the point of view of a Miller or a Rodriguez, and to do so even when the gesture is tentative: "I think that what Miller is saying is this. . . ." or "My sense of Rodriguez is that he would agree, or disagree, with Miller about this. . . .") The real test is to keep the assignment from becoming an empty formal exercise in comparing and contrasting. We insist that students make themselves present in the conversation. A revision, in fact, is often a way to invite students to do so.

EDWARD SAID

States e

When we first read *After the Last Sky*, we were struck by its combination of beauty and power. It is, as we said, a writing with pictures, and it was the writing that made the images both beautiful and powerful. The photographs themselves do not possess the beauty common to images in travel books or books of photojournalism, and yet, with the text that accompanies them (instructing you on how to look and what to notice), they become an opportunity to look through (or behind) the standard representations of Palestine and Palestinians. The license plate on the Mercedes in the opening photograph, the hands of the bride and groom, the relation of foreground to background—when you understand what you are looking at, these oddly ordinary scenes become memorable, and some, for us, unforgettable. The power of the essay's argument on behalf of the Palestinians resides in quiet attention to detail and to arrangement. The ability to read an image—for our students, the equivalent lessons were in art history classes—here is combined with political motive and a powerful argument for the importance of seeing beyond stereotype and thinking beyond formulas.

Having said all this, we should add that the chapter, "States," needed to be taught to our students. The most significant problem it presented in the classroom is the one that Said announces in the introduction to the book.

> Yet the problem of writing about and representing—in all senses of the word—Palestinians in some fresh way is part of a much larger problem. For it is not as if no one speaks about or portrays the Palestinians. The difficulty is that everyone, including the Palestinians themselves, speaks a very great deal. A huge body of literature has grown up, most of it polemical, accusatory, denunciatory. At this point, no one writing about Palestine—and indeed, no one going to Palestine—starts from scratch: We have all been there before, whether by reading about it, experiencing its millennial presence and power, or actually living there for periods of time. It is a terribly crowded place, almost too crowded for what it is asked to bear by way of history or interpretation of history.

We were working with *After the Last Sky* when Said's account of his experience in Palestine was being challenged in the press as false (see Justus Reid Weiner's article "'My Beautiful Old House' and Other Fabrications by Edward Said" in *Commentary*, September 1999). This was just a few months before the publication of Said's autobiography, *Out of Place: A Memoir*. We found the attack to be ugly and biased, an example of bad reading. It reminded us, however, that Said himself, at least in our circles, is also a "crowded place," almost too crowded for what he is asked to be by way of history or interpretation of history.

It would be foolish and wrong to teach the essay as though it had nothing to do with current events (whatever is happening in Israel, Syria, and Lebanon) or nothing to do with students' positions on or understanding of the Middle East, its history and crisis. At the same time, as Said warns us, current events and prior positions can make the essay unreadable. What we would suggest is that you use the passage above to frame and enable the discussion. What *can* one learn by pausing, by leaving the present and its polemics, and attending carefully to these photographs and texts? They, too, of course, have an argument to make. What is it? And what can be made of it?

We found it important to provide motive and context for careful attention to the text. It was also important to provide motive and context for students to learn about the history of Israel and the Palestinians and to have the chance to speak from their beliefs and concerns (particularly so as not to silence students identifying either with Israel or with the Palestinians). The background work is probably best done through group research and reporting, and the presentation of beliefs and concerns through an open discussion where you are at the front, using the blackboard and serving as recorder. Whether this should occur before or after close work with *After the Last Sky* was, on our campus, a matter of debate. We believe that the discussion will have a different and more useful focus (to establish a way of thinking from the text, perhaps in response to Said) if it comes after.

The other difficulty our students had with the essay was in simply learning to take time to read the photographs, to see them as something other than "illustrations" meant to provide nothing more than a moment's rest or to provide that one dominant impression to accompany the text (as in the standard textbook photo). We found it useful to call attention to the paragraphs following the opening three photographs, reading out loud and asking students to talk about what they see and what they heard. (And asking, "What is Said *not* noticing? What is outside his field of attention?") Then we would ask students (in groups) to prepare discussions of the relation of text to image in the subsequent pages.

Note: See page 347 for an essay by Tara Lockhart, "Thinking on the Page: Summoning Readers and the Uses of Essay."

QUESTIONS FOR A SECOND READING 🄴

1. This question is designed to address the problem identified above—the degree to which students are prepared either to ignore images in texts or to treat them as quick statements. To read this essay is to return to the photographs, to learn to see them by means of the discussions in prose. And, since one of the writing assignments asks students to prepare such a text, a combination of words and images, it is important for students to think about the *different* relationships Said establishes between text and photograph— sometimes writing from them; sometimes writing back to them; sometimes writing alongside, in adjacency. We found some exercises like this to be absolutely necessary. It allowed students to think about what it meant to *become* a reader of this text (rather than just reading it); and it produced pleasure in the text (and interest in what it was trying to do) that was crucially important when students began to write.

2. This question is a variation on the first, this time using Said's discussion of the necessity of an "alternative mode of representation" to call attention to style, method, and arrangement. It asks students to read the essay as an experiment, as a piece of writing set against the norms and conventions of, in Said's terms, journalism, political science, and popular fiction. For students, "States" can best be read against what they take to be the conventions of report and argument, usually represented by a term like "the essay." Questions about style and method are common in *Ways of Reading*, and this question is echoed in the "Questions for a Second Reading" following many of the selections: Anzaldúa, Griffin, and Wideman, among others.

    It has been important to us to teach students to see writing as "work," including a work against, or in response to, habit and convention, and for students to think about the ideology of style. Writing is not just fitting new content into standard forms. And, again, since one of the writing assignments asks students to write *like* Said, a discussion such as this can be crucial in allowing students to make the connection between what they read and how they write.

3. It has become increasingly important for us to send students to the library. (We don't have to send them to the Internet! They go there all too quickly.) And this essay, in particular, invites research projects. We know Palestine through the image of Yasir Arafat and young men throwing rocks. We know so little, generally, about Palestinian artists, intellectuals, and politicians that it is valuable to track down some of the names that

Said offers. It is our habit to insist on the library (and photocopies) as part of student presentations. As students turn to the Internet (and this is often a perfect way to begin), in this case more than most others, it is important to consider sources and the interests they represent. In the case of the Middle East, many sources that present themselves as balanced or objective are serving a particular point of view.

4. The book *After the Last Sky* teaches a reader to become observant, an observer. At the end of the book, Said questions the role he has been promoting. It is a striking challenge and stands as its own invitation to a second reading:

    I would like to think, though, that such a book not only tells the reader about us, but in some way also reads the reader. I would like to think that we are not just the people seen or looked at in these photographs: We are also looking at our observers. (p. 166)

    This question asks students to reread in order to think about how they have been positioned by the text, not only in relation to the photos (where they occupy the position established by the camera and its lens) but also in relation to the text (where Said assumes certain habits and predispositions). It is a wonderful opportunity to think about reading as reading and to think about entering and leaving a text. For students who are interested in doing more work with Said, it is a perfect introduction to *Orientalism*. This question is also useful for leading toward John Berger's "Ways of Seeing."

ASSIGNMENTS FOR WRITING 🅔

1. We have had great success with this assignment. Students are asked to compose a Said-like reading of a set of photos. The following assignment sentences are important and worth calling attention to in advance:

    These can be photos prepared for the occasion (by you or a colleague); they could also be photos already available. Whatever their source, they should represent people and places, a history and/or geography that you know well, that you know to be complex and contradictory, and that you know will not be easily or readily understood by others, both the group for whom you will be writing (most usefully the members of your class) and readers more generally. You must begin with a sense that the photos cannot speak for themselves; you must speak for them.

    Students, that is, are not just describing photos; they are using the photos to represent people and places, history and/or geography, to an audience unprepared to understand them. The selection and arrangement of photos is important, in other words. It is part of the work of writing this text. And the text that accompanies these photos should approximate the style and method in *After the Last Sky*. The prose is not simply captions, one after another. There should be an essay, a text with its own integrity, that is written with pictures. So, it is important to have students think about audience and occasion. What is the project? To whom are they writing? What is their relationship to subject and reader? And it is important to let students know in advance that they need to take time selecting the photographs and thinking about how they might be arranged. (It is useful to have them talk about what they left out and about plans they abandoned.) And they need to think about the writing. They are not writing captions; to think about what they might write, they can return to "States" to think about what it is that Said was doing and to think about how he did it. The writing can (perhaps should) be homage or imitation, an attempt to do something similar.

2. If you give students a choice of assignments, this will be a popular one. It is also the most difficult of the three. As Said remarks,

> For it is not as if no one speaks about or portrays the Palestinians. The difficulty is that everyone, including the Palestinians themselves, speaks a very great deal. A huge body of literature has grown up, most of it polemical, accusatory, denunciatory. At this point, no one writing about Palestine—and indeed, no one going to Palestine—starts from scratch. (p. 4)

Students who feel prepared for this essay will be prepared with arguments for or against the state of Israel. It is certainly in keeping with the spirit of "States" that these arguments should be engaged. The writing problem will be to work with the text; the pedagogical problem will be to make that work important, necessary, to ensure that the text is part of the project and not just a stepping-off point.

It is for this reason that we have asked students to begin with a summary. Summary and paraphrase are important skills to learn; they require attention to the text and, in particular, to those parts of the texts that are difficult, surprising, unexpected; and they require generosity, a willingness to enter into the text's argument. Summary and paraphrase, in our teaching, are always strategic; however, they are never ends in themselves. They allow a writer to position something he or she has read for work that will follow. In this assignment, we suggest that what follows might be statement, response, or extension. Students are asked, "As you are invited to think about the Palestinians, or about exile more generally, or about the texts and images that are commonly available, what do you think? What do you have to add?" You should not feel limited by the language of this section of the assignment. The work in your classroom might suggest other projects, not "statement, response, or extension" but something else—dialogue, appreciation, memorial, parody.

3. As we said above, the conclusion to the book *After the Last Sky* is both striking and challenging:

> I would like to think, though, that such a book not only tells the reader about us, but in some way also reads the reader. I would like to think that we are not just the people seen or looked at in these photographs: We are also looking at our observers. (p. 166)

This assignment asks students to think at length about what it means not only to read but also to be read by a text. It will be important for students to think differently about image and text. That is, the images alone position the reader as equivalent to the photographer (or, perhaps more appropriately, since there is little agency involved, as equivalent to the lens of the camera). The text positions them differently, both in relation to the images and as a reader. Said, in other words, makes certain assumptions about his readers, their habits, affiliations, and ways of seeing.

There are subtle distinctions to make, in other words, and students can be usefully assisted in making them. It is also important that they work from specific examples — long discussion of particular photographs and passages. We have found it important to insist upon extended discussions of a few examples (since students will most likely be drawn to brief discussions of several).

4. We will not repeat the entry for the first writing assignment, but it provides guidance for this assignment as well. We will say again that students should be reminded to work with "States," returning to it to think about what it is that Said is doing and to think about how he does it. The writing can, perhaps should, be homage or imitation, an attempt to do something similar.

MAKING CONNECTIONS e

1. The first of these assignments asks students to think of "States" as experimental prose, in which the experiment is a political necessity driven by the inadequacy of standard forms and styles available to a particular community. In this case, students are asked to think about the essay by Anzaldúa, "How to Tame a Wild Tongue." Other selections could be substituted here. The assignment can be assisted by the second of the "Questions for a Second Reading."

The assignment includes extended passages from the chapter and the introduction to *After the Last Sky*. Here, Said offers an account of the writing. There are similar passages in the selection from Anzaldúa and in the headnote and apparatus. It is important for students to try to work with these passages and their terms, to summarize and paraphrase, to deploy the key terms. But it is equally important that they work with the prose itself, with the arguments enacted in the ways of writing. Their essays, then, should also include long block quotations, foregrounding representative passages, and close discussion of what the prose does (not just what it says).

2. This assignment asks a lot from students. The task is straightforward — to compare the writing style of two authors. Although the assignment suggests other unconventional stylists among the authors in *Ways of Reading*, almost any would work. So, finally, students will need to read through several selections to find a writer whose style interests or puzzles them. We would suggest that students might first skim through the first three or four pages of selections from the list in the assignment, or they might choose from the table of contents. We'd ask students to do this after they have done considerable work with Said, perhaps after they have completed the third writing assignment, which echoes this one. They'll need some experience with writing about style. Once again, it will be difficult for them to focus on how writing works rather than on what it says. To take up the focus on style, they'll want to consider the Said piece (and their second selection) from a number of perspectives, including the overall organization, the author's use of such things as headings and subheadings, and the way the work proceeds (what comes first, second, and so on).

Students will also need to write about each author's sentences and paragraphs. How do they work? Are they long or short? Do they proceed from one thing to another like a train heading for a destination? Or do they linger, turn back on themselves, and move one way then another? Are they reflective? descriptive? argumentative? Do they report? invent? summarize? How, too, do the writers connect their ideas? their paragraphs? their sections or subsections?

It should be clear that some preliminary work with style can only benefit students, but how that proceeds will shape their writing for this assignment. We are almost always inclined to invite students to invent, imagine, and define. In this case, we might ask them what they take style to be in writing. To answer, to conjecture, they would work from moments in a particular piece—Said's "States" for this assignment. We'd be interested in hearing them invent terms to describe style at its various levels of enactment— whole selections, sections, paragraphs, and sentences. Only after students have had opportunities to do this work themselves would we deal in our understandings and readings of moments in Said's writing. And we wouldn't be heavy-handed about it. We'd want to see students using the language of their discussions, of one another's comments, in their writing for this assignment, so we'd track their comments on the board, highlighting the terms and examples they use, and recommend that they too take notes from the discussion to use when they finally write.

3. Said's "States" is, for this assignment, a case to further develop and test Pratt's notions of a contact zone in her "Arts of the Contact Zone" as social and intellectual space that is not homogeneous or unified and where understanding and valuing difference can occur. The object, then, is to read "States" as a project in light of Pratt's notions. Is there a way to write about Said's writing and the other writings represented in "States" as contact zones where difference is valued and understanding is the point? Is there a way to think about the cultures represented in "States," through Said's writing, as such contact zones? To figure this assignment, students will need to reread both essays. They'll need to work from moments in both as well. It is particularly important that students identify examples in "States" that they can use to test and further develop Pratt's ideas about the contact zone and what might happen there socially and intellectually, and, of course, in writing.

4. This "Making Connections" assignment is out of the ordinary, since it does not make connections with another selection from *Ways of Reading* (only an oblique connection to John Berger and "Ways of Seeing," since it refers to Berger's work with Jean Mohr). All the questions and assignments focusing attention on "States" focus on Said and his work. We wanted one assignment for students who were interested in Jean Mohr and who would like to think more about a photographer and photography and how and why it is valued by writers like Said and Berger. *A Seventh Man* is well worth the time it will take to locate and read it. Students should be encouraged to think about the differences between that project and the one represented in *After the Last Sky*.

5. This writing assignment, in some ways, asks students to do something that may already be familiar to them—to focus on the common themes between two texts. The prompt itself even outlines for students the common threads of exile, existence, and, as Butler

puts it, "the question of the human." But the assignment also asks students to think of the implications of these intersections between Butler and Said. What we like about this assignment is the possibility for students to reflect on their own experiences of "otherness." These experiences will not necessarily emerge in narrative or personal essay form but instead as a way of understanding, or sometimes challenging, the claims Butler and Said make about alienation, identity, and exile.

KATHRYN SCHULZ

Evidence (p. 362)

Being Wrong, the book from which this excerpt comes, was the first book Tony Petrosky and I (David) taught together in our first-year courses, the first one in a very long time. It was fun to teach, and after teaching it, we chose to use the chapter on "Evidence" for *Ways of Reading.* Let me take a minute to talk about the book itself. It is divided into four sections: "The Idea of Error," "The Origins of Error," "The Experience of Error," and "Embracing Error."

The opening section is, to my taste, dull and slow to get started. And the final section is a bit too sermonic, too Dr. Phil-like for my taste. But the middle sections are terrific, and the second section, on the "origins" of error, provides very interesting material for a course on rhetoric. It connects a history of thought with contemporary work in cognition and neuroscience. It is very nicely done, and Schulz has a wonderfully light and engaging touch as she moves through some pretty complicated material. We chose this book before Drew Gilpin Faust recommended it in the *New York Times Magazine.* She was asked what book she might recommend for the entering class at Harvard, where she is president, and she chose *Being Wrong* because, she said, it advocates "doubt as a skill and praises error as the foundation of wisdom." You can find Schulz talking about the book and about her research on YouTube and on TED.

Our goal in teaching the chapter was to give some depth and context for talking about "evidence," a term students have learned to use in thinking about writing, particularly in thinking about how paragraphs are constructed and what they do. And so our goal was to find ways of using Schulz's key terms or interesting examples to talk about the "evidence" presented in pieces of prose, their own and others'. I was surprised at how difficult it was to turn that attention to Schulz's prose. Frankly, I don't think Schulz (as a writer) follows her own program. Once she gets started, she moves pretty easily within the track defined by her argument. There isn't much "self-auditing" going on. She is not quick to call her own assumptions into question.

And I thought it would be interesting to turn Schulz's argument back on her style and method. But that turned out to be tougher than I thought. And it was tough *even* when students were quick to talk about the importance of "testing hypothesis," about the importance of a "paradigm shift," about the need to avoid the "confident bulldozer of unmodified assertions," about the importance of her message.

Why? Why the gap between saying and doing? I think this gap always exists. At least that has been in my experience as a teacher. And, frankly, I think the gap also exists here because Schulz writes so well. The prose seems seamless; students are charmed. They struggle (always) to see the "trick" in the forms of mastery that are part of how writing is taught and valued in the United States, forms of mastery they aspire to, that define their expectations and desires. It is always hard, and it takes tact and patience to know when and how to turn critical attention toward a kind of seamless, convincing prose whose values seem settled and, to be sure, whose values we also know how to share. As teachers, we are often urging students toward just that form of mastery. I know from my own teaching that when I am struggling to get a student to write a Schulz-like paragraph, I need to strategically forgo questions about what the paragraph is *failing* to do. Still, as I understand the mission of the first-year college writing course, it is my job to find time and space in the semester to raise just that question.

I would encourage you, then, to make this turn and to offer this challenge. The "Questions for a Second Reading," which I'll talk about below, open with exercises devised to assist this effort. What I can offer from a semester's experience with *Being Wrong* is this: It was much easier to use Schulz to create "adventuresome" revisions of student paragraphs than it was to develop a critique of her prose.

Note: We included a long preface Schulz added to her endnotes. We've placed it, as she did, at the head of those notes. It is a classic and has some very good things to say about Wikipedia.

QUESTIONS FOR A SECOND READING (p. 380)

1. The first of these questions is designed to direct a close reading. The prompt highlights two words—"we" and "explore"—and it says to students, "If you stop for a minute to think about these words, if you don't just skim past and take them for granted (or 'for granite' as one of my students was fond of saying), what do they assume, what kinds of meanings do they require? What do they require of you?"

    The "we" is an easy way in. It assumes that "we," the audience, are all the same and that, as people, we are also Schulz—sharing her knowledge, perspective, and assumptions. And it is not hard to get students thinking about how they might *not* be in that boat. Although race, class, and gender are available prompts for thinking about difference, my preference is to use age and history. There are important differences between John Kerry and Rene Descartes or between Albert Speer and Judge William Stoughton, and it is useful to consider them so as not to make an error about the timelessness or the "unsituatedness" of thought and action. And, of course, there are differences that students feel deeply between the "we" of high school, the "we" of the first year at college, the "we" of other young adults, the "we" of professors.

    I also found it useful to have students think about Schulz's method, here invoked through the reference to the act of "exploring" "our" aversion to uncertainty by looking to three figures: Hamlet, John Kerry, and the "undecided voter." I greatly admire the ease with which Schulz appropriates and manages her "cases." She brings together a range of material from classical literature, popular culture, acquaintances and interviews, and the newspapers. I want students to think that intellectual work can (and should) bridge these gaps. You don't "leave school," in a sense, when you leave the classroom. Your materials are all around you. And I think calling the term "explore" into question bring that idea forward. Just as I think it can call attention to the difference between the intellectual work represented by (and through) Schulz's chapter and the others forms of intellectual labor featured and valued in other places, other courses, other books, other institutions, and so on.

2. The chapter is full of references to historical figures, philosophers, scientists. The chapter invites a glossary and/or a set of extended Norton-Anthology-like footnotes. And the discussion of the text can certainly be enriched when students know something about, say, Descartes or Quine or Hume or Kuhn. This assignment, then, sends students out (perhaps in groups) on a mini-research project. I had students make presentations, usually working from a brief paragraph and including some visual materials.

    We often combine an exercise like this with a trip to the library and a session with a reference librarian on how to use a university library and its resources. A university library is a special and daunting place; it has tools well beyond what students will have encountered in their high school or neighborhood libraries. And students often quite literally need someone to take them across the threshold.

    Remember, though, that although it is important to have students track down, explain, and defend examples (here of research and of researchers) that lie beyond their immediate range of reference, it is equally important to have them come to class with examples that are close to them, that mean something to them, that are part of their own immediate cultural experience.

3. As I said above, I think it is important to turn Schulz's argument back toward her own prose, a prose (I would say) that does *not* practice a form of "self-subversive thinking." This prompt provides language—her language—language that can be deployed in a critical rereading of her prose.

ASSIGNMENTS FOR WRITING (p. 381)

1. This was the most successful of the writing assignments I taught in connection with *Being Wrong*. The key is to help students think about the example they might "bring to the table." Most of my students turned to their own experiences, times when they were found to be in error or found to be caught up in the error of others. I had two students who did the research (or had already done research) that enabled them to write about crucial moments in science. These were great and thoughtful papers, but they didn't attract the kind of attention as was given by the class to papers about divorce or racial identity (one set in Hawaii, for example) or drug and alcohol abuse or the decision to go to college—the familiar themes young adults bring to our classrooms.

    The assignment requires students to represent Schulz's essay through summary, paraphrase, and quotation (to represent it for readers who have not yet read it), to establish Schulz's position and then to respond. We never offer assignments that rely on summary alone. We want summary to function strategically and that is our goal here. Students will need to provide a rich and textured sense of what Schulz says in this essay (and what Schulz does there). This alone is a job of some complexity—and it might constitute a first draft. The most difficult part of the assignment, however, comes when the student writer needs to take center stage. We represent that moment in two ways—as a need to bring a new example to the table, something close to the student and his or her world, and as an invitation to extend or challenge Schulz's argument. This last part is the hardest. The student must take center stage, and the student must take center stage at (usually) the end of the essay—when they are tired and out of time. I always teach through revision. In fact, my assessment is always and only an assessment of what happens from draft to draft, where (as I say to my students) I can actually see them at work.

2–3. Most of our writing assignments also include a project where students extend the project of what they had read to some other context, here a piece of writing. In these two assignments, students turn either to a published piece of prose or to some of their own writing (and its revision) in order to talk about "due diligence" (I love that term) and "models of thinking."

The students struggled more with these assignments, as I suggested above. They are not yet adept at producing a "close reading" on the page. It takes times and much direct instruction to learn how to work with block quotations, for example, and how to see prose as *doing* or *enacting* rather than just *saying* something. Still, I think this is an important lesson. If I were to teach this material again, I would most certainly use these assignments.

4. This assignment is an afterthought. I didn't teach this. One of my students, actually, said that she had become a Schulz-like stalker, suddenly paying attention to how people got into trouble or out of trouble or avoided trouble as they were speaking. I wished that I had offered this assignment as an option when I sent students out to find written texts—either their own or others'—to use in assignments 3 and 4.

MAKING CONNECTIONS (p. 384)

1. For this question, see my comments above on assignments 1 through 3. This assignment brings Schulz-like attention to the prose of another selection in *Ways of Reading*. And it asks students to treat a section of this prose as an example they are "bringing to the table."

2. This is a broader and more open-ended assignment. It frees students from analyzing prose and invites them to engage in a general discussion of error.

The assignment provides a long list of selections in *Ways of Reading* that raise questions about error and its ways: Appiah, Berger, Butler, Foucault, Morris, Pratt, and Percy. We regularly feature assignments that ask students to read one essay in light of, or in reference to, another so that they can imagine that they are engaged in an ongoing project rather than just a little of this and a little of that—Schulz one week and Foucault the next.

We have always made it a point to insist that students use assignments like these to take a step beyond "compare and contrast," a method already (most likely) part of their toolkits. There is a technical side to using one text as a lens through which to view the other. One way to make this act of reading materialize on the page is to bring a paragraph or block quotation from one text—from Schulz, say—to a discussion that also requires a paragraph or block quotation from Pratt. What do you hear in each? Where and how do they speak to each other? Or not? As we ask students to visualize the page, we ask them also to imagine a space in the essay where they, the student writer, speaks, where they take a position and make an evaluative judgment about what they have read. (What is your favorite moment in all of this? Which text is most persuasive?) And we ask them to strike out on their own, either to develop an idea or to apply what they have found to a new situation or set of examples.

DAVID FOSTER WALLACE

Authority and American Usage (p. 388)

"Authority and American Usage" is a lively and playful essay that can nevertheless create some significant challenges for first-year students. For one thing, it's extremely long (the full version is forty-eight pages) and stylistically baroque. For another, the subject matter is not likely to be appealing to students at first glance. An extensive, heavily footnoted book review of a tome about American usage? Few students will find the prospect attractive. Yet Wallace's persona in this essay is so winning—precisely what he claims to be the case with Bryan Garner—that many students end up engaged with the text. And it can be quite helpful for their own work that Wallace discusses rhetorical success in terms of logos, pathos, and ethos. His argument is that the postmodern breakdown of authority means we can regain powerful voices as writers only by making an ethical appeal—that is, by convincing our readers that we are credible. Wallace notes that this is best accomplished by those "whose expertise is born of a real love of their specialty instead of just a desire to be expert at something," and in trying to convince us that such is the case with Garner, Wallace displays his own love of language.

Wallace's essay is in many ways an experiment and a comment on the essay as a form of writing. Note, for instance, the remarkable interchange between the colloquial and the formal in Wallace's language. He begins with a series of rhetorical questions addressing the lay reader directly (presumably someone who doesn't know about the Usage Wars), and his essay is filled with hilarious terms and anecdotes and interpolations, all of which serve to present him as a funny, wisecracking contemporary who is anything but pedantic. Indeed, his whole commentary on being a SNOOT ends up making him seem less so—or at least someone whose SNOOTism we can forgive as the charming oddity of a beloved relative. And yet at the same time, Wallace has to—and does—convince us of his own authority to comment at length on not just Garner's book but the Usage Wars in general. Hence the displays of grammatical erudition; references to other usage guides; use of lengthy footnotes; and so on. We come away with the sense that he knows this stuff and knows it well—not, perhaps, like a linguist, but for that very reason he is someone whom we can trust even more.

Wallace's experiment is to *combine* all of these things; he throws them together like ingredients in a big pot of stew whose smell you can savor down the hall. In other words, rather than seeing the essay as a hidebound form in which things happen in a predictable order, he approaches the essay as an opportunity to think his way through a set of problems, mixing his discourses along the way. Part of the excitement of teaching this text, then, is that students get to reflect on what constitutes an essay in the first place—how to address their readers; the value of interruptions and digressions; the ways in which they can "think on the page."

We came across an interesting essay by UCLA law school professor Eugene Volokh about correcting student papers using Garner's Dictionary. You can find it here: law.ucla .edu/volokh/errors.pdf.

Note: David Foster Wallace committed suicide in 2008. His death was covered extensively in the press; the links can easily be Googled. We chose not to mention the circumstances of his death in the headnote, since such a reference seemed more distracting than useful.

QUESTIONS FOR A SECOND READING (p. 415)

1. For some time now, we have been teaching students to "punctuate" their essays. It remains a remarkable discovery for students to learn that they can divide their essays into numbered sections or with subheadings. We teach this as a way of assisting the reader (which is how we teach all forms of punctuation). But we also teach it as a way of assisting the writer. The subsections provide places where a writer is able to stop and take stock, or to mark progress and direction, or to pause to catch a breath—and to pause, not only to rest but to see what has been left out, what counterexamples are possible, what new directions are not implied by the current track. Each pause is a moment to think about readers and what they might be thinking or where they might be confused. Wallace is, then, an exemplary writer, and the selection provides a ready lesson in punctuating the essay.

2. This question invites students to consider the *persona*, or character, that Wallace creates in the course of his essay. It might be helpful to remind students of the distinction between the first-person narrator of a novel and the author of that novel, since many may imagine that writers of nonfiction speak directly, without artifice, providing us with unmediated access to their thoughts. Wallace's text offers an opportunity to discuss the ways in which the essay as a genre—including essays students write in their courses—requires the invention of a speaker, a narrator, a character on the page whose ethos is crucial to how the piece gets read. We encourage students to locate specific passages in the text where Wallace's character appears especially visible or audible. What kind of figure does he seem to be? What are his traits and habits? And why would he want to be seen in these ways?

3. One of the most prevalent themes in Wallace's essay is the value of rhetoric—a notion that students may find odd, since the term "rhetoric" tends to be used pejoratively in public discourse. Complicating things further is Wallace's repeated praise for Garner's "totally sneaky" approach to persuading his readers, for rhetoric is generally associated with sneakiness of a sort that provokes condemnation rather than congratulation. This question asks students to work on this conundrum. Why does Wallace extol Garner's sneakiness? What does he find valuable in a rhetorical conception of language? In addressing these issues, we've asked students to make use of a block quotation from Wallace's essay—a quotation they are to introduce and discuss in a single long paragraph. Not only does this lead them to ground their discussion of Wallace's ideas about rhetoric in a passage from his text, but it also helps prepare them for the kind of work they'll do when writing a more extensive analysis of his essay. In class, students can share their paragraphs in small groups and discuss different (rhetorical? sneaky?) approaches to quotation.

4. Wallace's essay is long and structurally complex, so we've found it useful to have students chart its movement. Wallace is especially playful with the notion of a "thesis" or "thesis statement," which he mentions on several occasions—though not in the opening paragraph, where students may be used to looking for it. (Indeed, he doesn't reveal what he calls the "real thesis" of Garner's book until the final sentence of his essay.) Here again, we've asked students to write a long paragraph that includes a block quotation and that explains what seems to be Wallace's central argument—which is one way for them to begin to identify, amid all the interpolations and digressions, what's most crucial to his essay. These paragraphs can be shared and debated in class, and students might also work on a visual representation of Wallace's text—perhaps a map of the journey we take as readers as we follow Wallace's trail from the beginning to the end of his piece.

5. *Dilige et quod vis fac* (Love, and do what thou wilt). At first glance, this epigraph seems to have little to do with the text that follows—which is all the more reason for having students explore the potential connections between the two. If students need assistance, you might ask them where else Wallace mentions love in his essay. Who, among those Wallace describes, demonstrates love for his work? In what ways? And what does "do what thou wilt" have to do with Wallace's argument (especially since he writes against the permissiveness of the Descriptivists)?

6. This is an exercise we like to do with various texts throughout the semester. Having students locate and copy sentences they find grammatically striking is one of the best ways we know to engage them in discussions of style, rhetoric, rhythm, punctuation, and meaning. Here again, small-group work can be particularly effective. Students share their sentences, discuss their attributes, and choose one to write on the board. When the class reconvenes, each group describes the virtues of (and/or problems with) the sentence they've selected. Then, toward the end of class, each student chooses a sentence to imitate, creating his or her own content for a statement with the same amount of words, phrases, and forms of punctuation as the sentence from the original text.

7. We added this as an invitation for students who would like to see the essay in its entirety. (In our experience, this does happen, although not generally. Enough is enough! We regret the shortsightedness of some at Wallace's publisher, however. Somehow they have it in their heads that our textbook will compete with their list when, in fact, we are paying them to provide an advertisement.)

We often combine an invitation like this with a formal trip to the library and a session with a reference librarian on how to use a university library and its resources. A university library is a special and daunting place; it has tools well beyond what students will have encountered in their high schools and communities. And students often quite literally need someone to take them across the threshold.

ASSIGNMENTS FOR WRITING (p. 417)

1. This assignment asks students to respond to Wallace's argument about Standard Written English (SWE) and its place in a course on writing. Wallace admits that, when he teaches, he finds it very important to insist on SWE in students' papers, so much so that he often interrupts his original plans for his courses in order to spend several weeks on lessons in usage and grammar. He finds it regrettable that the ideology of the linguistic Descriptivists has led to an educational system that no longer places much emphasis on grammar instruction, and he believes that all students, regardless of their home dialect, should become fluent in SWE.

Wallace's argument about SWE is complex, and it will be important for students to acknowledge this complexity. Some students will be tempted to turn Wallace into a straw man—say, an elitist grammar hound who's simply afraid of cultural change—in order to contest his views. But Wallace admits that "SWE is the dialect of the American elite," and he's well aware that alternative dialects have their own integrity. Students who choose to challenge his position will need to account for such things, and they'll need to represent his text in ways that do justice to its intricacies. To prepare them for this assignment, you might have students locate passages in Wallace's essay where he says something about SWE, and then have them take note of nuances, shifts in direction, and apparent contradictions. By identifying a number of passages in advance, students will bring a more multifaceted understanding of Wallace's position to their writing.

In their essays, it will also be crucial for students to locate their own experience as speakers and writers in Wallace's work. We suggest that they focus on a particular occasion when they experienced or observed a struggle with SWE in the classroom, and then read what occurred with or against the grain of Wallace's argument. After examining this occasion in some detail, what do they have to say to Wallace about his views on usage and grammar in a writing course?

2. The most striking feature in Wallace's writing is the way the figure of the writer, as evidenced in the text, does and does not inhabit the conventions of academic writing. The point of this assignment is to give students the opportunity to think about style in

terms of ethos, a term introduced in the essay, and to think about the embodiment of the intellectual represented by the conventional and unconventional stylistic features in Wallace's essay. And it asks students to think about the differences in relation to their own intellectual styles, current and future.

Students can be helped toward this essay if you build class discussion around the first, second, and/or fourth "Questions for a Second Reading." Sending the class back to the text and then using class time to gather a set of examples will give students a common stockpile of material to work with, and it will free them to focus attention on the questions they want to pose or the arguments that make sense to them.

The use of examples is key here. Students need to learn to think about writing as an intellectual project, more than a rehearsal of opinion or writing off the top of their head. They need the sense of a workbench, with materials on it. One way to help them visualize the page is to insist that they include, at two or three key moments, a block quotation from the text. As we ask students to visualize the page, we ask them to also imagine a space in the essay where they, the student writer, speak, where they take a position and make an evaluative judgment about the essays (Which is their favorite? Which is more persuasive?), and where they strike out on their own, either to develop an idea or to apply what they have found to a new situation or set of examples.

3. This is a standard assignment in *Ways of Reading*. We ask students to read an essay closely and to pay attention to its stylistic features, to the shape and sound of its sentences, to the "voice" that emerges from the text. We also ask students to notice the oddities of form and structure, the nuanced departures from what we might otherwise expect from an essay. In other words, we want them to get a strong sense of the creative dimensions of a particular essay and the choices the writer has made in order to produce a text that challenges conventional procedures. Then we say to our students: "OK, now you give it a try. Take these methods and make them your own; bring them to a subject that is yours, not Wallace's, and see what emerges when you make use of his habits of mind and style as a writer."

Wallace's writing is especially suited to this kind of assignment, for it illustrates a number of highly visible traits and strategies that students can locate in class and list on the board: interpolations, interruptions, digressions, footnotes, and so on. More tricky will be helping them to identify and imitate his *tone* or *mood*—the ways that he argues and cajoles and reflects and criticizes. It's a complex performance, one that Wallace makes seem easier than students are likely to find it. Wallace has done his homework—he brings a scholarly erudition to his subject—and while we don't expect our students to be as knowledgeable as he is, the assignment asks them to include other writers in their essay. Like Wallace, students need to recognize and enter a conversation that precedes them, rather than assume they have the first (or last) word on the subject. Indeed, this is one way they might launch their essay—by turning to the words of another, just as Wallace has turned to Garner's book on American usage.

MAKING CONNECTIONS (p. 418)

1. This assignment asks students to notice the similar anxieties that inform the essays by David Foster Wallace and Richard Miller. Students can prepare for the assignment by discussing these essays alongside each other, identifying the particular concerns that trouble each writer. They might also consider the figure whom Wallace calls the SNOOT—a figure who appears, surprisingly, in the form of Eric Harris in Miller's essay. Why are SNOOTs so annoyed when others don't speak "correctly"? What does the "proper" use of language signify for them? Is there something of the SNOOT in all of us, depending on the social context?

   Following such a discussion, we ask students to write an essay that examines their own thoughts on the state of American literacy. This is a huge, complex question, so it's important for students to focus on a particular moment or two in their own experience or observation that speaks to Wallace's and/or Miller's fears about the future of reading and writing. Based on their own practices (and perhaps those of their friends and family), do students believe that reading and writing are likely to wane in the ways these writers worry they might? Why or why not? Are there crucial differences between reading on the Internet and reading print in a book or newspaper or journal? Is there something about the changes wrought by new media that writers like Wallace and Miller fail to understand? These are some of the questions students might address in the course of their essays.

2. We regularly feature assignments that ask students to read one essay in light of, or in reference to, another—so that they can imagine they are engaged in an ongoing project rather than just a little of this and a little of that, submitting essays on schedule. This assignment asks students to think about "style" in the essays by Wallace and Appiah. The most striking feature in Wallace's writing is the way the figure of the writer, as evidenced in the text, does and does not inhabit the style of scholarly writing exemplified by a writer as distinguished, elegant, and magisterial as Appiah. And it asks students to think about the differences in relation to their own intellectual styles, current and future.

   We have always made it a point to insist that students use assignments like these to take a step beyond "compare and contrast," a method already (most likely) a part of their toolkits. There is a technical side to using one text as a lens through which to view the other. One way to make this materialize on the page is to bring a paragraph or block quotation from one text, from Wallace, say, to a discussion that also requires a block quotation from Appiah. As we ask students to visualize the page, we ask them to also imagine a space in the essay where they, the student writer, speak, where they take a position and make an evaluative judgment about the essays (Which is their favorite? Which is more persuasive?), and where they strike out on their own, either to develop an idea or to apply what they have found to a new situation or set of examples.

JOHN EDGAR WIDEMAN

Our Time (p. 442)

This excerpt from *Brothers and Keepers* tells such a compelling story with such a power-ful voice that students are easily drawn into it. Wideman's younger brother, Robby, is in prison for his role in a robbery and murder. The excerpt picks up the story near the end and focuses on Robby's friendship with Garth; his growing up in Homewood, a black neigh-borhood in Pittsburgh; and his mother and his grandfather, John French. Throughout the selection, Wideman asks himself how this could have happened to Robby, how he could end up in prison and Wideman a Rhodes scholar and a college professor with a national reputation as a writer. The problem of writing about Robby bothers Wideman, especially since the book is an occasion for him to get to know his brother for the first time in his adult life, and because Wideman questions his own motives. Am I, he asks, exploiting Robby, or am I telling his story, or is it something else I am up to?

QUESTIONS FOR A SECOND READING (p. 459)

1. "Our Time" is about Robby and Homewood, about a family and a community, but it is also about the act of writing, and in this sense, it is primarily Wideman's story. This question points to moments when John interrupts the text to talk about its composition. It asks students to consider why he would call attention to the text as a text. It asks them to consider how Wideman might be said to address the problems he faces as a writer. Students will not have any trouble identifying these sections once they reread with these questions in mind. They will, however, have trouble understanding just what Wideman's problems are, and what they have to do with writing. And they will have trouble finding a position on the question "Why?" If he does not want to tell his story, if he does not want to deflect attention from Robby, then why does he do so? And what does he do to overcome the ways in which writing inevitably makes Robby's story his own? Are the author's intrusions a solution? What about the use of fictional devices? and the sections in Robby's voice? All of these are questions that allow you to bring forward the problems of reading and writing as they are represented in the text.

2. There are major passages in this selection where Wideman speaks in Robby's voice, offering talk that might be said to be Robby's but is, in fact, Wideman speaking to us in the voice of his brother. Students will need to locate those moments and to use sections of them that represent Robby's point of view. How do these passages reveal Robby's view of the world? What do they tell you about how he understands and represents the way the world works?

    Once students have discussed these questions, they'll need to turn to passages where John is speaking. Direct them to pay attention to the language, not so much to the subject of the talk. They'll need to look at the differences in Robby's and John's language. What aspects of the ways they use language, the ways they use their voices, can you point to as indicating differences in how they understand and represent them-selves? the worlds they live in? You might ask students to think about the voices. How does the voice in the passages where Robby talks treat his subjects, his readers, and himself? Who talks like this? For what reasons? To whom? And what about John's voice? What does the voice in his passages tell you?

3. To answer the questions on the differences it would make if Wideman started the story with different episodes, students will need to turn to the way he does start the story — with Garth's death. They'll need to reread, looking for moments in the beginning that frame the rest of the selection. You might ask them to look for passages later that use or rely on the opening to present a point of view. Students will need to discuss the point of view of the given opening. What does the passage on Garth's death do for the rest of the story? How can you demonstrate what it does by showing how other passages rely on that opening for their sense or impact?

    Once students have discussed the opening, they can turn to the other sections in the selection — the house in Shadyside and Robby's birth — that might be used to begin. They'll have to imagine those episodes starting the piece, and from there, try to say how those passages would change or alter the point of view. What would those moments do to other major moments in the selection if they were used to begin it? Students will want to generalize after imagining other beginnings, and you should press them to relate how their readings of specific passages in the selection change when the beginning changes.

ASSIGNMENTS FOR WRITING (p. 459)

1. This is the written response to the first of the "Questions for a Second Reading." If you haven't already, you might want to see what we say about those questions and the reasons for asking students to think about the author's intrusions into the narrative.

    We've taught this assignment several times, and we've found it important for students to work directly from passages in the text. The first thing they need to do is to reread the selection and choose their material. The assignment asks them to choose three or four passages; this may turn out to be too many. Once they have located their material, students do not have great difficulty describing it. They do, however, have trouble turning the discussion to the issue of writing — either the writing of "Our Time" or writing as a general subject. In their first draft, students should be encouraged to turn from their material to the question of *why* Wideman interrupts the narrative. We have found that students write well and at length about *what* Wideman says, but, when the space is open for them to comment or explain, they feel they have nothing to say. Students can imagine several routes to this question, several ways of imagining their authority. They can talk as fellow writers, imagining from that perspective why a writer might want to bring forward the problem of writing. They can talk as readers, explaining the effects of these intrusions. Or they can talk as students — that is, through their knowledge of other attempts to represent an understanding of race, family, crime, drug addiction, or the black community.

    For revision: Our experience with this assignment suggests that students can best use the time allotted for revision to work on the general issues raised in this paper.

What might they say about Wideman's narrative intrusions? More particularly, what might this have to do with the writing they are doing—or might do—as students in the academy? What would the consequences be of producing a text that calls attention to itself as a text, as something produced?

2. This assignment turns to "Our Time" as first-person sociology, pushing to the side the question of the text as text. It asks students to use Wideman's account of Robby's family and neighborhood as a way of framing an answer to Wideman's underlying question: What is Robby's story? The question can be rephrased in a number of ways: Who is Robby? How can you explain the differences between Robby and John? In what ways is a man or woman the product of family and environment? How did Robby end up in jail?

    Ideally, students will be working closely with the text. The evidence they have is here—not in whatever generalizations they can dredge up about crime or the ghetto. And students will need to do more than retell what they find in the text: they will need to assume a role similar to John's. In fact, one way students might get started on the project is to measure their sense against John's, to set themselves apart as someone who can see what he can't.

3. In order for students to step into Wideman's methods as a writer and write their own Wideman-like piece, they need to be familiar with the selection, and they need to spend some time studying and discussing Wideman's methods. We use the first two of the "Questions for a Second Reading" for class discussions that focus on the methods of this selection, and after two or three sessions our students seem ready to begin this writing project. Most students will write about their neighborhoods and family, and this works fine, we think, as long as they demonstrate an allegiance to Wideman's methods by writing in different voices, or at least in two voices, the voice of the narrator and the voice of one other person whose story is being told, at one point, and who, at other points, is telling his or her own story. Students can break their essays into sections, as Wideman does, either while they're writing or as the work of revision. They should ask themselves why they think Wideman has broken his piece as he has, and they should have reasons for breaking theirs. They can use different typefaces to signal different voices or the "essay" part of their writing. And, as Wideman does, they should allow their voices as narrators to be heard, to show their thinking about how to tell the other voices' stories, about how to do justice to the other voices. For most students this will mean "thinking aloud" in paragraphs about the problems they encounter as they try to evoke other voices with depth and credibility. This speaking aloud on the page is an important part of this project, as it allows students to do the kind of self-reflective thinking and writing that writers must do when they re-create others through their representations of their voices, as Wideman does. Students won't have great success with this reflective writing in their early drafts, and you should anticipate that this part of the project, and the telling of others' stories in their own voices, will be a large part of the work of the revision for this assignment.

    We have found it useful with this kind of assignment to turn students' attention regularly, throughout the students' work, to self-reflective questions about this kind of "mixed" writing. It's helpful for them to think about what this kind of writing can do that a more traditional essay can't. In this light, we ask them how it might serve them as students. Where, in what situations, might they want to write like Wideman? And why, do they suppose, is this kind of writing not taught in school?

MAKING CONNECTIONS (p. 46)

1. Much more challenging for students than it first appears to be, this project puts them in the position of doing a large share of the work for it on their own. To begin with, they'll have to study Wideman's selection closely for its methods. Much of this work can be done as a class with the first two of the "Questions for a Second Reading." Once they have spent two or three classes discussing Wideman's piece in terms of method, they need to select another piece from the assignment's listing to read alongside Wideman. Students will pick different selections and will need to find a way to examine the selections' methods. We have grouped students by twos or threes according to the selections they chose so that they could help each other. We have directed individual students and groups to the second-reading questions for their selections so that they might start with a set of method-related questions to open up their readings. And at other times, we have limited the selections to two or three from the list so that we can then assign students to groups and plan on some class work with each selection.

   Whatever approach you take, students will need to write essays in which they explain their two chosen projects and their methods to readers who have not read the selections; this requires a fair amount of summary. They also need to comment on each selection so that these naive readers can understand their thinking about what each selection's author is able to accomplish through experimental writing. These two tasks—summarizing and commenting on the accomplishments of each piece—are not separate, and students who treat them as such will get themselves tangled in long, unwieldy essays. Students need to know from the start that the examples they choose to summarize for readers unfamiliar with the selections should also serve as the examples they'll refer to when they comment on what each selection does or gains or accomplishes through its experimental work.

2. We regularly feature assignments that ask students to read one essay in light of, or in reference to, another so that they can imagine that they are engaged in an ongoing project rather than just a little of this and a little of that—Appiah one week and Wideman the next. This assignment asks students to use Appiah's account of racial identity (and identification) to think about John Wideman's family history. For Wideman, the difficulties of representation are present in the text as acts of memory and invention. And they are there as polemic, in his argument about the usual representation of African American male identity.

3. Questions of representation and truth are writing problems, problems that all writers must wrestle with at some point. Wideman's writing might be considered to be more explicitly engaged with these questions, while Miller's piece is more implicitly engaged, suggesting through its particular movement the problem of representation and reality. Miller, like Wideman, makes the stories he tells his own, bending and molding them for the purposes of "The Dark Night of the Soul." Whether we're writing

about ourselves or someone else, we must always choose what to include and exclude, where to begin and end, what portrait we will paint for our readers. On what basis do we decide, and what are the consequences of our decisions? We are always faced with the limits of language and representation, the limits of our perspective, the limits of any piece of writing to capture the complexities of identity. What kinds of ethical dilemmas do we face when we decide to write about others? What can we ever claim to really know about others? Are some representations more true, just, or valuable than others? By what means can we make such judgments responsibly? This assignment asks students to consider the difficulties of representation. In this essay, not only will students have a chance to offer an analysis of what Wideman and Miller suggest about representation and truth, but they will also have the opportunity to offer their own theories of truth, thinking carefully about the term, its definitions and its relevance to their own writing.

Part III. Working with the Assignment Sequences

For a complete commentary on the selections in each sequence, please be sure to read each essay's selection in this manual, particularly the opening discussion. While we will cull materials from the discussions of individual assignments, we won't reproduce the introductions. And, while the sequences provide writing assignments, you should think about the advantages (or disadvantages) of using the "Questions for a Second Reading." In every case, students should read the headnotes in the textbook, which are designed to serve the assignments and sequences.

• • ● • •

SEQUENCE ONE

Exploring Identity, Exploring the Self (p. 469)

Explorations of identity and inquiries into the construction of "the self" have been at the center of theoretical discussions and conversations about writing, of course, for quite some time. So, in many ways, a sequence like this one is not new. But it seems particularly urgent and relevant for students to be thinking about these questions of race, ethnicity, nation, gender, class, and sexuality in our present moment.

This sequence not only invites students to think about these aspects of identity, but it also asks them to contend with the overlaps, and perhaps even conflicts, as these aspects of identity come into contact with one another. What we admire and find productive about the writers we've included in this sequence is their attention to these many categories or characterizations of identity at once. And each writer in this sequence, in one way or another, explores his or her own identity as a writer, onlooker, theorist, family member, citizen, and also as a complex representation of perceived identity categories. Despite their commonalities in terms of the complicated layers of identity formation at work and under examination, the writers here have very different approaches, styles, and even audiences.

Some students will have particular political or ideological challenges to manage as they read and write about these texts. And, of course, there is no one way for instructors to navigate the sensitivities and prejudices that could arise when identity is explicitly part of class writing, class workshops, and class discussions. However, we have found that students (despite their nervousness or even resistance) are hungry to have these kinds of discussions—discussions about who we are, where we are, and how we have come to understand ourselves and others as we move through our lives. In teaching sequences like this, we find it is important to articulate to students that we are, in fact, in a writing course such as ours, uninterested in whether or not they agree or disagree with a particular author and that we are more invested in their abilities to consider both the positions of the authors and the questions posed to them in each of the assignments. Some instructors might be inclined to engage students in debate about many of the texts in this sequence, but we have found it most beneficial to keep students engaged in the act of inquiry rather than the act of argument.

ASSIGNMENT 1

Narrative and Identity [Appiah]

This has been one of the most interesting and productive assignments in our teaching in the last few years. We often ask students to extend the argument of an essay to materials or narratives central to their own lives. Here, the focus is more clearly on the narrative itself. Although our students aren't familiar with terms like "narrative nonfiction" or "creative nonfiction," we encourage them to write as though they were writing a story—with an emphasis on scene, character, and dialogue. The more people speaking, we say, the better. And we have received impressive papers in return—impressive in their length, their ambition, and their seriousness. This assignment always leads to a revision, and so we are quick to bring the most ambitious papers to class for discussion. Their example has provoked impressive revisions from students whose first drafts were mechanical or perfunctory.

We also, however, think of this as a critical exercise. We don't demand (or even prompt) direct reference to Appiah in these papers. In the assignment, however, we make it clear that this is an Appiah-like exercise. It is not an open invitation to a personal essay. It is an invitation to think through, as we say, the "competing demands of a life and a 'script,' of the personal and the collective, of individual freedom and the politics of identity."

ASSIGNMENT 2

Identity and Representation [Said]

The conclusion to the book *After the Last Sky* is both striking and challenging:

I would like to think, though, that such a book not only tells the reader about us, but in some way also reads the reader. I would like to think that we are not just the people seen or looked at in these photographs: We are also looking at our observers. (p. 166)

This assignment asks students to think at length about what it means not only to read but also to be read by a text. It will be important for students to think differently about image and text. That is, the images alone position the reader as equivalent to the photographer (or, perhaps more appropriately, since there is little agency involved, as equivalent to the lens of the camera). The text positions them differently, both in relation to the images and as a reader. Said, in other words, makes certain assumptions about his readers, their habits, affiliations, and ways of seeing.

There are subtle distinctions to make, in other words, and students can be usefully assisted in making them. It is also important that they work from specific examples—long discussion of particular photographs and passages. We have found it important to insist upon extended discussions of a few examples (since students will most likely be drawn to brief discussions of several).

ASSIGNMENT 3

The Concept of Human [Butler]

Butler provides a number of productive questions, as ways to introduce issues, as a hypothetical, or as a way of grappling with an unsolvable problem. Locating questions and lingering on their implications is a way of reading Butler, giving students something to *do* with Butler's essay, and something they will likely have immediate success in doing.

ASSIGNMENT 4

The Politics of Dehumanization [Butler, Said]

This writing assignment, in some ways, asks students to do something that may already be familiar to them—to focus on the common themes between two texts. The prompt itself even outlines for students the common threads of exile, existence, and, as Butler puts it, "the question of the human." But the assignment also asks students to think of the implications of these intersections between Butler and Said. What we like about this assignment is the possibility for students to reflect on their own experiences of "otherness." These experiences will not necessarily emerge in narrative or personal essay form, but instead as a way of understanding, or sometimes challenging, the claims Butler and Said make about alienation, identity, and exile.

ASSIGNMENT 5

Interconnectedness and Identity [Griffin]

Although the work students must do for this essay echoes the work they are asked to do in the second-reading questions, it is more determined, more focused. Students receive an invitation here to take a given trajectory through Griffin's text, and it's a key one: to understand her claims for the ways we are all connected in a matrix or a field or a common past.

In order to do this work, students will need to reread the selection looking for those moments when Griffin directly writes about interconnectedness or the key terms that the assignment presents them. They will also need to reread the "white spaces" between her fragments for the implications, the connections, that she implies. She never tells us, for example, how she thinks through RNA and DNA as metaphors that stand for growth or change, for instance, but she clearly implies that these metaphors have something to do with her thinking about these subjects and, too, about secrets. This has been the most difficult work for our students. They aren't accustomed to reading for implications or inferring between the lines, and they need to participate in discussions in class that seem to us like occasions for them to convince themselves that it's legitimate to infer or speculate about what something in the text, say Griffin's use of the DNA metaphor, might stand for or represent. These discussions seem to be essential, a part of the work of learning to read between the lines, and we encourage them whenever students appear skeptical or uncertain about their right to do such reading.

It's a difficult assignment because it steps right past the kinds of questions students will want to begin with—What is "Our Secret" about? What is Griffin saying?—and moves immediately to questions about the project as a project—What is she doing? Why does she write this way? It may be best to assign a preliminary writing assignment or to work with some of the "Questions for a Second Reading." Or it might be useful to precede or follow this assignment with one that asks students to write like Griffin, where students are allowed to think about her project in terms of their own practice as writers. This assignment worked best for us when we made it clear to students that they should think about Griffin's writing in terms of the usual education offered young writers in the United States. They should begin, that is, not with the language of literary analysis ("image" or "metaphor") but with the language of the composition classroom ("topic sentence," "paragraph," "organization," "footnotes," and "three-by-five notecards").

ALTERNATIVE ASSIGNMENT

A Writer's Identity, A Writer's Position [Wideman]

This is the written response to the first of the "Questions for a Second Reading." If you haven't already, you might want to see what we say about those questions and the reasons for asking students to think about the author's intrusions into the narrative.

We've taught this assignment several times, and we've found it important for students to work directly from passages in the text. The first thing they need to do is to reread the selection and choose their material. The assignment asks them to choose three or four passages; this may turn out to be too many. Once they have located their material, students do not have great difficulty describing it. They do, however, have trouble turning the discussion to the issue of writing—either the writing of "Our Time" or writing as a general subject. In their first draft, students should be encouraged to turn from their material to the question of *why* Wideman interrupts the narrative. We have found that students write well and at length about *what* Wideman says, but, when the space is open for them to comment or explain, they feel they have nothing to say. Students can imagine several routes to this question, several ways of imagining their authority. They can talk as fellow writers, imagining from that perspective why a writer might want to bring forward the problem of writing. They can talk as readers, explaining the effects of these intrusions. Or they can talk as students—that is, through their knowledge of other attempts to represent an understanding of race, family, crime, drug addiction, or the black community.

For revision: Our experience with this assignment suggests that students can best use the time allotted for revision to work on the general issues raised in this paper. What might they say about Wideman's narrative intrusions? More particularly, what might this have to do with the writing they are doing—or might do—as students in the academy? What would the consequences be of producing a text that calls attention to itself as a text, as something produced?

ALTERNATIVE ASSIGNMENT

What We Read and Its Connection to Who We Are [Miller]

Our students took these assignments personally, many making a case for a piece of writing either that they had loved for years or that had recently knocked them down. Because Miller is so focused on what kind of difference writing can make in school, in our public, these essays expressed a moving mixture of personal investment and public concern. Students chose a myriad of genres—children's books, song lyrics, magazine articles, novels, memoirs—and though different genres presented different challenges, the choice itself was central to the assignment's success. Many students were surprised by how much they needed to reread Miller despite the fact that the assignment asked them to focus on an outside source. Students must possess a deep understanding of Miller's definition of critically optimistic writing in order to make a case for the piece that they choose. The "Questions for a Second Reading" may help students develop this understanding, but this particular writing assignment asks them to move from broad argumentative strokes to specific aspects of writing. For example, what kinds of moves does Miller want authors to make? And what purposes does he hope underlie these moves? Thinking about Miller's writing style itself—his persistence in asking difficult questions, his refusal to shy away from "why" and "could"—can help students translate Miller's big ideas into writerly actions. Students tended to use Miller to discover the set of questions that they thought were most important to Miller's project and most relevant to the piece they had chosen. With the set of questions or concerns that they brought from Miller, students recast writing that they had enjoyed privately as publicly relevant: besides my liking this book, they asked, what could it be said to be good for?

ALTERNATIVE ASSIGNMENT

Representing Others [Wideman]

Questions of representation and truth are writing problems, problems that all writers must wrestle with at some point. Wideman's writing might be considered to be more explicitly engaged with these questions, while Miller's piece is more implicitly engaged, suggesting through its particular movement the problem of representation and reality. Miller, like Wideman, makes the stories he tells his own, bending and molding them for the purposes of "The Dark Night of the Soul." Whether we're writing about ourselves or someone else, we must always choose what to include and exclude, where to begin and end, what portrait we will paint for our readers. On what basis do we decide, and what are the consequences of our decisions? We are always faced with the limits of language and representation, the limits of our perspective, the limits of any piece of writing to capture the complexities of identity. What kinds of ethical dilemmas do we face when we decide to write about others? What can we ever claim to really know about others? Are some representations more true, just, or valuable than others? By what means can we make such judgments responsibly? This assignment asks students to consider the difficulties of representation. In this essay, not only will students have a chance to offer an analysis of what Wideman and Miller suggest about representation and truth, but they will also have the opportunity to offer their own theories of truth, thinking carefully about the term, its definitions and its relevance to their own writing.

ALTERNATIVE ASSIGNMENT

Who Is Talking? [Jamie]

Jamie's written conversations feature prominently in "Shia Girls." Our students commented on the ways in which they were unaccustomed to reading essays with many long conversations. They wanted to make sense of them quickly, to imagine that those conversations could be said to be making specific points, but that's not the nature of Jamie's presentations of the conversations. During class discussions of the conversations that they identified, we kept coming back to the question of why. Why does Jamie include them in such detail? What do they allow her to accomplish? After these discussions, students began to imagine that the conversations are her project, that they allow her to present her subjects in ways more complex than if she simply reported on them or on what they said. The conversations, as one student said, paint pictures of the people as people, as people with things to say about their situations and those of others they know.

This writing assignment pairs wonderfully with the fourth writing assignment that invites students to try their hands at imitating Jamie's creation of conversations. That too, though, has its challenges, since it asks students for more than just copied-down conversations. It asks them to interweave observations and comments into the conversations, as Jamie does, to present talkers as a journalist might.

• • **•** • •

SEQUENCE TWO

The Aims of Education (p. 477)

In the introduction to this sequence, we say that these essays confront the relationship between the individual and structured ways of thinking represented by schooling. The goal of the sequence is to give students the feel of what it would be like to step outside of the assumptions that have governed their sense of school, assumptions that would otherwise be invisible or seem like a "natural" part of an adolescent's landscape. The rhythm of the sequence has students moving in to look at textual problems in the essays—to look at the essays as methods, as ways of seeing and questioning education—and then moving out to apply this new frame of reference to their own familiar surroundings. The final assignment is, in the broadest sense, a revision assignment. The first six assignments lead students to develop a single-minded view of "alternatives" to conventional education. The last assignment is a "taking stock" assignment. It says, in effect, now that you have been studying a single problem for some weeks (we would think twelve or thirteen), let's see what you have to say if you stand back from what you have done and make a final statement. The alternative assignments ask students to imitate them to study an unconventional academic project (Griffin's), one created by a desire to understand but written outside the usual conventions of history or the social sciences.

ASSIGNMENT 1

Applying Freire to Your Own Experience as a Student [Freire]

The most powerful and accessible part of Freire's essay for students is the banking metaphor. They will be able to use (or explain) this long before they can speak or write well about "problem-posing education" or about the "structure" of oppression. Structural analysis of social systems is a method they will learn. The banking metaphor gives a way of imagining teachers and students not as individuals but as tokens bound into a social structure. The assignment begins, then, with what students will do best. It asks them to take this metaphor and use it to frame (or invent) an episode from their own schooling. In addition, the assignment asks students to try their hands at using some of Freire's more powerful (or puzzling) terms and phrases. We want students to see how they might understand terms like "alienation," "problem-posing," or "dialectical" by putting those terms to use in commenting on their own experience. The final paragraph of the assignment is really a carrot for the best students—those who will get inside Freire's frame of mind, make his argument, and then feel that they have been denied the fun of speaking back or carving a position of their own. So, in Freire's name, it says, "Don't just do this passively. If you are going to carry on his work, you are going to be expected to make your own contribution, even at the expense of challenging this new orthodoxy."

For revision: When our students have written this essay, their first drafts, at their best, tell lively stories of an individual's experience in school or provide a tightly organized demonstration that their experience shows that Freire was "right." The goal of revision, we feel, should be to open these accounts up, to call them into question.

Perhaps because they are often young adults, and perhaps because they are (by and large) Americans, students translate Freire's account of social, political, and historical forces into a story of individuals—a mean teacher and an innocent student. One way to challenge this interpretation in its revision, then, would be to send students back to Freire's essay to see how he accounts for "agency"—"who is doing what to whom" in Freire's account of education. Once students have reread the essay with this in mind, they can go back to their own piece, making this story of individuals a story of "representative" individuals, where teacher and student play predetermined roles in the larger drama of American education, where teacher and student are figures through which the culture works through questions about independence and authority, about the production or reproduction of knowledge, about the relationship of the citizen to the society.

It is also the case, however, that the first drafts make quick work of Freire. We asked one of our students how he was able to sum up everything Freire said in three tidy pages. He replied, "It was easy. I left out everything I didn't understand and worked with what I did." This is a familiar strategy, one that is reinforced by teachers who have students read for "gist." Another strategy for revision is to have students go back to the sections of Freire's essay that they didn't understand or couldn't so easily control and to see how they might work those sections into what they have written. This is an opportunity for students to have a dialogue with Freire—not a debate, but a chance to put his words on the page and to say, in effect, "Here is what I think you are saying." This revision will pressure students to be resourceful in including quotations and representing and working on text. It makes a big difference, for example, whether a student uses Freire to conclude a point or whether a student uses Freire's language as material to work on. And, we should add, these different uses of Freire provide handy illustrations for a discussion of "problem-posing" education.

ASSIGNMENT 2

The Contact Zone [Pratt]

This is a powerful assignment that gives students the opportunity to represent schooling through stories or images from their experiences. Pratt's argument for the classroom as a "contact zone," a place where oppositional discourses rub against each other, clashes with conventional notions of the classroom as a community of like-minded individuals working toward common purposes. As students begin to imagine the classroom as a contact zone, as they settle into the identification of experiences and images, they'll want to classify them as "community" examples or "contact zone" examples, and you'll want to push them to see the possibilities between the polarities that Pratt establishes, or to imagine other ways of representing their experiences that don't set up polarities.

Once students have read Pratt, it'll be difficult for them not to classify their experiences, but this assignment relies on them to present representative examples of their experiences and images of schooling, those that come to mind almost immediately when they think of school, and they'll first need to present those. When they turn to interpreting their examples in Pratt's terms, they'll have a way to push against her by taking up the question of what they have to gain or lose if they adopt her ways of thinking.

It might be helpful for students to do the initial draft of this assignment with most, if not all, of their attention focused on rendering the representative experiences of schooling that they want to work from. They'll want to create (or re-create) the people involved in the scenes, the dialogue, and the landscape. Most students aren't accustomed to this kind of detailed scene setting; they'll need to render it carefully enough for readers not familiar with their experiences to see the people at work and the kinds of interactions going on so that when they discuss the scene as representing (or not representing) a contact zone, readers will be able to discern the oppositions, resistance, and alternatives being played out. The same holds true if they are representing a community.

The second draft or revision could then focus more directly on students weaving their comments into or alongside the scenes. This would be the paper, then, where they read their experiences in Pratt's terms and come to conclusions about what they stand to gain or lose by seeing their schooling in her terms.

ASSIGNMENT 3

The Pedagogical Arts of the Contact Zone [Pratt]

For this assignment, students are asked to imagine their writing class, the one that has presented them with this assignment, as a possible "contact zone." To this end, they are invited to take one of the "exercises" that Pratt presents and discuss how it might work in their class. You'll want to be sure that students think about this invitation in terms of turning their classroom into a visible contact zone, into a place, that is, where differences are visible and taken as occasions for learning. So, for instance, if students decide to fold storytelling into their work, they need to say what kind of storytelling. What will the stories be about? What will they learn from them? How will the stories act to turn the class into a contact zone? The same need for definition holds true for whatever exercise students decide on. If they would like to critique, then they need to say what they would critique and how critiquing would act to establish a visible contact zone. For a number of the exercises that Pratt suggests (e.g., "experiments in transculturation," "unseemly comparisons"), students will need to imagine what these are and how they would work in a writing classroom. There's room to move here, but they'll need to read Pratt closely to flesh out her more abstract pedagogical arts.

If students decide to imagine comments a teacher would make on one of their papers so that its revision might be one of these exercises, they have the same problem of definition to deal with. What would the comments ask them, for instance, to tell a story about? How would the revision act to establish a visible contact zone? What would they learn from this kind of revision?

ASSIGNMENT 4

Ways of Reading, Ways of Speaking, Ways of Caring [Rodriguez]

Essentially, this assignment asks students to locate and characterize Rodriguez's methods, his "ways of speaking and caring," his ways, that is, of presenting and valuing what he presents. He's making an argument about being a scholarship boy and, finally, about the differences between the reflective and the "passionate and spontaneous" life. Students need to consider how he presents his arguments and his materials (Hoggart, his recollections, and so on) and how he thinks through them on the page. They need, too, to name and characterize the ways he "speaks" and to figure out what it is he cares about now, in this text, and what he cared about during the various stages of his education. What can he do now, in writing and in his thinking, that he says he couldn't do earlier, in other moments of his evolution into a "speaking and caring" guy?

ASSIGNMENT 5

A Story of Schooling [Rodriguez]

Here, students are asked to reinvest their lives by framing their stories in Rodriguez's terms. It becomes a more powerful exercise if students try to do it in Rodriguez's style. As an opening exercise, they might write out a paragraph of his, using the shape of his sentences but filling in the names and details from their own experience. There is no reason, however, why students cannot write a personal essay that is more loosely suggested by Rodriguez's. They might lay a Rodriguez-like commentary over it, or include one with it.

The revision process will differ in each case. If students are concerned first with telling their own stories and then in speaking of them in Rodriguez's terms, then that commentary may be the focus of revision. If the essay is more completely a stylistic revision, then we would reverse the emphasis. The first thing students want to attend to is the form that will enable the writing—sentences and paragraphs and the relationship of anecdote to commentary. Then, in revision, they can best attend to the richness and detail of their own stories. As Scholes says about autobiography, the tension is between beauty and truth. You want to shape a story but also to honor the details of memory and investigation. In the revision, we would ask students to try to honor the truth of the stories they are telling.

ASSIGNMENT 6

The Literate Arts [Miller]

Our students took this assignment personally, many making a case for a piece of writing either that they had loved for years or that had recently knocked them down. Because Miller is so focused on what kind of difference writing can make in school, in our public, these essays expressed a moving mixture of personal investment and public concern.

Students chose a myriad of genres—children's books, song lyrics, magazine articles, novels, memoirs—and though different genres presented different challenges, the choice itself was central to the assignment's success. Many students were surprised by how much they needed to reread Miller despite the fact that the assignment asks them to focus on an outside source. Students must possess a deep understanding of Miller's definition of critically optimistic writing in order to make a case for the piece that they choose. The "Questions for a Second Reading" may help students develop this understanding, but this particular writing assignment asks them to move from broad argumentative strokes to specific aspects of writing. For example, what kinds of moves does Miller want authors to make? And what purposes does he hope underlie these moves? Thinking about Miller's writing style itself—his persistence in asking difficult questions, his refusal to shy away from "why" and "could"— can help students translate Miller's big ideas into writerly actions. Students tended to use Miller to discover the set of questions that they thought most important to Miller's project and most relevant to the piece they had chosen. With the set of questions or concerns that they brought from Miller, students recast writing that they had enjoyed privately as publicly relevant: besides my liking this book, they asked, what could it be said to be good for?

ASSIGNMENT 7

Making Connections [Freire, Pratt, Rodriguez, Miller]

To repeat some of what we have said for assignment 6, this writing assignment asks students to move from broad argumentative strokes to specific aspects of writing. Thinking about Miller's writing style itself—his persistence in asking difficult questions, his refusal to shy away from "why" and "could"—can help students translate Miller's big ideas into writerly actions. Students are asked to pay attention to nuances of both Miller and the other writers—Freire, Pratt, and Rodriguez—and they will need to perform some careful close reading of both the passages here and their contexts in order to articulate not only the tensions among them but also how these authors seem interested in some of the same questions. This assignment might illuminate for students how writers—making no direct reference to one another and having written their respective pieces years apart—might be engaged in an intellectual conversation that began long before them and will continue long after; we hope that students might be able to see themselves as engaged in this conversation as well.

ALTERNATIVE ASSIGNMENT

Writing against the Grain [Griffin]

Our students had a great time with this assignment, and it produced some of the most interesting writing of the semester. They chose topics that ranged from parental influences, the relationship of machines and thinking, the struggle to be, as one young woman called it, in an unfriendly environment of violence, the replication of behaviors in men from different generations of the same family, and the various metaphors for space. The key to students having a successful experience with this assignment seems to lie in the subjects they choose to write about and the stories they tell. We have told them to write about stories they know or would like to research because they are curious about them, because they sense connections to other stories or examples that they may or may not need to research. The students' involvement in the writing will push them to do the kinds of thinking through and connecting that imitates Griffin's work.

This assignment demonstrates to them the kind of planning and care that Griffin's work required, and our students found that they could help themselves with outlines and charts or maps of the territories they wanted to cover. We allowed them class time, also, to test their plans with other students and with us. This proved to be time well spent, for it helped students see connections that others saw and it prevented anyone from being lost at sea for anything but a brief period. In this assignment, we also took students through multiple drafts, and we assigned students to pairs at different points so that they could continually test their work against the readings of others.

ALTERNATIVE ASSIGNMENT

The Task of Attention [Griffin]

To involve themselves in this assignment, students will need to reread Griffin to locate those moments when she reveals her methods. At times, she tells us exactly what she is doing (looking at an etching, studying an interview, thinking about her past, imagining her subjects in their pasts, and so on), and students should pay attention to those moments; at other times, students will need to infer (or imagine, as she imagines) the work she had to do (to learn, for instance, about the V-1 rocket development or about Himmler's childhood or record keeping as a Nazi). The weight of their work, though, should fall on the methods that Griffin reveals and directly writes about to her readers. How do the methods shape her study and make it hers? And students will need to consider, then, how her methods might be taught in a curriculum. What would they like to see taught? Why? What would they (and others) learn from it? Where might her work fit in a curriculum? in a particular subject-area course or courses? in English classes? as a part of the writing curriculum?

• • ● • •

SEQUENCE THREE

The Arts of the Contact Zone (p. 486)

The great pleasure of teaching Pratt's essay is watching students put to work the key terms of her interpretive system: "contact zone," "autoethnography," "transculturation." These terms allow students to "reread" or reconceive familiar scenes and subjects; they also provide a rationale (as well as tools) for working against the grain of the usual American valorization of "community." At first, her argument seems completely counterintuitive;

then it begins to make powerful and surprising sense. At least this was our experience when we taught the essay. It was difficult, in fact, to get students (at the end of their work) to stand at a critical distance from Pratt's position—that is, the image of the contact zone provided a perhaps too easy answer to the problem of difference; or it led students to an unexamined reproduction of "liberal" values: sympathy, respect, different strokes for different folks.

This sequence allows students to work at length with Pratt's essay, first with (and on) her terms, later in conjunction with the work of others. You can imagine the sequence working in two directions. It is, in keeping with a standard pattern in *Ways of Reading*, designed as an exercise in application. Students take the general project represented in "Arts of the Contact Zone," work those terms out through close reading and through application to an example from students' experience, and then apply it to essays in *Ways of Reading* that could be said to represent examples of the literate arts of the contact zone—essays by Anzaldúa, Wideman, and Said. Our goal in teaching this sequence, however, was also to invite students to begin to imagine that, through their work with these authors, they were in a position to talk back to Pratt—adding examples, perhaps counterexamples, testing the limits of her terms, adding new terms, thinking about Pratt's discussion of Guaman Poma and her discussion of "community," its usefulness and its limits in a more extended project, drawing not only on the resources of *Ways of Reading* but also on students' readings of documents drawn from their local communities.

If you wanted to shorten the sequence, you could drop one of the readings (Anzaldúa, Said, or Wideman). There is an alternative selection by Kathleen Jamie that could be substituted for one of those we have included here.

We chose the selections for this sequence because we wanted to focus the term "contact" on racial, ethnic, and linguistic differences. If you add other selections, you might want to focus attention on the range of differences (age, class, nation, institutional or intellectual status) that can be highlighted under the term "contact zone."

For a complete commentary on the selections in this sequence, please be sure to read each essay's selection in this manual, particularly the opening discussion. While we will cull materials from the discussions of individual assignments, we won't reproduce the introductions. And, while the sequences provide writing assignments, you should think about the advantages (or disadvantages) of using the "Questions for a Second Reading." In every case, students should read the headnotes in the text, which are designed to serve the assignments and sequences.

ASSIGNMENT 1

The Literate Arts of the Contact Zone [Pratt]

The first assignment is structurally a bit complicated. It offers two options, an "inventory" assignment (for which students collect examples of writing from a contact zone) and an "autoethnography" assignment (for which students imagine themselves as writers working in a contact zone). What complicates things is that the inventory assignment also offers two options. There are really three writing assignments listed here, grouped into two categories. You may want to make the choice of assignment for your students, depending on the goals of your course. The autoethnography assignment focuses the issues of Pratt's essays within students' self-representations, within the context of the "personal" essay. The inventory assignment focuses attention on students as readers (and archivists) of other writers' work. Whichever direction students take, we suggest letting them come back to revise their essays later in the semester. If you plan to work this way, it might be useful to tell students that they will be working on a draft they can come back to later.

1. The first of the two options in assignment 1 is an "inventory" assignment, asking students to collect documents that could stand, like the *New Chronicle*, as evidence of the literate arts of the contact zone. Pratt's essay provides a frame to organize the search (a frame students should imagine that they can break—that is, they can take it as a challenge to find the document that would surprise Pratt, that she would overlook or never think of), and it also provides the terms for a discussion of the material they collect (or representative examples from that material).

The assignment suggests two ways of conducting the inventory. The first sends students to a library (or historical society) to find documents from the past. We tried to suggest the many possible moments of contact in local history (between slaves and owners, workers and management, women and men, minority and majority). This assignment was prompted by Jean Ferguson Carr's teaching at Pitt (her courses almost always include some kind of archival project) and Pat Bizzell's teaching at Holy Cross (where she has students research local accounts of European settlements written by Native Americans). We were frustrated by the degree to which students feel removed from library archives and the degree to which our teaching (and the textbook) seemed to enforce that remove. Needless to say, this option will seem to be the harder of the two, and students will need some prompting or challenge or rewards to choose it. One thing to remember is that an assignment like this will take more time than usual, since it takes time to find the library and spend enough time in the stacks to make the experience profitable, more than a quick search for the one book that will get you through the assignment. We've also found that we needed to make the process of search and selection an acknowledged part of the work of the course. We ask students to collect folders of material, to present them to others (to the class, to groups), and, in their essays, to talk about how they chose the material they chose to write about.

In the second "inventory" option, students might go out into their local culture to look for "documents" (which can be defined loosely to include music, like rap, transcripts of talk shows, films, documentaries, Web pages, and so on). Students should feel that they can follow Pratt's lead and turn to their brothers and sisters (or their children) and to educational materials, including papers they are writing or have written recently. You should think about whether or not you would want students to choose papers from your course. It is an interesting possibility, but it will be hard for students to write about you and your class as anything *but* a utopia, paradise on earth. You may be disappointed if you invite students to take your classroom as an example.

Taking either direction, students are asked to present their material as part of a project Pratt has begun. We have found it important to remind students that they need to present "Arts of the Contact Zone," even to readers who have read it. You cannot assume, we remind our students, that readers have it freshly in mind or that they will be willing to get the book off the shelf and turn to pages. And we have found it important to help students imagine the role they will play in this text. They will need, in other words, to do more than simply cite from or summarize what they have gathered in their inventories. They will need to step forward (as Pratt does) to teach, translate, make connections, explain, comment, discuss, think this way and that. Students, at least our students, are often too quick to let the wonderful material they gather speak for itself.

2. This assignment asks students to write an "autoethnography." The inventory assignments in this set ask students to use Pratt's term "contact zone" to read the work of others. This assignment asks students to write from the contact zone, to show how they understand Pratt's argument through their practice.

It is important, as a starting point, to ask students to imagine how this might be different from writing an autobiography. In a sense, autobiographies have historically been read as autoethnographies. But as these terms define a *writer's* motive, it will be important for many students to imagine from the outset that they occupy a position likely to be ignored or un-read or misread. It can be useful to think of the ways writers signal that they are "engaging with representations" others make of them ("many people would say . . . ," "I have been called . . . ," "some might refer to this as . . . ," "from a different point of view . . ."). This is also a good time to return to the lists Pratt offers of the literate arts of the contact zone ("parody," "unseemly comparisons," "bilingualism," "imaginary dialogue," etc.). These lists can serve as a writer's toolkit—or perhaps, as a way of beginning to imagine revision.

ASSIGNMENT 2

Borderlands [Pratt, Anzaldúa]

One of the pleasures of working with Pratt's essay is that it gave us a new way of reading our table of contents. There are several pieces that could stand as examples of writing from a contact zone (or that could be said equally to illustrate the "literate arts of the contact zone"). This assignment turns students' attention to the *mestiza* text *Borderlands/La frontera*. You could also use the selections by Rodriguez and Wideman.

This is an application assignment—it asks for a generous reading and extension of Pratt's work. As always, students should feel free to exceed their example—to argue with Pratt, to notice things she wouldn't notice, to add to her list of the literate arts of the contact zone. And as always, it will help to give students a sense of what they will need to provide for their readers. They will need to present Pratt's essay (to establish it as a context). They cannot simply assume that it is there, in full, in their readers' minds. And they will need to present their example, providing an introduction to (let's say) "Incidents" and working closely with the text, including passages in quotation. (Since Pratt does not provide examples of the close reading of passages in "Arts of the Contact Zone," it might be useful to provide supplementary examples.) We have worked with pages from "Scratches on the

Face of the Country" (from Pratt, *Imperial Eyes*). You might also help students prepare by working on a set passage from Anzaldúa in class.

For us, every assignment (or almost every assignment) in a sequence goes through at least one revision. We would, that is, spend two weeks on most assignments. If students revise this essay, we would suggest two prompts for their work. When they revise, they should begin by rereading Anzaldúa, looking for those parts of the text that have not been accounted for in the first draft. Students shouldn't simply be pasting in more examples but should be looking to see the interesting examples that were left out and asking why, on a first pass, these fell outside their range of vision/understanding/desire. And they should be looking for ways (or places) to speak from their own positions as authors/scholars. Students should, that is, be looking to see how and where they can find a place in their essays to speak from their own learning and concerns. Here is the place where students begin to talk about the limits and benefits, for them, of Pratt's work.

ASSIGNMENT 3

Counterparts [Wideman]

Whereas the other assignments in this sequence ask students to use Pratt's term "contact zone" in an intellectual project, this assignment asks them to write an "auto-ethnography" from the contact zone, to show how they understand Pratt's argument through their practice.

It is important, as a starting point, to ask students to imagine how this task might be different from writing an autobiography. In a sense, autobiographies have historically been read as "autoethnographies." But as these terms define a *writer's* motive, it will be important for many students to imagine from the outset that they occupy a position likely to be ignored or unread or misread. It can be useful to think of the ways writers signal that they are "engaging in representations" others make of them ("many people would say . . . ," "I have been called . . . ," "some might refer to this as . . . ," "from a different point of view . . ."). This is also a good time to return to the lists Pratt offers of the literate arts of the contact zone ("parody," "unseemly comparisons," "bilingualism," "imaginary dialogue," and so on). These lists can serve as a writer's toolkit or, perhaps, as a way of beginning to imagine revision.

ASSIGNMENT 4

A Dialectic of Self and Other [Pratt, Said]

Said's "States" is, for this assignment, a case to further develop and test Pratt's notions of a contact zone as social and intellectual space that is not homogeneous or unified and where understanding and valuing difference can occur. The object, then, for students is to read "States" as a project in light of Pratt's notions. How might they write about Said's writing, and the other writings represented in "States," as a contact zone where difference is valued and understanding is the point? How can they think about the cultures represented in "States," through Said's writing, as such contact zones? To figure this assignment, students will need to reread both essays. They'll need to work from moments in both as well. It is particularly important that students identify examples in "States" that they can use to test and further develop Pratt's ideas about the contact zone and what might happen there socially and intellectually and, of course, in writing.

ASSIGNMENT 5

On Culture [Pratt, Anzaldúa, Wideman, Said]

We often end our sequences with "retrospective" assignments. This one asks students to return to Pratt's essay and to the work they have been doing with it in order to represent that work to someone who is an outsider. For the first time, however, the issue has been represented through the more inclusive term "culture." This assignment is a way for students to connect the work they have been doing with Pratt with larger questions of culture and community, reading and writing. Directing the assignment at an audience new to this material allows students to work from their strengths and to imagine the distance between what they have learned to say and where they began. To this end, it is important for this assignment that students imagine their audience to be a group of peers, people like them who have not been in this course. Without this warning, students tend to represent the "intellectual other" as a child or a simpleton. The stakes have to be high for this paper to work—students need to imagine that they have to address and hold the attention of their sharpest and most intellectually impatient colleagues.

An alternative to this assignment would be one directed not to students but to Pratt. We often end sequences with this other retrospective, in which the goal, we say, is for students to take their turn in a conversation begun by Pratt. Here, the pressure on them is to achieve some critical distance from Pratt, to find a way of challenging or supplementing what Pratt says on the basis of what they (the students) have learned over the course of their work with this sequence.

As we suggested earlier, it might be useful to ask students to work again on the first assignment in this sequence in a second or third draft. That way, the issues as they have bearing on what students do (how they read and write) and not just on what they know (in summary statement) will be forward in their minds. From this, they can begin to write to Pratt, or to students, perhaps students who would be reading the same materials in this course next semester. After a semester, you will have some of these essays on file. We have handed them out at the beginning of the term as a preview, and then brought them forward again at the end, in a discussion framing students' work with this final assignment.

ALTERNATIVE ASSIGNMENT

Producing Place [Jamie]

Many of our assignments ask students to work with the idea that writing (and images, and perhaps even speaking) *produces* realities rather than just reflects them, which might be the more conventional way of understanding writing. This question is no exception. In becoming more advanced readers and writers, students learn how to think critically about the how and why of production, keeping construction and motivation at the center of their attention as they think through both authors' work. We have found that having more broad discussions about travel writing has helped students work with this assignment. For example, on one occasion, we brought in a typical travel guide (in this case, it was a guide from Italy). Students quickly saw that the language was about "selling Italy" and that the writing produced an exotic and romantic Italy. We found it was useful for them to begin with the question: So what is Jamie doing that's different? One student observed, for instance, that the guide to Italy contained very few references to actual Italian people living in Italy. This was an interesting moment to launch them into this assignment. Because the assignments in *Ways of Reading* are often difficult, it can always be useful to help students see that they already know how to do the kind of work the question asks of them.

$$\cdots\cdots\bullet\cdots\cdots$$

SEQUENCE FOUR

Autobiographical Explorations (p. 493)

People often speak of *Ways of Reading* as though it were an argument against "personal writing." It is certainly *not* an argument against having students write autobiographically, drawing their subjects and expertise from prior knowledge and experience; almost every selection is followed by such assignments. Nor is it an argument against the genre of the personal essay; several selections in the anthology belong to that genre. And the course we teach always asks students to write from "life" as well as from texts.

There are arguments here, however. For the moment, let us say that they have to do with (1) how students learn to imagine the sources of their autobiographical writing and (2) how they learn to imagine its revision.

In one tradition of instruction, autobiographical writing begins with a set of relaxation and self-awareness exercises. Take a deep breath. Pretend this isn't school. Look into your heart and write. If you look at the assignments in this sequence, they all argue (if indirectly) that a writer *begins* by imagining a genre (a history of autobiographical writing) and the problems of representation, problems that are easily overlooked (or suppressed) when writers write about themselves. In this sequence, students always begin with a prior text (part of a history of what we refer to as an "American" genre) and with a discussion of that text as an attempt to rework the genre, to experiment or to work on the problems of representation and problems of understanding.

We tend not to build the revision assignments into the sequence, but this sequence (like all the others) assumes regular revision, where students work on a first draft one week and a revision the next. In the look-into-your-heart school of instruction, revision is a search for greater authenticity—finding a voice, providing more grounding detail. In our courses, it is not unusual for us to direct attention to "voice" and "detail," but the position of the writer is more combative. Rather than asking students to seek a voice or to look for details, most of our instruction is instruction in reading—in learning how to read their own texts (and their colleagues') with the same close critical attention they have used for Rodriguez (or any of the "real" authors in the course). The assigned readings serve as models of writers' work *on* writing problems, problems represented by words like "voice" and "detail." And the work we do with them as a class teaches an attention to language that a writer can use to revise. Students, then, learn to see the work of revision as a work with (and against) the language of the first draft, not "finding" a voice but finding where the language on the page is "voiceless" or "voiced" in ways that are troubling, where "voice" becomes a useful term to describe a kind of work with sentences (and not a therapeutic search for a pure center).

In a sense, then, the assignments in this sequence provide a repeated exercise in in-authenticity. Students write like someone else, someone else writing with a deep sense of the problems of identity and representation; in doing so, they learn something about autobiographical writing. And they get to work with materials close to home and close to the heart. We couldn't imagine teaching a writing course where students didn't feel that something was at stake—with both the first offering and the work of revision. Locating the problems of writing for students in "my voice" and "my experience" is a powerful way of producing those effects.

ASSIGNMENT 1

Desire, Reading, and the Past [Rodriguez]

When our students wrote in response to this assignment, what they took from Rodriguez was a tone (elegiac, negative, brooding) and a theme, a frame for the story of their own experiences (using the themes of family and schooling). Some of the most interesting essays have followed Rodriguez's formal lead quite closely by including something the student writer had read (the student's equivalent of the Hoggart passage). Without question, these were the papers that most caught students' attention when we reproduced papers for class discussion. This device prompted students to think (with Rodriguez) about how thinking *like* someone else allows you to "be" yourself, but, more important, students took pleasure in realizing that personal experience can *also* be intellectual experience. It is *not* that students don't read books or have intellectual lives, but that the usual classroom genre of the personal essay puts a premium on action and consequence. Rodriguez's essay allowed students access to a different representation of the "personal," and this was both surprising and (for some) invigorating.

A quick note: If you are concerned with how quickly students cast themselves as Rodriguez in their first drafts, it might make sense to organize the revision around sorting out the differences.

ASSIGNMENT 2

A Photographic Essay [Said]

It has been important to us to teach students to see writing as "work," including a work against, or in response to, habit and convention, and for students to think about the ideology of style. Writing is not just fitting new content into standard forms. A discussion like this can be crucial in allowing students to make the connection between what they read and what they write.

This assignment uses Said's discussion of the necessity of an "alternative mode of representation" to call attention to style, method, and arrangement. It asks students to first re-read the essay as an experiment, as a piece of writing set against the norms and conventions of, in Said's terms, journalism, political science, and popular fiction. For students, "States" can best be read against what they take to be the conventions of report and argument, usually represented by a term like "the essay."

After this preparation, students are asked to compose a Said-like reading of a set of photos. In the assignment, the following sentences are important and worth calling attention to in advance:

> These can be photos prepared for the occasion (by you or a colleague); they could also be photos already available. Whatever their source, they should represent people and places, a history and/or geography that you know well, that you know to be complex and contradictory, and that you know will not be easily or readily understood by others, both the group for whom you will be writing (most usefully the members of your class) and readers more generally. You must begin with a sense that the photos cannot speak for themselves; you must speak for them.

Students, that is, are not just describing photos; they are using the photos to represent people and places, history and/or geography, to an audience unprepared to understand them. The selection and arrangement of photos are important, in other words. They are part of the work of writing this text. And the text that accompanies these photos should approximate the style and method in "States." The prose, in other words, is not simply captions, one after another. There should be an essay, a text with its own integrity, that is written with pictures. So—it is important to have students think about audience and occasion. What is the project? To whom are they writing? What is their relationship to subject and reader? And it is important to let students know in advance that they need to take time selecting the photographs and thinking about how they might be arranged. (It is useful to have them talk about what they left out and about plans they abandoned.) And they need to think about the writing; they are not writing captions. To think about what they might write, they can return to "States" to examine what it is that Said is doing and how he does it. The writing can (perhaps should) be homage or imitation, an attempt to do something similar.

ASSIGNMENT 3

The Matrix [Griffin]

This is another challenging assignment, but the fascination of the text will more than make up for it. Our students have always found relevance in this text, and although it is written in an unusual style of interspersed passages, the juxtapositions have engaged rather than troubled our students. Much of the compelling nature of this piece has to do with the subject matter and the mystery of the connections within it. Griffin writes about the makeup of a cell, of DNA and RNA, of herself, her family, Heinrich Himmler, various people subject to and complicit with Himmler's agendas, Käthe Kollwitz, and the development of the V-1 rocket. She interweaves segments of these various texts, so the effect is a collage, but it's one that compels students, and ours have always been eager to discuss and write about this selection. One of the central questions Griffin raises by the juxtaposition of these texts and their interrelated subjects, and in her commentary, has to do with who we are. She asks over and over: Who are we? Who are we who can do these things? Who are we who can suffer them? Who are we who can change them?

To answer this question with all of its nuances and twists and turns, students will need to read this text twice. The first reading should be done to become familiar with it, to see what she's doing, and then to discuss what they make of it. After they have had the opportunity to do this, they can read it a second time, noting the moments when Griffin seems to imply answers to this question of who we are by her juxtapositions, her allusions, and, of course, moments when she directly comments on the question. It would be a mistake for students to expect consistency or seamlessness here. They will have to tie things together, mark a trajectory through a lot of material, much of it with contrary indications.

ASSIGNMENT 4

The Experience of Thought [Miller]

This question focuses on the reader, on the kind of reader Miller seems to be in his essay, and the kinds of readers students might be as they read both Miller and the texts Miller interprets. This question also points students to the problem of what a reader does with a text when he or she writes about it. Students will be able to consider that once we start writing, we are revising the text we have read, following our own agendas, speaking in place of the text. This, of course, as the question suggests, is part of the broader project of *Ways of Reading* itself and a part of our understanding that reading and writing are intimately bound. This assignment blurs the distinctions between reading and writing and hopes to open an opportunity for students to explore that blurring.

ASSIGNMENT 5

The "I" of the Personal Essay [Rodriguez, Said, Miller]

This retrospective assignment asks students to review their work in this sequence, thinking it over in terms of its underlying argument. We've used assignments like this as a regular feature in courses we teach. While they are often a useful exercise, a way of taking stock or focusing on the "theory" in the course, they don't always produce good writing. The prose is sometimes mechanical or dutiful. For the writing to be good, students will need to be serious about working *with* their own prose. They will need to be as careful in selecting and presenting passages as they are when they work from passages in Rodriguez, Miller, or Said. Even though you have been their teacher and editor for several weeks, they must now imagine a reader needing an overview of their prose (or they need to be reminded that you have not committed their work to memory, nor do you keep it by your bedside). They need to think of this assignment as a *writing* assignment (and not just as an end-of-term exercise). We have identified this text as a preface. Since our students are also turning in a portfolio, the text becomes the lead-in to a collection of essays. The hard work is convincing students to think of us as readers and not simply as teachers who are about to give them a final grade.

ALTERNATIVE ASSIGNMENT

Old Habits [Wideman]

With this assignment our intent was to focus on features of the text that could be transported to students' writing — the provisional openings ("What if I started here?"), the use of italics to mark different ways of speaking, the line breaks in the text, the authorial intrusions. We wanted students to begin with formal concerns and, from those, to think about the life story or the family story. This is primarily a writing assignment, in other words, and only secondarily an exercise in "discovery" or "revelation." The goal was not to see what students could learn about their families but to see what they could learn about writing and "real" life by conducting a Wideman-like methodological experiment. This has been a particularly successful assignment for us. The use of italics seems to authorize students to bring other voices and points of view into their writing, and often with dramatic effect (where we hear two parents speaking rather than hearing about an abstraction, Parents). And students feel the power of the fragmented (as opposed to the hierarchically organized) text. It allows them to follow a train of thought through structures of elaboration usually excluded from the writing classroom. And it is wonderful to finesse the problem of the "beginning."

ALTERNATIVE ASSIGNMENT

Graphic Autobiography [Bechdel]

In some ways, Bechdel's comments about telling her story are linked to the ones Wideman makes in his essay. When we choose readings that might be characterized as "autobiographical," we always seek to select readings that complicate the notion of telling a story or telling "the truth" of what happened. The story Bechdel wants to tell, a story of a mother-daughter relationship, is a very familiar story. So this assignment invites students to think of Bechdel's narrative as a genre and to look for other examples of the genre.

Some students have latched on to the mother-daughter genre, while others think of Bechdel's work as being in a genre of art that is self-conscious about its own making. One student remarked, "Reading Bechdel is like watching one of those movies where someone narrates the story the movie tells, as though the movie was separate from the voiceover." When students recognize connections between the pieces we focus on in class and the narratives with which they are already familiar, they often see new things about the piece they are writing about. Learning how to read in order to write means always trying to find multiple entry points into a text, to open up a new way of seeing Bechdel so that readers might also experience that viewpoint.

· · ● · ·

SEQUENCE FIVE

Experts and Expertise (p. 500)

We use the metaphor of apprenticeship several times in the textbook. This is the assignment sequence that features this particular use of texts. The assignments invite students to take on the key terms and angle of vision of each essay, to imagine that each author has begun a project and that the students, once they have been given the tools and have gotten the hang of what is going on, are to carry it on in the spirit of the master. The last assignment, in the name of Walker Percy, asks students to look back at what they have done and to question just what is at stake or what can be gained by taking on someone else's way of thinking and speaking in just this way. While we want students to have the opportunity of looking critically at this kind of imitation, we also want them to feel the power of it. It is, as we say, heady work. Students are given ways of thinking and speaking that they would not invent on their own—at least not so quickly and not in such rapid succession. And they are given a sense of Appiah, Butler, and Said that goes well beyond an encyclopedia-like recitation of the authors' key ideas.

Note: In the case of each assignment, it would be a good idea to go to the sections in the manual on each author and review what we say there as well. There are statements about the essays and about writing assignments that have bearing on the sequence but that we won't repeat here.

ASSIGNMENT 1

Depicting the Intellectual [Appiah, Wallace]

This assignment asks students to assess depictions of the intellectual figures Appiah and Wallace construct in their essays by working closely with a few key moments in each text. The quality of the work will certainly be improved if students have a chance to revise this essay. Their energies in the first draft will be directed to understanding how Appiah and Wallace depict this figure. After students have formally completed this project, the essay will feel complete—or it has felt complete to our students. And so we have found it very useful to send them back to revise—not simply to improve what they had done (to make it more correct or self-contained) but to write new pages and develop new sections of the essay—ones that assess the figure of the intellectual in relation to their own educations and to the figures they intend to cut for themselves as well-schooled adults.

ASSIGNMENT 2

A Question for Philosophers [Butler]

Students seemed to need to move through Butler's essay slowly. We spent a good deal of time in the first few classes after students had read the essay asking them to identify passages from the essay that were particularly difficult to understand or follow so that we could move through them together and linger on their difficulties. This assignment works to complement the spirit of that close reading. Taking Butler's sentences one phrase, or sometimes one word, at a time helps students not only to make meaning from that specific sentence but also to learn how to read a Judith Butler sentence. One of the challenges with reading Butler and with the density of her work is that students can lose sight of the reading's connection to LGBTQ realities. This question also asks students to consider the political and personal implications of their close reading of Butler, calling attention both to Butler's project as a whole and to the significance of that project in context.

ASSIGNMENT 3

On Representation [Said]

It has been important to us to teach students to see writing as "work," including a work against, or in response to, habit and convention, and for students to think about the ideology of style. Writing is not just fitting new content into standard forms. An assignment like this can be crucial in allowing students to make the connection between what they read and what they write.

Students should first use Said's discussion of the necessity of an "alternative mode of representation" to call attention to style, method, and arrangement. They should reread Said's essay as an experiment, as a piece of writing set against the norms and conventions of, in Said's terms, journalism, political science, and popular fiction. For students, "States" can best be read against what they take to be the conventions of report and argument, usually represented by a term like "the essay."

After this preparation, students are asked to compose a Said-like reading of a set of photos. Students, that is, are not just describing photos; they are using the photos to represent people and places, history and/or geography—in this case, contemporary Palestinians— to an audience unprepared to understand them. The selection and arrangement of photos are important, in other words. They are part of the work of writing this text. And the text that accompanies these photos should approximate the style and method in "States." The prose, in other words, is not simply captions, one after another. There should be an essay, a text with its own integrity, that is written with pictures. So—it is important to have students think about audience and occasion. What is the project? To whom are they writing? What is their relationship to subject and reader? And it is important to let students know in advance that they need to take time selecting the photographs and thinking about how they might be arranged. (It is useful to have them talk about what they left out and about plans they abandoned.) And they need to think about the writing; they are not writing captions. To think about what they might write, they must return to "States" to examine what it is that Said is doing and how he does it. The writing can (perhaps should) be homage or imitation, an attempt to do something similar.

ASSIGNMENT 4

On Experts and Expertise [Appiah, Butler, Said, Percy]

Previous assignments repeat a basic pattern. They ask students to take on the ways of speaking and thinking of other powerful thinkers—to be apprentices. They imagine (with the aid of a text) an "Appiah," a "Butler," and a "Said," and then work in his or her spirit. This assignment invites students to reflect on what they have done, this time in the name of a "Walker Percy," who says that there is nothing more dangerous for a student than to get into the hands of an expert theorist. Students, in a sense, are being invited to fold their own stories into the anecdotes about students in the second section of "The Loss of the Creature." This will be a difficult assignment for students who have done no prior work on Percy. It might be useful, in fact, either to allow time for a preliminary assignment or to allow time for this essay to go through several drafts. Percy's argument lends itself so easily to cliché (partly because he refuses to come forward as a theorist and provide a useful analytical language of his own) that students will need to have a complicated sense of how his essay works if they are to do justice to this assignment. (You don't, in other words, want students to be trapped in the corner of talking about nothing more than "the need to be an individual.") It is also important that students focus in on their work in the previous assignments: they will need, that is, to have good stories of their own to tell as well as the encouragement to select and quote from their own texts.

ALTERNATIVE ASSIGNMENT

A Story of Reading [Miller]

Our students took this assignment personally, many making a case for a piece of writing either that they had loved for years or that had recently knocked them down. Because Miller is so focused on what kind of difference writing can make in school, in our public, these essays expressed a moving mixture of personal investment and public concern. Students chose a myriad of genres—children's books, song lyrics, magazine articles, novels, memoirs—and though different genres presented different challenges, the choice itself was central to the assignment's success. Many students were surprised by how much they needed to reread Miller despite the fact that the assignment asks them to focus on an outside source. Students must possess a deep understanding of Miller's definition of critically optimistic writing in order to make a case for the piece that they choose. The "Questions for a Second Reading" may help students develop this understanding, but this particular writing assignment asks them to move from broad argumentative strokes to specific aspects of writing. For example, what kinds of moves does Miller want authors to make? And what purposes does he hope underlie these moves? Thinking about Miller's writing style itself—his persistence in asking difficult questions, his refusal to shy away from "why" and "could"—can help students translate Miller's big ideas into writerly actions. Students tend to use Miller to discover the set of questions that they thought were most important to Miller's project and most relevant to the piece they had chosen. With the set of questions or concerns that they brought from Miller, students recast writing that they had enjoyed privately as publicly relevant: besides my liking this book, they asked, what could it be said to be good for?

ALTERNATIVE ASSIGNMENT

Models for Thinking [Schulz]

Most of our writing assignments also include a project where students extend the project of what they had read to some other context, here a piece of writing. In this assignment, students turn either to a published piece of prose or to some of their own writing (and its revision) in order to talk about "due diligence" and "models of thinking."

The students struggled more with this assignment. They are not yet adept at producing a "close reading" on the page. It takes times and much direct instruction to learn how to work with block quotations, for example, and how to see prose as *doing* or *enacting* rather than just *saying* something. Still, we think this is an important lesson for students to learn. If I were to teach this material again, I would most certainly use this assignment.

ALTERNATIVE ASSIGNMENT

Short Talks [Carson]

This kind of assignment is not uncommon in *Ways of Reading*—assignments that ask students to imitate, mimic, or work in the spirit of another writer in order to learn something about that particular writer's project or sensibility. However, Carson's collection of short talks is not exactly an essay. In fact, we are not quite sure what it is. Some teachers may even feel nervous about this assignment because students will produce writing that is not measurable as an essay, per se. But, of course, we find this ambiguity to be one of the joys and possibilities of both Carson's work and the work students will do in trying to take on a short talks project of their own. Students will likely surprise you and themselves with their creativity. An assignment like this allows for the kinds of writing that emerge when the process itself is so strange and unfamiliar.

• • • **•** • • •

SEQUENCE SIX

Reading Culture (p. 506)

As we say in its introduction in the text, this sequence asks students to imagine culture as a large organizing force, one in which they are situated and implicated, one that shapes, organizes, and controls the ways we think, speak, act, and write. There is a power in this form of analysis that students can feel and share, but it comes at the expense of the usual celebrations of freedom, free will, and individuality. The usual ways of talking about experience will be displaced by this sequence. You and your students will have to work hard from the opening moments of the course to keep a watchful eye open for vestiges of the "old" ways of speaking; to stop, now and then, when you hear it at work in language, for instance, about what is "natural" or "true" or "obvious"; to bracket it; to put its key terms on the blackboard; and to imagine why it is attractive and how one might understand its limits. The pattern in this sequence is fairly straightforward. Students read the work of several critics, and they are asked to reproduce (or revise) their methods in critical writing of their own.

The sequence moves back and forth between summary and application. Students are asked to reproduce a form of critique (extending Bordo's project, for example) and then to work closely with the assumptions behind a critical project (like Berger's and Foucault's), asking fundamental questions: How do they do their work? Why? How might their projects be thought of as similar? The final assignment asks students to bring all of the work together, to select, edit, and revise, and to write a longer, more finished essay.

ASSIGNMENT 1

Looking at Pictures [Berger]

The Berger assignment is designed to familiarize the exotic (by asking students to "converse" with high art). Berger argues that criticism should turn to everyday language, to force connections between life and art. Berger turns against "academic" criticism to represent what he would like us to believe is the human reality of art and the perception of art. This is both compelling and problematic. Berger speaks in a voice students admire. It is difficult, however, to get students to read against that voice, to question the ease with which Berger assumes he knows the reality of history or the ease with which he assumes a kind of universal human experience, one that he understands because he has cut through the crap.

We've had a good deal of success with this assignment. Ideally, students should have ready access to a museum. Berger talks about the ways we have come to experience paintings in museums, and a trip to a museum to look at a painting will give students a way of adding to or reflecting on Berger's argument. But he also talks about reproductions, so we felt justified in adding the option for students to go to art books in the library. If you can reasonably expect your students to get to a museum, however, we think the trip will hold some interesting surprises for you. We usually schedule a class meeting at the museum—just to get the students in and walking around to think about which painting might be "theirs." Warn students against docents and taped tours—for your purposes, these prepared readings of paintings will be a real barrier to writing.

The students who have had the most success with this assignment have been fairly literal in their sense of what it means to have a "conversation" with a painting. Their essays, that is, have not read as museum-guide-like interpretations but as more open-ended and speculative pieces, sometimes cast as a narrative with dialogue, sometimes as pure dialogue. The key is to invite students to "talk" to the painting, to ask questions, and to imagine rich and ambiguous responses. It is best to have students avoid papers that begin with an idea of what a picture is about and simply impose that reading on the material. The painting needs to be imagined to talk back, to counter or open up a student's desire to master and control.

For revision: In some cases we've found that we needed to send students back to the painting and the original assignment, usually because students were more concerned to push through a single reading than to have a conversation with their material. In most cases, however, we used the revision as the occasion to send students back to the Berger essay. As they become involved with the museum assignment, students (in a sense) forgot about Berger, and so we used the revision to send them back, to see what use they can make of his way of talking about paintings or about the museum. (For example, "How could you use the example of your essay to explain what Berger might mean when he talks about 'history'?") The idea here is to engage them in a conversation with Berger, where your students can draw on their expertise to enter his argument.

ASSIGNMENT 2

Berger and After [Berger, Bordo]

To use Bordo's essay in a reconsideration of Berger's, students will obviously need to work with both essays. This is the kind of assignment that makes considerable demands on students, particularly of their close readings of Bordo's and Berger's examples as representatives of their respective arguments about the readings and uses of images. Because this is the case, students will need to do preliminary work both in discussions of their readings of each essay and in at least one piece of writing for each in which they work through a set of two or three images and discuss the ways each author uses those images to promote arguments and positions. What are each author's arguments and positions on readings and uses of images?

From this preliminary work, students will be ready to put the two essays next to each other to consider whether they're doing the same work and saying the same things. The key, of course, is to be certain that students are working from at least two images for each text, so that their arguments will be grounded in those and develop, then, as minicases. When students consider the relation of Bordo's work to Berger's, they'll need to imagine that Bordo is in some way extending and transforming Berger's. Berger came first, but it's not a cause-and-effect relationship. Bordo uses Berger, so students will need to imagine that she is on her own trajectory through the reading of the images that have caught her attention. Berger offers her a way to read and understand them. What material of Berger's does she use? How does she transform Berger's ideas? How, finally, might their work be understood to be similar and different?

ASSIGNMENT 3

Reading the Body [Bordo]

The invitation here to students is to extend Bordo's project, to present readers with at least the outlines and fundamental terms of her work in this essay, to read a set of ads as she does, using her methods, and to locate themselves as subjects with positions that are relative to them. It's a challenging piece of work, and you will want to begin it by giving students opportunities to discuss the assignment itself. You might ask students: "What are you being asked to do? What do you need to do in your essay? How do you identify and write from your subject position?"

If students have already completed the fourth second-reading question for the Bordo selection (which we recommend as prefatory work for this assignment), they will have collected the examples from which they can work. If not, then they'll need to set about doing this with an eye to identifying ads that allow them to make claims for the ways the ads promote specific notions of "what it means to be a man," as Bordo puts it.

It would be fun to extend this project beyond the boundaries of representations of the male by asking students to complete a second part in which they do a Bordo-like study of ads that represent particular ways of being a woman. Their methods of working would be similar, and once they had done both, they could imagine, for instance, the ways in which their own gazes define their subject positions toward men and women in these ads. How much of this defining is being manipulated by the ad? How much of it do they bring to the ad?

ASSIGNMENT 4

Animating Revolt [Halberstam]

One way to get inside the meaning of an author's project is to take on his or her project, to move its methods to another object of study. Students have taken on some complex critical lenses as they watch the film they choose to analyze, and they've had fun doing so.

One student, taking his cue from Halberstam, performed an interesting exploration of the film *Brave*, concluding that the film is not a symbol of revolution and challenging Halberstam's claim by writing, "Anything can look revolutionary, but that doesn't mean it is." This student, rather than reading for revolution, read for the normalizing functions of the film *Brave*. The class workshop focused on his paper and engaged in a fascinating discussion about whether something "counts" as queer or revolutionary if some aspects of its story are quite traditional. In short, the class was doing the kind of work Halberstam invites them to do, thereby taking on Halberstam's way of reading texts and employing some of their own strategies as well.

ASSIGNMENT 5

Combining Biases [Schulz, Halberstam]

Schulz's and Halberstam's texts are an engaging combination—both writers value the concept of *going against the grain*. This assigment asks students to see the ways the two authors think about "evidence that challenges our beliefs." As readers, we don't necessarily notice that we are responding to a text in a given way because it moves against our most basic logics or assumptions. In completing this assignment, students will have to think about the ways Halberstam might move against common belief systems. And because the question asks them to consider Schulz as well, students are invited to value rather than resist evidence that challenges their beliefs.

It is conventional for readers who are reading in order to write to see their reading as a means of looking for "evidence" that *supports* their beliefs. That rhetorical strategy is something many of our students are familiar with from their writing experiences thus far. Reading for kinds of evidence that might challenge their beliefs is likewise an important exercise not just for reading but for writing as well. The best writers are able to see many dimensions and contradictory ideas at once, and they learn to recognize and engage with how our beliefs affect our reading and writing practices.

ALTERNATIVE ASSIGNMENT

What Is It Good For? [Miller]

Our students took this assignment personally, many making a case for a piece of writing either that they had loved for years or that had recently knocked them down. Because Miller is so focused on what kind of difference writing can make in school, in our public, these essays expressed a moving mixture of personal investment and public concern. Students chose a myriad of genres—children's books, song lyrics, magazine articles, novels, memoirs—and though different genres presented different challenges, the choice itself was central to the assignment's success. Many students were surprised by how much they needed to reread Miller despite the fact that the assignment asks them to focus on an outside source. Students must possess a deep understanding of Miller's definition of critically optimistic writing in order to make a case for the piece that they choose. The "Questions for a Second Reading" may help students develop this understanding, but this particular writing assignment asks them to move from broad argumentative strokes to specific aspects of writing. For example, what kinds of moves does Miller want authors to make? And what purposes does he hope underlie these moves? Thinking about Miller's writing style itself—his persistence in asking difficult questions, his refusal to shy away from "why" and "could"—can help students translate Miller's big ideas into writerly actions. Students tended to use Miller to discover the set of questions that they thought were most important to Miller's project and most relevant to the piece they had chosen. With the set of questions or concerns that they brought from Miller, students recast writing that they had enjoyed privately as publicly relevant: besides my liking this book, they asked, what could it be said to be good for?

ALTERNATIVE ASSIGNMENT

Standard English in a Democratic Culture [Wallace]

This assignment asks students to respond to Wallace's argument about Standard Written English (SWE) and its place in a course on writing. Wallace admits that, when he teaches, he finds it very important to insist on SWE in students' papers, so much so that he often interrupts his original plans for his courses in order to spend several weeks on lessons in usage and grammar. He finds it regrettable that the ideology of the linguistic Descriptivists has led to an educational system that no longer places much emphasis on grammar instruction, and he believes that all students, regardless of their home dialect, should become fluent in SWE.

Wallace's argument about SWE is complex, and it will be important for students to acknowledge this complexity. Some students will be tempted to turn Wallace into a straw man—say, an elitist grammar hound who's simply afraid of cultural change—in order to contest his views. But Wallace admits that "SWE is the dialect of the American elite," and he's well aware that alternative dialects have their own integrity. Students who choose to challenge his position will need to account for such things, and they'll need to represent his text in ways that do justice to its intricacies. To prepare them for this assignment, you might have students locate passages in Wallace's essay where he says something about

SWE, and then have them take note of nuances, shifts in direction, and apparent contradictions. By identifying a number of passages in advance, students will bring a more multifaceted understanding of Wallace's position to their writing.

In their essays, it will also be crucial for students to locate their own experiences as speakers and writers in Wallace's work. We suggest that they focus on a particular occasion when they experienced or observed a struggle with SWE in the classroom, and then read what occurred with or against the grain of Wallace's argument. After examining this occasion in some detail, what do they have to say to Wallace about his views on usage and grammar in a writing course?

ALTERNATIVE ASSIGNMENT

Representing Race [Baldwin]

The point of this assignment is a comparison with contemporary text, and it makes the question of the style and method of "Notes of a Native Son" a secondary concern. The success of this assignment will depend upon the time and care students give to presenting and developing examples. It is not easy to write about music or a music video or a film or a television show. Students should not underestimate the task. In fact, if you are working with draft and revision, it will most likely be the case that the work of revision will be to further develop the examples and to further articulate the comparison with Baldwin.

· · ● · ·

ADDITIONAL SEQUENCE ONE 🄴

Deliberate Acts of Discovery

One of the most intimidating (sometimes even frustrating) aspects of reading difficult texts for students is running into references and terms that are unfamiliar to them. Many readers who are used to reading inactively will skip over or ignore these references. This sequence works to illuminate for students the possibilities for understanding and enrichment that become evident if we do the work to learn the text's language and to make sense of its references. The sequence connects quite well with the ideas in our Introduction, so it is often useful to have students read sections of the Introduction in preparation for the sequence.

We have found in teaching this sequence (or others like it) that at first many students seem uninterested in the work, identifying moving outside the text as "doing research," — something a good number of students have come to think of as "boring" or "busy work." However, we have also noticed two important aspects of the sequence. First, beginning with Lethem is quite useful because the references he makes are often compelling ones for students. And second, once students begin to see the ways their research allows them new doorways through which to enter the texts, they seem more willing to embark on research journeys. One student even posted a section of Lethem's essay to our online course space, adding actual hyperlinks to the references Lethem used. The other students really liked reading this way, and it also sparked interesting class discussion about how digital reading and writing is changing the way we interact with texts or, put another way, is highlighting the ways we've always interacted with texts.

All of the essays we've selected for this sequence make use of a variety of materials and terms that students can learn more about as they research. In their course evaluations, students often mention that assignments like these helped them learn how to engage with texts more fully. And it also helps them see that even their teachers (who they often believe are experts on the texts of the course) do not know every reference in a single essay well. As teachers, through our students' research, we also learn more about the texts we teach.

ASSIGNMENT 1

Creating Hyperlinks [Lethem]

We found that classroom discussions on Lethem's essay were advanced by having students track down some of his examples—"The Wasteland," for instance, and any commentaries on the work as borrowing or appropriation or plagiarism. This assignment sends students out on a mini-research project. We often combine an exercise like this with a trip to the library and a session with a reference librarian on how to use a university library and its resources. A university library is a special and daunting place; it has tools well beyond what students will have encountered at the libraries in their high schools or neighborhoods. And students often quite literally need someone to take them across the threshold.

Remember, though, that although it is important to have students track down, explain, and defend examples that lie beyond their immediate range of reference, it is equally important to have them come to class with examples that are close to them, that mean something to them, that are part of their own immediate cultural experience.

ASSIGNMENT 2

Zoning In [Jamie]

This question will result in a tapestry of discoveries that coheres when the entire class discusses their findings for a class meeting. Students had images on their computers and phones that they shared, definitions from multiple sources, and out of all these, we concluded our discussion with a reflection on what we could say that we learned to prepare us for our next reading of "Shia Girls."

ASSIGNMENT 3

Field Research [Berger]

Students will be asked to do multiple pieces of work for this essay. They might think of it as a case report of peoples' perceptions of the Caravaggio painting. First, they'll need to study the painting themselves without turning to art critics or other sources. They might think of it as a thought or perception experiment.

The first part of the experiment is their own two- to three-paragraph explanation of what the painting means to them. To be clear, they need to write about what they see in the painting, but they also need to attribute meaning to what they see. The assumption here is very much from Berger—that viewers make meaning of paintings.

The second part of the experiment is to imitate Berger's discussion of the painting with a small group of people. The video example seems to take a heavy hand in framing or perhaps leading the children to see things in certain ways. Students can do better than this by asking their small group of three or four people to do what they did. What do they see in the painting? What catches their attention? How do the details cohere into a whole from which they can take or draw meaning? What is that meaning?

Finally, after working on these two aspects of the experiment, students can write their essays in which they report on their study of their perceptions of the Caravaggio and the meanings they attributed to it and their groups' perceptions of the painting and the meanings they drew from it. Do they agree with Berger about the way the Caravaggio speaks to people based on their study? What would they conclude about what the others saw and they didn't and vice versa? Finally, what would they conclude about what it means for a painting to speak to its viewers? Would they agree with Berger on this?

ASSIGNMENT 4

Becoming an Expert Reader [Foer]

This assignment produced some very interesting essays from students in our classes. The question of being an expert in memory seemed to intrigue them. On the one hand, they find the memory work Foer describes quite impressive. On the other hand, they also raised questions about whether merely remembering facts or details makes one an expert in something. One student asked, "Doesn't being an expert mean you not only remember stuff but you fully understand the way things work? Just because you know a bunch of dates and facts doesn't mean you know how or why stuff is connected."

Students, like many of us, feel implicated at times by Foer's inquiry. After all, part of the experience of reading Foer's piece is to understand ourselves as forgetters. So certainly part of their impulse in challenging the idea that memory champions are experts is something of a defensive posture, but there is something more to it—an articulation of the distinction between remembering details and understanding connections. And that articulation, particularly in the context of the project of *Ways of Reading*, is an important one.

ASSIGNMENT 5

Building Your Own Frame of Reference [Lethem, Jamie, Berger, Foer]

It can be very useful to begin this assignment by asking students to do some brainstorming about subjects, places, people, music, books, or films that they are interested in. For example, we asked students to make a list of ten specific things that interest them. Here is one student's list: forensic shows about crime, The Beatles, the Catholic religion, golden retrievers, Harry Potter, knitting, American Idol, Facebook, *Perks of Being a Wallflower*, my hometown of Boise, and animal rights. Once students make these lists, they can begin to think about how some of these references might have ideas in common, or about what these interests might say to them about what they are interested in writing about. This student, for example, composed an essay about the ethical treatment of animals. The essay took the song "Blackbird" by the Beatles and discussed its implications for how personifying animals doesn't seem to lead us to treat them as people. It was quite an interesting essay and also made use of facts about dog ownership, the treatment of animals in rural Idaho, and a scene from one of the *Harry Potter* books. Students seem to get some enjoyment out of this assignment both because it allows them to produce the connections but also feels, as one student put it, "like solving a riddle."

ALTERNATIVE ASSIGNMENT

Frame of Reference [Halberstam]

Because it is easy for students to get lost in the pop-culture familiarity of Halberstam's references, this assignment asks them to pay attention to what is *un*familiar. We then ask students not only to research unfamiliar ideas or terms but to think about why they have not had exposure to these terms before. This question can spark interesting discussions about how our personal experiences shape our reading practices and the ways our environment shapes what we know. Students choose terms like "Marxist" or "animal husbandry" or even "human exceptionalism." These terms provide another entry point to Halberstam's essay, an alternative to taking the familiar route of the films themselves.

ALTERNATIVE ASSIGNMENT

Key Figures [Schulz]

The chapter is full of references to historical figures, philosophers, scientists. The chapter invites a glossary and/or a set of extended Norton-Anthology-like footnotes. And the discussion of the text can certainly be enriched when students know something about, say,

Descartes or Quine or Hume or Kuhn. This assignment, then, sends students out (perhaps in groups) on a mini-research project. I had students make presentations, usually working from a brief paragraph and including some visual materials.

We often combine an exercise like this with a trip to the library and a session with a reference librarian on how to use a university library and its resources. A university library is a special and daunting place; it has tools well beyond what students will have encountered in their high school or neighborhood libraries. And students often quite literally need someone to take them across the threshold.

Remember, though, that although it is important to have students track down, explain, and defend examples (here of research and of researchers) that lie beyond their immediate range of reference, it is equally important to have them come to class with examples that are close to them, that mean something to them, that are part of their own immediate cultural experience.

ADDITIONAL SEQUENCE TWO 🄴

On Difficulty

Difficult texts, like the ones in this sequence, present students with problems they are not accustomed to solving. They will see writers at work, thinking on paper and working through complex ideas. For most students, even the idea of working with texts like these will be challenging and new. Traditionally, educational enterprises "dummy down" texts for students, and that has been one of the great failures of American education. Rather than teaching students how to work with and how to write difficult texts, the educational community has moved farther and farther toward providing students with easier and easier texts as the solution to students' problems with reading. The underlying assumption of presenting students with easy texts, texts that students can "get" in one reading, is that reading is easy, that problems, then, are indications of a writer's or a reader's failures. This sequence begins with the assumption that difficult texts often present students with challenging, complex thinking, and that for students to develop into complex, critical thinkers, they need to learn the work of reading and writing difficult texts. The metaphor for this sequence is "work." The work students will do here is textual, and the experience of that work is designed to teach them that a great deal of important reading is hard work and not at all easy or instantaneous.

The assignments in this sequence invite students to consider the nature of several difficult texts and how the problems they pose might be said to belong simultaneously to language, to readers, and to writers. It is assumed that these texts are difficult for all readers, not just for students, and that the difficulty is necessary or strategic, not a mistake or evidence of a writer's (or a reader's) incompetence.

Since the sequence was designed to serve teachers interested in having their students study the problems of difficult texts, it might be helpful to think of using it (or some of the assignments) after students work with these selections either in class discussions (using the second-reading questions or the writing assignments as discussion questions) or in writing assignments or in some combination of both. You could also use the kinds of questions posed by these assignments for other difficult texts that students work with.

ASSIGNMENT 1

Foucault's Fabrication [Foucault]

Students don't usually have trouble with Foucault's examples—the stories he tells about the plague, for instance, or his elucidations on examples of the Panopticon. This assignment picks up on his examples and the way Foucault uses them throughout the selection to create an argument for the relationship of surveillance, control, power, and knowledge. Students will need to focus on Foucault's examples, and they'll need to invent a way to trace the examples from the beginning of the text through to the end as they summarize Foucault's developing arguments on surveillance and power. This task will be difficult. The writing is more exploratory, more thinking on the page, than it is summative, and even the most attentive students (and instructors) will find the last section, on power and knowledge, challenging and elusive. But this is an occasion for students to work at the problem (rather than to "get" it or to get it right); they can find a way into it by studying Foucault's examples of surveillance—particularly how they might or might not be similar—and the way in which he uses them to represent control and power. The students' summaries should proceed by examples, following Foucault's text if they wish, because it is through the examples that they'll be able to draw out and ground his arguments about the relationships of control and power and knowledge.

ASSIGNMENT 2

Concept and Example [Butler]

We think it is important to remind students that reading theory or philosophy is difficult work for any reader, regardless of the reader's intelligence or level of education. Encountering a new theoretical essay, or an essay outside our field of expertise, can feel like reading an entirely new language. Its key terms feel strange and empty. The assumptions and subtext are hidden from us, at first. In a sense, we begin reading as if in the dark, feeling around for something that is familiar, for something that evokes an image, a point of reference, a moment of connection. And then, we hang on to that moment as we read on, waiting for another. This assignment offers students one way to approach the difficulties of reading a highly theoretical work. Reading theoretical work, we think, is productive not just for its ideas but for the ways that it defamiliarizes language, making it strange and new all over again. This is an important experience for students because of the way it makes them aware of their blind spots and assumptions. When students begin to write their own essays engaging with Butler, they, too, have the burden of defining and contextualizing their concepts and key terms for their readers. They cannot simply take a word such as *agency*, for example, for granted, even if they think they know what it means. Reading philosophy reminds us that language attains meaning through its usage, through its repetition in context.

ASSIGNMENT 3

A Reader-Friendly Text [Appiah]

It has always been our concern that students see the selections as offering writing lessons—lessons as well as topics or ideas or arguments. And so we try to highlight features in the text as examples of "technical" achievement, something a student writer can bring into his or her own texts. Here, we focus attention on the ways Appiah engages and addresses his readers, the ways he brings them into the text or prepares them to work with difficult ideas or passages. And we insist that this is not magic or inspiration or brain surgery but a relatively simple technique. The key is to know how and when and where to apply it, how not to be cloying or patronizing, but these are lessons learned through experience, through trial and error. You can develop a working list of these strategies, perhaps online or on the blackboard or in a handout. In our experience, you'll see the effects of this lesson in student papers for the rest of the semester.

ASSIGNMENT 4

The Figure of the Writer as an Intellectual [Wallace]

The most striking feature in David Foster Wallace's writing is the way the figure of the writer, as evidenced in the text, does and does not inhabit the conventions of academic writing. The point of this assignment is to give students the opportunity to think about style in terms of ethos, a term introduced in the essay, and to think about the embodiment of the intellectual represented by the conventional and unconventional stylistic features in Wallace's essay. And it asks students to think about the differences in relation to their own intellectual styles, current and future.

Students can be helped toward this essay if you build class discussion around the first, second, and/or fourth "Questions for a Second Reading" following the essay. Sending the class back to the text and then using class time to gather a set of examples will give students a common stockpile of material to work with, and it will free them to focus attention on the questions they want to pose or the arguments that make sense to them.

The use of examples is key here. Students need to learn to think about writing as an intellectual project, more than a rehearsal of opinion or writing off the top of their head. They need the sense of a workbench, with materials on it. One way to help them visualize the page is to insist that they include, at two or three key moments, a block quotation from the text. As we ask students to visualize the page, we ask them to also imagine a space in the essay where they, the student writer, speak, where they take a position and make an evaluative judgment about the essays (Which is their favorite? Which is more persuasive?), and where they strike out on their own, either to develop an idea or to apply what they have found to a new situation or set of examples.

ASSIGNMENT 5

A Theory of Difficulty [Foucault, Butler, Appiah, Wallace]

Students are asked in this assignment to produce a guide that might be useful to other students who will be asked to work with difficult texts and assignments. It's important for students to understand their stance in this piece of writing. Although they are writing a guide that offers advice, they must write from examples of their reading and writing. The examples must come from their past work on this sequence, and they should feel free to cite and explain everything—from class discussions to note-taking to revising papers. The danger with retrospective assignments like this one is that students will turn immediately to generic platitudes, that they'll say what they think is expected of them ("Be prepared to work hard," "Don't see difficult texts as your failure or the writer's failure"). To push against these kinds of moves, you'll need to ask students to work from those moments in their past work that highlighted (for them) ways of reading and writing difficult texts, ways that might help other students who haven't done the kinds of work that they have. Here again they might use double-entry notebooks, first to identify the moments in their work they want to discuss, then to explain what that work stands for or taught them about difficult texts. In their papers or in a third column, they can begin those discussions that tie together what they have to say into a theory of difficulty. Whatever they do with their note-taking, they'll need it to stand as an example of good practice in reading and writing about difficult texts. And it's from those examples and illustrations that they should derive their theories of difficulty. While a theory is drawn from generalizations, these in turn are drawn from or anchored in illustrations or cases. So if students don't work from the examples they have at hand, their theory will be based on generalizations alone and will be a string of platitudes instead of an argument rooted in example.

ALTERNATIVE ASSIGNMENT

The Graphic Challenge [Bechdel]

This assignment asks students to be self-reflexive readers, to observe themselves reading and interacting with Bechdel's work in order to learn something about how the work is constructed and what it demands of its reader. Students are often unaware that they bring with them to the page a set of reading habits, approaches, and strategies. But sometimes a text that is unconventional in form can help students highlight for themselves the various ways they engage with a particular reading. We have begun this assignment many times by asking students first to think together, in a class discussion or small group discussion, about the question: *What is a reading strategy?* Students may, at first, not be able to identify what a reading strategy might be, or they may suspect there is some set of reading strategies they are supposed to remember from prior schooling but do not. It is useful to remind students that they are identifying and naming these strategies, and that their reading strategies are unique to them. Students can begin with small things: that they read with a pen in their hand or while listening to music, for example. But hopefully the discussions can lead them to larger questions about their approach, questions like: *Are you a skeptical reader with a hesitant approach? A gullible reader with a lazy approach? Are you used to reading with images? Does your approach allow the images to enrich your reading experience, or do the images distract from it?*

ALTERNATIVE ASSIGNMENT

Creating Hyperlinks [Lethem]

The classroom discussions were advanced by having students track down some of Lethem's examples—"The Wasteland," for instance, and any commentaries on the work as borrowing or appropriation or plagiarism. This assignment sends students out on a mini-research project. We often combine an exercise like this with a trip to the library and a session with a reference librarian on how to use a university library and its resources. A university library is a special and daunting place; it has tools well beyond what students will have encountered at the libraries in their high schools or neighborhoods. And students often quite literally need someone to take them across the threshold.

Remember, though, that although it is important to have students track down, explain, and defend examples that lie beyond their immediate range of reference, it is equally important to have them come to class with examples that are close to them, that mean something to them, that are part of their own immediate cultural experience.

ALTERNATIVE ASSIGNMENT

A Story of Reading [Wideman]

This assignment asks students to take an unusual stance toward Wideman's selection—to read it as a text that wants to break readers' habits—and it asks them to take an unusual stance toward themselves as readers and writers—to write down and comment on how they read Wideman's text. Students might begin by identifying moments in the text that they want to refer to, moments when they feel Wideman is deliberately working on his readers, defying their expectations and directing their responses. They'll also need to comment on what it was like for them to read those passages, and to this end, they might help themselves with a version of a double-entry notebook, or rather a triple-entry notebook, because the assignment also asks them to comment on what Wideman is doing and why he's doing it. The first column of their notebook might note in some way the passages they've identified where Wideman seems to be deliberately working on his readers.

The second column could tell the story of their reading those sections (in the context of their reading the entire selection), and the third column could indicate their thinking about what Wideman is doing, why he seems to be doing it, and how it affected them as readers. Students will need to read the selection at least twice, but they should begin their note-taking for the story of how they read it the first time through so that they can record their reactions to those sections where Wideman seems to be working on his readers. Once they've got their notes fleshed out, students will then need to tell the story of their reading, with careful reference to those passages they identified and with careful accounting of their reactions to their first reading of them. They'll need to continually step aside, so to speak, in their writing—as Wideman does—to comment on the habits Wideman assumes in his readers and why he wants to break them. For students, this paper is a story of reading with references to the Wideman text, narratives on their reactions to it, and asides commenting on Wideman's demands on readers. This, then, is an assignment to read a challenging text and to create another challenging text in response to it.

— • • • • • • —

ADDITIONAL SEQUENCE THREE ⓔ

The Uses of Reading (I)

This sequence focuses attention on authors as readers, on the use of sources, and on the art of reading as a writer. It combines technical lessons with lessons on the rhetoric of citation. The first assignment, for example, calls attention to the block quotations in Richard Rodriguez's essay "The Achievement of Desire." On one level, Rodriguez provides students with a useful example of how (strategically as well as technically) to use a block quotation. Our concern has also been to call attention to the ways in which (as in the case of Rodriguez) a writer need not always identify with the words of others. We make much in our teaching about the space that comes before and after the block quotation. Here is where a writer has work to do—setting a reader up and providing a way of reading, including critical reading. The next assignment looks at writers from different moments in history, with different relations to their sources and to the culture represented by those sources: Bordo and Berger. This provides an example of revisionary work that students can imitate as well as describe. Imitation will take them outside the conventions of "academic writing," at least as that is represented by term papers.

The last assignment turns back on the introduction to the textbook. This is a way for students to think again, to think retrospectively, about the book and the course. It would be lovely to believe that over the next few years, as students are assigned material to read, they continue to read as writers, asking not only "What does it say?" but "What does it do?" and "Would I want to do something like that?"

ASSIGNMENT 1

The Scholarship Boy (I) [Rodriguez, Hoggart]

This assignment asks students to turn Rodriguez's argument about education—about the relationship between students and teachers—back on the essay by considering the relationship between Rodriguez and Hoggart as a case in point. The general question is this: Is Rodriguez still a scholarship boy? Is he still reading "in order to acquire a point of view"? The earlier general discussion explains why we send students to look at the use of quotations. There are other ways of talking about the relationship between these two writers, but our concern is to make these problems textual problems—problems that hold lessons for readers and writers.

This can be a more complicated question than it appears, depending on how far you want to push it. Some students will argue that Rodriguez is still a blinkered pony. Some will take his argument on its own terms and argue that he rejects Hoggart in the end for being "more accurate than fair" to the scholarship boy. There is the larger question of Rodriguez's use of Hoggart's book *The Uses of Literacy*, a book about the class system which strives to speak in the general and not to sentimentalize individual stories. It is possible, if you and your students have the time, to send students to Hoggart's book in order to construct a more complicated and comprehensive account of this reading. An extract from it follows in the alternative assignment at the end of this sequence.

ASSIGNMENT 2

Sources [Bordo, Berger]

To use Bordo's essay in a reconsideration of Berger's, students will need to work with both essays. This is the kind of assignment that makes considerable demands on students, particularly of their close readings of Bordo's and Berger's examples as representatives of their respective arguments about the readings and uses of images. Because this is the case, students will need to do preliminary work both in discussions of their readings of each essay and in at least one piece of writing for each in which they work through a set of two or three images and show the ways each author uses those images to promote arguments and positions. What, then, are each author's arguments and positions on readings and uses of images?

After this preliminary work, students will be ready to put the two essays next to each other to consider whether they're doing the same work and saying the same things. The key, of course, is to be certain that students are working from at least two images for each text so that their arguments will be grounded in those and develop, then, as minicases. When students consider the relation of Bordo's work to Berger's, they'll need to imagine that Bordo's is in some way extending and transforming Berger's. Berger's came first, but it's not a cause-and-effect relationship. Bordo uses Berger, so students will need to imagine that she is on her own trajectory through the reading of the images that have caught her attention. Berger offers her a way to read and understand them. What material of Berger's does she use? How does she transform Berger's ideas? How, finally, might their work be understood to be similar and different?

ASSIGNMENT 3

Ways of Reading [Bartholomae, Petrosky, and Waite]

Over the years, we have heard from many readers about the usefulness of the introduction to *Ways of Reading*. This assignment asks students to work closely with its language and its argument and to use it retrospectively about your course and about learning to write in a college or university setting. If students do particularly well with this, we would be interested in receiving copies of essays. We can't promise to respond (we get many letters from students); we might, however, include copies in the instructor's manual for the next edition.

ALTERNATIVE ASSIGNMENT

The Scholarship Boy (II) [Rodriguez, Hoggart]

Rodriguez makes extensive use of Hoggart's work in his presentation of the scholarship boy, and the extended section of Hoggart's discussion of the scholarship boy makes an interesting contrast both to Rodriguez's notion of a scholarship boy and to his presentation of Hoggart's ideas. Needless to say, students will need to come to an understanding of how both Rodriguez and Hoggart create and use this notion of a scholarship boy. You might consider asking students to do this kind of work from their readings of the individual pieces (Rodriguez's and Hoggart's) before they begin working directly with the sequence assignments. This first assignment is straightforward, and if students follow its sequence of directions and questions, they'll see that initially they need to understand how Rodriguez uses Hoggart. The important question they need to deal with has to do with what Rodriguez says Hoggart is saying about scholarship boys. The third paragraph of the assignment lays out the questions that can help students read from outside Rodriguez's point of view to establish a sense of how he could be said to be revising Hoggart while using his text and ideas. Our students, for example, have been quick to point out that Hoggart's working-class scholarship boy is British and living in a culture quite different from Rodriguez's or from most Americans. Our subsequent question back to them then asks how this distinction (being British and working-class) makes Hoggart's scholarship boy different not just from the one Rodriguez imagines but also from the boy Rodriguez imagines Hoggart to be.

The fourth paragraph of the assignment turns students' attention to what they might attribute Rodriguez's strategy in using and revising Hoggart. We assume, as is evident from the assignment, that Rodriguez does reimagine and revise Hoggart, so it's a question of where, how, and why he does. The case isn't clear-cut, of course, because Rodriguez doesn't completely rewrite Hoggart, and students should have a good deal of leeway to make their cases for the where, how, and why of Rodriguez's revision of Hoggart's text. The excerpt from Hoggart is lengthy and substantive enough for students to do the kind of comparison readings this assignment calls for; and Hoggart's tone, or stance, along with his notions of the scholarship boy and how he comes into being and acts out his role, is apparent and detailed. More than anything, though, this assignment is designed to introduce students to the notion of authors working under others' influences and to the idea of the malleability of the past. Both Rodriguez and Hoggart serve as good examples of these.

$\cdots\bullet\cdot\bullet\bullet\bullet\cdot\cdots$

ADDITIONAL SEQUENCE FOUR 🄴

The Uses of Reading (II)

This sequence presents an alternative set of readings for the previous sequence. Like the earlier sequence, this one focuses attention on authors as readers, on the use of sources, and on the art of reading as a writer. It combines technical lessons with lessons on the rhetoric of citation.

ASSIGNMENT 1

Sources [Butler, Foucault]

This essay question is an expansive one, giving students the opportunity to think about how writers turn to each other to think through problems and to challenge each other's (and in some cases their own) notions of epistemology. This question also presents the possibility for thinking of research in new ways, suggesting to students that they might look through the books of Butler and Foucault — and those who write about them — to develop a sense of their work. This aspect of the assignment can also be done in group work by giving each group of students several of these texts, asking them to look around in the books and note what strikes them, how it might be connected to their assignments. This also allows for a kind of collaborative research — putting students in dialogue with one another not only about what they found in these texts but also about the meaning of what they found.

ASSIGNMENT 2

Reading and Memory [Foer]

In this instance, students return to some of the work they started in the first "Questions for a Second Reading" assignment. We've been told by teachers and by reviewers of *Ways of Reading* that many instructors *do* make use of the Introduction to the book as a way of preparing students for the kinds of reading and writing they will be asked to do in a course that is focused on essay writing. So in this edition, we've designed a few prompts that make use of the Introduction as it connects to the selections in the book. Students have commented that moving back to the Introduction for a later writing assignment helped them to see why they had read the Introuction in the first place. All of us would likely agree that when reading the introduction to something we identify as a textbook, we sometimes experience that reading as merely introductory, and we perhaps skim the text because we see ourselves as ready to read what's "really the book." We found that in returning to the Introduction again later in the course, students had more to say about it and had more reading experience to connect back to the piece.

ASSIGNMENT 3

Ways of Reading [Bartholomae, Petrosky, and Waite]

Over the years, we have heard from many readers about the usefulness of the introduction to *Ways of Reading*. This assignment asks students to work closely with its language and its argument and to use it retrospectively about your course and about learning to write in a college or university setting. If students do particularly well with this, we would be interested in receiving copies of essays. We can't promise to respond (we get many letters from students); we might, however, include copies in the instructor's manual for the next edition.

ALTERNATIVE ASSIGNMENT

A Story of Reading [Miller]

Our students took this assignment personally, many making a case for a piece of writing either that they had loved for years or that had recently knocked them down. Because Miller is so focused on what kind of difference writing can make in school, in our public, these essays expressed a moving mixture of personal investment and public concern. Students chose a myriad of genres—children's books, song lyrics, magazine articles, novels, memoirs—and though different genres presented different challenges, the choice itself was central to the assignment's success. Many students were surprised by how much they needed to reread Miller despite the fact that the assignment asks them to focus on an outside source. Students must possess a deep understanding of Miller's definition of critically optimistic writing in order to make a case for the piece that they choose. The "Questions for a Second Reading" may help students develop this understanding, but this particular writing assignment asks them to move from broad argumentative strokes to specific aspects of writing. For example, what kinds of moves does Miller want authors to make? And what purposes does he hope underlie these moves? Thinking about Miller's writing style itself—his persistence in asking difficult questions, his refusal to shy away from "why" and "could"—can help students translate Miller's big ideas into writerly actions. Students tended to use Miller to discover the set of questions that they thought most important to Miller's project and most relevant to the piece they had chosen. With the set of questions or concerns that they brought from Miller, students recast writing that they had enjoyed privately as publicly relevant: besides my liking this book, they asked, what could it be said to be good for?

- - • ● • - -

ADDITIONAL SEQUENCE FIVE 🄴

The Art of Argument

Short and experimental texts, like the ones in this sequence, present students with new kinds of challenges. In the pieces they will be asked to examine in this sequence, students will encounter writing that might not, at first, appear to be making any arguments at all—writing that seems to break many rules in terms of form, persuasion, and focus. Many students will have studied aspects of argument before coming into your class, and much of what they have learned is likely to follow the rhetorical tradition, with an emphasis on clearly stated premises and conclusions. It is precisely this prior experience that causes students to struggle in talking about the arguments of these pieces. You and your students will have to develop a new language, a language that suits these more experimental writings in order to talk about both what their arguments might be and how they are made. The work students will do here asks them to notice and speculate about what it might mean to make an argument, and ultimately, students are asked to revise and expand their thinking about what arguments are and how they might find new ways to make arguments in their own writing.

Since this sequence is designed to engage students in looking for arguments, it might be helpful for you, as the teacher, to first take a kind of inventory of what students already know about arguments—perhaps asking them to discuss with you what arguments look like, how they know if they see an argument, or what words or phrases might signal arguments. From this basic discussion, it may be productive to have follow-up discussions, once students have read one or more of the short pieces several times, in which you ask them to think about how these pieces challenge, revise, or add to their experience with arguments. These discussions will help students as they approach some challenging assignments.

ASSIGNMENT 1

Short Talks [Carson]

Students can find Carson's *Short Talks* baffling at first. The pieces are not clearly categorizable in a particular genre, and Carson can appear to be what students might call "random" or "arbitrary." This assignment asks students to read for and look for the arguments that might be embedded in Carson's work. Students can choose to look at one specific short talk, or they can think of the pieces as one whole essay or argument. In asking students to read for the features of argument, in some ways this assignment makes reading Carson's work more manageable. Rather than feeling the pressure of understanding Carson as they read, students are asked to look for features of argument and to imagine what the arguments might be. This is an occasion for students to think about how arguments are made and to examine a text that does not announce or outline its arguments. You'll find that students respond well to this assignment because it asks them to do a familiar kind of work (look for arguments), but this familiar work will lead them to new insights about what counts as argument and will lead them, ideally, to the beginning of a new language in which to talk about arguments. We have found that students are very inventive in thinking of words and terms that try to name the kinds of moves Carson makes.

ASSIGNMENT 2

Animating Argument [Halberstam]

Many assignments ask students to focus on the central or main idea of an essay, and doing so is certainly a useful way of reading. But this question focuses on the peripheral ideas in Halberstam's essay, inviting students to read for what isn't at the center. Students can sometimes find assignments like this one difficult because they are so used to looking for and reading for that main idea. But once they go searching (and perhaps this is work you might do collaboratively as a class by making a list of subjects *other* than the films), students often find subjects that intereest them and assumptions that Halberstam makes in order to construct that central argument in the first place. This is a key learning experience in how essays are made, and often students begin to see possibilities for their own writing or the assumptions they, too, make when they compose.

ASSIGNMENT 3

Secondhand Ideas [Lethem]

This assignment asks students to engage with the essay as an essay — to enter the conversation Lethem has begun (or joined or appropriated or highjacked!).

It is a more conventional assignment; it asks students to represent Lethem's essay through summary, paraphrase, and quotation (to represent it for readers who have not yet read it), to establish Lethem's position, and then to respond. We never offer assignments that rely on summary alone. We want summary to function strategically, and that is our goal here. Students will need to provide a rich and textured sense of what Lethem says in this essay (and what Lethem does there). This alone is a job of some complexity—and it might constitute a first draft. The most difficult part of the assignment, however, comes when the student writer needs to take center stage. We represent that moment in two ways—as a need to bring a new example to the table, something close to the student and his or her world, and as an invitation to extend or challenge Lethem's argument.

ASSIGNMENT 4

A Magic Path to Truth [Morris and one other]

The "Making Connections" questions all ask students to use Morris to reread another text in *Ways of Reading*. The first question uses Schulz's essay to consider the status of the photograph as "evidence" and its relation to error.

We regularly feature assignments that ask students to read one essay in light of, or in reference to, another so that they can imagine that they are engaged in an ongoing project rather than just a little of this and a little of that—Morris one week and Bordo the next.

We have always made it a point to insist that students use assignments like these to take a step beyond "compare and contrast," a method already (most likely) a part of their toolkits. There is a technical side to using one text as a lens through which to view the other. One way to make this act of reading materialize on the page is to bring a paragraph or block quotation from one text—from Schulz, say—to a discussion that also requires a paragraph or block quotation from Morris. What do you hear in each? Where and how do they speak to each other? Or not? As we ask students to visualize the page, we ask them also to imagine a space in the essay where they, the student writer, speaks, where they take a position and make an evaluative judgment about what they have read. (What is your favorite moment in all of this? Which text is most persuasive?) And we ask them to strike out on their own, either to develop an idea or to apply what they have found to a new situation or set of examples.

• • • • • •

ADDITIONAL SEQUENCE SIX 🔲

Working with Metaphor

In the introduction to this sequence, we say that metaphors are indispensable to thoughts and language. Often students do not yet recognize this, and it is very helpful to prepare students for this sequence by talking about the ways metaphor already functions in their ordinary uses of expressions and phrases. You can even begin by asking students to list some of these. You might find them providing examples like "put a lid on it" or "hit the road" as idiomatic expressions that make use of metaphor. This discussion can help students see that metaphor is not some strange literary device used only by poets and novelists, but that metaphor is inextricably linked not only to our writing but also to our everyday communications and understandings of our world.

The assignments in this sequence ask students to begin by looking closely at metaphor and how it becomes part of the work of each writer. With each writing assignment, students will be asked to add a layer to their understanding of metaphor, moving from one text to another and eventually developing a central metaphor of their own. We have found that students develop more complex understandings of metaphor through writing as well as reading. They begin to see the challenges and interpretative possibilities of writing away from the literal, of leading your reader through a series of figurative comparisons.

ASSIGNMENT 1

The Memory Palace [Foer]

While many students will have had discussions about metaphor prior to our particular writing course, we find it especially useful to prepare students for this assignment by conducting a class discussion on the topic. Students will usually know, literally, what a metaphor is and will be familiar with other terms connected to metaphor like "simile" or "figurative language." But it is often necessary to illuminate precisely *how* metaphor works to think through a problem or question. Short poems that use one central metaphor can be helpful in leading this kind of discussion. We have used poems such as Yehida Amichai's "Like a Ship's Captain" or Ruth L. Schwartz's "The Important Thing" to this end.

Fully understanding what metaphor makes possible and what limitations it might have sometimes requires pulling a specific metaphor apart and seeing how it works. When students get to that final question about why Foer chose the palace as opposed to another metaphor, oftentimes they actually begin thinking about metaphors Foer might have used instead, and this work is critical as well as creative.

ASSIGNMENT 2

Metaphorical Moments [Anzaldúa, Doyle, Griffin]

We find that students often have had exposure to similar contexts—meaning most students have some sense of what metaphors are and how they are different from, for example, similes or other what might be called "literary devices" or "figurative language." But we also find that students recognize metaphor most readily when it is obvious (like:

love is a piano) and less readily when the metaphor is part of a larger project or is implied in dialogue, echoes, or images in readings. This assignment invites students to first expand and complicate their own notions of metaphor. Once they've done that work as readers, the assignment invites them to write about that experience. A few students, surprisingly, have been really playful with this assignment—using, for example, metaphor to talk about metaphor. The final question in this prompt is perhaps the most important question for students to think through as they work on the assignment. Our goal is for students to understand that metaphor is not just for "fancy-ing" up one's prose or making it more vivid (though it can certainly do those things), but that it can also be used for layering and complicating the subject at hand like Griffin does in her treatment of the missile alongside the cell. We have noticed also that after students have completed this particular assignment, there is often an increase in their own experimentation with metaphor and noticing of metaphor in other readings from the book. This is especially useful for helping students become readers of all the readings in the collection.

ASSIGNMENT 3

On Your Own [Doyle, Carson]

Students have two options from which to choose for this assignment, but both choices are challenging ones. While this assignment is difficult, students often write very innovative and powerful essays in response. For this assignment, students can draw from their own archive of images and experience as they try to imitate the specific stylistic metaphoric elements of Doyle or Carson. What might prove useful to students before taking on this challenge is a longer discussion of how these writers do the work of metaphor, focusing on *how* Doyle and Carson write more than on *what* they write. We have found that if students have a complex and rich understanding of the moves each writer makes, they have a better chance at writing complicated and sophisticated essays of their own. To prepare, you might group students according to which essay they want to imitate and then ask them to work with their peers to describe the ways each piece moves, and how they might mimic or try out those particular moves.

ASSIGNMENT 4

Scripting Identity [Appiah]

This has been one of the most interesting and productive assignments in our teaching in the last few years. We often ask students to extend the argument of an essay to materials or narratives centralo to their own lives. Here the focus is more clearly on the narrative itself. Although our students aren't familiar with terms like "narrative nonfiction" or "creative nonfiction," we encourage them to write as though they were writing a story—with an emphasis on scene, character, and dialogue. The more people speaking, we say, the better. And we have received impressive papers in return—impressive in their length, their ambition, and their seriousness. This assignment always leads to a revision, and so we are quick to bring the most ambitious papers to class for discussion. Their example has provided impressive revisions from students whose first drafts were mechanical or perfunctory.

We also, however, think of this as a critical exercise. We don't demand (or even prompt) direct reference to Appiah in these papers. In the assignment, however, we make it clear that this is an Appiah-like exercise. It is not an open invitation to a personal essay. It is an invitation to think through, as we say, the "competing demands of a life and a 'script' of the personal and the collective, of individual freedom and the politics of identity."

ALTERNATIVE ASSIGNMENT

Parts and Wholes [Griffin and one other]

Should you want students to engage with a longer, more sustained project that relies heavily on metaphor, Griffin's essay is a good place to turn. This assignment asks students to pay attention to metaphor in Griffin's essay, noting the ways the essay's various parts complicate Griffin's larger project. In turning then to one of the other writers in the sequence, students can explore the ways this writer's use of metaphor helps to develop and layer his or her essay. Students can read this assignment as a familiar task, thinking that the prompt asks them to "compare and contrast" Griffin's essay with another. And while this is true to some extent, it might be worth the time to ask students to talk with you before they write about their assumptions or expectations about this kind of essay. You will want to direct students away from creating a straightforward list of similarities and differences between two essays. Instead of thinking about what is the same and what is different about two works, you might ask students to think about what a compare-and-contrast essay might *do*. Having students articulate these possibilities helps them write essays that do stronger interpretive work rather than merely identifying examples.

· · ● · ·

Additional Assignment Sequences

Here are eight additional assignment sequences. You are welcome to duplicate the materials for your students.

· · ● · ·

WRITING WITH STYLE

John Edgar Wideman
Kwame Anthony Appiah
John Berger
Susan Griffin
David Foster Wallace
Susan Bordo

This sequence is a set of exercises designed to encourage close attention to detail. Skilled readers need to know how to read closely for meaning and effect—to see detail and not just the gist of the text, or the "big picture." The exercises are designed to help you be a better reader. They are also, however, writing lessons. Skilled writers need to know how to attend to subtleties in phrasing and punctuation that assist in the organization of complex, multivocal sentences.

Each exercise provides (or asks you to select) a sample sentence or paragraph from the text, one that is characteristic or exemplary of the author's style. It asks you to imitate that sentence or paragraph (that is, to write in parallel). And it asks you to describe sentences, not through textbook terms (subject, predicate, direct object), but in terms of what the sentence *does*. The prose statement calls attention to writing as *action*, as a way of doing something with words.

The following examples can be extended to any of the selections in *Ways of Reading*. They serve as writing exercises, but also as exercises in close reading. It is unlikely that anyone could carefully read all of the selections in this sequence in a single term or semester. Your instructor may cut some to allow extra time, or you may be asked to skim or to read selectively. Skimming, scanning, reading selectively—these are ways of reading used often by serious scholars, who need to know how to pay attention to the surface as well as how to read deeply.

ASSIGNMENT 1

Language, Rhythm, Tone [Wideman]

To read Wideman's prose, a reader needs to learn to pay close attention to his "rules of etiquette," his "thumbnail character sketches," his "history of the community" — that is, Homewood. At several points in "Our Time," Wideman comments on the importance of language to life in Homewood ("a further inflection of the speaker's voice could tell you to ignore the facts, forget what he's just reminded you to remember").

Below are two passages from "Our Time." Listen for tone and inflection; pay attention to the rhythm and shape of the sentences.

Garth looked bad. Real bad. Ichabod Crane anyway, but now he was a skeleton. Lying there in the bed with his bones poking through his skin, it made you want to cry. Garth's barely able to talk, his smooth, medium-brown skin yellow as pee. Ichabod legs and long hands and long feet, Garth could make you laugh just walking down the street. On the set you'd see him coming a far way off. Three-quarters leg so you knew it had to be Garth the way he was split up higher in the crotch than anybody else. Wilt the Stilt with a lean bird body perched on top his high waist. Size-fifteen shoes. Hands could palm a basketball easy as holding a pool cue. Fingers long enough to wrap round a basketball, but Garth couldn't play a lick. Never could get all that lankiness together on the court. You'd look at him sometimes as he was trucking down Homewood Avenue and think that nigger ain't walking, he's trying to remember how to walk. (p. 423)

Wideman writes carefully here, paying attention to rhythm and idiom, and placing his speaker carefully in relation to Garth and to his community. The language moves from writing to speech and back again. How would you place the language — is this Black English? Homewood English? Wideman's English? And the fragments (the incomplete sentences), why are they there? What is Wideman doing?

Here is a second example. In this one, Wideman presents the French girls. If the previous passage was built from fragments, in this one a sentence seems to run past its boundaries. And again, the language moves from writing to speech and back again.

A French girl was somebody who lived in Cassina Way, somebody you didn't fool with or talk nasty to. Didn't speak to at all except in certain places or on certain occasions. French girls were church girls, Homewood African Methodist Episcopal Zion Sunday-school-picnic and social-event young ladies. You wouldn't find them hanging around anywhere without escorts or chaperones. French girls had that fair, light, bright, almost white redbone complexion and fine blown hair and nice big legs but all that was to be appreciated from a distance because they were nice girls and because they had this crazy daddy who wore a big brown country hat and gambled and drank wine and once ran a man out of town, ran him away without ever laying a hand on him or making a bad-mouthed threat, just cut his eyes a certain way when he said the man's name and the word went out and the man who had cheated a drunk John French with loaded dice was gone. Just like that. (p. 434)

Write two passages with exactly the same number of words, the same phrasing, and the same punctuation as these two. (We'll call them parallel passages and sentences.) You provide the subject matter. The words, of course, should be different. When you are done, write a one-sentence description of what you are *doing* in those passages.

Finally, go back to "Our Time"; choose two or three additional examples that seem characteristic of Wideman's prose, examples you find interesting and worth discussion. Write a brief, one-page essay in which you think out loud about why Wideman's project would require (or produce) such writing.

ASSIGNMENT 2

Depicting the Intellectual [Appiah, Wallace]

Both Kwame Anthony Appiah's "Racial Identities" and David Foster Wallace's "Authority and American Usage" have distinctive styles, voices, and methods. A character emerges in each essay, a figure representing one version of a well-schooled, learned, and articulate adult, an intellectual—someone who reads widely, who thinks closely and freshly and methodically about big questions, someone with ideas and with style, someone who is defined in relation to sources, to books and other writers, and someone who takes pains to engage his readers. This is an intellectual, then, who has a desire to reach others, to address them, to bring them into his point of view.

Write an essay in which you discuss the figure of the intellectual represented in these two essays. You'll need to work closely with a few key and representative moments in the texts. Your essay should assess this figure in relation to your own education—better yet, in relation to the kind of figure you yourself intend to cut as a well-schooled adult, as an intellectual, as a person with ideas and knowledge and something to say.

ASSIGNMENT 3

Character, Point of View [Berger]

In *Ways of Seeing*, John Berger argues that in order to understand art from the past, we should situate ourselves in it. He demonstrates what he means by that in his essay with his reading of the Frans Hals paintings. He also demonstrates what it means in the two additional selections, "On Rembrandt's *Woman in Bed*" and "On Caravaggio's *The Calling of St. Matthew*." Here's a lengthy passage from the latter:

The Calling of St. Matthew depicts five men sitting round their usual table, telling stories, gossiping, boasting of what one day they will do, counting money. The room is dimly lit. Suddenly the door is flung open. The two figures who enter are still part of the violent noise and light of the invasion. (Berenson wrote that Christ, who is one of the figures, comes in like a police inspector to make an arrest.)

Two of Matthew's colleagues refuse to look up, the other two younger ones stare at the strangers with a mixture of curiosity and condescension. Why is he proposing something so mad? Who's protecting him, the thin one who does all the talking? And Matthew, the tax-collector with a shifty conscience which has made him more unreasonable than most of his colleagues, points at himself and asks: Is it really I who must go? Is it really I who must follow you?

How many thousands of decisions to leave have resembled Christ's hand here! The hand is held out towards the one who has to decide, yet it is ungraspable because so fluid. It orders the way, yet offers no direct support. Matthew will get up and follow the thin stranger from the room, down the narrow streets, out of the district. He will write his gospel, he will travel to Ethiopia and the South Caspian and Persia. Probably he will be murdered.

And behind the drama of this moment of decision in the room at the top of the stairs, there is a window, giving onto the outside world. Traditionally in painting, windows were treated either as sources of light or as frames framing nature or framing an exemplary event outside. Not so this window. No light enters by it. The window is opaque. We see nothing. Mercifully we see nothing because what is outside is bound to be threatening. It is a window through which only the worst news can come. (*The Calling of St. Matthew*, paras. 12–13)

Berger is trying to do what he claims a viewer of art should do. The act, as represented here, is an act of writing. Berger stages a dialogue between a viewer and a painting, and he does this to provide a lesson in seeing. It is also, of course, a writing lesson.

Write a brief essay in imitation of (or as a critical revision of) Berger's brief essays on *Woman in Bed* and *The Calling of St. Matthew*. You'll need to find a painting as your subject, and you'll need to make that painting available in some way as part of your essay. (You could include a photo or a postcard or a reproduction.)

After you have written your passage, briefly discuss its writing. What were you expected to do? What, for example, were its pleasures and possibilities, the risks or liabilities of writing this way?

ASSIGNMENT 4

The Paragraph, the Essay [Griffin]

It is useful to think of Griffin's prose as experimental. She is trying to do something that she can't do in the "usual" essay form. She wants to make a different kind of argument or engage her reader in a different manner. And so she mixes personal and academic writing. She assembles fragments and puts seemingly unrelated material into surprising and suggestive relationships. She breaks the "plane" of the page with italicized intersections. She organizes her material, but not in the usual mode of thesis-example-conclusion. The arrangement is not nearly so linear. At one point, when she seems to be prepared to argue that German child-rearing practices produced the Holocaust, she quickly says:

Of course there cannot be one answer to such a monumental riddle, nor does any event in history have a single cause. Rather a field exists, like a field of gravity that is created by the movements of many bodies. Each life is influenced and it in turn becomes an influence. Whatever is a cause is also an effect. Childhood experience is just one element in the determining field. (p. 238)

Her prose serves to create a "field," one where many bodies are set in relationship.

It is useful, then, to think about Griffin's prose as the enactment of a method, as a way of doing a certain kind of intellectual work. One way to study this, to feel its effects, is to imitate it, to take it as a model. For this assignment, write a Griffin-like essay, one similar in its methods of organization and argument. You will need to think about the stories you might tell, about the stories and texts you might gather (stories and texts not your own). As you write, you will want to think carefully about arrangement and about commentary (about where, that is, you will speak to your reader *as* the writer of the piece). You should not feel bound to Griffin's subject matter, but you should feel that you are working in her spirit.

ASSIGNMENT 5

Italics, Footnotes, Digressions, Interpolations [Wallace]

David Foster Wallace's essay "Authority and American Usage" makes regular (and antic) use of many of the features of scholarly writing: footnotes, digressions, "interpolations," numbered lists, italics. (Is this serious scholarship? ironic scholarship? a parody?) Some of these are designed to be helpful; some, you might say, are deliberately designed to get in a reader's way.

As you reread, take note of the places where Wallace employs the conventions of scholarly writing. When you are done, go back over your notes to see if there are distinct strategies, to see if your examples cluster into types. Give them a name and prepare a brief essay on Wallace as a scholar or an intellectual, as a person who thinks carefully and honors his sources. What, as a writer, is Wallace doing in this essay? Why would Wallace, the writer, present himself (or enter the conversation) in just these ways? What was at stake for him? What are the consequences for a reader? What attracts your attention?

ASSIGNMENT 6

The Pleasure of the Text [Bordo]

For this assignment, we will use Susan Bordo's essay "Beauty (Re)discovers the Male Body" to think about timing and pacing. The chapter is long, but, for many readers at least, it is compelling and a pleasure to read. The writing operates under a set of expectations that does not value efficiency. The writing says, "It is better to take time with this, better to take time rather than hurry, rather than rushing to say what must be said, rather than pushing to be done. Slow down, relax, take your time. This can be fun." While there is attention to a "thesis," the organizing principle of this essay is such that the real work and the real pleasure lie elsewhere. Work and pleasure. As you reread, pay particular attention to how Bordo controls the pace and direction of the essay, where she prolongs the discussion and where and when she shifts direction. Think of this as a way for her (and you) to get work done. And think about it as a way of organizing the pleasure of the text.

And this is a long essay divided into subsections. The subsections mark stages in the presentation. The subsections allow you to think about form in relation to units larger than the paragraph but smaller than the essay. As you reread, pay attention to these sections. How are they organized internally? How are they arranged? How do they determine the pace or rhythm of your reading, the tonality or phrasing of the text? Which is the slowest, for example? Which is the loudest? Why? And where are they placed? What do they do to the argument?

Take time to reread and to think these questions through. It has become common for scholars and teachers to think about the pleasure, even the "erotics," of the text. This is not, to be sure, the usual language of the composition classroom. Write an essay in which you describe the pleasures (and, if you choose, the problems) of Bordo's writing. Describe how it is organized and how it organizes your time and attention. Describe how it works (or doesn't) for you as a reader, how it works (or doesn't) for her as a writer and thinker. You can, to be sure, make reference to other things you are reading or have read or to the writing you are doing (and have done) in school.

ASSIGNMENT 7

A Classroom Lesson [Hacker]

Most composition courses require a handbook of rules and models for writers. And most writers keep a handbook as a ready desk reference. Here is a sample from *A Writer's Reference* by Diana Hacker.

E1

Parallelism

If two or more ideas are parallel, they are easier to grasp when expressed in parallel grammatical form. Single words should be balanced with single words, phrases with phrases, clauses with clauses.

A kiss can be a comma, a question mark, or an exclamation point.
—Mistinguett

This novel is not to be tossed lightly aside, but to be hurled with great force.
—Dorothy Parker

In matters of principle, stand like a rock; in matters of taste, swim with the current.
—Thomas Jefferson

E3-b Place phrases and clauses so that readers can see at a glance what they modify.

Although phrases and clauses can appear at some distance from the words they modify, make sure that your meaning is clear. When phrases or clauses are oddly placed, absurd misreadings can result.

MISPLACED The king returned to the clinic where he underwent heart surgery in 1992 in a limousine sent by the White House.

REVISED   Traveling in a limousine sent by the White House, the king returned to the clinic where he underwent heart surgery in 1992.

The king did not undergo heart surgery in a limousine. The revision corrects this false impression.

Given the work you have done with these exercises, prepare a response to the handbook as a writer's guide. You could write a brief review, perhaps directed at college students who will be using a handbook; you could write your own alternative or parodic handbook entries. Your goal is to bring together what you have done in the form of advice for writers that can stand next to the advice provided by the handbook.

· · ● · ·

EXPERIMENTS IN READING AND WRITING

Susan Griffin
Edward Said
John Edgar Wideman
Gloria Anzaldúa

ALTERNATIVES:
David Foster Wallace
Alison Bechdel
Richard E. Miller

This sequence offers you opportunities to work with selections that are striking both for what they have to say and for the ways they use writing. In each case, the writer is experimenting, pushing against or stepping outside of conventional ways of writing and thinking. The sequence is an opportunity to learn about these experimental ways of writing from the inside, as a practitioner, as someone who learns from doing the very thing that he or she is studying. You will be asked to try out the kinds of writing you've read in the course. For example, the first assignment asks you to step into Susan Griffin's shoes, to mix personal and academic writing, and in doing so, you are challenged to do a kind of intellectual work on subject matter to which you feel strong (though maybe contrary and paradoxical) ties.

The remaining assignments direct your work with a series of intellectual projects that are also writing projects. Thinking differently means writing differently; in fact, some people would argue that the order should be reversed: writing differently enables one to think differently. All of the selections in this sequence stand outside the usual assumptions of school writing, assumptions which (in their most conventional form) put a premium on order, clarity, restraint, objectivity, and the thesis. From the point of view of most freshmen composition textbooks, for example, the writing here is outrageous, extravagant, indulgent. The final assignment provides the occasion to think about the connections (real and imagined) among experimentation, writing, and schooling.

ASSIGNMENT 1

A Mix of Personal and Academic Writing [Griffin]

I have come to believe that every life bears in some way on every other. The motion of cause and effect is like the motion of a wave in water, continuous, within and not without the matrix of being, so that all consequences, whether we know them or not, are intimately embedded in our experience. (p. 254)

—Susan Griffin
Our Secret

It is useful to think of Griffin's prose as experimental. She is trying to do something that she can't do in the "usual" essay form. She wants to make a different kind of argument or engage her reader in a different manner. And so, she mixes personal and academic writing. She assembles fragments and puts seemingly unrelated material into surprising and suggestive relationships. She breaks the "plane" of the page with italicized intersections. She organizes her material, that is, but not in the usual mode of thesis-example-conclusion. Nor does she only represent people's stories, including her own. The arrangement is not nearly so linear. At one point, when she seems to be prepared to argue that German child-rearing practices produced the Holocaust, she quickly says:

Of course there cannot be one answer to such a monumental riddle, nor does any event in history have a single cause. Rather a field exists, like a field of gravity that is created by the movements of many bodies. Each life is influenced and it in turn becomes an influence. Whatever is a cause is also an effect. Childhood experience is just one element in the determining field. (p. 238)

Her prose serves to create a "field," one where many bodies are set in relationship.

It is useful, then, to think about Griffin's prose as the enactment of a method, as a way of doing a certain kind of intellectual work, a work to which she has strong personal and emotional ties. One way to study this, to feel its effects, is to imitate it, to take it as a model.

For this assignment, write a Griffin-like essay, one similar to "Our Secret" in its methods of organization and argument. You will need to think about the stories you might tell, about the stories and texts you might gather (stories and texts not your own), stories to which you are drawn by an emotional and intellectual curiosity. As you write, you will want to think carefully about arrangement and about commentary (about where, that is, you will speak to your reader as the writer of the piece). You should not feel bound to Griffin's subject matter, but you should feel that you are working in her spirit with subjects that matter to you.

ASSIGNMENT 2

Unconventional, Hybrid, and Fragmentary Forms [Said]

Here are two extended passages from the introduction to Edward Said and Jean Mohr's *After the Last Sky* followed by a passage from the chapter "States," which we selected for *Ways of Reading*.

Its style and method — the interplay of text and photos, the mixture of genres, modes, styles — do not tell a consecutive story, nor do they constitute a political essay. Since the main features of our present existence are dispossession, dispersion, and yet also a kind of power incommensurate with our stateless exile, I believe that essentially unconventional, hybrid, and fragmentary forms of expression should be used to represent us. What I have quite consciously designed, then, is an alternative mode of expression to the one usually encountered in the media, in works of social science, in popular fiction. . . .

The multifaceted vision is essential to any representation of us. Stateless, dispossessed, de-centered, we are frequently unable either to speak the "truth" of our experience or to make it heard. We do not usually control the images that represent us; we have been confined to spaces designed to reduce or stunt us; and we have often been distorted by pressures and powers that have been too much for us. An additional problem is that our language, Arabic, is unfamiliar in the West and belongs to a tradition and civilization usually both misunderstood and maligned. Everything we write about ourselves, therefore, is an interpretive translation — of our language, our experience, our senses of self and others.

The striking thing about Palestinian prose and prose fiction is its formal instability: Our literature in a certain very narrow sense *is* the elusive, resistant reality it tries so often to represent. Most literary critics in Israel and the West focus on what is said in Palestinian writing, who is described, what the plot and contents deliver, their sociological and political meaning. But it is *form* that should be looked at. Particularly in fiction, the struggle to achieve form expresses the writer's efforts to construct a coherent scene, a narrative that might overcome the almost metaphysical impossibility of representing the present. (p. 494)

As you reread "States," think about form and the arrangement of image and text. What *is* the order of the writing in this essay? (We are calling it an "essay" for lack of a better term.)

How might you diagram or explain the structure of the piece? The essay shifts genres—memoir, history, argument, documentary. It is, as Said says, a "hybrid." How might you describe the author's strategy as he works on his readers? And, finally, do you find Said's explanation sufficient or useful—that the experience of exile produces its own inevitable style of report and representation?

Write an essay in which you think about "States" as a writing project that revises what you take to be the usual conventions of the essay. Be sure to talk about why you think Said does what he does, and be sure to take a position. Do you value what he has done? And if so, why?

ASSIGNMENT 3

Turning This Way and That [Wideman]

"Our Time" is a family history, but it is also a meditation on the problems of writing family histories—or, more generally, the problems of writing about the "real" world. There are sections in "Our Time" where Wideman speaks directly about the problems he faces as a writer. And the unusual features in the prose stand as examples of how he tried to solve these problems—at certain points, Wideman writes as an essayist, at others like a storyteller; at certain points, he switches voices and/or typeface; the piece breaks up into sections; it doesn't move from introduction to conclusion. Think of these as part of Wideman's method, as his way of working on the problems of writing as practical problems, where he is trying to figure out how to do justice to his brother and his story.

As you prepare to write this assignment, read back through the selection to think about it as a way of doing one's work, as a project, as a way of writing. What are the selection's key features? What is its shape or design? How does Wideman, the writer, do what he does? And you might ask: What would it take to learn to write like this? How is this writing related to the writing taught in school? Where and how might it serve you as a student?

Once you have developed a sense of Wideman's method, write a Wideman-like piece of your own, one that has the rhythm and the moves, the shape and the design of "Our Time." As far as subject matter is concerned, let Wideman's text stand as an invitation (inviting you to write about family and neighborhood), but don't feel compelled to follow his lead. You can write about anything you want. The key is to follow the essay as an example of a *way* of writing—moving slowly, turning this way and that, combining stories and reflection, working outside of a rigid structure of thesis and proof.

ASSIGNMENT 4

A Crazy Dance [Anzaldúa]

In looking at this book that I'm almost finished writing, I see a mosaic pattern (Aztec-like) emerging, a weaving pattern, thin here, thick there. . . . This almost finished product seems an assemblage, a montage, a beaded work with several leit-motifs and with a central core, now appearing, now disappearing in a crazy dance. The whole thing has had a mind of its own, escaping me and insisting on putting together the pieces of its own puzzle with minimal direction from my will. It is a re-bellious, willful entity, a precocious girl-child forced to grow up too quickly, rough, unyielding, with pieces of feather sticking out here and there, fur, twigs, clay. My child, but not for much longer. This female being is angry, sad, joyful, is Coatlicue, dove, horse, serpent, cactus. Though it is a flawed thing—clumsy, complex, grop-ing blind thing, for me it is alive, infused with spirit. I talk to it; it talks to me.

—Gloria Anzaldúa
Borderlands/La frontera

Gloria Anzaldúa has described her text in *Borderlands/La frontera* as a kind of crazy dance; it is, she says, a text with a mind of its own, "putting together the pieces of its own puzzle with minimal direction from my will." Hers is a prose full of variety and seem-ing contradictions; it is a writing that could be said to represent the cultural "crossroads" which is her experience/sensibility.

As an experiment whose goal is the development of an alternate (in Anzaldúa's terms, a mixed or *mestiza*) understanding, write an autobiographical text whose shape and mo-tives could be described in her terms: a mosaic, woven, with numerous overlays; a mon-tage, a beaded work, a crazy dance, drawing on the various ways of thinking, speaking, understanding that might be said to be part of your own mixed cultural position, your mixed sensibility.

To prepare for this essay, think about the different positions you could be said to oc-cupy, the different voices that are part of your background or present, the competing ways of thinking that make up your points of view. Imagine that your goal is to present your world and your experience to those who are not necessarily prepared to be sympathetic or to understand. And, following Anzaldúa, you should work to construct a mixed text, not a single unified one. This will be hard, since you will be writing what might be called a "forbidden" text, one you have not been prepared by your schooling to write.

ASSIGNMENT 5

Writing and Schooling [Griffin, Said, Wideman, Anzaldúa]

You have written four assignments so far, all of them looking at, thinking about, and practicing forms of writing that could be described as experimental. The selections are all different, to be sure, but none of them followed the usual guidelines for school writing. They pushed the limits. They didn't do what essays are supposed to do, at least by certain standards. They were frustrated by limits of the usual ways of doing things with words. In a sense, the authors saw "good" writing as a problem, a problem they could work on as writers. Most likely, the same things could be said about your writing in this sequence. You did things that stood outside of (or that stood against) the forms of writing most often taught in school.

Read over your work. What were you able to do that you wouldn't, or couldn't, have done if you had written in a more conventional style? Be as precise as you can. How and where does this writing differ from the writing you have been taught in school? Again, be as precise as you can — go to old papers, textbooks, or syllabi to look for examples of "good writing" and the standard advice to young writers. Given what you have seen, where and how might more experimental writing be used in the schools (or in schooling)? What role might it play in courses that are not writing courses? What role might it play in a young writer's education?

Write an essay in which you use the example of your work in this sequence to think about writing and the teaching of writing in our schools.

ALTERNATIVE ASSIGNMENT

Working by Association [Miller]

In the final chapter of *Writing at the End of the World*, Miller says the following about his own writing:

> While the assessments, evaluations, proposals, reports, commentaries, and critiques I produce help to keep the bureaucracy of higher education going, there is another kind of writing I turn to in order to sustain the ongoing search for meaning in a world no one controls. This writing asks the reader to make imaginative connections between disparate elements; it tracks one path among many possible ones across the glistening water. (e-Pages)

We can assume that this is the kind of writing present in "The Dark Night of the Soul."

Reread "The Dark Night of the Soul" with particular attention to Miller's method, which is, in simplest terms, putting one thing next to another. Pay attention to the connections Miller makes, to the ways he makes them, and to the ways as a reader you are (or are not) invited into this process. And write a Miller-like essay. To give the project some shape and limit, let's say that it should bring together at least three "disparate elements," three examples you can use to think about whatever it is you want to think about. You don't need to be constrained to Miller's subject — writing, reading, and schooling — although this subject might be exactly the right one for you. Your writing should, however, be like Miller's in its sense of urgency. In other words, write about something that matters to you, that you care about, that touches you personally and deeply.

ALTERNATIVE ASSIGNMENT

The Sentence [Wallace]

According to Bruce Weber, writing for the *New York Times*, David Foster Wallace's sentences show the "playfulness of a master punctuater and the inventiveness of a genius grammarian." As you reread "Authority and American Usage," choose a sentence that might fit this description. Type it out; and then create a sentence of your own in direct imitation—the same length, punctuation, grammar, and rhythm, but with new words and a different topic. When you are done, write a brief essay about what a sentence like this *does*—not what it says but what it *does*—the sentence as a gesture, an action, a deed in words.

ALTERNATIVE ASSIGNMENT

Composing Graphic Memoir [Bechdel]

Compose a piece of graphic memoir. Your piece need not be as long as Bechdel's, but you should think of yourself as imitating Bechdel, taking on her ways of composing. You can come up with your cartoon frames by either drawing them or, if you know how, constructing them digitally in whatever ways you can.

Once you've composed seven to ten frames, write an afterword in which you explore what you discovered in the process of trying to compose like Bechdel does. What was it like? How did the process reveal something to you about your own methods of composing? What did you learn from trying Bechdel's approach?

ALTERNATIVE ASSIGNMENT

Consider the Hummingbird [Doyle]

Here is a group of sentences that form the opening paragraph of Doyle's essay. Reread them three or four times. Notice the length and syntax of each one. Notice how the last sentence does very different work as a sentence from the others.

> Consider the hummingbird for a long moment. A hummingbird's heart beats ten times a second. A hummingbird's heart is the size of a pencil eraser. A hummingbird's heart is a lot of the hummingbird. *Joyas voladoras*, flying jewels, the first white explorers in the Americas called them, and the white men had never seen such creatures, for hummingbirds came into the world only in the Americas, nowhere else in the universe, more than three hundred species of them whirring and zooming and nectaring in hummer time zones nine times removed from ours, their hearts hammering faster than we could clearly hear if we pressed our elephantine ears to their infinitesimal chests. (p. 147)

Now write your own paragraph with your own topic or subject, but stay as close as you can to the kinds of sentences Doyle writes and the order in which they appear in the paragraph. Write a paragraph, in other words, like his. After you've done that, write another paragraph or two in which you explain how your sentences, like his, work. What do the opening sentences do? How does the final sentence work in relation to the others before it? What's a paragraph that is created like this good for?

·· ● ··

WAYS OF SEEING (I)

John Berger
Susan Bordo

This sequence works closely with John Berger's "Ways of Seeing" and his argument about the relationship between a spectator (one who sees and "reads" a painting) and knowledge—in his case, a knowledge of history. Assignment 1 asks for a summary of Berger's argument. Assignment 2 asks you to put Berger to the test by extending his project and producing a "reading" of a painting of your choice. Assignment 3 turns again to Berger, this time to his use of paintings by Rembrandt and Caravaggio. You are asked in assignment 4 to use the work of Susan Bordo, whose work also depends on a close reading of images, to think again about ways of reading visual images. The final assignment is a revision of your reading of a painting, this time with additional commentary to theorize and contextualize the work that you have done.

ASSIGNMENT 1

Ways of Seeing [Berger]

We are not saying that there is nothing left to experience before original works of art except a sense of awe because they have survived. The way original works of art are usually approached—through museum catalogues, guides, hired cassettes, etc.—is not the only way they might be approached. When the art of the past ceases to be viewed nostalgically, the works will cease to be holy relics—although they will never re-become what they were before the age of reproduction. We are not saying original works of art are now useless. (para. 60)

—John Berger
Ways of Seeing

Berger argues that there are barriers to vision, problems in the ways we see or don't see original works of art, problems that can be located in and overcome by strategies of approach. For Berger, what we lose if we fail to see properly is history: "If we 'saw' the art of the past, we would situate ourselves in history. When we are prevented from seeing it, we are being deprived of the history which belongs to us" (para. 12). It is not hard to figure out who, according to Berger, prevents us from seeing the art of the past. He says it is the ruling class. It is difficult, however, to figure out what he believes gets in the way and what all this has to do with history.

For this assignment, write an essay explaining what, as you read Berger, gets in the way when we look at paintings, and what it is that we might do to overcome the barriers to vision (and to history). Imagine that you are writing for someone interested in art, perhaps preparing to go to a museum, but someone who has not read Berger's essay. You will, that is, need to be careful in summary and paraphrase.

ASSIGNMENT 2

A Painting in Writing [Berger]

Original paintings are silent and still in a sense that information never is. Even a reproduction hung on a wall is not comparable in this respect for in the original the silence and stillness permeate the actual material, the paint, in which one follows the traces of the painter's immediate gestures. This has the effect of closing the distance in the time between the painting of the picture and one's own act of looking at it. . . . What we make of that painted moment when it is before our eyes depends upon what we expect of art, and that in turn depends today upon how we have already experienced the meaning of paintings through reproductions. (para. 61)

—John Berger
Ways of Seeing

Although Berger describes original paintings as silent in this passage, it is clear that these paintings begin to speak if one approaches them properly, if one learns to ask "the right questions of the past." Berger demonstrates one route of approach, for example, in his reading of the Hals paintings, where he asks questions about the people and objects and their relationships to the painter and the viewer. What the paintings might be made to say, however, depends on the viewer's expectations, his or her sense of the questions that seem appropriate or possible. Berger argues that, because of the way art is currently displayed, discussed, and reproduced, the viewer expects only to be mystified.

For this paper, imagine that you are working against the silence and mystification Berger describes. Go to a museum—or, if that is not possible, to a large-format book of reproductions in the library (or, if that is not possible, to the reproductions in this essay)—and select a painting that seems silent and still, yet invites conversation. Your job is to figure out what sorts of questions to ask, to interrogate the painting, to get it to speak, to engage with the past in some form of dialogue. Write an essay in which you record this process and what you have learned from it. Somewhere in your paper, perhaps at the end, turn back to Berger's essay and speak to it about how this process has or hasn't confirmed what you take to be Berger's expectations.

Note: If possible, include with your essay a reproduction of the painting you select. (Check the postcards at the museum gift shop.) In any event, make sure that you describe the painting in sufficient detail for your readers to follow what you say.

ASSIGNMENT 3

Berger Writing [Berger]

If the new language of images were used differently, it would, through its use, confer a new kind of power. Within it we could begin to define our experiences more precisely in areas where words are inadequate. . . . Not only personal experience, but also the essential historical experience of our relation to the past: that is to say the experience of seeking to give meaning to our lives, of trying to understand the history of which we can become the active agents. (para. 68)

—John Berger
Ways of Seeing

As a writer, Berger is someone who uses images (including some of the great paintings of the Western tradition) "to define . . . experiences more precisely in areas where words are inadequate."

In a wonderful book, *And Our Faces, My Heart, Brief as Photos,* a book that is both a meditation on time and space and a long love letter (if you can imagine such a combination), Berger writes about paintings to say what he wants to say to his lover. We have included two examples, descriptions of Rembrandt's *Woman in Bed* and Caravaggio's *The Calling of St. Matthew.*

Read these as examples, as lessons in how and why to look at, to value, to think with, to write about paintings. Then use these (or one of them) as a way of thinking about the concluding section of "Ways of Seeing" (paras. 61–69). You can assume that your readers have read Berger's essay but have difficulty grasping what he is saying in that final section, particularly since it is a section that seems to call for action, asking the reader to do something. Of what use might Berger's example be in trying to understand what we might do with and because of paintings? How is his writing different from yours? Would you attribute these differences to training and education? What else?

ASSIGNMENT 4

Writing Berger [Bordo, Berger]

In *Ways of Seeing* John Berger says:

According to usage and conventions which are at last being questioned but have by no means been overcome, the social presence of a woman is different in kind from that of a man. A man's presence is dependent upon the promise of power which he embodies. If the promise is large and credible, his presence is striking. If it is small or incredible, he is found to have little presence. The promised power may be moral, physical, temperamental, economic, social, sexual—but its object is always exterior to the man. A man's presence suggests what he is capable of doing to you or for you. His presence may be fabricated, in the sense that he pretends to be capable of what he is not. But the pretence is always towards a power which he exercises on others.

By contrast, a woman's presence expresses her own attitude to herself, and defines what can and cannot be done to her. Her presence is manifest in her gestures, voice, opinions, expressions, clothes, chosen surroundings, taste—indeed there is nothing she can do which does not contribute to her presence. Presence for a woman is so intrinsic to her person that men tend to think of it as an almost physical emanation, a kind of heat or smell or aura.

To be born a woman has been to be born, within an allotted and confined space, into the keeping of men. The social presence of women has developed as a result of their ingenuity in living under such tutelage within such a limited space. But this has been at the cost of a woman's self being split into two. A woman must continually watch herself. She is almost continually accompanied by her own image of herself. Whilst she is walking across a room or whilst she is weeping at the death of her father, she can scarcely avoid envisaging herself walking or weeping. From earliest childhood she has been taught and persuaded to survey herself continually.

And so she comes to consider the *surveyor* and the *surveyed* within her as the two constituent yet always distinct elements of her identity as a woman.

She has to survey everything she is and everything she does because how she appears to others, and ultimately how she appears to men, is of crucial importance for what is normally thought of as the success of her life. Her own sense of being in herself is supplanted by a sense of being appreciated as herself by another.

Men survey women before treating them. Consequently how a woman appears to a man can determine how she will be treated. To acquire some control over this process, women must contain it and interiorize it. That part of a woman's self which is the surveyor treats the part which is the surveyed so as to demonstrate to others how her whole self would like to be treated. And this exemplary treatment of herself by herself constitutes her presence. Every woman's presence regulates what is and is not "permissible" within her presence. Every one of her actions—whatever its direct purpose or motivation—is also read as an indication of how she would like to be treated. If a woman throws a glass on the floor, this is an example of how she treats her own emotion of anger and so of how she would wish it to be treated by others. If a man does the same, his action is only read as an expression of his anger. If a woman makes a good joke this is an example of how she treats the joker in herself and accordingly of how she as a joker-woman would like to be treated by others. Only a man can make a good joke for its own sake.

One might simplify this by saying: *men act* and *women appear*. Men look at women. Women watch themselves being looked at. This determines not only most relations between men and women but also the relation of women to themselves. The surveyor of woman in herself is male: the surveyed female. Thus she turns herself into an object—and most particularly an object of vision: a sight. 🅮

Like Berger, Susan Bordo is concerned with how we see and read images; both are concerned to correct the ways images are used and read; both trace the ways images serve the interests of money and power; both write to teach readers how and why they should pay a different kind of attention to the images around them.

For this assignment, use Bordo's work to reconsider Berger's. As you reread each essay, pay particular attention to how they read the images. What do they notice? How do they write about images? How do they connect the images to history? Mark instances that you might be able to put into interesting conversation with examples from *Ways of Seeing*.

When you have completed this work, write an essay in which you consider Bordo and Berger and the ways that they read images. Berger's essay precedes Bordo's by about a quarter of a century. If you look closely at their examples, and if you look at the larger concerns of their arguments, are they both saying the same things? doing the same work? If so, how? And why is such work still necessary? If not, how do their projects differ? And how might you explain those differences?

ASSIGNMENT 5

Revision [Berger]

For this assignment, go back to the essay you wrote for assignment 2, your representation of a painting, and revise it. You should imagine that your work is both the work of reconsideration (rethinking, looking again, changing what you have written) and addition (filling in the gaps, considering other positions and points of view, moving in new directions, completing what you have begun). As you do this work, you can draw on the comments you have received from your instructor and (perhaps) from other students in your class.

$\cdots\bullet\bullet\bullet\cdots$

WRITING PROJECTS

Edward Said
Michel Foucault
Judith Butler
Jonathan Lethem

ALTERNATIVES:
Kathryn Schulz
Kathleen Jamie
Richard Rodriguez

The purpose of this sequence is to invite you to work closely with pieces of writing that define substantial intellectual projects, with particular attention to a writer's method. Although you will be writing separate essays for each assignment, you should work on a single subject, or set of related topics, each time employing a new method, a new set of key terms, a new angle of vision, and new examples. (Each assignment can become part of something bigger, in other words.) Connecting the sections formally is not necessary — that is, you don't need to worry about transitions or continuity of style. (We have found that this can be an unnecessary burden.) You are not necessarily writing a book; think of it rather as a collection of essays. The final assignment asks you to reflect on the work you have done.

ASSIGNMENT 1

Words and Images [Said]

The first three paragraphs of Edward Said's essay "States" provide a "reading" of the opening photograph, "Tripoli, Badawi camp, May 1983." Or, to put it another way, the writing evolves from and is in response to that photograph. As a way of preparing for this assignment, reread these paragraphs and pay close attention to what Said is doing, to what he notices, to what prompts or requires commentary. How would you describe and explain the writing that follows? What is he doing with the photo? What is he doing as a writer? What is he doing for a reader? (How does he position a reader?)

It might be useful to begin by thinking about what he is *not* doing. It is not, for example, the presentation one might expect in a slide show on travel in Lebanon. Nor is it the kind of presentation one might expect while seeing the slides of family or friends, or slides in an art history or art appreciation class.

Once you have worked through the opening three paragraphs, reread the essay, paying attention to Said's work with all the photographs. Is there a pattern? Do any of the commentaries stand out for their force, variety, innovation?

For this assignment, compose a similar project, a Said-like reading of a set of photos. These can be photos prepared for the occasion (by you or a colleague); they could also be photos already available. Whatever their source, they should represent people and places, a history and/or geography that you know well, that you know to be complex and contradictory, and that you know will not be easily or readily understood by others, both the group for whom you will be writing (most usefully the members of your class) and readers more generally.

You must begin with a sense that the photos cannot speak for themselves — you must speak for them.

ASSIGNMENT 2

The Effects of Power [Foucault]

About a third of the way through his text, Foucault asserts, "The Panopticon is a marvelous machine which, whatever use one may wish to put it to, produces homogeneous effects of power." Write an essay in which you explain the machinery of the panopticon as a mechanism of power. Paraphrase Foucault and, where it seems appropriate, use his words. Present

Foucault's account as you understand it. As part of your essay, and in order to explain what he is getting at, include two examples—one of his, perhaps, and then one of your own.

ASSIGNMENT 3

A Philosophical Question [Butler]

The opening lines of Judith Butler's essay "Beside Oneself: On the Limits of Sexual Autonomy" might be understood as an invitation to participate with her in one of the traditions of philosophy. She writes:

> What makes for a livable world is no idle question. It is not merely a question for philosophers. It is posed in various idioms all the time by people in various walks of life. If that makes them all philosophers, then that is a conclusion I am happy to embrace. It becomes a question for ethics, I think, not only when we ask the personal question, what makes my own life bearable, but when we ask, from a position of power, and from the point of view of distributive justice, what makes, or ought to make, the lives of others bearable? Somewhere in the answer we find ourselves not only committed to a certain view of what life is, and what it should be, but also of what constitutes the human, the distinctively human life, and what does not. (p. 114)

Write an essay that takes up this invitation—and that takes it up in specific reference to what Butler has offered in "Beside Oneself: On the Limits of Sexual Autonomy." You will need, then, to take some time to represent her essay—both what it says and what it does. The "Questions for a Second Reading" following her essay should be helpful in preparing for this. Imagine an audience of smart people, people who may even know something about Butler, but who have not read this essay. You have read it, and you want to give them a sense of how and why you find it interesting and important.

But you'll also need to take time to address her questions in your own terms: What makes for a livable world? What constitutes the human? Don't slight this part of your essay. Give yourself as many pages as you gave to discussing Butler. You should, however, make it clear that you are writing in response to what you have read. You'll want to indicate, both directly and indirectly, how your thoughts are shaped by, are indebted to, or are in response to hers.

ASSIGNMENT 4

Ranges of Reference [Lethem]

These are the final words of Lethem's essay:

> As for canons, why should it be that to valorize reuse indicated, of all things, an enmity to canons? I was a fiend for canons. Sampling was "Ancestor worship," according to D.J. Spooky. Let a million canons Bloom. Only, canons not be authoritarian fiat but out of urgent personal voyaging. Construct your own and wear it, an exoskeleton of many colors. (para. 136)

Write an essay that is composed as Lethem's essay is composed, built out of pieces you've read elsewhere. Take a subject that matters to you. Work with texts you care about and want to read (or to reread). Please take into mind Lethem's sense that his was an act of "urgent personal voyaging"; it was an "ecstatic" act, not just a fishing expedition. Is such urgency possible for you? At least make it a goal of your work on this project.

When you are finished, you will need to provide a "key," as Lethem does. This is a necessary way to indicate that what you have done is a form of cut and paste (since what you have done could very easily be misconstrued and get you into a heap of trouble). It is also an opportunity for you to think about the process and the consequences, and all it has meant to you to write this way.

ASSIGNMENT 5

Commentary [Said, Foucault, Butler, Lethem]

This is the final assignment in the sequence. It is the occasion for you to revise and reflect on what you have written through these assignments. Gather the writing you have prepared in a folder. These may be chapters in a linked piece; they may be separate pieces collected as part of a more general project. And write a brief essay in which you comment on the work you have done. You could think of this essay as an introduction or an afterword to the work in your folder. Or you could think of it as a plan for revision. You could also think of it as the occasion to write about the relationship of this kind of writing, schooled writing, to the world you imagine outside this classroom—the world of work, the rest of the curriculum, the community, the nation, a close circle of family, friends, and companions.

ALTERNATIVE ASSIGNMENT

Models for Thinking [Schulz]

Schulz says the following about evidence in "Evidence":

Descartes was right to fear that this way of thinking ["believing things based on paltry evidence"] would cause us to make mistakes; it does. Since he was interested in knowing the truth, and knowing that he knew it, he tried to develop a model for thinking that could curtail the possibility of error. . . . In fact, curtailing error was the goal of most models of optimal human cognition proposed by most thinkers throughout most of history, and it is the goal behind our own broadly shared image of the ideal thinker. Some of these models, like Descartes', sought to curtail error through radical doubt. Others sought to curtail it through formal logic—using valued premises to derive necessarily valid conclusions. Otheres, including our shared one of the ideal thinker, seek to curtail it through a kind of general due diligence: careful attention to evidence and counterevidence, coupled with a prudent avoidance of preconceived notions. (p. 364)

"Due diligence," "a model for thinking," and the "ideal thinker." Over time, writing has been one of the ways human beings have tried to find forms and methods to represent (and preserve and transmit) models for thinking. You've received these models through instruction. Topic sentence, example, conclusion—these comprise a model for thinking. And every time you have been assigned something to read (and every time you have chosen something to read), you were presented with a "model for thinking," a model in practice.

For this assignment, we'd like you to find a piece of prose (somewhere in length from a paragraph to a page or two, no more). It can be ancient or it can be recent; it can be academic or it can be from outside the academy. We'd like you to think about it as a model for thinking, and we'd like you to think about it, at least for a brief period, through the lens of this chapter in *Being Wrong*.

Remember—you need to present your example to readers who are not familiar with it. And you'll need to present Schultz's chapter to people who have not yet read it. There will be some work you will need to do to prepare your reader for what you want to say. The most important part of your essay, however, will be the sections where you take the stage and present what you have to add to the conversation.

ALTERNATIVE ASSIGNMENT

Re-creating Conversation [Jamie]

Please reread the conversation between Jamie and Rashida starting with paragraph 150 and ending with paragraph 167. **e**

This section serves as a good example of the unique style Jamie employs when re-creating conversation. The essay is peppered with conversations that unfold in a "she-said, I-said, I-noticed-this, she-said, I-said" movement. It's a way of writing conversation that also allows her to comment on what she notices during the dialogue.

For this assignment, try your hand at imitating this aspect of Jamie's writing. You'll need to create or re-create a conversation with at least one other person that you can write out in the way Jamie does. Your goal is to produce at least a page of text equivalent in length to Jamie's. Write to capture the language of the person or people speaking so that readers can distinguish speakers. Be sure as well to work your own quick observations into the conversation the way Jamie does.

ALTERNATIVE ASSIGNMENT

The Achievement of Desire [Rodriguez]

Rodriguez insists that his story is also everyone's story. Take an episode from your life, one that seems in some way similar to one of the episodes in "The Achievement of Desire," and cast it into a shorter version of Rodriguez's essay. Your job here is to look at your experience in Rodriguez's terms, which means thinking the way he does, noticing what he would notice, interpreting details in a similar fashion, using his key terms, seeing through his point of view; it could also mean imitating his style of writing, working with quotations from other writers, doing whatever it is you see him doing characteristically while he writes. Imitation, Rodriguez argues, is not necessarily a bad thing; it can, in fact, be one of the powerful ways in which a person learns.

Note: This assignment can also be used to read against "The Achievement of Desire." Rodriguez insists on the universality of his experience of leaving home and community and joining the larger public life. You could highlight the differences between your experience and his. You should begin by imitating Rodriguez's method; you do not have to arrive at his conclusions, however.

· · ● · · ·

READING WALKER PERCY

Walker Percy
Richard Rodriguez
Errol Morris

This sequence is designed to provide you with a way of reading Walker Percy's essay "The Loss of the Creature." This is not a simple essay, and it deserves more than a single reading. There are six assignments in this sequence, all of which offer a way of rereading (or revising your reading of) Percy's essay; and, in doing so, they provide one example of what it means to be an expert or a critical reader.

"The Loss of the Creature" argues that people have trouble seeing and understanding the things around them. Percy makes his point by looking at two exemplary groups: students and tourists. The opening three assignments provide a way for you to work on "The Loss of the Creature" as a single essay, as something that stands alone. You will restate its argument, tell a "Percian" story of your own, and test the essay's implications. Then Richard Rodriguez and Errol Morris provide alternate ways of talking about the problems of "seeing." And, in addition, they provide examples you can use to extend Percy's argument. The last assignment is the occasion for you to step forward as an expert, a person who has something to add to the conversation Percy began and who determines whose text will speak with authority.

ASSIGNMENT 1

Who's Lost What in "The Loss of the Creature"? [Percy]

Our complex friend stands behind his fellow tourists at the Bright Angel Lodge and sees the canyon through them and their predicament, their picture taking and busy disregard. In a sense, he exploits his fellow tourists; he stands on their shoulders to see the canyon.

Such a man is far more advanced in the dialectic than the sightseer who is try-ing to get off the beaten track—getting up at dawn and approaching the canyon through the mesquite. This stratagem is, in fact, for our complex man the weariest, most beaten track of all. (p. 300)

—Walker Percy
The Loss of the Creature

Percy's essay is not difficult to read, and yet there is a way in which it is a difficult essay. He tells several stories—some of them quite good stories—but it is often hard to know just what he is getting at, just what point it is he is trying to make. If he's making an argument, it's not the sort of argument that is easy to summarize. And if the stories (or anecdotes) are meant to serve as examples, they are not the sort of examples that quickly add up to a single, general conclusion or that serve to clarify a point or support an obvious thesis. In fact, at the very moment at which you expect Percy to come forward and talk like an expert (to pull things together, sum things up, or say what he means), he offers yet another story, as though another example, rather than any general statement, would get you closer to what he is saying.

There are, at the same time, terms and phrases to suggest that this is an essay with a point to make. Percy talks, for example, about "the loss of sovereignty," "symbolic pack-ages," "sovereign individuals," "consumers of experience," "a universe disposed by theory," "dialectic," and it seems safe to say that these terms and phrases are meant to name or com-ment on key scenes, situations, or characters in the examples. You could go to the dictionary to see what these words might mean, but the problem for a reader of this essay is to see what the words might mean for Percy as he is writing the essay, telling those stories, and looking for terms he can use to make the stories say more than what they appear to say (about a trip to the Grand Canyon, or a trip to Mexico, or a Falkland Islander, or a student at Sarah Lawrence College). This is an essay, in other words, that seems to break some of the rules of essay writing and to make unusual (and interesting) demands on a reader. There's more for a reader to do here than follow a discussion from its introduction to its conclusion.

As you begin working on Percy's essay (that is, as you begin rereading), you might start with the stories. They fall roughly into two groups (stories about students and those about tourists), raising the question of how students and tourists might be said to face sim-ilar problems or confront similar situations.

Choose two stories that seem to you to be particularly interesting or puzzling. Go back to the text and review them, looking for the small details that seem to be worth thinking about. (If you work with the section on the tourists at the Grand Canyon, be sure to acknowl-edge that this section tells the story of several different tourists—not everyone comes on a bus from Terre Haute; not everyone follows the same route.) Then, in an essay, use the stories as examples for your own discussion of Percy's essay and what it might be said to be about.

Note: You should look closely at the differences between the two examples you choose. The differences may be more telling than the similarities. If you look only at the similarities, then you are tacitly assuming that they are both examples of the same thing. If one example would suffice, presumably Percy would have stopped at one. It is useful to assume that he added more examples because one wouldn't do, because he wanted to add another angle of vision, to qualify, refine, extend, or challenge the apparent meaning of the previous examples.

ASSIGNMENT 2

Telling a "Percian" Story of Your Own [Percy]

The situation of the tourist at the Grand Canyon and the biology student are special cases of a predicament in which everyone finds himself in a modern technical society—a society, that is, in which there is a division between expert and layman, planner and consumer, in which experts and planners take special measures to teach and edify the consumer. (p. 309)

—Walker Percy
The Loss of the Creature

For this assignment, you should tell a story of your own, one suggested by the stories Percy tells—perhaps a story about a time you went looking for something or at something, or about a time when you did or did not find a dogfish in your Shakespeare class. You should imagine that you are carrying out a project that Percy has begun, a project that has you looking back at your own experience through the lens of "The Loss of the Creature." You might also experiment with some of his key terms or phrases (like "dialectic" or "consumer of experience"), but you should choose the ones that seem the most interesting or puzzling—the ones you would want to work with, that is. These will help to establish a perspective from which you can look at and comment on the story you have to tell.

ASSIGNMENT 3

Complex and Common Readings of "The Loss of the Creature" [Percy]

I do not refer only to the special relation of layman to theorist. I refer to the general situation in which sovereignty is surrendered to a class of privileged knowers, whether these be theorists or artists. A reader may surrender sovereignty over that which has been written about, just as a consumer may surrender sovereignty over a thing which has been theorized about. The consumer is content to receive an experience just as it has been presented to him by theorists and planners. The reader may also be content to judge life by whether it has or has not been formulated by those who know and write about life. (p. 304)

This dialectic of sightseeing cannot be taken into account by planners, for the object of the dialectic is nothing other than the subversion of the efforts of the planners. (p. 300)

—Walker Percy
The Loss of the Creature

Percy charts several routes to the Grand Canyon: you can take the packaged tour, you can get off the beaten track, you can wait for a disaster, you can follow the "dialectical movement which brings one back to the beaten track but at a level above it." This last path (or "stratagem"), he says, is for the complex traveler. "Our complex friend stands behind his fellow tourists at the Bright Angel Lodge and sees the canyon through them and their predicament, their picture taking and busy disregard. In a sense, he exploits his fellow tourists; he stands on their shoulders to see the canyon." (p. 300)

When Percy talks about students studying Shakespeare or biology, he says that "there is nothing the educator can do" to provide for the student's need to recover the specimen from its educational package. "Everything the educator does only succeeds in becoming, for the student, part of the educational package." (p. 310)

Percy, in his essay, is working on a problem, a problem that is hard to name and hard to define, but it is a problem that can be located in the experience of the student and the experience of the tourist and overcome, perhaps, only by means of certain strategies. This problem can also be imagined as a problem facing a reader: "A reader may surrender sovereignty over that which has been written about, just as a consumer may surrender sovereignty over a thing which has been theorized about."(p. 304)

The complex traveler sees the Grand Canyon through the example of the common tourists with "their predicament, their picture taking and busy disregard." He "stands on their shoulders" to see the canyon. What happens if you apply these terms—"complex" and "common"—to reading? What strategies might a complex reader use to recover his or her sovereignty over that which has been written (or that which has been written about)?

For this assignment, write an essay that demonstrates a common and a complex reading of "The Loss of the Creature." Your essay should have three sections (you could number them).

The first two sections should each represent a different way of reading the essay. One should be an example of the work of a common reader, a reader who treats the text the way the common tourists treat the Grand Canyon. The other should be an example of the work of a complex reader, a reader with a different set of strategies or a reader who has found a different route to the essay. You should feel free to draw on either or both of your previous essays for this assignment, revising them as you see fit to make them represent either of these ways of reading. Or, if need be, you may start all over again.

The third section of your paper should look back and comment on the previous two sections. In particular, you might address these questions: What does the complex reader see or do? And why might a person prefer one reading over another? What is to be gained or lost?

ASSIGNMENT 4

Rodriguez as One of Percy's Examples [Percy, Rodriguez]

Those who would take seriously the boy's success—and his failure—would be forced to realize how great is the change any academic undergoes, how far one must move from one's past. It is easiest to ignore such considerations. So little is said about the scholarship boy in pages and pages of educational literature. Nothing is said of the silence that comes to separate the boy from his parents. Instead, one hears proposals for increasing the self-esteem of students and encouraging early intellectual independence. Paragraphs glitter with a constellation of terms like *creativity* and *originality*. (Ignored altogether is the function of imitation in a student's life.) (p. 352)

—Richard Rodriguez
The Achievement of Desire

"The Achievement of Desire" is the second chapter in Rodriguez's autobiography, *Hunger of Memory: The Education of Richard Rodriguez.* The story Rodriguez tells is, in part, a story of loss and separation, of the necessary sacrifices required of all those who take their own education seriously. To use the language of Percy's essay, Rodriguez loses any authentic or sovereign contact he once had with the world around him. He has become a kind of "weary traveler," deprived of the immediate, easy access he once had to his parents, his past, or even his own thoughts and emotions. And whatever he has lost, it can only be regained now—if it can be regained at all—by a complex strategy.

If Percy were to take Rodriguez's story—or a section of it—as an example, where would he place it, and what would he have to say about it?

If Percy were to add Rodriguez (perhaps the Rodriguez who read Hoggart's *The Uses of Literacy* or the Rodriguez who read through the list of the "hundred most important books of Western Civilization") to the example of the biology student or the Falkland Islander, where would he put Rodriguez, and what would he say to place Rodriguez in the context of his argument?

For this assignment, write two short essays. For the first essay, read Rodriguez's story through the frame of Percy's essay. From this point of view, what would Percy notice, and what would he say about what he notices?

Rodriguez, however, also has an argument to make about education and loss. For the second essay, consider the following questions: What does Rodriguez offer as the significant moments in his experience? What does he have to say about them? And what might he have to say to Percy? Is Percy one who, in Rodriguez's terms, can take seriously the scholarship boy's success and failure?

Your job, then, is to set Percy and Rodriguez against each other, to write about Rodriguez from Percy's point of view, but then in a separate short essay to consider as well what Rodriguez might have to say about Percy's reading of "The Achievement of Desire."

ASSIGNMENT 5

Encountering Experience [Percy, Morris]

Errol Morris's photographic essay "Will the Real Hooded Man Please Stand Up?" shares many of Percy's concerns. In fact, it is easy to imagine Morris using "The Loss of the Creature" as a title for his own essay. Percy is broadly concerned with all experience, with how we do (or don't) encounter what is there before us. Morris's primary concern is with how we encounter photographic images specifically. He says:

> Photographs attract false beliefs the way flypaper attracts flies. Why my skepticism? Because vision is privileged in our society and in our sensorium. We trust it; we place our confidence in it. Photography allows us to uncritically think. We *imagine* that photographs provide a magic path to truth.

> What's more, photographs allow us to think we know more than we really do. We can imagine a context that isn't really there. (paras. 58–59) [e]

Morris and Percy ask similar questions, and they write with similar urgency. Let's take their projects' similarities as a starting point. What are they? Make a brief list. Then, as you reread the essays, think primarily about the differences. Both are concerned with loss. What, for each, has been lost? What are the reasons? What are the consequences? What options are available for restoration?

Write an essay in which you use Percy's or Morris's point of views as a starting point. Then, consider the other's understanding of loss, its origins, and its consequences.

ASSIGNMENT 6

Taking Your Turn in the Conversation [Percy, Rodriguez, Morris]

> I refer to the general situation in which sovereignty is surrendered to a class of privileged knowers, whether these be theorists or artists. A reader may surrender sovereignty over that which has been written about, just as a consumer may surrender sovereignty over a thing which has been theorized about. The consumer is content to receive an experience just as it has been presented to him by theorists and planners. The reader may also be content to judge life by whether it has or has not been formulated by those who know and write about life. (p. 304)
>
> —Walker Percy
> *The Loss of the Creature*

It could be argued that all of the work you have done in these assignments has been preparing you to test the assumptions of Percy's essay "The Loss of the Creature." You've read several accounts of the problems facing tourists and students, people who look at and try to understand what is before them. You have observed acts of seeing, reading, and writing that can extend the range of examples provided by Percy. And you have, of course, your own work before you as an example of a student working under the guidance of a variety of experts. You are in a position, in other words, to speak in response to Percy with considerable authority. This last assignment is the occasion for you to do so.

For this assignment, you might imagine that you are writing an article for the journal that first printed "The Loss of the Creature." You can assume, that is, that your readers are expert readers. They have read Percy's essay. They know what the common reading would be, and they know that they want something else. This is an occasion not for summary, but for an essay that can enable those readers to take a next step in their thinking. You may challenge Percy's essay, defend and extend what it has to say, or provide an angle you feel others will not have seen. You should feel free to draw as much as you can on the writing you have already done, working sections of those papers into your final essay. Percy has said what he has to say. It is time for you to speak, now, in turn.

· · ● · ·

A WAY OF COMPOSING

Paulo Freire
John Berger
Alison Bechdel

This sequence is designed to offer a lesson in writing. The assignments will stage your work (or the process you will follow in composing a single essay) in a pattern common to most writers: drafting, revising, and editing. You will begin by identifying a topic and writing a first draft; this draft will be revised several times and prepared as final copy.

This is not the usual writing lesson, however, since you will be asked to imagine that your teachers are Paulo Freire, John Berger, and Alison Bechdel and that their essays are addressed immediately to you as a writer, as though these writers were sitting by your desk and commenting on your writing. In place of the conventional vocabulary of the writing class, you will be working from passages drawn from their essays. You may find that the terms these teachers use in a conversation about writing are unusual—they are not what you would find in most composition textbooks, for example—but the language is powerful and surprising. This assignment sequence demonstrates how these writers could be imagined to be talking to you while you are writing, and it argues that you can make use of a theoretical discussion of language—you can do this, that is, if you learn to look through the eyes of a writer eager to understand his or her work.

Your work in these assignments, then, will be framed by the words of Freire, Berger, and Appiah. Their essays are not offered as models, however. They are offered as places where a writer can find a vocabulary to describe the experience of writing. Writers need models, to be sure. And writers need tips or techniques. But above all, writers need a way of thinking about writing, a way of reading their own work from a critical perspective, a way of seeing and understanding the problems and potential in the use of written language. The primary goal of this assignment sequence is to show how this is possible.

ASSIGNMENT 1

Posing a Problem for Writing [Freire]

Students, as they are increasingly posed with problems relating to themselves in the world and with the world, will feel increasingly challenged and obliged to respond to that challenge. Because they apprehend the challenge as interrelated to other problems within a total context, not as a theoretical question, the resulting comprehension tends to be increasingly critical and thus constantly less alienated. Their response to the challenge evokes new challenges, followed by new understandings; and gradually the students come to regard themselves as committed. (pp. 222–23)

— Paulo Freire
The "Banking" Concept of Education

One of the arguments of Freire's essay "The 'Banking' Concept of Education" is that students must be given work that they can think of as theirs; they should not be "docile" listeners but "critical co-investigators" of their own situations "in the world and with the world." The work they do must matter, not only because it draws on their experience but also because that work makes it possible for students to better understand (and therefore change) their lives.

This is heavy talk, but it has practical implications. The work of a writer, for example, to be real work must begin with real situations that need to be "problematized." "Authentic reflection considers neither abstract man nor the world without men, but men in their relations with the world" (p. 223). The work of a writer, then, begins with stories and anecdotes, with examples drawn from the world you live in or from reading that could somehow be said to be yours. It does not begin with abstractions, with theses to be proven or ideas to be organized on a page. It begins with memories or observations that become, through writing, verbal representations of your situation in the world; and, as a writer, you can return to these representations to study them, to consider them first this way and then that, to see what form of understanding they represent and how that way of seeing things might be transformed. As Freire says, "In problem-posing education, men develop their power to perceive critically *the way they exist* in the world *with which* and *in which* they find themselves; they come to see the world not as a static reality, but as a reality in process, in transformation" (p. 223).

For this assignment, locate a moment from your own recent experience (an event or a chain of events) that seems rich or puzzling, that you feel you do not quite understand but that you would like to understand better (or that you would like to understand differently). Write the first draft of an essay in which you both describe what happened and provide a way of seeing or understanding what happened. You will need to tell a story with much careful detail, since those details will provide the material for you to work on when you begin interpreting or commenting on your story. It is possible to write a paper like this without stopping to think about what you are doing. You could write a routine essay, but that is not the point of this assignment. The purpose of this draft is to pose a problem for yourself, to represent your experience in such a way that there is work for you to do on it as a writer.

You should think of your essay as a preliminary draft, not a finished paper. You will have the opportunity to go back and work on it again later. You don't need to feel that you have to say everything that can be said, nor do you need to feel that you have to prepare a "finished" essay. You need to write a draft that will give you a place to begin.

When you have finished, go back and reread Freire's essay as a piece directed to you as a writer. Mark those sections that seem to offer something for you to act on when you revise your essay.

ASSIGNMENT 2

Giving Advice to a Fellow Student [Berger]

Yet when an image is presented as a work of art, the way people look at it is affected by a whole series of learnt assumptions about art. Assumptions concerning:

> Beauty
> Truth
> Genius
> Civilization
> Form
> Status
> Taste, etc. (para. 11) 🄴

> —John Berger
> *Ways of Seeing*

Berger suggests that problems of seeing can also be imagined as problems of writing. He calls this problem "mystification." "Mystification is the process of explaining away what might otherwise be evident." One of his examples of the kind of writing he calls mystification cites a reference to

Hals's unwavering commitment to his personal vision, which enriches our consciousness of our fellow men and heightens our awe for the ever-increasing power of the mighty impulses that enabled him to give us a close view of life's vital forces.

This way of talking might sound familiar to you. You may hear some of your teachers in it, or echoes of books you have read. Teachers will also, however, hear some of their students in that passage. Listen, for example, to a passage from a student paper:

Walker Percy writes of man's age-old problem. How does one know the truth? How does one find beauty and wisdom combined? Percy's message is simple. We must avoid the distractions of the modern world and learn to see the beauty and wisdom around us. We must turn our eyes again to the glory of the mountains and the wisdom of Shakespeare. It is easy to be satisfied with packaged tours and *Cliffs Notes*. It is more comfortable to take the American Express guided tour than to rent a Land Rover and explore the untrodden trails of the jungle. We have all felt the desire to turn on the TV and watch *Dallas* rather than curl up with a good book. I've done it myself. But to do so is to turn our backs on the infinite richness life has to offer.

What is going on here? What is the problem? What is the problem with the writing—or with the stance or the thinking that is represented by this writing? (The student is writing in response to Percy's essay "The Loss of the Creature," one of the essays in the text. You can understand the passage, and what is going on in the passage, even if you have not read Percy's essay. Similarly, you could understand the passage about Frans Hals without ever having seen the paintings to which it refers. In fact, what it says could probably be applied to any of a hundred paintings in your local museum. Perhaps this is one of the problems with mystification.)

For this assignment, write a letter to the student who wrote that paragraph. You might include a copy of the passage, with your marginal comments, in that letter. The point of your letter is to give advice—to help that student understand what the problem is and imagine what to do next. You can assume that he or she (you choose whether it is a man or a woman) has read both "The 'Banking' Concept of Education" and "Ways of Seeing." To prepare yourself for this letter, reread "Ways of Seeing" and mark those passages that seem interesting or relevant in light of whatever problems you see in the passage above.

ASSIGNMENT 3

Writing a Second Draft [Freire, Berger]

Problem-posing education, as a humanist and liberating praxis, posits as fundamental that the people subjected to domination must fight for their emancipation. To that end, it enables teachers and students to become Subjects of the educational process by overcoming authoritarianism and an alienating intellectualism; it also enables people to overcome their false perception of reality. The world—no longer something to be described with deceptive words—becomes the object of that transforming action by men and women which results in their humanization. (p. 226)

—Paulo Freire
The "Banking" Concept of Education

There is a difference between writing and revising, and the difference is more than a difference of time and place. The work is different. In the first case, you are working on a subject—finding something to say and getting words down on paper (often finding something to say *by* getting words down on paper). In the second, you are working on a text, on something that has been written, on your subject as it is represented by the words on the page.

Revision allows you the opportunity to work more deliberately than you possibly can when you are struggling to put something on the page for the first time. It gives you the time and the occasion to reflect, question, and reconsider what you have written. The time to do this is not always available when you are caught up in the confusing rush of composing an initial draft. In fact, it is not always appropriate to challenge or question what you write while you are writing, since this can block thoughts that are eager for expression and divert attention from the task at hand.

The job for the writer in revising a paper, then, is to imagine how the text might be altered—presumably for the better. This is seldom a simple, routine, or mechanical process. You are not just copying-over-more-neatly or searching for spelling mistakes.

If you take Freire and Berger as guides, revision can be thought of as a struggle against domination. One of the difficulties of writing is that what you want to say is sometimes consumed or displaced by a language that mystifies the subject or alienates the writer. The problem with authoritarianism or alienating intellectualism or deceptive words is that it is not a simple matter to break free from them. It takes work. The ways of speaking and thinking that are immediately available to a writer (what Berger calls "learned assumptions") can be seen as obstacles as well as aids. If a first draft is driven by habit and assisted by conventional ways of thinking and writing, a second can enable a writer to push against habit and convention.

For this assignment, read back through the draft you wrote for assignment 1, underlining words or phrases that seem to be evidence of the power of language to dominate, mystify, deceive, or alienate. And then, when you are done, prepare a second draft that struggles against such acts, that transforms the first into an essay that honors your subject or that seems more humane in the way it speaks to its readers.

ASSIGNMENT 4

Writing about Writing [Bechdel]

Writing and reading are major themes in Bechdel's work. There's the story of Bechdel writing the very work we are reading. There is her journaling, her mother's journaling, and Bechdel's references to writers like Virginia Woolf and Sylvia Plath. So one way of reading "The Ordinary Devoted Mother" is to understand the piece as being about reading and writing and perhaps also about the life of the mind.

If you think of the piece as being about the work of reading and writing, what does Bechdel seem to suggest about what writing does, where it comes from, and what it is for? What is Bechdel's philosophy on reading and writing as far as you can tell? What does her work tell you about the process of its own making? Write an essay in which you offer Bechdel's theory of composition, making an argument for how Bechdel understands the creative process of writing.

ASSIGNMENT 5

Preparing a Final Draft [Freire, Berger, Bechdel]

Their response to the challenge evokes new challenges, followed by new understand-
ings; and gradually the students come to regard themselves as committed. (pp. 222–23)
— Paulo Freire
The "Banking" Concept of Education

A piece of writing is never really finished, but there comes a point in time when a writer
has to send it to an editor (or give it to a teacher) and turn to work on something else. This
is the last opportunity you will have to work on the essay you began in assignment 1. To
this point, you have been working under the guidance of expert writers: Freire, Berger,
and Bechdel. For the final revision, you are on your own. You have their advice and their
example before you. You have your drafts, with the comments you've received from your
instructor (or perhaps your colleagues in class). You should complete the work, now, as
best you can, honoring your commitment to the project you have begun and following it
to the fullest conclusion.

Note: When you have finished working on your essay and you are ready to hand it in,
you should set aside time to proofread it. This is the work of correcting mistakes, usually
mistakes in spelling, punctuation, or grammar. This is the last thing a writer does, and it is
not the same thing as revision. You will need to read through carefully and, while you are
reading, make corrections on the manuscript you will turn in.

The hard work is locating the errors, not correcting them. Proofreading requires a
slowed-down form of reading in which you pay attention to the marks on the page rather
than to the sound of a voice or the train of ideas, and this form of reading is strange and
unnatural. Many writers have learned, in fact, to artificially disrupt the normal rhythms of
reading by reading their manuscripts backward, beginning with the last page and moving
to the first; by reading with a ruler to block out the following lines; or by making a photocopy, grabbing a friend, and taking turns reading out loud.

· · • · ·

WAYS OF SEEING (II) :e

John Berger

This sequence asks you to examine claims that John Berger makes about our ways of
seeing art. The first assignment invites you to consider what he says about how we look at
paintings, pictures, and images, and what all this has to do with "history." The second asks
you to write about a painting, giving you an opportunity to demonstrate how the meaning

of this piece of art from the past belongs to you. The third assignment then turns you back on your own writing so that you can examine it for the expectations and strategies that came into play when you wrote about the painting you chose. The final assignment invites you to review your first paper in the sequence so that you can enter into conversation with Berger about what gets in the way when we look at pictures, paintings, and images, and what all this might have to do with "history."

ASSIGNMENT 1

Berger's Example of a Way of Seeing [Berger]

We are not saying that there is nothing left to experience before original works of art except a sense of awe because they have survived. The way original works of art are usually approached — through museum catalogues, guides, hired cassettes, etc. — is not the only way they might be approached. When the art of the past ceases to be viewed nostalgically, the works will cease to be holy relics — although they will never re-become what they were before the age of reproduction. We are not saying original works of art are now useless. (para. 60) 🄴

—John Berger
Ways of Seeing

Berger argues that there are problems in the way we see or don't see the things before us, problems that can be located in and overcome by strategies or approaches.

For Berger, what we lose if we fail to see properly is history: "If we 'saw' the art of the past, we would situate ourselves in history. When we are prevented from seeing it, we are being deprived of the history which belongs to us" (para. 12). It is not hard to figure out who, according to Berger, prevents us from seeing the art of the past. He says it is the ruling class. It is difficult, however, to figure out what he believes gets in our way and what all this has to do with "history." 🄴

For this assignment, write an essay explaining what, according to Berger, gets in the way when we look at pictures, paintings, or images, and what this has to do with history.

ASSIGNMENT 2

Applying Berger's Methods to a Painting [Berger]

A people or a class which is cut off from its own past is far less free to choose and to act as a people or class than one that has been able to situate itself in history. This is why — and this is the only reason why — the entire art of the past has now become a political issue. (para. 69) 🄴

—John Berger
Ways of Seeing

Berger says that the real question facing those who care about art is this: "To whom does the meaning of the art of the past properly belong? To those who can apply it to their own lives, or to a cultural hierarchy of relic specialists?" As Berger's reader, you are invited to act as though the meaning of the art of the past belonged to you. Go to a museum or, if that is not possible, to a large-format book of reproductions in the library (and if that is not possible, to the reproduction of Vermeer's *Woman Pouring Milk* that is included in the essay). Select a painting you'd like to write about, one whose "meaning" you think you might like to describe to others. Write an essay that shows others how they might best understand that painting. You should offer this lesson in the spirit of John Berger. That is, how might you demonstrate that the meaning of this piece of art from the past belongs to you or can be applied in some way to your life?

Note: If possible, include with your essay a reproduction of the painting you select. (Check the postcards at the museum gift shop.) In any event, you want to make sure that you describe the painting in sufficient detail for your readers to follow what you say.

ASSIGNMENT 3

A Way of Seeing Your Way of Seeing [Berger]

What we make of that painted moment when it is before our eyes depends upon what we expect of art, and that in turn depends today upon how we have already experienced the meaning of paintings through reproductions. (para. 62) 🄴

—John Berger
Ways of Seeing

Return to the essay you wrote for assignment 2, and look at it as an example of a way of seeing, one of several ways a thoughtful person might approach and talk about that painting. You have not, to be sure, said everything there is to say about the painting. What you wrote should give you evidence of a person making choices, a person with a point of view, with expectations and strategies that have been learned through experience.

For this assignment, study what you have written and write an essay that comments on your previous essay's way of seeing (or "reading") your painting. Here are some questions that you should address in preparing your commentary:

1. What expectations about art are represented by the example of the person you see at work in your essay?

2. What is the most interesting or puzzling or significant thing that the viewer (you) was able to see in this painting? How would you characterize a viewer who would notice this and take it as central to an understanding of the painting?

3. What do you suppose the viewer must necessarily have missed or failed to see? What other approaches might have been taken? What are the disadvantages of the approach you see in the essay?

4. Is there anything you might point to as an example of "mystification" in that essay? ("Mystification" is the term Berger uses to characterize writing that sounds like this: "[referring to] Hals's unwavering commitment to his personal vision, which enriches our consciousness of our fellow men and heightens our awe for the ever-increasing power of the mighty impulses that enabled him to give us a close view of life's vital forces.") Is there anything in your essay you might point to as an example of mystification's opposite?

5. Berger says, "If we 'saw' the art of the past, we would situate ourselves in history." As you look back over your essay, what does any of what you wrote or saw (or failed to write or see) have to do with your position in "history"?

6. Berger says that what you write depends on how you have already experienced the meaning of paintings. What are the characteristic features in the work of a person who has learned from Berger how to "experience the meaning of paintings"? If you were to get more training in this—in the act of looking at paintings and writing about them—what would you hope to learn?

ASSIGNMENT 4

Reviewing the Way You See [Berger]

Now that you have had the opportunity to work with Berger's examples of "seeing" and with your own examination of a painting (and your way of seeing it), this final assignment invites you to return to the first paper you wrote in this sequence, to review it with an eye to revising what you had to say about what gets in the way when we look at pictures, paintings, or images. When you first worked on this assignment, you were untangling Berger's ideas about what gets in the way. This assignment is an occasion for you to speak with him, comment on his ideas, or challenge them. You know more now, after having written about a work of art and then studied that writing for what it could be said to show about your expectations and strategies. You have firsthand experience now with the problem Berger poses, and that experience should inform your review.

Write an essay in which you revise your first essay for this sequence. This time, you are in a position to add your response. Your revision, in other words, will do more than tighten up or finish that first attempt. The revision is an opportunity for you to come forward as both a speaker and an authority. Berger's text becomes something you can use in an essay of your own. Or, to put it another way, in this draft you are in a position to speak with or from or against Berger. He will not be the only one represented. Your revision should be considerably longer than your first draft, and a reader should be able to see (or hear) those sections of the essay which could be said to be yours.

— • • ● • • —

WORKING WITH FOUCAULT

Michel Foucault

This sequence is designed to give you a chance to work your way through "Panopticism" by summarizing Michel Foucault's argument, by interrogating the summary (as it does and doesn't "capture" Foucault), and by putting Foucault to work in a Foucauldian analysis of primary materials. The first two assignments are summary assignments, in which you grapple with Foucault's argument. You will be asked to look for what you missed or left out on a first reading and to account for these absences as meaningful rather than simply accidental or "mistakes." And you will be asked to consider the consequences of a project whose goal is to "master" an author who is a critic of mastery. The second two assignments ask you to apply Foucault's terms and methods to material outside his text. The final assignment asks you to reread Foucault once again, to discuss his essay and your work with it.

ASSIGNMENT 1

Foucault's Fabrication [Foucault]

About three-quarters of the way into the chapter, Foucault says,

> Our society is one not of spectacle, but of surveillance; under the surface of images, one invests bodies in depth; behind the great abstraction of exchange, there continues the meticulous, concrete training of useful forces; the circuits of communication are the supports of an accumulation and a centralization of knowledge; the play of signs defines the anchorages of power; it is not that the beautiful totality of the individual is amputated, repressed, altered by our social order, it is rather that the individual is carefully fabricated in it, according to a whole technique of forces and bodies. (p. 200)

This prose is eloquent and insists on its importance to our moment and our society; it is also very hard to read or to paraphrase. Who is doing what to whom? How do we think about the individual being carefully fabricated in the social order?

Take this chapter as a problem to solve. What is it about? What are its key arguments? its examples and conclusions? Write an essay that summarizes "Panopticism." Imagine that you are writing for readers who have read the chapter (although they won't have the pages in front of them) and who are at sea as to its arguments. You will need to take time to present and discuss examples from the text. Your job is to help your readers figure out what it says. You get the chance to take the lead and be the teacher. At the same time, you should feel free to acknowledge and write about sections you don't understand.

After you have written a draft, go back over it and Foucault's chapter. What did you leave out or miss? What did you pass over or ignore? Why? What questions might you ask to open these sections up and make them "readable"?

Write a one-page "coda" to your essay in which you account for these omissions as evidence of a "technology" (perhaps unacknowledged) for dealing with a difficult text. You are not apologizing for the omissions but describing what might otherwise seem a natural or inevitable way of responding to a difficult text.

ASSIGNMENT 2

The Technology of Mastery (A Revision) [Foucault]

After rereading "Panopticism" and taking note of what you left out of your summary for assignment 1 (and taking note, perhaps, of what other students in your class or group left out), go back and revise your summary. Again, you should feel free to acknowledge and write about sections you don't understand. You can make understanding tentative, provisional ("I'm not sure what Foucault means in this passage, but I think it is . . ."). Again, your goal is to provide a summary that will be useful to others who have read this chapter (although, again, they won't have the pages in front of them and hence you will have to include passages in quotation). You may want to translate difficult terms and turn to examples that are local and familiar for your audience.

When you are done, reread your revision and write another one-page "coda." This time, use the coda to talk about the technology of mastery and control. What is it that allows you to begin to control, to discipline, this unruly and resistant text? In assignment 1 you looked at Foucault again to see what you left out. Here, you will be looking at your text to see how and where you establish your authority as a reader.

ASSIGNMENT 3

Prisons, Schools, Hospitals, and Workplaces [Foucault]

Perhaps the most surprising thing about Foucault's argument in "Panopticism" is the way it equates prisons with schools, hospitals, and workplaces, sites we are accustomed to imagining as very different from prison.

At the end of the chapter, Foucault poses two questions (which he leaves unanswered) about the relationship between prisons and the other institutions:

> Is it surprising that the cellular prison, with its regular chronologies, forced labor, its authorities of surveillance and registration, its experts in normality, who continue and multiply the functions of the judge, should have become the modern instrument of penalty? Is it surprising that prisons resemble factories, schools, barracks, hospitals, which all resemble prisons? (p. 208)

For this assignment, take the invitation of Foucault's conclusion. No, you want to respond, it is not surprising that "experts in normality, who continue and multiply the functions of the judge, should have become the modern instrument of penalty." No, it is not surprising that "prisons resemble factories, schools, barracks, hospitals, which all resemble prisons." Why isn't it surprising? Or—why isn't it surprising if you are thinking along with Foucault?

Write an essay in which you speak from your work with Foucault. In that essay, work out the resemblances he points to, and then assess the significance of those resemblances. Are the resemblances significant? superficial? In relation to what? And what are the important differences you note? How would you argue their significance to an audience concerned with "experts in normality" or the key sites for surveillance and control?

ASSIGNMENT 4

Writing, Surveillance, and Control [Foucault]

At the end of this assignment, you will find four essays written by twelfth graders in 1923 as part of an evaluation project. The project was designed to normalize grading practices in English departments across the country. Teachers, it was proposed, would all assign the same topic. The question for the essays included here was this: Write an essay describing how you learned a lesson. All students would write under the same conditions, for fifty minutes in class under a teacher's supervision. All the essays would be graded against a set scale, one that could be used by teachers anywhere in the United States. The following essays were chosen to establish the scale. They represent the lowest possible score (1), the middle scores (5 and 6), and the highest possible score (10).

For this assignment, treat these student essays as examples chosen by "experts in normality," by judges, perhaps, who would want them to stand as a centralization of writing evaluation, and use them as a way of talking, after Foucault, about control, normality, constraint, and surveillance.

You can assume that even though methods of evaluation may have changed since these essays were written, the order of the essays (the hierarchy of value) would be preserved by schools and agencies across the country. The order 1 through 10 represented here, in other words, would be taken for granted as natural, right, inevitable. Your job is to jolt your reader out of the "natural" view in order to see it as representing a particular agenda and set of values. This is not an easy job—to step out of the discourse of the normal, the usual way of thinking, speaking, valuing. Here are two sets of questions you might ask to interrogate this material:

1. Imagine, for a minute, that you can become an English teacher and adopt an English teacher's values. How would you explain and justify the order of these essays? What terms are available? What arguments? What assumptions about writing and schooling and intelligence and mastery? Now, ask yourself why it is so easy for you to adopt that point of view. And ask what it would take to step out, to see the "popo bush" essay as preferable to the "Grub Hollow" essay. How many alternative orders can you imagine? How would you explain or justify or rationalize them? What light do they throw on the explanations

that belong to "English"? How, in fact, do they allow you to argue with or throw new light on "English" and its technologies of value and order?

2. Think about how and where you can bring passages or examples from Foucault to bear on your examples. You may need to work back through the text to do this. Remember—Foucault points to connections between prisons and schools. You are working with and not against Foucault if you make these associations. In particular, see how you can bring his discussions of control and surveillance to bear on these essays and their order. What knowledge is represented in incremental stages by the order in these essays? What does it have to do with "hierarchical surveillance" and "classification"? What knowledge is represented by this method of analysis—that is, what knowledge is represented by the expert judgment that chose these essays and ordered them? What might it have to do with control and constraint? What knowledge of writing is excluded here? What alternative accounts of mastery and expertise are excluded?

Write an essay that presents these examples and uses them to develop an argument about knowledge and constraint, about control, supervision, and classification. You can assume that your readers will have read Foucault's chapter but that they will need your help to see its application to these materials. You should assume that they do not have the examples of these essays in front of them, that you have come across them in an old book in a back quarter of the library. Part of your work, and not a small part, will be to present the examples so that a reader can understand and be interested in them.

How I Learned a Lesson (1923)

_____

SAMPLE 1

When I chewed tobacco and they found it owt they whipped me for about fifteen minnutes with popo bush. they broke ten switches out on me. but i kept on chewing. they found it out and my papa and Mamma whipped me for abowt twenty minnutes and learn me a lesson.

Score: 1

_____

SAMPLE 2

It is said that experience is a dear teacher and *that* is one of the lessons I learned along with the real lesson.

One day I came home from school (as I have been in the habit of doing for the past eleven years) to find the house locked. When our house is locked up and the family go out there are just two ways I know of to get in. The first and by far the easiest is to get the particular key that belongs to the lock in the front door and after inserting it in the lock, turn it, push forward and the door will come open. If a key cannot be obtained there is just one way left, as I know of (and I have had years of experience) and that is to get a good heavy brick and heave it thru the window. Not that I have ever tried this method but it's the only sure remidy left as I *have* tried all the others my brain could conjur up.

Score: 5

SAMPLE 3

Two years ago I worked for a meat shop. Every day I spent a good deal of money on such things as soft drinks, ice cream, and other good things. I did this all summer. My mother warned me against it, but I kept indulging in these things.

By the time school commenced I began to have stomach trouble. Mother made me quit eating anything I wanted, and kept me on a diet. Finally I was cured of the trouble. Since then I do not "eat drink and be merry" as much as then.

Score: 6

SAMPLE 4

When I sat down to think over the experiences of my life that have been profitable to me my memory wandered back to one of the big lessons I learned when I was yet a little child.

I was in the sixth grade in a little country school. Here I mingled with children from all stations in life and made friends with them all. There was, however, something insincere with my friendship for the poorer children. It was due, I now believe, to a feeling of superiority over them. I resented the ravenous manner in which they ate the lunches I divided with them; I detested their furtive glances when we talked; and I could not tolerate their tendency to lie. In all, they had an uncouth bearing that I could neither understand nor forgive.

That spring our teacher invited me to go with her while she took the enumeration. After visiting a number of homes we came to a place called Grub Hollow where several of our school patrons lived. In one little shack we found the family huddled around a little stove, the walls and floors bare, and everything most squalid and depressing. In another, a dirty, miserable hovel, we found a blind father, an indolent, flabby mother, and three mangy children. Finally we found a family of fourteen living in one room amid unspeakable conditions.

On our way home Miss Marxson was strangely silent, and, child that I was, tears stood in my eyes. I had heard "the still sad music of humanity," and it had given me a new understanding. Never again did I feel haughtily toward those children; and all through life that experience has modified my judgment of human conduct.

Score: 10

ASSIGNMENT 5

The Two-Step [Foucault]

This assignment has two parts. For the first, go back to your summary of Foucault's chapter in assignment 2. Once again, go back to the chapter to see what you have skipped, ignored, missed, or, from your new vantage point, misrepresented or misunderstood. Mark the passages that continue to befuddle you, that seem to defy understanding, and ask, Why? What makes them difficult? What would it take to make them available to you? Then go to those passages you now feel you understand. Again, why? What has made them available? Write a short essay, two to three pages, in which you use the example of Foucault's chapter to talk about difficulty and mastery, about the process of coming to command a difficult text.

Once you have completed this essay, go back for the last time (at least in this sequence) to revise that summary. As before, you should try to write the kind of summary that acknowledges (rather than ignores or finesses) the parts of the text that seem to defy summary. You should focus on (rather than write over) the difficult sections, doing what you can to translate, explain, provide additional examples. You could imagine, in other words, that you have learned to write a different kind of summary in this sequence, and that its final version is represented here.

Part IV. On *Ways of Reading*

· · ● · ·

Some of the essays that follow were written by current and former graduate students in our department as part of their work in a seminar on the teaching of composition. We include them here because we thought it would be helpful for you to hear from people who had taught for a year, and in some cases for the first time, from *Ways of Reading*. We hope that the discussions of their teaching and their experiences with selected readings and sequences will be helpful to you as you teach from our book. We would also like their essays to stand for the kind of work people can do in graduate seminars that make use of *Ways of Reading* for the study of the teaching of composition and literature.

Edward Said in the Classroom in the Era of Globalization

Rashmi Bhatnagar

The kinds of difficulty posed by the reading of "States," the chapter from Edward Said's *After the Last Sky* excerpted in *Ways of Reading,* can also serve as opportunity for strong writing and self-conscious reading for first-term composition students. Toward this end I discuss the assignment titled "A Photographic Essay" in *Ways of Reading,* which shines the light on the student's chosen photos that "represent people and places," challenging the student to narrate their stories and read their visual portraits and thus give them value, with the added complication of imitating the styles of Said in a "Said-like reading of a set of photos" (Bartholomae). Imitation writing shifts the student writer from a place of confusion and perceived lack of authority into a position of confidence about her writing. The student may be unfamiliar with the histories, languages, literatures, and politics of the human subjects photographed by Jean Mohr and described in Said's prose. This is not a deterrent because the student draws from the reading whatever appeals to her and serves her project in the photo essay assignment; she returns for a closer look at the reading after the first draft of her essay.

I also discuss the work of revision—second readings, teacher's comments on the first draft, peer review, revision guidelines—as tasks that work well with class discussion of the work that lays shadowily behind the "States" chapter, namely, Said's acclaimed work *Orientalism.* Much of what I say here draws from twenty-odd years of association with Edward Said's work as a postcolonial scholar who has taught Said in the U.S. academy and at Delhi University. This experience does not make me the source for the correct reading of "States." At best it makes me a careful reader of students' readings of Said's work. For instance, over the course of teaching the Said assignment in *Ways of Reading* in composition classes at the University of Pittsburgh and Boise State University, I learned two lessons from student papers. I learned that imitation of "States" enables student writers to discuss new Orientalisms in language, cultural artifacts, media images, and consumer products. The second lesson is a corollary to the first, namely, that new Orientalisms are not an obsolete remnant of earlier eras; rather they are a prominent feature of globalization.

In the process of learning from student papers, I often wonder if I could have done things differently in the classroom. For this reason the final section of the present essay offers a critique of my own comments on students' first drafts and shares my rethinking as a teacher. Second drafts for the Said assignment in *Ways of Reading* might be better served with revision suggestions that guide the student writer to engage with the logical second step of imitation writing, namely, attentiveness to those aspects of "States" that constitute style—styles of argument and styles of representation through word and image.

Imitation and Student Writing

Imitation is covert operations enacted at the site of a text. We enter a text's machinery and open its valves. We fuel our writing with vital energies of the imitated text. Yet the joke is on us, for the energies channeled into our imitations are in reality our own knowledge and our own powers of decoding and reassembling what we read in accents of parody, postmodern pastiche, or photo essay. The Said assignment in *Ways of Reading* taps into two sources of writing—imitation and visuality—and makes them available to student writing. The writer apprehends the reading through his own knowledge and powers of decoding and reassembling his chosen stories and photos and through his individual perspective on people, places, history, and geography that he knows well.

Precisely because the student writer is not asked to write directly about the reading, he notices more and he notices differently. In the context of dominant narratives of globalization, the Said assignment poses the problem of reading globally for composition students. After turning in a photo essay on the Depression era, my student John had more to say about the reading. Therefore, John adds this narrative as an appendix to his essay. Imitating Said in the photo essay makes him aware of reading as an experience with many layers. As John reads "States," he recalls earlier scenes of reading and viewing news broadcasts:

> As an American college student in the early twenty-first century I have
> long held a negative stereotype of the Palestinian people. Quite frankly, I viewed
> them as many of my peers and the media had projected upon me. Having been
> an avid viewer of both the local and national news broadcasts since a young age,
> I cringed every time I heard of a new suicide bombing or attack on innocent
> Jewish citizens. Developing into maturity during the post–9/11 era, I believed
> strongly that this was the face of "evil" or terror. Had it not been for personal
> experiences reading Edward Said's "States," I believe I would still harbor these
> disgusting notions. Said was able to persuade me more toward a view that it is
> neither the Jew nor Palestinian in this conflict that is victimless. Both people
> have suffered immensely, and when it comes down to it, neither is to blame.

In this passage John rehearses some of the moves of good writing. For instance, he connects his own lived experiences to his reading, constructs a word picture, and provides a narrative concerning the evolution of his thoughts. The work of imitation and in particular the work of imitating Said enables John to do something more with these standard moves. In the first sentence of the passage John locates himself in relation to his reading; this self-location is in terms of his identity "as an American college student." These moves in John's paper are rapidly done and stay within the realm of clichés. The reason I place emphasis on these moves in John's paper is that without recognizing either the terminology or the knowledges called Orientalism, the student writer seems to execute some of the work of critical thinking.

Later in the passage John makes another self-locating move, this time to identify with an age group that developed "into maturity" in a modern climate of thought. In John's words, "I viewed them [the Palestinians] as many of my peers and the media had projected upon me" and he names this project "the face of 'evil' or terror." By analyzing the ways the media "projected" a group of people as the face of evil, John names a key feature of the climate of thought in globalization: information technologies compose narratives, these narratives are instantaneously relayed through captions and repetitive images in cyberspace, the end result is that viewers interpret the relayed images and words through the culture of fear. Thus, my point about John's paper is that when and if student writing discusses new Orientalisms without the proper name of Orientalism, the teacher can convert this into an opportunity to discuss fresh perspectives for revision work.

Orientalism as Segue into Revision Work

In my class lectures and discussion assignments for the Said assignment I find the following aspects of Said's book *Orientalism* useful. At the moment in their academic lives when students enter introductory classes, they are equipped for critical reading and strong writing through awareness of the complex relations between academic disciplines and images about the Orient. Students grasp the idea that academic knowledge can either reinforce or challenge images of the Oriental Arab that represent him as antimodern, fanatic, misogynist, and an object of our fear. The Foucauldian element in Said's work has this advantage: it allows students to perceive the academy both as a place of multiple scholarly traditions that contest one another and as a place of intellectual choice, as well as an institutional site that is invigorated by scholarly disagreements.

Relationships between language and Orientalism are relevant to the composition class since much of our work involves attention to the operation of language in writing. Students both resist and are intrigued by the Saidian view of language. In his introduction to *Orientalism*, Said warns us: "One ought never to assume that the structure of Orientalism is nothing more than a structure of lies or of myths which, were the truth about them to be told, would simply blow away" ("Introduction to Orientalism" 1280). Is the stereotype of the Oriental woman as an image of passivity and victimage a lie or objective truth? In Said's view, when a sufficient number of people possessing scholarly authority or political power transmit a certain image in words, painting, and media, a discourse forms that is internally consistent and that has the power to construct its own reality. Thus, our view of the Oriental woman is influenced by Orientalist discourse to such an extent that we notice only those elements that reinforce our belief in her passivity and victimage; we do not notice other dimensions of her social and family life, which foreground her agency. It is in this context that Jean Mohr's photographs of women in "States"—standing beside her husband, sitting beside her husband on a sofa, striding across the refugee camp, leaning on the table to write a letter, giving a message to the local official seated in the car—counter the dominant Orientalist idea of women's dependency and seclusion.

Said's book *Orientalism* contends that the division of the world into Orient and Occident, West and non-West, has contoured the simplest grammatical relation between the pronouns "we" and "they" whenever the pronouns are used to designate the relation between *we* as students and teachers in the West and *they* as Israeli and Palestinian people in particular and the global refugee, internally displaced populations, and disposable poor in general. To underscore this point, Said examines "ideas about what 'we' do and what 'they' do and what 'they' cannot do or understand as 'we' do" ("Introduction to Orientalism"). Said's provocative thesis is that the ways our writing, speech, and media represent "they" determines in large part the construction of "we" in our society. "Indeed, my real argument is," notes Said, "that Orientalism . . . as such has less to do with the Orient than it does with 'our' world" ("Introduction to Orientalism" 1284). This aspect of Orientalism is relevant to the Said assignment because the assignment invites students to construct through imitation relationships between the student writer and the people described in "States" and between students' photo essays and Mohr's photographs of the Palestinian people.

Finally, Orientalism and Said's subsequent work is relevant to composition class work. It offers us ways to think about how we, as users of language and in our role as spectators of traditional and old media, have a choice either to accept and conform to the conventions of Orientalism or to feel stifled by the prison of Orientalist language. Alternately, we can return to "States" for directions that permit other ways of describing ourselves in relation to the Near East. The introductory writing class is a place where an institutional requirement of small class size and emphasis on class discussion, workshopping, and revision provide the opportunity for students' lived knowledges, received ideas, and "street smarts" to collide with the accumulated common sense of the poets, photographers, scholars, and critics compressed into their textbook. This collision activates critical thinking. Thus, revision of the Said assignment through class discussions of Orientalism enables rather than distracts a composition class from its designated tasks of reading and writing.

Student Writing and New Orientalisms in Globalization

Can students in first-term composition classes comprehend Orientalism? I would like to suggest that they are in fact active users of language and image codes of Orientalism; students are surrounded by that discourse. My contention is borne out in the common refrain in writings by my students John and Pervez and in the work of the Saidian scholar Aamir Mufti. Both the beginning writers and the senior scholar associate reading of Said with the problematic of public fear. Mufti's point is that debates about the culture of fear are precisely debates about Orientalism in its present form. "Orientalism may now be read fruitfully," observes Mufti, "as a sustained warning about the global atmosphere of fear that is now our everyday experience" (Mufti).

Reading Said through the theme of fear in public places is also a key motif in the photo essay submitted by a Pakistani-American student. The photographs Pervez chose were of his family chatting, eating, and visiting an amusement park. The part of "States" that he chose to imitate were the ways Mohr's photographs capture ordinary and routine activities. At a certain point in the essay, Pervez broke off into an account of what was not contained in the photographs:

> Said is trying to portray life in a war-torn Palestinian community. . . .
> Said, in his essay, is not showing the reader how things happened, instead he
> is making you believe you are there. . . . Speaking as a Muslim man, I am sick
> and tired of the word terrorist and Islam used in the same sense. . . . We lead the
> same life as many Americans. For example, we go to amusement parks to have
> fun just like anyone else. This particular instance we went to Kennywood Park
> located in Pennsylvania. . . . As we were boarding one ride, an arrogant white
> man yelled: "Go home you terrorist, you are destroying our country." At that
> point I felt embarrassed and did not continue to stay in line for that ride.

The *Ways of Reading* assignment presents the student writer with a paradox—how can the Saidian narrative about loss of community provide resources for a story "about people and places"? Both John and Pervez resolve this paradox by deploying the Said assignment as a vehicle to articulate their lived experiences of *fractured* community. Each is located differently: John sketches himself viewing media images and cringing, and Pervez describes his embarrassment when his family's enjoyment is marred by hate speech. Imitating Said means that the student writer does not confine himself to mere description of the experience of panic. John reflects on media images that produce fear, and Pervez narrates the specific way hate speech produces fear and embarrassment. Fear gives way to John's sense of the common suffering of "both people" and the conviction that the globally distant story concerns communities and community life in which "neither is to blame." These are small moves in the writing by John and Pervez, yet their significance lays in the fact that both student writers describe the dominant machinery of new Orientalisms and also imitate the Said–Mohr project of dismantling mainstream media imagery and language.

To Mufti's updating of Orientalism I add the following modification based on my teaching experience. If we define Orientalism not only as the body of scholarship by Orientalists but also as linguistic currency in everyday speech, media captions, radio shows, music lyrics, and television news, then an examination of new Orientalisms reveals that undergraduate students are the target audience for consumer products that reassemble Orientalism in marvelously creative ways. In the course of analyzing how the "clash of civilizations" thesis is a post–Cold War mapping of the globe, Said comments on the modus operandi of globalization's Orientalisms. Said criticizes the "sense of cutting through [of] a lot of unnecessary detail" and "boiling" the cognitive map of the globe down into "a couple of catchy, easy-to-quote-and-remember ideas, which are then passed off as pragmatic, practical, sensible, and clear" ("The Clash of Definitions" 573).

The official story of globalization is that it is post-Orientalism, that it is free of prejudices that constituted classical imperialisms of the nineteenth century and mired decolonizations of the twentieth century in violence. The proof is that globalization dispenses with divisions of Orient and Occident and carves the world as markets and the free flow of commodities, with knowledge and social interaction serving as one commodity among many. Contradicting the official story, Said comments on the hyperlucid condensations of language and thought in "easy-to-quote-and-remember" catchphrases like "clash of civilizations." Division between civilized and savage gives way to division between nations that are economic success stories and debt-ridden national economies teeming with slums.

One of the charges laid on Said by the critic Aijaz Ahmad is that his view of Orientalism is monolithic. This is pertinent to beginning students because they are unsure if they can write around or against such a monolith. Students find it enabling to return to the reading and examine Jean Mohr's role in light of this issue. Clearly the Swiss photographer was able to see his Palestinian subjects through the camera lens without turning them into the figure of the Oriental Arab. I ask students, What is it that Mohr's photographs do that is outside the box? Students comment that the Mohr photographs seize on saturated media images of the visually encoded Arab Palestinian, his *djellaba*, the Muslim woman's *burqa*, and Palestinian children. Mohr's images emphasize ordinariness and everydayness in Palestinian men, women, and children clothed predominantly in Western-style clothes and hand-me-down t-shirts or wedding gowns.

Moreover, the Mohr photographs perform self-location by claiming their Palestinian subjects and the accompanying written text by Said as brother texts. This phrase derives from my student Cairon's photo essay where he says at one point: "As an American, I see the Palestinians as brothers and sisters in a great struggle." Instead of hierarchic relation, the Mohr photos succeed in establishing interesting conversations with Said's words, persuading the reader that photos and writing are brother texts in the common project of bearing witness to the suffering of the refugee.

One of the pitfalls of the Said assignment in *Ways of Reading* is that the histories, suffering, families, oppression, and visual records of the Palestinian people function as a silent and passive landscape on which the student writer superimposes her story of her friends or family. What can the student writer do to prevent this superimposition, and how can she construct a brother text? In his lifetime's work Said indicated certain directions for combating reinventions of the Oriental Arab. One of those directions is pursued in *Ways of Reading* assignments on experimental writing and forms the subject of the final section of this essay.

Globalization as Style versus the Styles of Said

One direction toward which Said's work points as antidote to new Orientalisms is style. Experimentations by poets, novelists, photographers, and artists of film, news media, music, and painting might show the way to new subjectivities, human realities, new ways of imagining time and space, location and dislocation and resistances. In both *After the Last Sky* and a later essay titled "After Mahfouz" Said analyzes writing not in terms of the rationality of ideas but in terms of the logic of form and the logic of image. In the course of his analysis of a Palestinian writer, Said notes that the story is undermined as a narrative "by the novel's peculiarly disintegrating prose, in which within a group of two or three sentences time and place are in such an unrelenting state of flux that the reader is never absolutely certain where and when the story is taking place" ("After Mahfouz"). This description might well fit one of the styles of disintegration in *After the Last Sky* and affords us a clue concerning one of the chief modes of Saidian resistance.

Said's work on visuality also runs counter to the dominant trend in globalization within which intellectual debate is reduced and compressed to matters of style both in the sense of technology and in the sense of fashion. Contrarily, Said argues in an essay on the collaboration between John Berger and Mohr that the photograph "because of its peculiar status as a quotation from reality containing traces of the historic world . . . is not so easily co-opted" ("Bursts of Meaning" 150). If the styles of Said constitute a gateway to politics and intellectual life of the future, conversely, styles of globalization constitute an escape from the realm of politics, history, and social justice.

When student papers resist the Said reading, what is at stake is as much an argument about contrasting styles as an argument about political and social life. Students' resistance to revising the Said assignment is not the issue here—that is to be expected in an introductory class—but rather the *particular forms* for students' language of resistance. What follows is an attempt not so much to bring resistant readings in line with the approved reading of Said, but rather to listen to their words and look for that opening in their work where resistance turns into strong writing. For instance, students draw on phrases like "pity me writing" to display the ways they are inured to writing that invites them to enlarge their capacities for imaginative knowledge and compassion. For history-laden essays, students often have a simple one-rule formula—look to the future, get over it. As a case in point, my student Michelle states:

> In his essay "States" Edward Said focuses on how the Palestinians had
> lost their homeland. . . . And while this does make the reader feel compassion
> for the people of Palestine it does create a problem. Throughout the whole essay
> Said focuses only on the bad and on the past and never looks at how people have
> dealt with the changes presented to them. . . . They need to find a way of moving
> on and dealing with the problem. And even though Said makes valid points about
> how much the Palestinians have had to deal with he needs to realize that they
> need to get out of the past.

To illustrate her argument, Michelle composes a photo essay about a group of friends who are presented in images that stress their enthusiasm for future years at college. In retrospect I read her first draft as providing a clue to the problems specific to teaching the Said reading. For students, to read Said on the Palestinian people is to confront a disorienting picture of a part of the globe that signifies ancient histories and origins of world religions. Palestine signifies the presentness of several pasts in a volatile present. What may be at work in Michelle's critique as well is students' ambivalence about Saidian aesthetics of sadness; typically students respond positively to individualized romantic sadness but are overwhelmed by texts that portray the same emotion in a collective.

A prominent feature of globalization discourse appears in and through Michelle's words. At a broader level of generality, globalization theorists have described this notion as a component of the end-of-history thesis by Francis Fukuyama, a thesis criticized publicly by Said and modified in Fukuyama's later work. The eternal present and the sense of having arrived at the end of history delineate the principal tenet of the style, in the fullest sense of the word, of globalization. It is a style that can be glimpsed in Michelle's sense that the way to address the past is to "get out of the past." It would be more useful if I, as her teacher, staged my comments on her first draft as a contest of styles. In one style, global citizenship requires us to view the past as that which we must get over and move on from. In the other style, adopted and developed by Said, the past is evoked in its presentness, and Said's enduring preoccupation with Proustian meditations on time conveys his sense that the seed of the future lies in mining the past for insight and understanding.

My shift from content to form as a way of negotiating resistance in student writing resulted from my conversation with Carissa. In her retrospective Carissa looked at her Said paper with pride because she received an A grade on her final revision. I had encouraged her to develop her opinion that "States" does not present the Israeli side. In her first draft Carissa wrote a strong polemic, and I wrote back in my comments:

> I support your project about telling "their story about the land that is theirs" but I
> am not sure what evidence you offer that Said says anywhere in the essay that the
> land does not belong to the Israeli people, or that he supports the "random acts of

violence" against the people. You seem to conflate Said and his essay with those acts of violence, which seems to me to be a stereotype. One way to address this is to go back to the essay and reexamine those sentences, stories, and photographs which include this Israelis, and then discuss what else Said should have done to present the Israeli side of the story.

My comments laid emphasis on a return to the text to read more carefully and comment on its inclusiveness. I now think that my comments should have directed her to considerations of style. For instance, when Carissa writes about Israeli people in her paper, one way to strengthen her revision is to shift her discussion from justificatory polemic and dwell instead on imitating the cartographic imagination in "States." Referring to *After the Last Sky*, the critic Salah Hassan observes: "Said visits and revisits in his writing Arab places to produce a map of the region" (Hassan). Carissa might conceivably execute a Said-like reading of her chosen subject—the people of Israel—by imaginatively visiting Israeli towns and settlements. Style can function therefore as a bridge for Carissa. She can imitate the Said text without abandoning her pro-Israeli and anti-Said polemic while exploring the imaginative resources of language to make her argument.

In her response to my comments excerpted above, Carissa makes excellent use of the text through quotations. She then makes a remarkable move. She locates a place in the text where she sees Said describing how Palestinians are forced to carry identification cards. Carissa comments that in this passage Said constructs the Palestinian condition as a parallel to the Jewish persecution in the Holocaust. After acknowledging the parallelism, Carissa proceeds to dismiss it. It is the grounds of Carissa's dismissal that are of interest to me here. She argues that "many students will not realize this hidden side" and then concludes: "They (the Israeli Jews) need a louder voice than a parallel [in Said's writing]."

I suggest that Carissa is in effect making an argument about style. In this case, the contest over styles hinges on whether "the other side" (the title of Carissa's paper) ought to be presented "in a louder voice" or in the muted style of parallel histories. Student papers that are overtly critical of "States" seem to speak from the vantage point of a *style* of thought about history, compassion, and aesthetics of sadness in narrating the dispossession of a whole people. Codes for visuality, for relations between image and caption, for the correct pitch at which a writer might tell the other side of a story, undergird a student writer's resistance to Said. Might a combination of the photo-essay assignment and the style assignment in *Ways of Reading* serve these students better, provide their resistant readings the stimulant for good writing?

It is an error to believe that composition students cannot grasp the styles of Said or that they would fail to "get" what Said means by disintegrating prose and its relevance to the many styles in "States." Here, for instance, my student Cairon analyzes a paragraph in the Said reading that discusses form:

> The Palestinian author struggles to "achieve form" because his/her own world has no form. Their environment has no specific form, no structure, no permanence. How can one express form when they themselves have never experienced stability.

All three students—Michelle, Carissa, and Cairon—engage with the reading as style. Although the first two disavow the aesthetic principles of Said's styles, Cairon adopts a sympathetic stance and accepts the point Said makes about the relation between form and historical conditions. What I am arguing here is that the revision of the photo essay is best negotiated through attention to matters of style. I do not mean to diminish the substantive arguments a student writer makes in her criticism of Said by turning it into a question of form. Styles contain condensed markers for a range of arguments; in this sense globalization's styles are highly compressed arguments in themselves. To discuss student papers on Said as an argument about style allows student writers to mine their highly evolved and sophisticated understandings of the formal grammar of the discourses that surround them.

The teaching of reading and writing is a historically situated and geographically determinate activity, not a timeless craft or *techne* that transmits a set of skills and an essential body of knowledge. Assuming such a definition of the work of the composition classroom, it follows that we learn the problems and possibilities of globalization not only from scholarship and theory but also from student–teacher interactions as a microcosm of social space and political discourse. Each composition teacher has to resolve the terms in which she or he defines the relevance of *After the Last Sky* in the context of globalization. Without that preparatory work, Edward Said in the classroom takes on the glamour of an aging rock star whose work must be taught in a hushed voice because he speaks to our settled past and has nothing to do with our turbulent present. If the teaching of Said is delayed until undergraduates reach upper-level writing and literature classes or graduate study, we may risk losing the diverse literacies they bring into the introductory classes. Well-informed readers and self-conscious and self-critical writers constitute a time-honored recipe for a fearless citizenry, vitalized democracy, and public debate about social justice.

WORKS CITED

Bartholomae, David, and Anthony Petrosky. *Ways of Reading: An Anthology for Writing.* 7th ed. Boston: Bedford/St. Martin's, 2005.

Hassan, Salah D. "Other Places: Said's Map of the Middle East." *Paradoxical Citizenship: Edward Said.* Ed. Silvia Nagy-Zekmi. New York: Rowman & Littlefield. 221–28.

Mutfi, Aamir R. "Critical Secularism: A Reintroduction for Perilous Times." *boundary2* 31.2 (2004): 1–9.

Said, Edward W. "After Mahfouz." *Reflections on Exile and Other Essays.* Cambridge, Mass.: Harvard University Press, 2000. 317–26.

———. "Bursts of Meaning: On John Berger and Jean Mohr." *Reflections on Exile and Other Essays.* Cambridge, Mass.: Harvard University Press, 2000. 148–52.

———. "Introduction to Orientalism." *The Critical Tradition: Classic Texts and Contemporary Trends.* Ed. David H. Richter. New York: Bedford/St. Martin's, 1998. 1278–92.

I would like to thank Jonathan Arac, Steve Carr, and Pankhuree Dube for valuable commentary on earlier drafts of this essay. I also thank the students for permission to quote from their papers. Names of student writers are pseudonyms in accordance with students' wishes.

We Got the Wrong Gal: Rethinking the "Bad" Academic Writing of Judith Butler

Cathy Birkenstein

It is hard to think of a writer whose work has been more prominently upheld as an example of bad academic writing than the philosopher and literary theorist Judith Butler. In 1998, Butler was awarded first prize in the annual Bad Writing Contest established by the journal *Philosophy and Literature*, and early in 1999, was lampooned in an editorial in the *Wall Street Journal* by Denis Dutton, one of the chief architects of the contest. Quoting Butler's award-winning sentence, Dutton claimed that Butler's "inept," "jargon-laden" prose was typical of the obscurantist writing being admired and emulated in the most elite circles of today's academic humanities:

> The move from a structuralist account in which capital is understood to structure social relations in relatively homologous ways to a view of hegemony in which power relations are subject to repetition, convergence, and rearticulation brought the question of temporality into the thinking of the structure, and marked a shift from a form of Althusserian theory that takes structural totalities as theoretical objects to one in which the insights into the contingent possibilities of structure inaugurate a renewed conception of hegemony as bound up with the contingent sites and strategies of the rearticulation of power. (Qtd. in Dutton)

Passages like this, Dutton argued, show that Butler and the other allegedly incomprehensible writers targeted by his contest are mere "kitsch theorists" who, unlike genuine philosophers like Kant and Aristotle, "hope to persuade audiences not by argument but by obscurity." Such writers, Dutton claimed, only "mimic the effects of rigor and profundity without actually doing serious intellectual work." Butler's sentence, Dutton wrote, "beats readers into submission and instructs them that they are in the presence of a great and deep mind. Actual communication has nothing to do with it."

The way Dutton pitches the story, this is a classic emperor-has-no-clothes moment. Though Butler, like her other tenured radical colleagues, is supposed "to teach students how to write," she herself, Dutton suggests, cannot put together a coherent sentence. Her writing, despite its high pretentiousness, Dutton charges, seems incapable of delivering "genuine insight."

These, of course, are familiar charges that have been leveled against difficult academic writing, and sometimes against all writing in the academic humanities. They raise questions about which there still remains little consensus, even a full decade after *Philosophy and Literature* discontinued its Bad Writing Contest in 1999, and six years after Butler and several of her defenders answered the critics of difficult academic writing in a volume in 2003 (Culler and Lamb). Is "bad" academic writing in the humanities as reader-repellent as is charged? Is the difficulty of this writing merely a pretentious bluff—an attempt to divert attention from its lack of content? Do writers who produce this ostensibly unreadable prose

This essay first appeared in *College English*, volume 72, number 3, January 2010.

betray their obligation to address lay, nonspecialist audiences? Or, as its defenders reply, is the apparent difficulty of this writing justified or even necessary for expressing its challenging, heterodox content? Are difficult writers like Butler being true to ideas that would only be compromised by being reduced to popular forms and conventional registers?

In 1999, the same year Dutton took Butler to task in the *Wall Street Journal*, the feminist moral philosopher Martha Nussbaum published a harsh, widely cited critique of Butler in the *New Republic*, claiming that Butler's "ponderous and obscure" writing, like that of other postmodern feminists, breaks with the normal communicative practices that characterize "both the continental and Anglo-American philosophical traditions" (38). Since Nussbaum spends over half of her review quarrelling with the specific arguments that Butler advances in her books, one might have expected Nussbaum to concede that Butler does make comprehensible arguments that readers can discern well enough to either agree or disagree with. Nevertheless, like Dutton, Nussbaum claims that readers, including herself presumably, are "baffled by the thick soup of Butler's prose" (38). Instead of "trad[ing] arguments and counter-arguments" (40), Nussbaum insists, Butler enacts a rhetorical "mystification that eludes criticism because it makes few definite claims" (38). According to Nussbaum, Butler writes in a "teasing, exasperating way," presenting herself as "a star who fascinates, and frequently by obscurity, rather than as an arguer among equals." Echoing Dutton, Nussbaum concludes that Butler "bullies the reader into granting that, since one cannot figure out what is going on, there must be something significant going"—though again, Butler's alleged lack of clarity did not prevent Nussbaum from vigorously disagreeing with her (39).

These critiques had been anticipated in 1998 by Susan Gubar, who argued in *Critical Inquiry* that Butler's "obscurantism" is so "at odds with normative syntactic procedures" that it hinders the "tolerance and understanding needed for open dialogue" and separates "feminists within the academy [from] [. . .] women outside it" (894, 880–81).[1] And two years earlier, the journalist Katha Pollitt, writing in the *Nation*, complained that Butler and other "silly" "pseudo-leftists" combine a reckless rejection of "reason, logic, [. . .] and other Enlightenment watchwords" with an annoying "penchant for bad puns and multiple parentheses." According to Pollitt, Butler and other "self-infatuated" "humanities profs" write so poorly that even they themselves

> don't really understand one another's writing and make their way through the text by moving from one familiar name or notion to the next like a frog jumping across a murky pond by way of lily pads. Lacan . . . performativity . . . Judith Butler . . . scandal . . . (en)gendering (w)holeness . . . Lunch!

From across the political spectrum, then, and both inside and outside the academy, Butler and other difficult writers are accused of being elitists who, despite their egalitarian pretentions, promote a discourse that values flash over substance, and obfuscation over lucid argumentation.

Defenders of such writing have not sat by idly in the face of these accusations. In perhaps the most concerted response to date, several literary and cultural theorists, including Butler herself, came together in the 2003 volume *Just Being Difficult?: Academic Writing in the Public Arena*, edited by Jonathan Culler and Kevin Lamb. The contributors argue that the attacks on difficult writing rest on a set of double standards: that they target writers like Butler who are influenced by post-structuralism and postmodernism, while saying nothing about those who write in equally opaque ways in non-continental, analytic and empirical traditions; furthermore, that the accusers apply a standard of transparency to writers in the humanities that would never be applied to writers in the sciences, law, or medicine, where opacity and jargon are often expected if not demanded.

Yet one thing is curious about many of the defenses of Butler's alleged difficulty. Instead of refuting the charge that this writing is in fact bad and opaque, as one might expect, these respondents concede the substance of the charge or even embrace it. That is, many of the contributors to *Just Being Difficult?* agree that Butler's type of writing *is* deeply inaccessible, but insist that this inaccessibility is necessitated by the ideologically laudable goal of disrupting our culture's normative, sedimented ways of thinking, questioning the status quo, unsettling readers, and ultimately leading them to new insights.

Margaret Ferguson, for instance, whose essay opens the collection, sets the tone by quoting favorably the following passage by Theodore Adorno, which is also quoted favorably by several of the collection's other contributors. Lamenting how most consumers approach communication in mass, commercial society, Adorno writes,

> Only what they do not need first to understand, they consider understandable; only the word coined by commerce, and really alienated, touches them as familiar. (Qtd. in Ferguson 19)

In other words, Adorno suggests, commercial society tends to reject anything that does not reinforce conventional common sense—its preexisting vision of what the "understandable" and "familiar" look like. Conversely, Adorno suggests, unconventional language that refuses to conform to the already familiar has the subversive potential to jar us out of this complacency into new, unexpected, and more productive ways of understanding.

Citing this Adorno passage in her own essay in *Just Being Difficult?*, Butler argues that "the demand that language deliver what is already understandable appears to be a demand to be left alone with what one already knows." Indeed, Butler even sees in the demands for clear, accessible, popular writing a parochial defense of "self-satisfied-ignorance":

> What does it say about me when I insist that the only knowledge I will validate is one that appears in a form that is familiar to me, that answers my need for familiarity, that does not make me pass through what is isolating, estranging, difficult, and demanding? (203)

Although Butler does concede that there are merits to writing lucidly for a broad, popular audience, she insists that such writing tends ultimately to reinforce pernicious "relations of subordination and exclusion," while language that is "ruled out as [. . .] unintelligible" can be a "resource [. . .] to rethink the world radically"—or, as she puts it in a *New York Times* article answering her critics, "to [. . .] provoke new ways of looking at a familiar world" ("Values of Difficulty" 201; "'Bad Writer'" A27).

Along similar lines, Michael Warner defends difficult theoretical writing in the humanities on the grounds that it "keep[s] alive an alternative that may be reanimated in some distant future," even if it is unclear to mainstream readers today (119). Taking a different tack, Rey Chow sees the difficulty of theoretical, postmodern writing not as an elitist attempt to prevent communication with nonacademics, as the "anti-theory moralists" suggest, but as a laudable attempt to resist capitalist globalization—as a "heroic, if Sisyphisian effort to obstruct the path of a sweeping global instrumentalism," which requires language to "become more clear, more accessible, and more useable [for] [. . .] the developing nation" (99, 102). Obfuscatory prose, in short, strikes a blow for the proletariat! And finally, John McCumber sees the "suspect" call for clarity as a "misguided effort" to "force us all to remain in ancient and oppressive habits of thought" (69). Though he himself writes in a register that is itself unexpectedly intelligible and clear, McCumber argues that, instead of maligning the "seemingly unintelligible words" of Butler and those she summarizes and quotes, we should celebrate such words as "emancipatory" expressions of "playfulness, improvisation, and freedom itself" (69).

Surprisingly, then, many who defend Butler's writing and the type of theoretical discourse it represents agree with Butler's critics that her writing is inaccessible when judged by normative standards of accessibility. While Dutton, Nussbaum, and others condemn Butler's alleged inaccessibility to mainstream readers, Butler and many of her allies praise that alleged inaccessibility on the grounds that it has the subversive potential to liberate those very same readers. But is Butler's writing really that inaccessible and unintelligible? Does her writing really depart from common standards and conventions of clarity? My own view is that, far from breaking from recognized standards of intelligibility, Butler's writing conforms to those standards in ways that are missed by both her detractors and most of her defenders, Butler included. Though Butler's writing certainly does have unclear moments, it would not have had the wide impact it has had were it not for its ability to consistently make recognizable arguments that readers can identify, summarize, and debate. Butler's writing has succeeded in circulating as widely as it has in academic circles and beyond not because it breaks with the traditional pattern of "trad[ing] arguments and counter-arguments," as Nussbaum insists (40), but precisely because it makes systematic use of this classic argumentative pattern, and does so in ways that all writers (and readers) can learn from.

• • • ● • • •

I am not the first to notice Butler's rhetorical adeptness. In his essay in *Just Being Difficult?*, Jonathan Culler defends the difficulty and opacity of some philosophical writing, but rightly insists that these terms do not describe the sentence that won Butler the Bad Writing Prize and that Dutton mocked as incomprehensible in his *Wall Street Journal* article. Culler argues that, when Butler's sentence is restored to the context of the three-page essay that surrounds it, it actually makes a lot of sense. After quoting the award-winning sentence, Culler states,

> This is difficult writing, certainly, although not excessively so once one understands a few key terms and has in mind some particular illustrations of the process at stake. My undergraduate students quickly become able to handle it. (47)

Culler observes that "despite the high level of abstraction," the essay represents "quite pedagogic writing," in that "key points are rephrased and repeated, so that if you don't catch on the first time around, you have another chance when they come around again" (47). To Dutton's claim that Butler merely "mimic[s] the effects of rigor [. . .] without actually doing serious intellectual work," Culler retorts, "I think this is complete rubbish, actually. I wonder who it is who has failed to do serious intellectual work—such as read Butler's three page article" (45). Although "rubbish" might not be my word of choice, Culler, I think, is absolutely right. Butler's writing is far more lucid than her detractors (and many of her defenders, I would add) imagine. Though I will analyze Butler's award-winning sentence shortly, I now want to extend Culler's insight about Butler's rhetorical skillfulness by showing that she not only uses terms clearly and makes key points in a consistent, coherent, helpfully repetitive (or "pedagogic") fashion, but also organizes her points in the very argumentative, pro/con pattern that she has been condemned and praised for avoiding.

To see what I mean by this unnoticed polemical pattern in Butler's writing, let us start with the opening two sentences of what many consider one of Butler's most difficult books, *Gender Trouble: Feminism and the Subversion of Identity*:

> Contemporary feminist debates over the meaning of gender lead time and again to a certain sense of trouble, as if the indeterminacy of gender might eventually culminate in the failure of feminism. Perhaps trouble need not carry such a negative valence. (vii)

The passage does contain some jargon ("the indeterminacy of gender" and "negative valence"), and the second sentence lacks the kind of transition (a "But" or "However") that would signal that it is challenging the views summarized in the first. Yet I would argue that not only is there nothing fundamentally unclear about this passage, but that it contains a great deal rhetorically to commend it. Through the parallel use of "trouble," Butler twice echoes the key term of her book's title, signaling that these opening sentences are offering a helpful introduction to what the book as a whole will be about. And what it appears to be about is how this "gender trouble" need not, in Butler's view, "carry such a negative valence" as is ascribed to it by those engaged in the "contemporary feminist debates" referred to in the opening sentence. In other words, these opening lines suggest that, while those engaged in "contemporary feminist debates" worry that "the indeterminacy of gender" will undermine feminist activism, I, Judith Butler, will be arguing in this book that this indeterminacy need not be feared—or, as is asserted later in the book, that it should in fact be actively courted as the basis of a feminist politics that is even more radical and far-reaching than that of the trouble-fearing feminists I am responding to. To translate the passage into even more blunt terms: "Although many feminists are troubled by the inability to define *woman*, I believe that this trouble may be precisely what feminism needs"—or, "Though many feminists fear that the 'indeterminacy of gender' will undermine feminism, I assert that this indeterminacy is precisely what feminism needs to fuel its most radical projects."

It is true that Butler might have avoided some of the criticisms of her writing had she spelled out her point as bluntly as I just have. But what she does write, far from being opaque and esoteric, could still stand as a model for all academic writing, much of which may be superficially clearer at the sentence level but lacks Butler's polemical dexterity. Not only do Butler's two opening lines contain something much academic writing sorely lacks—a clear, overarching argument or thesis—but they usefully contextualize that argument by framing it as a challenge to some commonly held belief. Hence, before readers have advanced more than an inch down the opening page of her book, Butler not only has provided them with a succinct preview of her book's central argument (that what many see as bad news for feminism should not be seen so negatively), but also has suggested why that argument matters, which she does by indicating who thinks otherwise, and what other arguments her own is responding to or correcting. In so doing, Butler's writing acquires not just clarity but an underlying motivation and exigency that are woefully absent in the work of many less trendy, traditional writers.

Furthermore, as *Gender Trouble* progresses, Butler does not forget the essential contrast she has established in these opening lines between her own argument and the one she is answering. In keeping with Culler's observations about her repetitive, "pedagogic" style, she keeps returning to and extending this contrast as she moves through the rest of her text. In case readers do not grasp the opposition on their initial encounter, Butler gives them several more chances to process it by returning to it, reframing and redescribing it with a difference in modified terms.

In the following passage, for instance, Butler rearticulates her opening contrast as one between a humanist, foundationalist, origin-seeking position that she is challenging and a "genealogical critique" that she endorses and credits to the work of Michel Foucault. Using the classic road-mapping term *rather* to signal this opposition, Butler states,

> A genealogical critique refuses to search for the origins of gender, the inner truth of female desire, a genuine or authentic sexual identity that repression has kept from view; **rather**, genealogy investigates the political stakes in designating as an *origin* and *cause* those identity categories that are in fact the *effects* of institutions, practices, discourses with multiple and diffuse points of origin. (viii–ix; bolding added)

Echoing this opposition a bit later and marking it with another road-mapping cue, *instead*, Butler writes,

> [I]t is no longer clear that feminist theory ought to try to settle the question of primary identity in order to get on with the task of politics. **Instead**, we ought to ask, what political possibilities are the consequences of a radical critique of the categories of identity? (ix; bolding added)

Passages like these go far toward refuting the charge made by Dutton, Nussbaum, and others that Butler is a pretentious, hollow writer who simply "bullies readers" or "evades" argumentation. On the contrary, these passages suggest that Butler goes out of her way to make her central argument almost impossible to miss—not just by restating it numerous times in a variety of formulations, but by highlighting its presence with clear direction markers, as is further underscored by the *but* and *ought also* in the following passages[2]:

> For the most part, feminist theory has assumed that there is some existing identity, understood through the category of woman, who not only initiates feminist interests and goals within discourse, but constitutes the subject for whom political representation is pursued. **But** *politics* and *representation* are controversial terms. (1; bolding added)

> It is not enough to inquire into how women might become more fully represented in language and politics. Feminist critique **ought also** to understand how the category of "woman," the subject of feminism, is produced and restrained by the very structures of power through which emancipation is sought. (2; bolding added)

In light of such passages, it is hard to agree with Nussbaum's charge that Butler "makes few definite claims" and refuses to posit an "audience of specialists eager to debate (38)," or with Gubar's charge that Butler thwarts "the tolerance and understanding needed for open dialogue" (880–81). If ever there were a rhetoric aimed at fostering "open dialogue" and creating an "audience [. . .] eager to debate," Butler's would be it.

Again, this is not to deny that *Gender Trouble* contains stretches that are so filled with "recondite abstractions," as Gubar calls them (896), that readers can get lost. In Butler's summaries of Luce Irigaray, Simone de Beauvoir, and Monique Wittig in her Introduction, for instance, it is sometimes hard to tell whether Butler is agreeing with these thinkers, disagreeing, partly agreeing and disagreeing with them, or using one to critique the others. Even then, however, these challenging moments tend to be contained, since Butler, given what Culler lauds as her repetitively "pedagogic" manner, inevitably returns to some restatement of the central opposition that structures her book. So even though readers may lose Butler's thread for a paragraph or two, she repeats her book's central structuring opposition often enough that, with a little effort, they can always find their way back to it.

A related set of "not X but Y" contrasts structures the text that contains the sentence for which Butler won the 1999 Bad Writing Award: her 1997 article, "Further Reflections on Conversations of Our Time," a sympathetic exposition of the theories of Ernesto Laclau and Chantal Mouffe. In one classically contrastive sentence, Butler states,

> "patriarchy" or "systems" of masculine domination are **not** systematic totalities bound to keep women in positions of oppression, **but, rather,** hegemonic forms of power that expose their own frailty in the very operation of their iterability. The strategic task for feminism is to exploit those occasions of frailty as they emerge. (14; bolding added)

In this sentence, as in so many others, one can virtually hear Butler talking to skeptics standing by her side, telling them, "No, no, people, please, don't be mistaken. Patriarchy *is not* a system that operates in such and such a way (in a way that is hopelessly unchangeable), *but rather* one that works in such and such a way (that, as Laclau and Mouffe suggest, inadvertently creates opportunities for its own subversion)." In the following passage, this dialogue continues:

> **I would clearly agree** that the incorporative and domesticating possibilities of capital are immense. **But I would also argue** that any theory that fails to think the possibilities of transformation from within that "systematic" formation is itself complicit with the idea of the "eternal" character of capital that capital so readily produces. (13–14; bolding added)

In other words: "**Sure, dear friends, I concede that** [. . .] capitalism is extremely powerful. **But I would point out that** [. . .] we only aid those powers if we see them as immutable."

It is this basic opposition or dialogue—between those who see hegemonic powers as immutable and Butler's own view of them as transformable—that renders accessible the 1998 award-winning sentence that Dutton scorned as so obviously impenetrable, and that I will now quote again:

> The move from a structuralist account in which capital is understood to structure social relations in relatively homologous ways to a view of hegemony in which power relations are subject to repetition, convergence, and rearticulation brought the question of temporality into the thinking of structure, and marked a shift from a form of Althusserian theory that takes structural totalities as theoretical objects

to one in which the insights into the contingent possibility of structure inaugurate a renewed conception of hegemony as bound up with the contingent sites and strategies of the rearticulation of power. (Qtd. in Dutton)

To be sure, nobody would claim that this is a concise, economical sentence. But as Culler points out, it has been so prepared for by its surrounding context that, with a little effort, reasonably educated readers can be expected to understand it. What I would again add to Culler's insight is that, like all of the other Butler passages quoted above and many others I could cite, even this admittedly cumbersome sentence conforms to a conventional pattern of polemical argumentation and counter-argumentation that, in its purest form, can be reduced to a schema like "We need to stop doing this and start doing that instead," or "I agree with X and Y because, in contrast to those who assert __, they assert __." Or, to hug up even more closely to Butler's own sentence structure itself,

> The move from __ to __ marked a shift from __ to __, which has in turn inaugurated a renewed conception of __.[3]

Though Butler's sentence has been widely read as incomprehensible, it contains no fewer than four road-mapping phrases that highlight its dialectical structure: (1) *move from __ to __*; (2) *shift from __ to __*; (3) *inaugurated*; (4) *renewed conception*. Far from flouting standard conventions of argumentation, Butler's supposed disaster of a sentence has a very clear goal: to argue that Laclau and Mouffe, whose views about the iterability of power she had been championing throughout her essay, have ushered in an important new way of thinking that sees hegemony in less static ways than had earlier Marxist theorists and that, in emphasizing repetition and temporality, presents hegemony not as fated or inevitable, but as productively open to renegotiation and change.

Butler, then, is not an impenetrable, esoteric writer who rejects conventional communicative practices, as both her detractors and defenders suggest. Instead, she is a powerful rhetorician who commands the most important of these practices, not only, as Culler points out, by repeating concepts frequently and explaining her references, but also by conforming very closely to the classic rhetorical pattern that Kenneth Burke characterizes as dialecticism, negation, or "perspective by incongruity." This practice involves pushing off against other views, developing one's

> [p]hilosophy [. . .] partially in opposition to other philosophies, so that tactics of refutation are involved, thus tending to give [one's] calculus the stylistic form of a lawyer's plea. (113)

What Burke says of literary works—and of a great variety of everyday "symbolic actions" like praying, consoling, seeking freedom, and scapegoating—applies well to Butler's writing: it presents its central assertions "not in isolation, but as the answer or rejoinder to assertions current in the situation in which it arose" (109).

This habit of answering "assertions current in" her "situation" fits surprisingly well with Butler's postmodern, post-structuralist agenda. Granted, Butler's use of this conventional, dialectical form does contradict her suggestion that "forms that are familiar to me" reinforce the status quo and are to be avoided. But Butler claims that gender norms saturate our everyday lives, and that we cannot simply reject them. She opposes the idea that one could simply dispense with gender norms, as if "one woke in the morning, perused the closet or some more open space for the gender of choice, donned that gender for the day, and then restored the garment to its place at night" (*Bodies* x). Finally, then, Butler's adherence to classical argumentative norms is compatible with what she says about gender norms, since both reside not in dispensing with forms altogether, but in embracing them, watching for instabilities in their repetition and finding ways to use them to our advantage.

Furthermore, I would argue that the specific rhetorical form of "trad[ing] arguments and counterarguments" (Nussbaum 40) that Butler relies on as a writer fits well not just with such Enlightenment notions as universalist normativity, global instrumentalism, linguistic transparency, and the liberal marketplace of ideas that both her critics and defenders associate it with, but also with her own post-structuralist commitment to difference, conflict, alterity, and listening to the voice of the Other. That Butler's dialectical writing aligns with her vision of progressive political action and subjectivity can be seen in the following statement from her 1992 essay "Contingent Foundations: Feminism and the Question of Postmodernism":

> [T]his "I" would not be a thinking, speaking "I" if it were not for the very positions that I oppose, for those positions, the ones that claim that the subject must be given in advance, that discourse is an instrument of reflection of that subject, are already part of what constitutes me. (9)

Butler's claim that she is "already" constituted by the "positions" she "oppose[s]" suggests that she engages her critics not just as a matter of rhetorical practice, but also on some level as a matter of theory. As she says in the passage above, there would be no reason for her to state her own views were it not for those "current in [her] situation," in Burke's terminology (109), who hold the contrary position that the subject is a self-generating entity "given in advance" and that "discourse is an instrument of reflection."

The essay from which I just quoted, "Contingent Foundations: Feminism and the Question of Postmodernism," presents a particularly strong model for writers of how this answering of counter-positions can operate. Once again refuting those who see her as simply "bullying readers" and evading standard norms of argumentation, Butler proceeds by repeatedly summarizing those who disagree with her pro-postmodernism position and see it as "dangerous" and "irrational," as she herself puts it on the article's opening page:

> I know the term [postmodernism] from the way it is used, and it usually appears on my horizon embedded in the following critical formulations: "if discourse is all there is . . . ," or "if everything is a text . . . ," or "if the subject is dead . . . ," or "if real bodies do not exist. . . ." The sentence begins as a warning against an impending nihilism, for if the conjured content of these series of conditional clauses proves to be true, then, and there is always a then, some set of dangerous consequences will surely follow. So "postmodernism" appears to be articulated in the form of a fearful conditional or sometimes in the form of paternalistic disdain toward that which is youthful and irrational. (3)

After defending postmodernism against these "critical formulations," Butler returns to another version of these formulations when she writes, "A number of positions are ascribed to postmodernism [. . .]: discourse is all there is [. . .]; the subject is dead, I can never say 'I' again; there is no reality, only representations" (4) Then, after several more rounds in which Butler again defends postmodernism, returns to her critics, and then states her own position again, she gives her critics still more air time:

> There is the refrain that, just now, when women are beginning to assume the place of subjects, postmodern positions come along to announce that the subject is dead [. . .]. Some see this as a conspiracy against women and other disenfranchised groups who are now only beginning to speak on their own behalf. (14)

So unwilling is Butler to coerce or bully readers that she persistently gives the objections to her own positions a fair hearing, thereby risking that readers will find these objections more persuasive than her own refutations.

Perhaps the ultimate instance of Butler's making herself vulnerable to objections can be found in the 1993 book *Bodies That Matter*. In the seven paragraphs that open the Preface, Butler devotes herself not to advancing her own argument, but again, as should not be surprising by now, to ventriloquizing the views of those who find her central argument to be so misguided as to be foolishly naïve, if not ridiculous. Because, as Butler explains, she "persist[s] in this notion that bodies were in some way constructed," she keeps encountering those who want to "take [her] aside" and, knowing her arguments about the constructed nature of sexuality and gender from her previous work, repeatedly ask her in "exasperated," "patronizing" tones, "What about the materiality of the body?" and again, with even greater exasperation, "What about the materiality of the body, *Judy*" (ix)?

Butler explains:

> I took it that the addition of "Judy" was an effort to dislodge me from the more formal "Judith" and to recall me to a bodily life that could not be theorized away. There was a certain exasperation in the delivery of that final diminutive, a certain patronizing quality which (re)constituted me as an unruly child, one who needed to be brought to task, restored to that bodily being which is, after all, considered to be most real, most pressing, most undeniable. [. . . I]f I persisted in this notion that bodies were in some way constructed, perhaps I really thought that words alone had the power to craft bodies from their own linguistic substance?
> Couldn't someone please take me aside? (ix–x)

What is interesting about the voice of the particular interlocutor that Butler engages in this passage is that it could just as easily be that of an Average Jane or Joe on the street as that of a seasoned academic. Put another way, the skeptical voice that Butler engages in this passage belongs no more to academic culture than it does to the common sense of mainstream culture, to average folk who want to construct Butler not as an authoritative professor but as an "unruly child" — or, perhaps, a bungling, head-in-the-clouds philosopher — in need of *their* superior guidance. "Come on, *Judy*!" they say. "The body isn't constructed. Get real!" Or, as Butler herself puts it later in yet another paraphrase of their countervoice,

> For surely bodies live and die; eat and sleep; feel pain, pleasure; endure illness and violence; and these "facts," one might skeptically proclaim, cannot be dismissed as mere construction. Surely there must be some kind of necessity that accompanies these primary and irrefutable experiences. (xi)

One way of reading *Bodies That Matter* is as an elaborate explanation of why these "irrefutable experiences" do not tell us "what it might mean to affirm them and through what discursive means" (xi).

Rather than walling herself off from mainstream culture's dominant common sense, then, Butler engages it ("bodies are real"; "the category of 'woman' is unproblematic"), though in a way that ultimately challenges instead of capitulates to it. I would argue that a central reason Butler's writing circulates as widely as it does is not that it "beats readers into submission" (Dutton) and evades the conventions of argumentation, but that it enacts these conventions expertly, inviting into its pages readers from a broad range of educational backgrounds and ideological perspectives, specifically those inclined to disagree with her. And it not only encourages those readers to debate her, but goes so far as to provide them with arguments and techniques for debating her in case they are not sure how.

My response then, to those who see Butler as a bad, incomprehensible writer: you got the wrong gal. The academic world may indeed harbor many mystifying, incomprehensible writers, but Butler is not among them. The real culprits we should be concerned about are not Butler, Fredric Jameson, Homi Bhabha, and other theorists typically accused of bad writing, but the many academic writers, whether traditional or theoretical, whose work fails to register on readers because it lacks a discernible argument or point. These are speakers and writers often encountered at conferences and in the pages of journals who may be exceedingly intelligent, knowledgeable, and well-read, and may even be perfectly lucid from sentence to sentence, but who fail to offer an overarching argument or claim, or if they do, fail to suggest who disputes that claim and thus *why* it needs to be offered in the first place.

$$\cdot \ \cdot \ \bullet \ \bullet \ \cdot \ \cdot$$

In the end, then, Butler's example challenges some major misconceptions about the nature of academic writing. First, it challenges the idea that difficult academic writing must adopt a form that is itself difficult or impenetrable—or, more precisely, that challenging, complex academic contents can be conveyed only through writing that itself avoids simple or conventional rhetorical forms. More specifically, my analysis suggests that the most difficult, complicated academic writing that has a wide impact does not avoid binary oppositions and other conventional polemical structures, but is itself polemical, dialectical, and binary. Even writers who wish to challenge or deconstruct binary oppositions must rely on such oppositions, if only the opposition between those who rely on binary opposition themselves. Second, Butler's example challenges the idea that writing that follows a dialectical, "I argue X as opposed to Y" format must necessarily result in texts that are reductive, simplistic, mechanistic, or overly antagonistic—or, as McCumber argues, inherently reactionary or "oppressive" (69). Indeed, the many passages taken from Butler's writing above suggest that this "not X as many argue but Y" format can produce texts that, even while taking a strong position, are democratic models of many-sided dialogue and debate—of listening respectfully to what others think, rather than repressing or maligning it. And third, Butler's example refutes the idea that challenging common sense means flouting traditional dialectical patterns, as many defenders of difficult academic writing suggest. On the contrary, Butler's writing shows that a text's revolutionary impact will be blunted unless it can be read in terms of a sharp "X not Y" contrast—unless, that is, readers can see what commonsense belief is being challenged or revolted against.

Ultimately, then, Butler's writing suggests that all the provocativeness and sophistication of academic writing will be lost on readers unless it is framed by a clear dialectical structure—that without this structure, difficult academic writing will be just plain difficult and have a limited impact on readers. As Burke suggests, writing, in order to move readers, needs some polemical operation to perform, some alternate view to correct, displace, or add to; and this means situating itself within a larger conversation, engaging democratically with alternate viewpoints, supplying an underlying motivation or reason for being, and thereby answering all-important questions like "Who says otherwise?" or "Who needs to hear this?" Ultimately, then, polemical argumentation and counter-argumentation are not the death of academic complexity, but its underlying foundation.

NOTES

[1] Gubar herself builds on Linda Charnes's complaints about Butler's "jargon clotted [. . .] prose" (896).

[2] My argument here about the role of contrastive signal terms builds on John Schilb's point about how academic writers create exigence in their writing, defined by Schilb as the writer's "purpose for writing, the contribution she will make to scholarship." In analyzing a specific example of literary criticism, Schilb shows how the critic uses a contrastive signal term like *but* to help her establish this exigency. This "little word," Schilb writes, helps the critic show that she "is moving beyond familiar truths or easy insights into deeper levels of analysis" (142).

[3] This point that dialogical formulas underlie persuasive writing is heavily indebted to the work of David Bartholomae, Irene Clark, and John Swales and Christine Feak. Distancing himself from notions of writerly "self-expression" and "authenticity," Bartholomae emphasizes the schemas and conventions that academic writers learn to master, and claims that his own writing was greatly improved as an undergraduate when a teacher suggested he use the following "machine": "While most readers of __ have said __, a close and careful reading shows that __" (641). Clark offers graduate student writers patterns for "entering the conversation" (24–25) of other scholars, rather than stating their views in isolation, while Swales and Feak offer scholars formulas for engaging in what they call the "obligatory practice" of "Creating a Research Space" for their own claims by "introducing and reviewing items of previous research" (243–44).

These ideas about the schematic, dialogical nature of persuasive discourse have been crystallized in a textbook that I co-authored with Gerald Graff, *"They Say/I Say": The Moves That Matter in Academic Writing.*

WORKS CITED

Bartholomae, David. "Inventing the University." 1985. *Cross-Talk in Comp Theory: A Reader.* Ed. Victor Villanueva. 2nd ed. Urbana: National Council of Teachers of English, 2003. 623–53. Print.

Burke, Kenneth. "The Philosophy of Literary Form." *The Philosophy of Literary Form: Studies in Symbolic Action.* Berkeley: U of California P, 1973. 1–137. Print.

Butler, Judith. "A 'Bad Writer' Bites Back." *New York Times* 20 Mar. 1999: A27. Print.

———. *Bodies That Matter: On the Discursive Limits of "Sex."* New York: Routledge, 1993. Print.

———. "Contingent Foundations: Feminism and the Question of 'Postmodernism.'" *Feminists Theorize the Political*. Ed. Judith Butler and Joan W. Scott. New York: Routledge, 1992. 3–21. Print.

———. "Further Reflections on Conversations of Our Time." *Diacritics* 27.1 (1997): 13–15. Print.

———. *Gender Trouble: Feminism and the Subversion of Identity*. New York: Routledge, 1990. Print.

———. "Values of Difficulty." Culler and Lamb 199–215.

Chow, Rey. "The Resistance of Theory; or, The Worth of Agony." Culler and Lamb 95–105.

Clark, Irene. *Writing the Successful Thesis and Dissertation: Entering the Conversation*. Upper Saddle River: Prentice Hall, 2007. Print.

Culler, Jonathan. "Bad Writing and Good Philosophy." Culler and Lamb 43–57.

Culler, Jonathan, and Kevin Lamb, eds. *Just Being Difficult?: Academic Writing in the Public Arena*. Stanford: Stanford UP, 2003. Print.

Dutton, Denis. "Language Crimes: A Lesson in How Not to Write, Courtesy of the Professors." *Wall Street Journal* 2 Feb. 1999: W11. Print.

Elbow, Peter. "Methodological Doubting and Believing: Contraries in Inquiry." *Embracing Contraries: Explorations in Learning and Teaching*. New York: Oxford UP, 1986. 253–300. Print.

Ferguson, Margaret. "Difficult Style and 'Illustrious' Vernaculars: A Historical Perspective." Culler and Lamb 15–28.

Graff, Gerald, and Cathy Birkenstein. *"They Say/I Say": The Moves That Matter in Academic Writing*. New York: Norton, 2006. Print.

Gubar, Susan. "What Ails Feminist Criticism?" *Critical Inquiry* 24.4 (1998): 878–902. Print.

McCumber, John. "The Metaphysics of Clarity and the Freedom of Meaning." Culler and Lamb 58–71.

Nussbaum, Martha. "The Professor of Parody: The Hip, Defeatist Feminism of Judith Butler." *New Republic* 22 Feb. 1999: 37–45. Print.

Pollitt, Katha. "Pomolotov Cocktail." *Nation* 10 June 1996: 9. Print.

Schilb, John. "Composing Literary Studies in Graduate Courses." *Disciplining English: Alternative Histories, Critical Perspectives*. Ed. David Shumway and Craig Dionne. Albany: State U of New York P, 2002. 137–48. Print.

Swales, John M., and Christine B. Feak. "Constructing a Research Paper II." *Academic Writing for Graduate Students: Essential Tasks and Skills*. 2nd ed. Ann Arbor: U of Michigan P, 2004. 242–86. Print.

Warner, Michael. "Styles of Intellectual Publics." Culler and Lamb 106–25.

"*La Conciencia de la Mestiza*":[1] Cultural Identity and the Politics of Personal Writing[2]

Bianca Falbo

When I decided to put the excerpts from Anzaldúa's *Borderlands* on the syllabus for my General Writing Women's Studies class, I was worried about two things. One was the difficulty of having students work with the essay itself—not only the shifting languages (since I was fairly sure students could understand how this is inherent to the point Anzaldúa is making about the politics of negotiating cultural identity), but in addition I was uncomfortable with the implications of my asking students to imagine themselves as something other than unified subjects. To the extent that such an idea could be empowering, I knew it could also seem threatening. Consequently, I was worried about how I'd know whether I was challenging students' assumptions or simply alienating them.

The second thing that worried me came from my own resistance to assignments that ask for "personal" writing. In my experience as a teacher, I've come to realize that the "personal" is not readily available to students, that their "own experience" is not simply there for them to write about, that, in fact, it's difficult for students to write interestingly and purposefully about their own lives. This is not to say that their lives are uninteresting, but that the dominant paradigms for writing about a life—the ones students tend to come to college knowing how to produce or, at least, imagine they need to reproduce—do not generate the kind of "academic" writing I imagine as part of the project of General Writing, the kind of writing that they will be expected to do in the university courses they go on to take, writing that engages with, appropriates, and extends someone else's critical project.

This is an essay about how the experience of working with my students on Anzaldúa's text challenged my ideas both about what I imagined my students' experiences to be and about the place of and possibilities for personal writing in an academic classroom. I'll look first at the writing my students produced in response to the assignment, and then at their comments later on in the course about what it was like to work with Anzaldúa's text. For my part, I hope readers will find the glimpse into someone else's classroom practices (as well as anxieties, mistakes, and oversights) useful.

• • • • • •

Let me begin, though, by giving you some background about the work that preceded our work with Anzaldúa. In the spring of 1994, I had put together a sequence of *Ways of Reading* essays that included the selections from Jacobs's "Incidents in the Life of a Slave Girl," the chapters from Limerick's *Legacy of Conquest*, the Anzaldúa chapters, and Rich's

---

[1] My title is taken from a *Borderlands* chapter ("*La Conciencia de la Mestiza*/Towards a New Consciousness") that appeared in the third edition of *Ways of Reading*. In this chapter, [Gloria] Anzaldúa imagines the development of a new kind of consciousness—one that permits, among other things, a tolerance for ambiguity, the juggling of cultures, the breaking down of paradigms.

[2] A version of this article was presented as part of a panel on the uses of personal writing in the classroom at the Tri-State Teaching Women's Studies Conference, Indiana University of Pennsylvania, March 11, 1995.

"When We Dead Awaken."[3] The point of the reading and writing assignments was to think about the problems of writing from a position outside the dominant culture or some traditional paradigm (i.e., Jacobs writing as a slave, Limerick as a revisionist historian, Anzaldúa writing out of or toward a *"mestiza"* consciousness, Rich as a woman poet writing into a tradition defined by men). The Anzaldúa essay assignment (the first of the "Assignments for Writing") was third in the sequence, and we hit it about midway through the term—just after midterm grades—so many of my students were feeling anxious and worrying about improving their grades in the second half of the course. And then I was feeling anxious myself not only because of my ambivalence toward personal writing, but also because this would be the first time I'd worked with Anzaldúa's text.

In preparation for this assignment—and, to be honest, because I was concerned that students would lose patience with the text because it looked difficult—I asked them to come to class prepared to talk about the third of the "Questions for a Second Reading":

> Although Anzaldúa's text is not a conventional one, it makes an argument and proposes terms and examples for its readers to negotiate. How might you summarize Anzaldúa's argument in these three chapters? How do the individual chapters mark stages or parts of her argument? How might you explain the connections between the chapters? As you reread this selection, mark those passages where Anzaldúa seems to you to be creating a case or argument. What are its key terms? its key examples? its conclusions? (pp. 86–87)

I split the class into groups to discuss the responses they had prepared and asked them to decide, as a group, on two or three exemplary passages from the text where, as the assignment proposes, Anzaldúa seems to be "creating a case or argument." It was my hope that this kind of close, specific work on the text would help students think about how to construct their own "mixed" narratives.

From the discussion that followed once the individual groups reconvened as a class, it seemed as though students weren't necessarily having any more difficulty articulating a first response to Anzaldúa than they had with any of the other essays we'd read up to that point in the term. In fact, students seemed to be looking forward to writing about themselves and when, during the last ten minutes of class, we turned to discuss the essay assignment, they had a lot of questions about what they were being asked to do and on what terms. (This is a situation I always take as a sign that students are thinking seriously about their work.) I directed their attention to the last paragraph of the assignment since it offered them a way to begin thinking about the project:

> To prepare for this essay, think about the different positions you could be said to occupy, the different voices that are part of your background or present, the competing ways of thinking that make up your points of view. (p. 87)

In response to my reading this passage aloud, one student raised her hand and said she didn't understand the part about occupying different positions. What did that mean? Another student—Jenna, a junior taking the class for her women's studies certificate, whose familiarity with the discourse of feminist theory often intimidated other students in the class—preempted my response and said emphatically, gesturing with her arms, "FIRST of

---

[3] Some of these chapters appeared in previous editions of *Ways of Reading*.

all, you're a woman! A WOMAN! Don't you see?" The first student, Cheryl, looked puzzled and remained silent.

It was a particularly uncomfortable moment—exactly the situation I wanted to avoid. If, on one hand, students needed to consider the different positions they saw themselves occupying, on the other hand, I didn't want them to feel pressured, by me or their class-mates, to see themselves through one lens more so than another. If a student didn't see herself positioned in terms of her gender, I didn't want her to feel her success in the course depended on doing so. The point of the assignment was for students to use their writing to explore and examine the complicated nature of their cultural identity—not fit themselves into prescribed slots and preordained oppressions.

Because Jenna's perceived "expertise" often gave her comments in the class discussion a certain authority, I realized it was important for me to step in here, and so I did what I knew how to do—I turned the question back out to the class. "What would it mean to say that being a woman is occupying a particular cultural position?" I asked. In spite of the fact that we had just talked about Anzaldúa's essay in similar terms, students had little to say about this when pushed to examine their own lives.

"I'm not sure if this is what you're looking for, but are you saying you want us to write about what it means to be a woman?" someone asked.

I tried to explain that the richness of Anzaldúa's writing came from her examination of the ways in which the *different* positions she occupied inflected and contradicted one another. But then I've been teaching long enough to know that talking at students—summarizing, condensing, clarifying—is infinitely less successful than having students struggle with the text (assignment, question, problem) themselves. I also know that no matter how much an assignment is discussed ahead of time, the moment of truth comes when students sit down and put pen to paper (or more likely fingers to keyboard), but I was feeling pressed for time since our class was nearly over and so I tried to fashion some nugget they could take away with them. Using my own experience as an example, I explained how I could imagine writing an essay about the conflicts among my identities as a woman and as an academic, as well as someone who is the product of a middle-class, Italian American, Roman Catholic family.

Not surprisingly, class ended on a disappointing note: students were frustrated because they didn't have a handle on what I *wanted* (through my attempts to pare down the assignment, I'd come to be identified with its expectations) and I went home fairly sure that yet another personal essay assignment was doomed to failure.

· · · ● · ·

As it turned out for most students, though, the writing they produced in response to Anzaldúa proved to be the most interesting and complicated work they did all semester. The set of first drafts I received was both surprising and troubling—surprising for the variety of ways they'd found to make Anzaldúa's project meaningful to them, but troubling for what was revealed about my students' experiences of prejudice and alienation. And so I had to think carefully about how I wanted to respond.

Here are two first drafts with my comments. In my opinion, they are good working papers because of the ways the writing appropriates and extends the kinds of gestures Anzaldúa makes. In addition, they're typical of the ways my students were working to figure out what it would mean to construct a nonlinear, nonstraightforward narrative. As you read through them, you'll notice that my comments focus primarily on these aspects of the writing. In addition, I try to call attention to the moves they're making as writers trying to read their own experience.

Jakrita S. Sherman
March 18, 1994

"I'll Fly Away"

Thus saith the Lord, the heaven is my
✓ *throne*   (thrown) *and the Earth is my footstool:*
Where is the house that ye build unto me?
And where is my place of rest?

—*Isaiah*

<u>Black:</u>   1. adj. without light, or not able to reflect it || colorless or so dark as to appear colorless || <u>the opposite of white</u> || lowering, black clouds || <u>not hopeful,</u> *the prospects look black* || (rhet.) <u>sad,</u> *a black day for our team* || <u>angry, sullen or disapproving,</u> *a black look* || <u>very dirty</u> || (rhet.) <u>wicked,</u> *black villainy* || <u>evil,</u> *black magic* || <u>dark skinned, belonging to a race with dark pigmentation</u> || <u>reflecting discredit,</u> *a black mark* || <u>illegal,</u> *black market* || inveterate, a black Republican, a black liar || (Br.) not to be handled or worked in by trade unionist while other trade unionists are on strike || (of the members of a religious order) wearing a black habit || of or concerning black or blacks   2. n. a black pigment, fabric etc. || <u>dirt, soot</u> || (board game) <u>the dark-colored men or pieces or the player having these</u> || <u>a person whose natural skin color is black</u>   3. v.t. to make black || to polish with blacking || v.i. to become black, blacken to black out to darken, cause to give out or receive light || (esp. of pilots of planes pulling out of a dive or very sharp turn) to lose consciousness or memory usually temporarily (*BLACKOUT)

<u>White:</u>   1. adj. of the color sensation stimulated by a combination of all the wavelengths of visible light, or resulting from combinations of certain pairs of wavelengths, <u>being the color of e.g. milk</u> || (of hair) gray or silver || (of hair) very blond || (of wines) very pale yellow || <u>free from sin, pure</u> || pale, white with terror || <u>of or relating to the Caucasian division of mankind</u> || covered with snow || blank, not printed upon, leave the rest of the page white || (of silver and other

metals) unburnished || (of the members of a religious order) wearing white to bleed (someone) white to get money from (someone) until there is no more to be had   2. n. a white pigment, fabric etc. || a member of the Caucasian division of mankind || the white part of the eye surrounding the cornea || any of various breeds or species of white hog, white horse, white butterfly etc. || (printing) a blank space between words or lines || (archery) the outermost ring of a target || (archery) that shot that hits this ring || (board games) the light-colored man or pieces, or the player having these || (pl., pop.) leakoiihea

An effective
beginning

—New Webster's Dictionary and Thesaurus
of the English Language, copyright 1992

Ode to a Genius

The history of man begins at a place of uncertainty. No one really
✓ knows how [it,] life / was [all] started or where it all began. We are born by the fertilization of an egg and we die because of a physical shutdown of the systems of the body, but when did this cycle first originate and when will it end? <u>Some</u> people believe that an all-powerful, all-knowing entity created man and the universe by the motion of a thought. Other believe that a scientific phenomenon marked our creation. I agree with <u>Some</u>.

Man and his home came from the mind of the ultimate genius. *God* created the idea of man and produced a prototype in which he housed a program of regeneration of the being in different forms. He set these forms on a platform called Earth and surrounded it with other creatures and other worlds. I have believed in <u>*God*</u> for most of my life, doubting him only on occasions of emotional distress. I was born to believe in him.

History can only be written by the survivors.

God has been a comfort to <u>black</u> Americans for hundreds of years. As a people we were severed from our original beliefs, culture, speech, heritage, and homes. When some <u>blacks</u> accepted <u>*God*</u> in the terms dictated to them by <u>Europeans</u> they discovered a means of survival. They
✓ took the reality of <u>*God*</u> and made it their own by seeing ~~their selves~~ *themselves* as not the property of their white captors but as children of <u>*God*</u>. However, there were black people who after conforming to <u>Euro-American</u> thought

became even more self-hating because they started to believe that _God_
hated them or even, in some cases, that the _devil_ made them while whites

✓ were made by _God_. As time passes ~~both feelings~~ both feelings continue
                              latter
✓ to flourish, but the ~~later~~ is well disguised. Now it is not easy for everyone   _Why not —
to recognize the self-hate within blacks as being an attribute to the past._   _what are you
                                                                            getting at?_

    In my American history class in high school I was told about
white people and their heroes, conquerors; their fight for freedom from
British rule, their inventions, their innovations, philosophers, scientists, doctors, builders, fighters, etc. I also heard about a few popular
black people, Martin Luther King, Nat Turner, Harriet Tubman, and
Thurgood Marshall. I would estimate that such issues as Slavery and
The Civil Rights Movement were covered in only three of the thirty-six
weeks spent in school. I learned about Malcolm X and Marcus Garvey
through a black history program I was in that consisted of about ten
other black students. My high school was thirty percent black.

                    but? (Is this misquoted?)
The eyes see not thyself ~~for~~ in reflection.

    There have been studies done on the mentality of black children
and how they view themselves. Many black girls when given a choice   _On what
to play with either white or black dolls would choose the white dolls._   _do you
When my mother was a child there were no black dolls made available   base this?_
to her, so she, like most poor black girls, would make dolls out of tall
weeds, grass, and string.

    There is a product that many black American women use on their
hair, to make it straight, called _Relaxer_. As a young lady, if you are fortunate, you can get your hair straightened by _relaxer_ so that your hair can
be manageable. I got my first _relaxer_ or _permanent_ in the third or fourth
grade. I remember fondly how my hair was before this incident. It was
dark and thick and it hung down my back. There was a boy that liked
me and he used to pull my hair. My sister would fix my hair in pony tails
or braids with colorful beads. After my _perm_ clumps of my hair fell out
because the beautician left the "white cream" on my hair for too long.
It took a while for my hair to grow back and of course it will never be
the same again. I get a _touch up_ (the perms that you receive after your
first one) almost every month now. My hair is addicted to the chemicals

in the *relaxer*. If I do not get a *touch up* my hair will break off and become too <u>unmanageable</u>. I wonder how my <u>black</u> female ancestors dealt with their untamed hair. The only way that I can return my hair back to its natural state is to shave it all off and start over. I do not yet have the inner courage it would take to do that. We, <u>black</u> <u>girls</u>, <u>are</u> <u>taught</u> that in order to be considered somewhat beautiful your hair has to be nice and

✓ straight. Sometimes it is hard to see myself as beautiful. My dark skin, big

✓ lips, protruding mouth, large feet, and other <u>"black features"</u> have not been pronounced to me as <u>"naturally beautiful."</u> I ~~was~~ taught [through
1   2   3   4
example, history, tradition, and unspoken criticism] that my looks are
[1, 2, 3, 4]
inferior to that of <u>white</u> women. It takes a conscious effort on my part to ignore this deceit that has been embedded in my psyche since birth.

By whom? In what con-text? In what ways/forms has this been presented to you as the norm?

In what ways does that effort mani-fest itself?

A child cannot be dangerous.

In my home *God* was a given and it was an automatic rule that we were to believe in him. It was inconceivable or intolerable for anyone not to. However, I did not grow up attending church. I do not know whether it was because my mother did not have time to take me, for she worked two jobs and had an illness that kept her preoccupied, or because she did not have faith in the "institution of churches." My mother stressed education through schools and the strengthening of the mind so that one day you can be very successful. <u>Success</u>, <u>by her</u> <u>definition</u>, means having an excellent career that affords you the privi-lege of obtaining certain luxuries, once unattainable by <u>blacks</u>.

What pre-cedes this?

This definition is a reasonable one and it is definitely a welcome substitution for the all-too-common scenario of <u>blacks</u> doing the hard and dirty work while receiving no benefits. It is also better than the gang-bangin, <u>black</u>-on-<u>black</u>, self-destructive behavior that many of our <u>black</u> youth are participating in these days. In my opinion, though, success as my mother defines it is not the solution. We as <u>black</u> people <u>need to find our way back</u> to our natural state. We need to start over from the beginning <u>through our children</u> by instituting in them the things that were denied to us by history. Those things are: <u>self-respect,</u> <u>dignity, self-worth, self-love, pride, peace, inner happiness, unity,</u> <u>truth, knowledge, power, freedom,</u> etc. We need to give our children

Is your pro-posal related to G.A.'s proposal for a "mestiza" conscious-ness? Look back at what she says — can you use her here?

Does she give you a way of extending your argument about education here? the vision to see themselves clearly through their own perceptions and not those of others, <u>white</u> or <u>black</u>. The more fortunate children, <u>white</u> children, need to be <u>taught</u> as well, but we cannot wait for the "<u>individuals in power</u>" to change. To do that is to say that they are in control of our futures and only God occupies this position.

Taught what?

I'm going to heaven and I'll take my bear with me!

When I was eight or nine years old I went Christmas shopping with my mother at Macy's Department store. We were in the toy department when I saw this shelf full of stuffed animals. I went to reach for one when I looked up and saw <u>Herbert</u>, a medium-sized brown teddy bear with big <u>black</u> eyes, who at the time looked huge. I pulled him down and started hugging him. I begged my mother to buy him, but she said that she did not have enough money. Herbert cost nearly a hundred dollars.

✓ At this time my family and I were living in a place called La*ke* Lucerne, which sounds like a nice place to live, but it was just the opposite. Lake Lucerne is a deteriorating housing complex in <u>Miami</u> with only <u>one way in and the same way out, which was convenient for the local police because it made it easier to catch the drug dealers or other such unsavory characters that lived there.</u> There were many nights when my family and I would be woken up by the sound of gunfire. My mother would always make us sit in her closet in her bedroom. She had a huge walk-in closet that made a perfect hiding place.

Effectively put

After my sisters and I finished opening our presents that Christmas morning, my mother told me to go into her room and get something out of her closet. I walked into my mother's room with my head down low and my eyes drooping because I was sad that I had not gotten <u>Herbert</u> for Christmas, but I walked out of the room screaming with my eyes bulging out of my head squeezing <u>Herbert</u> tight in my arms. I named my bear <u>Herbert</u> after Herbie Hancock, who was one of my older sister's favorite musicians at the time. <u>Herbert</u> has been with me ever since. He has been the one constant in my life that I never had a genuine fear of losing. I could take him everywhere with me if I wanted. He will never die, like my grandmother, or he will never get so sick that I am afraid that he is going to die, like my mother, and he will never abandon me, like my father. Till this day, that moment when I saw <u>Herbert</u> sitting on my mother's closet floor was one of the happiest moments of my life.

The day will come when my happiness will know me and I will know it.

Use quotation marks to clarify

"The day will come when my happiness will know me and I will know it" is a phrase that I wrote some time ago when I was feeling optimistic about my status in this world that we exist in. I have a tendency to vacillate between stability and instability as far as the level of tolerance of the intolerable I have. I remember one time in the tenth or eleventh grade a boy in my French class (who was, by the way, extremely attractive) came up to me and said, in a rather serious tone of voice, "You are too serious for your own good." There are lots of times that I wish that

These seem very different but your sentence structure denies that.

my mind was filled with <u>shallow and immature</u> thoughts, or at least with <u>a profound</u> dedication towards accuracy, good grades, and success, instead of the worries and emotional burdens of everything. Life is a bad dream that one person is having. I wish that person would wake up-- I wrote that saying in high school during one of my down spells. However, despite my history, the parts that came before and after my birth, and my present, which is filled with fear and hope ("Where there is fear

This seems a less interesting ending gesture than your argument about education two sections earlier.

there is hope"), <u>I know that I am going to be okay, that everything is going to be okay in the end.</u>

To the man with no future,

To the man with no future I bid you peace for I have somewhere to go and people are waiting for me there.

—<u>me</u>

21 March

Jakrita —

This is thoughtful and interesting writing — nice going. I've made more specific comments in the margins and you should come talk to me if you have questions/comments.

If you choose to work further on this, consider developing in particular your argument about education (see comments in the last section).

Thanks for your work.

Bianca

Christine Schrodi
Assignment #3
3/18/94

SELF-UNDERSTANDING

Solo figure on crowded ground
Her stubborn chin held high,
Asking nothing, receiving nothing
Defiance in her eye.[1]

I guess one could say that I grew up in the average middle-class neighborhood. It was tucked away in a nice suburban area surrounded by beautiful farm land--fifteen minutes from the city yet a world away. It appeared that I had all the advantages with a supportive and loving family and an education from a good school. From the outside everything looked comfortable and safe . . . simple. But, even with all the advantages, there were and still are hurdles I have to overcome, situations that need to be understood, and experiences that need to be lived. I can't seem to go through these things unscathed. I always find some internal conflict.

Delicate child who's seen too much
Who's learned to hurt too soon,
Letting loose, a wild dance
Here beneath the moon.
She swings her head, her body moves
frustration drains away;
She can't forget the angry words
The things that people say.

I am an American citizen. Because of the fact that I am Asian, I never really feel accounted for and accepted.

Once, while I was at work, a woman asked me if I celebrated Easter in my country. Isn't America my country? I am a citizen.

Her pounding feet refuse to stop;
A tear slides down her face;
She clings to her compassion as
Hatred tries to steal the place.

The more people alienate me from this country, my home, the more I want to be accepted. The more I want to be accepted, the more I hate myself. Why would I ever want to be part of a country where I feel as though I am an outsider to the dominant culture, the white culture? Some even have the idea that I can't speak English. English is my first and primary language. So I am Asian.

> Whipping round, her back is arched
> Her hands attack the sky;
> She gives so much to others
> No return, she wonders why.

There is a saying in Korea that it is not enough to be born in Korea, but one has to be socialized as a Korean. I was socialized as an American. So I am an American.

America says I am Asian. Gloria Anzaldúa says that "to be close to another Chicana is like looking into the mirror. We are afraid of what we'll see there. Pena. Shame" (43). I also feel shame when I encounter other Asian people. At first, this was because I was ashamed of being Asian. Now, it is because I am not. I may look Asian, but I grew up in an Irish/German/Polish/white family. This is what was presented to me, and this is how I was raised.

G.A. is talking specifically about feminists, no? Does that change your use of her here?

Can you elaborate? How are you defining "white culture?" or "Irish/German/Polish"?

Learning about being Asian has been a learning process for me, it is not something that comes natural on a subconscious level of understanding. But just as African Americans feel pride in their culture and heritage, so do I as an Asian American.

Can you say something about the way in which this manifests itself?

> Beating heart pumping blood;
> One thousand eyes, they stare
> as silently her body leaps to slice the heavy air.

White culture has always dominated my life. It is my parents, a large percentage of my classmates, and most of my teachers. I still have not had an Asian teacher. Because of this situation, I feel as though I have assimilated into the white culture. But this is the same culture which excludes me. This is the culture which tells me I am Asian yet sometimes punishes me for it.

What would you expect to learn from her?

This is a nice laying out of the issue.

Landing light, she cannot breathe;

She longed for just one chance,

The moon retreats behind a cloud

Let lonely dancer dance.

Am I proud to be Asian? Yes, because that is who I am. I finally realized that being Asian doesn't make me less American, <u>it only adds one more dimension</u> to my person. It is to my advantage because I have more than one viewpoint. In a country like America, we have to realize that not all white people are the devil, that black is beautiful, and that not all Asians carry cameras. I'm just glad that <u>my experiences have allowed me to do just that.</u>

In G.A.'s sense of a "mestiza" consciousness?

You haven't really shown this — why mention it at the end here?

Note

1. All poetry excerpts from "Lonely Dancer" by Jen Niemeyer.

23 March

Christine —

This is interesting and thoughtful work — I really enjoyed reading it. I had thought about xeroxing it for class but hesitated in the end because I figured your classmates would know it was yours, and I wasn't sure how you'd feel about that since this is a more "personal" essay than we have so far written.

I've made more specific comments in the margins and you should come talk to me if you have any questions/comments. In general, I think your paper gets at the key issues raised by Anzaldúa's text. If you would like to take this further, you should think about working in sections — you have several powerful anecdotes/stories to offer here and they might be more productively developed into individual sections. In addition — while I like the way you weave Niemeyer's poem into your text — you might consider other kinds of texts (cultural myths, e.g., or legends, traditions, or customs) on which you could draw to represent your "mixed sensibility."

Thanks for your work,

Bianca

Both Christine and Jakrita reproduce Anzaldúa's project in terms of issues of racial identity. Although this is a somewhat reductive reading of Anzaldúa's project (she is concerned more broadly with cultural identity), it's clear from the ways in which the writers are working to produce "mixed" texts that, like Anzaldúa, they are trying to imagine that identity in terms of conflicting pressures. Jakrita's text is, perhaps, more self-consciously mixed in its use of multiple cultural texts—the biblical epigraph, dictionary definitions, stories of school experiences, bits from her diary. And then all of this is emphasized by her use of bold and italic type and separately titled sections (both of which echo gestures Anzaldúa makes).

Christine's story is intertwined with only one other text, but I think her use of that text is striking for the way in which it can be read as a commentary on or frame for her own story. See, for example, the way the lines "She can't forget the angry words / The things that people say" introduce

> Once, while I was at work, a woman asked me if I celebrated Easter in my
>
> country. Isn't America my country? [manual p. 287]

In addition, the repetition of "So I'm Asian" / "So I'm American" emphasizes the fact that she is simultaneously part of and alienated from two cultures.

To my mind, these are already strong papers even though they're only first drafts, because it's clear to me that they depend on the writers' careful observation of Anzaldúa's characteristic ways of working. In trying to figure out how I wanted to comment on these pieces, I decided that my responsibility would be to try to bring out the kinds of gestures—some more direct than others—students were already making toward putting their project into some kind of relationship to Anzaldúa's. This is usually a priority I have when commenting on student papers. For the Anzaldúa papers, it proved particularly useful because, in calling attention to the kinds of formal gestures students were making as readers and writers and in focusing on their writing as a rereading of Anzaldúa's text, I didn't put myself in the position of commenting on the (often) intensely personal material they were exploring in their writing.

Because I wanted to focus my comments in this way, another thing I noticed about these two papers was the way they entertain the possibility of the kind of educational project Anzaldúa proposes in her section *"La Conciencia de la Mestiza* / Towards a New Consciousness"* [which appeared in the third edition of *Ways of Reading*]. Anzaldúa puts it in these terms:

> Through our literature, art, *corridos*, and folktales we must share our history with [middle-class whites] so that when they set up committees to help Big Mountain Navajos or the Chicano farmworkers or *los Nicaragüenses* they won't turn people away because of their racial fears and ignorances. They will come to see that they are not helping us but following our lead.

Jakrita proposes something like this in her essay:

> We need to give our children the vision to see themselves clearly through
>
> their own perceptions and not those of others, <u>white</u> or <u>black</u>. The more fortunate
>
> children, <u>white</u> children, need to be taught as well. . . . [manual pp. 284–285]

And Christine makes a similar kind of move in the last paragraph of her paper: "In a country like America, we have to realize that not all white people are the devil, that black is beautiful, and that not all Asians carry cameras" [manual p. 289]. On one hand, I couldn't be sure whether these imitative gestures were intentional—Christine's paper, in particular, only gives the whole idea a sentence or two. But on the other hand, I thought these places would bear further exploration, and so in my marginal comments I pushed each writer to define her project more specifically in relation to Anzaldúa's.

In my General Writing course, students can revise a paper as many times as they want. Although Christine and Jakrita both wrote two more drafts of their papers, most of the changes were local ones and very little was altered in terms of the original structure. In spite of my final comments to Christine, she chose neither to work in separate sections nor to incorporate different kinds of cultural texts. And neither Christine nor Jakrita did significant work toward thinking through the idea of the national education project alluded to in their first drafts.

In fact, like many of my students, Christine and Jakrita were not only invested in their Anzaldúa papers, they were adamant about their intentions. This isn't so unusual in writing courses when it comes to the issue of revision—although I try to represent it as an occasion (an invitation, even) to imagine their papers as works in progress, students tend to see the work of revision as more burden than opportunity. With the Anzaldúa papers, however, it was clear to me that something more was at stake. Although most students could imitate Anzaldúa's methods, there were some, like Christine and Jakrita, whose investment in composing their "own experience" in a way that seemed to break the rules for conventional narrative also prevented them from undertaking a substantive revision. This is the opposite response from that of the student who refuses to revise a personal essay because "that's the way it happened." Rather it seemed that because students already felt they were operating outside "the system," they had more license to resist my suggestions for revision.

Now I'd like to turn to Staci's essay, one where revisions turned out to be more substantial, because I think that paying attention to the ways in which it was revised—what was changed, struggled over, added, left out altogether—says something more about students' attempts to work with Anzaldúa than is perhaps visible in the previous papers. Staci's first draft is written entirely in the first person: although she acknowledges her conflicted identity, she doesn't use her writing to exploit that. The intentions behind my comments to Staci are the same as in the preceding essays by Christine and Jakrita, but I'm also more overtly concerned with questioning and disrupting the seamlessness of the writing.

Staci Wenitsky

Assignment #3

3/18/94

My Positions in Society and in Life

✓   What exactly is my role in society? A woman, a Jew, a student()

they all apply, but what do they mean? While having no control of how

✓   or ~~under~~ the circumstances *under* ~~in~~ which I was born, I have to use my indi-

vidual characteristics to not only adapt to society but also to overcome

its hurdles. *positions?*

✓   My <u>position</u> in society is one that <u>can be stretched to whatever</u>   *Not sure*

<u>situation may arise at that particular time.</u> By being a woman I have   *how you*
mean this.

had to work to extreme limits in order for me to attain my goals. Prob-

lems such as racism and prejudice have arisen which only occurred for

the mere reason that I am Jewish and I am a woman. Being a woman in the United States has become easier throughout the years, but (it) *what?* should not be underestimated, and being a Jewish woman can in some instances make (it) *what?* that much harder.

✓   With the upsurge of the woma(ns) movement throughout the seventies, women today in the United States are finally working side by side with their male counterparts as equals. Who would have ever

✓   thought twenty years ago that my mother would be a neurologist(.) Sometimes when people ask me what my parents do, they give me a funny look after I tell them that my mom is a neurologist and my dad is a teacher. It seems kind of funny that their gender roles have been switched according to our society. Twenty years ago a woman was certainly not expected to be a doctor -- her role was probably a teacher or else raising her children at home while her husband worked nine to five.

Do you have a specific incident in mind? What would it mean to retell it as a personal anecdote that you then analyze in terms of how it has shaped/ informed your notion of cultural identity?

Being a woman in today's society has had both its advantages and disadvantages. Of course some attractive women may get a little *Again does* farther in life, but it also can backfire. Throughout high school I have *G.A. give you a way to re-* seen people I know being called stupid, ignorant terms such as jap *late a more* and princess. For what reason? For being a woman? For being a Jewish *specific e.g.?* woman? I have had people look at me because I have worn a star upon my *What would it mean to* neck for the sole reason of being proud to be a strong Jewish woman. *expand this*

¶ into its My identity in society will change as time goes on, but my beliefs *own section?* and intuitions as a woman I will have for a lifetime. I believe that as a woman I think and observe the world differently than my male counter-part. Some may call my ideals slanted or strange, but as a woman in *why may?* American society my convictions are important not only to my views of the world, but how I live them. My views as a woman are strong yet I am sometimes timid when sharing them with others.

What pro-duces this belief? How can you tell? What moments in your life would you point to? Are there other kinds of texts that sup-port your claim here?

When I was thirteen years old I got to express my pride and knowl-edge of the Jewish faith at my Bat Mitzvah. It was on this day that I told *If this is im-* to a large congregation of family and friends just how important being a *portant, why* Jewish woman was. *only a two-sentence ¶?*

I recall just a few years ago a conversation that I had with my parents about marriage. I was told that marrying within the Jewish heritage was very important to them. My aunt had married a man who was not Jewish and it ended in divorce. My mom told me that I must

raise my children Jewish or she would have nothing to do with them.
My views on Judaism are strong, but certainly not as strict. [I think, be-
cause my parents were raised in times where segregation ~~was~~ *, prejudice, and racism were* still quite
evident and people believed that Jewish people had horns growing out
of their heads, that their views have not changed *along* with the times. But
if we are discriminated against as Jews, and they know how it feels,
then why must they discriminate against other minority groups? This
is where I differ greatly with the views of my family. My uncle married
a Filipino woman and faced a large amount of hostility from my grandparents and his brothers and sisters. But why? Being Filipino is a
minority group just as much as being a Jew is.]

What do you mean?

[All in all, your race, ethnic background, gender, ~~and~~ little
positions such as being a brother, sister, daughter, father, etc., help
to mold you into your own individual. Each person perceives their role
in society and even in life in a different perspective than others may
perceive them. Everybody is equally as special and important in their
own way whether they are within the minority or the majority.]

So, are there other positions you've chosen not to consider here?

21 March

Staci —

This is thoughtful and interesting work. You've begun to suggest in powerful ways how being a woman and being Jewish are neither easily reconciled nor wholly opposed. You have also gathered together a number of very interesting personal anecdotes. Now I'd like to see you turn your narrative into the kind of "mixed" text that Anzaldúa writes. What would it mean to reconceive what you have here into separate sections that, as hers do, mark stages or parts of a larger argument about cultural identity? What would it mean to construct your paper not as a straightforward narrative but rather as a "mosaic" or "montage"? What other kinds of texts (poems, e.g., cultural myths or stereotypes) could you draw on? What other languages and/or ways of seeing do you have at your disposal as a result of the different positions you see yourself occupying?

If you have comments/questions about anything I've said here or in the margins, I'll be happy to talk further with you.

Bianca

Like many of my students, Staci had a number of interesting stories to tell. Additionally, her essay is ambitious for the set of cultural histories it tries to link together with her
own story: the rise of the women's movement, her parents' experience growing up Jewish
in the mid-twentieth century. Consequently, I tried to use my comments to help her work
with the interesting material she had already compiled—pushing her to use Anzaldúa as
a model for reimagining the overall shape of her essay.

Here is her second draft:

Staci Wenitsky
Assignment #3
3/24/94

My Positions in Society and in Life

My parents decided when I was four years old and my sister was six years old to move our family to a suburb called Richboro.

"It is in our best interest to move," my mom told me.

"But why, Mommy? I'm going to miss all of my friends," I replied.

That didn't seem to matter. Our family picked up to relocate to a very large house as opposed to the so-called lower-class neighborhood that I had grown up in thus far in my life. There was a huge field behind my house leading to absolutely nothing. The block was empty instead of clustered as I was used to. I knew nobody. My sister and I played together, not knowing any of the other children in the neighborhood.

later?

Race and Religion. I ~~latter~~ was old enough ~~to be able~~ to understand the reason for the move. My parents wanted a good education for me and my sister. Both of my parents had never had the opportunity to go on to a higher schooling such as college and they wanted better for their children. The school system that I would have been raised in was the Philadelphia School District. When people think of Philadelphia they may think of the city of "Brotherly Love," but my parents believe *or* Philly was more ~~of~~ less ~~as~~ a city of crime. There were a lot of black people moving into my old neighborhood.

Prejudice: Negative or hostile attitudes toward, and beliefs about a group of people.

And how do you under-stand this? I never thought of my parents as racist, but rather <u>they described their views</u> as being cautious and looking out for "our best interest."

Not sure what you mean. While having no control of how or the circumstances under which I *beliefs?* was born, I have to use my <u>individual characteristics</u> to not only adapt to society but also overcome its hurdles. I am a white Jewish woman. That is the obvious. I can't hide behind this, nor would I want to. I am proud to be what I am. Although I was born into these conditions I feel it is important to learn about what I am ethnically and to take pride in it.

✓   Problems such as racism and prejudice have arisen <u>in which only occurred</u> for the mere reason that I am Jewish and I am a woman. With the upsurge of the women's movement throughout the seventies, women today in the United States are finally working side by side with their male counterparts as equals. Twenty years ago most people would be surprised at the fact that my mother is a neurologist.

Do you mean to underline this?

[Grade school.]Boys hated girls and vice versa. Children were selfish and spoiled. It was my first day being a "big shot" third grader. We had to get to know our classmates and I was paired with a boy. The question he asked me was what my parents did. When I replied that my mom was a neurologist he laughed at me and made fun of me. I know that it seems kind of funny that their gender roles have been switched according to our society, and I guess that is why the boy laughed at me. Twenty years ago a woman was certainly not expected to be a doctor-- her role was probably a teacher or else raising her children at home while her husband worked nine to five.

<u>Anti-Semitism</u>: prejudice and discrimination against Jews. This is something that I believe (every) Jew has faced at some point in (their) life. I was lucky to be raised in an area populated heavily with Jewish people.

Watch pronoun agreement

"Oh, you live in Little Israel," my friend Meredith replied to me as I gave her directions to my house.

Nice juxta-position

This was the term ~~that~~ ^for^ the development in which I live. ~~in is labeled as.~~ Other words such as calling me and my friends JAPs (Jewish American Princesses) were hostilely used to put me down throughout high school. I have had people look at me because I have worn a star upon my neck for the sole reason of being proud to be a strong Jew.

<u>Reading from the Torah</u>: the whole body of Jewish religious literature at my Bat Mitzvah allowed me to express to a congregation of friends and family my pride in my religion. I had been studying Hebrew and learning about the history of the Jews for about four years now.

✓ The pride in my relativ(es)eyes on this day made all of my hard work worthwhile. Relatives of mine were killed in the Holocaust and I felt a

This sounds like an important experience for you — is there more you can do with it? Other ways to draw on it?

sense of necessity to be Bat Mitzvahed as my way of showing the world that I was proud to be a Jew.

Marriage is a sacred thing. It has been strongly expressed to me by my parents that I should marry a Jewish man. My mom refuses to have contact with her grandchildren unless they are raised Jewish. My views towards my ethnicity are strong, but certainly not as strict. <u>I think that because my parents were raised in times when segregation, prejudice, and racism were still quite evident, their views have not changed along with the times.</u> But if we are discriminated against as Jews, and they know how it feels, then why must they discriminate against other minority groups? This is where I differ greatly with the views of my family. My uncle married a Filipino woman and faced a large amount of hostility from my grandparents and his brothers and sisters. But why? Being Filipino is a minority group just as much as being a Jew is.

This is very nicely developed — you give a thoughtful account of your conflict.

<u>My identity in society</u> will change as time goes on, but my beliefs and intuitions as a white Jewish woman I will have for a lifetime. All in all, your race, ethnic background, and gender help to mold you into your own individual. Each person perceives their role in society and even in life in a different perspective than others may perceive them. <u>Everybody is equally as special and important in their own way whether they are within the minority or the majority.</u>

Not sure how you mean this.

Not sure why you want to end with this. What — at this point — is your sense of your larger project?

Staci,

This is a nice revision. You've really reimagined the shape of your paper, and I can see how you're working hard to develop/explore ideas introduced in your first draft. I've made more specific comments in the margins, and you should come talk to me if you have any questions.

Thanks for your work,

Bianca

Although her sentences seem awkward and tangled at times (due, I think, to attempts to overcorrect them), and although the writing still lapses into uninteresting generalities, Staci is working hard in her second draft to construct a "mixed" narrative. The way she juxtaposes the sections of her essay, as well as smaller sections within the bigger ones (although at times it's hard to distinguish separations) is very effective. For example, her parents' concern that "there were a lot of black people moving into my old neighborhood" is directly followed by a dictionary definition of "prejudice" [manual p. 294]; similarly, her comment "I was lucky to be raised in an area populated heavily with Jewish people" is immediately undermined by her friend's remark about "Little Israel" [manual p. 295]. I was also intrigued by the way Staci uses stories in the second draft to selectively amplify particular moments from the first draft: for example, she begins the second draft with a story that inflects the questions she raises in the first draft and then carries over in the second about her parents' prejudices; also, the paragraph in the first draft on the women's movement is divided into two separate sections in the second draft, one of which is an anecdote about explaining her mother's unusual occupation to a classmate.

Obviously there is still much more that Staci could do here, but in my opinion the fact that the changes she's made have opened up more possibilities is precisely what makes this a productive revision. In addition, because the moves she makes in the second draft—the way she juxtaposes modes of telling (stories, definitions, dialogue)—echo the kinds of moves that can be observed in the *Borderlands* essays, Staci's revisions also reflect her revised understanding of Anzaldúa's project.

· · ● · ·

Whether or not students managed successful Anzaldúa revisions, when, at the end of the semester, they had to write a retrospective essay about their work as writers in the course, nearly everyone had something positive to say about how this assignment freed them up from conventional essay writing. Tamarrah explained it this way:

> In all of my years of English composition, I was always told to write a five-paragraph essay. This included an introduction, three supporting ideas, and a conclusion. With my Anzaldúa assignments, I was asked to write a mixed text, which could include poems, quotes, stories, a combination of languages, or sporadic sentences here and there. This helped me a great deal, for when I sat down to write my essay, I felt more in control of my paper. I could pick and choose from many different creative options. . . .

Another student, Cheryl, wrote, "This assignment, unlike the others, gave me the freedom I felt I had previously been denied" (3–4). And Christine, the author of "Self-Understanding," explained, "We had to take everything that we had learned, technically, about writing and leave it in the gutter" (3–4).

At the same time that Anzaldúa's essay represented a kind of freedom, though, students —often within the space of the same essay—also reverted to very familiar metaphors for talking about personal writing as opposed to "academic" writing and as a direct representation rather than re-presenting of their experiences and feelings. "I am very proud of my efforts with [the Anzaldúa] paper," one student admitted. "It is raw and straight from my gut" (Bulawa 4–5). And another student who had written about her family's experience immigrating to America explained, "The freedom that I felt when writing this paper was unlike anything else. The fact that creativity was encouraged instead of suppressed made it possible for me to truly and freely express what was on my mind" (Nemirovsky 4).

Notwithstanding my students' enthusiasm, I was intrigued by the way these discussions obscured not only the point I think Anzaldúa is trying to make about the limitations of any single language or sign system to represent her identity, but more interestingly the successes my students had experimenting with multiple voiced narratives. When I think about why this might be the case, my sense is that it has less to do with students' sophistication, or insight into their own writing practices, than it does with the kinds of assumptions students have about personal writing in the first place, before they ever walk into General Writing. Ideas about the importance of self-expression, about the autonomous, free-thinking individual in society, are deeply embedded in American culture. So, to the extent that Anzaldúa's writing forces us to question these kinds of assumptions about the possibility of a unified identity, it's not surprising that students would still struggle with how to talk about the consequences of asking such questions.

But, I need to say that if students didn't have the theoretical language to articulate what was different about the writing they produced in response to Anzaldúa, the experience did, nonetheless, refocus their attention on issues that were central to the course. In the comments I quoted above, for instance, there is the sense that, writing into or out of a tradition, a writer necessarily makes choices about how to proceed. Additionally, in our class discussions and in the comments I wrote on their papers, thinking about Anzaldúa's writing in terms of different kinds of "strategies" gave us a way to talk about her writing, and consequently their writing, as negotiable, as a way of working out/through complicated ideas, as imagining (facilitating, complicating, undermining) the role of the reader.

These are all reasons I would teach Anzaldúa again, if the opportunity arose. They are also reasons that I've been forced to reconsider my own assumptions about the value of personal writing. And finally it's on these terms that I can begin to account for my students' success with Anzaldúa—and I do think their efforts were successful. In asking students to think and write about the traditions/ideologies Anzaldúa was responding to, what proved to be valuable was the way it brought to the surface the class's assumptions—mine included—about the limitations and possibilities for writing about personal experience.

WORKS CITED

Bartholomae, David, and Anthony Petrosky. *Ways of Reading: An Anthology for Writers.* 4th ed. Boston: Bedford/St. Martin's, 1995.

Bulawa, Jenny. "The Final Analysis of a Never-Ending Process." Unpublished, University of Pittsburgh: 1994.

Nemirovsky, Vita. "Growth and Development." Unpublished, University of Pittsburgh: 1994.

Schrodi, Christine. "Retrospective." Unpublished, University of Pittsburgh: 1994.

——. "Self-Understanding." Unpublished, University of Pittsburgh: 1994.

Sherman, Jakrita. "'I'll Fly Away.'" Unpublished, University of Pittsburgh: 1994.

Thomas, Tamarrah. "Reseeing My Own Writing." Unpublished, University of Pittsburgh: 1994.

Wenitsky, Staci. "My Positions in Society and in Life." Unpublished, University of Pittsburgh: 1994.

All student papers are used with the permission of their authors, to whom I am grateful.

I would also like to acknowledge the help of Pitt English Department colleagues David Bartholomae, Angie Farkas, and Kurt Simonds, who kindly offered valuable advice as I worked on this paper.

Public Writing and *Ways of Reading* in First-Year Composition

Hannah Gerrard

Deeply-held convictions about the importance of a deliberative, civic rhetoric have long underwritten the work of composition instruction. A piece that neatly distills some of the discipline's commonplaces is John Duffy's recent "Virtuous Arguments" in *Inside Higher Ed*, where Duffy argues that first-year writing is a (widespread, if marginalized) project to improve the public discourse "debase[d]" by politicians and the media. Despite the misperception of this work as remedial instruction, Duffy argues that the teaching of composition is "a well-organized, systematic, and dedicated effort taking place each day to promote an ethical public discourse grounded in the virtues of honesty, accountability, and generosity." Key for Duffy is academic writing's attachment to a community of participants, standards of proof and reasoning, and acknowledgement of complexity and counter-argument. Such an imaginary persists, despite several decades of the field questioning how "the public" or "public writing" might be the aim or object of instruction.

As Christian Weisser discusses in *Moving Beyond Academic Discourse: Composition Studies and the Public Sphere*, "public writing" is an increasingly popular theme for teaching and theorizing in composition studies, perhaps even threatening "academic writing" as the central object of instruction. For Weisser, the advantages of "real" exigencies over staged, "artificial" exigencies for student writers are clear, and the kind of engagement offered by academic writing is cast into this problematic realm of the artificial. This has not been an uncontested position. Scholars have critiqued this move to public writing as concerned to enhance the field's status at the expense of teaching academic conventions (see Ervin). And while some public writing scholars have argued that any public exigency for writing is inherently more valuable than one "staged" in the classroom, others have proposed more cautious and complex versions of public writing pedagogies, accompanied by caveats.

Much of the work on public writing pedagogies to date at least complicates the idea of a citizen-rhetor whose agency is demonstrated through rational discourse that then has direct effects (see, for example, Wells). Given significant shifts in civil society, pedagogically proposing a new or a nostalgic infrastructure for public discourse through the valorization of a particular mode of argument becomes perhaps less important than enacting a pedagogical space where relations to potential public spaces are opened up. Manuel Castells' analysis, for example, suggests the importance of attention both to local participatory spaces and to building or sensing relations that enable the work of decentralized, networked social movements to occur. Indeed, a number of scholars have looked to re-emphasize circulation and delivery as part of moving composition studies towards "public writing." We might think of, for example, the work of John Trimbur or Paula Mathieu and Diana George, or how this concern has only become more central to the field with the rise of multimodal pedagogies, where anticipating circulation is increasingly part of the work of composition and design (see Ridolfo and DeVoss.) Circulation becomes crucial, as Philip E. Agre argues, because while spaces of deliberation still exist, they "are thoroughly embedded in longer-term, multiply scaled political processes that extend far beyond the walls of any given meeting-house," and rather than fostering deliberation, the "main democratic potential of technologies like the Internet . . . rests mainly in their ability to support the work of issue entrepreneurs: identifying and researching emerging issues, distributing analyses of current events to an audience, organizing events, and networking with other entrepreneurs in the issue lattice" (213–4). In this model, Agre argues, the work of the citizen becomes, crucially, one of coordinating circulation, and this kind of "issue-networking" should thus be part of the curriculum in many educational domains (214). This questioning of the nature of agency in public spaces, as well as the boundaries that delineate public from private, has also led rhetoric and composition scholars to build on critiques of the Habermasian public sphere, in problematizing consensus as the aim of deliberative practice, and validating experimental or oppositional discourse in the classroom not circumscribed by a notion of audience.

In this context, we might ask: what is the public work, or value, of the elaborated, critical essay that, with the research essay, is a common manifestation of "academic writing" in the first-year course? Can this be recast as other than a luxury, or as a diversion from the "real" work of public writing? And can it be seen as something other than a nostalgic nod to a rational-critical public sphere, as is it in Duffy's "Virtuous Arguments"? Few today would question the value of teaching multimodal composition, for example, in order to have students produce "public writing," but the relationship between the critical essay and civic work is more often taken for granted than explored.

I'll admit — I think I have always taught with the suspicion that there is value in public terms, in the critical student essay. This is a feeling that comes from reading my first-year students' work and finding more in it to admire than increasing facility with academic gestures or prose style, or inventive reading and interpretation. I will also admit, however, that my sense of what "the critical essay" entails is very flexible, grounded as it is in a tradition of teaching composition perhaps best known through *Ways of Reading*, where the academic essay is a site to both negotiate and challenge academic conventions and to engage in stylistic innovation and collage.

This does not mean, of course, that issues of "academic literacy" are of no concern to first-year composition, as I understand it. While it may be difficult in a first-year course to account comprehensively for writing's variation across the disciplines, such a course might examine certain values embodied in literate practice that broadly characterize academic literacy, and that are imagined to characterize an ideal public culture. The first-year course can thus be imagined as a theater for the confrontation of these values and practices with those that students bring to the university. Teachers can foreground academic writing as engagement in a restricted public culture, creating a sense in the classroom of a public conversation about intellectual concerns into which students can enter, albeit in restricted ways. I try to make clear to students that the values I bring to the assessment of their work often have to do with "responsible" participation in this conversation: not misrepresenting a reading or a classmate's argument, for example; reading "generously"; taking care to support assertions; making evident "what's at stake" in an argument or analysis, how it addresses an issue of public concern (however narrowly one wants to define one's "public"). This would seem to echo Duffy's values of virtuous argument, albeit without the idea that teaching this kind of argument will rehabilitate a degraded public sphere. But I can well remember the first class I took as a student in which a professor talked about student work as if it were knowledge-generating, as if it were partaking in a critical enterprise involving a community of scholars, and in which I regularly read the work of my peers — this class was a revelation to me. There is, of course, a significant strain of idealism in associating this with public participation more broadly, but the power of the vocabulary this professor used to conceptualize student work remained.[1] I was a graduate student at this point, but I wonder what my undergraduate experience might have been like had I had this understanding of academic work then — a sense of that work tending outward, looking beyond the narrow path to the professor in the name of assessment.

I would agree with Gerald Graff's argument in *Clueless in Academe*, then, that the academic "culture of ideas and arguments" (2) is not entirely distinct from that of the broader public domain, and there is value in making this evident to students; I also share his sense of an educator's responsibility to the larger culture, of needing to prepare students for "public life" and to explicitly problematize what this might mean with them. At the same time, I would resist Graff's simplification of this "culture" — even as I acknowledge that, to some degree, we are bound to teach toward an idealized public culture rather than to try to replicate in the classroom anything like the complex structures of differential access and mediation that actually characterize public life. Graff himself expresses cynicism about the efficacy of public argument, and his vision for the work students might do in the composition classroom rests on a faith that such public arguing might find new efficacy in new forms (57–58). For his recommendations to hold good, however, these new forms will have to retain many of the dimensions of traditional academic argumentation, which casts their "newness" in a problematic light.

We might see more relevance in writing assignments that demonstrate both situated reflection on public issues, and the blurring of traditional boundaries concerning public and private writing that characterizes much composition with new media, not to mention shifts in journalism and non-fiction in recent decades — as these qualities define much public engagement today. One way to approach a more complex rendering of public life in the classroom, then, is to give more prominence to students' self-implicating, self-examining moves — not merely as moves to make an argument more effective, as Graff would suggest with his nod towards the argumentative force of "good stories" (4), but as recognition that argument in the public sphere is always situated, always calling into being particular discursive identities. This thinking influenced my choice of a chapter from Richard Rodriguez' *Hunger of Memory*, "The Achievement of Desire," for a final unit when teaching Seminar in Composition in Spring 2009. This excerpt is an example of writing that investigates the nature of the writer's identity in order to engage with matters of public concern, and public policy; having students work with "The Achievement of Desire" and write in response to it was, for me, a way of demonstrating how both they and professional writers can negotiate public argument without pretense of neutrality, or even without an orientation to consensus, in response to pressing concerns from one's own experience, and as a way of constructing that experience discursively.

---

[1] All credit to Roger Nicholson, University of Auckland.

My central assignment for the unit adapts a *Ways of Reading* assignment as follows:[1]

> He has used education to remake himself.... Those who would take seriously the boy's success—and his failure—would be forced to realize how great is the change any academic undergoes, how far one must move from one's past.
>
> "The Achievement of Desire," 559–560

In "The Achievement of Desire," Richard Rodriguez presents an account of his own education that theorizes about education more broadly: particularly, the ways in which the culture of schooling can prescribe change to "the person" (559)—to a person's identity and to how that person understands his or her identity—even as it prescribes a body of knowledge to be learned. In presenting a narrative that associates educational achievement with pain and loss, Rodriguez challenges the commonplace representation of education in American society as a straightforward path to unambiguous "success."

> With these arguments in mind, write an essay in which you discuss Rodriguez' essay in the context of your own experience as a student. You can make reference to an experience that took place on a single day, or to your development over a number of years, or something in between—whichever seems most useful for your purposes. *In any case, you should take care to present the reader with specific, detailed scenes from your education, as Rodriguez does, to generate and/or ground your analysis of his argument.* You will need to consider how your representation of yourself will shape your interpretation of Rodriguez (and any "others" who might be represented in your paper). As you illuminate how your experience both intersects with and diverges from Rodriguez' discussion of the process and aims of education, you should also contextualize your position with reference to another scholar whose work we have discussed this semester: Edward Said, Mary Louise Pratt, or Susan Griffin.

The essay assignment asks students to discuss "The Achievement of Desire" with reference to both their own experience as students and the work of another writer we read earlier in the term. The openness of the key term "discuss" was a deliberate move late in the semester, after a series of more directive assignments. That is, while setting up an argumentative framework within which students can work, the essay assignment does not isolate which elements of Rodriguez' text the students should bring into conversation with their own experience. In class, we discussed the necessity of narrowing the focus to a few key elements of Rodriguez' essay, rather than attempting to account for the whole. For me, this is important work for students to do consciously: acknowledging what falls outside the scope of a writing project, in conjunction with isolating what is significant to that project and making explicit the reasoning behind that choice. Such work explicitly calls for awareness of writing as an act that embodies a tension between boundaries and responsibilities: the

---

[1] This assignment is similar in some ways to the second "assignment for writing" in *Ways of Reading*, which asks students to imitate Rodriguez' style of description and analysis to represent an experience from their own lives (564–565). I retained something of this imitative-critical mode, by requiring students to represent particular scenes, but otherwise made the essay assignment more argumentative, and expanded its scope by requiring reference to the work of another writer.

responsibility to represent Rodriguez and one's own experience fairly, fully, is in tension with the limits of the length and scope of the paper and the perspective of the writer. I also mandated the key dimensions of academic literacy built into *Ways of Reading* in the form of the "Making Connections" sections after each reading, that is, drawing disparate texts into dialogue, and recursive reading.

With these gestures to broad academic values acknowledged, I do think that their invocation in a general composition course offers additional resonance with "public writing" pedagogy. Looking at the sheer variation in syllabi and approaches across the United States, I think of the first-year course as an oddly free curricular space. This might seem a peculiar way to think of a space that is so often assumed to contain quite a narrow pedagogical exercise by people outside the field, including various institutional actors with stakes in its work; certainly, I would not make light of the constraints under which many teachers of composition work. In my experience with relative freedom over classroom activities and assignment sequences, however, an odd openness emerges in first-year composition. I think here of Alexander Reid's account of how his pedagogy takes up his notion of the composition process, derived from Lessig's "rip, mix, and burn," as characterized by citation, "proliferation," and stabilization regardless of mode (130–131)—i.e. even in print—and directs it towards "the pedagogy of the event" (170). This pedagogy is crucially concerned with open-endedness—a new focus on process without the same notion of an author or project's goals, a "learning to unfold in unpredictable ways" (178). Reid is clear that an open-ended pedagogy is difficult to instantiate in the institution, and certainly there are broad "goals" for Seminar in Composition. The relationship between the arc of coursework and these goals is hardly direct or predetermined, however.

In the university, composition instruction is one rather unique place where, to use Elizabeth Ellsworth's terms, the hierarchy of curriculum and instruction is questioned, indeed where Ellsworth's challenge "to make something else of pedagogy—not simply to make pedagogy's subordination to curriculum obsolete but to think pedagogy in ways that make pedagogy encompass curriculum" (12)—has been taken up. I think this in several ways. The first is in composition's problem with "content," of course—the fill-in-the-blanks curriculum that surrounds so much attention to strategies of instruction, designing and sequencing assignments, and responding with some degree of spontaneity to a particular class, their progress, the projects they've chosen. The second, less obviously, is in teaching an act rather than a subject, there is a kind of learning-as-immediacy, or as-immersion, that is assumed. Hence that oddly reverent way of talking about "the composition classroom" as a kind of abstracted place—talked about in scholarship as a kind of public place, transversed by educational imperatives of testing and grading and all the rest, and by public imperatives, too, but also as a gateway, a place of intersection or where things happen (not so much where something is taught).

This is not to challenge Ellsworth's critique of the way that education maintains its narrow sense of what is and is not relevant to its enterprise, but to wonder whether acknowledging composition's rather unique—I say "rather," as art, design, and multimedia instruction might also work in this way—curricular space is key to thinking of it as civic pedagogy with all the resonance that Ellsworth finds in her "places of learning":

This brings us back to the paradox at the heart of pedagogy. If teaching is about think-ing and not complying with the one who holds the superordinate knowledge . . . then for pedagogy to put us in relation with each other in ways we have never been be-fore, for pedagogy to be a democratic civic pedagogy, it must create places in which to think about "we" without knowing already who "we" are. It must keep the future of what our engagements with those places make of us open and undecided. (94–5)

With such relations in mind, Ellsworth follows Brian Massumi in critiquing critique, or at least its taking time away from "augmenting" or "fostering" (128). The critical essay in more conventional argumentative forms, then, might seem to circumvent more open relations between writer and subject by prescribing a particular writerly position, even in the context of a classroom environment where students develop ideas through writing, in accordance with their own emerging projects.

To explore some of the civic possibility lurking in the critical essay, however, I'll dis-cuss here an essay written by my student Maria Bruno, in response to the assignment mentioned earlier. Here it is reproduced in full:

The Measure of Achievement

In *The Achievement of Desire*, Richard Rodriguez analyses his academic success. He addresses the meaning of a "successful student." Being a very "successful" stu-dent, he did not find himself worthy of all the praise that he'd received. He points out, "Always successful, I was always unconfident. Exhilarated by my progress. Sad. I became the prized student—anxious and eager to learn. Too eager, too anxious—an imitative and unoriginal pupil" (Rodriguez, 546). This self-analysis intrigues me, because I was always on the opposite side of this social norm.

Rodriguez noted his lack of inquiry. He never questioned his teachers, and they much appreciated his unwavering respect for their authority. I was surprised to learn that many teachers were unprepared for the possibility of a student en-quiring "Why?" I, myself, have always been a why-er. For me to learn and absorb information best, I not only needed to memorize the theory, I needed to know why the theory exists. I didn't just want to know the facts, I wanted to understand them. Rodriguez, perhaps due to his different home-life than myself, did not in-quire at all. "I came to idolize my grammar school teachers, I began by imitating their accents, using their diction, trusting their every direction. The very first facts they dispensed, I grasped with awe. Any book they told me to read, I read—then waited to tell me what books I enjoyed" (Rodriguez, 549). Rodriguez was the star pupil because he was the most convincing clone of his teachers. I have always been more resistant, and both of us had suffered consequences due to the extent of our stubbornness.

I was the stubborn one—too analytical, too inquisitive. Astute—or delu-sional—by nature, I concluded that the teachers that were not fond of me often felt threatened by me. I was often told to accept the answer, "because I said so." This effort to institutionalize and standardize the student body often frustrated me. In *Arts of the Contact Zone*, Mary Louise Pratt analyses the goals—and limited results—of this kind of standardized teaching. She cites her son's fourth grade paper, "Despite the spelling, the assignment received the usual star to indicate the task had been fulfilled in an acceptable way. No recognition was available, however, of the humor, the attempt to be critical or contestatory, to parody the structure of authority" (Pratt, 509). Pratt questions the nature of modern academic education, saying "Are teachers supposed to feel that their teaching has been most successful when they have eliminated such things and unified the social world, probably in their own image? Who wins when we do that? Who loses?" (Pratt, 509).

Pratt raises an interesting question about the pros and cons of standardizing education. Who does win? Our society today has a large emphasis on equality, as it should. However, there is a very fine line between being fair and being inflexible. Teachers are constantly judging both concepts. They try to avoid confrontation with parents while still attempting to provoke students to think. Teachers must help facilitate and mold a child's creative mind without imposing their points of view. Some have a tough time finding this balance.

Many of my teachers took a very passive route. Perhaps this is the way school district's policies were framed. Teachers often favored the kids with involved parents. This, I infer, has more to do with the teacher's fear of student complaints than with their desire to educate. My teachers often responded to my challenges of authority in two ways: they sent me to the office, or conceded to my every request. Were teachers really more willing to act radically than to risk a possible dispute with parents? The truth is: yes. Most teachers act out of submission to the school's rules. However, some are audacious and disagree with the school's policies, and therefore appreciate atypical opinions and challenges. My favorite teachers were the ones that chose to facilitate my creativity rather than suppress it. I respected them, and they respected me. It was a simple and effective relationship.

Rodriguez's favorite teachers, and his relationships with them, were very different. "To his teachers he offers great satisfaction; his success is their proudest achievement" (Rodriguez, 558). He was his teachers' trophy, whereas I was my teachers' challenge. Rodriguez and I seemed to have entirely different social experiences due to our different academic ones. He became the subject of ridicule for his ambition, and was often called the "kiss ass" (Rodriguez, 558). I, however, was always better known as the spokesperson for the students. Though other students did not have the nerve or wit to effectively participate in my coup, I often found myself with an army of support, as they repeated and rallied behind my argument.

Rodriguez and my stubbornness stems from different—perhaps opposing—reasons. I admired, and admire still, the courage and originality of my father. He's strong, moral, helpful and extremely intelligent. He has always been my Atticus Finch, the embodiment of moral character. He is aggressive but not mean, strong but not a bully. He has always chosen doing what's right over what's easy. That is who I want to be. Rodriguez saw his parents in a less praising manner. He saw his parents as an embarrassment, admitting "A primary reason for my success in the classroom was that I couldn't forget that schooling was changing me and separating me from the life I enjoyed before becoming a student" (Rodriguez, 547).

He saw school as a means of separating himself from his parents, whereas I saw it as a chance to grow up just like mine.

While our resistance towards social norms seemed to be entirely opposing, Rodriguez and I had much in common. Both he and I suffered from a common illness: abnormal self-awareness. He realized that his admiration of his teachers alienated him from his peers, while I knew that my questioning of education practices could lead teachers to dislike or punish me. I, respecting my father's (and in turn, my) opinion more than my teacher's, often doubted my teachers. He, on the other hand, lacked confidence in his parents' (and his) opinions, and always took his teacher's word over his parents'. We both saw the flaws of this. His ability to analyze and witness his own speech and mimicking opinions left him feeling unconfident. I struggled with contradicting expectations to think independently and accept direction, and often struggled balancing being educable and keeping my own point of view.

Rodriguez noted the adjustments he eventually had to make when he studied at a collegiate level. He says, "He even repeats exactly his professor's earlier comment. All his ideas are clearly borrowed. He seems to have no thought of his own. He chatters while his listeners smile—their look one of disdain. . . . the scholarship boy makes only too apparent his profound lack of *self*-confidence (Rodriguez, 559). He had a hard time adjusting to the expectation to think on his own. Rodriguez was not prepared to question his teachers or fellow students. He was not ready to be seen as an equal in the eyes of his professors. While in high school I was constantly told to accept the standards, in college I am often praised for my ability to doubt. My concerns are now noted as original, not undermining. Professors do not mind that I don't always agree with them.

Our different reactions to college are just more proof of our different expectations of education. Rodriguez wanted formal education to tell him what is important and what is not. He wanted to know the facts, and be taught what to conclude from them. I, however, wanted to know the facts, and then infer my own conclusions. He thought of academic theories to hold the same irrefutable truth of statistics, while I thought of theories as one possible explanation. There are flaws to both of these extreme views.

Who is more right? While it is not wise to assume that all theories are fact (note the world is flat theory proved to be entirely false and laughable), it is also not wise to assume that all theories are made up. Most theorists have studied facts, statistics, and patterns of their subjects. There is often at least some truth to these theories, but it is important to balance inquisitive questioning and respect towards experts. It comes down to balance. It is important to know when to question and when not to. This is a learned skill, and both Rodriguez and I are learning more with age.

On an initial read, Maria's essay might seem too mired in comparison and contrast, with its back-and-forth between shared and divergent experiences, and not yet moving from this to a fully developed argument—which, with its moments of nascent systemic critique even amongst the more flippant remarks, the essay certainly has the potential to do. I did, I think, invite such a writerly movement, with the phrase "illuminate how your experience both intersects with and diverges from Rodriguez' discussion" in the assignment text. However, in my initial comments to Maria, I focused on how she might elaborate and refine her complication of Rodriguez' ideas, perhaps with specific attention to his sense of "success," or the importance of imitation, or the significance of interaction between students—and abstract more from her experience, to generalize towards systemic critique.

On reflection, however, I want to value precisely this work of "comparison and contrast," and the relationship Maria establishes between the writerly persona and Rodriguez—which, because of the lack of movement towards argument, works more at the level of exploration of common cause than at the level of sustained critique. Rather than castigating Rodriguez as some of my students did—for not "relaxing," or for "exploiting" his point of difference, and so on—and thus taking a definitive position, Maria positions herself-as-student and Rodriguez as interlocutors considering a system from different perspectives. She may be overwhelmed by all the differences, but does not try to resolve these away: the question "who is more right?" indicates the temptation to end this way, but she resists it, and keeps the conclusion undecided. Without the burden of argument, the essay can meander to a more vulnerable writerly position.

The writerly vulnerability here is resisted in turn by the equalizing gestures, which put Maria and Rodriguez on the same footing; given that for my students, Rodriguez is both authoritative, educated writer and academic *and* disadvantaged student, his authority is an interesting question to begin with, but by considering his story as largely a matter of "views" or "experiences" or "expectations," rather than a story of disadvantage connected to class and ethnicity, Maria is better able to draw herself into a position from which to compare and contrast. This might seem a problematic elision, but through juxtaposition, Maria implicates herself in a system that allows and disallows authority in complex ways—even if she does not convey this through an "argument" in response to Rodriguez. Rather than, say, an accounting of static disadvantage or privilege, an idea of shared experience is being composed here, an account of shifting positions in relation to authority in the educational setting. This might not be work towards a "stronger reading" of Rodriguez, in the sense of a more precise drawing out of the nuances of his argument, but it's a companion project nonetheless. Thus I think it is possible to read an essay such as Maria's as "augmenting" or "fostering" (to use Ellsworth's terms) as much as it is taking something down or apart.

More broadly, I see the notion so central to *Ways of Reading*, the idea of seeing one's own experience anew through someone else's terms, or using one's own experience to put pressure on someone else's terms, as a kind of training in public thinking. But more than a passive empathy, the connection has to be forced a little, through the act of writing something like "argument" or analysis. We could see this thinking as connected to the kinds of public writing emerging to put pressure on "virtuous argument." In some ways, the kind of work involved in the "issue lattice" civic action described by Agre is oddly modeled by Maria's essay, where she sees moments of connection and potential paths by which to take up Rodriguez' ideas, but in a way more open-ended than if she presupposed a thesis and an audience. We might replace or supplement James Crosswhite's notion of including more and more diverse viewpoints into one's argument—trying to get the agreement of larger and larger audiences—by considering the sphere of circulation, bounded by notions of capacity, power, and language, as itself expanding, malleable, so the juxtaposition offered in Maria's essay becomes a particularly meaningful mode. Not all my students' essays were particularly innovative, or particularly strong analyses of Rodriguez, but the extent to which they enact a moment of saying, here is disparate yet connected experience, a kind of fellow-feeling across time and space, a kind of relation, is as powerful as speaking for or to a public: it is speaking as part of a public. I'm interested in considering public writing pedagogy in this way—as concerning the establishment of kinds of relations, even if the writing is not (yet) projected out into circulation—in contrast to only seeing the worth of public writing pedagogies as measured by the degree of direct social engagement or effects. At the least, such an expanded view allows us to make visible how *Ways of Reading* offers its students ways of writing in public.

WORKS CITED

Agre, Philip E. "The Practical Republic: Social Skills and the Progress of Citizenship." *Community in the Digital Age: Philosophy and Practice*. Eds. Andrew Feenberg and Darin Barney. Rowman and Littlefield, 2004. 201–223. Print.

Bartholomae, David, and Anthony Petrosky. *Ways of Reading: An Anthology for Writers*. 8th ed. Boston: Bedford/St. Martin's, 2008. Print.

Bruno, Maria. "The Measure of Achievement." Unpublished Essay. Seminar in Composition, University of Pittsburgh, Spring 2009.

Castells, Manuel. *The Power of Identity. The Information Age: Economy, Society and Culture* Vol. 2. Malden, MA: Blackwell, 1997. Print.

Crosswhite, James. *The Rhetoric of Reason*. Madison: U of Wisconsin P, 1996. Print.

Duffy, John. "Virtuous Arguments." *Inside Higher Ed* March 16, 2012. Web.

Ellsworth, Elizabeth. *Places of Learning: Media, Architecture, Pedagogy*. New York: Routledge, 2005. Print.

Ervin, Elizabeth. "Composition and the Gentrification of Public Literacy." *The Locations of Composition*. Eds. Christopher J. Keller and Christian R. Weisser. Albany: State U of New York P, 2007. 37–53. Print.

Graff, Gerald. *Clueless in Academe*. New Haven: Yale UP, 2003. Print.

Mathieu, Paula, and Diana George. "Not Going It Alone: Public Writing, Independent Media, and the Circulation of Homeless Advocacy." *College Composition and Communication* 61.1 (2009): 130–149. Print.

Reid, Alexander. *The Two Virtuals: New Media and Composition*. West Lafayette, IN: Parlor Press, 2007. Print.

Ridolfo, Jim, and Dànielle Nicole DeVoss. "Composing for Recomposition: Rhetorical Velocity and Delivery." *Kairos: A Journal of Rhetoric, Technology, and Pedagogy* 13.2 (2009). Web.

Rodriguez, Richard. "The Achievement of Desire." *Ways of Reading: An Anthology for Writers*. 8th ed. Eds. David Bartholomae and Anthony Petrosky. Boston: Bedford/St. Martin's, 2008. 545–563. Print.

Trimbur, John. "Composition and the Circulation of Writing." *College Composition and Communication* 52.2 (2000): 188–219. Print.

Weisser, Christian. *Moving Beyond Academic Discourse: Composition Studies and the Public Sphere*. Carbondale: Southern Illinois UP, 2002. Print.

Wells, Susan. "Rogue Cops and Health Care: What Do We Want from Public Writing?" *College Composition and Communication* 47.3 (1996): 325–341. Print.

Riding the Seesaw: Generative Tension between Teaching Models

Gwen Gorzelsky

In the end we're all freshman writers. This is a notion I've absorbed through many conversations with fellow University of Pittsburgh writing teachers, though it suggests different implications to its different hearers and users.

Let me begin to explain my sense of the implications through a short digression. Recently, I've watched my husband work on a pencil portrait based on an old black-and-white photo of his mother holding his infant sister. Because the photo itself is an unflattering representation—its lighting draws harsh lines and pales the woman's and child's faces—my husband subtly alters some of its aspects in his penciled version. The piece evolves through his process of working back and forth between the ideal of exact imitation and the ideal of artistic embellishment aimed at producing a more aesthetically pleasing effect. Like writing, drawing entails a combination of manual and intellectual activities that generates a material product. Like drawing, writing entails a set of back-and-forth moves between particular intellectual practices.

I like the portrait metaphor because it embodies the relationship between, on one hand, the back-and-forth moves between intellectual practices (here, the use of various artistic ideals as guides to ways of seeing and ways of drawing) and, on the other hand, the generation of a material aesthetic product. But there are other, more concrete comparisons that can serve as a shorthand to express the notion of a back-and-forthness between intellectual practices. A friend who swing dances has explained to me how the dancers simultaneously pull away from and hold onto one another to produce the couple's pirouettes. She says that this combination of seemingly conflicting motions generates a "creative tension" that enables the dance itself. Similarly, kids on a seesaw work simultaneously against and with each other's balance and weight to generate the material experience of the seesaw's sustained motion. This generative tension of the swing dance and the seesaw is a combination of moves that seems crucial to me in both the activity of writing and the use of models in theorizing writing and its teaching.

Because this generative tension, in the form of back-and-forth moves between intellectual practices, is as much a part of "freshman writing" as it is of "advanced composition" or of professional and scholarly writing, I see the term "freshman writing" as sort of a misnomer. That is, so many of the issues with which freshman writers grapple are issues that beleaguer experienced writers as well. An easy example is the tendency of writers to get balled up in sentences expressing complex thoughts and, as a result, to produce confused grammatical structures. (And my writing should certainly stand as an instance.) But there are issues—like finding and explaining the "right" piece of evidence, pitching a piece to your audience, developing the complexities of an argument, and hammering out that felicitous turn of phrase—that dog experienced as well as freshman writers. For me, the term "freshman writing" doesn't stand for a set of preliminary skills but for a set of complex issues that are problems, in different ways, for *all* writers. In a sense, I hear the phrase as an argument against a developmental model of freshman writing.

309

Others, though, hear the term as compatible with the developmental model. And conversations with some of these folks have pushed me to think about how different models might be useful.

And for the moment, what seems most useful to me is a set of back-and-forth moves between models, the generative tension of the seesaw and the swing dance. This kind of back-and-forthness is one of the things I like about Dave Bartholomae's essay "The Tidy House: Basic Writing in the American Curriculum." I see it as similar to the back-and-forth between producing narratives and producing critiques, which is one of the moves I read in "The Tidy House," or the back-and-forth between generous readings and against-the-grain readings.

My back-and-forth in models of freshman writing is this: on one hand, I believe in complex reading and writing assignments and in class discussions that address this complexity; on the other hand, I use commenting practices that draw on a developmental model. One way to explain this is to acknowledge that my comments have gotten more directive over the past year. As I'm a relatively new teacher, this might just be part of a developmental trajectory. On the other hand, I taught basic writing, a course sometimes seen as "prior" to the usual freshman writing course, for the first time this year. I often found myself writing, in response to a general, unsubstantiated claim about a text, versions of this comment: "*First*, you need to show readers evidence by quoting a place in the text. *Then*, you need to show us your interpretation of that quote and how that interpretation enables you to make your claim." This kind of comment certainly suggests a developmental model to me, and I must admit that I find it not just useful but indispensable.

The danger of such prefab comments, though, is when they become automatic, when they're the only response I can make, or bother to make, to a paper. The back-and-forth I'm striving for demands that I look for ways to intersperse these prefab comments with other kinds of comments that respond with real questions to an intellectual issue, problem, argument, or question raised in the paper.

To talk about why it's so important to me to hang onto complex reading and writing assignments and to engage actively in intellectual discussion with student texts, I want to read through sections of a paper by a student of mine, John B———. The assignment that prompted the student's writing follows:

Wideman Paper Assignment

Step One in class M 2/6, W 2/8, F 2/10

Step Two due M 2/13

Step Three due M 2/20

Step Four due W 2/22

Step Five due F 2/24

Step One

Choose a passage that seems significant to you, one in which Wideman shows his problems with representations, with reconstructing events and people's lives through writing. Quote this passage using the correct format. (Use your handbook or check with me if you need to.) Then, do an interpretation of the passage. (Your interpretation should be at least two or three substantial paragraphs.)

Step Two

Go back to your interpretation and reread it. Then, choose two or three places from *Brothers and Keepers*. These should be places where you see Wideman trying to cope with the difficulties of writing described in your interpretation. What kinds of writerly techniques does he use to do this coping? You can discuss broadly things Wideman does throughout the book (e.g., things like using both ghetto dialect and academic English), but be sure to interpret in detail two or three passages from the book.

Step Three

Reread your own identities paper (the paper was modeled on Wideman's book). Explain your paper's problems with representation, with reconstructing events and people's lives through writing. Then, choose two or three places from your paper where you, as a writer, are trying to cope with these problems. What kinds of writerly techniques do you use to do this coping? You can discuss broadly things that you do throughout the paper, but be sure to interpret in detail two or three passages from your paper.

Step Four

Reread your interpretations of *Brothers and Keepers* and of your own paper. For each text, discuss the effectiveness of the writer's attempts to cope with her or his particular problems with representing the world through writing. Use the passages that you've interpreted from each text. Build on your interpretations to explain how and why the writer's attempts to cope with her/his problems are and/or aren't effective.

Step Five

Reread all of your work from the previous steps of this assignment. Based on your work, what do you think are effective ways for both writers and readers to deal with the problems of representing the world through writing? Be careful to use the work you've done up to this point to build your argument and support your conclusions.

The combination of the above assignment and the assignment for the identities paper, which this assignment's Step Three requires students to reread, asks them to seesaw, to move back-and-forth, between different practices of reading and writing. John B————'s response to Steps Three and Four of the assignment follow.

III

In the biography *Brothers and Keepers* we saw that there was a problem with reconstructing people's events and lives in a totally unbiased way. This runs true throughout most biographies including the biography of John B———— and

Lauren D——. In order to compensate for these problems I try to cope with bias to make it the best interpretation as far as dealing with unbiased goes.

The general problem with this biography, and most other biographies in general, is the selective memory of the author. Surely there are many events that I choose not to remember or that I modify in my brain. When I retell the events that shaped our lives, this will make the re-creation highly unreliable. What needs to be considered as well is that there could be events that shaped my life that were more important than the ones listed, but this just needs to be understood by the reader and he or she needs to keep this in mind when reading any biography, including my own.

The language of the paper is going to be written in a manner of a freshman engineering student since that is my identity. The part that deals with the dialog from Lauren's childhood will definitely suffer from this. I try to compensate for the difference by working with Lauren for using phrases that she and her mother were likely to use back then. Lauren's interpretation is better than mine alone, but it also has the same selective-memory problem.

The other method of coping is in my part of the biography. I still go fishing with my dad, so many of the events and feelings of the first day have become ritualized. I can therefore cope by using my present-day recollections from the event of fishing. I therefore am not detached from the whole ceremony and this makes it a more accurate retelling of events.

I also tried to cope by mentioning a number of times that it was not the fishing ritual so much that was important as was the decision to follow my dad. This also runs true in Lauren's biography when at the end of the painting scene I dropped in the idea that the event could have been anything, just as long as Lauren was with her mom. This releases the stress of the importance of the exact details and points to the decision that was made during these two activities in our lives.

IV

Gwen, my feelings towards the usefulness of coping are expressed below. I did not answer the question in the way that it was asked, but I spent a good portion of the paper dealing with why coping is self-defeating. I do at the end talk about coping in my John Wideman papers but did not expand. I just wanted to test the waters and see if you think that my reasoning is good enough to make valid not including big explanations on effectiveness in coping. Please give me your input on this approach. If you think it is still necessary let me know if I should expand the coping effectiveness at the end!

It is my opinion that the human is formed from a complex series of experiences. Each experience either reinforces or contradicts a previous one. In the early stages of our lives we learn the most important things we will ever learn. I believe that it is an effect of childhood experiences in why we like some things and shun others. I also believe that no two people are even closely alike. There are many things that go unsaid, perhaps more things than are said. In light of the complexity and variety of every human there is no way to form a biography that everyone can relate to or understand. It is therefore my thought that a writer should not attempt to deal or cope with bias from his paper.

The reason that I feel so strongly about this is that when an author copes he is altering in some way the emotions conveyed by the paper to suit a certain audience. It is impossible to please everyone so when writing a biography I feel that when you cope you are again making a bias towards the story.

The author is shaped by certain events. If he or she is free to express them as he or she remembers them then they are more accurate than if he makes an attempt to recreate them exactly. This may sound a bit skewed but let me reason it out.

A person experiences thousands of events in their lives. Each event offers some aspect on life and a way of acting towards it. When I live through an event I interpret it and store it how I feel it can assist me in making myself a better person. When I recall stories that shaped my personality I need not cope with my bias, because it is with this bias I live. If I were to cope, this bias would not be part of the image I drew of myself and therefore would be false. Since the point of a biography is to create events that shaped my life I need to include the events in the way I interpreted them and remembered them not the way they factually happened.

The methods of coping used by both John Wideman and myself were done in such a manner that they drastically changed the event as it was interpreted not as it historically happened. Wideman is trying to write a biography of his brother. This is the reason that the book was published, but I assert that the real reason is to figure out why he is not in the big house. His family was never really that close and he wanted to see if there were differences in himself and Robby. Wideman oftentimes finds himself not listening to Robby. He does not say that he changed his final draft and if he asked Robby to repeat this missed stuff. I am assuming that it never was and it is better off not because Wideman at first was looking to find himself and his relationship to his brother. Since this is the case the stories that Robby tells are not as important as what Wideman writes since it is Wideman's head that we need to get into. There is no point when Wideman begins to write in order that others may experience what he and his brother have, the keepers and the prison system. Before this point though there is no need for coping because Wideman is dealing with a personal issue so any bias adds to what is in his head.

There is need for coping in the way Wideman tries to express Robby's hate at the end of the book, though, and he does this by including Robby's poems. This is a direct path into Robby and is an effective manner of coping because it gives us a firsthand look into Robby's head.

In my biography the coping occurs in the events retold. This coping does not affect the point, since the point is that Lauren and I decided to be like our parents not the actual event that happened on those two respective days. The coping is indifferent to the point of recollections.

In these paragraphs, John B———'s paper is working against the grain of class discussions that emphasized objectivity as Wideman's problem and "objective" depiction of Robby as the standard by which to measure the effectiveness of Wideman's solutions. John B———'s paper determinedly insists on *not* "addressing the assignment" and instead on redefining the problem.

A straight developmental model of freshman writing would, I think, argue that I should never have asked my students to read a complicated, controversial text like Wideman's, much less given them such a complex assignment. John B———'s paragraphs display difficulty with sentence structure and boundaries, with constructing logic in ways a reader can follow. Surely a developmental model would hold that its writer is far from ready to call the terms of his assignment into question. But it's precisely that thoughtful, provocative line of questioning I'd like to encourage for freshman writers, for all writers.

I'm not making any claims for John B———'s status as an example of the kind of resistant, excluded student described in "The Tidy House." In traditional terms, he's probably the "best socialized" student I've ever had: unasked, he presented me before the fact with absence excuses signed by his commanding officer and submitted typed homework and copies of in-class writing assignments. During discussions, he spoke enthusiastically, thoughtfully, confidently, politely. He never deviated in the slightest from class rules without first seeking permission. I wouldn't mark him as a resistant student.

Nonetheless, these paragraphs mark him as a freshman writer in institutional terms. But these freshman writing paragraphs also make the move of using an idea that John B——— insists is important to him as a way of questioning class discussion and the terms of the assignment. "It is . . . my opinion that the human is formed from a complex series of experiences." He *acknowledges* that this is his belief, not a premise he's proven, and then uses that belief as a frame to develop his critique and an argument about the text, an argument shaped by a belief and an approach in which he has significant stake.

This move seems crucial to me. I believe in the project of prompting our students and ourselves to question foundational assumptions. But I think that the kind of negotiation between students and the academy called for in "The Tidy House" demands that students find ways to bring their foundational assumptions *into* their academic writing projects. I can't imagine producing a paper that was more than a mechanical exercise in conventionality without working in and through my foundational assumptions. The generative tension between bringing foundational assumptions *into* academic writing, on one hand, and questioning those foundational assumptions, on the other, is a crucial instance of the back-and-forth intellectual moves that make successful pieces of writing pirouette so that they push readers' ways of thinking and seeing.

So whether John B——— is a "disfranchised" student or not, whether he's a freshman writer, an advanced composition student, or a professional or scholarly writer, his is the kind of move I want to encourage. While students' production of critiques of texts in response to assignments, class discussions, and/or teacher comments can be a valuable learning experience, that move isn't the same one John's text performs. The teacher-prompted critiques are moves that, in one sense, are obedient responses to authority. John B———'s paper is thoughtful, engaged questioning of the framework provided by authority. A notable move. And, I think, a way of interacting with texts, with teachers, with authority's frameworks that I don't know how to solicit but would certainly like to promote. It is a way of writing that intersects with ways of seeing and of being in the world.

Now, I continue to struggle with how to mediate between models, between kinds of comments, class work, and assignments. I'm striving to work out a balance between teaching calculated to help enable students "to negotiate the full range of expectations in the university" ("Tidy House" 20) and teaching calculated to help enable students to pursue, develop, and push on their texts' ideas and moves. This struggle for balance—for the seesaw's and the swing dance's generative tension—might, I hope, be useful to students in defining new ways of relating to authority and its frameworks. I'm working with two models: one of development and one of writing as a means of social transformation. Both enable particular kinds of work. Both produce problems. As I mentioned above, the developmental model can become automatic and thus prevent teacher engagement with the intellectual work happening in student texts. The social transformation model can prompt a focus on student papers' potentials and successes and allow teachers to lose sight of the real and extensive pressures students face to learn and use academic conventions.

So I'm suggesting a model of how to use models, a model of back-and-forthness, of sustained efforts to move into and out of models, using, critiquing, and perhaps improving, them. In the end, we all struggle with problems of articulating complexities and of negotiating between our own agendas and academic conventions. We're all freshman writers.

WORK CITED

Bartholomae, David. "The Tidy House: Basic Writing in the American Curriculum." *Journal of Basic Writing* 12.1 (1993): 4–21.

On Teaching *Ways of Reading*

Bill Hendricks

Imagine the beginning: the class has met three or four times. The teacher has introduced the course to her students, talked about her expectations, about what will be required of the students, about classroom procedures. The students have read the introduction to *Ways of Reading*, and the teacher has assigned a first reading, say, the Walker Percy essay. The students have read "The Loss of the Creature" and used the "Questions for a Second Reading" in their rereading; they've talked about those readings in class. Today the students handed in a paper for one of the "Loss of the Creature" writing assignments. The teacher sits down in front of this first stack of student papers and thinks about how the course has gone so far.

She was pleased with the class conversation about the introduction. She had been apprehensive that the students would be puzzled by, maybe even hostile to, an essay on reading that deemphasizes information-gathering, summarizing, and reading for main ideas in favor of "strong reading," an aggressive and challenging way of reading that few students are likely to have thought much about. But, happily, the students seemed intrigued, and a little flattered, to imagine reading as enabling them to pursue academic projects that they are responsible for not only maintaining and shaping but, in some ways, initiating. "I like the idea of being able to begin with what I notice," one student said, "of not just having to throw in a couple of sentences at the end of a paper about whether I agree or disagree with what I've read." True, some students objected to Bartholomae and Petrosky's claim that reading is a social interaction, but other students insisted that to deny that claim is really to affirm it. "How can anybody object to this essay's saying that reading is a social interaction," one student said, "without doing exactly what the essay talks about—making a mark on it and talking back to its writers?"

At the next class meeting, when the class discussed readings of "The Loss of the Creature," several students wanted to talk more about the course introduction, saying that the Percy essay reminded them of it. "I'm not sure I know just who a 'consumer' is," said one student, "but he probably isn't a 'strong reader.' The consumers Percy talks about seem pretty passive." The teacher noted this student's use of one text as a frame for understanding another, and she felt generally hopeful about the class's readiness to see acts of reading as involving construction and struggle.

Thinking about these class conversations, the teacher anticipates a satisfying semester, and she begins to read the student papers in front of her with high expectations. Many of these papers, she suspects, will offer rich readings of the problem Walker Percy investigates in "The Loss of the Creature." "The society of today is mechanical," begins the first paper, "and so are the people of this society. They do what they are told, when they are told, and how they are told to do it." The teacher pauses, taken aback by a reading of "The Loss of the Creature" that reduces the dilemmas Percy works with to terms of universal authoritarianism and regimentation—and marveling at how easily this writer has managed to free himself from such pervasive constraints. The teacher begins a second paper, less portentous than the first, which talks about the writer's success in eluding the preformed symbolic complexes that have threatened him: "the solution is to keep an open mind." But the writer seems to think that this formula needs no explanation. The slogan, maddeningly, stands alone. The teacher turns to a third paper, one which begins with what seems like a commitment to look closely at Percy's essay: "In 'The Loss of the Creature,' Walker Percy tries to understand some very important problems," the paper begins. "Such as," it continues, "how to see the Grand Canyon. This is important because if everyone saw the Grand Canyon in the same way the world would become a very boring place to live."

The teacher reads on. A few of the papers seem more promising, better ways to begin the difficult work on reading and writing she has in mind for the semester, but she finds none of the papers very satisfying. She is surprised most by how little most of the readings notice. Few readings notice Percy's distinction between "experts" and "planners"; no one wants to do anything with "dialectic." Many papers make no attempt to bring forth Percy's key terms and examples through direct quotation, relying instead on paraphrases that do not so much translate Percy's language into the writer's as translate it out of existence: "According to Percy, until people actually make an experience their own, or express their own ideas in their own words, the problem of missing the gift will not be solved, and people will be left merely to admire all the pretty packages." Here, quite neatly, the writer avoids the puzzle of what to do with Percy's "preformed symbolic complexes" by implying that "loss of sovereignty" is a dilemma only for the morally lazy: be true to yourself, and the creature is recovered. There are too many papers willing to portray the problems of the social construction of perception as cartoon conflicts: the expert or planner or "society" is plotting to cheat "individuals" of their rightful claims to authentic experience, and we all need to resist these encroachments through keeping an open mind and appreciating how special and unique we and our surroundings are. But few papers want to extend this fervor for resistance to doing a little resisting of Percy. The teacher finds only two or three papers that question Percy's conclusions about what Cárdenas or Terre Haute tourists see in the Grand Canyon; she finds no papers at all that question the liberating potential of apprenticeship to "great men" or majestic educators.

And she wonders: given the promise of the first few classes, how is it that this first batch of papers is so disappointing, so thin? And what is she going to do next?

Reading and Writing

In every course I have ever taught, there has been a moment like this. Always my students' first papers have been not what I hoped for, less than I wanted. Stubbornly, I continue to be a little surprised by such moments ("This semester," I have told myself, "things will be different"). But at least I have gradually developed, I think, ways of understanding the disparity between my expectations for my students and their initial performance—and strategies to narrow the gap by the end of the semester.

Even if *Ways of Reading* is being used for a first course in college reading and writing, students come to the book with considerable experience as readers and writers. But most students will not have been prepared by that experience for a course in which reading and writing are so tightly bound together—in which, for example, students' readings of an essay are validated largely through what they can do with that essay in writing essays of their own, and in which, further, the writing thus produced is ordinarily responded to with a request that the students validate it through going back to do more work on reading, and so forth. This back-and-forth movement between reading and writing creates, I think, special challenges and opportunities for both students and teachers of *Ways of Reading*. In this essay, I am not suggesting that there is a "right" way to teach the book and that I know what it is. I offer just one teacher's reading of the book, of the questions I imagine *Ways of Reading* posing for teachers and students, and the ways my teaching experience suggests to me to work with those questions.

Like the rest of us, students are practiced at getting along. As you together discuss their readings of the introduction to *Ways of Reading*, your students may well cheerfully assent to Bartholomae and Petrosky's ideas about new ways of looking at reading—partly because of the excitement of thinking about reading as a powerful tool for intellectual achievement, partly because of the great respect for students evinced by Bartholomae and Petrosky, and partly because *Ways of Reading* is your students' textbook and you're their teacher. The temptation is very strong: "Yes, now I see. Here's how I can be a better reader and writer and get more out of reading and writing." But as they write their first papers, your students will be relying on what they already know how to do, and what they know how to do probably does not include a way of treating reading as a constructive activity extending over time, as a process.

Reading and writing are not inevitable, not "natural." What people learn when they "learn to read" depends on their culture's (or cultures') ways of teaching and valuing reading. Much in your students' education has probably suggested to them that reading is a highly unusual form of interpretation: while one's parents or friends may inspire baffling mixtures of comfort and irritation, a well-written book is perfectly clear; while two workers may have good reasons for their conflicting evaluations of the same job, if two readers disagree, one of them is probably a better reader; while people may make very different judgments, over time, of their children, their neighborhood, their country, the meaning of a text is properly fixed, unalterable; life is a process, reading happens all at once.

For students to pursue the questioning and aggressive reading process suggested by *Ways of Reading* is difficult, moreover, because their education has often seemed to imply that intellectual pursuits, especially in school, are bounded by fairly rigid categories. It is not just reading and writing that have been presented as separate activities. Disciplines and texts and courses of study have also often been seen as self-contained, discrete, each in its predetermined place: tenth-grade biology, eleventh-grade chemistry, twelfth-grade physics; *The Scarlet Letter* "belongs to" American Literature, but not to History of Psychology; students are expected on a final exam in their Systems of Government course to "know the material," but are probably not asked how they could apply what they have learned to improving the governments around them. The student who identifies "how to see the Grand Canyon" as a significant problem presented by Walker Percy's essay, significant because "if everyone saw the Grand Canyon in the same way the world would become a very boring place to live," is probably not in the habit, as a reader, of seeing one thing in terms of something else. A metaphor is something that poets use.

As the students in your course work at being more self-conscious about and critical of their reading and writing, you can expect that they will become increasingly articulate about their reading and writing processes. The student quoted earlier who talked about Percy, the gift and its trappings, wrote midway through the semester:

> Generally I play one of two roles as a reader. For an essay based on an assigned reading, I take what I call the everything-fits-in-a-neat-little-package-and-you-can-tie-it-all-up-in-a-bow approach; for an essay based on personal experience, I use what I refer to as the sounds-like-I-know-what-I'm-talking-about-but-I'm-lying approach. The names are long but quite easily understood.
>
> The systematic everything-fits-in-a-neat-little-package-and-you-can-tie-it-all-up-in-a-bow approach is best applied in essays which analyze the assigned text of any author. My favorite example: "According to Percy, until people actually make an experience their own, or express their own ideas in their own words, the problem of missing the gift will not be solved, and people will be left merely to admire all the pretty packages." In a way, it is somewhat incredible if you stop to consider what I did. In one slightly longer than average sentence, I wrote what it took Walker Percy ten-and-a-half pages to say! I summed up an entire essay, all its examples, problems, and complications, in one sentence. How? I omitted anything he said that confused me and pretended that the complications didn't exist. That way I sounded as though I had Percy all figured out lock, stock, and barrel, case closed, the end. Granted, it is good to have a strong idea and to go somewhere with it, but in the process, I killed Percy. Not really; but I do sound as though I learned everything there was that Percy had to offer, used him up, and am finished with him. That is awful because I am probably sacrificing a lot of interesting ideas in my attempt to appear so conclusive. Perhaps if I dared to explore what confused me, I could have generated some new ideas even if they were not all neatly resolved in the end.

But your students' capacity to be reflective about and modify their ways of reading won't emerge quickly. To work at reading by writing takes opportunity and practice, repeated attempts, time.

It isn't that your students initially can't conceive of the interrelatedness of reading and writing, abstractly considered. They can, but different students will arrive differently (and take varying lengths of time) at ways of putting this interrelatedness to work for them. You can expedite this in part through the language in which you conduct your class, referring, for example, to class conversations and student papers as "readings" of the subject or assignment at hand, but the process of learning to see reading and writing as aspects of a single activity probably won't proceed far until students see the advantages, in the contexts of particular acts of reading and writing, of honoring the interconnectedness. For example, the student who writes, "People do what they are told, when they are told, and how they are told to do it" can be questioned about how he has conceived the relation between reading and writing. This student can write, and he can read, but he is trapped by acting as if there were only the slenderest of connections between reading and writing. He has read the Walker Percy essay, noticed that it could be said to have something to do with conformity, mentally scanned the commonplaces he has stored under "Conformity," and written a perfectly lucid sentence that makes nonsense of Percy and his own experience. He could use his sentence to prove that he has read the essay, or to prove that he can write correctly, but he couldn't use it to show why anybody, himself especially, should take his reading seriously. If, now, this student is asked to account for the reading his sentence represents, he will need to write better sentences, but he can't do that unless he simultaneously makes a better reading and goes to work on his and Percy's texts.

Reading here, writing over there: *Ways of Reading* is designed to help students work against such fragmentation. This is obviously true of the "Making Connections" assignments and the extended assignment sequences, which ask students to write about how two or more essays or stories might illuminate both each other and academic projects that they can be made to further extend. But it is also true of the "Questions for a Second Reading" and the initial "Writing Assignments," where students are asked, for example, to apply Paulo Freire's term "problem-posing" to their own educational experiences. There are a number of ways that you can reinforce your students' efforts to practice this sort of constructive, amalgamative reading and writing. For example, in introducing a writing assignment on, say, John Berger's *Ways of Seeing*, you might bring forward a student comment from your class discussion of Berger that wondered whether Emerson's original audience for the "American Scholar" oration[1] might be seen as having been in a position analogous to the audiences for art before mass reproduction. And both in class discussions and in your marking of student papers, you can attend to and encourage comments in the form of "*X* reminds me of *Y*" — the sort of comment that may have been dismissed as irrelevant in your students' previous school experience with reading.

Rewriting, Rereading

But while for most readers to notice that one part of their experiences can be connected to another part, that one text recalls another, that "*X* reminds one of *Y*," is by no means irrelevant, it is of only rudimentary usefulness.

In order to read or write a text, any reader, any writer, makes many linguistic connections. Students who in high school have read long books and made A's on tests on those books, and who have written correct and coherent papers in a number of courses, have a legitimate claim to a certain expertise as readers and writers. And even if (maybe especially if) students coming to a course in college reading and writing have been very successful in high school, they won't necessarily be discouraged by a comment on their work that says, in effect, "That's wrong." (They have, after all, a lot of experience in setting things "right," and college is supposed to be harder than high school.) But they may well be baffled and angered by a response to their work that says, in effect, "So what?" "How do you account for this reading? What passages or moments in the text might you use to bring it forward?

---

[1] Emerson's essay appeared in the fifth edition of *Ways of Reading*.

What is it good for? What does noticing that X reminds you of Y allow you to do that you haven't done already? What's the next step?" Suddenly for such students "to reread" must mean something other than reading an essay twice, and "to rewrite" must mean something other than fixing errors or being clearer—but just what these "others" might be will not be immediately apparent. What lies beyond one more academic hurdle successfully negotiated, one more teacher's approval duly registered?

In trying to assist students to sort out for themselves what might be "in it for them" to pursue writing and reading as ongoing, open-ended, and mutually supporting activities, I have found that I need to combine a number of considerations. Any group of student papers addressed to some question or questions about an assigned text will encompass a great variety of readings. Teachers of college reading and writing encounter, every day, the problem of trying to see these readings on their own terms, different as those terms may be from what the teachers themselves might have chosen to do in addressing the assignment. And this problem is likely to be more acute than usual in a course based on *Ways of Reading*, partly because these essays and stories resist easy pigeonholing or categorization (and thus the variety of student readings may be unusually broad) and partly because in almost every writing assignment students are asked to try to see one thing in terms of some other thing or things—a Percian reading of Clifford Geertz's travels in Bali, a progression in the creative development of Adrienne Rich's poetry[2] seen through the language of John Berger. Thus, a teacher is faced with a multiplicity of readings of complex cases. Both in commenting on student papers and in class discussions, I struggle (not always successfully) to suspend the strong readings I myself have made of these cases sufficiently to see what my students' readings have attended to. In class discussions, I often find it enormously tempting to propose my own reading of an assignment question or problem my students are working with. But when I have succumbed to the temptation, I have almost always regretted it. ("Well," too many students think—or at least act as if they do—"that settles it. He's paid to know what he's talking about.")

Usually I can resist the lure, but the more interesting pedagogical problem is how to tie the various readings that emerge in a classroom discussion to further acts of reading and writing. One of the most fruitful class discussions I've been involved in recently had to do with how students read the phrase "the end of education" in Richard Rodriguez's "The Achievement of Desire." Some students argued that the "end" of education means a formal stopping point, Rodriguez's way of acknowledging the completion of his academic training. Other students insisted that "end" here means "goal" or "object," that Rodriguez is identifying the aim of education as an ability to reconcile present and past. Still other students proposed that the phrase suggests a renunciation, Rodriguez's recognition that to desire the past would entail his no longer being able to participate in what he had been calling "education." The class discussion had begun in response to one of the "Questions for a Second Reading" that you'll find after the Rodriguez essay in *Ways of Reading*, but it seemed to me, as I listened to students forcefully articulate these competing responses to a troubling moment in "The Achievement of Desire," that here was an occasion to do more than acknowledge the variety and richness of readers' reactions to a powerful text. It seemed to me that the right move now was to draw on the excitement and energy of this

---

[2] Geertz's essay and Rich's poetry appeared in the eighth edition of *Ways of Reading*.

discussion by turning the reading question into a writing problem, by sending students back to the essay to see how they might work out, through writing about yet another reading, their interpretations. The resulting set of student papers was one of the strongest I have received lately. Whatever interpretations they were able to articulate in their writing, all students, as they went back to read Rodriguez's essay again, had somehow to take into account—acknowledge, react against, incorporate, consciously ignore—the other voices they had heard in our discussion.

In a course that provides opportunities for students to read and respond to their classmates' writing students will get further experience in seeing not only the anthology pieces but their own papers as subject to multiple interpretations. However, as I have suggested, it is probably naive to think that students will hear a teacher's comments as only one more voice in the dialogue. Teachers are readers, but they are also their students' teachers; they are responding from a privileged position, even if they wish that this were not so. But I think that it is possible for teachers to take advantage of the power relations implicit in institutional writing to become their students' allies in resisting the silence to which it is all too easy for readers and writers to acquiesce. Later in this essay, I show my marking of a sample student paper on Rodriguez, a paper that I thought was—though coherent and sometimes arresting—distressingly silent just when it most needed to speak up. For now, let me offer a few general remarks on how I approach helping students to become more articulate about what their readings have revealed to them.

Often I get papers in which an odd paragraph stands out, something that is hard for me to integrate with the rest of the paper; not what I'd call a "silent" paragraph exactly, but a paragraph that is speaking poorly—perhaps verbose, or seemingly extraneous or misplaced. Some years ago, when I would routinely comment on such a paragraph—with something like "Is this paragraph necessary?" I'd get back revisions with the offending paragraph (that's how students heard my questions) obediently cut. But it seems to me now that though teachers can always shut students up, they ought to be more than a little nervous about deciding to do so. And now I am generally concerned to encourage students to say more, not less. They aren't writing an essay about Percy or Geertz just to prove that they can do it and end there. I try in my comments to help students advance the work on projects which they have begun or might begin, asking them to make connections, in their revisions, with other essays and stories, or with other papers they have written, or among various parts (especially odd paragraphs) of the paper I am commenting on. And I am more likely than I used to be, faced with a puzzling paragraph, to ask questions about it that direct the student back into the essay of which it is a reading.

After one or more revisions of a paper, students may indeed decide that some sentence or paragraph or section of the paper is extraneous, that it doesn't advance the project they are working on. But rather than knowing what they are going to say or how they are going to say it before they begin to write, students will work out what they have to say as they write and rewrite. In order to write about a text, students have to listen to what an author says and then, in their turn, talk back to the voice they hear. And then a teacher speaks to the voices in the students' papers, commenting both about ways of reading and ways of writing. And though, as I have implied, I think that it is possible for a teacher to say too much too soon about a paper's rhetorical effectiveness, some of my ways of asking students to be more articulate are very much in keeping with traditional rhetorical concerns. On the most basic level, if I read a sentence or paragraph that seems to me so tangled that I can only respond, "I don't understand," I tell the student that I don't understand. I consider this to be providing the student with humble but useful information. And certainly I often request that a writer extend some remark by supplying elaboration or qualification or specific illustration. My problem, always, is to balance my desire, as a reader, for a stronger argument, against my perception, as a teacher, that there are other lines of argument that might also be profitably pursued—or lines of argument that, though hesitantly or confusedly, the writer might in fact *be* pursuing. "The text provides the opportunity for you to see through someone else's language, to imagine your own familiar settings through the images, metaphors, and ideas of others," students of *Ways of Reading* read. Ideally, this model of reading applies not just to students reading assigned texts.

Teachers respond in their comments not only to a particular paper addressed to a particular assignment, but also to what they know about the student's reading and writing development. I have found that my acknowledging a new direction, a new achievement—something that a student has not been able to do before—can have considerable effect in motivating that student to sustain and increase his or her articulateness. This may entail my praising something that, were I to notice it in the writing of a colleague or a professional writer, I would not ordinarily remark on. It isn't plausible that students will in the course of a semester become as expert as professional writers. But expertise is not really the issue. The essays and stories in *Ways of Reading* "leave some work for a reader to do. They require readers willing to accept the challenge and the responsibility, not experts; perhaps the most difficult problem for students is to believe that this is true." For students to improve as strong readers and writers requires that they take some risks; a teacher can honor their risk taking.

Before I turn to a discussion of some representative student papers and my marking of one of them, I want to say that I think teachers commenting on student papers have to develop some way to mediate between all that they *might* say about a paper and what they *do* say about it. Perhaps you have had the experience, as I have, of responding to a student paper with more words than the student wrote: comments snake about everywhere, densely interlining the text, crawling down every margin, turning corners to the back of the page; end comments expand into small essays. I now think that for students, unless they are already unusually good readers, trying to interpret so much commentary may mean that they can't interpret anything; staring at so many words may mean, strangely, that they can't *see* any of them. And, for the teacher, who doesn't have just one student but twenty (or forty or sixty), such mammoth expenditure of time and energy can quickly sink a labor of love into a dispiriting and debilitating trap. I think that the improvements students make in a college reading and writing class will occur gradually, over time—and continue, at the best, long after they have finished with the class. Certain kinds of instrumental writing may be totally successful at once: a grocery list gets the goods, a memo may be recognized by all concerned as having accomplished some purpose. But I think that most acts of strong reading and writing entail dissatisfactions of compromise. Understanding in reading is never complete; the performed understanding represented by a piece of writing may occasion, for its writer, just as much anxiety over what it has failed to accomplish as satisfaction in what it achieves. Paradoxically, this dissatisfaction probably increases along with skillfulness. The stakes keep going up. Writers' consciousness that some goal has been achieved, their *knowing* that they know, is often accompanied by a sense of further goals fleeing before them. As a teacher, I ask myself what I can reasonably expect my students to achieve in one semester and try to pitch my comments accordingly. And I try not to ask students to achieve everything at once. One thing I do to restrain the urge to speak volumes on a single paper is to keep a record (very brief) for each student of the accomplishments and problems I note on their growing portfolios of papers. This way I have a firmer sense of what each student has done so far as I sit down to read and comment on a fresh batch of student papers. And I'm more likely to be able to assist them in moving from the writing they have done so far to the writing they might do next.

Ways of Reading and Revising: Some Sample Student Papers

Reading begins with predispositions. When students read "The Achievement of Desire," they do so having already read a headnote that says something about Rodriguez's background and educational concerns, and something about the reception of Rodriguez's book *Hunger of Memory*. In addition, they begin to read with certain assumptions (different for different readers) about the purposes of education, about Chicanos and working-class families, about autobiographies. Further, students come to "The Achievement of Desire" with characteristic ways of reading, strategies that have worked for them in the past in making sense of texts in academic settings. Readers never notice everything that might be noticed; what they notice when they come to a text for the first time largely depends, then, on what they are predisposed to notice. Moreover, in rereading, as students try to articulate what they have noticed about a text through writing a text of their own, they can't write about all they have noticed. Even given the focusing instrument of an assignment question or problem, their rereading, their writing, will have to attend to some things that they might say about the question or problem and ignore others. This narrowing of the field of vision need not be seen as merely confining; it can also be seen as empowering. The selective and structuring acts of attention required by writing can transform what students have noticed into texts they must account for, the beginning of a performed understanding.

In commenting on a student's reading of an assigned text with an eye to having the student revise, I am commenting both on the understanding of what the paper represents, asking that it be strengthened and extended, and on the way of reading that the paper brings forward, asking about what it allows the writer to do and about how alternative ways of reading might enable the student to construct further, possibly more satisfying or complete, readings.

Let me illustrate by looking at some student papers written in response to an assignment that asks students to talk about Richard Rodriguez as a reader by examining the ways Rodriguez makes use of Richard Hoggart's *The Uses of Literacy* in writing "The Achievement of Desire." The assignment is closely similar to the first "Assignment for Writing" on Rodriguez in *Ways of Reading*. Here is the first paper.

> Rodriguez used Hoggart's "scholarship boy" as a role model to a certain
> extent. Rodriguez modeled his education around what Hoggart made the
> "scholarship boy" out to be. After he read Hoggart, Rodriguez thought he might
> become all the more educated and know so much more if he followed the ideals
> of the "scholarship boy."

In the beginning, Richard's education and learning became his first priority. He often resorted to hitting the books because his family life was folding around him. The isolation which he felt became the obsession for his hard work and constant classroom participation. The time spent on schoolwork made the division between his social and secluded life apparent. The lack of understanding and support he felt that was not coming from his parents made him draw further away as his family life fell to pieces. The only way for him to escape the confinement which he believed was around him was to view his teachers in astonishment. His admiration stemmed from their praise of his work and dedication. His work and efforts were directed toward some mystical goal, the goal to be like the "scholarship boy."

In conclusion, I understand and admire Rodriguez's perseverance and dedication to learn. I once wrote in a speech, "Anything of any worth or value has to be worked for. Oftentimes it is a struggle, but when you persevere and you reach your goal, there is a sense of accomplishment. And I do feel that sense of accomplishment." And so does Rodriguez.

Ways of Reading assumes that the essays and stories it asks students to read are worth the active questioning and recasting they require of their readers; and *Ways of Reading* also assumes that student papers written in response to these texts are worth similar effort. As I read and respond to papers my students have written, I am trying to see what their readings have noticed and trying to suggest ways in which, when they revise, they might do more with what they have attended to. When I begin to read a set of student papers, the question that guides my first reading is usually: "Which of these papers represent readings that grow out of acts of attention?" Or, as the question could also be put, "Which of these papers do some work with a text, and which don't?" That is, I believe that some papers are not worth revising, and this paper on Rodriguez is one of them.

Consider this sentence: "[Rodriguez's] work and efforts were directed toward some mystical goal, the goal to be like the 'scholarship boy.'" I was puzzled by the sentence, initially, because I couldn't understand how this writer is imagining the young Rodriguez to be pursuing a goal he had never heard of. It occurred to me, of course, that the sentence might represent this writer's way of saying that, retrospectively, the mature Richard Rodriguez was renaming his past through Richard Hoggart's language. (And the same thing could be said, hypothetically, about the sentence "Rodriguez modeled his education around what Hoggart made the 'scholarship boy' out to be.") But I had no way of reconciling these conjectures with the sentence "After he read Hoggart, Rodriguez thought he might become all the more educated and know so much more if he followed the ideals of the 'scholarship boy'" followed by a paragraph describing the young Rodriguez trying to become more educated. Bizarrely, the paper suggests that Rodriguez used *The Uses of Literacy* not as a way of retrospectively framing his experience but as a sort of twentieth-century conduct book guiding, *while* it was occurring, his education.

What way of reading does this paper represent? I believe that this writer has read "The Achievement of Desire" at breakneck speed, probably only once, and attended to very little, grasping at just enough to dash off a paper to hand in—never mind the assignment or trying to become engaged by the text. He has a paper, but he hasn't given himself a chance to make sense out of a puzzling text or a challenging problem. He begins with an assignment asking him to discuss Rodriguez as a reader of Hoggart; he scans the text for the first reference to Rodriguez reading Hoggart and finds this: "Then one day, leafing through Richard Hoggart's *The Uses of Literacy*, I found, in his description of the scholarship boy, myself. For the first time I realized that there were other students like me . . ."); and he goes on to grab enough from the essay to prove that, yes, Rodriguez found himself in the "scholarship boy." The student will not be swayed by assignment language that asks him to "look closely at Rodriguez's references to Hoggart's book," to "compare Rodriguez's version of the 'scholarship boy' with Hoggart's," or to examine "the way Rodriguez handles quotations, where he works Hoggart's words into paragraphs of his own"; he has no time to elaborate on his intriguing claims that "[Rodriguez] often resorted to hitting the books because his family life was folding around him" or "the lack of understanding and support he felt that was not coming from his parents made him draw further away as his family life fell to pieces"; and he especially gives himself no opportunity to wonder about what use Richard Rodriguez is making of Richard Hoggart's *The Uses of Literacy*.

In commenting on this paper, I said to the student, in greatly abbreviated form, what I have just said here, and asked him to go back and write a paper on the assignment. I did not ask him to "revise" his first paper because, for one thing, I believed that to do so would trivialize my idea of revision, a re-seeing of some act of attention. Also, I believed that to ask this student for a rewriting of his first paper would be to patronize him. I think that I would have been saying, in effect, "Sorry, you're just not bright enough to read Rodriguez or do this assignment, but maybe you can polish your prose a bit."

"The Achievement of Desire" is especially suitable to a study of the practices of academic reading and writing because of the many ways in which it could be said to suggest that intellectual achievement, as recognized by (contemporary American) academic communities, involves a continuing mediation between invention and imitation, between freedom and constraint. Students engaged in most academic projects are expected to articulate well-considered personal positions within limits not of their own choosing—limits that, unfortunately, probably cannot even be seen *as* limits in the absence of particular acts of reading and writing. That is, teachers cannot resolve their students' reading and writing dilemmas in advance. And students cannot resolve them until they experience them, until they begin, for example, to work at reading an essay through articulating in an essay of their own what their reading has paid attention to. "What strong readers know is that they have to begin regardless of doubts or hesitations."

I think that, in contrast to the first writer, the writer of the following paper has begun a project that she might usefully revise.

> Richard Rodriguez finds himself in Richard Hoggart's *The Uses of Literacy*.
> I thought I identified parts of myself in my psychology texts, but I was not so feverish about finding them. The anxiety in Rodriguez's life makes his reading of Hoggart more dynamic.

His unease can be seen in the way he jumps from thought to thought throughout "The Achievement of Desire." On almost every page, there is an example of Rodriguez questioning himself. The power that is bound to his anxiety is shown by the emphasis that he puts into his confession.

> What I am about to say to you has taken me more than twenty years to admit: *A primary reason for my success in the classroom was that I couldn't forget that schooling was changing me and separating me from the life I enjoyed before becoming a student.* That simple realization!

He sets the confession apart to give it more emphasis and throws in the italics and exclamation for good measure. It is this angst that characterized Rodriguez before he reads Hoggart.

When the author finally finds Hoggart, it is a relief for him. He gets much satisfaction from being identified. The description of a "scholarship boy" is held up as a theme to his life. "Then one day . . . I found, in his description of the scholarship boy, myself." For most of "The Achievement of Desire," there is a pattern to Rodriguez's use of Hoggart. He gives an excerpt of Hoggart's description and then tells of his early experiences. The way Hoggart is employed almost convinces me that Rodriguez based his life on the writing of Hoggart.

I must point out that the writer is able to distinguish himself from the generality. In my psychology courses, I would read about the different personality traits and think that I was an example of all of them. Under close inspection, though, I was able to see that I was more complex than any one category could portray. Rodriguez shows reservations about committing himself, too. He adds qualifications to Hoggart's view of the "scholarship boy." One instance of setting himself apart comes when he says that Hoggart only "initially" shows "deep understanding." Throughout the essay, we go from Hoggart's concept of a "scholarship boy" to the more specific reality of the author's life. Rodriguez sees the differences between the two, but he is content to call himself "a certain kind of scholarship boy."

Why is it so important for him to call himself a "scholarship boy"? He is not content to trust his own words to describe himself. The revelation was made by himself, but he felt a driving need to find "mention of students like me." This insecurity parallels his problems as a youth. I have to wonder if he has really come very far from the imitator he was. In an autobiography, we expect to hear an account in a personal, original, and direct manner. Here we get Rodriguez's life framed in the work of Hoggart. I do not want to say that using Hoggart is not effective for our understanding of a powerful part of his life. There are so many ways of presenting the subject, however, and his choice strikes me as being odd. He is very willing to give up his authority to an "expert."

He felt that he *must* find himself in the reading. A great deal of energy was bound to his feelings of loss. He had to pacify his anxiety. Hoggart gave a description that was close enough for identification and Rodriguez jumped at it. The reason that he gives us for reading Hoggart is that it gave him a measure of his change, but I see it as proof that he has changed very little.

When I got this paper, which was submitted for the same assignment in the same class as the paper I looked at earlier, I saw it as a worthwhile opening move in the construction of a strong reading. The tack that this writer takes in this reading, her insistent emphasis on Rodriguez's "anxiety," was not a direction that most of her classmates chose to pursue, nor one that I would have chosen myself, but it seemed to me that this paper, as I interpreted it, did grow out of an act of attention, one that I felt it worth my time and hers to ask her to question and extend.

Our class had already worked with reading and writing assignments based on Walker Percy's essay "The Loss of the Creature," and I noted this writer's allusion to Percy at the end of the fifth paragraph. I also noticed that the allusion was *only* that, not a genuine recasting of experience through new language. It was what we had been calling a "gesture." Certainly, I thought, her re-seeing her paper in conjunction with Percy's treatment of authority might give this writer more to say about Rodriguez-as-anxious-reader. At the same time, I did not want to overemphasize what for this reader might be seen as only tangential, an issue which, if she pursued it strenuously, might serve to turn her paper into my paper.

We had also, in our class, talked about readers' "roles," and it seemed to me that at times this paper (notably in the last sentence of the fourth paragraph) might profitably be questioned on the basis of the limiting roles it was asking me to assume as a reader — particularly since, in the fourth paragraph, the writer herself speaks of having declined to be limited by a certain kind of reading.

One of my strongest reactions to the paper was, as you might imagine, unease at the paucity of demonstration, illustration, and qualification of the claims being made — even though I was quite taken by a number of the claims. Here the task ahead will sound familiar: to deploy my own variants of the writing teacher's old refrain, "Show me." (Our class's term for unexplored assertion was "labeling.") This is how I responded to the paper.

Richard Rodriguez finds himself in Richard Hoggart's *The Uses of Literacy*. I thought I identified parts of myself in my psychology texts, but I was not so feverish about finding them. The anxiety in Rodriguez's life makes his reading of Hoggart more dynamic.

Significant? Why have you chosen not to demonstrate this in your paper?

His unease can be seen in the way he jumps from thought to thought throughout "The Achievement of Desire." On almost every page, there is an example of Rodriguez questioning himself. The power that is bound to his anxiety is shown by the emphasis that he puts into his confession.

What I am about to say to you has taken me more than twenty years to admit: *A primary reason for my success in the classroom was that I couldn't forget that schooling was changing me and separating me from the life I enjoyed before becoming a student.* That simple realization!

O.K., a reader can grant that you recognize his confession as worth noticing. So how do you account for its significance? Why not give us the interpretation? (The "angst" is not self-explanatory.)

He sets the ⟨confession⟩ apart to give it more emphasis and throws in the italics and exclamation for good measure. It is this angst that characterized Rodriguez before he reads Hoggart.

True? Important? Where's your reading?

When the author finally finds Hoggart, it is a relief for him. He gets much satisfaction from being identified. The description of a "scholarship boy" is held up as a theme to his life. "Then one day . . . I found, in his description of the scholarship boy, myself." For most of "The Achievement of Desire," there is a pattern to Rodriguez's use of Hoggart. He gives an excerpt of Hoggart's description and then tells of his early experiences. The way Hoggart is employed almost convinces me that Rodriguez based his life on the writing of Hoggart.

This is the one paragraph in your reading that parallels the "dynamic" reading you say Rodriguez makes of Hoggart. Here your Rodriguez can discriminate; elsewhere he is overwhelmed.

What can you make of this split?

I must point out that the writer is able to distinguish himself from the generality. In my psychology courses, I would read about the different personality traits and think that I was an example of all of them. Under close inspection, though, I was able to see that I was more complex than any one category could portray. Rodriguez shows reservations about committing himself, too. He adds qualifications to Hoggart's view of the "scholarship boy." One instance of setting himself apart comes when he says that Hoggart only "initially" shows "deep understanding." Throughout the essay, we go from Hoggart's concept of a "scholarship boy" to the more specific reality of the author's life. Rodriguez sees the differences between the two, but he is content to call himself "a certain kind of scholarship boy."

And then?

What role are you asking a reader to play when you imply that the quoted phrase contradicts Rodriguez's ability to see differences?

Well?

Why is it so important for him to call himself a "scholarship boy"? He is not content to trust his own words to describe himself. The revelation was made by himself, but he felt a driving need to find "mention

Only labels of students like me." This insecurity parallels <u>his problems as a youth. I have to wonder if he has really come very far from the imitator he was.</u>

In an autobiography, we expect to hear an account in a personal, origi- *How is it effective?* nal, and direct manner. Here we get Rodriguez's life framed in the work of Hoggart. I do not want to say that <u>using Hoggart is not effective</u> for our understanding of a powerful part of his life. There are so many ways of presenting the subject, however, and his choice strikes me as *Do you have something in* being odd. <u>He is very willing to give up his authority to an "expert."</u> *mind by the allusion to* He felt that he *must* find himself in the reading. A great deal of *Percy? Can* energy was bound to <u>his feelings of loss.</u> He had to pacify his anxiety. *You need to say more* *you make this more of* Hoggart gave a description that was close enough for identification and *a gesture?* Rodriguez jumped at it. The reason that he gives us for reading Hoggart is that it gave him a measure of his change, but I see it as proof that he has changed very little.

> *I admire your willingness to see Rodriguez's achievement at an advanced stage of his education, his way of reading Hoggart, as having roots in long-standing feelings and habits. But I don't think your essay yet demonstrates the reading it wants to claim. Your word "category" struck me. What categories besides "anxiety" could you incorporate in your reading of Rodriguez's relation to Hoggart?*

And here is the revision that the student handed in the following week.

In Richard Rodriguez's essay "The Achievement of Desire," we get a sort of record of how Rodriguez responded to reading a book by Richard Hoggart called *The Uses of Literacy*. But what I can't understand is how to separate how Rodriguez reacted to *The Uses of Literacy* when he first read it in the British Museum from how he is reading it when he's a professional writer writing an essay he wants to publish.

In the British Museum, Rodriguez says, he found in Hoggart's description of the scholarship boy, "myself." "For the first time I realized that there were other students like me, and so I was able to frame the meaning of my academic success, its consequent price--the loss."

At various points in "The Achievement of Desire," we see Rodriguez working out how what he read about the scholarship boy helps him understand why he feels so bad about his academic success. "Good schooling requires that any student alter early childhood habits," Rodriguez paraphrases Hoggart, and then Rodriguez remembers how "after dinner, I would rush to a bedroom with papers and books. As often as possible, I resisted parental pleas to 'save lights' by coming to the kitchen to work." Rodriguez wasn't as upset as his parents were about his need to be alone to study. When he first entered school, he remembers, "what bothered me . . . was the isolation reading required." But gradually, as he was tutored by one of the nuns, he began to feel the "possibility of fellowship between a reader and a writer," not *"intimate,"* but *"personal."* And he also started to want a power he sensed in reading: "Books were going to make me 'educated.'" So that eventually, Rodriguez often enjoyed being alone with his books--but the enjoyment made him feel guilty and anxious: "Nervous. I rarely looked away from my book--or back on my memories." His parents, he knew, were not "educated."

Hoggart helps Rodriguez interpret his past, but as he writes "The Achievement of Desire," Rodriguez is not always grateful for Hoggart's descriptions of the scholarship boy. Rodriguez quotes a passage from *The Uses of Literacy* in which Hoggart says that the scholarship boy "begins to see life as a ladder, as a permanent examination with some praise and further exhortation at each stage. He becomes an expert imbiber and doler-out." Here, says Rodriguez, Hoggart's "criticism" is "more accurate than fair." When I first read "The Achievement of Desire," I wasn't sure what Rodriguez meant by calling Hoggart's description here "criticism." After he quotes Hoggart's remarks, Rodriguez restates them in a way that makes me think he sees them as a good description--but he's worried about how "fair" they are. In reading the essay again, I noticed Rodriguez's saying that the scholarship boy "realizes more often and more acutely than most other students--than Hoggart himself--that education requires radical self-reformation." How does Rodriguez know how much Hoggart realizes? I haven't read *The Uses of Literacy*, and maybe if I did I would find out that Hoggart was not himself a scholarship boy, and this might be related to how much Rodriguez says Hoggart "realizes." Or maybe there are parts of *The Uses of Literacy* that show Hoggart not understanding what Rodriguez sees--but I don't see that Rodriguez quotes them.

I said earlier that I couldn't figure out how to separate Rodriguez's first reading of Hoggart from all the rereadings of Hoggart he must have done before he wrote and published "The Achievement of Desire." I still think, as I wrote in a previous paper, that Rodriguez "felt that he must find himself" in reading Hoggart, but I also think now that Rodriguez also became anxious *not* to find himself in Hoggart's book. Maybe I started to feel this way after Sylvia pointed out in class something that I hadn't noticed before: Hoggart says that the scholarship boy is unusual, not a typical working-class student, not even a typically *successful* working-class student. Most successful working-class scholarship students "manage a fairly graceful transition," Rodriguez paraphrases Hoggart. It is only the exceptional working-class scholarship student -- perhaps "intellectually mediocre" (Rodriguez's paraphrase of Hoggart) and maybe "haunted by the knowledge that one chooses to become a student" (Rodriguez's interpretation of Hoggart -- I think) -- who becomes a "scholarship boy." I think that Rodriguez found in Hoggart's idea of the scholarship boy something he thought he could use to help him understand his own anxieties about his success. But I also think that Rodriguez must have understood at some point (when I'm not sure) that Hoggart's description of the scholarship boy didn't completely correspond to his own situation. (Does Hoggart talk about race as well as class? Does Rodriguez really believe that he was himself of only average intelligence?) When Rodriguez reacts against Hoggart's description, then, you could say that it is Rodriguez, not Hoggart, who is not being "fair." But I prefer to say that Rodriguez, as he writes "The Achievement of Desire," is being what in our class we've called a "strong reader."

When Rodriguez says,

> *A primary reason for my success in the classroom was that I couldn't forget that schooling was changing me and separating me from the life I enjoyed before becoming a student,*

I read him to mean that his being unable to forget that his education was making him lose something he valued in his relationship with his family kept him continually anxious to be a big success as a student. If he were only a little successful, he would have "lost" his family without gaining anything in return. I'm not saying that as a boy Rodriguez was conscious of this (he says the "realization" took him twenty years), but I do think this is how he sees it as he writes "The Achievement of Desire." Partly, Rodriguez *wanted* to separate himself from his parents; he wanted to become "educated." What he found in books became what guided his feelings about who he was. But I don't think that it's exactly right to say that Rodriguez wanted, in Walker Percy's words from "The Loss of the Creature," to "surrender" his "sovereignty" to "experts," his teachers and the authors of the books he read. At some point, Rodriguez had to see that his way of pursuing education only made sense if *he* became the expert. In a way, I know that when I read my psychology texts and find myself there, I am only playing at psychology. Even when I realize that I am more complex than any one psychological "category" can portray, I also know that I don't yet know enough psychology to feel very sure about just where I do or don't fit into the language being used. And I could understand someone's saying that I am still caught up in believing, in Walker Percy's words, that "the thing is *disposed* of by theory." But I also suspect that if I want to become a psychologist (and I do), I can't just ignore psychological theory. I can't just go *around* the words and categories of "psychology"; somehow I have to go *through* them. And I think that Rodriguez was doing something like this when he reread Hoggart. In the British Museum, he wanted an "expert," somebody his education had taught him to respect, to give him a handle on his life. But he was also anxious, as he wrote "The Achievement of Desire," to go beyond Hoggart, to show that his expertise was greater than Hoggart's. He needed to show that he was better able to explain his own life than his teacher was. I think that if Richard Hoggart were to read "The Achievement of Desire," he might feel both complimented and astonished.

When I compared this revision to the original paper, one of the things that struck me was the change in the writer's manner of using quotations. In the original, the material quoted is all drawn from a cluster of three pages in "The Achievement of Desire"; in the revision, the writer has ranged through much of Rodriguez's essay for her citations. In reading the original, I felt a disjunction between phrases like "on almost every page," "for most of 'The Achievement of Desire,'" "throughout the essay," and the nonarticulation of readings those phrases only gesture at. In the revision, it seemed to me, the writer has needed to lean less on summarizing assertions because she has demonstrated her readings through a much closer working relationship with Rodriguez's text.

But I would not want to say that I think the revised paper "supports" its "points" better than the original (though I can certainly imagine a teacher's saying something like that). Ways of reading that emphasize repeated readings and writings, that posit back-and-forth movements between reading and writing, are probably not well served by talking about "support" (supporting "thesis" statements, for example, by "adding detail"). Students can learn fairly quickly how to generate and support theses; but to present that activity as a goal of writing about readings can mean that that's all students will learn. To write a paper is to perform a reading. Strong reading is dependent on attentiveness, on curiosity; if students see their job as primarily to support a thesis, attention declines, curiosity withers.

I do not think that the writer of the original paper has seen her reading as simply supporting a thesis. She's done more than that. A strong reading of "The Achievement of Desire," one that allows itself to be curious, is likely to end up with a proposition different from the one it begins with. And to some extent this is what happens in the original version of the paper. Like the writer of the first Rodriguez paper I looked at, this writer, in her original paper, begins with Rodriguez's claim to have found himself in Hoggart's description of the "scholarship boy." But she hasn't approached Rodriguez's declaration blankly; she hasn't, that is, adopted the role of a reader who is content to take Rodriguez at his word, a reader who has been entrusted with the key to the essay and need now only locate and assemble all those instances in the text that show that the key works. In fact, almost immediately, the writer decides that her reading of "The Achievement of Desire" will tease out not *that* or *how* Rodriguez finds himself in Hoggart, but *why* he chooses to do so. And this project is further modified by the writer's incorporating a comparison between a reading of her own experiences and Rodriguez-as-reader-of-Hoggart, which leads to her becoming (if only temporarily) cautious about and critical of what she is doing: "I must point out that the writer is able to distinguish himself from the generality. . . ." Throughout the essay, we go from Hoggart's concept of a "scholarship boy" to the more specific reality of the author's life.

But, I think, the writer does not sustain her strong reading. Perhaps daunted by the work she senses it would take to follow up on the differences between Hoggart's "concept" and Rodriguez's "specific reality," or perhaps feeling impelled to conclude her reading unwaveringly, she ties up loose ends with her final sentence: "The reason that he gives us for reading Hoggart is that it gave him a measure of his change, but I see it as proof that he has changed very little." I like the sentence. I find it gutsy and intelligent. But I also think that the sentence is a kind of giving up. It indicates, to me, a writer who does not yet have a way of reading that allows her to be more than sometimes curious about what she is saying.

In the revised paper, the writer takes the risk of beginning with a puzzle that she is not going to be able to solve—no more than any reader could. My guess is that the risk is calculated: that though she knows there is no way to separate with certainty Rodriguez's early and late readings of Hoggart, she recognizes that the problem she poses is one that leaves room for multiple strong interpretations. And it's the sort of problem that she can tie to more ways and acts of reading than Rodriguez's reading of Hoggart in the British Museum. While making a strong reading of Rodriguez, she is also beginning readings of the relations between reading and writing, between reading and rereading, between individual and collective participations in language. Interestingly, these connections emerge (and, yes, they are mostly implicit—there are more papers to be articulated here), I think, *because* she has decided to work curiously and attentively with reading and rereading Rodriguez. In strong reading, the commonplace "You can't see the forest for the trees" makes little sense. For strong readers, the forest is not a given but a field of possibilities, and whatever possibilities are realized require detailed attention to lots of trees.

Talking about Reading and Writing

As they work through the reading and writing assignments of *Ways of Reading*, students will have many opportunities, in a variety of contexts, to attend to the construction of meaning. Occasionally they will be asked to paraphrase or reconstruct a difficult passage. More often, they will be asked to interpret what they have read, with some specific purpose in mind: framing something in their own experience with the key terms and methods of another writer, in order to learn more about both that writer's methods and their own experience; or turning an essay back on itself by testing out its claims or reconsidering its examples; or seeing how they might use one text to interpret another. Frequently, students will be asked for revisions of their papers, revisions in which they can continue projects suggested by the assignments and their responses to the assignments. Always students are asked, implicitly or explicitly, to reread what they have written, to rewrite what they have read.

Much of this work will go on in the classroom. Students' dormitory rooms or library carrels or kitchen tables are not their only arenas for making meaning; the assignments and anthology pieces, the papers students write and the comments a teacher makes on those papers, are not a class's only forums for engaging in the conversations of reading and writing. What happens in the classroom can reinforce or redirect those other exchanges—and serve to make them more fruitful.

I find that class conversation is facilitated when a class begins to develop early its medium of exchange—a language about language that can be shared. Whatever ways students have, individually, for talking about reading and writing, they probably bring with them to a course in college reading and writing a sort of lingua franca from their various high school English courses: "coherence," "organization," etc. Certainly college teachers and their students may choose to draw on these terms to talk about the work of reading and writing, but I have often been surprised at how slippery this seemingly stable language can be. A couple of years ago, for example, when I returned a set of student papers on which I'd commented to some writers that they were "summarizing," two students approached me after class. The first said that he had just reread the assignment carefully and didn't see it asking him anywhere to "summarize," and that that was certainly not what he had done in his paper, though he could have if he'd been asked. The second student thanked me for the comment but wondered if I'd found anything "wrong" with his paper. Both students, that is, revealed to me that my class had not so far provided a context for these readers to do anything with the word "summarizing." In the absence of our class's having worked out a distinction between "summarizing" and, say, "interpreting," these students could only conclude that "summarizing" meant exactly what they knew it meant: a routine performed by students in English classes—ordinarily when asked but sometimes, miraculously, unbidden.

What I like to try to do is have my reading and writing classes construct—gradually, accretively—a language for language that has had to be interpreted, a language for which we have had to make sense. Many terms in my marking of the student paper discussed earlier—"labels," "gesture," readers' "roles," "demonstrate," writing about a text as "reading" it—are terms that that class had been slowly accumulating since the beginning of the semester. Generally these terms first surfaced in class discussions. Sometimes they were first proposed by me, sometimes by students, as linguistic tools for our class to use to make sense of some text before us. Sometimes the terms first appeared in an assignment. Obviously not all classes will fashion the same tools, and one semester's key terms, metaphors, are not likely to be identical to what gets used the next semester. In redeploying these terms to comment on student papers, a teacher models a version of what students are engaged in as they read and respond to the pieces in *Ways of Reading*—seeing their own projects through the frame of language they have had to come to terms with, redefining preexistent language and routines for their own purposes.

I think that there are certain benefits in devoting much of a class's time together to discussions of student papers. Students whose papers are being discussed get multiple responses to what they have written, and possibly insights into how they might revise. The whole class gets a chance to look at other writers struggling with dilemmas similar to those that they themselves have been wrestling with in their own papers.

Classroom discussion of their papers gives students opportunities to explore the possibilities and problems involved in moving from writing to rewriting, from a reading that has noticed something significant to a reading that can better articulate and account for the significance of what has been noticed. The revised paper on Rodriguez I looked at earlier grew not only out of what the writer was able to do with my comments on her first version but also, as it happened, out of a class discussion of the original paper. Students generally liked and were impressed by the paper, but they were puzzled at times by the reading. One student wondered what the writer meant by saying that Rodriguez "jumps from thought to thought" in "The Achievement of Desire." A second student said that, whatever the writer meant, she should have shown how this "jumping" works. Someone else said that she wasn't sure why Rodriguez's jumping from thought to thought, if he does, might be important in the first place, but a fourth student said that obviously it could indicate, as the writer says, Rodriguez's "unease," an "anxiety," just as Rodriguez's "questioning himself" could—provided the writer demonstrated that. "But self-questioning doesn't always mean anxiety," said a fifth student. "I don't think I'm very anxious, and I question myself all the time. Self-questioning could mean that a person doesn't know enough." "Right," said another student, "or that he knows too much." The conversation continued. This sort of discussion provides not so much a chance for writers to hear that they haven't said what they meant (though it may do that), as an occasion for writers to become more curious about just what they *do* mean. The writer of this paper, as she learned from the discussion, couldn't do a rewriting of her paper, not in any important sense, without doing some more reading, getting back into Rodriguez's text and hers.

And class discussions of the papers students write can offer substantiations of the assumption that there are multiple ways, and many good ways, to read. I talked earlier about a class discussion in which students argued about the interpretation of the phrase "the end of education" that concludes Rodriguez's essay. When I read the set of papers that came in for the writing assignment I made, I picked out and duplicated three of them for class discussion. The first writer argued that his interpretation of "the end of education" as the completion of Rodriguez's academic training derived from noticing that "The Achievement of Desire" is constructed as a series of commentaries on important moments in an academic's schooling; that Rodriguez speaks early on of trying to figure out—"in the British Museum (too distracted to finish my dissertation)"—what that schooling amounts to; and that by the last words of the essay, "the end of education," Rodriguez has come to a resolution—though, this writer conceded, he could also see that Rodriguez retained some unfulfilled "desires." The second writer insisted, also quite convincingly, that, according to her reading, "the end of education" must be the accomplishment the essay's title foregrounds—"The Achievement of Desire"; that the significant incidents in Rodriguez's education can be read (she gave readings) as his holding the past at arm's length; and that Rodriguez is able to stop this repression only when he becomes secure enough in his "educated" identity that it can't be undermined by regret for what he has sacrificed; so that, finally, he can turn "unafraid to desire the past." The third reader, in her paper, while saying that she understood the "end" of Rodriguez's education to be in one sense its completion, thought it most important to notice that Rodriguez calls his schooling, early and late, "miseducation," and that, whatever Rodriguez learns in school, he can't understand himself until he gets outside the boundaries of schooling ("too distracted to finish my dissertation"); so that, as this writer reads the essay, "education" is opposed to both "desire" and understanding. I don't do these readings justice with this outline, but I thought that one of the most interesting outcomes of our class discussion of them was several students' remarking that, since they found all three papers persuasive, they judged that not only do different readers read differently, but a single reader might read a text in various ways. Discussions of student papers, texts articulating readings of other texts, parallel the practice of looking at one thing through something else, which most of the course's assignments ask students to perform. For a class to examine student papers with the same attention and care brought to discussions of the anthology selections by themselves augments students' belief in the value of the strong reading they are being asked to pursue.

A teacher's decisions about how to use student papers in class — which papers to use, how much student text can be profitably addressed in a single class period, what questions to use in guiding the discussion, just how a discussion of some particular paper or papers serves broader discussions of reading and writing — all depend on a teacher's experience, agenda for a course in college reading and writing, and way of imagining how *Ways of Reading* fits into that agenda. I'll end here with just a few more notes from my own experience. I have found that student papers duplicated for distribution and class discussion can focus on the acts of reading and writing represented by the papers rather than on uneasy exchanges governed by diffidence about or defense of the emotional investments that the papers also represent. Generally speaking, students adapt to the convention of authorial anonymity quickly and easily. As much as possible, I try to choose papers for discussion that will give the class opportunities to notice, wonder about, and question efforts at performed understanding — rather than papers that I think exhibit little effort, nonperformance. Ideally, I want my students to see a discussion of papers as an occasion not for sniping at lousy work but for talking about how good work might be extended. For example, I can imagine my using the first Rodriguez paper I looked at earlier only in an early semester class discussion — using it as a way of talking about nonreading, perhaps pairing it with a much stronger paper. But after the first few weeks of a semester, I would think that that paper no longer has a place (and, indeed, its writer did not seek a place) in our class conversations.

If you are teaching *Ways of Reading* along with other teachers at your college, and if some of you have made similar selections from among the scores of assignments available in the book, you might want to share some student papers along with the other things you are sharing about teaching the course, thus giving each of you a bigger pool from which to draw the kinds of papers you want for class discussion.

Restless and Hopeful: Teaching toward Difficulty in Freire's "The 'Banking' Concept of Education"

Jennifer Lee

Each semester, I step into the General Writing classroom with a strange mixture of romantic idealism and anxiety. Part of me imagines the twenty-two mostly first-year students and myself embarking together on what Paulo Freire calls the "restless, impatient, continuing, hopeful inquiry" that makes us human. The other part of me remembers that General Writing is a required course—few students manage to "test out"—and for many incoming freshmen, the prospect of a semester spent reading and writing rarely elicits excitement. Some students hope General Writing will provide them with useful skills, but few envision finding the course particularly stimulating. If I forget, momentarily, this divergence between my expectations for the course and students', I am reminded when I read the first batch of essays. How, I ask myself again, will I get students to "open up" the way they read and write? How will I get students who carry eighteen credit hours, maybe work at night, invested in the process of reading and writing their way into difficult and complex terrains? How will I enable them to see the limitations of writing only about what they understand, or make it possible to see writing as something that rather than capturing its subject moves toward it?

On the first day of class, I ask students to respond to an excerpt from the introduction to *Ways of Reading*, one in which the editors talk about reading as "social interaction"—"You make your mark on a book and it makes its mark on you"—and set this approach against "finding information or locating an author's purpose" (*Ways of Reading* 1). As we look at samples of their responses during the next class, I ask students what it would mean, or for that matter what it would look like, for a writer to actually make her mark on a text. In one form or another, we will circle around this notion all semester. But one of the most important ways I suggest that making a mark might be possible is by reading toward difficult moments in a text. A significant part of students' work will be to write "difficulty papers," informal responses to the assigned readings where students think through a moment they find particularly confusing, hard to understand or decipher, or a passage that surprises or angers them. These "difficulty papers" then serve as the center of class discussions, students reading selections during class and using them to lead us in and out of the text at hand.

At the same time, I ask questions in the margins of their essays and attempt to trouble their assumptions by playing devil's advocate, trying to get them to tease out their ideas. Combined, these strategies usually initiate dialogue about writing that continues all semester, a conversation with difficulty and uncertainty at its heart. As students become familiar with the routine and we establish a rhythm of work, their essays get progressively messier. By midsemester, the five-paragraph essay has all but disappeared. Paragraphs lengthen, sometimes taking up a full page. Comma splices begin to appear in the writing of students who, at the beginning of the semester, were fine-sentence boundary managers. Things begin to feel a little out of control. When I read essays at this point in the term, there is a discernable momentum to the way students think through their ideas on the page, and with it, a kind of chaos. No longer attempting to present what they know in neat little packages, there are redundancies, digressions, moments of ambivalence and uncertainty.

At least, that was the story until this past spring when my tried-and-true methods just didn't work. It was only by way of working with Paulo Freire's essay "The 'Banking' Concept of Education" that I was forced to slow the process of reading down, both for my students and for myself, forced to make visible the way a reader forges her path through a difficult text. What I found was that, in a sense, Freire's text demands a certain attention and humility. It is nearly impossible for a reader to wave her hand and say simply, "I get it." In light of the essay's complex, abstract language, any attempt to "sum up" the essay's main idea feels conspicuously incomplete. Each reading elicits textual nuances and meanings that surface only after a second, third, or fourth reading, and while this may be true for any text, Freire's essay makes the notion of layered meanings impossible to ignore. Students cannot help but notice the partial nature of their work, something they do not readily see when reading "easier"—meaning more narrative, more "straightforward"—texts. As they attempt to control Freire's essay by summing it up, they know they are leaving so much out. The idea of shaping an explicitly partial reading begins to make more sense. Besides, students readily admit, attempts to account for the whole leave them with little to say. What Freire's essay made possible for my students and me, just as the class seemed to be grinding to a painful halt, was actually *seeing* what writing and reading toward difficulty could accomplish. Working on Freire's text over the course of three weeks, we began again, this time taking small, creaking steps toward making a mark.

It was midsemester by the time we made it to "The 'Banking' Concept of Education," and as I read through the students' essays, I encountered one attempt after another to read for Freire's "main point." I could almost hear the sentences putting one foot in front of the other, playing themselves out along a script. *Do this, then this, now go here and there.* Many of the essays were quite short. In their introductions, writers often reiterated the assignment prompt: "The banking concept of education describes how in the classroom, students are transformed into 'containers' and are 'filled' with information by their teachers." They provided an example from their own educational experiences, as they were asked to do, and shaped their stories to illustrate the "banking" concept of education. Everything fit. The textures of the students' experiences, their ambiguities and conflicts, the complicated ways they did, and did not, play out Freire's theories, were lost. Students made sweeping proclamations: "This is wrong," or "Freire makes very powerful statements." It seemed these quick appraisals of Freire's argument were self-evident and should, without further embellishment and with little fanfare, make perfect sense to the average reader. Their analyses skipped across the surface of Freire's ideas like stones across water. I panicked. Now, looking back at the essays they had written up to this point in the semester, I could see ways the class had moved forward, but compared to other General Writing classes I'd taught, we hadn't made it very far into the land of gritty intellectual work. The silence in the room, both literal and figurative, was palpable. The essays seemed almost numb. It wasn't just that students persisted in writing along familiar, perhaps more comfortable, models, but that they seemed unengaged in the work, bored. The Freire essays were not so much a step backward as a moment in which I saw just how far we hadn't come.

Something else that caught my attention was the way many students actually quoted the same paragraph-long passage, in spite of the fact we had not yet discussed Freire's essay in class. This move was something I associated with responses written after class discussion of a text. I went back to Freire and back to the assignment prompt and found, not surprisingly, that students had chosen to represent Freire's argument by including the passage from which the assignment's language is drawn. Jillian's essay, excerpted below, represents the way many students approached the assignment, including the passage many of them quoted:

> This common way of teaching is stripping the information being taught of its significance and meaning. Paulo Freire, a radical educator of our time, believes the methods of teaching must be changed. The student never truly understands what he/she is learning, and in doing so, the information is stripped of any life, substance, meaning. Often a student sits in a classroom taking notes on the facts the teacher lectures about, carefully involved in making certain nothing is missed. But in effect, something is missed. The teacher lectures and tells the student what he/she must memorize in order to be "successful" and ultimately enlightened and intelligent. Freire stated:
>
> > Narration (with the teacher as narrator) leads the students to memorize mechanically the narrated content. Worse yet, it turns them into "containers," into "receptacles" to be "filled" by the teacher. The more completely she fills the receptacles, the better a teacher she is. The more meekly the receptacles permit themselves to be filled, the better students they are. (318)
>
> This is true in classrooms in every society. The student takes on the role of memorizer, focusing not on what the meaning behind events are, but mainly on the precise facts. They don't ask why, they just listen and memorize. The better the teacher gets the students to memorize the information, the better their grades are on the tests, and the more successful the student and the teacher feel. He is considered to be an excellent teacher if students memorize enough of the information to pass. The students that memorize what the teacher tells them to memorize receive good grades and therefore are considered good students.
>
> I can easily recall sitting in the front seat of my tenth grade American history class. My teacher, Mr. G——— walks in at the sound of the bell. . . . "Get your notebooks out" he states, and everyone responds simultaneously to his direction. The routine has been reinforced by its daily occurrence. "Today we will finish up our lesson on the roaring twenties and then follow up with a review for the test that will be taking place tomorrow in class." The students look around at each other and begin to smile, for we all know that the underlying meaning of "reviewing for the test" is finding out what is exactly going to be on it. After forty minutes of taking notes on the facts that Mr. G——— states robotically, we

switch notes and turn to the review. "Now if I were you, I would pay very close
attention to the words I say," Mr. G——— says with a wink. . . .

 Each student received a good grade on the test making Mr. G——— look
like a "fabulous teacher who could get even the worst students to pass." In
reality none of us actually learned anything or showed a desire to learn more.
We just memorized and repeated what the teacher told us to. It was actually
quite easy . . . a little time spent . . . what could be better?

Later in the semester, Jillian would tell me she'd worked hard on this essay, and I certainly
noticed her attention to developing an example, the way she moves carefully through her
general reading of Freire. In fact, I chose Jillian's essay to duplicate and distribute for class
discussion because her essay was not only representative but, I thought, a comparatively
good effort. Like her classmates, Jillian shapes her reading of Freire around the notion of
memorization, not just as a symptom of the "banking" concept, but as its very definition.
Everything explicitly drawn from Freire's text comes from the first page and a half of his
essay—the language included in the assignment prompt, memorization as a key term.

 News writers rely on a story structure called the inverted pyramid, in which the most
crucial information, the who, what, when, how, and why, is crammed into the first and perhaps second paragraphs. This way, so the reasoning goes, a reader can get what's most important and, if time or attention are short, quit midway through the story without missing
anything important. When I read the essays on Freire, I wondered if students had similarly
quit before making it to the end of the essay, or if they figured the essay's essential points
could be found right up front, the remainder of the text just reiteration, unnecessary elaborations. But in each essay, I also saw hints of other ways of reading, threads that echoed
moments in Freire's text not talked about explicitly. Jillian, for example, focuses on narration in her work with Freire, but her example is as much about the complicity between
student and teacher as it is about narration and memorization. She has, it seems to me,
both a more particular reading of Freire to assert and an argument against his text. What
she will name, in her second version of this essay, the "easy work bond" between teacher
and student, their mutual sense of satisfaction, she only hints at here. Mr. G——— may
be lecturing "robotically," but it's clear from the smiles and winks that the students and
teacher like one another and that both parties enjoy their unspoken pact.

 If Jillian's paper represents the majority of student responses to Freire, then Nick's
paper, which I also handed out to the class for discussion, represents something like the
kind of work I'd expected, or hoped, students would do:

 It was pounded into my head that America was the greatest place on
earth and was hardly ever wrong and I believed every word of it. I did not think
to question my teachers and they did not question me as to what I thought of
America. Even if they had I would have only responded with a rehashing of what
they had taught me because that is all I knew. Freire states, "The capability of
banking education to minimize or annul the students' creative power and to
stimulate their credulity serves the interests of the oppressors, who care neither

to have the world revealed nor to see it transformed. The oppressors use their 'humanitarianism' to preserve a profitable situation" (Freire 320). By this pounding of patriotism into our heads at a young age the United States government is playing the role of the oppressor trying "to preserve a profitable situation" by using the banking concept of education. . . .

As I got older I began to see contradictions in what was taught to me by my elementary school teachers. My reality had always been that America was always right, but now I was finding things outside of school that transformed this reality. I saw people on television arguing over whether we should have dropped the atom bomb on Japan or whether we should have fought in Vietnam. . . . When I saw these contradictions I began to question my teachers. I began to shape my own reality. That is when I began to engage in the act of, as Freire would call it, my own "humanization."

Though I would say Nick misreads Freire in a sense, assigning full responsibility for the "banking" concept to government, it might also be said that he is forging a strong reading, actually extending and reshaping Freire's argument. He agrees with Freire—he reads generously—yet his conspiracy theory approach also risks leaving the assignment prompt behind. He utilizes Freire's notion of education as a *system*, which he conflates with "the government," then grabs hold of contradiction as a way out. Nick, more than most of his classmates, tackles difficult and not so obvious moments in Freire. He reads beyond the main point as it is set forth in the assignment prompt, and toward the link Freire makes between education and humanization.

I also included, in the essays I reproduced for class discussion, a piece in which the writer, Rae, disturbed by what she sees as Freire's assertion that she has been duped by "banking" education, asserts, "*I* think that I have a firm grasp on reality." Rae continues:

Perhaps Freire's "banking concept" does exist during the foundation part of education, but it certainly does not continue for very long. If it did, the essay "The 'Banking' Concept of Education" that I have just read would have acted as my teacher, making "deposits which [*I*] the students [should] patiently receive, memorize, and repeat" (318). However, if I were merely this "receptacle" for information or also someone else's opinion, how would I ever be capable of writing anything that remotely argues against the teacher?

What struck me about Rae's essay was the way it questioned Freire—she was the only writer to do this—as well as the way Rae asserts herself in the piece—italicizing the "I" and inserting herself right into Freire's language. Her difficulty with Freire's text is made explicit and placed at the center of her response. What I found myself unable to discern finally was why, poised at midterm and having familiarized ourselves with the notion of using difficulty to read and to write, I hadn't received more essays like Rae's and Nick's.

My decision to place these three essays on the table for discussion was not intended to play the good essay/bad essay game. As a matter of fact, I considered all three pieces to be quite "good" in certain ways. I felt as if I'd lost perspective and I needed a litmus test. I wanted to gauge the students' relationship to the work of General Writing, and because so many essays looked like Jillian's, I fully expected the class to see hers as the strongest. I was no longer sure what the class would say about Nick's and Rae's.

In preparation for the discussion of Jillian's, Nick's, and Rae's papers, I asked students to mark in each essay moments when they saw the writer most actively engaging with Freire's ideas. Once they had read all three essays, they were to write about a moment in one of the essays that was particularly "illuminating or surprising" in its reading of Freire. My language, drawn directly from difficult paper assignments and class discussions, was by this time familiar to students. Much to my surprise, the class reacted to Jillian's essay with little enthusiasm. While some students liked her description of Mr. G———'s class, most wrote about moments in Rae's essay as most interesting. Her argument, many of them said, was right on target. On the other hand, students reacted negatively to Nick's essay. While they liked the writer's work with contradiction—like Rae's argument, it articulated the difficulty many of them were having with the lack of agency assigned to students—they didn't buy Nick's assertion that the government influences education. Ultimately, their discomfort with Nick's essay had less to do with seeing it as misreading Freire—only one student wondered aloud if Freire really meant the government was responsible for "banking" education—as it did with the fact that the essay seemed lopsided, that it "harped" on the notion of oppression.

With ten minutes left before the end of class, I interrupted what had become a lively discussion and asked students why their objections to Freire's ideas were so conspicuously absent from their own essays. One student responded by saying, "Well, maybe we just fit our experiences into Freire's ideas, even if they didn't really go all the way. I guess that's what we thought we were supposed to do." A few students laughed, some looked sheepish. On the way home that day, I thought about how this insightful comment wasn't, as I first presumed, merely the admission of a "good student." The class had not been simply "following orders" as they wrote their essays on Freire. Rather, I came to read this moment as evidence of the fact that I had not yet *taught* students to read their way into difficulty. The Freire essays were not anomalous at all, but indicative of the fact that students didn't know how to work their way through a text, except by summing it up. While I had made gestures toward teaching them to make a mark, I had duped myself into believing these overtures were enough. Only my students' "failure" in the face of "The 'Banking' Concept of Education," their trouble digging into its overt complexities, finally foregrounded my own short-sightedness.

For the next class I asked students to reread Freire, this time stopping at moments or phrases they had "missed," or even purposely glossed over in their first reading. I asked them to notice unfamiliar words or difficult phrases and suggested that while a dictionary would certainly help, they would also need to work contextually. I suggested they work toward a passage's meaning by reading around it and then by moving to other places in the essay where Freire seemed to be chewing on the same idea. In this way, I was asking students to be conscious of themselves as readers, to notice where they "tuned out" or avoided part of the text, and to give this occurrence a tangible weight. Then, I wanted to get them tracing that moment through Freire's essay, following a particular thread of argument rather than trying to account for the essay as a whole.

When students read from their journal entries in class, many of them isolated particular words, *dichotomy* for instance, which led one student to notice Freire's assertion that the banking concept creates a fissure between the student and the world. Someone else singled out *conscientização* and tried to figure out its relationship to both *banking* and problem-posing education. One student returned to the notion of oppression after the workshop and talked about the idea that the "banking" concept oppresses by instilling student "credulity." Often, students had little trouble tracing the thread itself through Freire's essay, but when they turned to talking about what the passage *meant* exactly, they tended to resort to generalizations, like the student who noted a series of moments when Freire talked about "reality," then wrote that "'Reality' is not one thing, at least it is something different for each person who is aware of it." None of the journal entries were revelatory; students did not suddenly "understand" the nuances of Freire's complex argument. There were entries that seemed to lead to greater confusion: "Conscientização refers to taking action against contradictions, like against the banking concept. . . . The banking concept is conscientização because it's the more natural way of doing things and therefore more responsible for social, political, economic contradictions." But for the first time that semester, students were moving into the text at hand. It was as if the difficult terms themselves had finally hooked students into understanding the value, and sometimes the necessity, of close reading.

Important to note here is the fact that this day's conversation was facilitated by a group of three students. While they had already prepared a set of discussion questions for Freire's essay, I asked them if they would be willing to use this most recent set of journal entries as part of the conversation. More than I had during other classes led by students, I worked hard this time to recede from the conversation. Given the reluctance of students to make their own ways through Freire's essay, it seemed vitally important that I avoid providing any sanctioned reading. One student led us to "praxis" by providing first a series of dictionary definitions, then taking us into the text itself to work around the passage. This in turn initiated a conversation about Freire's phrase "Education as the practice of freedom," and led students to move around the essay as they tried to discern what exactly the "practice of freedom" meant. Dissatisfied with Freire's lack of concrete examples, students turned to a hypothetical discussion of what problem-posing education might actually look like.

When I asked students to write at the end of class about a moment they had found particularly productive during the course of discussion, many noted the way focusing in on praxis had helped them define, or "draw a line," between the "banking" concept and problem-posing education, or they talked about how defining praxis led to provocative arguments about education as dehumanizing. What happened, in other words, was that students moved in and out of attending closely to Freire's text and thinking about their own stake in his arguments. Because "The 'Banking' Concept of Education" is such a challenging text, I think students were able to see how, by slowing down and biting into difficult moments, they actually reaped tangible rewards. The more students worked with Freire's difficult terms, the more they teased out the specifics of his argument, the more invested they became in the conversation. There was a sense that day that students had "opened" the text; not that we had finally arrived at the *real* meaning, but that we had truly worked our way past numbing summary and into something more substantial.

Not that any of this was really new. I had, after all, tried to *tell* students about "taking charge" of a text. But as is often the case, I found myself confusing the act of telling with the act of teaching. Until this part of the semester, I hadn't been forced to slow the process down enough to make it fully visible to my students. Of course, the revisions students produced soon after were not miraculous transformations. Many writers continued to focus on memorization, keeping, in fact, the language of the assignment intact in their essays. I wish I could say the work they did in their reading journals made it directly into their revisions, but for the most part it didn't. What did happen was that their essays, finally, began to fall apart. Their arguments digressed, weaving in and out of Freire's essay as students zoomed in on particularities. Jillian, for instance, focuses on the pact between student and teacher, and though she follows the notion of passivity through Freire's text and her own example, she never does much with the sense of satisfaction she'd noticed in her first draft. She responds to my question in the margin by saying only "at the time I liked the idea of simply memorizing information to receive a good grade, now I understand all the important information that I missed." But later in the essay, Jillian does extend her example to talk about how, while she was taught about flappers, she was never taught about the dangerous conditions in 1920s era sweatshops, which, she asserts, might have caused students to draw connections to "the sweatshops owned by Nike sneaker companies today."

Another student, Adam, revised his essay around the phrase "consciousness as consciousness of consciousness," which, in fact, he had written about in his journal. In this second version of his essay, he talks directly to his reader, making the *process* of thinking through difficult ideas on the page visible. His argument may be repetitive, even circular at moments, but he is working it out:

> Freire, as well as myself, believes that a person's reality, like their identity, is
> a learned and developed perception. A person develops their own identity, just
> as students should develop their own way of perceiving the world. Freire states,
> "They [students] may perceive through their relations with reality that reality
> is really a *process*, undergoing constant transformation" (Freire 320). In this
> sentence, Freire shows that each and every student develops their own reality,
> their own perception of the world around them and how they fit into it. Yet, by
> using the banking concept, by directing what students learn, a teacher ultimately
> shapes his pupils' reality. Another way to explain this would be, if all you know is
> what I have shown you, then you are a product of that, you are only able to see
> the world through my, the teacher's, eyes. This holds true in my biology class, I
> am shown only what my professor deems necessary or proper to learn. My reality
> has had boundaries made for me since I was little. The trick lies here, because if
> all I am able to learn is what people deem necessary for me to learn, then how
> can I see beyond those boundaries? A quick, maybe not so good analogy for this
> would be, I, the student, am like a horse with blinders on, except that I do not
> know that I am wearing blinders. Therefore, all I see is what I am shown. Freire

believes that "a teacher's most crucial skill is his or her ability to assist students' struggle to gain control over the conditions of their lives, and this means helping them not only to know but 'to know that they know'" (Bartholomae and Petrosky 243). I believe that it is knowing that they know, such as understanding that you or I exist in a reality created by the society that governs us, that teachers should ultimately strive to teach and show to their students.

Many of the revisions looked like this: long paragraphs (sometimes lengthening out beyond a single page), comma splices linking a series of successive ideas together. Rather than seeing this as carelessness, what I saw was evidence of minds at work, writers grabbing hold of ideas and chewing on them. Elsewhere in the essay Adam turns to the reader and asks questions, anticipates objections: "What in the world did you say? I said the same thing at first." He takes on the role of both teacher and student, approaching the notion of consciousness from first one angle and then another: "Another way to explain this . . ." or "A quick, maybe not so good analogy would be . . ." Like his classmates, Adam has not yet organized his ideas because they are still in transit, the writing still working toward its subject.

A teacher of mine once asserted that all good writing can be condensed to a single sentence. I remember the way my heart leaped into my throat, the way I felt queasy and thought, *If this is what it means to read and write, I want none of it.* Though the teacher was most likely talking about finding focus, I also knew that this kind of reduction—of ideas, people, experiences—to a "main point," this erasing of textual difficulty and contradiction and question, was exactly what I worked against *as a writer.* When I opened the end-of-term evaluations for this General Writing course, I discovered—and this time I was not surprised—that students had consistently cited Freire's essay as the text they found most useful. One student wrote, "it was difficult because he really 'beat around the bush' a lot . . . that was confusing if you weren't giving the essay *all* of your attention." Because I value, and want to teach students to work their way through, the messiness of texts that "beat around the bush," I am inclined to begin next semester with "The 'Banking' Concept of Education." I know that Freire's text will once again force us to slow down and grapple with difficulty from the start. Then, I imagine, we might move on to "easier" texts, better able to dig in and push the kind of "beach reading" so many students are inclined to do. But considering how uncomfortable and confusing I found teaching last semester, I can't help but think I don't much enjoy mucking around in difficulty either (except, of course, when what is difficult for students is comparatively easy for me). And I wonder if falling apart in the middle of the semester isn't itself inevitable, in one form or another, or at least part of the praxis of teaching writing. As one student put it, "Even though I got frustrated with the repetition of staying with it for so long, it was kind of a 'gateway' piece for me."

WORK CITED

Bartholomae, David, and Anthony Petrosky. *Ways of Reading.* 5th ed. Boston: Bedford/St. Martin's, 1999.

Thinking on the Page: Summoning Readers and the Uses of Essays

Tara Lockhart

> [T]he irreducible pleasure of putting pen to paper with black ink is a way of trying out thought, or expressing ideas, of trying to reach people I otherwise couldn't reach. In a certain way, it's a refusal of the silence that most of us experience as ordinary citizens who are unable to effect change in a political and economic society that is obviously moved by larger forces than individuals.
> —Edward Said
> *Edward Said and the Work of the Critic: Speaking Truth to Power*

Perhaps what I admire most about Edward Said's writing is the way you can see his thinking on the page, from word to word, sentence to sentence, idea to complicated idea. When I work with Said in my writing classes, this is one of the first things I ask students to notice. How does he use writing to think? How does he use writing to complicate his own thinking—to think *beyond* the first, familiar thoughts to come to mind? And why, I ask my writing students, do you think Said uses the form of the essay (and the photographic essay, in particular) to do this work?

At the beginning of the semester the essay has a bad rap for many students. Often schooled in a sort of makeshift essay—the standardized five-paragraph version which serves a specific educational goal (often testing)—the college-level student finds that the critical, academic essay presented as a model of writing is different indeed. Essays like Said's don't aim to simplify an issue or make a black and white argument; they don't end back exactly where they began. Instead, they grow. They question. And they demonstrate a different history of essay-writing by illustrating the essayist's habits of mind: self-awareness, intellectual curiosity, flexibility of thought, detailed observation, openness, reflexivity.

One of the reasons I teach Said's writing, then, is to get students to practice developing similar habits of mind. Another reason is to work with a writer who uses writing as a way to engage the world in all its complexity, and who summons the reader along for the ride. An essay like "States" is a particularly good example of this kind of writerly address to a reader, an address which asks readers to acknowledge, to complicate, to challenge, and even to implicate themselves. This summoning and inclusion of the reader is heightened all the more by Jean Mohr's accompanying photographs—photographs which not only ask students to be savvy readers of images, but photographs which enact a complex relationship with both the written prose and the readers by "looking back."

Said's longtime friend and fellow scholar W. J. T. Mitchell, in his book *Picture Theory*, describes this type of relationship we see between words and images in an essay like "States" as a relationship based on three primary qualities: equality, independence, and collaboration. That is, the image and word must exist equally, they must have an element of independence from the other, and yet they must at the same time collaborate (288). Mitchell writes that the "text of the photo-essay typically discloses a certain reserve or modesty in its claims to 'speak for' or interpret the images; like the photograph, it admits its inability to appropriate everything that was there to be taken and tries to let the photographs speak for themselves or 'look back' at the viewer" (287). This complex interaction between word and image helps each medium to "look back" at the other, instead of forcing itself over and above the other — a dialogic interrelation that is also mirrored in the content of the essay and its invitation to its readers.

Constructing a Project, Enacting an Essay

Sharing the context for the publication of the full text of *After the Last Sky*, as well as what Said and Mohr wrote about the process of composing the book, is one way I've found to tap into students' natural interest in the relationship of the pictures to the essay's text. In the "Introduction" to the 1985 project, Said tells of his suggestion that photographs of Palestine and the Palestinian people be hung in the United Nations conference hall in Geneva. At the time, Said was serving as a consultant to the UN's International Conference on the Question of Palestine. The UN agreed to the proposal, and Swiss photographer Jean Mohr was sent to capture the images. However, when it came time for the photographs to be displayed, there was a distinct and unusual problem. Said writes:

> The photographs he brought back were indeed wonderful; the official response, however, was puzzling and, to someone with a taste for irony, exquisite. You can hang them up, we were told, but no writing can be displayed with them. No legends, no explanations. A compromise was finally negotiated whereby the name of the country or place (Jordan, Syria, Lebanon, West Bank, Gaza) could be affixed to the much-enlarged photographs, but not one word more. (3)

This "prohibition on writing" was particularly striking for Said. Although the issues surrounding Palestinian life should have been central to the International Conference on the Question of Palestine, what Said found instead was an uncomfortable response to those narratives or details about actual Palestinians.

After the Last Sky was the collaboration that emerged in the face of this episode. Choosing to confront the deluge of literature about Palestinians — most of it "polemical, accusatory, and denunciatory" — Said and Mohr relate that they decided to "use photographs and a text . . . to say something that hasn't been said about Palestinians" (4). The creation of such a text demanded careful representational choices. Said describes the construction of this type of text at some length, emphasizing its necessarily hybrid nature:

> Since the main features of our present existence are dispossession, dispersion, and yet also a kind of power incommensurate with our stateless exile, I believe that essentially unconventional, hybrid, and fragmentary forms of expression should be used to represent us. What I have quite consciously designed, then, is an alternative mode of expression to the one usually encountered. . . . The multifaceted vision is essential to any representation of us. (6)

By combining a range of genres and modes, Said and Mohr were thus able to construct a text that begins to do justice to the diverse lived realities of Palestinians. This hybrid text seeks to acknowledge, Said contends, that "whatever we are, we are dogged by our past, but we have also created new realities and relationships that neither fit simple categories nor conform to previously encountered forms" (5). Thus, the composition of *After the Last Sky*—and the subsequent reading that emerges as so much about Palestine continues to remain undecided—creates new possibilities (and hopefully new relationships) grounded in fresh interpretations of Palestine and its citizens.

Central to sparking such new relationships are the different audiences the authors hoped to reach with this project. Jean Mohr writes that one commitment he brought to the project was the desire to extend beyond the small, mostly academic audience his previous photos of Palestinians had reached. Likewise, although Said was already well known as a literary theorist and visible as a public intellectual, he, too, attempted to reach a wider audience by connecting narratives of his own cultural heritage to the divisive debates concerning the state of Palestine and its relationship to Israel. In choosing "essentially unconventional, hybrid, and fragmentary forms of expression" to represent Palestinians, and in constructing a complex, interactive relationship between the text's prose and its photographs, Said and Mohr thus attempted to ethically represent others without reducing complexity to the "habitually simple" (6).

Critics taken by Said's rich body of work agree that, given its flexibility, the essay is undoubtedly Said's primary genre. Mustapha Marrouchi, for example, describes Said's intellectual investment in the essay as stemming from the essay's versatility, its use of a unique author's "voice" to stitch the parts of the essay together, and the type of personal connection the essayist can establish with his material, himself as a thinker, and his audience. Much like the writing assignments offered in conjunction with "States," the essay offers Said a way of "writing back" to those voices which have simplified or misconstrued Palestinians. The essay offers writers a flexible way of making a particular project their own.

The ability of "States" to navigate the local and the worldly, the image and the word—putting them both into dialogue and weighing the results and implications—coupled with its inherent investigative and skeptical disposition, can be productively used as an example of how essay-writing can be used to challenge conventional thinking. One thing I return to with students is how Said enacts this "assaying," this testing and rethinking inherent in the essay form. As Said writes in *Beginnings*, the writer whose writing is "perpetually at the beginning" is intimately involved in thinking in and through the world: she writes to "take . . . up a subject in order to begin it, keep it going, create it" (74; 11). These acts of invention, reflection, and re-beginning—clearly seen throughout the text of "States"—thus provide an example of what a sophisticated essay might look like, as well as a potential model for composing one.

Summoning Readers

Although many students may be unfamiliar with the places Said and Mohr document, nearly all will have some familiarity with the strife present in the region. In fact, many might be surprised that this book was published twenty-five years ago instead of more recently. Students might thus approach "States" with a type of unfamiliar familiarity—a knowledge of Palestine and Palestinians that has been broadly disseminated but does not reach very deep. Many images and descriptions of Palestine and its people that students may have encountered are, as Said rightly notes, often nothing more than recycled stereotypes, a simulacrum of life in that region that does not do justice to the lived experiences or material realities of its people.

To engage readers in moving past these recycled representations, "States" must offer something more, and it must do so in a way that simultaneously challenges and invites. One way readers are drawn into the text is through the direct and powerful juxtaposition of words and images—a juxtaposition which occurs on nearly every page. Both images and words defy simple interpretations; both often address the reader through either a second-person address or, in the case of certain photographs, a head-on gaze back at the reader. When I've taught this essay, as well as other selections from *After the Last Sky*, this acknowledgment and confrontation of the reader/viewer has been one of the first things that catches students' attention. In viewing a photograph that ends the full volume, for example, student Lisa Crawford was struck by the image of two little girls, camera in hand, aiming their photographic gaze back at the reader. She likened this reaching through the book toward the reader as an expression of agency—on the part of the girls, as well as, perhaps, on the part of the Palestinian population in general. "They have taken the next step towards fighting back," she writes, "by 'shooting' right back at us in a standoff of cameras."

By noticing the way the photograph provides a way for Palestinians to "look back," this student homed in on a central idea of "States"—the shared failure of misrepresenting Palestine and its citizens and the shared responsibility of correcting that failure. By discussing the ways that the audience is called upon to acknowledge their own role in perpetuating misrepresentations of Palestinians, we can also discuss how the text then encourages readers toward rethinking their positions and taking action. And we discuss the ways that our texts could possibly prompt the types of powerful responses students identify in relationship to "States."

The next step is to build on students' engagement with the photographs by asking them to discern how the images and words work together. Take for example the conjunction of image and prose on facing pages 36 and 37 [see page 315], a place where the reader encounters two images which both contain an adult and a young girl of about the age of four or five. The adults look elsewhere, but both girls eye the photographer and thus the viewer: one shyly, one inquisitively. The layout of the spread locates the images diagonally across from one another, creating an axis along which the viewer's eyes travel. Thus, even as the reader moves to the text below the image on page 37—text in which Said describes finding one's place within a world constantly focused on erasure of the population to which you belong—it is difficult to remain solely focused on the description. Reading bits of sentences—descriptions of the "ephemera . . . we negotiate with, since we authorize no part of the world"—the reader's eyes cannot help floating up to take in the refugee writing a letter to her husband imprisoned elsewhere, the stare of the little girl, the direct implication of someone looking back across the page.

As the reader turns the page to the next prosaic vignette, Said shifts his description to the search for form across Palestinian writing:

> The striking thing about Palestinian prose and prose fiction is its formal instability: Our literature in a certain very narrow sense *is* the elusive, resistant reality it tries so often to represent. Most literary critics in Israel and in the West focus on what is said in Palestinian writing, who is described, what the plot and contents deliver,

STATES   Strip off the occasional assertiveness and stridency of the Palestinian stance and you may catch sight of a much more fugitive, but ultimately quite beautifully representative and subtle, sense of identity. It speaks in languages not yet fully formed, in settings not completely constituted, like the shy glance of a child holding her father's knee while she curiously and tentatively examines the stranger who photographs her. Her look conjures up the unappreciated fact of birth, that sudden, unprepared-for depositing of a small bundle of self on the fields of the Levant after which comes the trajectory of dispossession, military and political violence, and that constant, mysterious entanglement with monotheistic religion at its most profound – the Christian Incarnation and Resurrection, the Ascension to heaven of the Prophet Mohammed, the Covenant of Yahweh with his people – that is knotted definitively in Jerusalem, center of the world, *locus classicus* of Palestine, Israel, and Paradise.

STATES

Sidon, South Lebanon, 1983. A refugee writes out a message destined for her husband, a prisoner in the camp at Ansar.

Amman, 1984. Pediatric clinic.

A secular world of fatigue and miraculously renewed energies, the world of American cigarettes and an unending stream of small papers pulled out of miscellaneous notebooks or 'blocnotes,' written on with disposable pens, messages of things wanted, of people missing, of requests to the bureaucracy. The Palestinian predicament: finding an 'official' place for yourself in a system that makes no allowances for you, which means endlessly improvising solutions for the problem of finding a missing loved one, of planning a trip, of entering a school, on whatever bit of paper is at hand. Constructed and deconstructed, ephemera are what we negotiate with, since we authorize no part of the world and only influence increasingly small bits of it. In any case, we keep going.

their sociological and political meaning. But it is the *form* that should be looked at. . . . [T]he struggle to achieve form expresses the writer's efforts to construct a coherent scene. . . . Impelled by exile and dislocation, the Palestinians need to carve a path for themselves in existence, which for them is by no means a given or stable reality. (563–65)

Here, writing becomes not only a way to represent the conditions of Palestinian identity and survival, but also a survival strategy in and of itself—a way for people to "carve a path for themselves." Writing, in some ways, *is* the reality. This description recalls one of the images above where an adult writes as the child gazes back at the reader; as readers, we are drawn into this act of creation via writing by the child's gaze. This is a particularly fruitful moment to discuss how Said both describes and enacts using writing to "carve a path," to come to know and understand more fully and to take action.

Such moments ask readers to move fluidly between prose and image, finding ways to make each "mean" in relationship to one another. The procedure is accumulative, but because of the difference in media the materials "accumulate" differently, pointing the reader in new, unexpected directions and demanding an open interpretative capacity. Likewise, the power of an essay like "States" exists not only for Said—the author using composition as a way to create and maintain a place in this shifting world—but extends to the reader as well. In the final sentences of the essay, what has been a layered, polyphonic discourse negotiating memory, interpretation, speculation, and invitation shifts to the second-person plural, uniting the narrator with the reader/viewer and bringing her into the world of the text. The inclusion of the reader is reinforced by the invitation of "entering" the world Said and Mohr have presented through the final image; the concluding sentence reads: "Let us enter," and we imagine walking up the stairs to the door in the photograph (575). Suggesting that we make our way through the building's "openings that suggest rich, cool interiors which outsiders cannot penetrate," the narrator positions himself—and us, as readers—as insiders, capable of understanding and participation within the pleasures inside this world.

Responsible Readership: Invitations and Expectations

This invitation is not offered without expectation, however, and this is one of the text's primary achievements in terms of establishing a relationship with its audience. In "States," the prose consistently turns back on itself, sometimes after looking deeper into a photographic image, sometimes as the narrator attempts to sort out his own interpretative lenses and possible misunderstandings. Said uses the essay as a form of inquiry that pushes his thought further, but he also uses the images not only to demonstrate his conclusions but to complicate them or provide another direction of thought or interpretation. In this way, "States" suggests not only the rich possibilities of the hybrid essay, but also productive pedagogies for using reading and writing to generate increased understanding of both the selves and cultures. Said and Mohr's text is especially valuable, then, in that it widens "interpretation" beyond a sense of unidirectional communication to a sense of shared inquiry, even among those who perceive themselves as unconnected to the population under consideration.

To fully engage this text, then, it's important to discuss with students the type of reader that "States" imagines: What are we being asked to do as readers? How are we being called to action? Said is straightforward about one purpose of the text being to encourage readers to question the stereotypes and static representations of Palestinians they might hold. Yet in presenting a range of other, more complex representations, and in sometimes struggling to situate himself (as a doubly exiled figure) within these representations, Said opens up many possible entry points for readers to diversify their understanding of Palestine and its citizens. As the photos of Palestinians look back at us, as the prose intimately portrays Palestinian experiences and difficulties, as we are asked directly to confront the ways our understanding of this region is necessarily limited, the text both invites us in and holds us accountable. As Said writes in the final pages of *After the Last Sky*:

> I would like to think, though, that such a book not only tells the reader about us, but in some way also reads the reader. I would like to think that we are not just the people seen or looked at in these photographs: We are also looking at our observers . . . we too are looking, we too are scrutinizing, assessing, judging. We are more than someone's object. We do more than stand passively in front of whoever, for whatever reason, has wanted to look at us. If you cannot finally see this about us, we will not allow ourselves to believe that the failure has been entirely ours. Not any more. (166)

An important project of this text is thus not only to complicate and diversify the staid representations of Palestinians, but also to position Palestinians and the Palestinian gaze as participants in a dynamic, multidimensional relationship. That is to say, Palestinians are not, in Mohr's photos, as they often are in other media representations, "just the people seen or looked at." Said strengthens the intensity of this message in the penultimate sentence which once again shifts to second-person address, using the "you" to emphasize the necessity of this two-way dynamic.

Students readily describe the interaction between observer and observed and the way that these relationships are, in this instance, destabilized. Christy Galletta, for example, wrote in response to Said, drawing also on the work of W. J. T. Mitchell as a way to describe the text's project:

> Said tells us that he and his people will no longer accept full responsibility for our misunderstanding. . . . Instead we learn what we need to know by looking at the picture and reading the text, and then looking again at the picture for small ways (or large ways) that they interact or speak to each other. . . . By allowing the photograph to do more than just illustrate the text (simply to add visual interest) and instead to clash with the text, agree with the text, or elaborate on the text, Said has brought a complexity to his work that Mitchell values. This way, Said has created "that most ambitious of books, a nation-making text" (Mitchell 321).

Students are quick to notice the complex ways the text and photographs interact to create richer meaning than either would singly. Galletta, for example, notices the ways that the words and images are both "technically unrelated" and yet "speak to each other." She reads the photograph as illustrative of the ways the project allows Palestinian citizens—through Said and Mohr—to "take a stand." Finally, Galletta is able to recognize the "nation-making" ability of *After the Last Sky*, by which Mitchell means not only the capacity for (re)creating a nation in the eyes of others, but the making of a nation for the citizens themselves. Focusing on not only the "message" of essays like "States," but the way such essays are composed to achieve particular purposes and erect a particular relationship with their audiences, helps students both to attend to their own compositional choices and to imagine the projects that their own texts can construct.

In inviting us to take part in this project of re-representation, "States" creates a powerful reversal of sorts in which we, the readers and viewers, become the center of attention and all eyes are on us. All eyes wait now for our next move. In my classes, this next move (or a move that exists in tandem with reading) is the construction of photographic essays that take, as their impetus, the same intellectual goals we see in "States": a mutually sustaining and provocative relationship between words and images, a critical and reflexive scrutiny, an attempt to connect acts of writing and self-representation to an outside audience. This is a project which students can feel excited about—it's a type of work (and a type of essay) that is real, useful, and potentially quite powerful. I challenge students to think of Said's essay in terms of the way he shaped the genre to his own purposes, both rhetorical and representational: How might they think through their compositional choices in similar ways to produce a text with its own most appropriate structure, a hybrid text for which hybridity is a "necessity"? And how might they take up some of the habits of mind they see reflected in this text for their own purposes and projects? Whether using the assignments in *Ways of Reading* to think with students about exile, subjecthood, representation, or the interaction of words and images, "States" can help students grapple with what it means to use essays to discover, reflect, and engage with readers in a dialogic way. And writing such essays with their own intellectual projects in mind can help teach students how they might summon their audiences to engage difficult issues and complex realities, while also teaching them ways to intellectually and ethically engage the diversity of our different experiences across the spaces of our increasingly global world.

WORKS CITED

Bové, Paul A., ed. *Edward Said and the Work of the Critic: Speaking Truth to Power.* Durham, NC: Duke University Press, 2000.

Marrouchi, Mustapha. *Edward Said at the Limits.* Albany: SUNY Press, 2004.

Mitchell, W. J. T. *Picture Theory.* Chicago: University of Chicago Press, 1994.

Said, Edward. *After the Last Sky: Palestinian Lives.* New York: Pantheon, 1986.

———. *Beginnings: Intention and Method.* New York: Basic Books, 1975.

———. "States." *Ways of Reading: An Anthology for Writers.* 9th ed. Ed. David Bartholomae and Anthony Petrosky. Boston: Bedford/St. Martin's, 2011. 541–75.

Fault Lines in the Contact Zone

Richard E. Miller

On the cover of what has turned out to be the final issue of *Focus*, a magazine "for and about the people of AT&T," there's a tableau of five happy employees, arranged so that their smiling faces provide an ethnically diverse frame for a poster bearing the slogan "TRUE VOICE." Although the cover promotes the image of a harmonious, multicultural working environment, one gets a slightly different image of the company in the "Fun 'n' Games" section at the back of the magazine. In the lower right-hand corner of this section, beneath a quiz about AT&T's international reach, there is a drawing of a globe with people speaking avidly into telephones all over the world: there's a woman in a babushka in Eastern Europe; there's a man with a moustache wearing a beret in France; and, following this theme and the telephone lines south, there is a gorilla in Africa holding a telephone (50). A gorilla?

Although Bob Allen, AT&T's CEO, has acknowledged in a letter to all AT&T employees that this was "a deplorable mistake on the part of a company with a long, distinguished record of supporting the African American community," he has so far met with little success in his attempts to manage the crisis caused by the distribution of this illustration to literally hundreds of thousands of AT&T employees worldwide. First, the art director who approved the cartoon and the illustrator who drew it were dismissed; commitments were made to hire more minority artists, illustrators, and photographers; a hotline was opened up for expressing grievances and making suggestions; AT&T's Diversity Team was instructed to make recommendations "for immediate and long-term improvement"; and, as a cathartic gesture, employees were encouraged to "tear that page out and throw it in the trash where it belongs," since they wouldn't want "AT&T material circulating that violates our values" (Allen). Then, when the hotline overheated and the battle raging across the company's electronic bulletin board continued unabated, Allen pulled the plug on the entire *Focus* venture and assigned all its employees to other posts. This is certainly one strategy for handling offensive material: declare solidarity with those who have been offended (Allen's letter is addressed "To all AT&T people"); voice outrage (it was "a deplorable mistake"); shut down avenues for expressing such thoughts (fire or reassign employees, dismantle the magazine). While this approach undoubtedly paves the way for restoring the appearance of corporate harmony, does it have any pedagogical value? That is, does the expulsion of offending individuals and the restriction of lines of communication address the roots of the racist feelings that produced the image of the gorilla as the representative image of the African? Or does it merely seek to ensure that the "deplorable mistake" of having such an image surface in a public document doesn't occur again?

"What is the place of unsolicited oppositional discourse, parody, resistance, critique in the imagined classroom community?" Mary Louise Pratt asks in "Arts of the Contact Zone" (39). In Pratt's essay, this question is occasioned not by an event as troubling as the cartoon discussed above, but by the fact that Pratt's son, Manuel, received "the usual star" from his teacher for writing a paragraph promoting a vaccine that would make school attendance unnecessary. Manuel's teacher, ignoring the critique of schooling leveled in the paragraph, registered only that the required work of responding to the assignment's questions about a helpful invention had been completed and, consequently, appended the silent, enigmatic star. For Pratt, the teacher's star labors to conceal a conflict in the classroom over what work is to be valued and why, presenting instead the image that everything is under control—students are writing and the teacher is evaluating. It is this other strategy for handling difficult material, namely, ignoring the content and focusing only on the outward forms of obedient behavior, that leads Pratt to wonder about the place of unsolicited oppositional discourse in the classroom. With regard to Manuel's real classroom community, the answer to this question is clear: the place of unsolicited oppositional discourse is no place at all.

Given Pratt's promising suggestion that the classroom be reconceived as a "contact zone," which she defines as a social space "where cultures meet, clash, and grapple with each other, often in contexts of highly asymmetrical relations of power" (34), this example of the kind of writing produced in such a contact zone seems oddly benign. One might expect that the writing Pratt's students did in Stanford's Culture, Ideas, Values course, which she goes on to discuss, would provide ample evidence of more highly charged conflicts involving "unsolicited oppositional discourse, parody, resistance, critique." Unfortunately, however, although Pratt avows that this course "puts ideas and identities on the line" (39), she offers no example of how her students negotiated this struggle in their writing or of how their teachers participated in and responded to their struggles on or over "the line." Instead, Pratt leaves us with just two images of writers in the contact zone—her son, Manuel, and Guaman Poma, author of the largely unread sixteenth-century bilingual chronicle of Andean culture. Both, to be sure, are readily sympathetic figures, obviously deserving better readers and more thoughtful respondents, but what about the illustrator who provided what might be considered an unsolicited parody or critique of AT&T's "Common Bond values," which state that "we treat each other with respect and dignity, valuing individual and cultural differences"? What "Arts of the Contact Zone" are going to help us learn how to read and respond to voices such as this? And what exactly are we to say or do when the kind of racist, sexist, and homophobic sentiments now signified by the term "hate speech" surface in our classrooms?

In focusing on a student essay that, like the *Focus* cartoon, is much less likely to arouse our sympathies than Manuel's inventive critique, my concern is to examine the heuristic value of the notion of the contact zone when applied not only to student writing, but also to our own academic discussions of that writing. The student essay I begin with was so offensive that when it was first mentioned at an MLA workshop on "Composition, Multiculturalism, and Political Correctness" in December 1991, provisions were quickly made to devote an entire panel to the essay at the 1992 Conference on College Composition and Communication, and this, in turn, led to a follow-up workshop on "The Politics of Response" at CCCC in 1993. Thus, I would hazard a guess that this student essay, entitled "Queers, Bums, and Magic," has seized the attention of more teachers, taken up more institutional time, and provoked more debate than any other single piece of unpublished undergraduate writing in recent memory. Before beginning my discussion of "Queers, Bums, and Magic," I should note, however, that in what follows I have intentionally allowed the content of the student's essay and the wider sweep of its context to emerge in fragments, as they did in the contact zone of the national conferences, where competing modes of response served alternately to reveal and obscure both the text and information about its writer. This partial, hesitant, contradictory motion defines how business gets transacted in the contact zones of our classrooms and our conferences, where important questions often don't get heard, are ignored, or simply don't get posed in the heat of the moment, with the result that vital contextual information often either is never disclosed or comes to light very late in the discussion. I believe that following this motion provides a stark portrait of the ways in which dominant assumptions about students and student writing allow unsolicited oppositional discourse to pass through the classroom unread and unaffected.

"Queers, Bums, and Magic" was written in a pre-college-level community college composition class taught by Scott Lankford at Foothill College in Los Altos Hills, California, in response to an assignment taken from *The Bedford Guide for College Writers* that asked students to write a report on group behavior. One of Lankford's students responded with an essay detailing a drunken trip he and some friends made to "San Fagcisco" to study "the lowest class . . . the queers and the bums." The essay recounts how the students stopped a man on Polk Street, informed him that they were doing a survey and needed to know if he was "a fag." From here, the narrative follows the students into a dark alleyway where they discover, as they relieve themselves drunkenly against the wall, that they have been urinating on a homeless person. In a frenzy, the students begin to kick the homeless person, stopping after "30 seconds of non-stop blows to the body," at which point the writer says he "thought the guy was dead." Terrified, the students make a run for their car and eventually escape the city.

It's a haunting piece, one that gave Lankford many sleepless nights and one that has traveled from conference to conference because it is so unsettling. When Lankford discussed it at CCCC in his paper entitled "How Would You Grade a Gay-Bashing?" the engaged, provocative, and at times heated hourlong discussion that followed provided a forum for a range of competing commitments to, as Pratt might say, "meet, clash, and grapple" with one another. What was clear from this interchange was that part of what makes "Queers, Bums, and Magic" so powerful is that it disables the most familiar kinds of conference presentations and teacher responses. Here is writing that cannot easily be recuperated as somehow praiseworthy despite its numerous surface flaws, writing that instead offers direct access to a voice from the margins that seems to belong there. The reactions given to Lankford's request to know how those present "would have handled such a situation" (5) varied considerably, both in intensity and in detail, but most of them, I would say, fell into one of three categories: read the essay as factual and respond accordingly; read the essay as fictional and respond accordingly; momentarily suspend the question of the essay's factual or fictional status and respond accordingly.

In the first category, by far the most popular, I place all suggestions that the student be removed from the classroom and turned over either to a professional counselor or to the police. Such a response, audience members argued repeatedly, would be automatic if the student had described suicidal tendencies, involvement in a rape, or having been the victim of incest. To substantiate this point, one member of the audience spoke passionately about Marc LeClerc, saying that the Canadian gunman had revealed his hatred of women to many of his college professors prior to his murderous rampage. As compelling as such examples seem, it is important to realize that this line of argumentation assumes that the essay records a set of criminal events that actually occurred or, at the very least, evidences the fantasy life of a potentially dangerous person. This assessment of the student essay is striking because the audience members had little to go on beyond the kind of brief outline that has been provided here. In other words, although no one in the audience had actually read the student's essay, many felt quite confident recommending that, based on brief excerpts and a summary of the essay's content alone, the student ought to be turned over to either the legal or the psychological authorities! These respondents, starting with the assumption of a stable and unified subjectivity for Lankford's student, went on to construct a student writer capable of dissimulation. Within such a paradigm, the actual text the student produced was of secondary importance at best in relation to a hasty and, as we will see, partial summary of the text's contents.

Lankford chose another route entirely, electing "to respond to the essay exactly as if it were a fictional short story" (4). What this meant in practice was that he restricted himself to commenting on the student's word choice, querying the student about his imagined audience, acknowledging the text's "reasonable detail," and "favorably comparing the essay to *A Clockwork Orange* in its straightforward depictions of nightmarish 'megaviolence' and surrealistic detail" (4). According to these criteria, Lankford determined that the essay merited a low B. Although this strategy provoked the wrath of a large portion of the audience, Lankford argued that it was not without its virtues: by focusing only on the formal features of the essay and its surface errors, Lankford was able to successfully deflect the student writer's use of his writing to "bash" his professor, with the unexpected result that the student not only stayed in the course, but actually chose to study with Lankford again the next semester. Thus, despite Lankford's own assessment of his approach as "spineless," he was in a position to insist that it was nevertheless a "qualified success," since the student in question "learned to cope with an openly gay instructor with some measure of civility" (5).

Among those present who had access to the student's paper, there were those on the panel who agreed with Lankford's approach but disagreed with the grade assigned. These respondents spoke of the essay's faulty organization, the problems evident in its plot development, the number of mechanical errors. On these grounds alone, one panelist assured the audience, the paper ought to have received a failing mark. If the first category of response displays a curious willingness to dispense with the formality of reading the student's essay, Lankford's strategy asks teachers to look away from what the student's writing is attempting to do—at the havoc it is trying to wreak in the contact zone—and restrict their comments to the essay's surface features and formal qualities, affixing the "usual star" or black mark as the situation warrants. Such a strategy itself invites parody: would changing the word choice/spelling errors/verb agreement problems/organization really "improve" this student's essay? Would such changes help inch it toward being, say, an excellent gay-bashing essay, one worthy of an A?

I intend this question to be deliberately troubling and offensive. The problem, however, is not that this approach is "spineless." To the contrary, in Lankford's hands, this kind of response made it possible for both the teacher and the student to remain in the contact zone of his classroom, allowing them to negotiate the difficult business of working with and through important issues of cultural and sexual difference. By suggesting that his difficulty in responding to the student's essay is a personal problem, that it revolves around a question of "spine," Lankford obscures the ways in which the difficulty that confronted him as he struggled to find a way to respond to "Queers, Bums, and Magic" is the trace of a broader institutional conflict over what it means for a teacher to work on and with student writing. Lankford and the others who spoke of responding to the essay as "a piece of fiction" did not suddenly invent this curiously decontextualized way of responding to writing, this way that can imagine no other approach to discussing a piece of writing than to speak of how it is organized, the aptness of the writer's word choice, and the fit between the text and its audience. Such an approach to writing instruction has been proffered in the majority of grammars, rhetorics, and readers that have filled English classrooms since before the turn of the century: it has been around for so long that, despite the grand "turn to process" in writing instruction, it continues to suggest itself as the most "natural" or "reasonable" way to define the work of responding to student writing. All of which leaves us with this profoundly strange state of affairs where the discipline explicitly devoted to studying and articulating the power of the written word gets thrown into crisis when a student produces a powerful piece of writing.

To sum up, then, these two lines of response to the student essay—one recommending the removal of the offending writer from circulation and the other overlooking the offensive aspects of the student text in order to attend to its surface and structural features—taken together dramatize how little professional training in English Studies prepares teachers to read and respond to the kinds of parodic, critical, oppositional, dismissive, resistant, transgressive, and regressive writing that gets produced by students writing in the contact zone of the classroom. This absence of preparation, I would argue, actually comes into play every time a teacher sits down to comment on a student paper: it's just that the pedagogical shortcomings of restricting such commentary to the surface features and formal aspects of the writing aren't as readily visible in a response to an essay on a summer vacation as they are in response to an essay about beating up the homeless. Unfortunately, recent efforts to reimagine the work of responding to student writing provide little guidance for addressing this particular problem. Edward White's *Teaching and Assessing Writing*, for instance, argues for holistic scoring, but offers no suggestions on how to go about holistically scoring essays that are racist, homophobic, or misogynistic. And, similarly, the NCTE's *Writing and Response: Theory, Practice, and Research*, which asserts that "real, substantive response is in one form or another fundamental to language development" (Anson 4), never gets around to the business of discussing how to produce a "real, substantive response" to the kind of unsolicited oppositional discourse discussed here. Since this is uncharted territory, it is not surprising that we often find ourselves at a loss, not knowing what to do, where to go, or what to say once we cross this line.

One has to wonder why it is that, at a time when almost all of the current major theories on the rise celebrate partial readings, multiple subjectivities, marginalized positions, and subjugated knowledges, nearly all student essays remain essentially illegible, offered forth more often than not as the space where error exercises its full reign, or, as here, the site where some untutored evil shows its face. There seems, in other words, to be little evidence of what one might call "poststructural" or "postcolonial" trickledown, little sign that the theoretical insights that carry so much weight in our journals actually make themselves known in the pedagogical practices deployed in classrooms across the country. There were, however, a few respondents to Lankford's presentation who saw a way to smuggle some of these insights into the classroom and thereby propose more fruitful responses than either expelling the student or ignoring the content of his essay. In proposing that "Queers, Bums, and Magic" be reproduced alongside legal definitions of hate speech for the entire class to read and discuss, one panelist found a way to pull the paper out of the private corridor running between the student writer and the teacher and move it into the public arena. This approach turns the essay into a "teachable object," enabling an investigation of the writing's performative aspect—how it does its work, what its imagined project might have been, and who or what might be the possible subjects of its critique. By situating the essay in relation to legal definitions of hate speech, this approach also puts the class in a position to consider both how words can work in the world and how and why that work has been regulated.

The prospect of having such a discussion would, no doubt, frighten some, since it would promise to be an explosive, tense, disturbing interchange. Some students would undoubtedly agree with the treatment meted out to the disenfranchised; others might speak of it as being funny; others might point to the references to "Elm Street," "nightmares," and "magic" in the essay to argue that it was a piece of fiction; and still others might be horrified by the essay and express their feelings to the class. Such a discussion would, in other words, place one squarely in the act of teaching in the contact zone where, as Pratt says, "No one [is] excluded, and no one [is] safe" (39). The point of having such discussions, however, is neither to establish a community where a simple pluralism rules and hate speech is just one of its many voices, nor to create an environment that is relentlessly threatening, where not feeling safe comes to mean the same thing as feeling terrified. Pratt, in fact, is careful to maintain the importance of establishing "safe houses" in the curriculum, courses where a different kind of talk is supported and sustained. But for those courses that take as their subject how language works in the world, the central concern should be to provide students with moments taken from their own writing as well as from the writing collected in published texts where the written word is powerful. In such classrooms, "teaching the conflicts" is not simply an empty slogan plastered over a practice that means "business as usual," but an actual set of practices whereby the conflicts that capture and construct both the students and their teachers become the proper subject of study for the course.

This third category of response argues for the necessity of seeing the way we structure our courses and the kinds of texts we read with our students as potential resources for commenting on the writing our students produce. Thinking along these lines, another member of the audience suggested that the best way to respond to this essay was with a revisionary assignment, where the student would be required to rewrite the story either from the perspective of the gay man whom the students had harassed on Polk Street or from the perspective of the homeless person whom the students had beaten in the alleyway. This strategy of having the student do some more writing about this event seems particularly appropriate in a discipline that believes in the heuristic power of the composing process, and the further requirement to have the student shift perspective provides a meaningful avenue for re-seeing the described events. As useful as I believe it is to see the assignment of revision as a way of responding to student writing, though, I think the response called for in this instance is so obvious that it is most likely to solicit a seamless parody, one of those acts of hyperconformity regularly produced by those writing in the contact zone. In other words, while producing a writing situation where the student is advised to mime the teacher's desired position would probably succeed in sweeping the most visible manifestations of the student's hateful thoughts and actions out of the classroom, it would not, I think, actually address the roots of that hatred. That hatred would simply curl up and go underground for the duration of the course.

At this point, it may seem that in assessing the range of reactions to "Queers, Bums, and Magic" I am holding out for some magical form of response that not only would make this student stop writing such things, but would actually put an end to his thinking them as well. My central concern, however, is not with this particular student essay or with what the student writer, as an individual, thinks, but with what this student essay and the professional activity that surrounds it can tell us about the cultural, political, and pedagogical complexities of composition instruction. With this distinction in mind, I would go so far as to argue that adopting any classroom strategy that isolates this essay and treats it as an anomaly misreads both the essay's cultural significance and its pedagogical possibilities. As the recent debate over military service has made abundantly clear, Lankford's student has not expressed some unique or private hatred of gays, nor, to be sure, has he voiced some peculiar antipathy for the homeless. Rather, the homophobia this student articulates and the violence he describes himself as perpetrating against the disenfranchised are cultural commonplaces. For these reasons, it involves articulating, investigating, and questioning the affiliated cultural forces that underwrite the ways of thinking that find expression in this student's essay—a classroom, in short, that studies the forces that make such thoughts not only permissible but prevalent.

From this perspective, one could say that the only truly surprising thing about "Queers, Bums, and Magic" is that it voices this particular set of cultural commonplaces in the classroom, since most students practiced in the conventions of reading teacher expectations know not to commit themselves to positions their teachers clearly oppose. In this regard, the following facts are not insignificant: the student writer grew up in Kuwait; English is his second language; he was writing during the onset of the Persian Gulf War. An outsider himself, Lankford's student almost certainly did not understand what was intended by the examples that accompanied the assignment in the *Bedford Guide* to: "Station yourself in a nearby place where you can mingle with a group of people gathered for some reason or occasion. Observe the group's behavior and in a short paper report on it. Then offer some insight" (41). Following these instructions, the student is informed that one writer "did an outstanding job of observing a group of people nervously awaiting a road test for their driver's licenses"; another observed a bar mitzvah; another an emergency room; and another a group of people looking at a luna moth on a telephone pole "(including a man who viewed it with alarm, a wondering toddler, and an amateur entomologist)" (42). Unschooled in the arts of reading the textbook, this student failed to pick up on the implicit directions: when you write this essay, report only on a group from which you are safely detached and on behavior unlikely to disturb others. Had the student been able to read the cues in the suggested examples, he might well have selected a less explosive topic and thereby kept his most familiar ways of knowing the world out of view.

If the examples direct students to topics guaranteed not to provoke offense, the assignment, by refraining from using any kind of critical terminology, further guarantees that the students will not wander beyond the business of reporting their immediate experience. In lieu of inviting students to work with any of the central terms from anthropology, sociology, or cultural studies, say, the assignment merely informs the students that, after observing the behavior of their selected group, they are "to form some general impression of the group or come to some realization about it" (42). They can expect, the assignment concludes, that it will take at least two written pages "to cover" their subject. Grasping the import of these directories, Lankford's student did even more than was required, performing the kind of hyperconformity I suggested earlier characterizes one of the arts of the contact zone: he wrote, as required, for his "fellow students" (41); he handed in not two, but four typed pages; and he made sure his essay concluded with "some insight." His final paragraph reads as follows:

> Although the night was supposed to be an observation on the people of the streets, it turned out that we were walking on "Elm Street," and it was a "nightmare." I will always remember one thing, next time I see bums and fags walking on the

streets, I will never make fun of them or piss on them, or anything like that, because they did not want to be bums or fags. It was society that forced them out of their jobs and they could not beat the system. Now when I think about that bum we beat up I can't understand how he managed to follow us the whole time, after being kicked and being down for so long. I think it was one of two things; he is either psychic or it was just plain magic.

In miming the requisite better understanding that is supposed to come from studying groups, the student's essay concludes by disrupting all that has come before: did the beating actually taken place, or has the writer simply fabricated it, recasting the assignment within the readily narrative frame of *Nightmare on Elm Street*? Is the student having one over on the system, manufacturing both the material for his response and his consequent realization, and thus, in one fell swoop, parodying, resisting, and critiquing the values that hold the classroom community together? Or, and this is obviously the more frightening possibility, is his conclusion some kind of penitential confession for events that really did happen?

These questions, slightly rephrased, are of central importance to any writing classroom: How does a writer establish authority? How does one distinguish between fact and fiction in a written document? What does it mean to read and to write dialogically? And yet, it is important to realize that, had the assignment worked as it was supposed to, these questions would never have surfaced with the urgency they have here. That is, had Lankford's student been a better reader of classroom norms and textbook procedures, he might well have written about beekeepers or people at hair salons and left the surface calm of the educational community undisturbed. If we step back from "Queers, Bums, and Magic" for a moment and consider the fact that the mixture of anger, rage, ignorance, and confusion that produced this student essay are present in varying degrees on college campuses across the country, what is truly significant about this event is not that it occurred, but that it occurs so rarely. This, surely, is a testament to the immense pressures exerted by the classroom environment, the presentation of the assigned readings, the directions included in the writing assignments, and the range of teaching practices which work together to ensure that conflicts about or contact between fundamental beliefs and prejudices do not arise. The classroom does not, in other words, automatically function as a contact zone in the positive ways Pratt discovered in the Stanford course, where, she asserts: "Along with rage, incomprehension, and pain there were exhilarating moments of wonder and revelation, mutual understanding, and new wisdom—the joys of the contact zone" (39). As the conclusion of Pratt's article makes clear, and the foregoing discussion of "Queers, Bums, and Magic" vividly illustrates, there is still a great deal of work to be done in constructing the "pedagogical arts of the contact zone." Thus, in setting aside the important but what is for us irresolvable question of whether or not "Queers, Bums, and Magic" is a factual or fictional account, I would like in the remainder of this essay to discuss my own efforts to reconfigure the power relations in my classroom so that more contact between the competing interpretive systems of the classroom and the worlds outside the classroom might occur and become available for discussion.

There is a paradox, of course, in trying to establish a classroom that solicits "unsolicited oppositional discourse." There is, also, an attendant danger of a kind of "intellectual slumming," where investigating the disjunction between the ways of knowing fostered inside and outside the classroom might inevitably result in students deeming the former kind of knowledge "artificial" and the latter "authentic." Rather than perish in the abyss created by this killer dichotomy or put myself in the pedagogically questionable position of inviting my students to vent their feelings on the page for us to discuss afterwards, I have tried to develop a pedagogical practice that allows the classroom to function as a contact zone where the central activity is investigating the range of literate practices available to those within asymmetrical power relationships. My primary concern as a composition instructor, in other words, is with the kinds of issues raised in Pratt's article and Lankford's student's essay in so far as they shape the ways of reading and writing that occur inside and outside the classroom and our ways of talking about that reading and writing. Given the heightened racial tensions following the Rodney King beating, the ongoing fear and ignorance about AIDS and the means of its transmission, the backlash against feminism, and a climate of rising unemployment and violence, it has not been difficult to find material around my campus that meets those requirements.

Most recently, for example, I have become interested in a battle being waged at my campus along what I have come to call the "textual corridors"—the walkways to and from the main libraries, the mailboxes and newspaper dispensers, the bus stops and lampposts. In these spaces, all well away from their classrooms, one or more students or perhaps competing groups of students have been carrying out a heated, accusatory, and highly coded discussion about rape, feminism, and sexual politics. Early in the semester, the following poster affixed to the lid of a garbage can caught my attention:

> DON'T MAKE
> YOUR
> MOTHER
> HAVE TO TELL
> HER FRIENDS
> THAT YOU'RE
> A
> RAPIST

Copies of this poster stayed up for a couple of days before being ripped down or papered over with campaign flyers for the upcoming student elections. Then, a few weeks later, the following poster appeared:

> WHO aRE ~~you? Go~~
> TRA~~de your~~ MoPs
> ~~for a~~ BIT ~~of~~ CHange
> ~~Be a w~~HOLE ~~woman~~
> ~~becauSe~~ LITtle ~~else~~
> Will ~~ev~~EN CHange.
> DefY, Kill, ~~Even~~
> TrEAt SomE ~~as~~
> DOGS.
> RevolUtioN
> RevolUtioN

While I found the rhetorical tactic of the first poster fairly straightforward, this one stumped me: I simply could not figure out how to read it or what it might be saying. Was it written by the same person or group of people who had distributed the first poster? Or was it written in response to the first poster, demanding to know who was making such anonymous accusations? What sense was to be made of the play between the text under erasure and the subtext placed in the foreground? And, how, finally, was one to read the question in much smaller type at the bottom of the poster: "what are you, a feminist?"

My inability to decode the interaction between these posters ceased to be a simple matter of curiosity for me that weekend, when I read in the local paper that one of our students had been abducted and raped on her way home from a party. Because I found this event so upsetting and felt that it, in some way, was connected to the posters, I brought the broadsides into my composition classroom as texts to be read. We had just finished working through what Pratt might mean when she defines autoethnographic texts as "heterogeneous on the reception end as well as the production end" (36–37), and I felt that discussing these two posters might bring this definition to life. Here was writing from the contact zone that was simultaneously oppositional, parodic, resistant, and critical: how, I asked, were we to read it? One student described the first poster as "sneaky": instead of just coming out and saying that rape was wrong, it asked a rhetorical question. When I asked her to turn that rhetorical question into a statement, she replied: "It says, 'We know who you are and we're going to catch you,' but it says it in a way that makes you stop and think. It's like a threat, almost." While the students had up to this point expressed a healthy suspicion of "hidden meanings" in general and had specifically criticized Pratt for "reading too much into" the writings of her son and Guaman Poma, they found little to object to in this assessment of the first poster's strategy and its "message." And although there was some disagreement about whether the "you" in the poster signified all men or just those men who were or had the potential to be rapists — about whether the poster was produced by "one of those male-bashing feminists" or by a "politically committed artist" trying to make a better world — the students were united in condemning the act of rape. Given the combination of the context and the location of this discussion and the spell cast by the rhetorical structure of the first poster, it is hard to see how they could have said anything else.

The second poster problematizes the dependable uniformity of this response, however, since, to a certain way of reading, it seemed to make an open call for violence against women. From this perspective, the second poster responds to the first, asking "Who are you?" in an effort to discover the identity of its anonymous and threatening author. The poster then parodies a feminist call to arms — "go trade your mops for a bit of change" — and culminates in a command to "defy, kill, even treat some [men presumably] as dogs." The poster, in effect, transforms the feminist revolution into license to talk back to, discipline, and, ultimately, kill their oppressors. This is a multivocal poster, however, deploying the clumsy Derridean device of erasure to speak its two positions simultaneously: beneath the parodic call to arms rests the undistilled anger of the author or authors, unleashed in a catalogue of derogatory terms for women as it builds to the frightening transformation of "revolution" into a series of commands to "Run, run." In the context of the kidnapping and sexual violation that had occurred on campus over the weekend, I was both convinced that this was what the poster intended and horrified by what I read. To my mind, and to some of the students in the class, the second poster openly defied the threat of the first poster, providing an involved, but nonetheless clear, assertion of the second writer's determination to go on a rampage.

A number of the students in the class resisted this take on the second poster, however, arguing that it was probably by the same person who produced the first one. Making a case for a wholly ironized text, these students insisted that the writer was miming the voice of "the angry male" and through this process mocking that voice. This reading, in effect, reverses the foreground and the background of the previous reading, making the list of derogatory terms the literal or surface meaning and the call to arms embedded in and amongst the letters of this list the hidden promise of a better world. Thus, where the voice of the "angry male" commands "Run, run," the creative genius of the writer/artist sees the possibility of "revolution, revolution." As clever as I found this approach to the text and as persuasive as many of the members of the class deemed it to be, I was not, in the end, convinced that the second poster was just "more of the same" from the writer of the first poster. Although this discussion ended up releasing a flood of stories from the students about the daily acts of violence they experienced in the dorms and parking lots, at football games and dance parties, on and off campus, it did not lead to any sort of consensus about which reading of the poster was "correct." This is one of the hazards of allowing students to work with writing in the contact zone: the meaning of a text is seen to be up for grabs; the students, drawing on their local knowledge, may prove to be better readers of certain texts than their teacher; and the teacher's ability to insist upon a certain reading will be diminished. In a place of a community of uniform and obedient students, one finds a contestatory space where the vertiginous possibilities of the multivalent, multivocal text become at least momentary reality in the hands of a loosely federated, heterogeneous group with widely divergent reading abilities and political commitments.

As exciting as it can be when students are arguing in an engaged way about how best to interpret a text, such moments mark for me a starting point in the work of a course on reading and writing rather than an end point. That is, while such exercises do serve to introduce students to the idea that texts may be interpreted to have a range of meanings, there is always the danger that such work will quickly produce a classroom situation where any reading is seen to be as good as any other reading. Thus, when the third poster appeared a month later, it was difficult to get the students to move beyond developing an interpretation of the poster to staking out a position in relation to their interpretation, despite the poster's deliberately provocative declaration:

NOT ALL

MEN RAPE

SOME OF US

JUST

WATCH

By this point in the semester, we were reading Stanley Fish's "How to Recognize a Poem When You See One," and the students had become fairly adept at detecting and exploiting ambiguities in a text. Some of the students had also read an interview with the author of the first poster, entitled "Guerilla Feminist Kicks Some Ass," in the university's self-described "common, degenerate tabloid." In this interview the student, whose anonymity is maintained, stated, "I put these flyers up because art has an obligation to be dangerous and political" (Mulligan). With Fish and the interview in mind, the students quickly produced three overlapping readings of this poster: the broadside, written by the author of the first poster, either accuses all men of being involved in rape in one way or another or, more inclusively, indicts an entire culture for standing by while rape occurs; or, some students suggested, the poster, conversely, could have been written by a male parodying the feminist critique. . . . What had started as an exciting discussion that led to a number of insights into the dynamics of the contact zone quickly devolved into a predictable trotting out of interpretations. The students, it seemed, had learned what they could *in the classroom* about the advantages and disadvantages of the conventions governing this particular interchange in a textual corridor outside the classroom. But they also recognized that the anonymity of the participants deprived the interchange of the kind of depth necessary to sustain discussion, with the significant result that a strategy to produce public art designed to be "dangerous and political" ended up being dismissed as the work of cowards afraid to make their position clear. This, too, is one of the inevitable perils of writing in the contact zone: the rhetorical approach designed to deliver a critique or parody may simply lead to the material being cast aside as nonsense. These is always the possibility, as Pratt observes, that the letter will not reach its intended destination.

This is not an insignificant lesson to learn in a course devoted to thinking about writing as a process, since it both introduces the possibility of a range of ways of responding to a writing assignment and, at the same time, drives home the importance of balancing the strengths and weaknesses available within any given rhetorical approach. To return to the example of the posters, anonymity may buy the writer or writers the freedom to express opinions and prejudices openly, but it does so at the cost of undermining the credibility or significance of what is being said. It also, in the name of fostering a heightened awareness of violence against women, helps to create an environment of suspicion and hostility: "What if," one of my students asked, "the people producing these posters are in this class?" The conventions governing the interchange, in effect, guarantee only that the described situation will continue: in this sphere, anonymous threats and ambiguous slogans combine to produce a kind of political paralysis, where nothing happens because nobody knows where anybody stands. The value of pursuing such issues in a writing course is that it helps to illustrate the fact that no writing situation is without its conventions, nor is any writer ever fully able to control those conventions. Once the student writer recognizes that all texts, in this regard, are heterogeneous in their production as well as their reception, it becomes possible to talk about the range and kinds of choices available during the acts of reading and writing, and this, I would argue, is the most important work that can be begun in a composition course.

If discussing the posters and the conventions of the interchange within this particular textual corridor allowed us to explore what can and cannot be achieved through the adoption of a uniformly confrontational stance, the assignment of Gloria Anzaldúa's "Entering into the Serpent" moved the class on to the business of developing alternate routes of response to a challenging and, for many of my students, threatening text. In "Entering into the Serpent," excerpted from Anzaldúa's *Borderlands/La frontera*, Anzaldúa shifts back and forth between Anglo-American English, Castilian Spanish, Tex-Mex, Northern Mexican dialect, and Nahuatl, writing in a mélange of languages to express the diversity of her heritage and her position as lesbian, feminist, Chicana poet, and critic. While Anzaldúa's multilingual text thus places special linguistic demands on its readers, it also makes relatively unique generic demands, moving between poetry and prose, personal narrative and revisionist history. Where the posters spoke in one or two voices, Anzaldúa occupies a range of positions, some of them contradictory, as she relates her efforts to reclaim the Aztec goddess Coatlicue, the "serpent goddess," split from the goddess Cihuacoatl by the "male dominated Azteca-Mexica culture" in order to drive "the powerful female deities underground" (26–27). After the Spanish Conquest, Cihuacoatl was further domesticated by the Christian Church and transformed by stages into the figure now known as the Virgin of Guadalupe. While Anzaldúa admires *La Virgen de Guadalupe* as "the symbol of ethnic identity and of the tolerance for ambiguity that Chicanos-*mexicanos,* people of mixed race, people who have Indian blood, people who cross cultures, by necessity possess" (29), she nevertheless insists on the importance of regaining access to Coatlicue, "the symbol of the dark sexual drive, the chthonic (underworld), the feminine, the serpentine movement of sexuality, of creativity, the basis of all energy and life" (33). Recovering this contact with the supernatural provides one with "*la facultad . . .* the capacity to see in surface phenomena the meaning of deeper realities, to see the deep structure below the surface" (36). Anzaldúa concludes this section by asserting that "those who are pounced on the most have [*la facultad*] the strongest—the females, the homosexuals of all races, the dark-skinned, the outcast, the persecuted, the marginalized, the foreign" (36).

Here's how one of my students described his experience of reading "Entering into the Serpent":

> Even though I had barely read half of the first page, I was already disgusted. I found myself reading onward only to stop and ask "What is she trying to prove?" Scanning the words and skipping over the ones that were not English, I went from an egocentric personal story to a femo-Nazi account of Central American mythology that was occasionally interrupted by more poems. . . .
>
> From what I gather, she is trying to exorcise some personal demons. Her feelings of inadequacy and insecurity drove her to project her own problems not only onto the world, but into history and mythology. I'm surprised she didn't call history "herstory." It seems that she had no sense of self or worth. To overcome this, she fabricated a world, a past, and a scapegoat in her own image. Although her accusations do hold some truth, her incredible distortion of the world would lead me to believe that she has lost touch with reality and is obsessively driven by her social psychosis. She views herself as a gallant and brilliant member of a great culture that has been oppressed by the world. Her continuous references to females, sex, and the phallic symbols of snakes is most likely brought out by the lack of a man in her life. Rather than admit her faults, she cherishes them and calls them friends.

This is not an uncommon response to my assignment that began by asking the students to discuss the difficulties they encountered reading Anzaldúa's essay. This student, having made his way past the language barrier of the text, confronts the description of a world and a way of being in that world that he finds personally repugnant. Beginning with a variant of Rush-Limbaughism, "femo-Nazi," the student then proceeds to document the many ways that "Entering into the Serpent" offended him: it contains Anzaldúa's effort to "exorcise some personal demons"; it includes "her incredible distortion of the world"; the writer claims to be "a gallant and brilliant member of a great culture" of which the student is not a part. Given this reading, it is not too surprising that the student concludes that all the faults in the text are produced by "the lack of a man in [Anzaldúa's] life."

Taking offense at this student's response to Anzaldúa's essay strikes me as being exactly the wrong tactic here. It is of paramount importance, I believe, to begin where students are, rather than where one thinks they should be, and this student, by my reading, is trapped between the desire to produce a stereotypical critique of any feminist text ("I'm surprised she didn't call history 'herstory'") and the necessity of responding to this particular feminist text. He negotiates the tension between this desire and this necessity by producing a fairly detailed outline of Anzaldúa's essay and, simultaneously, mocking its argument ("Rather than admit her faults, she cherishes them and calls them friends"). However rudimentary or sophisticated one deems this kind of multivocalic writing to be, it is, as I've said above, only a starting point for beginning more detailed work with Anzaldúa's text. For this reason, the assignment that solicited this response does not simply ask the students to revel in the difficulties they experienced reading Anzaldúa's essay, but also requests that they outline "a plan of action for addressing the difficulties [they] encountered." The goal, thus, is not to invite students simply to record their various levels of rage, incomprehension, and despair with an admittedly difficult text, but rather to have them reflect on how their own ways of reading are disclosed and complicated during this textual transaction.

The results of having the students read their own readings and chart out alternative ways of returning to the text can be startling indeed. Although this writer began by accusing Anzaldúa of being a "femo-Nazi," he concluded by reflecting on what he had done with her text in the following way:

> If not for searching for her hidden motives and then using them to criticize/bash Anzaldúa and her story, I would not have been able to read the story in its entirety. Although my view is a bit harsh, it has been a way that allows me to counter Anzaldúa's extremities. In turn, I can now see her strategy of language and culture choice and placement to reveal the contact zone of her own life. All of my obstacles previously mentioned, (not liking the stories, poems, or their content) were overcome by "bashing" them. Unfortunately, doing that in addition to Anzaldúa's ridiculous disproportionism and over-intense, distorted beliefs created a mountain which was impossible for me to climb. This in effect made it impossible to have taken any part of her work seriously or to heart. I feel I need to set aside my personal values, outlook and social position in order to escape the bars of being offended and discouraged. Not only must I lessen my own barriers of understanding, but I must be able to comprehend and understand the argument of the other. It is these differences between people and groups of people that lead to the conflicts and struggles portrayed and created by this selection.

This strikes me as being an extraordinarily astute assessment of the strengths and weaknesses of this writer's initial reading strategy: "bashing" Anzaldúa enabled a certain kind of work to be accomplished (the reading was completed, the writing assignment could be fulfilled), but it also prevented the writer from taking "any part of her work seriously or to heart." The writer's approach, in effect, only verified feelings he already had: it did not allow him to see or learn anything he didn't already know. Reflecting on his own reading practice, the writer finds himself compelled to reassess Anzaldúa's strategy, seeing at the end of this work that she has written in a way that will show "the contact zone in her life." Thus, by "bashing Anzaldúa," the student inadvertently ended up showing himself that her description of her trying experiences within the straight Anglo world was, at least partly, accurate. The writer's proposed solution to this problem—setting aside his "personal values, outlook and social position"—attests to the magnitude of the challenge Anzaldúa's position holds for him. Whether or not this proposed solution proves in practice to be a workable plan is something that emerges when the writer returns to Anzaldúa's essay to begin his revision. What is important to notice here, however, is that the writer's plan does make returning to her text an imaginable activity with an unforeseeable outcome. Given the way this student's essay began, this is no small accomplishment.

Required self-reflexivity does not, of course, guarantee that repugnant positions will be abandoned. At best, it ensures only that the students' attention will be focused on the interconnections between the ways they read and the ways they write. This can be a salutary experience as in the example above, where it provided the student with an avenue for renegotiating a relationship with a difficult text and the wide range of concerns affiliated with that text, but it does not mean that this approach wields sufficient power to transform the matrix of beliefs, values, and prejudices that students (and teachers) bring to the classroom. This kind of wholesale transformation (or, to be more precise, the appearance of this kind of wholesale transformation) is only possible in classrooms where the highly asymmetrical relations of power are fully reinstated and students are told either implicitly or explicitly (as I was during a course in graduate school), "No language that is racist, sexist, homophobic, or that degrades the working class will be allowed in our discussions." Reimagining the classroom as a contact zone is a potentially powerful pedagogical intervention only so long as it involves resisting the temptation either to silence or to celebrate the voices that seek to oppose, critique, and/or parody the work of constructing knowledge in the classroom. By dismantling *Focus*, Bob Allen did not address the roots of the problem that produced the offensive cartoon; he merely tried to make it more difficult for another "deplorable mistake" of this kind to further tarnish the image of multicultural harmony the company has been at such pains to construct. Scott Lankford, on the other hand, achieved the kind of partial, imperfect, negotiated, microvictory available to those who work in the contact zone when he found a way to respond to his student's essay that not only kept the student in his course, but eventually led to the student signing up to work with him in another course as well. By having my students interrogate literate practices inside and outside the classroom, by having them work with challenging essays that speak about issues of difference from a range of perspectives, and by having them pursue this work in the ways I've outlined here, I have been trying to create a course that allows the students to use their writing to investigate the cultural conflicts that serve to define and limit their lived experience.

In the uncharted realms of teaching and studying in the contact zone, the teacher's traditional claim to authority is thus constantly undermined and reconfigured, which, in turn, enables the real work of learning how to negotiate and to place oneself in dialogue with different ways of knowing to commence. This can be strangely disorienting work, requiring, as it does, the recognition that in many places what passes as reason or rationality in the academy functions not as something separate from rhetoric, but rather as one of many rhetorical devices. This, in turn, quickly leads to the corollary concession that, in certain situations, reason exercises little or no persuasive force when vying against the combined powers of rage, fear, and prejudice, which together forge innumerable hateful ways of knowing the world that have their own internalized systems, self-sustaining logics, and justifications. For teachers who believe in education as a force for positive social change, the appropriate response to these new working conditions is not to exile students to the penitentiaries or the psychiatric wards for writing offensive, antisocial papers. Nor is it to give free rein to one's self-righteous indignation and call the resultant interchange a "political intervention." The most promising pedagogical response lies, rather, in closely attending to what our students say and write in an ongoing effort to learn how to read, understand, and respond to the strange, sometimes threatening, multivocal texts they produce while writing in the contact zone.

Coda: On the Teacher's Zone of Effectivity

When I finished writing "Fault Lines in the Contact Zone" nearly a decade ago, I opened a file called "Son of Fault Lines," where material for a future essay would be stored. Over the years, my file has grown fatter with stories about how lives are lived and lost at moments when power relations are inequitably distributed or deployed. In the New York area, these examples are everywhere ready to hand:

- Abner Louima, unarmed, is assaulted, then sodomized with a stick, by police officers while in custody, August 1997.

- Amadou Diallo, unarmed, is killed by police officers in a hail of forty-one bullets after reaching for his wallet, February 4, 1999. All four officers are later acquitted.

- Patrick Dorismond, unarmed, is shot and killed in a scuffle with undercover police officers, March 2000. Dorismond, the target of a sting operation, had refused to buy drugs from the undercover officers.

Then, there's O.J. and "The Crime of the Century"; Colin Ferguson strolling through the Long Island Railroad commuter, shooting thirty passengers and killing six on December 7, 1993; Lawrence Russell Brewer, Shawn Allen Berry, and John William King, white Texans, chaining James Byrd to the back of their pickup truck and then dragging him two miles until he was ripped to pieces in June 1998; and Eric Harris and Dylan Klebold killing twelve fellow students and a teacher before killing themselves at Columbine High, April 1999.

This list, which we might just as well label "Men (mostly white) killing others (mostly black)," could be extended almost indefinitely. In the world defined by these events, fear of contact and its consequences results in violent outbursts, murderous rage, death, and destruction. It is a world, it seems, always on the verge of apocalyptic collapse.

There's no reason to assume, of course, that the violence that has found such regular and full expression in the high schools during the past decade won't eventually make its way into our lecture halls, seminar rooms, and college dorms, but for the moment it is safe to say that most of us who teach in higher education do not inhabit this space of homicidal violence *while at work*. Indeed, the injustices that occur outside the academy are so clear and so great that they perpetually demand our full attention: we write about and get our students to write about the world *out there*, a world that roils with racism, prejudice of every kind, economic injustice, irrationality, and bureaucratic indifference. We write because we feel this experience has transformed us, we feel that it can and will transform our students so that, someday, there will never again be spaces of exclusion.

This is a noble goal, one that serves to enchant the work of teaching and make it appealing to those of us who have committed our working lives to helping others learn to read and write expository essays. But as I make my way through this hulking file, it is hard for me to see what this goal has to do with the daily workings of the educational system. There are the stories about the Greenwich High students who embedded the phrase "Kill All Niggers" in their yearbook; the Manhattan High School students who left notes for their teachers saying "Kill all Jewish People"; the student who was denied the role as class president because the word "crematoriums" appeared beneath his yearbook photo; the LSU administrator who awarded forty-nine of fifty-four minority fellowships to white students; the university president who was quoted as saying that minority students lack the "genetic hereditary background" to score well on college entrance tests. Public and private schools, colleges and universities: despite being inhabited with so many people of such good will, these institutions routinely create situations where power is abused by teachers, administrators, and students alike. The contact zones, thus, aren't just "out there" or just at the interface between school and the world outside the school yard; they also could be said to saturate and to define the educational environment, influencing all that gets said and done in these spaces.

The value of the "contact zone" concept rests with its ability to make these abuses into objects of study, thereby helping to bring to light the complex social and cultural histories that allow such abuses to go from being imaginable to being permissible. Unfortunately, this analytic concept is so perfectly suited to the work of identifying areas of conflict for analysis and critique that it can seduce us all into believing that producing such analyses or critiques (or lists of abuses for that matter) is of some consequence in and of itself. The danger in being so seduced is that giving ourselves over to the business of producing critique can serve to forever divert attention from the one zone where we have the best chance of exercising some real, sustained influence: our home institutions.

My growing dissatisfaction with the gap between the production of critique and the generation of viable plans of action is the reason that "Son of Fault Lines" never got written: I came to feel that the stories that fill the headlines come from worlds where I am unlikely ever to exercise any significant influence and that writing about them simply diverted my attention from the areas where I have some hope of effecting a measure of change. So, I grieve over these events that dominate the headlines, I can't get them out of my head, but I focus my attention on the work that can be done by a writing teacher—work on the curriculum at my institution, on our retention policies, on our support services, on teacher training, on accumulating the resources necessary for other teachers in our program to do a good job. These areas constitute the academic's primary zone of effectivity, and by concentrating my attention on this zone, I am able to engage more productively with the forces that are exerting an ever-increasing control over the form and content of higher education—local, state, and corporate funding streams, demands for greater teacher accountability and more accurate testing and placement of students, merit-based performance assessment, and the allocation of all available resources to technological initiatives. The notion of "the contact zone" helped me to see these forces and to name them for what they are, and this has value as long as it is a preliminary step in the process of learning how to act in the conflicted, contestatory curricular spaces that surround us all.

Focusing on curricular matters may seem quite distant from—and even trivial in comparison to—the racially charged events discussed above or the violent acts I wrote about in "Fault Lines." I would argue, though, that when we devote our energies to the curriculum, to better understanding the funding of higher education, to taking control of testing at our home institutions, and to plunging ourselves headlong into the technological revolution, we are working in direct and concrete ways to determine who gets access to higher education and what experience awaits them when they arrive. We are moving, in other words, from studying the contact zone to creating a zone of effectivity, a pragmatic space where our actions have discernable consequences. To commit to such work is to acknowledge that there is no academic space that is not a "contact zone" and thus that there are no battles, curricular or otherwise, that are ever over. In the end, all we have is the constant struggle to realize the elusive goal of creating wider, more supportive communities.

The formation and dissolution of communities, at least academic communities, is not the stuff that headlines are made of. Stanford's Culture, Identities, and Values course, which serves as the background to Pratt's article, was an exception to this rule, of course: its introduction into the curriculum made the front pages of papers around the country a decade ago. There just seemed to be something particularly newsworthy in the image of students chanting, "Hey, hey, ho, ho, Western Civilization's got to go." But, when the CIV course was dismantled and replaced with a series of more traditional humanities courses a few years back, hardly anyone took notice. Indeed, at a recent conference on General Education held at New York University, John Bravman, Vice Provost of Stanford University, stated that the CIV course was "a relic of our PC past" and sparked no response at all. And so, the curricular space that Pratt describes with such pleasure at the end of "Arts of the Contact Zone," that space of joy and peril, has been eclipsed by a competing vision of what first-year students should be reading and writing about.

How this came about is a longer story, but this much should be obvious to all: across the country, the first-year curriculum suddenly has the interest of administrators and funding organizations concerned with attracting and retaining students. For those who have learned how to work and live in the contact zone, this should not be perceived as a disaster but as an opportunity that we cannot afford to let pass us by. Having learned the arts of the contact zone, it's time we put them to use building curricula that not only assist our students in assessing what's wrong with the world at present, but that provide them with training in how to construct and plan for better futures for us all.

NOTE

I thank Scott Lankford for making this student essay available for discussion, Jean Ferguson Carr for providing me with materials related to this panel, and Mariolina Salvatori for introducing me to the idea of the "position paper" that appears here, in modified form, in my discussion of my students' responses to Gloria Anzaldúa's essay. None of these parties is, of course, to be understood as endorsing the position I have staked out here.

WORKS CITED

Allen, Bob. Letter to all AT&T employees dated September 17, 1993.
Anson, Chris, ed. *Writing and Response: Theory, Practice, and Research*. Urbana: NCTE, 1989.
Anzaldúa, Gloria, "Entering into the Serpent." *Ways of Reading*. 3rd ed. Ed. David Bartholomae and Anthony Petrosky. Boston: Bedford, 1993. 25–38.

Fish, Stanley. "How to Recognize a Poem When You See One." *Ways of Reading*. 3rd ed. Ed. David Bartholomae and Anthony Petrosky. Boston: Bedford, 1993. 140–52.

Focus. September 1993.

Kennedy, X. J., and Dorothy M. Kennedy. *The Bedford Guide for College Writers*. 2nd ed. Boston: Bedford, 1990. 41–42.

Lankford, Scott. "'Queers, Bums, and Magic': How Would You Grade a Gay-Bashing?" Paper presented at CCCC, Cincinnati, March 19, 1992.

Mulligan, Bartley. "Guerilla Feminist Kicks Some Ass." *The Medium* September 29, 1993: 1.

Pratt, Mary Louise. "Arts of the Contact Zone." *Profession 91*. New York: MLA, 1991. 33–40.

White, Edward M. *Teaching and Assessing Writing*. San Francisco: Jossey-Bass, 1985.

On the Critical Necessity of "Essaying"

Thomas E. Recchio

> Luck and play are essential to the essay. It does not begin with Adam and Eve but with what it wants to discuss; it says what is at issue and stops where it feels itself complete—not where nothing is left to say. Therefore it is classed among the oddities.
>
> —T. W. Adorno
> "The Essay as Form"

Starting this chapter has been more difficult than any writing I have done for years, probably because I am writing about something that will not stand still. My subject is the essay, but I am not concerned with the essay as product, as a configuration of words with particular formal features, stylistic characteristics, and rhetorical topoi. I am not concerned with the essay as a method of writing, the appropriate means through which one may render experience. Rather, I would like to discuss the essay as a writing practice whose fundamental ground is a critical orientation toward the object of inquiry and toward the subject, that is, the self. As Graham Good argues in *The Observing Self*, "The essay is an act of personal witness. The essay is at once the inscription of a self and the *description* of an object" (1988, 23). In other words, in essaying, the writer and the object of inquiry (an experience, an institution, a text, a disciplinary practice, or even one's self as that self is rendered in language) define and transform themselves reciprocally, aspects of each becoming understood in relation to the other (Good 1988, 8). My object of inquiry is the place of the essay in the teaching of writing; in writing this I hope to work toward a reconciliation between my professional commitments and personal values and between the conventions of academic writing and my desire to be heard as an individual. In exploring the relation between myself and our profession, I will be critical of both, my purpose less to draw a conclusion than to claim with Montaigne the privilege to "speak as one who questions and does not know . . . not [to] teach [but to] relate" (cited in Good 1988, 5).

I.

It is mid-winter in 1971. A twenty-year-old Marine sits in a windowless room on an American air force base on the northern tip of the main island of Japan. The Marine's F-4 Phantom jet squadron has been assigned to fly air cover for Navy spy ships off the Korean coast. The planes are launched infrequently, so the Marine's main job is to wait. He and his fellow Marines (all enlisted men with high school educations at best) spend most of their time playing pool, drinking beer, and smoking grass; service to country seems analogous to his capacity to tolerate high levels of alcohol and extended periods of boredom. Upon his enlistment he had been given a National Defense Service Medal, the Vietnam conflict still being "operative" (to borrow a Watergate word). Two and a half years later, he will feel that a Certificate of Merit from the Anheuser-Busch Brewing Company would have been more appropriate. Today he waits, somewhat queasy, fighting sleep.

In a moment of idle thoughtlessness, he reaches down and picks up a book from the end table next to his chair. The book is *The Brothers Karamazov* by Fyodor Dostoevsky. He recognizes the author's name as Russian, probably a commie, he thinks. He remembers having read histories and biographies voraciously when in high school, anything but the books assigned for class. He is out of the habit of reading, but he is also bored and out of beer. He opens the book and reads. He finds moments of hate-filled love between fathers and sons, spiritual desire mired in earthly passion, the "Grand Inquisitor" speaking for the military-industrial complex. The inarticulate stirrings of his intellectual and imaginative desires reawaken under the shaping pressure from the words on the page. The book seems to be reading his mind, to be, in fact, giving him a mind to read. He knows instinctively that his life will never be the same.

Over the next year, he reads nineteenth-century Russian literature with a passion; he is much taken with Dostoevsky's *Notes from Underground*, inwardly affirming the "underground" man's defiant "twice two makes five." He culls authors' names (from Gogol to Goncharov) and novel titles (from *Dead Souls* to *Oblomov*) from the introductions to every novel he reads. He begins to write too, first poetry (mawkishly philosophical stuff about village idiots, despite having never read Wordsworth) and later the beginning of a novel (embarrassingly autobiographical). After his return to the States and his release from the military, he spends his next ten years in college and graduate school, from North Carolina to California to New Jersey, his goal to understand what he later learns to call his epiphany. He stops writing "creatively" and starts writing "critically." He begins to understand his life as a kind of essay, a continual restless effort to compose a self in relation to his experience of the world and of language. Subsequently, he thinks of this effort in self-composition as an open-ended process, aspects of which are describable in retrospect but which do not culminate in a final product. He feels fortunate, even blessed, to have found a kind of work that seems to offer possibilities for wholeness, where his personal and professional lives can become one. He recalls the alienation of his military experience when wholeness was an illusion conceivable only through numbing both body and mind. He remembers his working-class father who always seemed either tired or drunk, emotionally distant because of his inarticulateness. He feels saved by words, by stories, by writing. He looks forward to future epiphanies.

· · · • · · ·

It is mid-winter in 1991. A fortyish professor of English Literature and teacher of writing is standing behind a podium under the irritating florescent lights of a run-down classroom. Wires dangle from the wall where a clock had once been. The professor holds a cheap paperback copy of Mary Shelley's *Frankenstein* in his hands. He talks about creation myths; he mentions feminist discussions of how Mary Shelley's anxieties about being a mother colored the language she used in describing the creation of the monster. He mentions William Godwin, the notion of *tabula rasa*, and John Locke's theories of education. He offers, he thinks enticingly, fragments of Shelley's biography: the circumstances of her marriage, the birth of her children, the early death of her husband. He quotes Percy Shelley's "Alastor" and parallel passages from *Frankenstein*, and suggests that Percy's wife Mary may have been trying to rewrite "Alastor" to correct her husband's naive faith in the radically creative powers of language and the renovating powers of the imagination. He describes the story-writing contest among Byron, the Shelleys, and a man whose name escapes him, which was the catalyst for the writing of *Frankenstein*. He tries to be witty, interesting, engaging. His students, many feeling queasy from the previous night's parties, are fighting sleep. They are more than tired; they are bored, waiting for class to end. They have better things to do.

When the class ends, the students rush from the room, one leaving his copy of *Franken-stein* on the floor next to his chair. The professor stuffs his notes and his book into his book-bag and walks briskly to his office, not bothering to bend down to retrieve the student's book. He sits at his desk, glances at the book-covered walls of his office, packs his pipe, and tries not to think. He thinks anyway. He's been trained to. His thoughts carry him to the past. He recalls his youthful intoxication with texts. He remembers midnight discussions in graduate school when he and his fellow students would sip wine, talk philosophy, and read Walt Whitman, T. S. Eliot, A. A. Milne. ("I contain multitudes." "I have shored these fragments against my ruins." "Halfway down the stairs is the stair where I sit. There isn't another quite like it.") He remembers wanting to share the excitement of such talk, its po-etic quality, its surprising juxtapositions of images, writers, and ideas. He recalls how hard he worked to grow as a teacher, to have a system of reading, to develop a coherent line of thought for every book and every poem he taught, to design writing assignments with clear, formal guidelines in order to help his students write with precision and power. He remembers his desire to become expert, as reader and writer, to be worthy of his profes-sion. He thinks he has achieved that; he knows his stuff. He feels worthy. But his students are beginning to make him feel the opposite. He is tempted, as he has heard so many of his colleagues do, to blame his students, to construct them as intellectually incorrigible, to consign them to the damned of the unlettered. His imagination is teased with apocalyptic visions, the decline of education, the decline of the West, the death of literate culture. He pushes those visions aside and resolves to do better. He wishes he knew how.

II.

One way to construe those two scenes (other than as epiphany and anti-epiphany) is to see them as marking central moments in my progress from novice to expert, from one who wants to know to one who thinks he knows (which is, in a sense, true), but I cannot avoid recognizing in that "progress" an obvious sense of diminishment and loss, a version of the literary trope of the movement from innocence to experience. More specifically, that loss could be understood as the result of a change from personal commitment to professional performance, from exploration to consolidation. In the first scene, reading and writing pro-vided an intellectual site where I could work on the human task of becoming, of forming and reforming a self; in the second scene, reading and writing provided a means of confirm-ing what I thought I had become. While it is true that performance and consolidation do not necessarily involve a diminishment of commitment or serve as roadblocks to one's becom-ing, I felt stalled. Perhaps the loss is related to a change in my attitude toward language; that is, I was losing a sense of the eventfulness of language, beginning to treat language as a kind of information. The loss signals a change from openness to closure, from a process to a product orientation toward language—toward learning, toward life.

Such a loss seems at times inevitable given the pressures toward specialization in the university and the fragmentation of personal and professional life. In that context, it would not be much of an exaggeration to say that my task of becoming has been turned into a ritual; in playing the role of teacher, of professor, I simply perform an institutional func-tion. The dissatisfaction evident in the second scene is both a sign of alienation from my work and a stimulus for change. But what form might that change take? How might it be conceptualized? In what medium might it begin to be realized? How possible is it to bridge the gap between the personal and professional, to begin to affirm one's humanness through one's work with others?

Reconsidering the essay as a critical orientation toward self and other can provide a starting point for exploring those questions. Consider the following, for example.

In German scholarship the essay is linked constantly to *Wissenshaft*, that is, "science," in the root meaning of "knowledge." It is the meeting ground between "pure literature" and "pure science," the mediator between "poetry" and "science." It is the means of overcoming the isolation of specialists, of bridging the gap between science and the rest of society, between natural sciences and humanities. It can provoke a synthesis of science and art at a "common third level," and on that level can seek to restore the "lost unity" of culture; to recapture a world-view (*Weltbild*); and to counteract the fragmentation of culture, the proliferation of isolated disciplines of learning—in a word, the disintegration of the mind. At this level it goes well beyond criticism in the ordinary narrow sense to become the criticism of life (*Lebenskritik*). (Chadbourne 1983, 142)

Note the key terms in that passage—*mediator, overcoming isolation, bridging the gap, synthesis, counteract fragmentation, Lebenskritik*—which, taken as a whole, suggest a working definition of the essay and, following Bruno Berger, what we might call the "essayistic spirit" (Chadbourne 1983, 142). Reflecting a critical orientation toward self and other, the essay, as both attitude and writing practice, is Janus-faced; it looks inward and outward simultaneously, implicitly and/or explicitly registering the relationship between the person writing and the object and the context of the writing. The "essayistic spirit" is self-conscious, aware always of the provisional nature of any discourse and the situatedness of any writer. On this latter point, Max Bense observes that "whoever criticizes must necessarily experiment; he must create conditions under which an object is newly seen" (cited in Adorno 1984, 166). And those conditions, despite the predetermined "intentions" of various discourses (Bartholomae 1985), are already implicit in the particular situation of the writer.

In creating such conditions through a recognition of one's personal situation, writers are not isolated from their objects; they establish a connection, albeit arbitrarily. Instead of masking arbitrariness through a putatively objective formal discourse, however, the essay takes "arbitrariness reflectively into its own procedure" (Adorno 1984, 166). The essay, then, provides a means through which our personal sense of and commitment to our professional lives can find expression in a public space; our texts can begin more openly to reflect our sense of self at the time of writing. Somewhat akin to Bakhtin's notion of the novel as an open form that offers a "distinctive social dialogue among languages" (1981, 263) rather than a genre as such, the essayistic spirit can shape writers' fundamental sense of their task whether or not the completed piece of writing is overtly reflexive.

III.

Change for me as a teacher of writing is beginning to find a conceptual center in the idea of the essay as a writing practice where self formation and cultural formation proceed together in a dialogical relation, with self dependent on culture for its potential forms and culture dependent on many selves for its composition. The idea of the essay hints at the possibility of realizing the potential interanimation of life and language, of one's person and one's work, as each informs the other in continually shifting configurations, a vague sense of which I have in retrospect constructed, somewhat naively and nostalgically, from my Marine experience. Realizing the potential of the essay in the Freshman English classroom, however, is a thorny problem, for writing pedagogy has been dominated by formalized, self-contained systematic thought where play, discovery, and recursiveness are squeezed out of discourse, and subordinated to a misleading, formalist consistency and clarity. This essay has survived in name only, its pleasures and dangers avoided, its spirit nearly dead. The pedagogy of rhetorical modes and of thesis-then-demonstration-argument still dominate the teaching of writing. Such a formalist pedagogy is hard to resist because it appeals to our desires for clarity and the minimization of risk. Nonetheless, I will add my voice to some others in order to suggest that writing instruction can be infused with the essayistic spirit.

Recently, I reviewed twenty years of *College English* issues to see how the "essay" has been addressed in the professional literature. Two articles in particular, Keith Fort's "Form, Authority, and the Critical Essay" (1971) and William Zeiger's "The Exploratory Essay: Enfranchising the Spirit of Inquiry in College Composition" (1985) discuss the essay in terms similar to my own. Fort concerns himself with what he calls the "prescribed structure" of critical essays on literature. "In the essay," he argues, "it would seem that [the] key rule is that there be a thesis which the essay proves" (1971, 631). He characterizes that key rule as the "[f]ormal tyranny of essay writing," a tyranny that "is based on the need of those who are in control to make the appearance of the expression confirm a desired idea of which there is *no doubt*" (1971, 631, my italics). Skepticism, uncertainty, openness to possibility have no place in such a form.

Zeiger echoes Fort on the tyranny of form in his discussion of the notion of "proof" in the expository essay. To *prove*, in the expository writing taught in Freshman English, he argues, is to demonstrate "a truth or [establish] the validity of a proposition," whereas for Montaigne (and other Renaissance writers) it is "to examine [an idea] in order to *find out* how true it [is]" (1985, 455). The former is the art of "demonstration," the latter the art of "inquiry" (1985, 456). Zeiger closes his article with the following: "Teaching the exploratory essay would contribute to the larger effort of revitalizing the humanities by restoring the spirit of inquiry to a place of currency and honor, and by educating people to communicate freely with one another" (1985, 464). While I share a concern about the potential continued tyranny of a rigid formalist pedagogy, and while I would dearly love to help to restore "the spirit of inquiry" throughout the university curriculum and, by extension, professional and social life, I am not convinced that the problem can be addressed by teaching the "exploratory essay." By bracketing the notion of exploration in a separate form, inquiry is ghettoized, the rigidity of other forms remains unchallenged and unchangeable, and the processes through which writing in any form is done get shortchanged. As the boundaries between and among academic discourses continue to blur (Geertz [1983] and Elbow [1990]), it seems more useful to consider the points of contact between the person writing and the available and changeable discourses within the writer and at the writer's disposal.

In other words, there is no neutral language available for purely personal expressive purposes, nor does any person writing merely deploy and transcribe an absolutely preconfigured language. As David Bartholomae puts it, in part, "I would say . . . that the person is erased in professional discourse. The person writing can be found in the work, the labor, the deployment and deflection (willed or otherwise) of the languages and habits of academic writing. The person . . . can be found in the figuring, not in the figure" (1985, 130). I would add, however, that the figuring can change the figure, though it does not always. Discourses, academic or otherwise, do not remain constant; figures (that is, conventions of discourse) change over time through an accumulation of nuance and inflection. People write. Boundaries blur. We shape language even as language shapes us.

At this point, I would like to evoke the work of Mikhail Bakhtin, not simply because his work helps to explain the relation between stability and change in the life of language, but also because his work has been emerging as a significant link between my past and my present personal and professional life.

I first encountered Bakhtin's work in 1974 in a shabby used bookstore called Olde York Books in New Brunswick, New Jersey. Books were piled everywhere in no particular order; the smell of canned spaghetti cooking on a hot plate and the site of ratty rattan chairs with ripped, overstuffed seat cushions randomly placed throughout the shop gave the place an aura of literary naturalism. George Gissing would have been at home there (I think now). My reading of Dostoevsky was still fresh, so when I saw the title *Problems of Dostoevsky's Poetics* I couldn't resist. Though confused by the title (Dostoevsky hadn't written poetry, had he?), I bought the book (the 1973 Rotsel translation published by Ardis). When I tried to read it, however, I was stumped. Sentences that now speak to me with clarity seemed non-sensical. "The new artistic position of the author vis-à-vis the hero in Dostoevsky's polyphonic novel is a *consequent* and *fully realized dialogical position* which confirms the hero's independence, inner freedom, unfinalizedness and indeterminacy" (Bakhtin 1973, 51). While I understood "independence" and "inner freedom," I did not know enough about Bakhtin's (or anyone's) theory of language to get a grasp on the nuance of those common terms, much less on the whole meaning of the passage. I felt, nonetheless, that somehow reading and writing must be essential in one's struggle to attain independence and inner freedom, and I now see that the struggle has something to do with one's individual effort to construct a voice for one's self, even if that effort can never be absolutely successful. For in language there is space for individual effort in a medium that by its nature depends on many individuals for its existence.

In "Discourse in the Novel" (1981) Bakhtin discusses this tension between the idea of a common language and the reality that individuals speak both as representatives of groups and as unique, unduplicatable beings. Bakhtin uses the term *heteroglossia* to define "languages that are socio-ideological: languages of social groups, 'professional' and 'generic' languages, languages of generations and so forth" (1981, 272), in short, the full range of particular jargons that distinguish one social group, profession, or whatever from another. He goes on to claim that a common language "makes its real presence felt as a force for overcoming this heteroglossia, imposing specific limits to it, guaranteeing a certain maximum of mutual understanding and crystallizing into a real, although still relative unity—the unity of the reigning conversational (everyday) and literary language, 'correct language'" (1981, 272).

Since social groups are composed of individuals, the nuanced language conditioned by personal experience injects another level of heteroglossia within social and professional languages. Language, in this view, always mediates between the life-world of the individual and the large and small unifying pressures of public and professional life. Although Bakhtin tends to value heteroglossia over a common language (for personal and historical reasons related to Soviet life in the first three-quarters of the twentieth century), he claims that every utterance reflects both. But rather than dichotomizing those forces, Bakhtin argues that they constitute another kind of unity. "It is possible," he argues, "to give a concrete and detailed analysis of any utterance, once having exposed it as a contradiction-ridden, tension-filled unity of two embattled tendencies in the life of language" (1981, 272). Such a unity has little to do with conformity to conventions even as it does not reject conventions. It is a "tension-filled" unity, played out in the consciousness of particular speakers and writers, an effort to reconcile contradictions that result not from some failure of internal coherence within a discourse (or from within a life) but from the very conditions of language in a fragmented, heteroglot world.

Bakhtin's theory of language outlines a context where the essayistic spirit can thrive, where almost every written utterance can contribute to the inscription of some aspect of the self through the disclosure of something "other" in a discourse. If we imagine the heterogeneous nature of contemporary culture manifested within individuals in addition to being diffused among various social and professional groups, we can understand the failure of formalist writing pedagogy as a failure to impose a unitary linguistic practice onto multi-linguistic (heteroglossic) consciousness. That is, the boundaries between and among the multidisciplinary and nondisciplinary verbal worlds we inhabit continually shift and blend in the mind; to use a key term from Bakhtin, the languages we experience and use in the world continually "interanimate" each other. Despite the compartmentalization of contemporary life, the various discourses at play in our consciousness tend to fuse together as we inevitably essay to construct a provisional coherence in the face of fragmented experience. Written products, then, carry traces of the linguistic, cultural, institutional, and personal contexts that surround and partially determine their composition. No writing is *sui generis*. It is deeply embedded in the history of language and of discursive practices. Writing products thus carry traces of personal and impersonal (or transpersonal) intentions, that is, the desires of the writer and the constraints of a discourse and/or discourses.

I would like to "read" the following passage, written by a student in Freshman English, in order to locate some of those traces and to speculate about what they might reveal about the interplay of the language of the student's social world and classroom discourse. The assignment asked for an interpretation of Clifford Geertz's "Deep Play: Notes on the Balinese Cockfight" in the context of Stanley Fish's argument about "interpretive communities" in "How to Recognize a Poem When You See One."

> Last week, while this assignment was plaguing my mind, I was listening to a particularly loud and obnoxious song whose lyrics reminded me of my own personal image of Stanley Fish. The lyrics to this song, "Eye of the Beholder" by Metallica, are strikingly similar to what I felt inside about Stanley Fish, but I just could not place those feelings into words. The song that helped me put this image to paper reads as follows: "Doesn't matter what you see, or into what you read, you can do it your own way, if it's done just how I say. Independence limited, freedom of choice is made for you my friend, freedom of speech is words that they will bend, freedom with their exception."

Who says heavy metal songs are useless conglomerations of satanic, destructive, and immoral lyrics? I do not want to appear to be digressing from the assignment by talking about my personal interests in music. The point I want to make is that the lyrics to this song helped me focus my perception on the ideas being discussed in the assignment. Similar to what the song says, Stanley Fish makes his students see what he wants them to see. To Fish, texts and objects do not exist. Rather the interpreter creates objects. It is here that Stanley Fish is wrong in his assumptions on interpretation and Clifford Geertz is wrong in his methods of interpretation of the Balinese.

The two most striking features of that passage are intelligence and anxiety: intelligence in the student's suspicious interpretation of Fish's argument and anxiety about the source of the student's insight, the heavy metal band Metallica. The writing reflects an uneasiness in its crossing of the boundaries separating the student's social language from classroom language. The language of rock music, defined by Michael Moffat as an emergent medium of "a common, classless, internationally defined youth culture" that "unmistakenly state[s] their antielitist sentiments" (1989, 50–51), and the language of the classroom reflect, though uneasily, a characteristically essayistic engagement, connecting the personal and the cultural in enacting their points of contact in the individual consciousness. What I call the personal here, however, is also, as suggested by Moffat's observation, cultural. Thus the passage reveals a clash of cultures, which the writer struggles to mediate. In this light, we might say that the personal is less a pure, contextless subject position, some domesticated version of Emerson's transparent eyeball, and more a multicultural construct, the configuration of which is unpredictable and subject to change. We can see traces in the passage of the student's effort to construct an authoritative position for himself, based on his "local knowledge," even as he simultaneously resists a discourse (the discourse of interpretative communities) that would give him a prefabricated authoritative position.

The authority in the passage, and essayistic authority more generally, is paradoxical. The apologetic moments ("I do not want to appear to be digressing . . . The point I want to make is that . . .") imply a distrust of personal authority, just as the judgment offered on Fish ("It is here that Stanley Fish is wrong") asserts a distrust of academic authority. This double distrust, a version of what Paul Ricoeur has called "hermeneutical suspicion," marks the writing as essayistic. The passage, in being critical of self and other, achieves the authority of a mind at work.

The sense of the essay that I am trying to approximate suggests that "essaying" is, at least implicitly, a subversive activity, for in its tentative and suspicious inscription of the self through an encounter with an object, the essay simultaneously stabilizes and destabilizes both. That subversive quality, I think, tends to give teachers of writing pause. By emphasizing the centrality of a critical orientation toward self and the texts of the academy, we fear that we may misrepresent the writing that students will have to do in other courses. They simply will not *need* to be critical in the introductory courses in the various disciplines, and it is questionable whether they will *need* to be critical, in the essayistic sense, in their major courses. To borrow Richard Rorty's terms, by encouraging an essayistic spirit in all student writing we may prematurely encourage students to produce an "abnormal discourse" when, in fact, they will be asked to write in the "normal discourse" of the academic disciplines (cited in Bruffee 1984, 647). To tilt the emphasis slightly: is it not necessary to know a discipline from the inside, to master its conventions in order to learn its possibilities and limitations, before earning the authority to be critical of it and of one's place in it?

I felt the force of that question recently in a discussion with a student who had asked me to read a paper she was writing for an education school graduate course. When I pointed out the lack of a critical dimension in the paper, she explained that her professor had told her that since she had not generated the statistics in the study she was responding to (or replicated the study to gather her own statistics), she had no grounds to be critical. Her task was simply to report. Of course, one can never simply report, for in reporting one has to select, and in selecting one judges relative value; one interprets. But I suspect her professor meant that in reporting, students have to mask the interpretative component of their work through a putatively objective language. Even though the student had studied statistics and knew how to interpret them, she was not permitted to exploit the knowledge she brought to her task. She had to hide what she knew and suppress her interpretative authority. From such a professor's point of view, to teach the essay in the terms of this chapter is to ask students to do too much too soon. But to begin with the simple is merely to put off an encounter with the complex, and as Adorno puts it, "Such a postponement of knowledge only prevents knowledge" (1984, 162). If the fundamental goal of freshman writing courses is to empower students as critical thinkers through writing, critical about their objects of study and about themselves, we need to invite them not just to look but to think, not simply to perceive but to probe, not to accept but to question, all qualities of the essay as a record of the mind at work.

· · **·** · ·

There are a couple of questionable assumptions implicit in the idea of a necessary deferral of criticism until a student has fully entered a discourse. One is that knowledge is something that one acquires (rather than makes) in an orderly, linear way, beginning with the simple and building up to the complex—as if in learning how to write we begin with individual sounds linked to letters, build to words, to phrases, to clauses, to sentences, to paragraphs, to papers. The other is that criticism can only be generated from within a discipline, by those who have mastered disciplinary practices and who accept the values of those practices—as if, for example, in criticizing the Catholic church we should look to priests to lead the way. If we grant that such assumptions underlie the idea of a normal discourse, the implications for what constitutes education are disturbing, for education would have to be in the service of the status quo, suffused with complacency. Its main task would be socialization in the most limited and narrow sense: socialization as uncritical conformity.

Of course, one could object that the very fact that I am writing this belies my point. Aren't I criticizing from the inside? Hasn't the institution given me a place from which to write, the authority to write, even, on some level, the words to write? And as a necessary consequence, haven't I already been co-opted? I feel the force of those objections, but to credit them as definitive would be to lapse into silence, and it would grant the institution a power that I don't think it has. While my language is both enabled and constrained by my institutional context, the institution does not totally determine what I write. As my discussion of Bakhtin's theory of language reveals, there are other, pre- and post-institutional languages at play in my consciousness, social languages from my experience and the languages of the students I have worked with. Thus, pressures for institutional change have complex sources that converge at points of intersection between institutional and non-institutional life. The precise contours of change are open, the future always an unanswered question.

If there is even a degree of truth in what I have claimed in my criticism of a necessary deferral of knowledge (and I grant that I have overstated the case, but not by much), it is imperative, I think, that the essay, understood as a critical orientation toward the object and the self, have a central place in writing instruction and in the university curriculum as a whole. Essayistic writing — writing as inquiry, writing as a way to understand — requires, as Adorno has it, that we begin "with the most complex . . . which is in every case the habitual" (1984, 162). The habitual, our habits of thought and the matter-of-course presentation of texts/objects of study, should themselves be the first objects of critique. In essaying to understand an object, a text, a discourse, we need to examine ourselves in relation to the object, to bring out in the open our assumptions about that object. Only after we have worked out what aspects of the object our assumptions and intentions toward it enable us to see can we begin to uncover our blind spots, to see more, to see differently, to come to a new understanding in establishing a new relation to the object.

This critical orientation, this essayistic spirit, enables a writer to work self-consciously within the margins of difference between subject and object, and, in confronting that difference, to change the relation between the two. Through the essay, subject and object inter-animate each other dialogically; they do not exist in stasis. The knowledge that comes through essaying unfolds; knowledge is not simply there, a given. The essay, in its very contingency, in its sensitivity to its specific contexts, and in its resistance to prescribed forms, is the most powerful means through which writers can negotiate an entry into the discourses of specific disciplines. (N.B.: Janus, in addition to looking before and behind, is also the god of doorways.) As a flexible, unmethodical orientation, the essay can exploit and animate any number of verbal formulations (discourse forms) without surrendering its critical dimension to the "normality" of a given discourse. The essayistic spirit carries the promise for writers to participate in and to change a discourse; it can thrive on the meeting ground between the person and the discipline where individual people participate in the work of understanding. Whether the writing practices of particular academic disciplines implicitly reject the essay or not — and I would argue that most, ideally, would not (although most on the introductory level assume a walk-before-run idea of learning) — should not constrain the highest pedagogical ambitions of freshman writing programs.

IV.

It has been a rather long (and I hope not too tedious) passage from my rendering of my Marine Corps epiphany to my grand claims for the place of the essay in writing instruction. My impulse now is to focus on the relation between the two, to draw a conclusion (for example, that the moments of personal narrative and of academic analysis and application in this chapter are equally essayistic); to make a detailed recommendation about, say, teaching practices (how can I do better as a teacher?); or, at the very least, to make a stylistic gesture that would create some sense of aesthetic closure. Even though I take on the tone of the teacher in the latter part of this essay, recall that with Montaigne my intent is to relate, not to teach. So I would like to back off from my effort to "recommend" the essay as *the* most desirable approach to writing instruction and relate something of my effort at self-understanding through both writing this essay and reading texts I hoped would help me in my task. I was not sure (and still am not completely) what the particular relevance of my Marine experience was to the idea of the essay as I started writing. The sentences in my Marine anecdote that address the idea of the essay are clearly imposed. But I did think in those terms at the time. The anecdote is a reconstruction, not a "true" rendering of thought and experience. I wanted to believe that the experience could be understood in the context of the essay because, quite simply, I wanted this chapter to be as much an essay as it is an academic argument. That is, I wanted to inhabit what I like to think *is* my own writing. But perhaps the idea of the essay I have been struggling to articulate is simply too utopian to be of much use. Perhaps not.

Let me draw on a short section from Robert Musil's three-volume *The Man Without Qualities* (1953) to help me out of this impasse. In a chapter with the wonderful title "The earth too, but Ulrich in particular, pays homage to the Utopian idea of Essayism" (the source of my utopian reference in the previous paragraph), Musil charts a change of perception in the thinking of his character, Ulrich. "From the earliest times of the first self-confidence of youth, which it is often so touching, even moving, to look back upon later, all sorts of once-loved notions lingered in his memory even today, and among them was that of 'living hypothetically.' This phrase still expressed the courage and the involuntary ignorance involved in a life in which every step is an act of daring without experience behind it" (296). For Ulrich, "living hypothetically" involves "[a] thrilling sensation of being destined to something" (296). Experience, however, changes his sense of destiny. After having desired to have "a character, a profession, a definite mode of existence," Ulrich "tries to reach a different understanding of himself." Musil renders that "different understanding" as follows:

> Later, as his intellectual capacity increased, this gave rise in Ulrich's mind to a notion that he no longer associated with the indeterminate word "hypothesis" but, for certain reasons, with the peculiar concept of the essay. It was approximately in the way that an essay, in the sequence of its paragraphs, takes a thing from many sides without comprehending it wholly—for a thing wholly comprehended instantly loses its bulk and melts down into a concept—that he believed he could best survey the world and handle his own life. The value of an action or of a quality, indeed their essence and nature, seemed to him dependent on the circumstances surrounding them, on the ends they served, in short, on the whole complex—constituted now thus, now otherwise—to which they belonged. (297)

As I read those lines, I felt, as I had with my reading of Dostoevsky, that I was reading myself. I too dreamed of a profession and of forming a stable "character." I too looked back at my "involuntary ignorance" with some affection and recognized a quality of "daring" in my lack of experience as a reader and writer. Dreams change; the desire for "large terms of reference" (296) and the utopian dream of free and full self-expression become transformed by experience, changed by circumstances, revised through interactions with others. "The peculiar concept of the essay" offers another kind of utopian dream, a dream where everyone can speak and write from where they are, where everyone has the authority of experience and the workings of their own minds. In the essay, we have a notion that refuses to see wholly, a notion that invites us to confront our situatedness, to look from where we are and then to shift, to see partially, and to look again ("constituted now thus, now otherwise"). The essay invites writers to resist absolutes, and it bestows on us the authority to write and rewrite in an effort to understand and, through understanding, to remake ourselves, our work, and our lives.

WORKS CITED

Adorno, T. W. "The Essay as Form." Trans. Bob Hullot-Kentor and Frederic Will. *New German Critique* (1984) 32: 151–71.

Bakhtin, M. M. "Discourse in the Novel." *The Dialogic Imagination*. Trans. Caryl Emerson and Michael Holquist. Ed. Michael Holquist. Austin, TX: University of Texas Press, 1981. 259–422.

———. *Problems of Dostoevsky's Poetics*. Trans. R. W. Rotsel. Ann Arbor, MI: Ardis Publishers, 1973.

Bartholomae, David. "A Reply to Stephen North." *PRE-TEXT* 11.1–2 (1990): 122–30.

———. "Inventing the University." In *When a Writer Can't Write*. Ed. Mike Rose. New York: The Guilford Press, 1985. 134–65.

Bense, Max. "Uber den Essay und seine Prosa." *Merkur* 3 (1947): 414–24.

Bruffee, Kenneth A. "Collaborative Learning and the 'Conversation of Mankind.'" *College English* 46.7 (1984): 635–52.

Chadbourne, Richard M. "A Puzzling Literary Genre: Comparative Views of the Essay." *Comparative Literature Studies* 20 (1983): 133–53.

Cohen, J. M., trans. *Montaigne: Essays*. Harmondsworth: Penguin, 1958.

Dostoevsky, Fyodor. *The Brothers Karamazov*. New York: New American Library, 1957.

———. "Notes from Underground." In *Great Short Works of Fyodor Dostoevsky*. New York: Harper & Row, 1968.

———. "Forward: About Personal Expressive Academic Writing." *PRE-TEXT* 11.1–2 (1990): 7–20.

Elbow, Peter. "Reflections on Academic Discourse: How It Relates to Freshmen and Colleagues." *College English* 53.2 (1991): 135–55.

Fish, Stanley. "How to Recognize a Poem When You See One." In *Ways of Reading*. Ed. David Bartholomae and Anthony Petrosky. New York: St. Martin's Press, 1993.

Fort, Keith. "Form, Authority, and the Critical Essay." *College English* 32.6 (1971): 629–39.

Geertz, Clifford. "Blurred Genres: The Reconfiguration of Social Thought." In *Local Knowledge: Further Essays in Interpretive Anthropology*. New York: Basic Books, 1983. 20–35.

———. "Deep Play: Notes on the Balinese Cockfight." In *Ways of Reading*. Ed. David Bartholomae and Anthony Petrosky. New York: Bedford, 1993.

Good, Graham. *The Observing Self: Rediscovering the Essay*. London: Routledge, 1988.

Kauffmann, R. Lane. "The Skewed Path: Essaying as Unmethodical Method." In *Essays on the Essay: Redefining the Genre*. Ed. Alexander J. Burtrym. Athens, GA: The University of Georgia Press, 1989. 221–40.

Lukacs, Georg. "On the Nature and Form of the Essay." In *Soul and Form*. Cambridge, MA: The MIT Press, 1974. 1–18.

Moffatt, Michael. *Coming of Age in New Jersey*. New Brunswick, NJ: Rutgers University Press, 1989.

Montaigne. *Selections from the Essays of Montaigne*. Trans. and ed. Donald M. Frame. Arlington Heights, IL: AHM Publishing Corp, 1971.

Musil, Robert. *The Man Without Qualities*. 3 vols. Trans. Eithne Wilkins and Ernst Kaiser. London: Secker and Warburg, 1953.

Torgovnick, Marianna. "Experimental Critical Writing." *Profession 90*. The Modern Language Association of America, 1990. 25–27.

Zeiger, William. "The Exploratory Essay: Enfranchising the Spirit of Inquiry in College Composition." *College English* 47.5 (1985): 454–66.

Good Difficulties and Not-So-Good Difficulties: Teaching Underprepared Students to Negotiate Theoretical Discourse

Christine Ross

It is easier to write a good paper about a difficult text than it is to write a good paper about a text that is "easy" or self-evident in what it says. If students leave their freshman course understanding why that is so, we have had a pretty good semester. There are, however, points of difficulty beyond which it is not productive for freshman students to venture without considerable assistance. "Problems with decoding" is a general heading under which to gather many if not all of the textual difficulties that are generally unproductive. Decoding difficulties are determined by something as mundane and as crucial as unfamiliar vocabulary and by things as complex and elusive as an unfamiliar set of discursive or linguistic rules. If students confront a page having a preponderance of words they have never seen before or following linguistic rules they have never heard of, they don't know enough language to read the text with the fluency requisite to making much, if any, sense out of it. Because I teach *Ways of Reading* to underprepared freshmen, decoding problems can be of some concern. Students in my course have a tenuous grasp, at best, on much of the abstract, technical vocabulary to be found in an essay such as Paulo Freire's "The 'Banking' Concept of Education," and they often understand language in instrumental terms as a transparent "window" on the world and the mind. For many students I have taught, academic or theoretical discourse does not pose simply "interpretive problems." It seems downright bizarre.

Significant decoding problems seem to represent an insuperable bar to the use of *Ways of Reading*. Its pedagogical orientation restores to students their authority to construct meaning as they read and write. If decoding problems are directly addressed by glossing a text to help students find their way through "tough vocabulary," for example, students' readerly rights and responsibilities are undermined. On the other hand, if decoding problems are not addressed, students can feel disabled rather than challenged or engaged by a plethora of alien terms. In the fall of 2003, as we piloted the use of *Ways of Reading* in our course for underprepared freshmen, I foregrounded, in more concrete terms, the shift in students' reading and writing habits that our course is designed to teach. I also borrowed techniques used to support second-language speakers of English to foster more fluent reading of the abstract theoretical language in Freire's "The 'Banking' Concept of Education." Because Freire appears first in the "Aims of Education" sequence I taught, I was particularly concerned that underprepared students would find Freirean language merely frustrating. The combination of early practical intervention in students' reading and writing practices and the use of ESL strategies permitted me to support greater immediate fluency in students' reading while respecting their interpretive authority. Surprisingly, as well, ESL strategies provided for sustained experience of language as a complex network of words, which allowed students to consider more deliberately why academics use language the way they do.

Concrete Changes in the Literate Habits of Underprepared Freshmen

The introduction to *Ways of Reading* outlines many of the assumptions about reading and writing that students bring to their freshman classes. They have often been taught to understand reading as a matter of hunting for bits of information: a "main idea" or the "key terms" of textbook exposition, perhaps the "theme" or "character flaw" located in a literary text. More generally, students have often been taught, through textbook instruction, that reading is episodic in the extreme and usually unnecessary. To judge from their high school experience with books (and for many of them, that is all they have to judge by), reading is done in comparatively short bursts of time in merely additive units that are attenuated over weeks, months, even an entire school year. Instead of reading *Lord of the Flies* or the narrative of their history textbook in one or two or three sittings, students' reading is distributed over a three-to-four-week "unit" or an entire academic year, during the course of which the teacher will "explain" or "give notes" on what the book "says" or "means." It is no wonder, then, that most students do not understand much about the role of fluency and sustained attention in successful reading. Sitting two to three hours to read before attending a class for discussion is not an experience that most students understand or have ever had.[1] Students enrolled in freshman courses therefore have very little basis for knowing anything about, let alone choosing to do, the habitual practices of careful, sustained reading, writing, revision, and rethinking that *Ways of Reading* requires.

In my courses for underprepared students, I directly teach and require, during the first weeks of class, the temporal-physical changes in practice that students need to engage in. Students are required to develop and use a system of annotation when they read, based on initial guidelines I give them. They make copies of their annotations, and I comment on them, as work in progress, in the same way that I comment on their written drafts in progress. During that first week, students are also required to keep a record of the amount of time they spend reading, annotating, and writing a typical journal response for our course. We discuss why I ask them to do that and begin to think through why they must set aside significant blocks of time, every week, so they can do their English assignments. I also give assignments in rereading based on what appear to be purely mechanical requirements: e.g., focus on something "unusual" or "new" in the assigned text that you did not talk about in your first journal entry; focus on some words in a quotation that you have not yet discussed. I require these seemingly "mechanical" revisions in students' habitual practices to foster a process of reading that is slightly different from the one described in the introduction to *Ways of Reading*.

Very fluent readers often do perform as the introduction indicates, by marking, in some way as they read, the passages that stand out as challenging, different, unusual, or interesting (7). In order to do that, however, fluent readers must also be translating parts of the text into something more or less connected to what they already know: a "region of being" or "topic" already articulated through prior reading with a well-known network of language and discourse; a set of readerly experiences with a particular genre; a kind of argument or style; a set of critical questions or problems already defined by an ensemble of accepted solutions or conundrums. To recognize (or read) something as unusual or mysterious presupposes that there are elements of a text—even long stretches of text—that are not new or mysterious but more or less familiar.

In order to support nascent fluency as well as teach underprepared students some of the skills and pleasures of rereading, I describe a process of "first" reading and annotation that proceeds in two apparently discrete steps rather than one fluent event. Just as do fluent readers, readers who struggle with comprehending a text attempt to translate it into the concepts, stories, experiences, and genres they already know. Beginning readers produce different results, of course, because their linguistic and discursive repertoire is based in some hybrid of their oral language use, their "schooled" print knowledge, and stories and concepts gleaned from popular media, rather than the disciplined networks that make a trained reader so powerful. But both beginning and expert readers translate an unfamiliar text into something they already know because if they could not, they could not read (recognize) anything at all. I therefore tell students that all readers begin by turning a text into something they already know. Skilled readers simply go to the next step and focus on the parts that are different from what they know. I also tell students that sometimes these two things—connecting to something familiar and discovering something unusual or new—happen at the same time. The annotation system I provide to students, as a "rough draft" they revise over the course of the semester, creates an index for what they, at first, find "clear" (clear), "different or unusual" (new), "interesting" (*), or "confusing" (?). These minimal marks allow students to remain fluent, while supporting rereading that develops their initial understanding as well as the "strong" reading that Bartholomae and Petrosky celebrate in their introduction.

In addition to learning to annotate, the first two weeks of class include a number of concrete assignments that ask students to discuss, for example, a passage that is unusual in some way (new) and to connect it to some other clear (clear) or interesting part of the text (*). Students are also asked to reread quotations used in their journal entries and to write about some part of the quotation that they have not yet talked about. I like to start with a range of assignments addressed to apparently mechanical or "concrete" practices such as these. Through them students can begin to experience the potential power of new ways of reading. I say "begin to experience" because, of course, the intellectual acts implied by these concrete changes are very difficult for students to do. Their struggle with that difficulty is a necessary point of departure for a semester-long process of revising and rethinking their literate practices.

Here is Steve, as he works on a journal assignment that asks him to connect something "new" to some other "clear" or "interesting" part of the introduction to *Ways of Reading*. Steve's response draws on a number of familiar figures for reading, such as "look below the surface" to "get down deep," as a way "to understand what the author is trying to say." Steve's focus on metaphors for comprehension is a frequent one among the underprepared readers I have taught, often coupled, as with Steve, with the license to come up with one's own meaning. Steve's response therefore shows him translating the introduction into something he already knows, but it also shows him engaged in new reading practices, in which he actively connects different parts of a text, identifies something that is new rather than familiar to him, and begins to create a "strong reading."

> In the introduction to the reading, "The Ways of Reading" written by David Bartholomae and Anthony Petrosky discusses the essentially different "ways of reading." One of the more important focal points is to make you as a reader a stronger, more critical reader. In other words the reading teaches one to look

past just the plain facts and to look below the surface of what they are reading and really get down deep into the text and try to understand what the author is trying to say. After doing so the reader will then be able to relate what he or she has just read to their everyday life. Knowing that all people are different in many ways, the way they interpret what they have read could and most likely will vary in many ways, even after reading the same text. Also, this reading discusses how something as simple as reading can change the way you as a person and or we as a society think about something.

People are very different. They differ in everything from their goals in life to the way they view certain topics. Being different and living different lives can lead people to interpret the same exact reading in a completely different way. "If ten of us read his essay, each would begin with the same words on the page, but when we discuss the chapter (or write about it) each will retell and interpret Rodriguez's story differently." ("Ways of Reading" Bartholomae and Petrosky) I found this "new" because I was not aware that just because you were brought up differently can change the way you interpret something you read.

Another aspect of the reading witch I found to be unusual or "new" was at the end of the introduction where it talks about new and different ways of reading, thinking and writing. It tells you how to become a stronger, and more critical reader. It does this by presenting a very helpful sequence, "The sequences allow you to participate in an extended academic project, one in which you take a position, revise it, look at a new example, hear what someone else has to say, revise it again, and see what conclusion you can draw about your subject." ("Ways of Reading" Bartholomae Petrosky)

The reason why I chose these sections of the reading is because I feel they are relevant in many ways. They play off of each other in the sense that if you as a reader are brought up a certain way and you have a different outlook on life then that of the person you are comparing information with, when you compare knowledge with them your final conclusion will differ.

As I read the introduction and learned about different ways of reading and learned how to interpret what I have read, by the end of the reading I was, well reading and interpreting the reading in a different more meaningful, more critical way.

Steve's journal performs a number of interesting moves that are not quite visible because he has not yet fully developed the role of quotation in constructing a reading. Nevertheless, the deep structure of his reading strategy appears to be "cause-and-effect" relationships. That deep structure appears to be motivated by the potential of the introduction to explain why reading happens as it does. Steve's first paragraph suggests that "digging down deep" causes reading comprehension, which in turn causes a reader to relate a text to his life, which in turn prompts the recognition that people's lives differ, which subsequently causes interpretations to differ. He concludes by juxtaposing this implicit causal chain with the new idea that reading can cause people and society to change, which Steve apparently gleaned from the discussion of Richard Hoggart and Richard Rodriguez. Although Steve does not return to this moment in his September 8 journal entry, his work over the course of the semester led him to return, repeatedly, to the potential power of reading to change people.

Steve's focus on "difference" in "upbringing" as a root cause of differences in interpretation would be his "strong reading" of the introduction. His choosing to quote a direct statement that readers' interpretations differ appears to be prompted by common instruction that a quotation is used to "prove" one's "point" or to offer "support" or "evidence." These legalistic metaphors often prompt students (not without reason) to (re)present the most dead obvious (or indisputable) statement as the best evidence for their reading of a text, which unfortunately prompts their using quotation where a summary statement would suffice. In any case, Steve quotes text directly stating that interpretations will differ rather than text that helps him explain why he believes there is a specific causal account for that difference. In the same textual vicinity of the passage he quotes, the introduction discusses readers' "own predisposition to see or read in particular ways" and a reader who sees a story "in his or her own way," which is followed by the observation that students "see themselves" in Rodriguez (2–3). Steve appears to interpolate his own understanding of what causes differences between people—how they are brought up—to account for why readers read differently, but not without a prompt from the introduction. Where common explanations for variable interpretations focus on the richness of the text, the introduction appears to consider the richness of the reader. A slight shift in accent, legible in the description of reading in the introduction to *Ways of Reading*, is apparently "magnetized" and surfaced by the prior experience of students who do not fail to recognize the continued focus on interpretive validity—a logic of "correct" and "incorrect" readings—in the claim that the unique qualities of literary texts alone account for variable interpretations. In the introduction to *Ways of Reading*, Steve hears the possibility of a different explanation that is "new" to him, prompting his "strong reading" of the text.

As he develops his journal entry, Steve goes on to connect the causal sequence in his opening paragraph to another part of the text that is focused on the "logic" of connections: the description of assignment sequences. Steve's connection to this part seems eccentric until one surfaces the deep structure of causal relationships. That deep structure "magnetized" and surfaced the part of the introduction that directly represents intellectual work as sequential and non-arbitrary. Steve continues his strong reading by suggesting that the "consequential" nature of sequenced work in reading and writing, coupled with the cause of differences in reading, will lead different people to draw different conclusions from the same sequence of assignments. His readerly project prompts and supports a connection that, again, the introduction does not quite make but that continues the thinking of the introduction in meaningful ways.

The changes in Steve's reading practice required by his journal assignment are not immediately routed through a specific hermeneutic task, such as "close reading," which is often further focused on "literary language" or "metaphor." The traditional, strictly her-meneutic focus of "close reading" is an instructional contradiction. It requires students to demonstrate mastery of the very task that instructional insistence indicates they have not yet achieved. Traditional instruction in close reading therefore proceeds as a vicious circle that continually faults and fails beginning readers who need guidance rather than repeated, merciless evaluation. Steve's journal assignment is organized by heuristic tasks that require him to process text differently while positioning him to select a hermeneutic focus of interest to him and implicitly, therefore, within his grasp. These heuristic tasks surface the implicit logic of close reading: focusing on "new" (or unusual) passages/elements followed by "mak-ing connections" with other passages/elements. Students have an opportunity, thereby, to gain readerly experience with practices that can support their becoming "close readers."

"Scaffolding" Exercises and "The 'Banking' Concept of Education"

I teach the introduction to *Ways of Reading* as a reading and writing assignment in my course. Students I have taught appear to like the introduction a great deal because it is organized around a respectful contrast between their high school training and the major figures of literate practice that the introduction has to offer: "strong reading," "construct-ing a reading," "reading with the grain" or "against the grain." These figures establish a common language that we can all use to frame the (new) practices that the course will teach as it repositions students with a degree of authority and a range of readerly options that sound engaging to them. Steve's first journal assignment on the introduction offers an explicit statement of what many students remark on with greater and lesser degrees of clarity: "This passage [from the introduction] has made me for the first time in my life ex-cited to read. Never looking at reading in any other way than to gather information I now am looking forward to having a 'conversation' with the author." Steve's focus on the figure of "conversation" suggests, I think, many students' desire for an experience of reading that is less alienated than those that have, very probably, resulted in their being placed in a class for underprepared freshmen.

The "vocabulary problem" that Paulo Freire's text represents to underprepared fresh-men is not reducible to knowing isolated definitions, which the list-like designs of diction-aries, thesauruses, or glossaries imply. Powerful language use is a function of complex networks of relationships between terms for which no list of definitions is a substitute. It is no wonder that students are often frustrated by the failure of a dictionary entry to illuminate the difficulty they have when they encounter texts constructed almost entirely out of words such as "narrative," "empirical," "existential," "transformation," "sonority," "significance," "dialectic," "praxis," as is Freire's. The alternative has been to encourage students to learn new language from the context in which it appears. This usually preferable strategy is short-circuited, however, for students who do not have a fairly substantial command of the words that organize that context. If there are too many unfamiliar words to figure out, then it is that very context that is lacking. Students with substantial "vocabulary problems" need the language and discourse of (the unreadable) context rather than a list of definitions.

Although students appear to lack the context assumed by an academic or theoretical idiom, they are not blank slates. They have often been taught to define a writer's lexical re-sponsibilities in terms of a need to "keep the reader interested" with accessible, varied, and attractive language. Language variety is solely decorative, in this model; it contributes to an affective response at most rather than any significant cognitive or semantic difference. Take, for example, the instruction that writers should avoid reader "bore[dom]" or textual monotony by "vary[ing]" the use of "signal phrases," which is a common response to students who make repetitive use of "says" and "writes" when quoting or summarizing (e.g., Maimon and Peritz 187). This kind of language training reduces the differences between "signal" verbs—in which an author "claims" or "suggests" or "proves" or "explains," etc.—to matters of solely aural "variety" rather than a (student) writer's judgment that the quoted text in question has "claimed" rather than "explained," for example. Similar instruction commonly addresses matters of diction or "word choice" as if a dictionary or a thesaurus were a giant book of synonyms rather than the palette of connotations, registers, and precise shades of difference available to a writer in English. Through this kind of handbook- and thesaurus-based literate practice, words become generic aural "chits" easily substituted, one for another, in relation to great slabs of inert, undifferentiated "meaning." The practical linguistics inculcated through this kind of instruction makes the precision and force of academic and theory-based uses of language virtually incomprehensible.

The following paragraph, from Stacey's first essay on Freire, suggests the depth of the problem academic discourse can pose to students who have been trained to understand language as a massive tissue of equally good synonyms for the same slabs of stuff:

> Paulo Freire *creates* and *explores* an interesting perspective on our educational system. He *warns* us of dangerous pitfalls in some teaching techniques which he calls the "Banking Concept." He *acknowledges* that being educated will get you far in life. However, Freire *asserts* that our present educational methods give a false representation of reality. He *informs* that by teaching students to memorize, educators are corrupting future generations; robbing them of important critical thinking skills. . . . *According to Freire*, this [the "incident" she will narrate in her paper] is a perfect example of the "banking concept." The teacher only deposited the information into my bank where it was stored. (italics added)

The first two sentences are perhaps closest to suggesting what Stacey understands Freire to perform in his essay: he "creates," "explores," and "warns." However, because Stacey's sentences are consistently launched through the verbal tic of varying the "signal phrase" in sentences that remain syntactically uniform in many respects, her essay increasingly draws on the empty aural "variety" that common instruction in the use of "signal phrases" implies. In addition to the "variety" of her first paragraph, above, Stacey's essay goes on to include the following: "Freire sees," "He suggests," "Freire points out," "Freire expresses strong feeling," "Freire believes." Stacey does not claim that "Freire expresses strong feeling" or "believes" or "suggests" as part of an argument or interpretation she is making about Freire's essay or what he performs. She uses the verbs, interchangeably, to introduce another line of apparent summary or flat statement. Nor does Stacey ever use the "signal phrase" that would perhaps be most appropriate: "Freire argues." In a similar fashion, the summary of Freire is an illusion created with verbal "chunks" borrowed from op-ed prose nowhere found in Freire. Stacey is not the author of any of the following popular phrases or phraseology, which she uses to stand for a summary of Freire: "an interesting perspective on our educational system," "dangerous pitfalls," "teaching techniques," "our present educational methods," "give a false sense of reality," "educators are corrupting future generations," "robbing them of important critical thinking skills." Just as Stacey substitutes one signal verb for another, so she substitutes chunks of op-ed prose in the syntactic slots of her sentences. Insofar as the formal consistency of Stacey's performance is evidence for training and habitual practice, it is not helpful to understand her text as a result of personal choice or preference or problems in "diction" reducible to "overuse of cliché" or "lack of specifics." The more or less autonomous force of habitual practice or discourse is suggested by the sentence that functions as a "thesis statement." Although it would be Stacey who is arguing that her "incident" is a "perfect example" of Freire's "banking concept," Stacey "introduces" her statement with yet another signal phrase: "According to Freire."

As they begin to negotiate academic discourse for the first time, students accustomed to handling language as a vast tissue of synonyms, as in Stacey's text, are confronted with a style of language use that often makes no sense to them. Why don't "they" just use words that everybody can understand? The words all mean the same thing anyway. Students' common use of this "they" signals the alienation that unusually difficult academic or literary language can prompt. If students are not provided with a way to think about why academic language works as it does, they are frustrated and bored by writing that seems alien to no purpose. ESL "scaffolding" offers a surprisingly concrete way to support students' exploration of academic language and discourse.

ESL scaffolding can be said to "work" to the extent it organizes immediate, rapid language acquisition. When used to support reading, scaffolding provides a means for students to construct a network of core terms before they read an essay employing it. Their reading is then more fluent, precise, and engaged. Scaffolding can also provide an occasion for students to stand back and observe the active construction of a linguistic network as they internalize it. As the class works on scaffolding exercises, I ask heuristic questions that invite students to see, in our construction, a model for how academic language or theory works as systems of relationships and connections rather than direct references to things. Although the scaffolding activity I am about to describe may sound dull because it appears to be "empty" of any story or argument, students have referred to it and activities like it, in course evaluations and reflective essays, as work that has been particularly helpful and enjoyable. They have argued that Freire would call these scaffolding activities a kind of problem-posing, and they have talked about how much they value their social nature, as the whole class constructs an understanding of words that had, initially, appeared strange or meaningless. One might say that students experience and value the negotiation and emergent consensus that organizes the social construction of "meaning."

One kind of scaffolding strategy begins with what appears to be a traditional vocabulary lesson: looking up words in a dictionary. Before students began to read Freire, they were put in small groups that worked together for five minutes. Each group was given a handout with two words/phrases and a question. Students were to look up the words in a dictionary,[2] to be prepared to define the words for the class in more or less familiar terms, and to answer their assigned question. The groups were given the following texts to work from: Group One: *narrative (go to definition number 2); empirical (go to definition number 4); What is the difference between learning through narrative and learning through the empirical?* Group Two: *alter; transform; What is the difference between altering something and transforming something?* Group Three: *sonority/sonorous; significance; What is the difference between the sonority of words and the significance of words?* Group Four: *alien; existential experience; What is the difference between something alien and existential experience?*[3] As each group reported out, definitions were recorded on the board and elaborated by the group's answer to the assigned question. A traditional vocabulary lesson might have stopped there. However, that degree of "exposure"—or opportunity to learn—is not sufficient to support meaningful internalization of new language. Building on the assigned questions, I invited sustained discussion of this small network of words for most of a class period. After each group reported out, the entire class was invited to illustrate each word with examples from their own experience. I then asked which of the two assigned words members of the class would prefer to have or do and why, following up with progressively more specific questions such as the following: Do you think your education has altered you or transformed you? When might sonority be important? As students responded to these and other questions, I invited them to consider why academics require precise attention to words. As the students accurately perceived, for example, it makes a big difference whether you say "alter" or "transform." Once we had all the definitions on the board, I also asked the entire class to look for relationships between all the words we had discussed. Do they see any terms that are opposite or similar, for example? Do some terms include or require the others? Students constructed relationships between "empirical" and "existential experience," for example. They said that these two terms seem to be about a person's "experience" and, for that reason, they are more about "reality." They decided that "transformation" would happen if you learned by "existential experience" but not by "narrative," because "narrative" is done by someone else and not yourself. As they articulated what appeared to be a list of words as a kind of linguistic system, they began to tease out how concepts or technical terms allow academics to "name" things without using whole sentences: "existential experience" is a way of saying a large number of things when it is articulated by its implicit relation to other terms, such as "narrative" and "empirical." We could then begin to consider why the network of words in a theory could work as a lens through which to see something new.

This forty-minute activity provided students with an opportunity to develop some of the linguistic repertoire that Freire assumes as he organizes his revelatory theoretical use of it. It also provided an occasion for students to conceptualize and account for some of the stark lexical difficulty they would soon encounter as they read. Freire's repertoire is not codified as a list of "vocabulary" but as a network of related terms (usually acquired through years of reading academic, philosophical discourse) that is part of the significance of individual words embedded in it. Students' work to create and reflect on the force of such a network could be especially meaningful because they developed and internalized it as language is usually internalized: through multiple experiences of using, hearing, interpreting, and relating, which slowly inscribes new words and relationships in the interstices of the fluent language one already has. After this scaffolding process, we used the remaining five minutes of class to take turns reading aloud from the opening paragraphs of Freire, students annotating as they read. Students then had the pleasure of reading and experiencing immediate verbal power. The text appeared alien—there were a lot of strange words—but it wasn't quite because the students understood enough to construct a meaning as they read: they experienced fluency.

The general principles of ESL scaffolding are evident in the exercise: students are supported by considerable experience using and manipulating core vocabulary before encountering it in a new text. That experience includes integrating new words within the linguistic repertoire of a distinctive cultural experience; (re)articulating that experience or "region of being" through multiple, varied use and exposure to new language; reflection on the relationship between the new words and what is already known. Because it creates a highly focused, social, linguistic activity centered on a core vocabulary, scaffolding can be understood as a mode of rapid language acquisition. And because that acquisition occurs in mature students who can reflect on what they do, scaffolding can also function as a "living" laboratory of how language works.

Reading and Writing with a Revised Linguistic Repertoire

Students' greater fluency as they read the opening paragraphs of Freire, together with their new reading practices, fostered greater facility with Freire's text and resulted in some of the most varied and detailed responses to his text that have ever been submitted in a course I taught. Significantly, most students appropriated and used words developed through the scaffolding exercise. Where students did not focus on those specific words, their responses were remarkable for singling out unusual or markedly frequent words for commentary: e.g., "biophily," "spectator," "communication." The range of differences made by scaffolding and concrete heuristic changes in reading and writing practices can be observed by comparing Steve's first journal assignment on August 27 with his fourth journal assignment on September 8.

On August 27, Steve wrote the following journal entry after reading the prefatory discussion of high school and university writing that appears in our freshman program's casebook of student-authored essays:

> There are many differences between the training received in high school
> in regards reading and writing as opposed to the training received at a university
> level. The biggest difference is in high school reading and writing are used to
> gather information about a topic, to find the authors purpose, and or to find the
> main idea. On the other hand university reading and writing are used to "make
> new knowledge." Instead of just finding and using the information to support
> a topic the information gathered while reading and writing at a university is to
> change the way someone feels about something, to motivate people to do some-
> thing, to provoke thought, and to once again to gain new knowledge.

Steve's paragraph reports, virtually verbatim, points made in introductory paragraphs of the assigned reading. More significantly, the final sentence attributes to university writing all the elements that the reading attributes to high school writing, Steve having created what is commonly understood as a significant "misreading." As did Stacey, Steve draws on the mechanical strategies for constructing textual order. His sentences approximate parallel structure and use repetition of "key terms" ("differences," "difference," "high school") as well as "transition phrases" ("On the other hand," "Instead of"). This composure is disrupted somewhat by the blurred syntax in the first sentence: "in regards to" is blurred with "as regards," which results in the faulty elision of "to." The oral structure of the second sentence, which elides "that" after "is" and drops the commas that would set off "in high school," also creates a jarring illusion of faulty syntax. Steve therefore has the same kind of control—using linguistic "chunks" of "key terms" and "transition" phrases as formal indices of "connection" and "continuity"—as appears in Stacey's use of "signal phrases" and semantic "chunking" and in the handbook rules both are following. Nevertheless, Stacey's or Steve's difficulties are perhaps not best understood solely in terms of "writing problems" or "reading problems." One might also consider the effects of an implicit, practical linguistics installed by prior training, which determines how print or school language is understood to "mean" or organize significance. Scaffolding appears to intervene in that practical linguistics by teaching a small archive of language that works according to different principles.

Four class periods after his first journal entry on high school and university writing, Steve wrote the following in response to Freire:

> "The Banking Concept of Education" in *Ways of Reading* by Bartholomae and Petrosky is Paulo Freire theory of education. His theory is that the student teacher relationship is one that is narrative. They learn from the experiences of the teacher, never giving the student a chance to make his or her own interpretations of what they are being told. Thus killing the significance of what is being taught. The students are nothing more than collectors of information, never having the opportunity to do anything with the things they learn.
>
> The students' heads are filled with the teacher's thoughts, which the students memorize and repeat. "Education thus becomes an act of depositing, in which the students are the depositories and the teacher is the depositor." (Page 260) They learn the teacher's knowledge and interpretations and have a chance to make their own. The student gets nothing besides the *sonority* of the teacher's words. What the teacher says to the students is nothing more than just sounds, no meaning, just fact, and no explanation why. Freire believes this to be a "misguided system" of learning, which leads to the lack of creativity and ability to make new knowledge.
>
> In order for proper education to exist there must be a relationship where the student learns from the teacher and where the teacher learns from the student. "The raison d'etre of libertarian education, on the other hand, lies in the drive towards reconciliation. Education must begin with the solution of the student-teacher contradiction, by reconciling the poles of the contradiction so that both are simultaneously teacher and student." (Page 244) The teacher teaches the student and the teacher then learns from the students' response.

Steve is actively engaged with Freire's text, wrestling with and using his technical terms, quoting passages that stand out for him, and beginning the work of paraphrase and interpretation. The continuity of his paragraphs is not grounded in mechanical "transition" phrases but in the deep structure of his work as a reader, which we first saw above in his journal on the introduction to *Ways of Reading*. In the present journal, the terms organizing that deep structure are becoming more textualized and available as the evident discourse of his writing. Steve begins by characterizing the student–teacher relationship through Freire's concept of "narrative" instruction. He connects that narrative instruction to "killing the significance" of what is taught. Replicating the nascent structure of cause-and-effect in earlier work, the concluding sentence of the first paragraph defines the effect of that loss: students are only "collectors" of thoughts who never get to "do anything" with what they learn. His second paragraph further explores the teacher–student relationship with a quotation and presents what is left if the significance is "killed": only the "*sonority*" of words. He again defines the effect of a loss, which mere "sonority" represents: "no meaning" and "no explanation why." Steve's focus on the difference between "sonority" and "significance," as Freire deploys it in his first paragraphs, perhaps foregrounds for critical reflection a "schooled" language that evidently taught Steve and Stacey to privilege "sonorous" variety over semantic force. His third paragraph begins to focus on the teacher–student relationship itself, and to connect the problem of "narration" to the "contradiction" that must be resolved. Steve offers his understanding of what that reconciliation would look like: the teacher and the student learn from each other. In short, after the scaffolding process and heuristic shifts in his reading practices, Steve was able to engage in traceable work with language as opposed simply to reproducing the set pieces of handbook training. For Stacey, whose literate habits were much more thoroughly schooled than Steve's, the emergence of that kind of work required two-thirds of a semester.

A large number of students made striking and quite distinctive uses of Freire's technical vocabulary as they developed their readings of the text. Michael, who had initial difficulty understanding the genre of argument as such, was nevertheless able to discern the outlines of that kind of discourse at the level of language use. He states "that in the 'Banking Concept' one has to alienate the students' thoughts so the student can develop the teacher's thoughts," while "'problem-posing education' wants to liberate its readers and learn off its existential experience." He goes on to say that Freire's "banking" theory is "altered from Bartholomae and Petrosky's view of education" and that one cannot "transform some concepts of ideas" within banking education. Danielle, on the other hand, used "transformation" to frame a distinctive trajectory through Freire's argument as she puzzled over what conditions the possibility for change:

> The student and teacher affect each other in many ways. Sometimes the student alters the way the teacher sees something they just taught, but they never thought of it that way. They work off of each other and bounce their ideas around which in turn make them realize things they never saw before. They affect the society as a whole when ideas are thrown around and people are allowed to see others points of view. The oppressed begin to transform and learn from what they are allowed to see. They become "beings for themselves." They

realize that society is constantly undergoing transformations and that the banking education is resisting them of their liberation. They are resisting them of the knowledge that is available to them in the world. Freire is basically trying to say that we learn from each other and realize things we did not see before.

Danielle has situated the teacher and student through a dependent relationship, in which the student inaugurates change because he or she "alters the way the teacher sees something they just taught." That alteration has force if the teacher and student proceed then to "work off of each other." Student creativity, in this view, is not oriented toward the student's private life but toward the teacher who apparently can choose, or not, to acknowledge that he or she has seen something new through the students' work. Danielle argues that a failure to acknowledge "alteration" prevents students from participating in a process of transformation, identifying a site of more local, practical "mystification" than those that motivate Freire. It appears to her that schooling does not allow students to "realize" something and that teachers' failure to reveal what they learn from students is the root cause of it.

Similarly, Kristyn begins her journal with the claim that "[t]he kind of education that classrooms lack is imagination, creativity, and transformation. [Freire] feels that the teachers are giving the students to many 'dimensions of reality,' and to much of their own 'existential experience.'" Remarkable, here, is Kristyn's recognition that "existential experience" is not simply the opposite of "narrative experience." When teachers narrate, they substitute their own "existential experience" for that of the students. Kristyn's recognition suggests an increasingly flexible use of language as a system rather than a list of signs that refer to discrete empirical things.

Kristyn returns to the idea of existential experience as she responds to a journal assignment that asks her to explore how Freire redefines the "human." She quotes and discusses Freire as follows:

> It is the people themselves who are filed away through the lack of creativity, transformation, and knowledge in this misguided system. For apart from inquiry, apart from the praxis, individuals cannot truly be human. Knowledge only emerges through invention and re-invention, through the restless, impatient, continuing, hopeful inquiry human beings pursue in the world, with the world, and with each other. (244)

> Freire makes a good point; he feels that any man or woman is not human unless they connect with the world and other humans in order to create their own experiences. The only way that this is possible is if they actually try new things over and over again, and work on one thing to make it become their own. This is how they can make it become nonalien and an existential experience. No man or woman can complete this goal unless they take time and are patient with themselves.

Kristyn's text exhibits the power of a language-maker increasingly extending herself into the linguistic networks that her work in the course has opened up for her. Her use of "non-alien" and "existential experience" is virtually fluent as her sentences integrate Freirean language with the common idea of learning through experience of trial and error. That commonsense view is so much transformed by Kristyn's treatment that it is barely legible beneath the surface of her reading. We might say that her sentences are increasingly "written" rather than ventriloquized from either Freire or her normal repertoire.

Of course, students did not translate their emerging linguistic power into writing assignments that easily recast their classroom experiences through Freirean language. When compared to their increasingly detailed engagement with Freire's text, their initial choice and discussion of examples appeared somewhat thin. However, when underprepared students have difficulty selecting and narrating an example that is comparable to the emerging force of their interpretation of Freire's words, they experience the kind of difficulty that is endemic to the assignment itself, given at the beginning of the "Aims of Education" sequence. To the extent freshman students generally understand language as a translucent window on the world, they do not easily understand stories they might tell as an interpretation of their experience through language. The challenge of the assignment is to disarticulate one's own experience from the familiar terms that determine it as a story and to rearticulate it in a new idiom that, when successful, should dramatically alter what one understands one's story to be or dramatically alter what one understands Freire to have (successfully) argued. The challenge to all students is to recognize the possible conflicts between two accounts of the "same" experience in "different terms." The negotiation is, implicitly, between idioms or languages rather than "experience" and "text." A possible pitfall, for all students, is therefore the degree to which the linguistics endemic to literate practices learned at school might prompt them to understand the commonsense idiom of their "experience" as simply equivalent to Freire's (an example of merely sonorous "variety" rather than significant difference). By supporting students whose literate skills may not be as robust as those of some of their peers, all freshmen can engage this assignment (and the assignment sequences in *Ways of Reading*) in a meaningful way, which might be considered one style of a literate rite of passage into academic discourse and the intellectual world of college.

NOTES

[1] This experience is not confined to underprepared students. I have taught students in freshman writing who describe themselves as having earned "A's in AP English," who also report with acute anxiety that they have never read a book from cover to cover or had to create an interpretation before it was discussed in class.

[2] I have done this exercise in a lab classroom with desktops and in a wireless classroom with laptops, both of which provided students access to an electronic version of the *OED*. This exercise could also be done with paper dictionaries, although part of students' engagement proceeded from the pleasure and fluency with which they use electronic media. I further represented the lesson as a way for them to promptly access an occasional definition when they read. Scaffolding does not replace that common use of a dictionary; it is a supplement where common use would not be sufficient.

[3] The original design of this exercise undermined an opportunity to support students in considering whether or not "alienated experience" can also be "existential experience." That would have been an interesting conversation to have had. As originally designed, it unfortunately supported a more conventional opposition.

WORKS CITED

Bartholomae, David, and Anthony Petrosky. *Ways of Reading*. 6th ed. Boston: Bedford/St. Martin's, 2002.

Maimon, Elaine P., and Janice H. Peritz. *Writer's Resource: A Handbook for Writing and Research*. New York: McGraw, 2003.

Reading Theory in Student Writing

Mariolina Salvatori

My work as a compositionist, like that of many others who came of age professionally in the 1980s, was irrevocably shaped by discussions of student language, of student learning, and of the centrality of student texts to the emerging scholarship of composition. I entered the field of composition because it valued, and made intellectually rewarding, to study the work of students whose cultural capital was not immediately recognizable in traditional terms. To study, rather than to expose, the shortcomings of student writing demanded that theorists and practitioners, in an act of intellectual consistency, be ready to reexamine the assumptions and to reassess the implications of traditional theories of reading and writing in light of what they learned from student work. A great deal of the writing in composition done at that time represents for me a responsible and thoughtful application, in Gadamer's sense of the word, of exciting new understandings of the reading process and its inter-connectedness with writing. The push toward, and the ability to read, nontraditional texts as critical reflections on what *constitutes* tradition, rather than as examples of the exotic, or of aberrant stylistic choices, or of conceptual approximations, was greatly aided by the de-stabilizing force that poststructuralist theories exerted on canonicity, intentionality, reader's function, and reader's relationship to writer, text, and context. Thus, in composition studies, at least in my experience, teachers' and theorists' inquiry of the steps that novice (nontra-ditional) readers take toward interpretation, and of the theories of interpretation that guide those steps, was recognized for what it was, and is—ethically responsible scholarly work.

In my department, at the University of Pittsburgh, this focus on student work led to consequential changes. It is worth noticing that these changes were first articulated within an extraordinary context: a "remedial," intensive, six-credit seminar in reading and writing, the seminar at the center of Bartholomae and Petrosky's groundbreaking *Facts, Artifacts, Counterfacts* (Boynton/Cook, 1986). But the field of composition at large did not sustain the production of sufficient scholarship of this kind: written, fully theorized, demystifying scholarship that would propose, test, and reassess the implications of poststructuralist theo-ries of reading for teaching composition and literature through an examination of student texts. The signal feature of *Facts, Artifacts, Counterfacts*, and the work it made possible for others to do, is not only the presence of student texts and the ways in which student work is read, interpreted, theorized, but also, in fact especially, the interrogation of established theoretical understandings of reading and writing on the basis of student work.

Although the field of composition studies at first embraced this way of doing scholar-ship, the field gradually began to promote a scholarship which theorized the reading and writing processes in ways that made students and their work invisible.

Several reasons for this erasure come to mind. One may have to do with the histori-cally resilient construction of teaching as practice, to be precise, with the construction of practice as at worst divorced from, or in opposition to, theory; at best, as ancillary to, or implementational of, theory. The problem with this construction is that even when teach-ing is theory-conscious, even when teaching is a rigorous enactment of theory, teaching is ultimately *talked to* by but cannot *talk back to* theory. Within this construction of teaching as just practice, seldom can teaching and teachers, and even less can students, expose, if and when necessary, the obliviousness of theories to the particular literacies of students.

At the beginning of this new millennium, I suggest, the field of composition is producing and expecting scholarly work that makes it unlikely to acknowledge how students and their work are instrumental in teaching us how to teach; in pointing out possible, albeit inadvertent, shortcomings in our teaching; in deepening or revising our understanding of how humans learn.

I want to move now to one example of student writing. It is very possible to read this text as an instance of failed attempts, errors, misreadings resulting from lack of knowledge, and/or resistance to new ideas; in short: inadequate, by certain well-entrenched criteria. I want to propose a different reading. I want to suggest that the features of this text that could be read as errors, failed attempts, misreadings are actually moments of incipient theorizing, fertile instances of an understanding struggling to emerge, and I want to foreground the possibilities for engaging student work such reading opens up.

The text was produced in a course in which the assigned text was *Ways of Reading*; this particular writing sample was produced in response to my Difficulty Paper assignment.[1]

> I found difficulty in understanding the last few sentences of the first
> paragraph in the introduction to *Ways of Reading*. The paragraph states that
> "you will begin to speak only when the authors are silent and you begin to
> speak in their place, sometimes for them--doing their work, continuing their
> projects--and sometimes for yourself, following your own agenda." This state-
> ment is somewhat confusing. Letting the author become silent means to stop
> reading. If I stop reading then how can I totally understand what the author is
> trying to say and what he is trying to portray or imply.
>
> Another confusing part is how I'm supposed to continue their work and
> projects. It seems impossible to me to continue the thought process of another.
> The author and myself have different views and ideas on certain topics or issues.
> He cannot think in the same way or style as I and I cannot think the same way

---

[1] The student text was written in response to the following assignment, one that I use regularly in every course I teach, whether in literature or composition:

> You can expect to write regularly in this course. In preparation for class discussion and writing assignments, you will write short (1/2 to 1 page) "difficulty papers": these are papers in which you identify and begin to hypothesize the reasons for any possible difficulty you might be experiencing as you read a/an _____ (poem, play, essay). Each week, you will write a difficulty paper on one or more of the assigned texts. Each week, I will select one or two of them as unusual or representative examples of the readings you produce. I will photocopy, distribute, and use them to ground our discussions. My goal, in doing so, is to move all of us from judging a difficulty as a reader's inability to understand a text to discerning in that difficulty a reader's incipient awareness of the particular "demands" imposed by the language/structure/style/content of a text.

as he. Knowing this, if I attempted to finish his work or project, it is possible that my conclusions would vary from those of the authors.

Through all of this confusion, I can make out what the introduction says about speaking in the author's place for myself and my own agenda. This is stating that I can create my own ideas and opinions about the author's subject rather than follow his ideas. Therefore, I am freeing myself to think in my own personal way. Doing this will allow myself to branch off and create more thoughts on similar and relevant topics.

Thus, there is much confusion on my part in the introduction of *Ways of Reading*. Hopefully, in reading the paragraph that confuses me over and over again, things will become more clear and tangible. -- Mark Costa[2]

The way Costa is testing, in fact putting pressure on, Bartholomae and Petrosky's highly metaphorical and difficult description of reading is remarkable. "Letting the author become silent means to stop reading," Costa writes, suggesting that he understands the act of reading as giving voice to an invisible, intangible author, an author who lives only through the text she has written, a text which, like its author, is mute unless a reader gives it voice. But what kind of reading does that? Costa is appropriating and "pushing against" the language of Bartholomae and Petrosky, just as the language of Bartholomae and Petrosky is appropriating and pushing against the language of Hans-Georg Gadamer. But of course Bartholomae and Petrosky are pushing against and silencing Gadamer from a theoretical place, that is, from a theory of reading that envisions and sustains this kind of dialectical agon. But Costa is not there yet. He needs the writer's voice "to tell him" how to understand what "the author is trying to say and what he is trying to portray or imply." He cannot do that difficult work on his own. He very possibly has never been asked to do so. His reading, in other words, is guided by a recognizable, and still well-entrenched, theory of reading that gives the author absolute authority over making meaning and controlling its reception. Within this theory of reading, "trying to say," Costa's language marks an author's precise volition rather than perhaps attempt, approximation (which is what allows a reader to speak back). And from within this theory of reading, it makes perfect sense for Costa to say, How can I begin to formulate, even less continue, the thought process of another? This is the question that author-centered theories of reading suppress, mystify, make irrelevant. And it makes perfect sense then that Costa should say, "If I don't reproduce exactly what the author intended, my conclusions will vary from his." This position is not to be invalidated, or prohibited. This position needs to be examined, its presuppositions need to be excavated and made visible so that he can understand how his thinking is shaped, so that he, not his teacher, can decide what to do about it. And this is not a question of "freedom." It's a question of "deep learning," a learning nobody can do for anybody else.

---

[2] "Mark Costa" is a pseudonym. I want to call attention to the fact that I refer to the author of this paper as "Costa" rather than "Mark." I have become increasingly sensitive to our referring to students by first name. In fact, I have argued that this convention is, albeit inadvertently, infantilizing and hierarchic. Mariolina Salvatori, "The Vanishing Presence of Students in Composition Studies," CCCC, Atlanta, GA, 1999.

In the next paragraph Costa tries to resolve his confusion. And the way he does may look familiar to many. Having called into question the possibility of a reader ever to be able to continue the author's work and projects, he interrupts the communication before it even starts, and opts for freedom of thinking in his own personal way, to branch off. But he does not seem to be convinced this is what is expected of him, or that this might be the wise thing to do. Thus, he returns, in the concluding sentences, to the position he started arguing from. His apparent solution? He will keep reading, over and over again, until things become clear and tangible. How? Who/what will make them clear? After how many readings?

The questions I have posed about Costa's paper, the comments I have made about it, stem — I suggest — from the kind of inquiry student writing can and should provoke.

It might be objected that in reading student texts the way I do I am actually "reading into" them, constructing their difficulties as productive of understanding when those difficulties are roadblocks to understanding, visible markers of error, of things improperly done, of lack of knowledge. Indeed, I am reading into student texts, the same way, using the same interpretive strategies I use when I read into established literary texts. With similar pleasure. And for similar reasons: to look for clues, directions, signs of work begun, if not fully developed and articulated; for markers, for directions on how to recognize, how to read, and how to enable students to mine the knowledge they bring to the classroom. Not to do so, I think, is to declare this knowledge irrelevant to, unworthy of, and insignificant for our scholarship.

Susan Bordo and Michel Foucault:
Teaching Close Reading a Moment at a Time

Dawn Skorczewski

When the teaching assistants I supervise select essays from *Ways of Reading* for their first-semester syllabus, they rarely choose Foucault. Many of them have struggled to read Foucault in a theory class the previous semester, and have been amazed at the discrepancy between what they understand of the text and what their brilliant instructor presents as her reading of it. They are not confident in their reading of Foucault's text, and they tend to be even less confident in the ability of the first-year student to reach any understanding of his work at all. Bordo's "Hunger as Ideology,"[1] on the other hand, tends to be one of their first picks. They rightly believe that students will have a lot to say about the topic of eating and the body, that students will be eager to find examples from popular culture to counter or confirm Bordo's argument.

These teachers' opinions of what might or might not work in a classroom rest on the assumption that we teach best what we know best—that if we are confused, our students will be similarly confused. They also presume a level of mastery of a text to teach it successfully. And for teachers who struggle to retain confidence in their own authority, this makes sense to me. But it also makes me a bit apprehensive about the dangers of staying within our comfort zones. What is excluded from the conversation when we do this? What are we prevented from learning with, about, or from our students when we feel that we have mastered or understood a text that they cannot? For these reasons, I suggest that new teachers attempt to teach a text they feel comfortable with alongside one that they do not. I urge them to use this Bordo/Foucault sequence as an opportunity to consider what might be learned from teaching reading and writing as processes of risk and discovery for both students and teachers.

I first designed this assignment, which asks students to read Foucault and then trace his influence on Susan Bordo's "Hunger as Ideology," to help me answer a genuine question I had in mind, a question which I did not know the answer to: how much has Bordo been influenced by Foucault? To my delight, semester after semester, students teach me new ways in which she has or has not adopted his ideas. As we work with these texts a moment at a time, I attempt to teach students the value of very detailed close work with a text that can yield answers to our questions and provoke new ones as well.

WRITING ASSIGNMENT

Theories of Power

Susan Bordo and Michel Foucault

[The Panopticon] is an important mechanism, for it automatizes and disindividualizes power. Power has its principle not so much in a person as in a certain concerted

---

[1] This essay appeared in the sixth edition of *Ways of Reading*.

distribution of bodies, surfaces, lights, gazes; in an arrangement whose internal mechanisms produce the relation in which individuals are caught up. The ceremonies, the rituals, the marks by which the sovereign's surplus power was manifested are useless. There is a machinery that assures dissymmetry, disequilibrium, difference. Consequently, it does not matter who exercises power. Any individual, taken almost at random, can operate the machine: in the absence of the director, his family, his friends, his visitors, even his servants. . . . Similarly, it does not matter what motive animates him: the curiosity of the indiscreet, the malice of a child, the thirst for knowledge of a philosopher who wishes to visit this museum of human nature, or the perversity of those who take pleasure in spying and punishing. The more numerous those anonymous and temporary observers are, the greater the risk for the inmate of being surprised and the greater his anxious awareness of being observed. The Panopticon is a marvelous machine which, whatever use one may wish to put it to, produces homogeneous effects of power.

—Michel Foucault
"Panopticism," 282–310

In "Panopticism," French philosopher Michel Foucault summarizes his theory of how power works through surveillance in the modern world. Foucault's theory has influenced innumerable thinkers, including feminist philosopher Susan Bordo. In this first assignment, you will trace the extent of Foucault's influence on Bordo. In short, you will closely read her essay "Hunger as Ideology" in relation to his theory of power articulated above in order to develop a thesis about how Bordo mimics, rejects, or expands upon Foucault's theory of "panopticism" in her essay. You will formulate your own thesis based on a careful analysis of Foucault's and Bordo's key terms, and, in Bordo's case, textual and visual examples.

Writing Skills

- Provide a *close reading* of Bordo's use or expansion of Foucault's key terms and concepts. "Close reading," as we will discuss in class, includes both detailed analysis of the text and the argument you make about the text, based on that analysis.

- At the beginning of your essay, *summarize* Foucault's theory of surveillance for the reader who is not familiar with "Panopticism." Begin your summary by identifying the author and the source, and state the main idea. Then present key supporting points. Don't evaluate; merely report. Use your own words and an occasional quoted phrase. Your summary should be less than a page.

- *Orient* the reader. You should address your essays to readers who have read the essay, but not recently and not in-depth. You will need to orient them with appropriate reminders (explanations of the context of quotations), always making sure these explanations serve a purpose in your essay as a whole (not just summary for its own sake). Your reader should always know where you are in the text, through the material you provide to jog their memories. As you close-read, never assume (1) that readers know what to look for, (2) that they'll read a passage in the same way that you do, and (3) that they'll draw the same conclusions. Your *analysis* of the *evidence* should persuade your readers of the validity of your claims.

- *Style*: limit your use of the verb "to be." To increase your awareness of "to be" verbs, underline every one you use in your draft and try to substitute active verbs when you revise. "To be" verbs include **is, are, was, were, be, to be, been,** and **being**. You should have no more than one per page; before you turn in an essay, be sure to circle the uses that remain.

DAY 1

"Panopticism": Is this written in English?

We begin with Foucault on a day when the students have just handed in an essay and have not read a word of "Panopticism." I ask them to open to his essay and find a sentence anywhere in it that makes sense to them—a sentence that sounds, I tell them, like it might be written in English. "Pretend for now that it is written in another language, that you are trying to find words that are familiar to you." Each student finds a sentence and presents it to the class. Together we map their sentences on the board, charting their paraphrase of Foucault's words. We write these paraphrases in order of their appearance in Foucault's essay. Once we have finished, we already have a general sense of the notion of the panopticon, and of Foucault's understanding of policing mechanisms that continually produce and reconstruct individuals' identities in relation to powerful experts.

Once we have a broad sense of what Foucault is going to be teaching us as we read him, we begin to sketch out the sections of his essay in the same way. This time students work in groups to present a paragraph of the first section of the piece. Again they present their readings, and again we chart them on the board. We discuss how to keep track of our readings of this difficult text in the margins or on yellow Post-its, and I suggest that I will be looking for their "maps" of Foucault's text when they arrive next time. They then go home to read the essay.

In this initial exercise I try not to impose my reading of Foucault on the students. When they suggest what seems to me to be a blatant misreading, for example, I simply ask them to show where in the text it says that. Sometimes I let it go, and wait for someone to contradict the misreading. Misreadings like those that often appear during a first class on Foucault very often give way to stronger and more textually based readings in the classes that follow, and I am more committed to my belief in the students' abilities to read a very difficult text on their own than I am concerned that they "get it right." "Getting it right," moreover, seems to me exactly the opposite of what we want to emphasize in a course in college writing.

DAY 2

Building readings of Foucault: The useable text

Exercise 1.1 due: *Identify, define, and discuss at least five of the key terms Foucault uses as he describes the nature and function of "panopticism."*

In our second class on Foucault, students have read the text and are generally more confused than they were in the last. We discuss how deepening our reading of a text, or our writing of our own texts, can result in an initial sense of loss. The easy understandings we had arrived at together in the previous class have been replaced by complications and nuances that we cannot reconcile with the meanings we generated in class. I argue that persisting in our examination of particular moments in the text and connecting these moments to each other will eventually yield another understanding of it, one that goes beyond what we initially formulated and one that connects more directly to our individual experiences as readings of the text.

Students work again in this class at mapping Foucault's text, section by section. Groups of students "teach" a section of the text to their classmates, writing on the board their most important points. They then compare notes. How does each section build on the last? What does it add to the conversation about how individuals are policed and produced by the panoptic mechanisms in contemporary culture? We also draw from their exercises to generate a vocabulary list of important terms in Foucault's discussion.

Finally, each group finds examples of what Foucault is talking about from their own lives, and presents them to the class. Some groups discuss the experts who sit in the center of the panopticon in our culture: doctors, lawyers, teachers, judges, parents, personal trainers at the health club, etc. This discussion prepares us to work with Susan Bordo's text in the next class.

DAY 3

Susan Bordo: Echoing, then speaking back

Exercise 1.2 due: Choose one quotation from each of the sections of Bordo's argument that discusses the ways in which advertisements work to shape our ideas about bodies, selves, food, and so on. Discuss what Bordo argues in the quotation, and whether you believe she is correct. Choose an ad from a magazine to support your case if you wish.

Students have many visceral reactions to Bordo's text, many of which oppose her readings of advertisements that students are familiar with. Many resist Bordo's readings because they identify ways in which unknowing consumers learn what it means to be embodied in our culture. They do not necessarily believe that they have been influenced in the ways Bordo describes. When we discuss Bordo, we usually begin here, with a listing and venting of reactions to her. I credit students for being active and critical readers at this point in the course, but I also caution that I am not certain that we are entirely doing justice to Bordo's arguments.

Once we have vented, it is time to "echo back" Bordo's arguments, to really listen to what she is saying rather than merely reacting to it. We discuss the article section by section, and students offer examples from their exercises to help us reconstruct and respond to Bordo's argument. I also ask students to bring in advertisements for this session, and we lay them out on the floor in the middle of our circle. As we discuss each section of Bordo's piece, we look on the floor for an ad that supports, refutes, or complicates what Bordo is saying. Students match quotes from Bordo with particular aspects of the ad they are studying. Often, other students use evidence from their sections of the piece to add to the conversation.

After this exercise, students are generally more fluent readers of Bordo's arguments, and they are often more generous readers of her as well.

DAY 4

Making connections: An in-class Ping-Pong game

Exercise 1.3 due: (1) *What evidence of Foucault's concept of surveillance appears in Bordo's essay? Choose 2–3 quotations from Bordo's essay and explain how they provide an example of Foucault's concept.*

(2) *What evidence does Bordo use to suggest a different or an expanded concept of how surveillance works and its limitations from the concept Foucault describes? Choose 2–3 quotations to support your argument.*

In this session, we begin to make connections between Bordo's and Foucault's texts. We are trying to figure out how, exactly, Bordo's text is in conversation with Foucault's. What has she learned or borrowed from him that informs her readings of contemporary culture? We play the "echo game" to help us decide. Students start with a quotation from Bordo; then they look for one in Foucault that somehow relates to Bordo's. (We begin with those they found when they did their exercises.) Once we have found one quotation from each text, we discuss in detail their relationships to each other. This gives us a chance to practice the close reading skills that will inform their work with evidence in the essay.

At the end of class, I ask students to write a test-run of the thesis paragraph of their essay. Here is what I ask them to do: "On the basis of your assessment of Bordo's debt to Foucault, write a paragraph in which you elaborate your own thesis about the implications of this debt. For example, does Bordo use Foucault's theory as her main lens, or way of seeing attitudes toward food and the body in contemporary culture? Do her examples make us see things that Foucault's theory does not account for or anticipate?"

Armed with evidence and a "dummy" first paragraph, the students are ready to compose their drafts.

DAY 5

First drafts: A writing workshop
(pink and yellow highlighters required for each student)

Assignment: see Writing Assignment above

ESSAY 1

Cover Letter (due with first version of your essay)

Write a letter, addressed to your readers, in which you answer the following questions and present any other concerns that you have. As with all letters you write in this course, this one should be typed and should be about a page long.

- What argument are you making about Bordo's relationship to Foucault? Please quote the thesis statement of your essay as you explain.

- What are the biggest problems you're having at this point in the writing process?

- What is your favorite part of your essay?

- What is the number one question about your essay that you would like your reader(s) to answer for you?

- What is your plan for revision?

For this class, two students arrive with enough copies to workshop with the entire class. The remaining students bring three copies each: one for me and one for each of their two readers, who write Readers' Letters for them to be delivered in the next class session.

In our workshop, each student highlights the following: quotations from Bordo (in yellow), quotations from Foucault (in pink). They then underline the sentences in which the writers discuss the relationships between the quotations. We discuss how the writer builds an argument based on analysis of the evidence as we workshop each piece.

If there is time, the writers highlight the copies of the two essays they will write Readers' Letters for (see below). It generally becomes clear during this workshop that the writers need more evidence to build their arguments and that they need to discuss that evidence in more detail if they are to persuade their readers of their interpretations of Bordo's debt to Foucault.

ESSAY 1

Readers' Letter (bring a copy for the instructor and the writer)

Revision literally means "seeing again." When experienced writers revise, they often radically alter their idea and reorganize the entire essay. By contrast, when inexperienced writers revise, they change a few words here or there but leave the essay essentially unaltered. Help your partners become experienced writers! They have several days to revise, so you can make comments that demand—and direct—a true revision. Try to make comments that you think will help the writer revise. (That said, please be respectful.)

Directions: As you carefully read and reread each essay, *draw a squiggly line* under the awkwardly expressed sentences and phrases whose meanings are unclear. Write *marginal notes* to the writer on anything that puzzles or interests you. After rereading, write a letter to the writers in which you answer these questions:

- In your own words, what is this paper about? (What's its *idea*?) Don't assume that the writer knows what his/her story is about. Mistrust the stated thesis (if there is one).

- Accept the writer's idea and try to extend the argument by providing additional examples, suggesting questions that provoke further thought, discussing parallels, and so on.

- Provide counterargument for the writer. If you did not accept this argument, what objections might you raise? Are there other interpretations possible? Provide one and discuss it briefly.

- In the cover letter, the writer has asked one or more questions. What answer do you have to offer?

- What is your favorite moment in this writer's essay?

DAY 6

Final Drafts

ESSAY 1

Self-evaluation Letter (due with final version of Essay 1)

This is the cover letter, addressed to me, that you should staple to the front of your revision. Each time you hand in a revision, you should attach such a self-evaluation letter. This time around, please answer the following questions and address any other concerns you have:

- What argument does this essay make?

- What do you like best about the essay overall? What specific parts work well?

- What were the two biggest problems for you in writing this essay? How did you address these problems?

- Discuss your use of evidence in your essay.

On a scale from 1 to 5, with 5 being high and 1 being low, how would you rate your final product? What's your reasoning for giving it this rating?

When students hand in the final copies of their essay, they submit the exercises, the draft (with cover letter attached), the Readers' Letters that they received, and the final essay, with a self-evaluation letter attached. After I respond to it, this collection becomes a piece in their final portfolios.

Ways of Reading Students' Ways of Writing: Imitations of Susan Griffin's Collage, "Our Secret"

Patricia Suzanne Sullivan

After we had spent quite a bit of class time reading, mapping, and discussing Susan Griffin's collage, "Our Secret," I asked the students in my first-year writing class to try their hand at the form, or as the assignment suggested, "to imitate it, to take it as a model . . . write a Griffin-like essay, one similar in its methods of organization and argument" (Bartholomae and Petrosky 348). We had read parts of Griffin's collage together and slowly, talking about how we saw connections between pieces. Students worked with the first "Question for a Second Reading" (Bartholomae and Petrosky 346–47) on their own, and then in groups in class. We covered two chalkboards with the result of all our efforts: lists of themes, elaborations on themes, the various sources Griffin uses, perspectives she offers, metaphors she employs, and visual representations of some of the connections we had made as readers (with lots of lines and arrows). Then they worked in small groups discussing their plans and materials (some more prospective than actually physically present in front of them). I circulated, fielding questions, asking questions.

Yet, at the end of the class, before they were to go home and write the first drafts of their collages, one student said, amidst the chatter of other students getting ready to leave, "So, then, anything goes, right?" I looked around at the chalkboards, densely packed with notes from our class discussions, and began to worry. Another student responded to the first student, "No, not anything goes, you can't just write a regular essay, you have to mess it all up, you have to confuse the reader, make it like a puzzle." "No, it's harder than that, you have to have different points of view and everything." "Well, it's not like you can do everything Griffin does, right? We only have a couple of pages and she had fifty something pages. So, Patricia, can we just pick one or two aspects of Griffin's essay and do it like that?" There is nothing like hearing students who have been participating in a thoughtful discussion about the complexities of Griffin's text, faced with the prospect of producing their own collages, suddenly reduce all that reading and writing work into one very pragmatic and seemingly doable suggestion: "You just write a regular essay and then break it up."

The assignments in *Ways of Reading* challenge many of the assumptions students make about reading and writing. As the introduction suggests, the writing and reading assignments are carefully worded to discourage students from doing exactly what my students were doing at the end of class, that is, oversimplifying the work before them:

> When we write assignments, our goal is to point students toward a project, to provide a frame for their reading, a motive for writing, a way of asking certain kinds of questions. In that sense, the assignments should not be read as a set of directions to be followed literally. In fact, they are written to resist that reading, to forestall a writer's desire to simplify, to be efficient, to settle for the first clear line toward the finish. We want to provide a context to suggest how readers and writers might take time, be thoughtful. And we want the projects students work on to become their own. (Bartholomae and Petrosky, "Introduction," 21)

Though several of my students were most likely trying to find "the first clear line toward the finish," it is also possible to see their comments otherwise, to see them as trying to use ways of writing they knew and with which they felt comfortable (e.g., the "essay") as the basis for leaping into completely new ways of writing (e.g., the "collage"): "You write an essay and then just break it up." An earlier assignment I had given to the same writing class had specifically and rather explicitly (at least in my teacherly eyes) cautioned students to be careful in their writing:

> Write an essay that focuses on a rich and illustrative incident from your own educational experience and read it (that is, interpret it) as Freire would. You will need to provide careful detail: things that were said and done, perhaps the exact wording of an assignment, a textbook, or a teacher's comments. And you will need to turn to the language of Freire's argument, to take key phrases and passages and see how they might be used to investigate your case.
>
> To do this you will need to read your account as not simply the story of you and your teacher, since Freire is not writing about individual personalities (an innocent student and a mean teacher, a rude teacher, or a thoughtless teacher) but about the roles we are cast in, whether we choose to be or not, by our culture and its institutions. . . . Use your example, in other words, as a way of testing and examining what Freire says, "particularly those passages that you find difficult or obscure." (Bartholomae and Petrosky 347)

Many, if not all, of my students had neglected some or the other key bit of advice embedded in the assignment's language: either they simply told the story of a teacher (sometimes evil, sometimes good) and a student (almost always good); or they managed to tell a complicated story from their educational past but tended to ignore Freire's text, avoiding, perhaps, the often more messy work they might produce in trying to figure out his difficult language and ideas. I mention this Freire assignment because it seems to me that if students get a sense that the assignment is asking them to do something different, it is also true that they don't know yet how to make those new and different moves. Instead, they find ways of making the complex assignments into things they know how to do, for example, compare and contrast their experience with Freire's ideas without really letting each affect the other, use their own experience to illustrate Freire, or attempt to hide their confusion or uncertainty by oversimplifying Freire. For many of my students, writing is still about showing what you know, not using writing to work out a response to a text.

I had tried to help students all semester (Griffin was the last assignment) as they revised their ways of reading and writing—took chances, faltered, resisted, forged ahead, fell back on old habits, tried out new approaches. The Griffin assignment which asked them to write a collage, however, seemed to send them a very clear message: one has got to do something very different, old ways of writing will not help (or at least that is how it might appear). What hadn't yet occurred to me at the time was that while my students would need to figure out new ways of writing, I as their teacher might need to figure out new ways of reading. Of course, as a graduate student in English studies, I had more experience and practice than my students with new and unconventional forms. But would this experience, along with Griffin as a model, be enough for me in reading students' texts? Would it be merely a matter of evaluating how well they had imitated Griffin's text, or would responsibly engaging with their writing require that like my students I too would have to develop my own project?

The first thing that became apparent to me when I received my stack of student collages was the difficulty students had in resisting the inexorable pull of familiar writing conventions. The Griffin assignment had by its very form taken what were originally writing goals to work toward and turned them into traps to be avoided. Even with all our preparation, I came to realize that those traps couldn't always be avoided, those familiar writing conventions were not always so easily dismissed. As I read some of the most "coherent" essays I had read all semester, my students' interpretations of the writing assignment echoed in my ears. One student wrote about her breakup with her boyfriend in the form of a linear narrative disrupted by descriptions of a roller coaster ride, clearly meant to be a metaphor for relationships. I imagined that all she had heard in the class discussion was the idea that you could write about what you wanted and then break it up a little. Another student's collage was so chaotic that I worked and worked to make connections and had finally given up. Had she decided that "anything goes," or that the whole idea had been to confuse the reader, to make the writing like a puzzle? And then there were some collages which had tried to find a balance, not too coherent, but not too confusing, moving toward the potential of a collage form, yet with traces of essay conventions in them. These were the kinds of collages I focused on in class discussions and the ones that I read here in order to highlight not only the ways in which students were and were not able to take on Griffin's project, but also the ways in which I struggled to learn how to read their attempts.

One of the first collages I read began with definitions of the words "racist" and "racism," and went on to discuss how difficult it is for people to talk about. As the collage never leaves the topic of racism, the opening clearly functions as an introduction. Another student collage by Cecilia Rodriguez, which focuses on the effect on the lives of Chileans under Pinochet, begins this way:

> Chilean Air Force Hawker Hunters fires 18 rockets straight into the 300-year-old presidential palace. By 2:45 p.m. there was total calm. President Allende was found dead at his desk, surrounded by the lifeless bodies of his 14 personal assistants.
>
> General Augusto Pinochet was at the head of this military coup. The General, assisted by the conservative right wing and the North American CIA, that considered Allende's left tendencies a threat to democracy, was able to organize the military and overthrow Allende's government. Despite scattered resistance, the left was crushed. Pinochet became president and the disappearances, tortures and assassinations began. Within 19 days of the coup 320 people were executed by the military, 13,500 were arrested and many were rounded up and tortured at Santiago's National Stadium. (Rodriguez 1)

Both students employ two familiar strategies of introductions: offering definitions as a way to introduce a topic ("racism") and providing necessary exposition (about Pinochet's military coup). As a class, we had discussed how Griffin's collage differed from more conventional essays, specifically in that it did not have what we usually thought of as an introduction, middle, and conclusion. Yes, we decided, it had an opening and an ending, and yes, there was movement (though not always linear) in the middle, but this was not the usual essay format. We had also discussed how the collage, as evidenced by Griffin's "Our Secret," had asked if not demanded that readers do more and different kinds of work than they were used to doing. Yet, here were some very clear "introductions" in my students' texts. Were they wary of asking their readers to do very much work or nervous about losing their readers? An important question about writing emerged: what might be the difference between an introduction and a beginning? Though we went on as a class to discuss opening moves for these student collages, when I think back now, I wonder about not just conventional introductions in terms of their effects on readers, but the role that conventions play in enabling (or disabling) the writing process: how does one start writing without an introduction? Could it be that the convention of an introduction actually helps writing begin, and if that is the case, then how does one decide where to begin when the requirements of the assignment seem to take away that enabling device? Or does one write an introduction in order to get started and then take it away later, or move it, replacing it with something more appropriate to the collage form — a story, an image, a text that works metaphorically? Here is an example of an opening from Bernadette Loftus's first draft that resists the conventional introduction (or puts it in the second slot?):

> As the corpse of the monstrous entity Chton sinks back into the lava whence it rose, you grip the Rune of Earth Magic tightly.
>
> Now that you have conquered the Dimension of the Doomed, Realm of Earth Magic, you are ready to complete your task. A Rune of magic power lies at the head of each haunted land of Quake. Go forth, seek the totality of the four Runes!
>
> I don't remember acknowledging or even caring much when I heard about the killings in Colorado. Violence in the news does not upset me much. Violence just kind of melds into other television programming. "What a shame," I remember saying. It was a shame. No one should have to die like that, especially kids. Monsters, I thought, tortured every day of their lives. They just couldn't take it anymore. (Loftus 1)

When we discussed this opening in class, some students thought the collage was going to be about computer or video games, and though they reported feeling a little disoriented, they said they had been curious to read on and see if they were right. When we discussed the next part — where Bernie relates her response to the news of the Columbine High School shootings in Colorado — students began debating. On the one hand, the thrill was gone for some students once they realized that the collage was most likely going to focus on the relationship between violent games and youth violence (a topic that had been much in the news at the time). On the other hand, some students argued that the predictability of the connection was mitigated by their surprise at reading about the writer's apparently indifferent attitude: "I don't remember acknowledging or even caring much . . ." Either way, my students recognized that Bernie had found a way to open her collage that was different from yet similar to Griffin's opening. Whereas Griffin had opened with a definition of a "nucleus," Bernie had chosen the discourse of a video game, *Quake*, to pull her reader in before going on to imitate Griffin's next move—the use of a personal narrative (for Griffin, an interview; for Bernie, a personal narrative showing her own reaction).

Through class discussion of the ways in which Bernie's and Griffin's openings had worked, students reconsidered how they had opened their own collages, seeing that for this new form an introduction might be undesirable. Yet, in looking back at Cecilia's "introduction" to her collage on Chile, I wonder now if advising Cecilia to take away her introduction and replace it with something else is a piece of advice more easily given than taken. One of the reasons that Bernie's opening seemed to succeed so well, according to my students, was because they recognized the passage as a video game (even if they were not familiar with *Quake*). Could Cecilia rely on her readers' knowing who Pinochet was or what happened in Chile in the same way that Griffin might be able to rely on her readers' familiarity with the Holocaust or in the same way that Bernie might be able to rely on her fellow students' ability to recognize a video game? I wonder now about how helpful some of my generic advice actually was to students when the subject of their collage might pose particular problems for them not answerable by suggesting that they review their notes on "Our Secret," or work harder to imitate Griffin's collage.

The attempts to not only imitate Griffin's moves but adapt them to the specificity of their own work is evident in all three of the collages I include here. For example, though Cecilia begins her collage with exposition, her next move employs Griffin's use of definition for a different effect:

> Within 19 days of the coup 320 people were executed by the military, 13,500 were arrested and many were rounded up and tortured at Santiago's National Stadium.
>
> *Fear: emotion caused by threat of some form of harm, sometimes manifested in bravado or symptoms of anxiety, and prompting a decision to fight the threat or escape from it. (Microsoft Encyclopedia '97).* (Rodriguez 1)

Later, after presenting an excerpt from a personal testimony of a man who watched his wife die as the result of a car bombing, Cecilia returns to the general idea of fear, this time invoking its physiological manifestation:

> It is a strange thing, living in permanent fear. Adrenaline is constantly pumping through your bloodstream. It makes your heart race, strengthens your muscle, raises your blood sugar, and boosts your sugar metabolism. This reaction is often called the "fight or flight" response; it prepares the body for strenuous activity. (Rodriguez 2)

If my class had decided that the scientific definitions and information (particularly of the cell) in Griffin's text could be read metaphorically, Cecilia's definitions instead seem to offer something different: a way for the reader—who ostensibly has felt fear or a fight or flight response at some point in his or her life—to connect to the specific cultural fear of people staying in Chile under Pinochet's rule.

Similarly, when I first read Tony Portis's collage on racism, I noticed how his collage as a whole imitated Griffin's "Our Secret" in that it provided multiple texts, sources, and perspectives: quotations from Malcolm X, job applications, movie reviews, Web sites, excerpts from newspapers and television news, examples drawn from his own experience, and so on. However, one way that Tony apparently makes Griffin's project his own is by inserting statements that look like inter-titles into his collage, which either name topics for parts of the collage—"Application and Workplace," "The Media," "Let's Go to the Movies," "Web Sites," "My Experience"—or comment on something just discussed or presented, "He Needed a Chance," "Don't Judge Me before You Know Me," "Why Do We Continue to Kill over Color?" "Give Me a Break" (Portis 2–8). Are these titles an instance of revising Griffin's work or another instance of the conventions of the essay emerging to prevent the different work of the collage as a form? The inter-titles seem to have at least two effects: first, as transitions, they work against imitating the kind of abrupt shifts evidenced in Griffin's text; second, the titles seem to be another example of my students' reluctance to risk losing their reader or their reluctance to risk being misunderstood. Moreover, I began to see these titles and their accompanying texts as creating mini-essays: a mini-essay on racism in the news media, a mini-essay on racism in the movies, a mini-essay on racism in sports, and so on. In a section titled *"Trading Places,* Eddie Murphy," Tony describes how difficult it was for football player Jason Shorn to play cornerback for the New York Giants since all the cornerbacks in the NFL were black at the time. Tony concludes this section with the inter-title: "He Needed a Chance," titles the next piece of his collage, "Shoe on the Other Foot," and describes playing basketball with his friends in the park:

> When we play basketball in the summer at Mellon Park and there are a
> couple of white guys wanting to play, we pick them up to show them we just
> want to play basketball. I have a few friends that might say it's us four and
> "white boy." I say to them, "Hey, he has a name; all you have to do is ask him."
> Just think, if the shoe was on the other foot--if it were four whites and the
> "nigger" you would be ready to fight. (Portis 4)

Similarly, in a section titled *"Let's go to the movies!"* Tony describes the controversy about the ways in which the character Jar Jar Binks in *Star Wars* is considered a racial stereotype. Immediately following this, in the next section titled "The Good," Tony offers an example of a movie, *Rosewood,* that shows "how racism is defeated by people of color coming together as one" (Portis 5). Though there is certainly a kind of collage created by all these mini-essays, and if Tony had adopted Griffin's ways of working with juxtapositions, Tony's collage lacks the kinds of associative connections present in Griffin's collage. If it doesn't seem to challenge a reader to read and think across parts (since related parts were so often adjacent to one another), could it be that Tony's collage achieves some other effect?

In fact, most of my students had clearly found this work of making associative connections, or asking a reader to think analogically across pieces, the most difficult work. Their collages were often very focused on a specific issue, or a set of clearly related issues. Surely, this was a missed opportunity and something I encouraged them to explore as part of their revision work, but was this absence of associative connections to be considered a failure? Or could it be that their collages were doing other things, going for other effects in an attempt to make Griffin's project their own?

To return to Tony's collage on racism, it had many of the markers of a conventional argumentative essay: an introduction which defined its terms, set forth the problem — "there's something about racism that puts people in denial, and they just don't want to deal with it" (Portis 1) — and a conclusion which acknowledged that racism "is one problem that just won't go away. People of today have to realize it is here and we have to deal with it" (Portis 8). In the end, Tony offers a list of suggestions about how to deal with it, including not prejudging and being respectful of others. One way my students had read Griffin — one path they had taken through her text — was to see her text as making an argument about the necessity of realizing we are all connected. With this in mind, many students thought that the collage form had allowed her to explore and represent the complex and often subtle nature of those interconnections. By providing a varied and critical mass of instances, perspectives, sources, and texts, Tony's collage realizes its argument by disallowing his reader's attempt to deny racism. There is a very real sense of immersion when reading his text, an immersion which challenges the reader to "deal with it," to look directly at instances of racism, rather than think about it as an abstract problem.

Similarly, when my class was discussing Bernie's collage on youth violence, one of my students asked whether or not Bernie's collage was making an argument or had an organizing theme or themes. The collage includes references to a video game, reactions to Columbine from the Internet, statistics, descriptions of the formation of two different planets (Earth and Venus), as well as Bernie's commentaries and personal narratives. All of the perspectives presented are those of teenagers and young adults, describing how ostracized, frustrated, and angry they felt during high school. If discussions in the media had seemed to ask how kids could suddenly murder other kids, Bernie's commentary has a way of putting her reader at ground zero, reminding us that while it might seem that kids just lose it (out of nowhere), in actuality, their actions are often the result of a long struggle:

> For many people school was a breeding ground for pain. Day in and day out, being tortured by peers while other students and administrators turned their back. How much can one person stand before crumbling, before wanting the world to end? It seems you have two choices: you can leave or they can.
>
> But what makes people choose the lives they choose? Hundreds of kids, *millions*, grow up in America tortured. Why do some of them go on rampages . . . Luke Woodham, 16, Pear, Mississippi, 10-1-97 2 students killed, 7 wounded, *Mother stabbed to death*
> and how do those who don't prevent themselves acting out their anger and pain? (Loftus 2)

It seems that the statistic here literally interrupts Bernie's thoughts because it interrupts her syntax, or that the statistic is offered as evidence to support the preceding phrase "go on rampages." Yet, it can also seem that Bernie's question surrounds the statistic, asking us to think not just about the kids who become statistics but about the many other kids who don't resort to murder, who are able to "prevent themselves [from] acting out their anger and pain."

If Bernie's text tries to defend troubled adolescents (or at least generate some compassion), there are also attacks on the adults whose attempts to help or handle troubled teenagers prove inadequate. For example, Bernie includes a long Internet testimony from "Dan in Boise, Idaho," in which he relates how his school advisor suggested students write about their feelings about what happened in Colorado. However, when Dan wrote an article for the school newspaper, arguing that it was wrong to blame "screwed up kids or the Net," and that perhaps it was the system that was to blame and that he felt sympathy for the boys who had done the shooting, his article was "killed" and he was sent home with a letter to his parents:

> So this is how they are trying to figure out what happened in Colorado, I
> guess. By blaming a sub-culture and not thinking about their own roles, about
> how fucked-up school is. Now, I think the whole thing was a set-up, cause a
> couple of other kids are being questioned too, about what they wrote. They
> pretend to want to have a "dialogue," but kids should be warned that what they
> really want to know is who's dangerous to them. (Loftus 4)

Bernie follows this with another statistic and with two pieces: in the first one (since this paragraph is in italics, it's not clear whether it is a quote or Bernie's writing), she wonders if Columbine had an effect on the "microculture of our own household"; in the second one, she recounts a recent conversation with her father about Columbine:

> But how many of us actually did anything differently? Spent more time
> with our children, or someone else's? Came home a little earlier? Skipped a
> meeting? Turned off the TV? Called other parents, called a teacher, volunteered
> to help with some after school activity--Girl Scouts, theater, baseball--that will
> happen only if enough grown ups show up?
>
> I sent my father three articles from the other side. He called me up to tell
> me he refuses to read them; he has made up his mind about the situation. I told
> him I understand these kids. I play *Quake*. I was tortured by others for being
> different. "Did you ever want to hurt them?" he asked. "Sure," I said, "all the
> time. But I knew better." "Oh, Bernie . . ." he said, his voice heavy with the tone
> of devastating disappointment. I could almost see him walk away from me like
> some leprous being. Has he forgotten? Have fifty-four years washed away the
> pain of adolescence? (Loftus 4–5)

The story Bernie tells here emphasizes the generation gap and the difficulty that adults and adolescents have talking with one another—the misunderstandings, the fear, the mutual suspicion, the "refusal" to read or listen, the mutual disappointments. But it is the language she uses to open this section which is perhaps most telling and which led my class into a discussion about what perspectives were present and not present in her collage. She writes, "I sent my father three articles *from the other side*" (emphasis mine). What we have here, she seems to be saying, is a matter of sides, one against the other, with a lot of space or static in between. Because at the time of the class discussion, I was still caught up in trying to respond to my students' texts in terms of how well they had imitated Griffin's project, I asked them (rather leadingly, I have to admit) if Bernie's collage needed more and different perspectives, for example, texts which quoted what the media was actually saying about the connections between video games and violence, or more texts which let the adults — teachers, administrators, parents — speak. My students were adamant: absolutely not. They argued that those perspectives were already implied by the texts Bernie had chosen as responses and that adding more texts would detract from the forcefulness of the material she had already chosen. I kept pushing, asking them to consider to what good uses multiple perspectives had been put in Griffin's "Our Secret," but to no avail. Apparently there was something more at stake here than students' reluctance to do the work of revision.

In my comments on her collage and in conversation with her, I encouraged Bernie to at least experiment with including other perspectives. It would make for a tidy story if I could report here that she acted on my advice, but she didn't. My motives for pushing her seem now rather tangled. I still value the work of revision, particularly exploratory revision. In retrospect, though, I wonder if I hadn't been clinging too much to Griffin's text as a model. To some degree, I felt that Bernie's collage had failed by not imitating more of Griffin's moves. I also felt that I had failed her as a teacher by not convincing her to try to do this work. Yet, both she and the class had made strong arguments for excluding those other texts and for respecting the project of the collage form as Bernie had realized it. Perhaps the mistake I had made was in holding on too tightly to the importance of students' taking on Griffin's project. And perhaps this looks like a slight mistake, a mere matter of emphasis. Yet, I am beginning to think that shifting one's emphasis might make the difference when trying to get students to take chances and write in new and different ways. Faced with a similar situation in the future, I would want to try to give more precedence to the student's writing, to be able to say, "Let me show how I see your text as different from Griffin's, and let's talk about how you might use some of her moves, adapt her moves, or create new moves in order to develop *your own project*."

When my students tried their hand at this new kind of writing, they sometimes fell back on old ways of writing. I, too, sometimes fell back on typical ways of reading which prevented me from seeing the nature of the difficulties they were having, or even the nature of their successes. The key for me is to make my ways of reading part of the classroom discussion. I don't mean to suggest that I make my problems their problems, but that as readers and writers trying to figure out a new form, it is important to acknowledge our shared obstacles and our shared achievements. If I wanted my students to "forestall a writer's desire to simplify, to be efficient, to settle for the first clear line toward the finish" (Bartholomae and Petrosky, "Introduction," 21), then I, too, had to move beyond the kinds of readings of student work which merely compared them to Griffin and evaluated the ways in which their texts measured up or failed to measure up. I had to resist my impulse to write quick remarks on their papers like "replace that introduction with a more collage-like fragment," "cut your transitions," "provide more perspectives." In the context of my own project as a teacher, those kinds of comments represent the easier work. The harder work for me is to take the time to be thoughtful, to be able to recognize when students need help revising their ideas about reading and writing, and when they are not necessarily failing but coming into their projects.

WORKS CITED

Bartholomae, David, and Anthony Petrosky. *Ways of Reading*. 5th edition. Boston: Bedford/St. Martin's, 1999.

Loftus, Bernadette. "Jocks Are from Earth, Oddballs Are from Venus." Unpublished, University of Pittsburgh, 1999.

Portis, Anthony. "Racism." Unpublished, University of Pittsburgh, 1999.

Rodriguez, Cecilia. "Truth and Reconciliation." Unpublished, University of Pittsburgh, 1999.

All student papers are used with permission of their authors, to whom I am very grateful.

I would also like to thank Keely Bowers, Juli Parrish, and Mari Pena-Jordan, who talked with me about my students' papers, or read drafts of my writing, or sometimes did both.

• • • • • ──────────────────────────────────────

The Retrospective Essay: "Making Progress" in a Writing Class

Steve Sutherland

> A Klee painting named "Angelus Novus" shows an angel looking as though he is about to move away from something he is fixedly contemplating. His eyes are staring, his mouth is open, his wings are spread. This is how one pictures the angel of history. His face is turned toward the past.
>
> —Walter Benjamin
> "Theses on the Philosophy of History, IX"

Halfway through the reading and writing course I teach at the University of Pittsburgh, and again at the end of it, I ask students to write a retrospective paper in which they look back upon the work that they've done in my class in order to "look for key moments and points of transition, for things that have changed and things that have remained the same" in their writing.[1] These two assignments could be said to stand as markers of "progress" or "development" in the class, as moments when students are afforded the opportunity to think about how their writing has changed and about how they have changed as student readers and writers. In other words, the opportunity for an act of retrospection aims at enabling my General Writing class to "see" change by constructing narratives about what has happened in the course.

In a memo to graduate students teaching at Pitt, Jean Ferguson Carr offers the following rationale for this act of retrospection: "The final retrospective assignment should direct your students to some significant rethinking of their practices and positions as readers and writers, as they have been influenced by this course, by your comments and classroom work, by their classmates, and by the texts they have read and the papers they have written. . . . This is a difficult assignment for your students, coming at a difficult time. It can be, however, a very important experience for them and a very telling assignment for you to evaluate." At first glance, the retrospective assignments might seem to offer tidy, historical evaluations of the course, mini-chronicles of what happened and failed to happen. Yet the histories that students write are "very telling" in other ways, since they are indeed functions of what Carr calls a "difficult time." This essay is about how teachers and students work within and against the constraints of that "difficult time." It's about the difficulty of writing in/about time.

Very often, the pedagogical gesture of asking students to write a midterm and final retrospective essay reinforces their sense of the course as an unfolding history of progress, a story about a time of growth. For example, many of their retrospective narratives are structured by notions of causality ("This occurred, and it then caused that to happen") that allow students to see a chain of influence running through their successive papers. The retrospective essays are almost always chronologically structured, so that successive moments of insight serve to reinforce a linear progression toward a conclusion in which the

─────────────────────────

[1] This essay refers to previous editions of *Ways of Reading*.

student frequently claims to have reached a kind of educational utopia. There is, I think, a sense in which the rhetorical demand of asking students to write these essays can often reinforce rather than challenge unproblematic accounts of history and of what it means to *become* educated. This is because the retrospective papers that my students write frequently participate in broader cultural narratives about change and progress.

For a moment, I'd like to problematize the popular notion of "course as narrative of progress" by entertaining a somewhat absurd notion of "course as Zeno's stadium." Zeno of Elea proposed the well-known "stadium paradox." Here is his scenario: If someone were to walk from one end of a stadium to another, it would be impossible to arrive at the other end. This is because the person would have to pass through an infinite number of points: halfway, quarter-way, and so forth, *ad infinitum*. Since it is impossible to pass through an infinite number of points in a finite period of time, it would be impossible to reach the end of the stadium or even to get to a halfway point. So much for end of term and midterm.

Since Zeno's account precludes any kind of change or movement, it seems necessary to refute his argument, not only because he is violating "common sense" in general but, more important, because his position calls into question some "commonsense" notions about teaching. Plato finds a way out by positing two worlds: one of unchanging, ideal forms, and another of change and illusion. This is a familiar Platonic position, which insists that the world of change (of "becoming") is only a reflection of a more substantial, unchanging world of "being." The argument allows Plato to account for change while still preserving an essentialist notion of an unchanging reality. According to his model, change is merely something that appears to be the case, an illusion. This illusory world is, for Plato, precisely what education should not be asking students to look at. In the *Republic* he writes, "Education then is the art of . . . this turning around, the knowledge of how the soul can most easily and effectively be turned around" in order to apprehend permanence in the world of forms (171). When Plato's students are asked to "look back," they look away from change and toward permanence—that is, in the opposite direction to my students. In fact, the whole of the *Republic* might be understood as an attempt to "look at" a utopian model "laid up in heaven" (238). Plato's moment of turning and looking (his retrospective act) fails to see change. And, I'd like to argue, this particular way of looking has pedagogical and political consequences, since it is a predictable prerequisite for establishing the kind of republic Plato desires: one that is free of change and conflict.

Although it's clear that Plato's notion of change is substantially different from that of Zeno, both arguments manage to turn change into an illusion. This way of accounting for change is of considerable importance because it allows the narrative to construct utopian spaces (like Plato's *Republic*) that are free of contradiction. Utopian fiction, for example, frequently offers mystical or unreliable accounts of the historical changes that brought utopia into existence. A kind of forgetfulness often frames utopian narratives. Since utopias are almost always narrated retrospectively (e.g., More's *Utopia* or Bellamy's *Looking Backward*), one might say that an unwillingness to engage with history can all too easily produce utopia.

I want to argue that a similar construction of change is often at work in my reading/writing class, both in discussions and in student papers, and that this construction of change frequently allows students to imagine an educational model that is free of complication, unproblematic, and utopian. I'll focus first on class discussions and then on student essays. During the course of the semester, students (most are in their first year of study) read five selected texts from Bartholomae and Petrosky's *Ways of Reading*, an anthology of essays for student writers. Each week, they write a paper (about five pages in length) in response to an assigned question on a particular text. These weekly assignments are sequenced and inter-related, asking students to consider among other things, the ways in which they are enacting a particular "reading/rereading" of each text. Our class discussions center on sample student papers, which I select and distribute ahead of time. I do not choose the "best" or the "weak-est" essays, neither models for imitation nor pitfalls to avoid. Instead, the samples are papers that I believe will lead the class into a productive discussion, perhaps papers that enact or raise issues that seem to crop up in many essays. I sometimes choose papers that might seem provocative, problematic, even absurdly Zenoesque. We then talk about these essays as a way of investigating student writing, and also as a way of thinking about how students are reading the assigned texts in the anthology. Two of these assigned pieces, Adrienne Rich's "When We Dead Awaken: Writing as Re-Vision" and Harriet Jacobs's "Incidents in the Life of a Slave Girl," regularly provoke conversations that can lead to important insight into the ways in which students discuss change.

Jacobs's text, an excerpted slave narrative written in order to further the abolitionist cause, is accompanied by a second-reading question which asks students, "What is Jacobs doing in this text? What might her work as a writer have to do with her position (as a female slave) in relation to the world of her readers?" (p. 390). The first writing assignment asks students to "consider the ways she [Jacobs] works on her reader . . . and also the ways she works on her material," emphasizing that students "will need to reread the text as some-thing constructed" (p. 391). In our class discussions, students usually see Jacobs's narrative not as a constructed account but rather as a kind of window into her life, one that allows her to "show" her story "just as it is." Students often use optical words (like "reveals") to describe Jacobs's work; they seldom use words like "selects" or "organizes." In this way, Jacobs's story is frequently seen as an accurate display of the truth, and as an autobiogra-phy that is *inevitable* in the sense that it is dictated solely by Jacobs's real life rather than by her choices as a writer. What students frequently do not see is precisely what the question asks them to see, namely, that Jacobs is a writer at work, constructing a text, making deci-sions, making changes to her material. What seldom gets discussed is the fact that Jacobs's narrative is not identical to her life; neither is it propelled by her life in an automatic or a deterministic manner.

Getting students to think about Jacobs's work as a writer might be done in various ways, but I think an effective method would probably entail managing a discussion about how Jacobs looks back on her life in a retrospective gesture that allows her to work with her ma-terial by selecting, emphasizing, ordering, or otherwise changing it. If we imagine Jacobs looking back, our account of her work can move beyond seeing only inevitability, and to-ward a recognition of how her narrative gets changed in the very act of writing it. Such a move can help students to acknowledge the critical choices that Jacobs makes. It's a move toward a nondeterministic/nonautomatic account of the text's production, toward seeing Jacobs as a writer who is both self-aware and aware of her choices. In this way, the absent moment, Jacobs's retrospective gesture in which changes are made, can be made present.

A similar discussion is often prompted by the two assignments on Adrienne Rich's essay, a piece about the changes she sees as she looks at a brief history of her poetry. This time, the first writing assignment asks students to choose a poem by Rich and to consider "the poem as an act of 'renaming'" by asking, "What is transformed into what? and to what end?" (p. 540). The second assignment (drawn from a previous edition) extends the first, asking students to "take three of the poems Rich offers as examples of change in her writing . . . and use them as a way of talking about revision." Both of these questions explicitly ask students to talk about "change" or "transformation." Nevertheless, the notion of change frequently disappears from our class discussions. Students are able to offer intelligent insight into the "meaning" of Rich's poetry or passionate opinions on her homosexuality. However, they seldom talk about change. When they do, they describe an almost self-evident development in Rich's poetry. A common way of accounting for the changes they see is to imagine change that takes place *between* the poems, in a chronology that exists prior to Rich's actual writing of the essay. While this account is undoubtedly somewhat accurate, it fails to account for the revision that gets enacted by Rich's essay itself.

In order to problematize this particular construction of "change," I ask students to construct a narrative of what they think Rich actually does as a writer. They respond by saying that she writes a poem, notices that it is somehow insufficient, then writes another poem that tries to solve the problems of the earlier poem. Subsequently, Rich sees the second poem as insufficient, and she goes on to make up for its inadequacies in the third poem, and so forth. This narrative, although addressing the issue of change, locates change outside (prior to) Rich's act of writing her essay. It thus offers only one, chronologically based understanding of what our class might mean by "re-vision."

Adrienne Rich's piece reminds us that "re-vision" is an act of "looking back." I want to argue that this act, this retrospective moment, which so often disappears in our discussions of Jacobs, partially disappears in our discussions about Rich. Students frequently do not examine the absent moment in which Rich looks back on her work with a gaze that selects, connects, exaggerates, or otherwise changes her material in the very act of writing about change. My role in the discussions about Jacobs and Rich is to recuperate the moment of change, to try turning students' attention toward the retrospective gestures that could otherwise manage to disappear. In this way, I hope to provoke a conversation about how Rich and Jacobs *use* chronology, about how they construct histories, and to move beyond a discussion that views chronology only as a self-evident determinant of the texts we read.

The same might be said of the texts we write. Of course, many of the texts we read are essays written by students in the class. Our discussion of these essays is intended to get students to think about how their writing both enacts and produces a particular reading. To a large extent, then, our class is about how acts of reading and writing are connected.

When students sit down to write their retrospective assignments, they occupy what I have called the moment of constructing change, of looking backward, the same moment they learned to identify as readers. The two retrospectives ask students to "review the work you've done . . . and describe what you see. . . . You might look . . . at what stands as evidence of your efforts and achievements as a writer." As students respond to these questions, they confront rhetorical tasks similar to those undertaken by Rich and Jacobs. Students, too, have to look back on the past and construct a text that accounts for changes. They, too, are writing history; and they are rereading the readings they produced in their essays. This affords them the opportunity to enact some of what they have learned in our class discussions.

However, what frequently happens at these moments is that students again ignore what they did not initially see in our discussions of Rich and Jacobs, namely, that writers of history do not merely report, but also construct their narratives. When we talk about the retrospective papers, then, I try to get student writers to push against conventional accounts of change driven by narratives of inevitability. I remind them of the work we performed as readers of Jacobs and Rich. In short, I try to get my students to produce writing that enacts a critically self-conscious retrospection rather than utopian narratives that either banish change completely or effectively neutralize the possibility of writing a critical account of change.

Sometimes students write utopian accounts—papers that, in looking backward, turn away from change and toward closure, permanence, the end of history. At the end of my first semester teaching at Pitt, I received final retrospectives that constructed change in this way. The conclusion of Amy's paper is an appropriate example of what I've called utopian closure. She writes, "Now at the end of the term, I feel confident that I have completed the wishes of Bartholomae and Petrosky and have proved myself as an open-minded and honest writer. I see myself as a well-rounded reader with the intelligence of knowing that there are many other ways of reading, seeing, thinking, and writing." In Amy's account, the work of the course is completely over, the agenda fulfilled, the goals achieved. It's almost as if Amy's paper functions as a kind of testimony that bears witness: "I have proved myself."

This is how she describes her essay in her opening paragraph: "While I was gathering ideas for a retrospective paper I had a feeling that this paper could be considered as a confession. What I have done on the following pages was to confess to my professor what I feel I have accomplished in his class." The purpose of Amy's confession is, in part at least, to claim that she has "satisfied the desires of Bartholomae and Petrosky" in what she calls "an effort to achieve the praise of B[artholomae] + P[etrosky] and to have the satisfaction for myself." I want to point out that her paper is an astute reading of the pedagogical scene in which she finds herself. Having been asked to write about how her work has changed in the course, she reads the assignment as a request for testimony, a chance to prove to the teacher that she has performed all of the requirements. In this act of writing, though, the retrospective gesture glosses over contradictions and complexities. She does not, for example, "read against" what she sees as the "desires of Bartholomae and Petrosky," even though she describes herself as a student who is becoming a "strong and critical reader."

Rather than a precise demonstration of the changes she identifies, Amy's paper offers only a claim: "I have changed." Her essay draws on broader cultural narratives about education as an almost total transformation of the student. As such, it constructs a conversion narrative—not necessarily because Amy feels that she has converted to the course's agenda, but because she feels that this is what she is required to say.

Felicia and Damian also employ narratives of change that are relatively predictable and unproblematic. Their papers offer accounts of developmental progress that are as inevitable as organic growth. Felicia's retrospective is called "Stages," and it employs the following model as a way of talking about the changes she sees in her writing: "Just as humans go through these different stages, I strongly believe as a writer that I have encountered these stages but in a different manner. First, there is the baby stage. . . ." Felicia then goes on to talk about the "teenage stage" and the "young adult stage," comparing teenage rebelliousness with a kind of rebellion in her writing. She reinforces this developmental metaphor, but also adds a more sophisticated reading of it in her conclusion:

> One semester can't transform my way of thinking. This can be compared
> to being raised; once your parents have told you to behave in a certain manner,
> if all of a sudden others tell you differently, it will take you a while to adjust to
> what they tell you. I believe that I have adjusted dramatically from the begin-
> ning of the semester, but I believe it will not stay.

While I admire both Felicia's fairly elaborate deployment of the "growing up" metaphor and her resistance to the utopian closure that operates in Amy's paper, I cannot help thinking that her account of change limits her ability to reflect critically on the work she has done in my class. Her narrative presents change as a matter of growing up, but she fails to problematize her metaphor by seeing its limitations or by acknowledging that the "stages" she relies upon are also socially constructed, culturally specific stages rather than phases that are chronologically inevitable. I think her metaphor disallows a critically useful construction of change because it locates change within the familiar, predictable, sequential framework of "growing up." For example, her metaphor prevents her from recognizing that she is at work in her retrospective, seeing developments or noting significant moments while she is engaged in the very act of looking backward.

Damian's paper also accounts for change, but he uses a similarly limiting metaphor, that of swimming. Looking back on his work, Damian writes, "I see this [his early work] as being shallow, but I had to start somewhere. After all, when one goes swimming at the beach, one starts off in the shallow water. It is not possible to start in the middle of everything." Perhaps Damian's swimming metaphor is suggested by the adjective "shallow," which he uses initially in a figurative sense and then employs literally in his description of wading into the water. I had hoped Damian's paper would enact an awareness of this particular move he makes as a writer, that it would trouble this metaphor of education as wading into water. It would be interesting, for example, to see a revision of Damian's paper in which he replaces the more progressive action of wading into the ocean with a less sequential metaphor like getting thrown in the deep end, or diving into water. It might certainly be argued that students begin their work in my class *in medias res*: the first text we read is Adrienne Rich's essay, which is not shallow by any means. How, then, might Damian account for change within less sequential narratives? This is the kind of question he does not pose.

My reading of retrospective essays like Damian's, Felicia's, and Amy's led me to conclude that the work of recuperating the retrospective moment—making it more explicit—does not necessarily result in students' ability to construct powerful or critical accounts of change when they write. Strong student readers who learn to identify the kind of work undertaken by Rich and Jacobs do not automatically become more aware of the work they are performing when they write retrospectives themselves. I had hoped to see students move away from narratives of utopian closure or from unproblematic accounts of educational "progress" and change toward constructions of change as problematic, constructions that might allow them to think about their work and their education in ways that are more critical, more self-aware.

In my second semester, I taught the same sequence of writing/reading assignments. This time I wanted to forestall utopian retrospectives by prompting my class to think about change and education from the beginning of the semester. My course description centered on a student's retrospective essay from the previous semester, which I asked the new students to read closely as a way of examining how a former student had accounted for my class and for the changes he and his work had undergone. I wanted them to see that change could be described in various ways, as something to be welcomed and also as something to be resisted.

At the end of that semester, I read the new set of retrospective essays with keen attention. All of them resisted utopian closure; all of them refused to engage in conversion narratives. Does this represent a success? I'm not sure if this change is because students now feel that they simply ought not to write such narratives, or because they are indeed able to see that such accounts do not allow for a complex assessment of what they've learned. Many of these papers still employ models of change as inevitable progress or growth. Laurie, for example, describes herself as "fifteen weeks old" at the end of a semester in my class. Her account echoes Felicia's paper; moreover, it assumes that a student entering my class is *tabula rasa*, or a newborn baby. I am troubled by this attitude, which strikes me as overly and uncritically forgetful.

As I come to the end of this my own retrospective paper, I feel perhaps the same as my students do: in need of utopian closure. How can I end with a story that might account for the ways in which my work works?

The most successful retrospective paper I received in the second semester was Steve's. What I admire most about his essay is that it troubles its own sense of accomplishment and questions the narrative of progress that it presents. It also problematizes and calls in question some of the pedagogical work I have described in this paper.

Steve begins his search for change in the following way: "I wondered how my writing might have improved . . . so a comparison between papers written before midterm and later essays seemed to be a good way to see if anything had changed. I wasn't sure what to look for." Using the midterm point as a marker, he constructs a careful discussion, which leads him to the conclusion that his earlier papers simply took for granted the kinds of implications that his words have. He explains: "In earlier essays I noticed I was using words . . . without any hint that they have many different contexts. I used them as easily as if I were talking to myself." He sees his later work as being more aware of the implications involved in using certain words. But then his retrospective takes an unusual turn, which I would like to quote at length:

> So there it is . . . I can now write about "writing." I once was lost but now I'm found . . . Halleluia, I've seen the light. All is fine with the world, right? Well, I'm not sure I'd go that far. I could just savor the important things I learned about writing, but I find myself with a sense of uncertainty about what happens next.
>
> I looked back at my writing, and as I said, my later essays said a lot more about the ways in which the texts were written. I felt my Wideman essays [the last in the sequence] were the best ones, but why then did I feel as I had once

again missed something? Was I simply operating in the "General Writing frame of reference"?

I looked again at my [John Edgar] Wideman papers . . . the author's use of language, frame of reference, and other aspects that we discussed throughout the term are important for understanding him, but just how much consideration do they deserve in the scope of the overall work and its moral implications in the "real" world? I made statements like "in Wideman, we have no such simple judgment," and "we have to face disturbing questions." Earlier in the semester I would have made a judgment or dealt with those questions, not just pointed out that Wideman presents them to us with some technique. I guess that in the "General Writing frame" this is progress, but I'm not sure about the "responsibility frame." Maybe the earlier papers were the better ones. So, you see my dilemma? Here I am with a collection of texts [by Rich, Jacobs, Berger, Tompkins, and Wideman] about oppression, slavery, morality, and racial injustice, and I'm spending more time discussing the language of the author than I am the issues that he or she has made it a point to write about. An increasing amount of my time has been spent writing about "writing." I'm just not sure this is progress. I don't know what the proper balance between ethics and semantics should be. Maybe that's what I missed.

In Steve's account, a definition of "progress" is itself context-bound, not to be taken for granted. He locates his definition first in the "General Writing frame" and then in what he calls the "responsibility frame." For him, the former represents a gain, and the latter involves a very troubling loss—troubling because it questions the "proper balance between ethics and semantics." I find this formulation of change provocative and insightful, and its attendant critique of the educational process in my class presents an important challenge to much of what I have argued in this paper. Perhaps the course, in insisting on its own frame (what Steve calls "writing about writing" rather than writing about the "real" world), ends up "talking to itself"? I'm not sure. I know that I could respond to Steve's paper by asking him to challenge his division between "ethics and semantics" by examining, for example, how these two categories are intertwined. This might also produce a different reading of his distinction between the "General Writing frame" and the "responsibility frame." After all, knowing how words are put together—how they mean—is precisely what enables us to make the kind of moral judgment that Steve wishes to make.

Because retrospectives like Steve's are produced at the end of term, at that "difficult time" in which students are asked to reconstruct the fifteen-week time period of the course, they have a tendency to escape the kind of thoughtful revision that is so central to my reading/writing class. When I began my second year of teaching at Pitt, facing a new set of students, Steve, Amy, and the others were not there to respond to my comments and questions about their papers. We were unable to "go back" and rework what had been done. I think students know this, and I think their knowing it reinforces their desire to write "end of history" essays. My concern is to seek and imagine ways of turning this desire into a self-reflexive and critical account of history that brings a retrospective understanding back into the work of the course—making it present rather than invisible.

When I present my syllabus to the next reading/writing class I teach, I hope to direct the new group back to the "very telling" retrospectives of my former students. I would like these narratives to help situate our work on a continuum of constant and repeated retrospection, to build an awareness of a course history that is already well under way. What might begin to emerge is a more self-conscious understanding of the ways in which we (students and teachers) work within and against very powerful notions of what it means to make educational progress.

I may well use Steve's piece in my next course description. In this way, his project will continue, not as the utopian end of history or the fullness of time, but as an involvement in ongoing critical, educational work. As in the story of Walter Benjamin's "angel of history," there is no utopian space that is exempt from criticism and change, or from the often thwarted desire not only to look backward, but also to use retrospection in order to think critically about how "progress" gets made.

> The angel would like to stay, awaken the dead, and make whole what has been smashed. But a storm is blowing from Paradise. . . . This storm irresistibly propels him into the future to which his back is turned, while the pile of debris before him grows skyward. This storm is what we call progress.

WORKS CITED

Bartholomae, David, and Anthony Petrosky. *Ways of Reading*. 4th ed. Boston: Bedford/St. Martin's, 1996.

Benjamin, Walter. "Theses on the Philosophy of History, IX" in *Illuminations*. Ed. Hannah Arendt. Trans. Harry Zohn. New York: Schocken Books, 1969. 257–58.

Bloom, Damian. Retrospective Essay. Unpublished, University of Pittsburgh, 1990.

Carr, Jean Ferguson. Memo on Final Retrospective Assignment 11/23/1990, University of Pittsburgh.

Gray, Felicia. "Stages." Unpublished, University of Pittsburgh, 1990.

Nicotra, Amy. "Confessions." Unpublished, University of Pittsburgh, 1990.

Plato. *Republic*. Trans. G. M. A. Grube. Indianapolis: Hackett, 1974.

Rich, Adrienne. "When We Dead Awaken: Writing as Re-Vision" in *Ways of Reading*. 549–62.

Sheaffer, Steven. "Looking Backward, Seeing Ahead." Unpublished, University of Pittsburgh, 1991.

All student papers are used with permission of their authors, to whom I am grateful.

I would like to thank Jean Ferguson Carr and Barbara McCarthy, who provided the retrospective assignment that I have cited in this essay.

I am also grateful to Phil Smith, Joe Harris, Paul Kameen, Mariolina Salvatori, and Dave Bartholomae, who gave me valuable suggestions as I worked on this paper.

Stories as Movable Definitions:
Narrating Queer Pedagogies

Stacey Waite

> By the risks of its writing, personal criticism embodies a pact . . . binding writer to reader in the fabulation of self-truth, that what is at stake matters also to others: somewhere in the self-fiction of the personal voice is the belief that the writing is worth the risk. In this sense, by turning its authorial voice into spectacle, personal writing theorizes the stakes of its own performance. . . . Personal writing opens an inquiry on the cost of writing—critical writing or Theory—and its effects.
>
> —Nancy K. Miller
> *Getting Personal: Feminist Occasions*
> *and Other Autobiographical Acts*

Reflection

Since the 2009 CCC Conference, where an earlier version of the following essay was given at a panel presentation entitled "Alternative Theories of Literacy: Making Waves through Narratives of the Classroom," I have been thinking very much about Miller's notion of "fabulation" raised in the epigraph to this piece—fabulation being a kind of invention of tales, the creation of "fantasy" or a kind of wakeful dreaming. And at first, it's difficult to swallow—to think of myself as involved in a constant fantastic invention of myself, of my students, of the classes I teach. I take my responsibility to my students quite seriously. I care very deeply about why and how teachers represent students. I care about the authorial respect and credit given to their writing, and I care about their privacy. I think of this piece (and of my work as a whole as I try to represent and learn from my students' thinking and writing) both as an inquiry into the intricacies or problems of this "fabulation" *and* as an opening up of deepening ethical possibilities for this *fabulation of self-truth* or of "other-truth." After all, Judith Butler, who is a touchstone for much of my thinking about identity and pedagogy, not only points to the importance of these possibilities, but also points in the direction of fantasy *as* possibility, and her work is now a part of the selection of writings in *Ways of Reading*. She writes: "Fantasy is part of the articulation of the possible; it moves us beyond what is merely actual and present into a realm of possibility, the not yet actualized or the not actualizable" (28). Perhaps narrative and the telling of the stories of classrooms is one significant way to think through what this kind of fantasy and imagination has to offer composition pedagogies. We can represent and invent our students and our teaching. We can become better teachers and writers in the process—that is, assuming we can accept and honor the both-at-once-ness always looming in the distance of that project. We represent *and* misrepresent, read *and* misread, speak *and* misspeak. To begin always with having already come to terms with these failures is to do justice to the complicated, reflexive, and troubling project of narration—narration that conjures up a student who learns, whether that student is a student in my class, or whether I myself *am* the student.

Narrative Attempt One

I had asked my students to read a chapter from Judith Butler's *Undoing Gender*. Danielle says Butler is impossible. Maria jokes: *Doesn't she have anything better to do than be completely impenetrable?* Johnnie says: "This woman does talk in circles, I'll give 'em that." I fear this is the start of the coup—the moment when my students forge an ever-strengthening uprising to overthrow the queer text they have been given. And by extension they seem to threaten to overthrow me, their queer teacher, and also to leave little room for the possibility of value in queer and difficult texts. I feel simultaneously angry and guilty. But I need to hurry, to decide what approach to take. There is, of course, the "eat your vegetables, they are good for you" approach, which I have to say usually ends with my students rightfully feeding my metaphorical vegetables to the metaphorical dog. There is the "therapeutic" approach; this is where I say, "Are you frustrated by this text?" and perhaps I make the ever-predictable move of "take us to a place in the chapter you found so difficult or frustrating to understand." There is also the "I hate 'the man' too" approach. In this approach, I validate their revolution. I say things like: "Yes, Judith Butler is impossible." I say: "Yeah, I don't know why this theory stuff has to be so dense on purpose." I say: "We want theory for the people!"

I can't say that I like the teacher in this narrative very much, even though this teacher is me. I can't say that I find the students compelling either—how could they be compelling when they are so erased by my own inner neuroses? What my students are saying to me is quite interesting, though because I categorize their response to Butler as "resistance" or even more problematically as a "coup," it can be difficult to see how their responses are interesting. Though I suppose my anxiety, which is what causes me to see their responses as a kind of "coup," does interest me. The anxiety speaks to some of the complicated questions of power present in all classroom scenarios. And as queer theory's interventions in pedagogy can tell us, power is not fixed; it is ever shifting, even in moments when we are reaching for its fixity. Knowing this, I need to find ways to work *with* the moments when I can feel the power shifting between me and my students, who can also feel power shift. My internal monologue amuses and disturbs me at once because if a shift in power is happening in this moment, none of the "approaches" I consider above seem to be conscious of that power shift. Each move is an attempt at taking power back, or asserting its fixity rather than moving *with* the shift of power in the direction of my students.

Narrative Attempt Two

When my students say Judith Butler is impenetrable, I laugh. I say: *Don't you think it's kinda ironic that we're calling a butch lesbian queer theorist "impenetrable"?* They look stumped. Finally, Johnnie says enthusiastically from the back: *Oh, I get it. Impenetrable, like won't be penetrated. Like by a man.* The students shift uncomfortably in their seats. *Something like that,* I say. I'm a little worried I've said something wrong, but hope I'm hiding it well. Hope I am teaching my students that penetration is a something we can collectively consider as an intellectual term. When my students then say Butler is *impossible*, I feel sad, defensive even. So I read from Butler, page 29: "Possibility is not a luxury; it is as crucial as bread." *Interesting, I say, that we are accusing a person who says possibility is as crucial as bread of being impossible. Does anyone else find this interesting?* From the back again, *It just proves her point,*

Johnnie says. I am sweating. I know in my mind that I have my clothes on, but my body feels naked. And Johnnie, the other visible queer in the classroom, is wearing his compassion on his sleeve. I can tell he wants to help me. We are of the same impossible body, after all. Him with his purple beret, his skinny girl jeans, and beautiful queer lisp. Me with my unruly chin hair and a voice that I can only describe as my father's. How will Johnnie and I lead the students out of impossibility? *This woman does talk in circles*, Johnnie says, *I'll give 'em that.*

I don't know about this teacher either. And clearly the representation of students is just as problematic as their erasure. I don't know if I should or how I should write about my students' bodies or if their bodies and fashion choices move the narrative in another theoretical direction. I don't know if I have the right to say what Johnnie's cooperation means. I do know there is always something different about a classroom in which there is a queer body, a queer sensibility. This narrative is about trying to make Butler *possible*—not accessible, or easy, or even pleasurable but possible. There is much at stake in recognizing her possibility. Because if she is *im*possible, I also am impossible. Johnnie is impossible. Queer bodies have certainly the potential for pushing up against what is possible; and this potential can cause us to be deemed *impossible*. This is not necessarily a problem; in fact, it is sometimes desirable to be impossible, illegible—to become the difficult text. Can this teacher, who is me, really make an ironic joke about penetration with first-year students? Is that even possible or ethical or "appropriate"? What context would a narrative need that says this? What teacher would we allow to say it? Narrative exposes our vulnerability as teachers (and often the vulnerability of our students) endlessly. Sometimes I wonder if it is the vulnerability itself that gives classroom story a bad wrap or turns narrative into the little brother many of us like to bully. But narrative almost always raises complicated questions about representation. And as queer theory also tells us: representation is already impossible before we even begin—identity itself is moving beneath our feet as we teach, as we write about teaching.

Let me try it once more.

Narrative Attempt Three

Much of my teaching is waiting. I try to be patient—I try to wait the way I wait for the bus. Confident it will arrive. Not exactly sure the precise moment, but soon. Each class a series of waitings. On this particular day, I am waiting for one of my students to make a comment *I* am able to see as possibility—the piece of a discussion that we will all remember because without it, the conversation might have fallen to pieces. They have read Judith Butler for the first time. There is the sense of struggling, maybe even of suffering in the room. Comments are made about difficulty, about big words, about density. One student even heckles Butler a bit. I am waiting still. *This woman does talk in circles*, Johnnie says, *I'll give 'em that.* By "them," he means the other students. He means he agrees with them about the denseness and difficulty of the text. But what I am interested in most are the circles. What it means for a writer to approach her task "in circles." *What shapes do people usually talk in?* I ask. At first, they seem to think a little that I am teasing. Then Danielle sees that I am not and says: *I think of essays more like boxes that connect.* On the board, I draw a picture of circles spiraling into one another and then boxes that connect. We end up drawing a geometrical diagram for every essay that follows (both the course readings *and* the students' essays);

we try to graph their shapes as a way of understanding the content. Some students grow to like the talking in circles—the way ideas slip back into one another again and again—and each time they are changed.

The composition course I am writing about here was titled "Human Psyche and Sexuality," and the students enrolled in this course had chosen this course theme through the University of Pittsburgh's Freshmen Studies program. It's hard, even for me, to see these three narratives as speaking about or telling the story of the same classroom moment. But each one does describe the same seventy-five-minute period of time. I move them *in* time. I begin at a different moment. I skip over time. Narrative time becomes as fluid and movable as power and identity. I offer these narratives not because I see them (or any narrative) as instructions for writing pedagogies, but because the questions that narrative produces for me are distinct and essential to teaching practice and to queer pedagogy as a theoretical field of inquiry. I thought to begin this paper by finding a teaching narrative in which someone attempted to record or describe queer pedagogies in composition. And each time I noticed the way I treated the narrative more like an object, like an opportunity for critique. I noticed myself pointing to the limits of narrative first before thinking about the possibilities of narrative. So I decided that I might raise some questions about my own teaching story, that it might be important or illuminating for me to risk my own narratives—to offer a moment when both narrative possibilities and pedagogical possibilities intersect. And I think every one of these narratives is problematic—narratives are never *not* problematic. But I am also interested in thinking about and asking questions about what narratives make visible. And as someone who is interested in the intersections between queer studies and composition studies, I am curious about the ways teaching stories are shaping understandings of what queer teaching is, or if there is even such a thing as queer teaching practices beyond the presence of queer teachers, queer students, or queer texts. I do, after all, agree with Judith Butler: "Possibility is not a luxury; it is as crucial as bread" (29).

WORKS CITED

Butler, Judith. *Undoing Gender.* New York: Routledge, 2004.
Miller, Nancy K. *Getting Personal: Feminist Occasions and Other Autobiographical Acts.* New York: Routledge, 1991.

Opening a Conversation with the Text, or "What Part of the Assignment Should I Write About?"

Kathleen A. Welsch

The question in my title was posed by one of my students after we had spent a class period closely reading and discussing one of the writing assignments in *Ways of Reading*. Although this student had been quite attentive and had dutifully taken notes during class, her frustration and exasperation at not having been told precisely what or how to write was reflected in her face and in the way she slammed her notebook closed at the end of class. She had come to class looking for answers, and what she got instead was a discussion about rereading and working with the text in preparation for writing. This didn't correspond to her previous writing experiences. For her, reading and writing were two distinctly separate activities. She'd read the text already; she knew the story; the reading was done. What she wanted now was a precise definition of what she should write about: What were the important points in the text? What did I (the teacher) see as its value for students? What kind of essay did I expect her to produce? As students filed out of the classroom, she approached me in a final effort to ask, "What part of the assignment should I write about?" Because she had come to class expecting to hear an answer, she had neither seen how class work related to what she might do on her own nor heard that what she might write depended on how *she* read, what *she* noticed, why *she* was interested in this passage or image and not that one. Her final question asked for a connection to the ways of knowing and doing papers that she had come to rely on and that had worked for her in the past. In this case, however, these old ways blocked her from understanding class work and discussions, making use of the information she'd taken down in her notebook, and, ultimately, from engaging in the challenge of the assignment at hand.

This student's question, though simply stated, reveals a set of assumptions about reading and writing that many students and teachers bring to assignments like those in *Ways of Reading*. To begin with, my student wanted a clearly stated topic to *write* about, for that's what she had come to expect of a writing assignment. How reading fit into that she couldn't imagine. Her question asked me to clear a path through all the reading and to identify the topic so that she could get to work on writing her essay. Prior experience had led her to assume that an assignment defined her choices as a writer, that it possessed an authority to which she had to submit rather than being the starting point for her own work. Her readiness to tell back what an assignment asked for clashed with this new assignment that challenged her to write about her reading of a text. She didn't grasp how she could use the assignment for her own purposes: to return to the text, to open it, question it, respond to it, and then write about *that* interaction. It didn't occur to her that writing about her reading might entail looking at what she'd noticed and why, what she'd skimmed over because it seemed difficult, and what she had found outright confusing or intriguing. It didn't occur to her because she assumed that this was the work of the assignment, not the writer. The assumptions about the roles of teachers, students, assignments, and texts embedded in her question worked to undermine her authority as a reader/writer. First, she imagined that the text presented a specific knowledge she needed to find; second, she expected the assignment to tell her what was important to find and write about; third, she assumed that I knew what it was she should focus on rather than her establishing that for herself. This last assumption frequently took the shape of the question "What do you want?" as if I could tell a student what she would notice, connect with, find confusing, or feel compelled to write about.

Assignments in *Ways of Reading* imagine that writing is more than reporting what the text says and that reading is more than finding a main point or getting the story. Students are challenged to write about their own acts of attention and making of meaning. This is no easy task, when one considers the level of complexity in each of the essays or the possibility that one might notice something new or have a deeper understanding with each rereading. The complexity of the essays is reflected in the complexity of the assignments in this book, and attempting to simplify either assumes that an essay's complexities can be reduced to a single most important point or lesson—something to be "gotten" quickly. Students and teachers who assume assignments should provide a path to a pre-established meaning (or who have grown comfortable with such an arrangement) may be confused by the nature of assignments in this book. For this reason, learning to read the assignments (making meaning of them as one would make meaning of an essay) is just as important as reading the essays before one can write a response. As I've talked with students and teachers about the essays and assignments in this book, I've encouraged them to recognize and question their assumptions about what it means to read or write an essay, and to imagine alternatives to these old ways of knowing. My plan for the rest of this essay is to discuss some alternatives in relation to three assignments that challenge both students and teachers to imagine possibilities in essays rather than the right answer; to open a subject to the range of directions it might take rather than close it down with conclusions, the main point, or the lesson; to notice not only the complexity of each project but how one might read, write, and make meaning in one project in a way that leads to rereading, rewriting, and rethinking meaning in relation to another project. The assignments I've selected address the work of Harriet Jacobs and Alice Walker.[1] They are based on "Assignments for Writing" and "Making Connections" questions in the book, but I have revised several questions for my course.

Assignments like the first Jacobs assignment for writing are particularly perplexing because they seem to say a lot about Jacobs's narrative and much less about what one should write. This particular Jacobs assignment opens with quotes by Jean Fagin Yellin, Susan Willis,[2] and Houston Baker, is followed by a statement about "gendered subjects" and a brief discussion of the public discourse of slavery, moves on to distinguishing between a life and a narrative, and shifts to observing how Jacobs's text reflects the circumstances of her life. All this before any writing objective is suggested, and this, too, is complicated by parenthetical remarks. In response to this mass of information, inexperienced students (and teachers) tend to grasp the one part of the assignment they understand best as their focus and generally disregard the rest. This isn't surprising, since most students have plenty of experience establishing a clearly stated topic and presenting an organized explanation of it.

---

[1] Jacobs's narrative "Incidents in the Life of a Slave Girl" and Walker's essay "In Search of Our Mothers' Gardens" appeared in the eighth edition of *Ways of Reading*.

[2] Willis's essay "Work(ing) Out" appeared in the third edition of *Ways of Reading*.

What they have less experience in is pursuing the numerous possibilities a text might offer. They tend to note what they understand, organize it, and keep it under control rather than consider how the one part of the assignment they do understand relates to the parts they don't seem to have a handle on. They are less practiced in the art of questioning what confuses them in order to make meaning; more commonly, students assume they didn't read thoroughly enough or that the material is simply beyond their comprehension.

My students and I have addressed this particular Jacobs assignment by beginning at the end—identifying the type of rereading the writing project suggests—and then turning to the rest of the assignment as a way to address that rereading. The final paragraph in the assignment states:

> Write an essay in which you examine Jacobs's work as a writer. Consider the ways she works on her reader (a figure she both imagines and constructs) and also the ways she works on her material (a set of experiences, a language, and the conventional ways of telling the story of one's life). Where is Jacobs in this text? What is her work? How do you know when you've found her? When you find her, have you found an "authentic voice"? A "gendered subject"?

In this assignment students are invited to write an essay in which they "examine Jacobs's work as a writer" by investigating how her text (chapters from *Incidents in the Life of a Slave Girl*) can be read "as something constructed." Since students have read Jacobs's text, they generally assume they know the material (the details of her narrative), and they generally assume that the narrative represents the "truth"; that is, that Jacobs doesn't deviate from or alter her experience as she writes it. To consider Jacobs's text as constructed, however, requires a different kind of reading, one in which the truth of a life is read through the truths of nineteenth-century social and literary conditions. An understanding of Jacobs's text and audience as constructed is crucial for a reader/writer who plans to reread Jacobs's narrative for the work she does as a writer. The reader needs to attend to *how* the story is told/constructed rather than being caught up in and carried along by the emotion and details Jacobs provides. The reader needs to ask: What does her text reveal about the decisions she makes as a writer with a purpose?

One way that my students and I begin talking about the kind of work one would have to do to reconsider Jacobs's story as something "constructed" is by reexamining the Houston Baker quote at the beginning of the reading from a variety of angles, since it provides a key to understanding Jacobs's text as something constructed. Baker writes:

> The voice of the unwritten self, once it is subjected to the linguistic codes, literary conventions, and audience expectations of a literate population, is perhaps never again the authentic voice of black American slavery. It is, rather, the voice of a self transformed by an autobiographical act into a sharer in the general public discourse about slavery.

The problem for many students lies in the fact that although they've read this quote, it remains an abstraction because they can't imagine how it might connect to Jacobs. So we discuss phrases that appear mystifying—"linguistic codes, literary conventions, and audience," "general public discourse"—and define them in terms of their own experience and understanding. We explore the meaning of the "unwritten self" by replacing the phrase with Harriet Jacobs's name and considering the differences between the unwritten and written Harriet Jacobs. When students have difficulty making this distinction, we shift to more personal terms by replacing the "unwritten self" with the word "student" so that they can consider what it means to them to be a written or unwritten self. For example, what linguistic codes, literary conventions, and audience expectations do they find themselves subjected to or restricted by when they go to write? We can take this question a step further by replacing the words "linguistic" and "literary" with academic codes and conventions and "audience" with teacher expectations. Such a discussion positions students to be more thoughtful about what it means to construct a text or about how what they write might be called a construction rather than a truth. We use the second paragraph following the opening quotes to establish an understanding of a "general public discourse" by exploring students' storehouses of general public discourse. The assignment explains that in Baker's formulation:

> [Jacobs's] voice shares in the general public discourse about slavery and also in the general public discourse representing family, growing up, love, marriage, childbirth, the discourse representing "normal" life—that is, life outside of slavery. For a slave the self and its relations to others has a different public construction.

Students begin to investigate what it means to participate in a public discourse by considering how they, too, are sharers in it. What do they know about slavery, life outside slavery, literary expectations for a writer like Jacobs who wants to be published? If necessary, we shift to the more personal again as students consider the public discourse that describes the life of students in the university and the academic expectations they must meet to be successful. A discussion such as this allows them to see and understand their own participation in public discourses. It also allows them to begin imagining how Harriet Jacobs participated in the general public discourses of the nineteenth century as a writer, while at the same time being positioned outside those discourses for the person she was—an African American, a slave, and a woman. We pursue this "inside but outside" conflict in Jacobs's narrative by mapping out on the blackboard the dichotomies identified in the third paragraph of the assignment.

> The passages from Baker, Willis, and Yellin allow us to highlight the gap between a life and a narrative, between a person (Harriet Jacobs) and a person rendered on the page (Linda Brent), between the experience of slavery and the conventional ways of telling the story of a life, between experience and the ways experience is shaped by a writer, readers, and a culture.

As a group students compose four parallel lists on the board that identify the differences they see between a life and a narrative, Harriet Jacobs and Linda Brent, the experience of slavery and how one is expected to tell one's life story, a lived experience and the ways in which experience becomes shaped by forces outside one's life. By the time students have completed this work, they have created a context that they can complicate and explore further by considering how the Willis and Yellin quotes relate to what Baker writes.

Students have accomplished a great deal of work by this point, but that work has not yet included writing the assignment essay. Instead, they have focused on using the assignment to work closely with Jacobs's text, rereading and rethinking it from a number of critical perspectives. Students begin to see that her text is no longer only the story of a life; it is also the story of a writer's work. For readers to arrive at this distinction, they need to be willing to see the text as something constructed rather than only the flow of the writer's memory. And that requires working with Jacobs's text more than once. When I describe the variety of ways my students and I discuss a text like Jacobs's (as I did in the previous paragraphs), I want to make clear that we aren't just talking off the top of our heads from what we remember. Our books are open; we search the text for specific passages; we go home and read it again and come back to class the next day to continue our discussion by turning to what we notice today that we didn't notice yesterday. It is only after we have worked with the text in this way that we go back to the final paragraph of the assignment where the writing project is outlined. At this point I ask students to notice the verbs in the assignment; we talk about ways they have already begun to "examine," "consider," and "reread" Jacobs's text and her notion of audience as something constructed and how they might continue this work on their own. As students construct readings of Jacobs during class discussion, they model the type of work they'll need to do to construct individual readings as they write their essays. Through class work they also identify an array of possibilities for reading the text; this task, in turn, gives them the writer's responsibility of focusing, selecting, and developing what interests them most about Jacobs's work as a writer.

Reading Harriet Jacobs's work as a writer—exploring what it means for a writer to "construct" a text—positions students to move on to investigating the work of other writers who not only have different projects but write in different contexts. Students are thus challenged to reconsider and complicate their understanding of a text as something constructed from still other critical directions. A sequence in which students move from Jacobs to Alice Walker invites a revision and complication of how they understand the choices a writer makes as she constructs a text. In the first writing assignment following Walker's essay "In Search of Our Mothers' Gardens," students are invited to write an essay in which they "discuss Walker's project as a creative endeavor, one in which she reconceives, or rewrites, texts from the past." Unlike the Jacobs assignment, there are even fewer directions here about what students should write in their essays. The question posed to them is simply: "What would you say . . . that Walker creates as she writes her essay?" Writing an essay that answers such a broad question entails some very specific reading; the second paragraph of the assignment offers a number of questions to begin investigating her project:

> How would you say that Walker puts that term, "contrary instincts," to use within her project? What does Walker's use of that term allow her to understand about the creative spirit of African American women, including Phillis Wheatley and her own mother? And if you consider Walker's position as an African American artist of today, what would you say the process of looking back at ancestral artists helped her to understand about herself?

Where students frequently encounter difficulties with such broadly stated assignments is when they focus on what to write rather than on constructing a reading through writing. Instead of using assignment questions to open a conversation with the text, some students shut down possibilities by writing essays that read like a checklist of the assignment's questions; that is, they devote one paragraph to answering each of the questions about Walker's project. Answering the questions, however, doesn't address the larger issue of what it is that

Walker creates as she writes. Before students write about Walker's project, they first need to read her text closely (as they did with Jacobs) for what the project is, what influenced its construction, and how it works.

When we talk about Walker in class, we begin by examining her revision of Virginia Woolf's passage in which she defines her key phrase, "contrary instincts." We use a strategy from our work with Jacobs as we draw up parallel lists on the board to illustrate the dichotomy between these two constructions of contrary instincts and to highlight how it is that Walker is revising a text from the past. Students test their understanding of Walker's revision by drawing up another list (in class or for homework) of all the women Walker names in her essay in order to identify each woman's creative gift and how it was or might have been subjected to contrary instincts. These discussions do not move students through the set of questions in the assignment; they do, however, provide students with ways to begin formulating answers and discovering how the questions lead to an understanding of the project. And by examining the array of women that Walker brings together and how each contributes to her revision of contrary instincts, students begin to see a process of creation. As they construct their understanding of this process through their own close reading, students don't need to rely on the assignment's questions to structure their essays. Instead, they can turn to their own authority as readers as they write about how they understand Walker's creation of a project.

Both the Jacobs and the Walker assignments challenge students to develop as strong readers—readers who notice what they pay attention to as they read—who respond to and interact with a text rather than repeating it. As they read and reread these texts, students develop a method of analysis and a set of key terms for looking at and talking about a writer's project—whether it's the work of Jacobs, Walker, or the student herself. Another type of writing assignment in *Ways of Reading* invites students to participate in a writer's project by extending it, either by connecting it to personal experience or by rereading one text through the frame of another. The first "Making Connections" assignment after the Jacobs piece calls for students to reread Jacobs through Walker's frame of contrary instincts and the creative spirit of African American women. To do this work, students need to extend what they already understand about these two texts. Instead of seeing them as separate projects, students need to reimagine each of them as contributing to a larger project: in general, how writers construct a text and, more specifically, how these two African American women construct texts within and against established discourses and traditions.

This assignment suggests that students "extend Walker's project by considering where and how Jacobs's work as a writer and artist would complement Walker's argument for the 'creative spirit' of African American women in the face of oppressive conditions." To do this, students will need to return to Jacobs's text for another rereading, this time in light of Walker's frame. And likewise, they'll need to return to Walker's text, rereading for places where Jacobs's work as a writer and artist would complement Walker's argument. The work students have done with these two pieces in prior assignments provides them with a level of familiarity with content; it can also be used as a starting point for reentering the texts, for beginning a new conversation with them.

This last point is important. It would be very easy to reenter the texts and repeat what one has already seen and said about them before. For example, the second paragraph of the assignment suggests that students note the choices Jacobs makes as a writer. They are to attend to

> her use of language, her selection of incidents and details, her method of address-ing an audience, the ways in which she negotiates a white literary tradition. Where for instance do you see her writing purposely negotiating a literary tradition that isn't hers? Who does she imagine as her audience? How does she use language dif-ferently for different purposes? Why?

Students have answered questions similar to these in their first essay on Jacobs. This set of questions, however, does not serve to reacquaint students with Jacobs's work but pro-poses that similar questions can be answered differently in relation to Walker's argument. In their first essay on Jacobs, students focused on her work on her terms; they read her text for how she constructs herself and her story in relation to traditions and public discourses that excluded her. The third paragraph in this new assignment asks them to extend this original reading by considering a new set of questions that incorporate Walker's terms:

> How would you say that the writerly choices Jacobs makes and enacts allow her to express a creativity that otherwise would have been stifled? What type of legacy does she create in her narrative to pass on to her descendants? And, as Walker writes in honor of her mother and Wheatley, what might Walker or you write in honor of Jacobs?

Answering these questions entails still more reading. This time, however, students reread Jacobs with an eye toward noticing what makes a particular writerly choice creative and how that creativity creates a legacy that Jacobs passes on to future generations. As they reread Walker, they need to attend to those places where her argument about creativity in the face of oppressive conditions relates to Jacobs's experience as a writer. The challenge of this assignment, then, lies in reseeing and rethinking both Jacobs's and Walker's work from new perspectives and in writing an essay that presents this revision.

One way that my students and I address this challenge is by identifying what we understand as the key terms or phrases in Walker's argument, for example, "contrary in-stincts," "creative spirit," "artist," "legacy," and "notion of song." We talk about why we chose them and how they help us understand Walker's project. We also use these terms to reread the quotes included in the first paragraph of the assignment.

> Of her mother, Walker writes: "Her face, as she prepares the Art that is her gift, is a legacy of respect she leaves to me, for all that illuminates and cherishes life. She has handed down respect for the possibilities—and the will to grasp them." And to the poet Phillis Wheatley she writes: "It is not so much what you sang, as that you kept alive, in so many of our ancestors, the *notion of song*."

Students consider how they understand the legacies created by Wheatley and Walker's mother—two women separated by time, living conditions, and legal status. From here stu-dents are prepared to shift to a discussion of how Jacobs, too, shares in and helps create this legacy out of a context and experience quite different from that of Wheatley and Walker's mother. It is when students have looked at all three of those women as possessing "creative spirits" and "contrary instincts," and as artists who have kept alive the "notion of song" and created a "legacy" that I invite students to consider what type of statement they would write in honor of Jacobs, as Walker has written in honor of Wheatley and her mother. I want students to try on Walker's way of thinking and working, to test her language in relation to Jacobs's creativity, to know where it works (or doesn't) and why, to consider how they would revise her project and why. In the end, I want my students to be responsible for constructing a reading in the essays they write rather than reporting what an author says.

My students and I devote a good deal of time to developing reading strategies for writing essays that present their understanding of a text. We read assignments closely for ways to enter the texts from different directions, work through confusions, understand complicated ideas, discover what they know, and make personal connections. One can't expect to just *do* these assignments — to go off and write a paper. It's important for both students and teachers to realize that one first needs to learn to read the assignments; they provide a guide or model of how one might go about rereading, interacting with, and responding to the essays in this book. They offer keys to opening conversations with texts, and it is these conversations that the reader writes about in response to the assignments.

Part V. Research and *Ways of Reading*

•••●•••

ENTERING THE ARCHIVE:
AN INTERVIEW WITH JEAN FERGUSON CARR
ON STUDENTS' LIBRARY PROJECTS

This is an interview with Jean Ferguson Carr about the freshman composition course that was taught at the University of Pittsburgh in 1993–94. Jean was part of a team directing multiple graduate student–taught sections of freshman composition using the History and Ethnography sequence in *Ways of Reading*. Two of the assignments in the sequence have research options: assignment 2, History; and assignment 5, Reading Others. In the interview, Jean talks about the logistics of preparing both freshmen and local librarians for the archival projects these assignments suggest.

DAVID BARTHOLOMAE: Jean, you and the people you work with made a decision to do the history and ethnography sequence in *Ways of Reading*. Can you talk to us a little bit about why you chose that sequence and what sorts of changes you made?

JEAN FERGUSON CARR: We wanted to have students doing some kind of work that took them outside the classroom, gathering materials and attempting to represent other lives, places, or times. So we were drawn to the double set of assignments in the sequence on history and ethnography. Students are in one case sent to the library to do archival work; in the other they gather materials from family, friends, or "contemporary documents from the print that is around" them. We liked the idea of doing two versions of this kind of project, one in connection with reading the essay by Limerick* and one in connection with reading Pratt. For the first assignment, we specified that students work with historical materials; for the second assignment, we gave them the choice of library work or community work, of materials from the past or from the contemporary scene. In both projects, we wanted students to have a stake in what they gathered and to see that forming their topic and constructing the material that would make the topic possible was part of the work of writing the paper.

That seemed imperative in this project, because they couldn't write the paper without having done some kind of gathering. It was very difficult for them to make up material, or to write without any preparation or reading.

---

* This essay, "Empire of Innocence," appeared in the fifth edition of *Ways of Reading*.

Indeed, the students who were irritated by these assignments were ones who habitually delayed, who therefore hadn't worked at gathering materials, and then found they couldn't write the paper.

DB: **Right. And as students were making a choice about where they would go to gather information for the material that they would work on, were there patterns? That is, were there obvious places that students went?**

JFC: Many of them wanted to write about what they saw as their ethnic or regional history. They wanted to write about various immigrant groups, for example, or about their town or school. They would go into the archives assuming that their town would be represented under a listing that said "my town." They were taken aback by finding themselves at a distance from what they saw as the "local," i.e., in a larger urban setting where perhaps they couldn't find their hometown newspaper or family records. Many of them did find ways to research something that had been important to their family. In some cases, that meant getting materials from home. One student, for example, wrote about a set of letters that his grandfather had written to his grandmother when he was off in World War II. Another student began with a picture of the Johnstown flood that had hung on her wall at home. Another worked from a family journal that described her grandparents' muck farm.

But they also came with a strong—in some cases, disabling—notion of what counted as "history." For many of them it had to mean a fairly big event—the Holocaust, race relations, wars, assassination attempts, the Depression. They had difficulties imagining one could write about ordinary people, and looked for documents about groups that seemed clearly marked as important historically—slaves, soldiers, politicians. Yet it was an interesting feature of doing this project in Western Pennsylvania that many of them assumed the importance of striking factory workers and of immigrants. Their sense of history was also shaped by their reading of Limerick, and so they followed her cue of representing undervalued histories of different kinds of people. One of the nice things about this assignment was that it provoked topics we would not have predicted for students. It showed interests and attitudes outside of widely shared claims about "today's student." Our sense of who the students were and what they found interesting was greatly expanded, and in many cases challenged, by this assignment.

When the students returned to archival work near the end of the course, in the context of the essay by Pratt and after reading Wideman's account of growing up in Homewood, many of them had a changed sense of what was appropriate to write about as "history." Their sense of being able to write about more ordinary people developed, which had something to do, I suspect, with moving away from Limerick (and naming their work "history") and toward using Pratt's category of materials from "the contact zone" (and so naming their work "culture").

DB: **So the first assignment was the Limerick assignment and the second was the Pratt assignment? Isn't there a point where they are asked to think back to Limerick as a historian? Did they? or did they in useful ways? You talked about the students having a sense of history—of what it was, where you found it, and how you wrote it. Did Limerick play into that evolving sense of what they were doing?**

JFC: It's hard to pinpoint how the students understood to use Limerick in their own work. Many of them referred back to Pratt's work with the letter of Guaman Poma (we had read Pratt at the beginning of the course, to introduce issues of representation and the politics of idealizing the past and others versus acknowledging the "arts of the contact zone"). Limerick seemed to challenge, in fairly serious ways, their prior sense of what a historian was and did. You can see this in the one-page memos students wrote at the end of their Limerick assignments, memos in which they were to tell Limerick something about the "experience of a novice historian that she might find useful or interesting." These memos were both wonderful and distressing in what they revealed about how the students understood the work of history. They were, however, always fascinating texts to read. Some students took the directive of offering Limerick something "useful," and wrote to inform her what she needed to learn to write history. One student, writing to "Patricia," encouraged Limerick to "keep up the good work as a professional historian"! Another explained politely about "some of the tactics . . . that you may find helpful." This student recognized the problem of writing as a novice to a professional, writing: "If you are trying to achieve what I have just state [*sic*], then please disregard it as a helpful suggestion and take it as a mere observation."

The assignment was forcing them to experience the difficulty of making absolute narratives, of negotiating different perspectives; you can see this in comments in the memos about specific problems they encountered. One mentioned the difficulty of retelling "what has already been said." Another wrote that "it's hard to write a history when you have so many different opinions and secondhand views." One student discovered that "you can't just write History you have to read into it first," or, as another student wrote, "It is excessively important to try to become a part of what you are researching." Their experience with the construction of history stayed in conflict with their previous sense of what it meant to be called a historian. Several students used the memo as an occasion to challenge the construction of history Limerick represented to them, a construction they were in many cases trying out themselves in their papers. One student wrote, "I failed to understand your work as a history. Maybe it is because I have a set definition of 'history' and do not believe your work was one." As this student suggested, Limerick upset their notion of what history entails. In class discussion, they attributed this to her willingness to reflect on her own authority, to resist the notion that a single history will suffice. Limerick's efforts to see historical narratives as always problematic, as always contested, made her somehow not a real historian, and so they offered her advice about how to do better at this thing they called history.

Despite this conflict, many of them were intrigued by isolated moments in Limerick where they could see her doing historical work. If they didn't initially engage with Limerick as someone who *owns* history, they did take from her a sense of concern about how to work with quotations or with objects left behind. Many of them, for example, mentioned the illustration of cans left behind by the miners as something needing to be noticed. They started to take on ways of imitating moments in the history, while at the same time remaining fairly troubled by the argument Limerick is making about history as constructed, as contested.

DB: **Can you give an example?**

JFC: The epigraph for the assignment on Limerick asks students to imagine "it is as if one were a lawyer at a trial designed on the principle of the Mad Hatter's tea party." The students homed in on the first part of this—the lawyer at the trial—and therefore saw their job as one of arguing a case, presenting the facts, representing pro and con positions. They were then adamant that there had to be two opposing points of view. This assumption became a major barrier in their search for appropriate documents. They would dismiss perfectly interesting documents because they weren't explicitly opposite or antagonistic, but simply represented slightly different positions or articulations of an event.

DB: **Right, because they weren't pro and con.**

JFC: They were unsettled by the second part of the epigraph, which refers to a trial "on the principle of the Mad Hatter's tea party." They didn't like the idea that things might change depending upon where you sat. They were looking for authoritative history. This became a problem in how they could talk with the librarians and of how they could recognize when they had found a useful document. For many of them it remained a problem through the whole assignment—they couldn't find their material because nothing looked like what they expected to find, what they assumed they were being instructed to find.

Let me give you a specific example. This assignment was exceedingly frustrating to a student who had decided he wanted to write on the assassination attempt on the industrialist Henry Clay Frick. As he wrote in his memo, he expected to find "personal diaries or any material of personal significance (not meant to be read by others by publishing or other means) toward the subject." When he couldn't find precisely these materials, he was surprised because, as he knew, "the Homestead strike was a controversial event." He looked for "autobiographies on Henry Clay Frick . . . so that I could get his story," and was disappointed when he "had to rely on a biography and some newspaper stories." He also used the accused assassin's prison autobiography, which he found "remarkable" in that it "leaves out a lot of information on the assassination attempt compared to other sources." This student expected to find a "private" (and never-before-published or used) account of an assassination, but expected the accused assassin to record a full version of the event, with as much information as he could read in professional histories. He couldn't negotiate the problem of writing before the fact or retrospectively, or the various constraints (legal, journalistic) under which people wrote. He imagined his only option was to tell the true story of what happened, rather than to derive an argument about attitudes or issues that could be said to lead to such an event. If he couldn't find the documents he expected, he felt he had nothing. This student never could complete the assignment. He hovered at the entry to the archive, with his preconceptions preventing him from looking at what he could have found (indeed, in many cases, what he did find but rejected as "wrong"). He ended up using an authoritative history of the attempt, citing its quotations as his "document."

Students had difficulty negotiating the difference between their expectations—of an already constructed narrative clearly delineating pro and con positions—and what they found. They were unnerved at having to write a history from a document that didn't already have a clear narration organizing its details.

DB: **What kind of documents did students end up using?**

JFC: Students used books of interviews and letters, published memoirs, and diaries. They worked from documents in the university archives, with newspaper accounts, family letters and journals, and, in one case, from architectural plans. Two students wrote on the Depression, using books of memoirs people had written looking back to the old days.

DB: **You mean interviews by Studs Terkel? That sort of oral history?**

JFC: In one case, clearly oral history interviews. Another student used a book of letters workers wrote during the Depression about their jobs, letters that were clearly instigated by journalists or social workers to "document" problems. They were working from relatively short accounts, mostly retrospective or written under specific prompts at the time. The gap in time became a central issue in our class discussion and to both of these students; one of them actually went back to look for more materials written from the time. Both students were concerned about writing from such limited sources. They felt responsible for a general, and authoritative, history of the Depression. When we discussed these two papers, the class was agitated about the students' "presumption" to write from small evidence and without knowing "what really happened." The student writers and their colleagues shared the notion that "what really happened" exists somewhere out there in textual form. These particular writers, I think, both turned this assignment around to see that they had a responsibility to account for even the few documents they had, and that this was a complicated job in itself. One had documents from two different people and saw that they remembered comparable events differently, to make different "stories." The other student used materials written at different moments (and out of different circumstances) in the Depression, and saw that such circumstantial differences altered what the writer saw as "his story." These were among the most successful archival projects. Neither of these students was a particularly expert writer, but both worked very hard, returning to reread these materials over and over, rewriting, and reorganizing. They both produced long, elaborate, and careful revisions of this assignment, which they—and their classmates—liked and cited in their final papers.

DB: **I want to go back for just a second to the assignment. In the process that you are describing, students learned (at least for the occasion of this course) that working as a historian means learning how to work on some materials they have gathered. Then that's unsettling because they think that history is a body of knowledge about a point in time, from which they would make an argument. That is, they would know what they need to know about the Depression, and from that they would argue to some material that was in front of them, rather than working from some material that was in front of them to some sense of what it would mean to speak for "The Great Depression."**

JFC: I think they are imagining the historian's work to be to find a fairly streamlined, relatively neutral narrative that manages to incorporate everyone's experience. Two comments kept coming up that show this conception: one was the notion of wanting to know "what really happened" and the other was of wanting to know "what happened in a nutshell." Both of these concerns show an anxiety about dealing with unruly detail, with multiple strands of an event or with multiple perspectives. Both propose, implicitly, a method of cutting away what is read as unimportant, distracting, off the target. In both cases, students push toward whittling out what they see as biased or individual perspectives to find what "really" happened—which somehow exists without agents, outside time or place. These represent strongly held beliefs about fact, objectivity, truth, beliefs that the Limerick assignment pressured tremendously. By suggesting that students might locate oppositional documents, which might, in turn, produce divergent accounts, the assignment challenged this need to "discover" what has already been authorized as the event.

DB: **That's right.**

JFC: These students had clearly learned a procedure for dealing with different opinions or accounts, but difference had to be clearly presented as pro and con. They were most comfortable when a situation had a very clear villain and victim, or a clear set of preconstituted oppositions: black/white, male/female, German/Jew. They were less comfortable when they were dealing with figures who seemed somewhat aligned, but yet reported events differently. Such situations forced them not to pare the accounts down to the "nutshell," to a consensus or neutral event, but to work closely with specific versions, trying to see how different interests or conditions might influence the construction of "the event."

DB: **If you were going to do this sequence once again, or if you were going to give us some advice for the book, would you set it up differently? Would you set it up the same way?**

JFC: Some of these difficulties are what you have to work through. It is important to recognize that you have to work through students' strong and pressured sense of what it means to write as a historian. That is simply part of what this assignment demands. This sense about writing history is connected with students' strong investment in issues of objectivity and fact, in concern about bias, prejudice, subjective perspectives. I would say, however, that the assignment's hint about opposing views at a trial is misleading, since students tend to disregard Limerick's qualifications about this as a peculiar—"mad hatter"—trial. You want to suggest multiplicity without necessarily suggesting the model of the trial.

DB: **Exactly.**

JFC: Once they had settled on the model of a trial, they didn't pay attention to the rest of the assignment (references to "problems of myth, point of view, fixed ideas," for example). The trial was a solution for many of them, and they grabbed on to it desperately. I would say the other problem is the degree to which they don't know what to do with the document. They imagine that they should summarize it, or that it is self-evident. They imagine they should boil it down to a simple position. The assignment asks them to treat a document as full of details, as potentially complex, as something you don't simply retell but study, question, wonder about. This is, of course, the problem posed in all the assignments in *Ways of Reading*. This assignment brings to the surface the problem of representing another's words or account in a particularly visible and pressing way—which is useful.

We tried to deal with this textual problem by having students bring in the documents they had found before they wrote their papers. We had them work in class from these documents, treating them as "texts" for study. I think it is probably useful in this kind of assignment to break it into parts or stages. Students have a lot of trouble finding something, and so that activity probably needs to be done as a separate part, where they discuss their ideas for a project, and their strategies for finding material, then discuss the documents they have found, and then work on how to use these documents to write "a history." I asked students to bring in their materials, with a preliminary account in which they described their document, discussed briefly the detail they found most intriguing, and indicated what they thought would need to be annotated to use this for "history." This accomplished a couple of things. It pressured them to find a document, and it also allowed them to share their work with their peers while they still had time to work on their materials. The brief written assignment helped them see that there were levels of description, that there was a difference, for example, between describing the document itself (e.g., what kind of document, how long, written by whom to whom, of what level of literacy or sophistication, etc.) and skipping over the document to describe "the event." The suggestion that they attend to specific details—and that details could be important because they provoked questions or were difficult to understand—usefully encouraged them to work within their documents, not to reduce them to a generic outline. And the request to begin imagining the document as needing annotation allowed us to discuss the problems of information, knowledge, and accessibility. Students began to negotiate the differences between what they didn't know because of the remove in time or situation and what most readers wouldn't know because of its private or local nature. This encouraged students to take some responsibility for the "larger" history available to them through reference guides and secondary histories without simply renouncing their own roles as readers of the past.

I copied out for class discussion many of these preliminary reports. In these preliminary discussions, it was wonderful to watch students teaching each other about their newly found expertise in library research. One of the nicest moments in my class was when a student explained to the rest of the class how to use the library's online catalog. He had not found what he wanted in the rare book collection, and so had taught himself how to use a "keyword" search to find a volume of Civil War letters. The other students were delighted at the idea of finding materials they could take home with them, and most seemed stunned at the idea that one could access the library's materials through such mechanisms. Similarly, students were greatly impressed at one writer's lengthy quotation from his document. Many had not located a full primary document but were instead working with dispersed quotations from a history or biography. The descriptions of documents helped such students considerably. The terms "document" and "first-person account" don't mean much to most students.

One of the major difficulties of this assignment is how their concept of the project limits their process of searching for documents. Students generally had difficulty knowing what to ask librarians, knowing how to describe what they needed or wanted, and knowing how to describe their idea for the paper in strategic terms (i.e., I want to write on Subject X, and therefore it would be useful to find these kinds of documents). I think it is probably important to work closely with the documents within the essays by Pratt or Limerick—to define discussion as coming from documentary work in specific ways. It is useful to work backwards from the essays to try to recuperate what archival work must have been done, to recover what the "evidence" might have looked like initially.

DB: **One of the things, just frankly, that I remember as a problem when I taught both Limerick and Pratt is that they don't present material very fully; they allude to material. Pratt does quite a lot with the Guaman Poma letter. In Pratt's book *Imperial Eyes*, you get these extended, really quite lovely close readings of block quotations that in many ways figure what you would want students to do. But they don't see enough of this in Limerick.**

JFC: Well, I think there are places in Limerick, although I agree with your sense of needing more explicit uses of documents. I have worked closely on Pratt's treatment of Guaman

Poma and on Limerick's account of Narcissa Whitman. One place we discussed at length was where Limerick quotes from the journal of a woman pioneer, beginning with the instruction: "Consider Mrs. Amelia Stewart Knight." That section allowed us to talk usefully about what Mrs. Knight did "record" and what she reported but did not discuss (the work of tending to seven children). Students were intrigued by Limerick's suggestion that "one simply has to imagine what some of her terse entries meant in practice," and that became the hinge for a discussion on what constrained a historian's "imagination" and on the value of trying to connect "entries" with "practice." The passage contains at least one marker to help account for Limerick's "work" ("The older children *evidently* helped out" [my emphasis]), and it shows how one can construct a pattern out of clustered details ("The youngest child, Chatfield, *seemed* [my emphasis] most ill-fated: 'Chat has been sick. . . . Here Chat fell out. . . . Here Chat had a very narrow escape"). One of the problems, though, might be described as graphic or visual. Because Limerick quotes in dispersed fashion, breaking up passages with her own commentary, students had difficulty "seeing" where she was using documents. We spent quite a bit of class time *literally* finding quotations, which proved a very hard search. We did a similar job in working on Pratt's section on Guaman Poma.

In the Pratt essay, students could see perhaps more readily that Pratt had gathered diverse "materials" to make her account: the Guaman Poma letters, her son's classroom materials, the Stanford course debates. It's useful in that case to think of each section as having its own materials. In class we looked carefully at what are the material bases for each argument, at what kind of "document" is used, and at how some of the "evidence" is based on nontextual materials such as conversation, which is then quoted and treated as a "document" (i.e., cited, retold, interpreted). But one of the problems is the ease with which Pratt moves from section to section, the eclectic nature of this particular piece. She, like the students, assumes at times that the texts speak for themselves; she doesn't belabor her interpretation of materials. This has to do, of course, with the occasion for this particular lecture, but it poses a problem for students trying to model historical work.

I think a teacher and a class have to work fairly closely on how to use these essays as models for archival work. One of the issues that suggested students' confusion was that they couldn't decide whether they were in Pratt and Limerick's roles or in the roles represented by Guaman Poma and the western pioneers. Students tended to see themselves more in relation to the historical figures, identifying, I suspect, with the difficulty of speaking and being heard, with the position of being an unknown and unarticulated subject. Part of what the assignment calls for is having students imagine themselves as also in Pratt's and Limerick's positions of authority, however much those positions are qualified or challenged by Pratt and Limerick as cultural critics.

DB: **This is the time that I should ask you to talk a bit about what remains for me one of the really remarkable achievements of this project of yours, which was that it wasn't just your twenty-two students doing this, but about twelve hundred Pitt undergraduates over two semesters. I'm imagining how they needed to make use of the region's resources to do documentary work.**

I guess there are several questions to ask here. One of them is to ask a very specific logistical question: How did you pull it off? The other question is, what led you to think that this was something you would want to do?

JFC: It was very useful for me to do this with a more dispersed group than my own class. I do considerable historical work myself and in my stand-alone courses, and I know the resources in this region fairly well. But it's very useful to figure out how to do such work with a set of teachers who are new to the area and, by and large, new to historical work.

DB: **And new to teaching.**

JFC: Yes. I was thinking about it partially as a way of showing me what is particularly difficult about this kind of work, what needs to be explained or facilitated. But I also wanted to try it out for the book, which presumably asks people to launch such historical projects without necessarily being historians, without being terribly familiar with the resources, and without time or particular interest in devoting a lot of energy to such a search.

And the book can't, of course, predict what will be available—or particularly interesting—in any particular region of the country, to any particular teacher or set of students. That is a problem, but it also seems to me a considerable advantage. It is a situation that makes apparent the kind of work teachers and students need to do to make the book useful, to make it locally appropriate. This assignment is very useful in how it challenges the model of teacher authority and knowledge. The assignment proposes that the teacher is no longer the sole resource person, the one who knows all the material best, but that students are going to have to learn how to use their own resources, to use library collections, to learn how to get help from other university experts—librarians, for example.

I think that's a useful thing. It is initially a very scary thing.

DB: **By teachers, in this case, do you mean teaching assistants? teaching fellows?**

JFC: In this case, the staff was mostly first-year teaching assistants and fellows. There were several faculty, advanced graduate students, and part-time faculty who volunteered to teach the sequence and make their classes available for observation. It was unnerving for teachers to undertake this assignment without knowing from their own experience what the library had. I think most experienced teachers' inclination was to go find out what the library had and bring back a list, or at least to try out the procedure of searching for themselves. Others set up special sessions with the library's instructional staff to teach students how to access books and periodicals. I think it's important to resist providing the students with too explicit a menu, with a list of targeted materials for them to go "find." This would certainly solve some of the logistical problems, but it doesn't necessarily teach students how to do a certain kind of work. And it limits the topics they can find to what the teacher or resource person imagines are their interests.

Some of what made this assignment difficult has to do with the social history of students' library use. Most of the students in my class had never used more than the reserve collection in the library and its study rooms. The library functioned for them as a large study hall with prescribed readings and marginal levels of quiet. They had never used a card catalog, or had much use for one since their books and articles had all been preselected for them. They didn't know that books can be taken out but manuscripts cannot. They didn't know that a researcher might have to make appointments for use of some collections or work within more limited hours. They didn't know that they might not be allowed to make a copy of a document or that they might need permission to quote from private papers. There was, in other words, a whole set of social conceptual problems that this assignment inherits. Simply getting students to the library and into rather rarefied collections was a challenge. Then on the other side, the assignment done on this scale posed quite a challenge to the librarians, most of whom (for archival and rare book collections) are used to dealing with scholars and professional visitors, not with freshmen.

DB: **And not with large numbers of them.**

JFC: And large numbers of them. Yes. Well, because the librarians are used to dealing with professionals, they're used to conducting a fairly elaborate question-answer interview with a prospective user. This kind of user knows what he or she wants to do and knows a lot about how to get at it or what it might look like; what this user doesn't know is the offerings of a particular collection. Librarians were initially imagining they needed to do a full-hour interview with each student, which, needless to say, overwhelmed them. These interviews stretched in some cases to two or three hours when librarians confronted the students' lack of experience with documentary collections, and their lack of understanding about historical procedure. Librarians were faced with students who didn't know what they wanted (and in many cases, couldn't explain why they wanted it). Or they were faced with students who wanted only one very specific thing and were indignant when the librarians couldn't produce it. The librarians described them as wanting the history of the world or a specific history never written. They had little sense of how to negotiate the topic, of how to find something approximate or comparable, of how to make use of a document to elaborate an interest. The librarians were concerned about students trying to do the work of professionals in amateur time (often fifteen minutes before the close of the archives) with amateur credentials.

DB: **What did you learn about working first with the librarians that was important to you? How did you prepare them?**

JFC: I learned as much about the librarians as I did about students in this project. I must say, our librarians were extraordinarily helpful, concerned, and knowledgeable, willing to put in far more time than they could spare to this project. It's very important for any teacher doing this project to meet with librarians ahead of time, to warn them that this is happening. Give them the sense of the scale and get some advice from them about how their system operates. I asked permission from each specialist librarian to include their particular collection on a memo and sent every participating librarian a copy of the assignments with the expected dates for student work. If I were doing this again, I would meet with the librarians ahead of time to discuss the aims and scope of the assignment, to show some sample papers, and to talk over what they should offer students and what they should encourage students to negotiate more independently. I wrote a memo to the students about the different libraries and what kinds of items were in each collection, about library hours, how to make an appointment, about using pencil when taking notes about a rare book. It's important to support the librarians' procedures.

DB: **How many different sites were involved? How many places were students potentially going to?**

JFC: There were about nine archive and book collections, as well as the general resources of the university and city library.

DB: **Can you name some of them?**

JFC: There's a rare book special collection, the university archives (a collection of materials about the founding of the university, about the construction of campus buildings, about university departments and organizations), the library science collection (which had an archive of children's materials, including periodicals and television programs), the local historical society (which had letters and documents), and the Labor Archives. Many students chose the university archives. They wanted to stick close to home and write about something they could visit or observe. Many of them used some kind of newspaper, periodical, or facsimile versions of local history papers. Few of them wanted to go beyond the university bounds to the historical society or city library, although they're very close to campus. Some of their choices had to do with ease of availability, with hours and location. That wasn't so much the case in the second project. They were more adventuresome after they'd done it once and were willing to go to more than one collection to find what they wanted. Once they adjusted to the idea, they respected the librarians' requests to make appointments; indeed they seemed reassured by the structure of scheduling official appointments, of going to a specific site, of physically gathering materials. The first time, the issue of scheduling was a disaster. Many students assumed they could go, en masse, to a special collection fifteen minutes before closing on a Friday and retrieve specialized materials from a collection. Many of them assumed they would enter an archive, be handed their own particular material, and take it home with them.

Several students were very angry at the librarians when they found this wouldn't work: they blamed the librarians for preventing them from carrying out their task. This greatly unnerved the librarians. They're used to arranging for scholars to get what they need. They're not used to disappointing people or having people refuse to come back later.

DB: **I just want to get you to talk for a few more minutes about the librarians' side of it. How did you establish, not only for yourself but for all of these other teachers and students, a set of working relationships with the librarians?**

JFC: I'd say that it goes two ways. One, you need to talk to the librarians to find out their procedures, their interests, and their materials. You need to prepare your students in some way ahead of time to negotiate these procedures. That was the aim of the handout I prepared. But the other thing that is important is to talk with the librarians about what you hope to get out of the assignment. It is easy to fall into a mentality of imagining the problems of such work and to avoid discussing the aims, the expectations, the possibilities. I gave the librarians copies of the assignments and copies of what the students had been reading. I talked to them about where these projects fell in the semester (the first one came at three weeks into the term; the second at eleven weeks), and I talked about how the first assignment might lead to a different level of work in the second. I talked with them some about the kinds of reading and writing students know how to do at this level but also about what they are learning but can't fully accomplish yet. In other words, you don't imagine that students become expert at such work with one try; you try to seed the ground for the second project, even for subsequent work in the curriculum. And you don't need to expect the project to fail because students stumble along the way. I talked with them not only about what students might know specifically about using libraries, but also about what they might know about formulating questions, articulating a topic, defining a document. This was an important part of the discussion.

Many of the initial difficulties we had arose from the librarians' assumptions of a certain kind of knowledge and experience and the students' assumptions of what librarians could (should?) offer or provide. Many of the students assumed that librarians could simply hand them what they needed, that they could read students' minds and concoct an appropriate source to satisfy the students' topics. Some students expected to be able to describe their interests very generally and then have the librarians fill in all the rest: out would come two opposing documents already annotated, legible, translated, etc. The librarians for the most part assumed students would know how to talk about a project, and they assumed that students knew what documents were available. Things improved considerably when I urged librarians not to take on the job of teaching students how to write their paper and not to write the paper for them. In the first go-round, I think many of the librarians were spending more time than they should with individual students and with large—and often inattentive—groups of students. They were trying to make up for lost time, to do remediation in library research, history, professional writing, etc. They tried to teach them how to read the document and produce a history the librarians knew was available. It was important to discuss how a course based on revision might differ from one with a single term paper at the end. Students in a revision-based course might be expected to reread their document, to go back later to see what else they could do with the material, to rethink their construction of history. Their first attempt didn't need to be imagined as all they could do.

It was important, then, to suggest that the students' difficulties were not just their unfamiliarity with library procedure. We could, in other words, teach them to use the card catalog, and we would still have many comparable problems to face. It was important to suggest how the problems students had negotiating the library were connected to problems in reading, in negotiating the academy more generally, in imagining themselves trying out what it means to work as a researcher. I urged the librarians to send really ill-prepared students back to their teachers, to stick to their sense of what procedure was important. I encouraged them not to feel they ought to be handing out documents at random to the twenty students who arrive at quarter to five, but that it was important to maintain their own procedures. It was useful for students to see how part of being a historian is an ability to imagine that a set of documents ought to be somewhere specific, not in some neutral reference shelf prepared for generic use. It was also useful for students to work at describing the kinds of documents they wanted to see. An experienced historian will enter an archive with a kind of confidence based on having visited other collections. She'll assume that there's likely to be something like this and it's likely to be in this kind of collection because she's found comparable documents elsewhere using similar search procedures. She'll be able to describe the kind of material she wants, even though the specific features are bound to be different in every collection she enters. She'll know that the catalogs for accessing special collections are full of information that might be hard to read initially, and she'll know how to ask for help in prying that information out of the particular format or tradition. We wanted, in part, to teach students some of that confidence, the confidence of being able to ask about what they don't know fully or absolutely. We wanted them to envision a library as a place to go to find out about what you only know parts of, or only know imperfectly.

DB: If we were to interview some of these librarians right now, would they say they had a good year? How would they remember this experience?

JFC: The initial onslaught of five-hundred-plus students in the fall term was a horror. I was surprised at how agitated the librarians were, and we were all deeply surprised at how much work this project entailed for them. I went in for an emergency meeting—twelve research librarians and me. I felt very much that I was being called on the carpet. At the same time, they were very willing to pursue the issue, to work to make it better. They did not simply want to complain or make the problem go away (although those sentiments did dominate the beginning of that first meeting). They were by and large sympathetic to the aim of getting students into the library.

As we talked, we considered a number of ways of easing the burdens, and we recognized how much we shared similar aims at the university. A lot of the initial problem was logistical: when they treated each student as a visiting scholar, the numbers soon overwhelmed them. We discussed the suggestion that we produce a model set of documents to put on reserve for all students to use; this seemed to promise to contain the chaos and to reestablish "our" oversight of the project (we could help students better because we would regain control of the materials, both physically and intellectually). The group divided on this issue, with the librarians of book collections expressing more reluctance about having inexperienced students in large numbers using their collections than did the librarians of archive collections. This is certainly understandable; the ethos of rare book collections makes one very aware of how fragile such materials are, of how each use, however careful, damages or potentially destroys irreplaceable materials. The university archivist argued, however, that we didn't want to solve the problem of library use by shutting inexperienced students out of "the library," i.e., by reproducing a set of materials to read in a reserve room. The transformation of "the library" into a study hall was an issue about which the librarians were very concerned. The debate revolved around getting students into the central collections of the library or warding them off with a prepared packet that would be used in the library or purchased for use in class. I offered to try this out. I can certainly imagine the use of a set of documents to use in preliminary discussions. But the university archivist held out, arguing, as I had, that a prepared packet doesn't get students into a part of the library (or of the academy) where they have both the intellectual and social experience of constructing a project for themselves.

The group of librarians came to agree that this was a desirable goal, and this discussion was an important one for us to have. They were willing to try the experiment a second time in the semester, as well as two more times the following semester. And we discussed how to build on this intensive project in subsequent courses across the curriculum. They saw the importance of getting students into the library in a substantive way early in their college careers, despite the difficulties and the logistical problems. There was very little turmoil in the second semester. I got joking reminders from librarians that they were undergoing extra work thanks to me. But they were pleased (and surprised) by the kinds of papers students produced out of the experience. They were pleased to imagine students might build on this experience to use the library in future work.

DB: Do you think they will?

JFC: I don't know. I think that for most students it was initially a very demanding, somewhat daunting experience; yet most students were proud of their accomplishments and recognized the substantive difficulty of the project. Many of them said it made them feel like scholars. They felt they were doing serious work, and it raised their sense of self-esteem that their university had such resources. They enjoyed questioning their families and looking for documents from their parents' or grandparents' past. They liked the sort of professionalism that the project encouraged.

Many of them spoke about the pleasure of finding their own material, of defining their own topic. We forget how much we control their work, even when we invite them to experiment, to speak their own opinion, even when we choose as texts what we imagine are "their" kinds of materials. Although this was in many ways a highly structured, disciplined project, in other ways the material was more fully theirs than are class texts. Students talked about being in "charge" of their materials, of bringing it to our attention, of bringing it into the public or the present. I think this project challenges in important ways issues of authority in the classroom. Teachers are necessarily less in charge of the material when they haven't chosen it and haven't in most cases read it. Students had more responsibility for describing, reporting, accounting for their materials. This was particularly useful for the beginning teaching assistants, although the project also caused moments of anxiety for many of them with its lack of a uniform text to order the class discussion. TAs found out how much more students could say or write when the text was not already the "property" of the teacher or of the class. In such a situation, teachers are not the ones who must persuade a resistant audience to find the material interesting or persuasive; they ask their students to explain what makes something worth reading, worth interpreting. In this case, it is a real question. This is often not the case, even when we've offered what count as "student" texts as a basis for our conversation.

DB: Can you talk about a set of rules or principles for getting students ready to work in the library?

JFC: I'd say one of the things that is important to do is not to send all students at the same time to work in a rare book or primary paper collection. Much of this work can be done in book collections or in microforms, using almost any college or city library. There are many books that reprint documents or narratives, government papers, letters, and diaries. Students who used books had the advantage of taking the book home with them, of being able to go back easily, of being able to read around their document, of reading more widely when they had the interest. I think for many students that kind of book work was very productive. Some students wanted to brave the challenges of the rare book collection or the archives, and I think for them this assignment was particularly exciting. It's useful to set up the project so students can sort themselves out, so that the most interested students can have access to look at manuscripts, to translate letters from Polish immigrants, or to read eighteenth-century handwriting. In some cases, students figured out their interests using books, and then turned to more specialized collections with their newly discovered expertise. Book sources aren't particularly easier than special collections for most students, but students are going to do less damage or be more dispersed in the general collection than when they are concentrated in special collections.

It is useful to offer some sort of general library orientation for students before the project begins, but most introductory library tours will not solve the problems this assignment recognizes. Most initiations in libraries are aimed at teaching students how to access material they can name already. This is a very different kind of project, introducing more sophisticated use of library resources. One could develop, with a librarian, a very useful one-hour session that would help students find material for this project. Such a session would have to address not simply research tools but a logic for searching and asking questions. This session might discuss using catalog searching to help develop a potential topic; it might teach students how to browse productively, how to examine a book as a possible source without reading it fully.

DB: So that would mean working with somebody who understood the project?

JFC: I would say to work closely with somebody familiar with archival projects and interested in the particular problems of inexperienced users.

DB: So, in most textbooks, all this work is represented through the mechanics of note-taking . . .

JFC: Term papers, collecting bibliography cards . . .

DB: Exactly. To what degree were your students in need of or coming to you for help with things like note-taking?

JFC: One of the things that happened that interested me in this project was that they taught each other what they needed to know. This turned into a fairly collaborative project, even though students had individual topics and materials. They ran into each other in the library and offered their different expertise. Some of them were willing to try out the interactive computer catalog and taught themselves how to access their materials through a subject index.

There is in general very little familiarity with using the library. Students had little experience with making distinctions between materials in a special collection and printed books, between facsimile letters and original manuscript documents. It is useful to work back from an essay like Limerick's or Pratt's to discuss what the documentary source must have looked like and to discuss the relationship of what is being quoted to the whole document. I can imagine it would be useful to add a packet of different kinds of primary materials as an appendix to the textbook. You could put in a facsimile letter, for example, or a section of a diary. One of the problems—and one of the pleasures—of working with original materials is dealing with handwriting, as well as working with items in multiple languages. Some students chose documents written in Lithuanian, Czech, or Slovenian. Because of the makeup of this region, some students had multiple language abilities, but they often had more difficulty with the handwriting than with the language itself. Another difficulty was reading texts without annotations. A letter would refer to something they didn't understand, and that would make them feel they couldn't continue. It is useful to teach students how to piece information together by reading the context, to continue reading even when something isn't perfectly clear. It's also useful to suggest how to begin annotating such materials.

DB: Let me move ahead to the second assignment you did. Limerick was the first archival assignment and Pratt came later. How did Pratt and the second assignment work for you? What were you and your students able to do with it?

JFC: The Pratt assignment pressured them to think more about how the document they picked represented a group's experience, and how that experience could be seen as contested.

DB: **You're referring to Pratt's discussion of the "contact zone"?**

JFC: Yes. Students worked with documents from groups trying to explain their positions to mainstream culture. That moved the issue of pro and con to considering the questions of audience, of multiple audiences, and to issues of persuasion and representation. They worked with the documents not as simply telling facts but also as a way of trying to marshal the material to speak to a difficult audience.

DB: **And to represent a position.**

JFC: Yes. Our sequence stressed issues of representation. How could a document represent a larger group? How does an individual speak for the experience of a diverse group? The issue of bias, which kept coming up in the first assignment—triggered in part by their reading of Limerick's radical position about institutional historical bias—became an issue students negotiated better through reading Pratt. For many students, any document written by an individual is biased simply because an individual wrote it.

DB: **Do they make the same assumptions about the authors in the textbook?**

JFC: They want to believe that texts written by an authority or historian attain neutrality and somehow suppress "personal" bias. Limerick upset this opposition by asking them to think about institutional or disciplinary bias or conventions. It was then useful to reconsider the issue in Pratt's terms about the contact zone.

DB: **Would you talk a bit with some examples about the kinds of materials students found to write about? Talk about the ones that seemed to you to be particularly a mark of success and the ones that seemed to represent the sort of problems you have when you do this kind of teaching.**

JFC: I've mentioned the problems of the student writing about the Frick assassination attempt and the productive efforts of the students working with Depression-era documents. I'd say the projects that were most successful were the ones where students found an array of materials from which they selected specific parts. The Pratt assignment asks students to "conduct" a "local inventory of writing from the contact zone." The task of conducting the inventory is very useful to spend some time on. I encouraged students to consider the relationship between the array of materials they looked at more quickly and the text they selected to focus on. In the first assignment, many of the more successful pieces involved such a broader survey to set a context for the closer attention to a single document. They read more than one document to make a substantive choice for focus and so had some basis for comparison. One student wrote about letters written home by a Civil War soldier; he selected this particular soldier after looking over a volume of comparable letters. Another student wrote about letters written by inmates of [Nazi] Germany's death camps, letters written, as it were, "to the world." My sense is these students were clearly more at ease with the work because they had some knowledge or previous interest in the general topic. Sometimes, of course, their previous understandings were challenged or contradicted, which was also interesting to them and to me.

The project challenged not just the inexperienced student researcher but also the ambitious student who embarked on the project with self-directed interest. One student, for example, wrote about H. P. Lovecraft, a science fiction writer he had long admired. This student began with five volumes of Lovecraft's letters and couldn't figure out how to leave anything out. He was very devoted to Lovecraft and felt anything he could write would falsify the totality he envisioned. He kept saying, "I don't know enough. How could I represent him out of these two letters? I'd have to read all of it." He worried about the necessity of having "an opposing view": he couldn't imagine how to "oppose" what Lovecraft himself said or how to credit as opposition the letters of any of his correspondents. He ultimately recognized that the letters don't simply speak for themselves, that there was considerable work he could do as a reader—even as a devoted reader—to read Lovecraft's self-descriptions against his more mundane accounts of daily life and to do that in a concentrated way focusing on a few letters rather than the whole collection. His became one of the most successful and satisfying projects, but it took a lot of work and rethinking.

DB: Did students tend to choose to do the historical option here? My memory of the Pratt assignment is that it gives you a choice between turning to the past or to your immediate environment.

JFC: Yes, that's true. For the Limerick assignment, students had the choice between library materials or materials from their family "archives." Most students chose the library work because of the logistics of getting materials from home. Many students returned to this history work for the Pratt assignment, but others understood the political issues Pratt raises as more evident in current materials.

Students had comparable problems with both options, except for the specific issues of gaining access to the library materials. Those who chose to read from current culture often had more problems than those who used the library. One student, for example, wanted to write about the founding of the university's Black Action Society but had considerable difficulty imagining what a primary document would be. She was concerned because everything she considered seemed to her to be secondhand knowledge (and she was right!). She was talking to people about their sense of what must have happened. She had difficulty perceiving that this was a different strategy (i.e., it let her investigate current *attitudes* about the past) from interviewing some of the people who were involved (which might have let her investigate different *accounts* of the past). She finally worked her way back to reading the student newspaper from the past (rather than the anniversary issue she had initially chosen, which basically preempted her work as investigator). This choice led her back—via a different interest and route—to the library. She announced one day that her problem was that she didn't have any place in the story, that there was nothing for her to do. She was right, and we had to work on what it would mean for her to construct a place for herself as a writer, as an observer, a place from which to write her own story rather than simply retell someone else's version.

DB: Were there students who chose a contemporary piece, say a piece produced by the Black Action Society in the month of September? or a piece from the student newspaper?

JFC: Most of my students who chose the current culture option focused on topics having to do with sports (Steelers Superbowls, for example). It was their sense of having partaken in history.

DB: **I see.**

JFC: These tended to be fairly unsatisfactory projects—not because of the topic per se, but because students were convinced they already knew the history of the event and wrote from memory rather than from sources.

Perhaps the opposite problem is exemplified by the student who wrote about the tearing down of Forbes Field, the baseball park, an event that he felt powerless to discuss because, as he said, "I wasn't there." He worked from a contemporary "retrospective" from a local newspaper, an account in which the reporter had in a sense already done his assignment, had gathered documents, quoted from interviews, sifted through memoirs. The student could not understand what role he could now play as a writer. He could not see that using the reporter's passages and narrative was plagiarism. He was trapped by his faith that the past had *happened* and therefore there could only be one set of "evidence" available and only one assignment carried out. He couldn't see that he might presumably tell a different story if he focused on different primary sources, or if he asked different questions of them. We went round and round on this. I don't think it was a case of unwillingness to do the assignment, or laziness about the work, but of deep incomprehension about what it means to produce "history." He would say that he could go back and read original accounts, but he wouldn't thereby change the "history" that was already there. The events, the quotes, the opinions, all already had a place in the narrative he imagined as fixed, permanent, unauthored.

DB: **What role did Pratt play in this work? Was it just an occasion for students to revise earlier work, or did she function strategically in particular ways?**

JFC: For some students, neither Pratt nor Limerick was sufficient—partially because they had difficulty reading their material in the fairly politically charged contexts of those two pieces. For several students, the key text in the sequence was Geertz's essay.* Students went back to Geertz to work out how to account for something that happened, how to take it through different analytic models. For others the key text was Wideman, who allowed them to see what stake individuals might have in negotiating the representations of the past.

Many students returned to these history papers several times, using every opportunity for revision or reuse of the materials. One student wrote five revisions of his historical project, moving from a one-page paper to a fifteen-page paper in the end. He wrote on *Black Elk Speaks*, a memoir about the days of Crazy Horse (this was one of the complications: was his work about Crazy Horse or about Black Elk, or about the mediator to whom Black Elk spoke?). He had a lot of difficulty untangling what in such a book counted as a "document." But that was crucial to his success with the project: the project began to work for him when he saw that parts of the book were derived from something someone saw, parts were legend, parts were official accounts, and parts were Black Elk producing a kind of counterhistory, indirectly challenging the other histories available. Pratt was a very useful text for him; indeed, his interest in the project began in our early class discussions of Pratt. Limerick helped him see how Black Elk had to negotiate a white narrative of history, how he had to struggle to be able to "speak" a different version of the past. Geertz helped him see he could

---

* Geertz's essay "Deep Play: Notes on the Balinese Cockfight" appeared in the eighth edition of *Ways of Reading*.

approach his project in several different ways, making it different without simply contradicting his earlier work. Pratt helped him pay close attention to how Black Elk told Crazy Horse's story, to consider specific language and narrative moves that implied a contest over meaning. He came to see Black Elk as trying to negotiate the representation of Indian culture. He came to treat Black Elk as an author rather than as a found object. He spent maybe seven weeks on this work. But it was important work for him to do intellectually.

DB: **As people say here — it was hard because it was hard.**

JFC: Many of the difficulties I have described show students grappling with what are extremely important issues in writing and reading. One difficulty is perhaps a literary issue, of seeing how to read a text closely, of how to use a text to locate a writer's positions and hesitancies. The other is perhaps more a cultural issue, that is, imagining that somebody you have understood as an object can have something to speak that may alter "history" as it has been previously narrated. Some students were struggling with the recognition that there are competing notions of what is culturally important, of what counts, of what "really happened." I count these as serious difficulties, but also as serious work to investigate.

DB: **Jean, we've been talking about the Limerick and Pratt assignments largely because I was interested in what you see as the problems and successes in sending students out to work with documentary and archival material. But I want to take a moment to ask you generally about the shape of the sequence you worked with. That is, I know that there are other readings or other kinds of writing students do, and I know that you and the group made some changes to the sequence so that it worked for you. Would you talk about the sequence and those changes?**

JFC: We worked with the history and ethnography sequence. We read the introduction to *Ways of Reading*, Pratt, Geertz, Limerick, Wideman, and then Pratt again. We used Pratt at the beginning to raise some of the problems of representation, to set these up as issues that are contested in the academy, that are difficult to negotiate — even for "professionals." Pratt usefully suggests how this problem crosses many lines, not resting in only one disciplinary site. For the first assignment of the semester, we added an assignment to the sequence. We had students write from the Pratt essay on the issue of community. (This is the third "Assignment for Writing" following the Pratt essay.) They were asked to write about an observed community in terms of Benedict Anderson's discussion about "imagined communities" and then in terms of Pratt's "contact zone." Many of them wrote about high school groups, community groups from their past. Another change we made was that we inserted more time before each archival assignment so students had time to discuss their searches and their documents before writing the minihistories. We built in time for students to go out to gather material and sometimes to do a small assignment to work from in class. This differed somewhat in various sections. My students had to produce a short position paper when they first described their documents.

The second assignment, reading Geertz, asked them to observe a group —

DB: **It says a group or subgroup, some part of the culture you know well.**

JFC: Yes — to do an ethnography, a reading of the activities of a group or subgroup and to consider what constitutes a group and its representations. Students tended to choose local

organizations, university groups, or work situations. We emphasized in this case the importance of going out now to observe, rather than relying—as many of them had for the first
assignment—on memory of a group. Then we did the Limerick assignment. Then we did
a revision, inviting students to choose any of their first three papers to revise (Pratt, Geertz,
or Limerick). We worked with the introduction to *Ways of Reading* as they were preparing to
revise and having midterm conferences.

Then we read Wideman. Instead of doing a writer's guide using Wideman, we composed an assignment more explicitly on the problems of representation in Wideman, considering how to put those into conversation with Pratt, Geertz, or Limerick. Wideman
usefully complicates their sense of who has problems of representation. They've been willing to imagine it as a historian's problem, or as a problem Geertz, for some reason, takes
on himself by going to Bali. When they hit Wideman, they begin to see it as a problem
anyone has with the past, with others—even with others as close as family. They see how
what they have understood as personal can be read as historical. Wideman quite usefully
revisits the work of ethnography begun with Geertz, and brings home the work of history,
as well as Pratt's concern with the arts of the contact zone. Wideman localizes and makes
visible what for the students was more abstract in Pratt, even in Limerick—the sense of
having different positions from which to speak, of having different authority as a speaker,
of needing to negotiate dominant narratives or perspectives. So, although it's a slightly different piece than the others in the sequence, it was crucial to how the sequence worked. It
was also useful for students to go back from Wideman to rethink how the other essays are
shaped by the disciplines they inhabit and critique, by history and anthropology, by being
offered as a lecture at a conference on literacy. After Wideman, we returned to Pratt and
worked with materials representing "the arts of the contact zone." Some students revisited
earlier materials, while others launched a new project at this point.

DB: **So, did some people who had started working on the Depression continue that?**

JFC: Some continued their archival projects through the Pratt assignment and into the final
project as well. I'd say maybe a third of the class revised the archival work a couple of times,
extending it, rethinking it.

DB: **Would you generalize from this that it would be a good idea for students to work
with fundamentally the same body of materials from beginning to end?**

JFC: I think that the difficulty of finding things in the first place is so great that it is useful
to continue with them when possible. On the other hand, you don't want to limit students
by what they can find in the third week of class. This places too much pressure on what
is already their sense that they have to find the right stuff to succeed. Some students did
find wonderful materials early on, and they mined these to great effect for the rest of the semester. Others learned from their first experiment how to find something of more interest to
them for the second foray. They were pleased at their growing confidence in searching, with
their ability to formulate more clearly what they might want to work on. Some students
used the historical assignment as a trial run for finding cultural materials. They saw then
the usefulness of having a document and not just relying on a generalized sense of culture
or on memory alone. They saw that one could document attitudes, that one could quote
material to work on intensively. So I think that the historical project was useful both for

students who caught the bug of archival work and for those who preferred to turn to more contemporary issues. I left it up to the students. I didn't want to force them to keep going with the history work unless they were so moved. But many of them were. Many of them saw it as their strongest writing, which may, of course, have had to do with my obvious interest in it. We ended the course with work on a class book. Each student contributed a revision of one of the assignments; we had these copied and bound as a book; and the students bought them to use as our text for the last two weeks of class. In some sections of the course students all revised one particular assignment, but in others students chose to revise material from the entire course. Many of these revisions were of papers we had discussed earlier in the semester, so students saw how their classmates' early work had changed. Students really seemed to enjoy having the book, reading the essays as stories or part of a book rather than as papers to edit.

DB: **So at the end of the course everybody had a book?**

JFC: Yes. Everybody had a book, and we used it to talk about issues of representation, about how they might represent their work as student writers or represent the project of the course.

DB: **May I have the title of this book?**

JFC: Mine was called simply "Classbook," but it had a nice table of contents.

Afterword

Joe Harris, Margaret Marshall, Jim Seitz, and I were the faculty responsible for planning the first-year course and the accompanying program for beginning graduate students. Rashmi Bhatnagar, Bianca Falbo, Jean Grace, and Steve Sutherland worked with me to oversee the course and the staff meetings. I also want to acknowledge the following teachers who used this sequence and allowed beginning graduate students to observe their classes: Rita Capezzi, Nick Coles, Joe Harris, Margaret Marshall, and Paul Kameen.

I want to thank the wonderful staff of archivists and special collection librarians at the University of Pittsburgh, and especially Charles Aston, Director of Special Collections at the University of Pittsburgh, who has long helped me carry out my pedagogical extravaganzas with library projects. He was instrumental in coordinating problems and solutions, in channeling complaints my way, and in working out plans for improvement.

I want to thank the students in my section of General Writing, Fall 1993, for permission to quote from their papers.

—JFC